Expert One-on-One
J2EE™ Design and Development

Rod Johnson

wrox

Programmer to Programmer

Expert One-on-One J2EE™ Design and Development

Published by
Wiley Publishing, Inc.
10475 Crosspoint Boulevard
Indianapolis, IN 46256
www.wiley.com

Library of Congress Card Number: 2003107067

ISBN: 0-7645-4385-7

Manufactured in the United States of America

10 9 8 7 6 5 4 3

1B/RQ/QW/QT/IN

For general information on our other products and services or to obtain technical support, please contact our Customer Care Department within the U.S. at (800) 762-2974, outside the U.S. at (317) 572-3993 or fax (317) 572-4002.

Wiley also publishes its books in a variety of electronic formats. Some content that appears in print may not be available in electronic books.

Trademark Acknowledgments

Wrox has endeavored to provide trademark information about all the companies and products mentioned in this book by the appropriate use of capitals. However, Wrox cannot guarantee the accuracy of this information.

Credits

Author
Rod Johnson

Commissioning Editor
Craig A. Berry

Technical Editors
Kalpana Garde
Niranjan Jahagirdar

Project Managers
Cilmara Lion
Abbas Rangwala

Author Agent
Nicola Phillips

Index
Adrian Axinte
Andrew Criddle
John Collin

Proof Reader
Chris Smith

Technical Reviewers
Simon Brown
John Carnell
Eric Eicke
Meeraj Kunnumpurath
Todd Lauinger
Eric Paul Schley
Andrew Smith
Tobin Titus
Tom Watkins
David Whitney
Dave Writz

Production Coordinators
Abbie Forletta
Manjiri Karande

Illustrations
Santosh Haware
Manjiri Karande

Cover
Dawn Chellingworth
Natalie O'Donnell

About the Author

Rod Johnson is an enterprise Java architect specializing in scalable web applications. Rod spent two years designing and delivering a J2EE solution for FT.com, Europe's largest business portal, before trekking to Everest Base Camp, parenting a baby, and writing this book. He would like to thank Tristan for providing the toughest of these challenges.

Rod completed an arts degree majoring in music and computer science at the University of Sydney. He obtained a PhD in musicology before returning to software development. With a background in C and C++, Rod has worked with both Java and J2EE since their release. He is currently a member of JSR 154 Expert Group defining the Servlet 2.4 specification.

Rod has contributed several chapters to other Wrox publications including *Professional Java Server Programming* (J2EE and J2EE 1.3 editions) and *Professional Java Server Pages* (2nd edition), and is a reviewer for Wrox Press. He has presented at international conferences including Times Java, Mumbai (2001), and his writing has been featured on java.sun.com.

An Australian, Rod is currently living and working in London.

He can be contacted at expert@interface21.com.

Although all authors seem to thank their families, I had no idea how richly such gratitude was deserved until I wrote this book.

Above all, I would like to thank my wife, Kerry, for her love and support throughout a lengthy and stressful process.

Others to give generous support include my parents-in-law, Don and Dana Jamieson.

Of those who have given practical help, I would like to thank my editor, Craig Berry, for helping me to distill a huge topic into a book; and my former colleague, Dominic Fisher, for his business insight and valuable help in formulating realistic requirements for the sample application.

O CEANUS

INSULÆ

PHILIP

ARC

Sinoe

Alinsu

Tunquan

I. Ainao

I. Philippo

Siley

Bulacos

Moro Hermoso

Pintados

Anson triste

G. de Matababambre

Pontam

Mandato

Parasalle

C. del Spirito Santo de Chos

Francisco Gomez

Ylhas del Primeiro

Sururidere

Puelhas

Abo camuoho Primeiro

Caburas

Abiso

Passage de S. Clera

I. de Mata clotes

I. dos Arecifes

Luco

Palo S. Polo

Doa Tanquero

Pracel

Enseada de Cauchin

Costa de Pracel

Sinoa

Cambo

Cambo ia

Palo Ciri

Palo Condor

Palo babe

Palo Tigao

Mon Practen

Palo de S. Maria

Calamianes

S. Michael

Pracel

I. Tecwole

Caragan

Damaon

Canal

MINDANA

Mindanao

A. de Resureicam

C. Buey

I. de S. Ioanne

I. da Palmeras

Malaguas

S. Clera

I. de la Matia

I. de S. Joana

Baguinaan

I. de Sagim

Carongao

I. de Talao

I. de Rao

I. di Din

I. los Graos

BOR NE O

Borneo

Melano

Puchauarni

Tomocaen

Tancaraboo

Lorc danla Say Manuel de Sina

Bentan

Banca

Bibilitam

Chinabato

Nosssira

Batupao Cadapali Nsoora

Brames

S

Mo Tidore

Tidore

Bachian

CELE BES

Ablas

Buorho

Xula

Burro

Batolina

Cabao

Porto Canam CEIRAM

Hie hybernae de Menezes

Aru

Agas in hernoe Martin Afonso de mela

Bentan

AVA, quæ et IAOA dicitur. Fiderda

Timor

Batolga Batolina

I. de S. Matheus

Terra alta Guliam

Guaon

LANT

DOL

Baixos

Table of Contents

Table of Contents

Table of Contents

Table of Contents

Table of Contents

Table of Contents

Table of Contents

Table of Contents

Introduction

I believe that J2EE is the best platform available for enterprise software development today. It combines the proven merits of the Java programming language with the lessons of enterprise software development in the last decade.

Yet this promise is not always fulfilled. The return on investment in many J2EE projects is disappointing. Delivered systems are too often slow and unduly complex. Development time is often disproportionate to the complexity of business requirements.

Why? Not so much because of shortcomings in J2EE as because J2EE is often used badly. This often results from approaches to architecture and development that ignore real world problems. A major contributing factor is the emphasis in many J2EE publications on the J2EE specifications rather than the real world problems people use them to address. Many issues that commonly arise in real applications are simply ignored.

When reading J2EE discussion forums, I'm struck by how little guidance and direction many developers find, and how much time and effort they waste as a result. In many cases, these developers have years of IT experience, and yet are finding it hard to come to grips with J2EE.

The problem is not a lack of information about J2EE components. Many books and web sites do a good job describing servlets, EJBs etc. Enabling technologies such as JNDI, RMI, and JMS are equally well served.

The problem is in getting to the next level – taking these construction materials and using them to build applications that meet real business requirements in a reasonable period of time. Here, I feel that much of the existing literature on J2EE is a hindrance rather than help. There is a gulf between the world of J2EE books – the world as it perhaps should be – and the real world of enterprise software projects.

This book aims to address this problem and provide clear guidance and direction on using J2EE effectively in practice. I'll help you to solve common problems with J2EE and avoid the expensive mistakes often made in J2EE projects. I will guide you through the complexity of the J2EE services and APIs to enable you to build the simplest possible solution, on time and on budget. I'll take a practical, pragmatic approach, questioning J2EE orthodoxy where it has failed to deliver results in practice and suggesting effective, proven approaches.

I feel that no existing book delivers this. The closest is probably *Core J2EE Patterns* from *Prentice Hall (ISBN: 0-130648-84-1)*, which generated much excitement on its release. Here at last was a book that addressed *how* to use J2EE components. *Core J2EE Patterns* is a good book and a valuable resource for J2EE architects and developers. In particular, the terminology it uses has become widely accepted, but it's a Sun publication, and can't help reflecting the "party line".

It also deals purely with the J2EE standards, paying little attention to issues encountered in working with real application servers. It fails to provide clear guidance: too often, it sits on the fence, presenting a variety of very different alternative "patterns". Readers able to choose confidently between them have little to learn from the book.

The more I considered the available publications, sample applications, and discussion forums, the more convinced I became that J2EE needed a healthy dose of pragmatism. J2EE is a great platform; unfortunately, many of the architectural practices promoted for it are not, and don't help to solve many common problems. Many J2EE sample applications, such as Sun's Java Pet Store, are disappointing. They don't face real world problems. They perform poorly, and their code often contains sloppy practices, providing a poor model.

I was also struck by the difference in outlook between developers new to J2EE and those who had actually used J2EE to build enterprise systems. A former colleague used the wonderfully evocative word "gnarly" to describe developers who've come to grips with practical challenges of working with a technology and bear the scars. While those new to J2EE sounded like J2EE evangelists, the "gnarly" developers told a different story. They had had to jettison some of the ideological baggage of the innocents to implement necessary functionality or achieve adequate performance. Like my colleagues and myself, they'd found that reality intruded harshly on the initial vision.

In this book I'll draw on my experience and industry knowledge to help you design and develop solutions that work in practice, without the need for you to go through a painful process of discovering the difference between J2EE theory and reality.

J2EE Myths

I believe that the causes of disappointing outcomes with J2EE can usually be traced to a few common myths, which underpin many explicit and implicit assumptions in development projects:

❑   J2EE is about portability, between application servers and databases.

❑   J2EE is the best answer to all the problems of enterprise development. If a problem that would traditionally have been solved using non-J2EE technologies, such as RDBMS stored procedures, can be solved with standard J2EE technology, it's always best to use the "pure" J2EE approach.

❏ J2EE servers take care of performance and scalability, leaving developers to get on with implementing business logic. Developers can largely ignore the performance implications of J2EE "patterns" and rely on acceptable performance in production.

❏ J2EE enables developers to forget about low-level problems such as data access and multi-threading, which will be handled transparently by the application server.

❏ All J2EE applications should use EJB, which is the essential J2EE technology for developing enterprise-class applications.

❏ Any problems with J2EE will soon be addressed by more sophisticated application servers.

Let's quickly consider each of these myths in turn.

Portability is a great bonus of the J2EE platform. As we'll see, portability *can* be achieved in real applications, but it's not the point of J2EE. The requirement of the vast majority of projects is to build an application that solves a particular problem well on one target platform. An application that runs badly on one platform will never be ported to other platforms (the application might be ported to another operating system that runs on more powerful hardware to gain adequate performance, but that's not the kind of portability that professional developers aspire to).

J2EE orthodoxy holds that an application should be portable across J2EE application servers and must be able to work with different databases. The distinction between these two goals is important, and sometimes missed. Portability between application servers may deliver business value and is usually a realistic goal. Portability between databases is much more fraught, and often provides no business value.

Portability is usually taken to mean *code portability*: the ability to take the application and run it on another platform without any change. I believe that this is an expensive misconception. Naïve emphasis on total code portability often leads to heavy costs in lost productivity and less satisfactory deliverables. **Write Once Run Anywhere (WORA)**, while a reality where Java itself is concerned, is a dangerous slogan to apply to enterprise development, which depends on a range of resources.

> *I'm not talking about the minority of projects to develop "shrink-wrapped" components (usually EJBs). This appealing concept is still to be proven in the market. Furthermore, I'm yet to see a non-trivial component that aimed for both, application server portability (which makes sense in this situation) and database portability (which will almost certainly be more trouble than it's worth).*

I prefer **Design Once, Re-implement a Few Interfaces Anywhere (DORAFIA)**. I accept that this is not so catchy, and that people are unlikely to leave Java One chanting it. This more realistic approach is widely used in other domains, such as windowing systems.

The portability myth has led to wide acceptance that J2EE applications can't use the capabilities of today's relational databases, but should use them only as dumb storage. This does great harm in the real world.

This is not to say that I don't believe that J2EE applications can or should be portable. I'm just arguing for a more pragmatic and realistic view of portability. We *can* design J2EE applications to be ported easily; we can't do the same thing with a proprietary technology such as .NET.

It's pleasant to imagine that J2EE is the final stage of the evolution of enterprise architecture; that finally, the application of object technology and the Java language has cracked problems the industry has wrestled with for decades. Unfortunately, this is not the reality, although it's implicitly assumed in many approaches to J2EE development. J2EE builds on many of the technologies that preceded it. It's a step forward, but it won't be the last and it doesn't address all the issues of enterprise software development.

Exaggerated emphasis on portability, along with this J2EE-centric attitude, has led to the assumption that if something can't be done in standard J2EE, it's a design error to do it. This is even creeping into the EJB specification with the introduction of EJB QL: a portable but immature query language that's more complex but far less powerful than the familiar, mature, and largely standard SQL that is available to the great majority of J2EE applications.

I like to think of a J2EE server as the conductor of a group of enterprise resources such as databases. A good conductor is vital to any performance. However, a conductor doesn't attempt to play individual instruments, but leaves this to skilled specialists.

Perhaps the most dangerous myth is that J2EE is the easy route to good performance and scalability, and that efficiency is a lesser concern than approved J2EE "patterns". This leads to naïve and inefficient designs. This is unfortunate, as outside the Java community Java has always been dogged by fears of poor performance. Today, the evidence is that the Java language offers good performance, while some popular J2EE "patterns" offer very poor performance.

We cannot assume that the application server can take care of performance and scalability. In fact, J2EE gives us all the rope we need to tie up not only our J2EE application server, but the database as well. Had optimal performance been the main goal of software development, we'd have been writing web applications in C or assembly language. However, performance *is* vital to the business value of real-world applications. We can't rely on Moore's Law to allow us to solve performance problems with faster hardware. It's possible to create problems that prevent adequate performance, regardless of hardware power.

The idea that the J2EE server should transparently handle low-level details such as data access is appealing. Sometimes it's achievable, but can be dangerous. Again, let's consider the example of relational databases. Oracle, the leading enterprise-class RDBMS, handles locking in a completely different way compared to any other product. The performance implications of using coarse or fine-grained transactions also vary between databases. This means that "portability" can be illusory, as the same code may behave differently in different RDBMS products.

Oracle and other leading products are expensive and have impressive capabilities. Often we'd *want* (or need) to leverage these capabilities directly. J2EE provides valuable standardization in such infrastructure services as transaction management and connection pooling, but we won't be saying goodbye to those fat RDBMS product manuals any time soon.

The "J2EE = EJB" myth can lead to particularly expensive mistakes. EJB is a complex technology that solves some problems well, but adds more complexity than business value in many situations. I feel that most books ignore the very real downside of EJB, and encourage readers to use EJB automatically. In this book, I'll provide a dispassionate view of the strengths and weaknesses of EJB, and clear guidance on when to use EJB.

Allowing the technology used (J2EE or any other technology) to determine the approach to a business problem often leads to poor results. Examples of this mistake include determining that business logic should always be implemented in EJBs, or determining that entity beans are the one correct way to implement data access. The truth is that only a small subset of J2EE components – I would include servlets and stateless session EJBs – are central to most J2EE applications. The value of the others varies greatly depending on the problem in hand.

I advocate a problem-driven, not technology-driven, approach (Sun's "J2EE Blueprints" have probably done as much harm as good, by suggesting a J2EE technology-driven approach). While we should strive to avoid reinventing the wheel, the orthodoxy that we should never ourselves implement something that the server can (however inefficiently), can be costly. The core J2EE infrastructure to handle transaction management, etc., is a godsend; the same cannot be said for all the services described in the J2EE specifications.

Some will argue that all these problems will soon be solved, as J2EE application servers become more sophisticated. For example, ultra-efficient implementations of entity bean **Container-Managed Persistence (CMP)** will prove faster than RDBMS access using raw SQL. This is naïve and carries unacceptable risk. There is little place for faith in IT. Decisions must be made on what has been proven to work, and faith may be misplaced.

There are strong arguments that some features of J2EE, such as entity beans, can *never* be as performant in many situations as some alternatives. Furthermore, the Promised Land is *still* just around the corner. For example, entity beans were soon going to provide brilliant performance when they were first introduced into the EJB specification in 1999. Yet the next two years revealed severe flaws in the original entity bean model. Today, the radical changes in the EJB 2.0 specification are still to be proven, and the EJB 2.1 specification is already trying to address omissions in EJB 2.0.

How is this Book Different?

First, it's an independent view, based on my experience and that of colleagues working with J2EE in production. I don't seek to evangelize. I advocate using J2EE, but caution against J2EE orthodoxy.

Second, it has a practical focus. I want to help you to implement cost-effective applications using J2EE. This book aims to demystify J2EE development. It shows how to use J2EE technologies to reduce, rather than increase, complexity. While I don't focus on any one application server, I discuss some of the issues you're likely to encounter working with real products. This book doesn't shy away from real-world problems that are not naturally addressed by the J2EE specifications. For example, how do we use the Singleton design pattern in the EJB tier? How should we do logging in the EJB tier?

This book doesn't seek to cover the whole of J2EE. It aims to demonstrate effective approaches to solving common problems. For example, it focuses on using J2EE with relational databases, as most J2EE developers face O/R mapping issues. In general, it aims to be of most help in solving the most common problems.

We'll look at a single sample application throughout the book. Rather than use an unrealistic, abstract example as we discuss each issue, we'll look at a small part of a larger, more realistic, whole. The sample application is an online ticketing application. It is designed not to illustrate particular J2EE *technologies* (like many sample applications), but common *problems* facing J2EE architects and developers.

This book is about quality, maintainability, and productivity.

This is the book I wished I'd had as I worked on my first J2EE project. It would have saved me a lot of effort, and my employer a lot of money.

My Approach

This book is *problem*-oriented rather than *specification*-oriented. Unlike many books on J2EE, it doesn't aim to cover all the many services and APIs. Instead, it recognizes that not all parts of J2EE are equally useful, or of interest to all developers, and focuses on those parts that are used in building typical solutions.

Software design is as much art as science. The richness of J2EE means that it is often possible to find more than one good solution to a problem (and many bad solutions). While I make every effort to explain my views (or prejudices), this book naturally reflects my experience of and attitude towards working with J2EE. I present an approach that I've found to work well. However, this doesn't mean that it's the *only* valid approach.

The book reflects my attitudes towards software development in general:

❑ I try to avoid religious positions. I've never understood the energy and passion that so many developers devote to flame wars. This benefits no one.

❑ I'm a pragmatist. I care about outcomes more than ideology. When I work on a project, my primary goal is to deliver a quality result on time and budget. The technology I use is a tool towards that goal, not an end in itself.

❑ I believe that sound OO principles should underpin J2EE development.

❑ I believe that maintainability is crucial to the value of any deliverable.

In keeping with this pragmatic approach, I'll frequently refer to the **Pareto Principle***, which states that a small number of causes (20%) are responsible for most (80%) of the effect. The Pareto Principle, originally drawn from economics, is highly applicable to practical software engineering, and we'll come across it repeatedly in approaching J2EE projects. For example, it can suggest that trying to solve all problems in a given area can be much harder (and less cost-effective) than solving just those that matter in most real applications.*

My approach reflects some of the lessons of **Extreme Programming (XP)**. I'm a methodology skeptic, and won't attempt to plug XP. This isn't an XP book, but I feel that XP offers a valuable balance to J2EE theory. In particular, we'll see the value of the following principles:

❑ Simplicity. XP practitioners advocate doing "the simplest thing that could possibly work".

- ❑ Avoiding wasted effort. XP practitioners don't add features they may never need. This approach is captured in the acronym YAGNI (You Aren't Going to Need It).

- ❑ Focus on testing throughout the development process.

Who this Book is for

This book is aimed at Java architects, developers already working with J2EE, and Java developers who have a basic knowledge of J2EE and expect to work on J2EE projects.

This book is not an introduction to EJBs, servlets, JSP, or J2EE. Readers unfamiliar with these areas might read this book while referring to a comprehensive reference (see *Recommended Reading* below).

Aims of this Book

This book aims to leave the reader comfortable making architectural and implementation decisions about J2EE development.

After working through this book, a developer familiar with the basic concepts of J2EE but who might not have any experience working with it would be confident in attempting a J2EE project. A more experienced architect or developer would benefit from the discussion of J2EE architecture and implementation from a practical perspective. The chapters on project choices, testing and tools might be of interest to managers trying to understand the implications of adopting J2EE technology.

What this Book Covers

This book covers:

- ❑ How to make key J2EE architectural choices, such as whether to use EJB and where to implement business logic

- ❑ J2EE web technologies, and effective use of the **Model-View-Controller (MVC)** architectural pattern in web applications

- ❑ How to use EJB 2.0 effectively, including the implications of the introduction of EJBs with local interfaces

- ❑ How to choose an application server

- ❑ OO development practices important to J2EE applications

- ❑ Using JavaBeans in J2EE applications, and how this can help develop maintainable and portable applications

- ❑ Using XML and XSLT in J2EE applications

- ❑ J2EE transaction management

- ❑ How to access relational databases efficiently in J2EE applications

- ❑ How to use generic infrastructure code to solve common problems and ensure that application code focuses on business logic in the problem domain
- ❑ How to test J2EE applications, and especially web applications
- ❑ How to design J2EE applications for satisfactory performance, and how to improve the performance of existing applications
- ❑ Packaging and deploying J2EE applications
- ❑ Aspects of leading application servers, such as BEA WebLogic and Oracle 9 Application Server, which may affect how we design J2EE applications
- ❑ Understanding the implications of fundamental design choices for scalability

This book also includes and discusses much generic infrastructure code that can be used in your applications.

Assumed Knowledge

The following knowledge is assumed:

- ❑ Strong Java language skills
- ❑ Solid grasp of OO principles
- ❑ Familiarity with classic OO design patterns
- ❑ Familiarity with servlets and EJB
- ❑ Some familiarity with JSP
- ❑ Familiarity with web and distributed object protocols such as HTTP and IIOP
- ❑ Understanding of fundamental underpinnings of J2EE such as RMI, JDBC, and JNDI

The following knowledge is desirable:

- ❑ Relational database fundamentals
- ❑ Understanding of transaction concepts (ACID properties and isolation levels)
- ❑ Basic understanding of XML and XSLT
- ❑ Basic understanding of UML, especially class and sequence diagrams
- ❑ Familiarity with basic Computer Science concepts such as data structures

Recommended Reading

This book refers to many of the 23 design patterns discussed in the classic book *Design Patterns: Elements of Reusable Object-Oriented Software* from *Addison Wesley (ISBN 0-201633-61-2)*. Although many of the patterns presented in this book merely codify the practice of any skilled OO practitioner, it provides a common language for architects and is essential reading for any serious developer. It is assumed that the reader has read, and has access to, this book.

I also use pattern names introduced in *Core J2EE Patterns: Best Practices and Design Strategies* from *Prentice Hall (ISBN 0-130648-84-1)*, as these are widely accepted. Although the present book can be read without reference to *Core J2EE Patterns*, it is recommended reading. Note, however, that I advocate a different approach in several areas. Also, some sections of *Core J2EE Patterns*, especially those relating to entity beans, are out-dated by the release of the EJB 2.0 Specification.

Some J2EE patterns are also discussed from *EJB Design Patterns* from *Wiley (ISBN 0-471208-31-0)*. Again, this is recommended, although not essential, background reading.

A good reference covering the J2EE 1.3 platform is essential. I recommend *Professional Java Server Programming J2EE 1.3 Edition* from *Wrox Press (ISBN 1-861005-37-7)*. Ed Roman's *Mastering Enterprise JavaBeans, (Second Edition),* from *Wiley (ISBN 0-471417-11-4)* is a good book on EJB.

Full Javadoc for the J2EE 1.3 platform is available online at
http://java.sun.com/j2ee/sdk_1.3/techdocs/api/index.html

Finally, all professional J2EE architects and developers should refer to the specifications that define the J2EE 1.3 platform, which are available from http://java.sun.com/j2ee/download.html. Throughout this book, I will refer to the relevant sections (such as EJB 17.4.1) of the following specifications:

- ❏ J2EE 1.3
- ❏ EJB 2.0
- ❏ Servlet 2.3
- ❏ JSP 1.2

Where relevant, I'll also refer to the J2EE 1.4 specification releases, now in public draft and also available from Sun: notably EJB 2.1, Servlet 2.4 and JSP 2.0.

What You Need for Using this Book

To run the samples in this book you will need:

- ❏ Java 2 Platform, Standard Edition SDK v 1.3 or above. We used the Sun JDK 1.3.1_02 to run all sample code.
- ❏ A J2EE 1.3-compliant application server. We used JBoss 3.0.0 for the sample application.

❑ An RDBMS. We used Oracle 8.1.7i for the sample application. A free evaluation copy of the "Personal Edition" is available from the Oracle site. Some changes (clearly identified in the text) will need to be made to the sample application to use a database other than Oracle 8.1.7 or above.

To run the sample application, you will need the following third-party libraries:

❑ Apache Log4j 1.2
❑ An implementation of the **JSP Standard Tag Library (JSTL)** 1.0

To use the testing strategies discussed in *Chapter 3*, you will need:

❑ JUnit 3.7 or above
❑ The Apache Cactus J2EE testing framework

To run all the web content generation examples in *Chapter 13* you will need:

❑ Apache Velocity 1.3
❑ Lutris XMLC 2.1
❑ The iText PDF generation library
❑ The Domify XML generation library

See *Appendix A* for information on how to install and configure these last four products.

All the third-party products and libraries discussed above are free and open source.

To build the source code you will need Apache Ant 1.4.1 or later, including optional task support.

The complete source code for the samples is available for download from our web site at http://www.wrox.com/. There are two versions of the download: one which contains all the binaries discussed above, and a much smaller bundle that includes only the source code and compiled code discussed in this book. Download the smaller version if you already have, or want to download, the third-party products listed above.

Conventions

To help you get the most from the text and keep track of what's happening, we've used a number of conventions throughout the book.

> **These boxes hold important, not-to-be-forgotten information, which is directly relevant to the surrounding text.**

While the background style is used for asides to the current discussion.

As for styles in the text:

- ❑ When we introduce them, we **highlight** important words
- ❑ We show keyboard strokes like this: *Ctrl-K*
- ❑ We show filenames and code within the text like so: `persistence.properties`
- ❑ Text on user interfaces and URLs are shown as: Menu

We present code in two different ways:

```
In our code examples, the code foreground style shows new, important, pertinent
code.
While code background shows code that's less important in the present context, or
has been seen before.
```

Customer Support

We always value hearing from our readers, and we want to know what you think about this book: what you liked, what you didn't like, and what you think we can do better next time. You can send us your comments, either by returning the reply card in the back of the book, or by e-mail to feedback@wrox.com. Please be sure to mention the book title in your message.

How to Download the Sample Code for the Book

When you visit the Wrox site http://www.wrox.com/ simply locate the title through our Search facility or by using one of the title lists. Click on Download in the Code column, or on Download Code on the book's detail page.

The files that are available for download from our site have been archived using WinZip. When you have saved the attachments to a folder on your hard-drive, you need to extract the files using a de-compression program such as WinZip. When you extract the files, the code is usually extracted into chapter folders. When you start the extraction process, ensure your software (WinZip) is set to use folder names.

Errata

We've made every effort to make sure that there are no errors in the text or in the code. However, no one is perfect and mistakes do occur. If you find an error in one of our books, like a spelling mistake or faulty piece of code, we would be very grateful for your feedback. By sending in errata you may save another reader hours of frustration, and of course, you will be helping us provide even higher quality information. Simply e-mail the information to support@wrox.com; your information will be checked and if correct, posted to the errata page for that title, or used in subsequent editions of the book.

To find errata on the web site, go to http://www.wrox.com/, and simply locate the title through our Advanced Search or title list. Click on the Book Errata link, which is below the cover graphic on the book's detail page.

E-Mail Support

If you wish to directly query a problem in the book with an expert who knows the book in detail then e-mail support@wrox.com, with the title of the book and the last four numbers of the ISBN in the subject field of the e-mail. A typical e-mail should include the following things:

- ❑ The **title of the book**, **last four digits of the ISBN**, and **page number** of the problem in the Subject field

- ❑ Your **name**, **contact information**, and the **problem** in the body of the message

We *won't* send you junk mail. We need the details to save your time and ours. When you send an e-mail message, it will go through the following chain of support:

- ❑ Customer Support – Your message is delivered to our customer support staff, who are the first people to read it. They have files on most frequently asked questions and will answer anything general about the book or the web site immediately.

- ❑ Editorial – Deeper queries are forwarded to the technical editor responsible for that book. They have experience with the programming language or particular product, and are able to answer detailed technical questions on the subject.

- ❑ The Authors – Finally, in the unlikely event that the editor cannot answer your problem, they will forward the request to the author. We do try to protect the authors from any distractions to their writing; however, we are quite happy to forward specific requests to them. All Wrox authors help with the support on their books. They will e-mail the customer and the editor with their response, and again all readers should benefit.

The Wrox Support process can only offer support to issues directly pertinent to the content of our published title. Support for questions that fall outside the scope of normal book support is provided via the community lists of our http://p2p.wrox.com/ forum.

p2p.wrox.com

For author and peer discussion join the P2P mailing lists. Our unique system provides **programmer to programmer**™ contact on mailing lists, forums, and newsgroups, all in addition to our one-to-one e-mail support system. If you post a query to P2P, you can be confident that it is being examined by the many Wrox authors and other industry experts who are present on our mailing lists. At p2p.wrox.com you will find a number of different lists to help you, not only while you read this book, but also as you develop your applications.

To subscribe to a mailing list just follow these steps:

1. Go to http://p2p.wrox.com/

2. Choose the appropriate category from the left menu bar

3. Click on the mailing list you wish to join

4. Follow the instructions to subscribe and fill in your e-mail address and password

5. Reply to the confirmation e-mail you receive

6. Use the subscription manager to join more lists and set your e-mail preferences

Why this System Offers the Best Support

You can choose to join the mailing lists or you can receive them as a weekly digest. If you don't have the time, or facility, to receive the mailing list, then you can search our archives. Junk and spam mails are deleted, and your own e-mail address is protected by the unique Lyris system. Queries about joining or leaving lists, and any other general queries about lists, should be sent to listsupport@wrox.com.

OCEANUS

INSULÆ

PHILIP

AR

PINÆ

Sinoe

I. Ainan

Philippina

Siley

Aiceos

Luzon

Moro Hermoso

Pintados

Ancon triste

G. de Matalahambre

Tunquin

Doa Tanquero

LUCO

Pinalan

Mandato

Paragalle

Cd. del Spirito Santo

de Elios

Enseada de Cauchon de Sinoa

Cochinchina

Costa de Pulo Cambi

MIAN

Pulo S. Polo

Francisco Gomez

Ylhas del Primero

Suegidera

Puelhas

Abo camacho Primero

Abigo

Caburac

Sian Diam el Odia

Anse Ogou

Cambo la

Cambo

Pulo Ciri

Pracel

Masilha

Pasage de S. Clara

Colasonianes

Damian

Cerigan

Malaga

Pulo Condor

Insula Pracatan

I. de S. Maria

I. des Arcifes

S. Michael

Pracel

Ternate

MINDANA

Mindanao

Pulo Tigao

Mon Praeras

S. Clara

A. de Resureicam

C. Bicay

I. de S. Ioannes

Borneo

Arabu

Matena

R. de Burne

Malana

Puchavara

Tanamacen

Tamrado

BOR NE O

I. de la Mata

I. de S. Joana

Baparenam

I. de Sagin

Carango

I. de Talao

I. da Palmeras

I. de Rao

I. de Dei

Do Moreno

Tidom

I. dos Greos

de Aguada

LUCCA

Bachian

Batachina

Porto Canan CEIRAM

Abias

CELE BES

Buero

As hybernat de Mente

Bintan

Banca

Saua Mango

Caracci

Machea

Portugal

Sofon

Ginoco

Buero

Batua

Sadagra

Xore

Buxos

Xula

Buero

Piolatan

Xsao Piro

Bibliotam

Chinabato

Nasfira

I. de S. Matheus

Tobi

Aru

Aqui in bernon Martin Afonso de mela

Batchu

Bantam

Pulo Timor

Pulo Ag

Terra alta Guillam

Ghaon

IAVA, quæ et IAOA dicitur. Fideuda

Timor

Buxor

E LANT

DOL

1

J2EE Architectures

J2EE provides many architectural choices. J2EE also offers many component types (such as servlets, EJBs, JSP pages, and servlet filters), and J2EE application servers provide many additional services. While this array of options enables us to design the best solution for each problem, it also poses dangers. J2EE developers can be overwhelmed by the choices on offer, or can be tempted to use infrastructure inappropriate to the problem in hand, simply because it's available.

In this book I aim to help professional J2EE developers and architects make the appropriate choices to deliver high-quality solutions on time and within budget. I'll focus on those features of J2EE that have proven most useful for solving the commonest problems in enterprise software development.

In this chapter, we discuss the high-level choices in developing a J2EE architecture, and how to decide which parts of J2EE to use to solve real problems. We'll look at:

- ❑ Distributed and non-distributed applications, and how to choose which model is appropriate
- ❑ The implications for J2EE design of changes in the EJB 2.0 specification and the emergence of web services
- ❑ When to use EJB
- ❑ Data access strategies for J2EE applications
- ❑ Four J2EE architectures, and how to choose between them
- ❑ Web tier design
- ❑ Portability issues

This book reflects my experience and discussions with other enterprise architects. I will attempt to justify the claims made in this chapter in the remainder of the book. However, there are, necessarily, many matters of opinion.

> **In particular, the message I'll try to get across will be that we should apply J2EE to realize OO design, not let J2EE technologies dictate object design.**

Familiarity with J2EE components has been assumed. We'll take a close look at container services in the following chapters, but please refer to an introductory book on J2EE if the concepts discussed are unfamiliar.

Goals of an Enterprise Architecture

Before we begin to examine specific issues in J2EE architecture, let's consider what we're trying to achieve.

A well-designed J2EE application should meet the following goals. Note that while we're focusing on J2EE-based solutions, these goals apply to all enterprise applications:

❑ **Be robust**
Enterprise software is important to an organization. Its users expect it to be reliable and bug-free. Hence we must understand and take advantage of those parts of J2EE that can help us build robust solutions and must ensure that we write quality code.

❑ **Be performant and scalable**
Enterprise applications must meet the performance expectations of their users. They must also exhibit sufficient **scalability** – the potential for an application to support increased load, given appropriate hardware. Scalability is a particularly important consideration for Internet applications, for which it is difficult to predict user numbers and behavior. Understanding the J2EE infrastructure is essential for meeting both these goals. Scalability will typically require deploying multiple server instances in a **cluster**. Clustering is a complex problem requiring sophisticated application server functionality. We must ensure that our applications are designed so that operation in a cluster is efficient.

❑ **Take advantage of OO design principles**
OO design principles offer proven benefits for complex systems. Good OO design practice is promoted by the use of proven **design patterns** – recurring solutions to common problems. The concept of design patterns was popularized in OO software development by the classic book *Design Patterns: Elements of Reusable Object-Oriented Software* from *Addison Wesley*, (*ISBN 0-201-63361-2*), which describes 23 design patterns with wide applicability. These patterns are not technology-specific or language-specific.

It's vital that we use J2EE to implement OO designs, rather than let our use of J2EE dictate object design. Today there's a whole "J2EE patterns" industry. While many "J2EE patterns" are valuable, classic (non-technology-specific) design patterns are more so, and still highly relevant to J2EE.

❑ **Avoid unnecessary complexity**
Practitioners of **Extreme Programming (XP)** advocate doing "the simplest thing that could possibly work". We should be wary of excessive complexity that may indicate that an application architecture isn't working. Due to the range of components on offer, it's tempting to over-engineer J2EE solutions, accepting greater complexity for capabilities irrelevant to the business requirements. Complexity adds to costs throughout the software lifecycle and thus can be a serious problem. On the other hand, thorough analysis must ensure that we don't have a naïve and simplistic view of requirements.

❑ **Be maintainable and extensible**
Maintenance is by far the most expensive phase of the software lifecycle. It's particularly important to consider maintainability when designing J2EE solutions, because adopting J2EE is a strategic choice. J2EE applications are likely to be a key part of an organization's software mix for years, and must be able to accommodate new business needs. Maintainability and extensibility depend largely on clean design. We need to ensure that each component of the application has a clear responsibility, and that maintenance is not hindered by tightly-coupled components.

❑ **Be delivered on time**
Productivity is a vital consideration, which is too often neglected when approaching J2EE.

❑ **Be easy to test**
Testing is an essential activity throughout the software lifecycle. We should consider the implications of design decisions for ease of testing.

❑ **Promote reuse**
Enterprise software must fit into an organization's long term strategy. Thus it's important to foster reuse, so that code duplication is minimized (within and across projects) and investment leveraged to the full. Code reuse usually results from good OO design practice, while we should also consistently use valuable infrastructure provided by the application server where it simplifies application code.

Depending on an application's business requirements, we may also need to meet the following goals:

❑ **Support for multiple client types**
There's an implicit assumption that J2EE applications always need to support multiple J2EE-technology client types, such as web applications, standalone Java GUIs using Swing or other windowing systems or Java applets. However, such support is often unnecessary, as "thin" web interfaces are being more and more widely used, even for applications intended for use within an organization (ease of deployment is one of the major reasons for this).

❑ **Portability**
How important is portability between resources, such as databases used by a J2EE application? How important is portability between application servers? Portability is not an automatic goal of J2EE applications. It's a business requirement of some applications, which J2EE helps us to achieve.

> The importance of the last two goals is a matter of business requirements, not a J2EE article of faith. We can draw a dividend of simplicity that will boost quality and reduce cost throughout a project lifecycle if we strive to achieve only goals that are relevant.

Deciding Whether to Use a Distributed Architecture

J2EE provides outstanding support for implementing **distributed** architectures. The components of a distributed J2EE application can be split across multiple JVMs running on one or more physical servers. Distributed J2EE applications are based on the use of EJBs with remote interfaces, which enable the application server to conceal much of the complexity of access to and management of distributed components.

However, J2EE's excellent support for distributed applications has led to the misconception that J2EE is *necessarily* a distributed model.

> **This is a crucial point, as distributed applications are complex, incur significant runtime overhead, and demand design workarounds to ensure satisfactory performance.**

It's often thought that a distributed model provides the *only* way to achieve robust, scalable applications. This is questionable. It's possible to cluster applications that **collocate** all their components in a single JVM.

Distributed architectures deliver the following benefits:

❑   The ability to support many clients (possibly of different types) that require a shared "middle tier" of business objects. This consideration doesn't apply to web applications, as the web container provides a middle tier.

❑   The ability to deploy any application component on any physical server. In some applications, this is important for load balancing. (Consider a scenario when a web interface does a modest amount of work, but business objects do intensive calculations. If we use a J2EE distributed model, we can run the web interface on one or two machines while many servers run the calculating EJBs. At the price of performance of each call, which will be slowed by the overhead of remote invocation, total throughput per hardware may be improved by eliminating bottlenecks.)

However, distributed architectures give rise to many tough problems, especially:

❑   **Performance problems**
Remote invocations are many times slower than local invocations.

❑   **Complexity**
Distributed applications are hard to develop, debug, deploy, and maintain.

❑   **Constraints on practicing OO design**
This is an important point, which we'll discuss further shortly.

Distributed applications pose many interesting challenges. Due to their complexity, much of this book (and J2EE literature in general) is devoted to distributed J2EE applications. However, given a choice it's best to avoid the complexities of distributed applications by opting for a non-distributed solution.

> In my experience, the deployment flexibility benefits of distributed applications are exaggerated. Distribution is not the only way to achieve scalable, robust applications. Most J2EE architectures using remote interfaces tend to be deployed with all components on the same servers, to avoid the performance overhead of true remote calling. This means that the complexity of a distributed application is unnecessary, since it results in no real benefit.

New Considerations in J2EE Design

The J2EE 1.2 specification offered simple choices. EJBs had remote interfaces and could be used only in distributed applications. **Remote Method Invocation (RMI)** (over JRMP or IIOP) was the only choice for supporting remote clients.

Since then, two developments – one within J2EE and the other outside – have had profound implications for J2EE design:

❑ The EJB 2.0 specification allows EJBs to have local interfaces, in addition to or instead of, remote interfaces. EJBs can be invoked through their local interfaces by components in an integrated J2EE application running in same JVM: for example, components of a web application.

❑ The emergence of the XML-based **Simple Object Access Protocol (SOAP)** as a widely accepted, platform-agnostic standard for RMI, and widespread support for **web services**.

EJB 2.0 local interfaces were introduced largely to address serious performance problems with EJB 1.1 entity beans. They were a last-minute addition, after the specification committee had failed to agree on the introduction of "dependent objects" to improve entity bean performance. However, local interfaces have implications reaching far beyond entity beans. We now have a choice whether to use EJB without adopting RMI semantics.

While some of the bolder claims for web services, such as automatic discovery of services through registries, are yet to prove commercially viable, SOAP has already proven its worth for remote procedure calls. SOAP support is built into Microsoft's .NET, J2EE's leading rival, and may supersede platform-specific remoting protocols. The emergence of web services challenges traditional J2EE assumptions about distributed applications.

One of the most important enhancements in the next release of the J2EE specifications will be the integration of standard web services support. However, several excellent, easy-to-use, Java toolsets allow J2EE 1.3 applications to implement and access web services. See, for example, Sun's Java Web Services Developer Pack (http://java.sun.com/webservices/webservicespack.html) and the Apache Axis SOAP implementation (http://xml.apache.org/axis/index.html).

> With EJB local interfaces and web services, we can now use EJB without RMI, and support remote clients without EJB. This gives us much greater freedom in designing J2EE applications.

When to Use EJB

One of the most important design decisions when designing a J2EE application is whether to use EJB. EJB is often perceived to be the core of J2EE. This is a misconception; EJB is merely one of the choices J2EE offers. It's ideally suited to solving some problems, but adds little value in many applications.

When requirements dictate a distributed architecture and RMI/IIOP is the natural remoting protocol, EJB gives us a standard implementation. We can code our business objects as EJBs with remote interfaces and can use the EJB container to manage their lifecycle and handle remote invocation. This is far superior to a custom solution using RMI, which requires us to manage the lifecycle of server-side objects.

If requirements don't dictate a distributed architecture or if RMI/IIOP isn't the natural remoting protocol, the decision as to whether to use EJB is much tougher.

EJB is the most complex technology in J2EE and is the biggest J2EE buzzword. This can lead to developers using EJBs for the wrong reasons: because EJB experience looks good on a resume; because there is a widespread belief that using EJB is a best practice; because EJB is perceived to be the only way to write scalable Java applications; or just because EJB exists.

EJB is a high-end technology. It solves certain problems very well, but should not be used without good reason. In this section we'll take a dispassionate look at the implications of using EJB, and important considerations influencing the decision of whether to use EJB.

Implications of Using EJB

One of the key goals of the EJB specification is to simplify application code. The EJB 2.0 specification (§2.1) states that "The EJB architecture will make it easy to write applications: Application developers will not have to understand low-level transaction and state management details, multi-threading, connection pooling, and other complex low-level APIs."

In theory, by deferring all low-level issues to the EJB container, developers are free to devote all their effort to business logic. Unfortunately, experience shows that this is not often realized in practice. Using EJB often *adds* at least as much complexity to an application as it removes. Moreover, it may be dangerous for developers to "not have to understand" the enterprise software issues that their applications face.

Introducing EJB technology has the following practical implications, which should be weighed carefully:

❑ **Using EJB makes applications harder to test**
Distributed applications are always harder to test than applications that run in a single JVM. EJB applications – whether they use remote or local interfaces – are hard to test, as they are heavily dependent on container services.

❑ **Using EJB makes applications harder to deploy**
Using EJB introduces many deployment issues. For example:

❑ Complex classloader issues. An enterprise application that involves EJB JAR files and web applications will involve many classloaders. The details vary between servers, but avoiding class loading problems such as inability to find classes or incompatible class versions is a nontrivial problem, and requires understanding of application server design.

❑ Complex deployment descriptors. While some of the complexity of EJB deployment descriptors reduces complexity in EJB code (with respect to transaction management, for example), other complexity is gratuitous. Tools can help here, but it's preferable to avoid complexity rather than rely on tools to manage it.

❑ Slower development-deployment-test cycles. Deploying EJBs is usually slower than deploying J2EE web applications. Thus, using EJB can reduce developer productivity.

Most practical frustrations with J2EE relate to EJB. This is no trivial concern; it costs time and money if EJB doesn't deliver compensating benefits.

❑ **Using EJB with remote interfaces may hamper practicing OO design**
This is a serious issue. Using EJB – a technology, which should really be an implementation choice – to drive overall design is risky. In *EJB Design Patterns* from *Wiley*(ISBN: 0-471-20831-0), for example, four of the six "EJB layer architectural patterns" are not true patterns, but workarounds for problems that are introduced by using EJB with remote interfaces. (The Session Façade pattern strives to minimize the number of network round trips, the result being a session bean with a coarse-grained interface. Interface granularity should really be dictated by normal object design considerations. The EJB Command pattern is another attempt to minimize the number of network round trips in EJB remote invocation, although its consequences are more benign. The Data Transfer Object Factory pattern addresses the problems of passing data from the EJB tier to a remote client, while the Generic Attribute Access patterns attempt to reduce the overhead of working with entity beans.)

The pernicious effects of unnecessarily using EJBs with remote interfaces include:

❑ Interface granularity and method signatures dictated by the desire to minimize the number of remote method calls. If business objects are naturally fine-grained (as is often the case), this results in unnatural design.

❑ The need for serialization determining the design of objects that will be communicated over RMI. For example, we must decide how much data should be returned with each serializable object – should we traverse associations and, if so, to what depth? We are also forced to write additional code to extract data needed by remote clients from any objects that are not serializable.

❑ A discontinuity in an application's business objects at the point of remote invocation.

These objections don't apply when we genuinely need distributed semantics. In this case, EJB isn't the cause of the problem but an excellent infrastructure for distributed applications. But if we don't need distributed semantics, using EJB has a purely harmful effect if it makes an application distributed. As we've discussed, distributed applications are much more complex than applications that run on a single server. EJB also adds some additional problems we may wish to avoid:

❑ **Using EJB may make simple things hard**
Some simple things are surprisingly difficult in EJB (with remote or local interfaces). For example, it's hard to implement the Singleton design pattern and to cache read-only data. EJB is a heavyweight technology, and makes heavy work of some simple problems.

❑ **Reduced choice of application servers**
There are more web containers than EJB containers, and web containers tend to be easier to use than EJB containers. Thus, a web application can run on a wider choice of servers – or cheaper versions of the same servers – compared to an EJB application, with simpler configuration and deployment (however, if we have a license for an integrated J2EE server, cost isn't a concern, and the EJB container may already be familiar through use in other projects).

These are important considerations. Most books ignore them, concentrating on theory rather than real-world experience.

Let's now review some of the arguments – good and bad – for using EJB in a J2EE application.

Questionable Arguments for Using EJB

Here are a few unconvincing arguments for using EJB:

- ❑ **To ensure clean architecture by exposing business objects as EJBs**
  EJB promotes good design practice in that it results in a distinct layer of business objects (session EJBs). However, the same result can be achieved with ordinary Java objects. If we use EJBs with remote interfaces, we are forced to use coarse-grained access to business objects to minimize the number of remote method calls, which forces unnatural design choices in business object interfaces.

- ❑ **To permit the use of entity beans for data access**
  I regard this as a poor reason for using EJB. Although entity beans have generated much interest, they have a poor track record. We'll discuss data access options for J2EE applications in more detail later.

- ❑ **To develop scalable, robust applications**
  Well-designed EJB applications scale well – but so do web applications. Also, EJB allows greater potential to get it wrong: inexperienced architects are more likely to develop a slow, unscalable system using EJB than without it. Only when a remote EJB interface is based on stateless session EJBs is a distributed EJB system likely to offer greater scalability than a web application, at the cost of greater runtime overhead. (In this approach, business objects can be run on as many servers as required.)

Compelling Arguments for Using EJB

Here are a few arguments that strongly suggest EJB use:

- ❑ **To allow remote access to application components**
  This is a compelling argument if remote access over RMI/IIOP is required. However, if web services style remoting is required, there's no need to use EJB.

- ❑ **To allow application components to be spread across multiple physical servers**
  EJBs offer excellent support for distributed applications. If we are building a distributed application, rather than adding web services to an application that isn't necessarily distributed internally, EJB is the obvious choice.

- ❑ **To support multiple Java or CORBA client types**
  If we need to develop a Java GUI client (using Swing or another windowing technology), EJB is a very good solution. EJB is interoperable with CORBA's IIOP and thus is a good solution for serving CORBA clients. As there is no web tier in such applications, the EJB tier provides the necessary middle tier. Otherwise, we return to the days of client-server applications and limited scalability because of inability to pool resources such as database connections on behalf of multiple clients.

- ❑ **To implement message consumers when an asynchronous model is appropriate**
  Message-driven beans make particularly simple JMS message consumers. This is a rare case in which EJB is "the simplest thing that could possibly work".

Arguments for Using EJB to Consider on a Case-by-Case Basis

The following arguments for using EJB should be assessed on a case-by-case basis:

❑ **To free application developers from writing complex multi-threaded code**
EJB moves the burden of synchronization from application developers to the EJB container. (EJB code is written as if it is single-threaded.) This is a boon, but whether it justifies the less desirable implications of using EJB depends on the individual application.

There's a lot of FUD (Fear, Uncertainty, and Doubt) revolving around the supposed necessity of using EJB to take care of threading issues. Writing threadsafe code isn't beyond a professional enterprise developer. We have to write threadsafe code in servlets and other web tier classes, regardless of whether we use EJB. Moreover, EJB isn't the sole way of simplifying concurrent programming. We don't need to implement our own threading solution from the ground up; we can use a standard package such as Doug Lea's util.concurrent. See http://gee.cs.oswego.edu/dl/classes/EDU/oswego/cs/dl/util/concurrent/intro.html for an overview of this package, which provides solutions to many common concurrency problems.

> EJB's simplification of multi-threaded code is a strong, but not decisive, argument for using EJB.

❑ **To use the EJB container's transparent transaction management**
EJBs may use **Container-Managed Transactions (CMT)**. This enables transaction management to be largely moved out of Java code and be handled declaratively in EJB deployment descriptors. Application code only needs to concern itself with transaction management if it wants to roll back a transaction. The actual rollback can be done with a single method call.

CMT is one of the major benefits of using EJB. Since enterprise applications are almost always transactional, without EJB CMT we will normally need to use the **Java Transaction API (JTA)**. JTA is a moderately complex API and it's thus advisable (but not essential) to avoid using it directly. As with threading, it's possible to use helper classes to simplify JTA programming and reduce the likelihood of errors.

Note that the J2EE transaction management infrastructure (for example, the ability to coordinate transactions across different enterprise resources) is available to all code running within a J2EE server, not merely EJBs; the issue is merely the API we use to control it.

> The availability of declarative transaction management via CMT is the most compelling reason for using EJB.

❑ **To use EJB declarative support for role-based security**
J2EE offers both **programmatic** and **declarative** security. While any code running in a J2EE server can find the user's security role and limit access accordingly, EJBs offer the ability to limit access declaratively (in deployment descriptors), down to individual business methods. Access permissions can thus be manipulated at deployment time, without any need to modify EJB code. If we don't use EJB, only the programmatic approach is available.

❑   **The EJB infrastructure is familiar**
    If the alternative to using EJB is to develop a substantial subset of EJB's capabilities, use of EJB is preferable even if our own solution appears simpler. For example, any competent J2EE developer will be familiar with the EJB approach to multi-threading, but not with a complex homegrown approach, meaning that maintenance costs will probably be higher. It's also better strategy to let J2EE server vendors maintain complex infrastructure code than to maintain it in-house.

> **EJBs are a good solution to problems of distributed applications and complex transaction management. However, many applications don't encounter these problems. EJBs add unnecessary complexity in such applications. An EJB solution can be likened to a truck and a web application to a car. When we need to perform certain tasks, such as moving large objects, a truck will be far more effective than a car, but when a truck and a car can do the same job, the car will be faster, cheaper to run, more maneuverable and more fun to drive.**

Accessing Data

Choice of data access technology is a major consideration in deciding whether to use EJB, as one of the choices (entity beans) is available only when using EJB. Data access strategy often determines the performance of enterprise systems, making it a crucial design issue.

Note that container support for data source connection pooling is available in the web container, not merely the EJB server.

J2EE Data Access Shibboleths

Many J2EE developers are inflexible regarding data access. The following assumptions, which have profound implications for design, are rarely challenged:

❑   Portability between databases is always essential

❑   **Object/Relational (O/R) mapping** is always the best solution when working with relational databases

I believe that these issues should be considered on a case-by-case basis. Database portability isn't free, and may lead to unnecessary complexity and the sacrifice of performance.

O/R mapping is an excellent solution in some cases (especially where data can be cached in the mapping layer), but often a "domain object model" must be shoehorned onto a relational database, with no concern for efficiency. In such cases, introducing an O/R mapping layer delivers little real value and can be disastrous for performance. On the positive side, O/R mapping solutions, if they are a good fit in a particular application, can free developers of the chore of writing database access code, potentially boosting productivity.

> **Whatever the data access strategy we use, it is desirable to decouple business logic from the details of data access, through an abstraction layer.**

It's often assumed that entity beans are the only way to achieve such a clean separation between data access and business logic. This is a fallacy. Data access is no different from any other part of a system where we may wish to retain a different option of implementation. We can decouple data access details from the rest of our application simply by following the good OO design principle of programming to interfaces rather than classes. This approach is more flexible than using entity beans since we are committed only to a Java interface (which can be implemented using any technology), not one implementation technology.

Entity Beans

Entity beans are a questionable implementation of a sound design principle. It's good practice to isolate data access code. Unfortunately, entity beans are a heavyweight way of achieving this, with a high runtime overhead. Entity beans don't tie us to a particular type of database, but do tie us to the EJB container and to a particular O/R mapping technology.

There exist serious doubts regarding the theoretical basis and practical value of entity beans. Tying data access to the EJB container limits architectural flexibility and makes applications hard to test. We are left with no choice regarding the other advantages and disadvantages of EJB. Once the idea of entity beans having remote interfaces is abandoned (as it effectively is in EJB 2.0), there's little justification for modeling data objects as EJBs at all.

Despite enhancements in EJB 2.0, entity beans are still under-specified. This makes it difficult to use them for solving many common problems (entity beans are a very basic O/R mapping standard). They often lead to inefficient use of relational databases, resulting in poor performance.

In Chapter 8 we'll examine the arguments surrounding entity bean use in detail.

Java Data Objects (JDO)

JDO is a recent specification developed under the Java Community Process that describes a mechanism for the persistence of Java objects to any form of storage. JDO is most often used as an O/R mapping, but it is not tied to RDBMSs. For example, JDO may become the standard API for Java access to ODBMSs. JDO offers a more lightweight model than entity beans. Most ordinary Java objects can be persisted as long as their persistent state is held in their instance data. Unlike entity beans, objects persisted using JDO do not need to implement any special interfaces. JDO also defines a query language for running queries against persistent data. It allows for a range of caching approaches, leaving the choice to the JDO vendor.

JDO is not currently part of J2EE. However, it seems likely that it will eventually become a required API in the same way as JDBC and JNDI.

JDO provides the major positives of entity beans while eliminating most of the negatives. It integrates well with J2EE server transaction management, but is not tied to EJB or even J2EE. The disadvantages are that JDO implementations are still relatively immature, and that as a JDO implementation doesn't come with most J2EE application servers, we need to obtain one from (and commit to a relationship with) a third-party vendor.

Other O/R Mapping Solutions

Leading O/R mapping products such as TopLink and CocoBase are more mature than JDO. These can be used anywhere in a J2EE application and offer sophisticated, high-performance O/R mapping, at the price of dependence on a third-party vendor and licensing cost comparable to J2EE application servers. These solutions are likely to be very effective where there is a natural O/R mapping.

JDBC

Implicit J2EE orthodoxy holds that JDBC and SQL (if not RDBMSs themselves) are evil, and that J2EE should have as little to do with them as possible. I believe that this is misguided. RDBMSs are here to stay, and this is not such a bad thing.

The JDBC API *is* low-level and cumbersome to work with. However, slightly higher-level libraries (such as the ones we'll use for this book's sample application) make it far less painful to work with. JDBC is best used when there is no natural O/R mapping, or when we need to use advanced RDBMS features like stored procedures. Used appropriately, JDBC offers excellent performance. JDBC isn't appropriate when data can naturally be cached in an O/R mapping layer.

State Management

Another crucial decision for J2EE architects is how to maintain server-side state. This will determine how an application behaves in a cluster of servers (clustering is the key to scalability) and what J2EE component types we should use.

It's important to decide whether or not an application requires server-side state. Maintaining server-side state isn't a problem when an application runs on a single server, but when an application must scale by running in a cluster, server-side state must be replicated between servers in the cluster to allow failover and to avoid the problem of **server affinity** (in which a client becomes tied to a particular server). Good application servers provide sophisticated replication services, but this inevitably affects performance and scalability.

If we do require server-side state, we should minimize the amount we hold.

> **Applications that do not maintain server-side state are more scalable than applications that do, and simpler to deploy in a clustered environment.**

If an application needs to maintain server-side state, we need to choose where to keep it. This depends partly on the kind of state that must be held: user interface state (such as the state of a user session in a web application), business object state, or both. Distributed EJB solutions produce maximum scalability with stateless session beans, regardless of the state held in the web tier.

J2EE provides two standard options for state management in web applications: HTTP session objects managed by the web container; and stateful session EJBs. Standalone clients must rely on stateful session beans if they need central state management, which is another reason why they are best supported by EJB architectures. Surprisingly, stateful session EJBs are not necessarily the more robust of the two options (we discuss this in Chapter 10) and the need for state management does not necessarily indicate the use of EJB.

J2EE Architectures

Now that we've discussed some of the high-level issues in J2EE design, let's look at some alternative architecture for J2EE applications.

Common Concepts

First, let's consider some concepts shared by all J2EE architectures.

Architectural Tiers in J2EE Applications

Each of the architectures discussed below involves three major tiers, although some introduce an additional division within the middle tier.

Experience has shown the value of cleanly dividing enterprise systems into multiple tiers. This ensures a clean division of responsibility.

The three-tier architecture of J2EE reflects experience in a wide range of enterprise systems. Systems with three or more tiers have proven more scalable and flexible than client server systems, in which there is no middle tier.

In a well-designed multi-tier system, each tier should depend only on the tier beneath it. For example, changes to the database should not demand changes to the web interface.

Concerns that are unique to each tier should be hidden from other tiers. For example, only the web tier in a web application should depend on the servlet API, while only the middle tier should depend on enterprise resource APIs such as JDBC. These two principles ensure that applications are easy to modify without changes cascading into other tiers.

Let's look at each tier of a typical J2EE architecture in turn.

Enterprise Information System (EIS) Tier

Sometimes called the **Integration Tier**, this tier consists of the enterprise resources that the J2EE application must access to do its work. These include **Database Management Systems (DBMSs)** and legacy mainframe applications. EIS tier resources are usually transactional. The EIS tier is outside the control of the J2EE server, although the server does manage transactions and connection pooling in a standard way.

The J2EE architect's control over the design and deployment of the EIS tier will vary depending on the nature of the project (green field or integration of existing services). If the project involves the integration of existing services, the EIS tier resources may impact on the implementation of the middle tier.

J2EE provides powerful capabilities for interfacing with EIS-tier resources, such as the JDBC API for accessing relational databases, JNDI for accessing directory servers, and the **Java Connector Architecture (JCA)** allowing connectivity to other EIS systems. A J2EE server is responsible for the pooling of connections to EIS resources, transaction management across resources, and ensuring that the J2EE application doesn't compromise the security of the EIS system.

Middle Tier

This tier contains the application's business objects, and mediates access to EIS tier resources. Middle tier components benefit most from J2EE container services such as transaction management and connection pooling. Middle-tier components are independent of the chosen user interface. If we use EJB, we split the middle tier into two: EJBs, and objects that use the EJBs to support the interface. However, this split isn't necessary to ensure a clean middle tier.

User Interface (UI) Tier

This tier exposes the middle-tier business objects to users. In web applications, the UI tier consists of servlets, helper classes used by servlets, and view components such as JSP pages. For clarity, we'll refer to the UI tier as the "web tier" when discussing web applications.

The Importance of Business Interfaces

Many regard EJBs as the core of a J2EE application. In an EJB-centric view of J2EE, session EJBs will expose the application's business logic, while other objects (such as "business delegate" objects in the web tier in the Business Delegate J2EE design pattern) will be defined by their relationship to the EJBs. This assumption, however, elevates a technology (EJB) above OO design considerations.

> **EJB is not the only technology for implementing the middle tier in J2EE applications.**

The concept of a formal layer of business interfaces reflects good practice, and we should use it regardless of whether we use EJB. In all the architectures we discuss below, the **business interface** layer consists of the middle-tier interfaces that clients (such as the UI tier) use directly. The business interface layer defines the contract for the middle tier in ordinary Java interfaces; EJB is thus one implementation strategy. If we don't use EJB, the implementation of the business interfaces will be ordinary Java objects, running in a J2EE web container. When we do use EJBs, the implementations of the business interfaces will conceal interaction with the EJB tier.

> **Design to Java interfaces, not concrete classes, and not technologies.**

Let's now look at four J2EE architectures that satisfy different requirements.

Non-distributed Architectures

The following architectures are suitable for web applications. They can run all application components in a single JVM. This makes them simple and efficient but limits the flexibility of deployment.

Web Application with Business Component Interfaces

In most cases, J2EE is used to build web applications. Thus, a J2EE web container can provide the entire infrastructure required by many applications.

J2EE web applications enjoy virtually the same access to enterprise APIs as EJBs. They benefit from the J2EE server's transaction management and connection pooling capabilities and can use enterprise services such as JMS, JDBC, JavaMail, and the Java Connector API. All data access technologies are available with the exception of entity beans.

The web tier and middle tier of a web application run in the same JVM. However, it is vital that they are kept logically distinct. The main design risk in web applications is that of blurred responsibilities between UI components and business logic components.

The business interface layer will consist of Java interfaces implemented by ordinary Java classes.

This is a simple yet scalable architecture that meets the needs of most applications.

The following diagram illustrates this design. The dashed horizontal lines indicate the divisions between the application's three tiers:

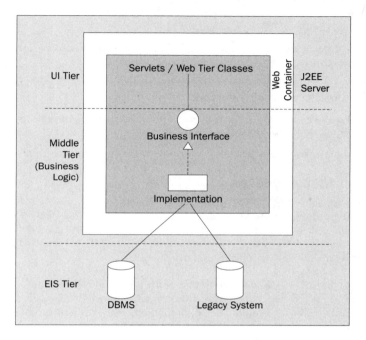

Strengths

This architecture has the following strengths:

- ❑ Simplicity. This is usually the simplest architecture for web applications. However, if transaction management or threading issues require the development of unduly complex code, it will probably prove simpler to use EJB.

- ❑ Speed. Such architectures encounter minimal overhead from the J2EE server.

- ❑ OO design isn't hampered by J2EE component issues such as the implications of invoking EJBs.

- ❑ Easy to test. With appropriate design, tests can be run against the business interface without the web tier.

- ❑ We can leverage the server's transaction support.

- ❑ Scales well. If the web interface is stateless, no clustering support is required from the container. However, web applications can be distributed, using server support session state replication.

Weaknesses

The following drawbacks should be kept in mind:

❑ This architecture supports only a web interface. For example, it cannot support standalone GUI clients. (The middle tier is in the same JVM as the web interface.) However, a layer of web services can be added, as we shall see later.

❑ The whole application runs within a single JVM. While this boosts performance, we cannot allocate components freely to different physical servers.

❑ This architecture cannot use EJB container transaction support. We will need to create and manage transactions in application code.

❑ The server provides no support for concurrent programming. We must handle threading issues ourselves or use a class library such as `util.concurrent` that solves common problems.

❑ It's impossible to use entity beans for data access. However, this is arguably no loss.

Web Application that Accesses Local EJBs

The Servlet 2.3 specification (SRV.9.11), which can be downloaded from http://java.sun.com/products/servlet/download.html, guarantees web-tier objects access to EJBs via local interfaces if an application is deployed in an integrated J2EE application server running in a single JVM. This enables us to benefit from the services offered by an EJB container, without incurring excessive complexity or making our application distributed.

In this architecture, the web tier is identical to that of the web application architecture we've just considered. The business interfaces are also identical; the difference begins with their implementation, which faces the EJB tier. Thus the middle tier is divided into two (business interfaces running in the web container and EJBs), but both parts run within the same JVM.

Two approaches can be used to implement the business interfaces:

❑ A **proxy** approach, in which a local EJB implements the business interface directly and web container code is given a reference to the EJB's local interface, without needing to handle the necessary JNDI lookup.

❑ A **business delegate** approach, in which the web-container implementation of the business interfaces explicitly delegates to the appropriate EJB. This has the advantage of permitting caching and allowing failed operations to be retried where appropriate.

We don't need to worry about catching `java.rmi.RemoteException` in either case. Transport errors cannot occur.

In this architecture, unlike an architecture exposing a remote interface via EJB, the use of EJB is simply an implementation choice, not a fundamental characteristic of the architecture. Any of the business interfaces can be implemented without using EJB without changing the overall design.

This is an effective compromise architecture, made possible by the enhancements in the EJB 2.0 specification:

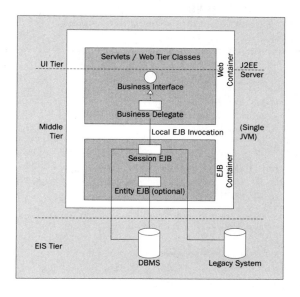

Strengths

This architecture has the following strengths:

- ❏ It's less complex than a distributed EJB application.

- ❏ EJB use doesn't alter the application's basic design. In this architecture, only make those objects EJBs that need the services of an EJB container.

- ❏ EJB use imposes relatively little performance overhead as there is no remote method invocation or serialization.

- ❏ It offers the benefits of EJB container transaction and thread management.

- ❏ It allows the use of entity beans if desired.

Weaknesses

Its drawbacks are as follows:

- ❏ It's more complex than a pure web application. For example, it encounters EJB deployment and class loading complexity.

- ❏ It still cannot support clients other than a web interface unless we add a web services layer.

- ❏ The whole application still runs within a single JVM, which means that all components must run on the same physical server.

- ❏ EJBs with local interfaces are hard to test. We need to run test cases within the J2EE server (for example, from servlets).

- ❏ There is still some temptation to tweak object design as a result of using EJB. Even with local interfaces, EJB invocations are slower than ordinary method calls, and this may tempt us to modify the natural granularity of business objects.

Sometimes we may decide to introduce EJB into an architecture that does not use it. This may result from the XP approach of "doing the simplest thing that could possibly work". For example, the initial requirements might not justify the complexity introduced by EJB, but the addition of further requirements might suggest its use.

If we adopt the business component interface approach described above, introducing EJBs with local interfaces will not pose a problem. We can simply choose the business component interfaces that should be implemented to proxy EJBs with local interfaces.

Introducing EJBs with remote interfaces may be more problematic, as this is not merely a question of introducing EJB, but of fundamentally changing the nature of the application. For example, business interface granularity may need to be made more coarse-grained to avoid "chatty" calling and achieve adequate performance. We will probably also want to move all business logic implementation inside the EJB container.

Distributed Architectures

The following two architectures support remote clients as well as web applications.

Distributed Application with Remote EJBs

This is widely regarded as the "classic" J2EE architecture. It offers the ability to split the middle tier physically and logically by using different JVMs for EJBs and the components (such as web components) that use them. This is a complex architecture, with significant performance overhead:

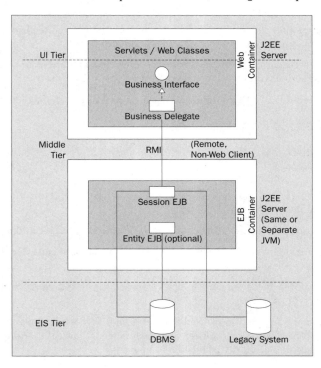

Although the diagram shows a web application, this architecture can support any J2EE client type. It is particularly suited to the needs of standalone client applications.

This architecture uses RMI between the UI tier (or other remote clients) and the business objects, which are exposed as EJBs (the details of RMI communication are concealed by the EJB container, but we still need to deal with the implications of its use). This makes remote invocation a major determinant of performance and a central design consideration. We must strive to minimize the number of remote calls (avoiding "chatty" calling). All objects passed between the EJB and EJB client tiers must be serializable, and we must deal with more complex error handling requirements.

The web tier in this architecture is the same as in the ones we've discussed above. However, the implementations of the business interface will handle remote access to EJBs in the (possibly remote) EJB container. Of the two connectivity approaches we discussed for local EJBs (proxy and business delegate), only the business delegate is useful here, as all methods on EJB remote interfaces throw `javax.rmi.RemoteException`. This is a checked exception. Unless we use a business delegate to contact EJBs and wrap RMI exceptions as fatal runtime exceptions or application exceptions, `RemoteExceptions` will need to be caught in UI-tier code. This ties it inappropriately to an EJB implementation.

The EJB tier will take sole charge of communication with EIS-tier resources, and should contain the application's business logic.

Strengths

This architecture has the following unique strengths:

- ❏ It can support all J2EE client types by providing a shared middle tier.

- ❏ It permits the distribution of application components across different physical servers. This works particularly well if the EJB tier is stateless, allowing the use of stateless session EJBs. Applications with stateful UI tiers but stateless middle tiers will benefit most from this deployment option and will achieve the maximum scalability possible for J2EE applications.

Weaknesses

The weaknesses of this architecture are:

- ❏ This is the most complex approach we've considered. If this complexity isn't warranted by the business requirements, it's likely to result in wasted resources throughout the project lifecycle and provide a breeding ground for bugs.

- ❏ It affects performance. Remote method calls can be hundreds of times slower than local calls by reference. The effect on overall performance depends on the number of remote calls necessary.

- ❏ Distributed applications are hard to test and debug.

- ❏ All business components must run in the EJB container. While this offers a comprehensive interface for remote clients, it is problematic if EJB cannot be used to solve every problem posed by the business requirements. For example, if the Singleton design pattern is a good fit, it will be hard to implement satisfactorily using EJB.

- ❏ OO design is severely hampered by the central use of RMI.

- ❏ Exception handling is more complex in distributed systems. We must allow for transport failures as well as application failures.

When using this architecture, don't subvert it. For example, Sun Java Center's "Fast Lane Reader" J2EE pattern (http://java.sun.com/blueprints/patterns/j2ee_patterns/fast_lane_reader/) advocates performing read-only JDBC access from the web tier so as to minimize the overhead of calling through the EJB tier. This violates the principle that each tier should only communicate with those immediately above on beneath it. It also reduces the deployment flexibility that is a key virtue of the distributed architecture. Now servers running the web tier must be able to access the database, which may necessitate special firewall rules.

Even if we use remote interfaces, most J2EE servers can optimize out remote invocations and substitute call by reference if EJBs and components that use them are collocated. This may greatly reduce the performance impact of using EJBs with remote interfaces but cannot undo the harmful effects that remote semantics introduce. This configuration changes the semantics of the application. For this configuration to be used, it's vital to ensure that the EJBs support local invocation (by reference) and remote invocation (by value). Otherwise, callers by reference may modify objects to be passed to other callers with serious consequences.

> **Do not let the use of EJBs with remote interfaces cause an application to be distributed unless business requirements dictate a distributed architecture.**

Web Application Exposing Web Services Interface

The emergence of web services standards such as SOAP means that J2EE applications are no longer tied to using RMI and EJB to support remote clients. The following architecture can support non-J2EE clients such as Microsoft applications:

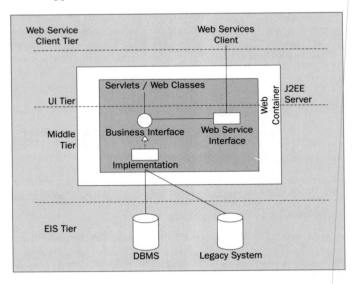

This architecture adds an object layer exposing the web services, and a transport layer implementing the necessary protocols, to any J2EE application. Web services components may either run in the same web container as a traditional web interface, or the web service interface may be the only one exposed by the application.

The object layer may be simply the application's business interfaces. The details of the transport layer will vary (J2EE does not presently standardize support for web services), but J2EE servers such as WebLogic make it easy to implement. Third-party products such as Apache Axis provide easy SOAP web services support on any J2EE server. For example, Axis provides a servlet that can be added to any web application and can publish any application class, including generating WSDL, as a web service. This is a very simple operation.

This architecture differs from the distributed EJB architecture we've just described not only in remoting protocol, but in that remote interfaces are typically added onto an existing application, rather than built into the structure of the application.

The diagram opposite shows web services being exposed by a web application without EJB. We can use this approach to add web services to any of the three architectures we've described (especially the first or second. The use of web services remoting removes one major reason to use EJBs with remote interfaces).

It's possible that web services protocols such as SOAP will eventually supplant platform-specific protocols such as RMI. This seems to be Microsoft's belief as it moves away from its proprietary DCOM remoting technology.

Strengths

These are the strengths of this architecture:

❑ SOAP is more open than RMI/IIOP. This architecture can support clients other than J2EE-technology clients, such as VB applications.

❑ Exposing a web services interface may be more beneficial for business than exposing an RMI/IIOP interface.

❑ Web services transport protocols run over HTTP and are more firewall-friendly and human-readable than RMI.

❑ The delivery of remote access is an add-on that doesn't dictate overall architecture. For example, we can choose whether to use EJB, based on the best way of implementing an application, rather than how it will be accessed.

Weaknesses

The weaknesses of this architecture are:

❑ Performance. The overhead of passing objects over an XML-based protocol such as SOAP is likely to be higher than that of RMI.

❑ If all client types use J2EE technology, this architecture is inferior to a distributed EJB architecture. In such cases, there's little justification for using a platform-independent remoting protocol.

❑ Marshaling and unmarshaling of complex objects may require custom coding. Objects will be passed down the wire in XML. We may have to convert Java objects to and from XML.

❑ Even though SOAP is now widely accepted, there is currently no standardization of Java web services support comparable to the EJB specification.

EJB applications can also expose web services. WebLogic and some other servers allow direct exposure of EJBs as web services.

Web Tier Design

Although J2EE allows for different client types, web applications are the most important in practice. Today even many intranet applications use web interfaces.

The four architectures discussed above do not differ in the design of their web interfaces, but in the manner that they implement and access business logic. The following discussion of web interface design applies to all four architectures.

The web tier is responsible for translating gestures and displays understood by users to and from operations understood by the application's business objects.

> It's important that the web tier is a distinct layer that sits on the middle-tier business interfaces. This ensures that the web tier can be modified without altering business objects and that business objects can be tested without reference to the web tier.

In a web application, the web tier is likely to be the part subjected to the most frequent change. Many factors, such as branding changes, the whims of senior management, user feedback, or changes in business strategy, may drive significant modifications in a web site's look and feel. This makes designing the web tier a major challenge.

The key to ensuring that the web tier is responsive to change is to ensure a clean separation between presentation on the one hand, and control logic and access to business objects on the other. This means making sure that each component focuses either on markup generation or processing user actions and interacting with business objects.

The Model View Controller (MVC) Architectural Pattern

A proven way of achieving separation between presentation and logic is to apply the MVC architectural pattern to web applications. The MVC architecture was first documented for Smalltalk user interfaces, and has been one of the most successful OO architectural patterns. It is also the basis of Java's Swing interface packages. MVC divides the components needed to build a user interface into three kinds of object, ensuring clean separation of concerns:

- ❑ A model data or application object – contains no presentation-specific code
- ❑ A view object performs screen presentation of model data
- ❑ A controller object reacts to user input and updates the model accordingly

We'll discuss the design of the web tier in detail in Chapter 12, but let's take a look at how a variant of the MVC pattern can be implemented in J2EE.

In J2EE applications, the web tier will be based on servlets. JSP pages and other presentational technologies such as XSLT will be used to render content.

A typical implementation involves having a standard **controller servlet** as a single point of entry into an entire application or subset of application URLs. This entry point chooses one of multiple application-specific **request controllers** to handle the request. (The mappings will be defined in configuration, outside Java code.) The controller servlet is effectively a controller of controllers. There's no standard term for what I call a "request controller" – the Struts web application framework calls such delegates **actions**.

A request controller or action corresponds to the controller in the MVC triad. It produces no output itself but processes requests, initiates business operations, optionally manipulates session and application state, and redirects requests to the appropriate **view**, where it exposes a model resulting from its processing.

Model, view, and controller objects map onto J2EE components as follows:

❏ A model is a JavaBean that exposes data. A model object should not know how to retrieve data from business objects, but instead, should expose bean properties that enable its state to be initialized by a controller. Thus, the rendering of a view will never fail because of reasons such as failure to retrieve data. This greatly simplifies error handling in the presentation tier (it is also possible to use XML documents as models).

❏ A view is a component that is used to display the data in a model. A view should never perform business logic or obtain data other than that which is made available to it in a model. View components in J2EE systems are most often JSP pages. Each view in this architectural pattern is analogous to one implementation of a simple contract ("display a certain set of objects"). Thus, each view can be replaced with another view that displays the same model differently, without altering the application's behavior.

❏ A controller is a Java class that handles incoming requests, interacts with business objects, builds models, and forwards each request to the appropriate view. A request controller does not implement business logic (this would impinge on the responsibilities of the middle tier).

Each component type is used to its strengths; Java classes (request controllers) handle logic, not presentation, while JSP pages focus on generating markup.

The following sequence diagram illustrates the flow of control. The controller servlet will be a standard class provided by a framework such as Struts (there is seldom any need to implement an MVC framework in house, since many implementations are available as open source). The request controller is part of the application's UI tier, and uses the business interface, as part of the middle tier in each of our four architectures. The view might be a JSP page:

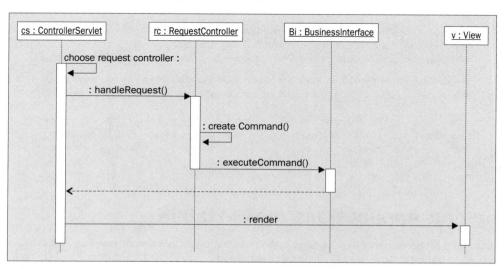

The sequence diagram overleaf shows the use of the Command design pattern, which encapsulates requests to a subsystem as objects. In J2EE web applications, the Command design pattern promotes clean connectivity between web tier and middle tier through non web-specific command objects. In this example, command objects are created to encapsulate the information contained in HTTP requests, but the same command objects could also be used with other user interfaces without any impact on business objects.

> *Readers familiar with the "Core J2EE Patterns" will note that I've described the Service-to-Worker presentation tier pattern. I don't recommend the Dispatcher View pattern, which allows data retrieval to be initiated by views. I discuss the drawbacks of this approach in Chapter 12.*

Systems built using the MVC approach tend to be flexible and extensible. Since presentation is separated from logic, it's possible to change an application's presentation significantly without affecting its behavior. It's even possible to switch from one view technology to another (for example, from JSP to XSLT) without significant change to application logic.

> **Use the MVC architectural pattern in the web tier. Use a web application framework such as Struts to provide a standard implementation of the MVC pattern, minimizing the amount of application code you will need to write.**

Connectivity Between the Web Tier and Business Objects

It's vital that the web-tier is cleanly separated from business objects. While the MVC pattern results in a clean separation between web-tier controllers and presentation objects (which hold formatting), it's no less important to separate web tier controllers (which are still tied to the Servlet API) from business objects (which are interface-agnostic).

In later chapters we look at infrastructure that promotes good practice in this respect. For now, let's consider the key goals:

❏ Web-tier components should never implement business logic themselves. If this goal is met, it is possible to test business logic without the web tier (making testing much easier). Meeting this goal also ensures that business logic cannot be broken by changes to the web tier.

❏ A standard infrastructure should make it easy for the web tier to access business objects and still allow business objects to be created and tested easily without the web tier.

> **In a well-designed J2EE web application, the web tier will be very thin. It will only contain code that's necessary to invoke middle-tier business interfaces on user actions and to display the results.**

Designing Applications for Portability

J2EE does an excellent job of standardizing middleware concepts in a portable manner. Java itself runs on almost all operating systems used in enterprise applications. Yet the J2EE specifications alone do not guarantee the infrastructure to help solve all real-world problems (J2EE 1.3 does, however, close the gap).

It's wrong to argue, as proponents of .NET do, that J2EE portability is meaningless. However, we do need to take care to ensure that we are able to retain as much portability as possible even if we choose or are forced to leverage the particular capabilities of the initial target platform. This can be achieved in three ways:

❑ Write code that complies with the J2EE specifications.

❑ Know the capabilities of the standard J2EE infrastructure and avoid using platform-specific solutions when a satisfactory standard alternative exists.

❑ Use loose coupling to isolate the use of platform-specific features, to ensure that the application's design (if not all its code) remains portable.

We use loose coupling to isolate the rest of our application from any parts of it that must be implemented in a platform-specific way through using an **abstraction layer**: an interface (or set of interfaces) that is itself platform-independent. These interfaces can be implemented for the target platform to take advantage of its special capabilities. They can be implemented differently without affecting the rest of the application if it's necessary to port to another platform.

> **We must distinguish between implementation portability ("this code runs without change on any application server") and design portability ("this application will work correctly and efficiently on any application server, if a small number of clearly identified interfaces are re-implemented"). Total implementation portability can be achieved in J2EE, but may not be a realistic or even a very worthwhile outcome. Design portability is achievable, and delivers most of the business value of portability. Even when portability is not a business requirement, design portability should flow from good OO design practice.**

At times in real-world situations, we might need to use vendor-specific extensions offered by our application server, or non-portable extensions offered by resources such as databases. Sometimes, there is no other way of implementing required functionality. Sometimes, performance requirements dictate a platform-specific solution. Such situations demand a pragmatic approach. J2EE architects and developers are, after all, employed to deliver cost-effective solutions that meet or exceed requirements, not to write "pure" J2EE applications.

Let's consider some typical issues that may force us to use vendor-specific extensions:

❑ **The limitations of EJB QL**
If we use EJB 2.0 entity beans with CMP, we're likely to encounter the limitations of EJB QL. For example, it doesn't offer aggregate functions or an ORDER BY clause. We will need to consider using database-specific functionality or vendor-specific enhancements in such cases (WebLogic, for example, offers extensions to EJB QL).

❑ **Access to proprietary features of EIS-tier components**
Quite rightly, the J2EE specifications don't attempt to address the requirements of different data sources. However, there are situations when we must use non-portable features of such resources. For example, there isn't a standard way of performing a batch update or invoking a stored procedure using CMP entity beans when the underlying data store is a relational database. Yet, these operations may be necessary for performance reasons.

The best way to preserve portability in such cases is to use a portable abstraction layer and a specific implementation for the target platform. In special cases, such as the limitations of EJB QL, we could gamble on standard support being in place before there is any need to port the application, or that other container vendors will also provide similar proprietary extensions.

> **Don't reject vendor-specific enhancements or EIS resource-specific functionality, which may produce significant benefits. Instead, ensure that these can be accessed without compromising design portability.**
>
> **Application portability results from good design. If we localize vendor-specific functionality and ensure that it is accessed through vendor-independent interfaces, we can take full advantage of valuable features of each target platform without compromising the portability of our overall design.**

Summary

In this chapter, we've taken a high-level look at J2EE architecture. We've considered:

- ❑ The advantages and disadvantages of adopting a distributed architecture. Distributed applications are more complex, harder to implement, test, and maintain than applications in which all components are collocated. Distributed applications can also exhibit disappointing performance, unless designed carefully. However, distributed applications can be more robust and scalable in some cases and a distributed architecture may be the only way to meet some business requirements. Thus deciding whether to use a distributed architecture is an important decision that should be made early in the project lifecycle. It's best to avoid a distributed architecture unless it delivers real advantages.

- ❑ The implications for J2EE architecture of the enhancements in the EJB 2.0 specification and the emergence of web services. EJB 2.0 allows us to access EJBs running in the same JVM using call-by-reference, through local interfaces. Thus EJB 2.0 allows us to use EJB without forcing us to adopt a distributed architecture. Web services protocols enable us to support remote clients without using EJB, as RMI-based remoting protocols are no longer the only choice for J2EE applications. Which of these approaches to remoting is preferable depends on the needs of any remote clients the application must support.

- ❑ Deciding when to use EJB. EJB is a complex, powerful technology that solves some problems very well, but is inappropriate in many applications. In particular, we should not let desire to use EJB make an application distributed when it is not otherwise necessary.

- ❑ Some of the major issues in data access in J2EE applications, notably:

  - ❑ Database portability. While J2EE can deliver portability between target databases, this does not always produce business value. Thus database portability may not justify any sacrifices in terms of performance or productivity.

  - ❑ Major data access strategies. We've discussed the choice between O/R mapping strategies such as entity beans and JDO, and SQL-oriented, JDBC-based persistence. Choosing the correct data access strategy for an application can have a huge impact on performance and ease of implementation.

❑ The importance of concealing the details of data access from business objects via an abstraction layer. If this abstraction layer will consist of ordinary Java interfaces, we are free to use any data access strategy and able to leverage proprietary capabilities of any target database without compromising the portability of our overall design.

❑ The importance of a tiered architecture, in which each architectural tier depends only on the tier immediately beneath it. This ensures clean separation of concerns and ensures that changes to one tier do not cascade into other tiers.

❑ Four J2EE architectures, their strengths and disadvantages:

❑ **Web application with business component interfaces**
This is a simple, performant architecture that meets the requirements of many projects. Although it does not use EJB, it still delivers a clean separation between business objects and web-tier components. A layer of business component interfaces exposes all the application's business logic to web-tier components.

❑ **Web application accessing local EJBs**
This is a slightly more complex architecture that allows us to use EJB container services to provide thread and transaction management without making the application distributed or suffering the performance overhead of remote method invocation.

❑ **Distributed application with remote EJBs**
This is a significantly more complex architecture that is ideal for meeting the needs of remote J2EE-technology clients. This architecture is more scalable and robust than the other architectures in some cases. However, it is harder to implement, maintain, and test than the simpler architectures we've discussed, and usually delivers inferior performance, compared to a non-distributed architecture meeting the same requirements.

❑ **Web application exposing web services interface**
This architecture enables us to support non J2EE-technology clients by adding a web services layer to an application that is not distributed internally. This architecture is normally a variant of the first or second architectures discussed above.

❑ Web-tier design issues, and the importance of using the MVC architectural pattern. Within the web tier, separation between presentation and logic is vital to the delivery of maintainable web applications that can respond to changing presentational requirements. It's also vital that the web tier should be a thin layer on top of a J2EE application's business interfaces and that as little of an application as possible should depend on the Servlet API.

> **Good OO design practice is fundamental to a sound architecture. J2EE technologies should be applied in pursuit of a sound object model, and should not dictate the object model itself.**

J2EE Projects: Choices and Risks

Enterprise software projects are often large and costly. The challenges they face may include:

❑ Integrating resources within an organization. Enterprise applications may need to access multiple data sources and legacy systems, using a variety of technologies. Integration of multiple technologies is inherently risky.

❑ Working with complex products such as application servers and databases.

❑ Meeting demanding expectations of quality of service, performance, and scalability.

❑ Developing and maintaining a large codebase.

❑ Introducing new technologies to an organization – for example, when a legacy application is web-enabled. Sometimes the technologies are themselves new, posing a risk that they may be unfamiliar or immature.

❑ Successful running of teams with a disparate skill set.

❑ Achieving rapid time-to-market in a competitive environment.

The J2EE platform helps us to address many of the problems of enterprise software development. However, choosing J2EE is just the first of many choices.

Choices made early in the development lifecycle – before any code has been written – have a vital influence on the success or failure of projects, and how investment is directed. Decisions taken in the inception phase of a project will determine how it unfolds.

It is also vital to manage risk in J2EE projects, especially where integration is involved.

In this chapter, we discuss some of the most important choices, besides software architecture, in J2EE projects. Many of these choices involve tradeoffs that will vary with the needs of each application. Often there is no single "right" answer. We'll try to cover some major issues and discuss the decision making process, though particular choices will be left to the reader.

In some projects, many of these choices will have already been made as part of an existing J2EE strategy. However, even architects and developers working on such projects should be familiar with the issues discussed in this chapter.

Developing a Policy on Specification Versions

The first decision to be made is your organization's attitude towards specification and language versions. Is it important to use the latest J2EE and J2SE features? This is a tradeoff between enhanced feature sets and proven functionality.

Decisive factors will include:

❑ **The nature of the application**
A minority of applications may benefit so much from the latest J2SE and J2EE features that there is little alternative to using them.

❑ **The length of the project**
For a large and lengthy project, it may be possible to predicate strategy on new, published features and defer the implementation of those parts of the application that need them until server support is more mature. For a short project, it will be most important to deliver a solution quickly using proven technology. Note that predicating even a lengthy project on new features in *non-final* J2EE specifications is very risky, and therefore inadvisable, even when "preview" implementations exist. The EJB 2.0 specification, for example, changed radically in successive public drafts.

❑ **The nature of the organization**
A "wait until it works" approach might be appropriate for an organization that prizes technological firsts, but inappropriate for a financial institution or other organization in which reliability is critical. The organization's skill base in the new technologies is another important consideration here.

❑ **Portability between application servers**
The later the specification versions adopted, the more problematic portability is likely to prove, as the choice of alternative servers implementing the same specification level will be limited.

Version choice will both influence and be influenced by the choice of application server.

New server and specification releases are likely during the lifecycle of large projects. It's also important to decide whether to upgrade when this happens. If the new release is a bug fix or point release, it may be a worthwhile and inexpensive undertaking. If it's a major upgrade, think carefully before committing, as there may be many implications, such as different tool requirements, new server bugs, and different support requirements. It's difficult to keep up with a moving target, and J2EE is still moving rapidly.

> To minimize risk, steer clear of new, unproven technologies, even if they seem attractive. One safe policy is to target the versions of the J2SE and J2EE specifications that are supported by the mainstream application server vendors at project inception, although some projects may need to take future server release schedules into account.

Choosing an Application Server

Choosing a J2EE application server is one of the most important IT decisions an organization will make. Adopting J2EE is a strategic decision, so how it's done will have a lasting effect. Many application servers are expensive, requiring significant outlay on licenses for large installations. However, the cost of the server is only a part of the story. Even when choosing a free server such as JBoss, we are making a significant commitment. Expenses over and above license costs are likely to include:

❑ Training costs. Server vendors usually offer product-specific training, and many application servers are complex enough to warrant purchasing it for key personnel. However, training is often expensive, unless offered as an incentive to purchase licenses.

❑ Consulting costs. It may be necessary to purchase consulting services from the server vendor or a third party while getting up to speed with the application server.

❑ Any support costs. With some vendors, support requires an additional contract, and adds to license costs.

❑ Loss of productivity while getting up to speed with a new server, along with the loss of developer time during training or mentoring.

The virtue of having a marketplace for servers is that different servers fit different requirements. Comparisons rapidly become outdated and misleading, and can't be kept up-to-date in book form. Hence we'll discuss the issues to be considered while making a choice here, rather than recommend or compare products. In this section we look at:

❑ When to choose an application server

❑ How to choose an application server

❑ Who should choose an application server

Note that the ideal is to standardize on a single application server throughout an organization. Maintaining multiple application servers will prove expensive throughout the software lifecycle, and should be avoided if possible. Usually, the use of several different application servers in an organization reflects historical accident or lack of a coherent strategy.

One of the few valid technical reasons for running more than one application server in an organization is when a few applications depend on a particular feature that is unavailable in the application server normally used: for example, when one application requires features from the latest release of J2EE and therefore must run on a recently released application server, while most applications run on a proven application server. In this case, the long-term aim will usually be to return to the use of a single server.

45

> In many cases, the application server will have been chosen before the project begins. For example, there may be an organization-wide policy regarding application server choice. In this case, try to work with the chosen server. Don't introduce another based on your or your team's preferences, complicating the organization's technology mix. If the chosen product is demonstrably inferior, and it's still realistic to abandon it, lobby to have the choice changed.

When to Choose an Application Server

It's wisest to choose an application server early in the project lifecycle. This has the following advantages:

- ❑ No effort is wasted working with the wrong server. Getting up to speed with an application server – even a new major release of the same product – takes time and effort. The more times we need to do it during a project, the less effort we can devote to designing and developing applications.

- ❑ The entire project lifecycle can be used to perfect a development, deployment, and administration strategy for the targeted server that meets the needs of your organization. J2EE application servers are complex, and achieving efficiency in this area is vital.

- ❑ There is more time to build a strong relationship with the server vendor.

It's important to recognize that the potential to port J2EE applications between servers does not mean that a J2EE server can be chosen at leisure. The same considerations apply as to other important enterprise products such as databases. The longer a choice is deferred, the more familiarization time is wasted and the less potential there is to make use of valuable features of the eventual choice.

The only advantage in choosing a server late is that the choice may be made after your team has gained J2EE experience. This is only a consideration if all team members are unfamiliar with J2EE, which itself is an unacceptable risk. Address this problem by hiring some J2EE specialists early in the project. A small pilot project is often a good idea to familiarize a team with both J2EE and a candidate server. Implementing a "vertical slice" of the planned application is also a good way of mitigating many other risks, such as inadequate performance.

> Choose an application server and other important software products such as a database as early as you can. Attempting to defer a choice because "J2EE applications are portable" is a recipe for wasting time and money.

While we should choose an application server early, we should still try to ensure that code is portable between application servers wherever possible. Working with a single server from early in the project lifecycle does mean that it is easy to write code that violates the J2EE specifications without realizing it. For example, many EJB containers allow violations of the EJB specification. However, undetected violations are a major cause of portability problems. There are good reasons why total code portability isn't always possible, but ignorance and carelessness aren't among them.

One strategy to avoid such inadvertent violations of the J2EE specifications is to deploy and test the application regularly on another server (it is much less likely that two servers will fail to detect violations). However, this strategy demands that resources are devoted to configuring the other server and mastering its deployment process, not merely testing the compliance of code. The J2EE Reference Implementation server is sometimes used for this purpose. However, as the Reference Implementation server is slow to start up and buggy, the open source JBoss server is probably a better choice if adopting this strategy. JBoss 3.0 does tight compliance checking and offers particularly simple application deployment.

A better strategy is to use the `verifier` tool that also ships with the J2EE Reference Implementation (available from http://java.sun.com/j2ee/download.html) to verify the compliance of all J2EE deployment units – WARs, EJB JARs, and EAR files. This tool gives excellent and helpful output. It can be invoked with commands like the following:

```
cd J2EE_SDK_HOME/bin
setenv
verifier -v  /path/to/ejb-jar-file.jar
```

The `-v` flag causes verbose output of all tests. The output will indicate either compliance (no failed tests) or list those tests that failed. A log file will be generated. The following is an example of log output on a failed test:

Test Name: tests.ejb.session.ejbcreatemethod.EjbCreateMethodFinal
Test Assertion: Each session Bean must have at least one non-final ejbCreate method test
Detailed Messages:

  For EJB Class [facade.ejb.JdbcReportEJB] method [ejbCreate]
  Error: A final [ejbCreate] method was found, but [ejbCreate] cannot be declared as final.

Verification can – and should – be integrated into the application build process, for example using the Jakarta Ant build tool (discussed below).

> **Regularly test the compliance of J2EE deployment units with the J2EE 1.3 Reference Implementation verifier tool. Integrate such verification into the application build process.**

Defining the Requirements

It's important that the process of server selection should be planned and transparent. Let's consider some of the steps and decisive criteria.

The first goal is to define the requirements of an application server. Unfortunately, few organizations do this. Many allow their selection process to be driven by vendor presentations and what they perceive as industry buzz. It's important to get past the marketing hype and to base the decision on the present and probable future needs of your organization.

Key criteria include:

❑   What are the performance and scalability requirements of the system? Be realistic. Many applications are never going to be the next Amazon, so may not require the most capable and scalable server.

❑   Does your organization prefer a commercial product or an open source product?

❑   What is the budget available for the application server choice and rollout?

47

We'll take a closer look at some of these below.

Evaluation Criteria

Let's take a look at some of the factors that should determine server choice.

Supported Specifications

Policy on specification versions (discussed above) will dictate how important a requirement is support of the latest J2EE specification (remember, however, that J2EE specifications are normally backward compatible – in the case of J2EE 1.3, wholly so):

❑ What level of the J2EE specifications (EJB, Servlet, JSP, J2EE) does the server implement?

❑ What is the vendor's strategy regarding specification releases? If the vendor simply doesn't bother to keep up, it may indicate that the product isn't viable. However, leading products have different strategies. BEA ensures that WebLogic supports each specification release as it appears. IBM, on the other hand, has traditionally adopted a more conservative policy with WebSphere, choosing to wait until the dust has settled on each specification release. (WebSphere seems to be picking up the pace since version 4.0, however.) Which approach is preferable depends on business need.

❑ Which version of Java does the server require? This may not necessarily be the same as the J2EE version. Java 1.4 offers significant language and library improvements, so it is a significant plus if the server is supported on JDK 1.4.

Sun Resources

Sun, as the custodian of the J2EE specifications, runs two application server evaluation programs: the **Compatibility Test Suite** and **ECPerf**. While the existence of these programs is important, as we'll see we cannot rely on them to guide our choice of server.

Let's look at the aims and practical value of these programs in turn.

The Compatibility Test Suite (CTS)

Sun publishes a J2EE CTS and maintains a list of products that have satisfied its requirements at http://java.sun.com/j2ee/compatibility.html. Products on this list may be marketed as "J2EE Compatible". The J2EE 1.3 CTS includes over 15,000 tests covering all classes and methods in the J2EE APIs, and interaction between J2EE services.

The CTS is a welcome development. In the early days of J2EE, no such guarantee was available, and servers often failed to deliver workable implementations of core J2EE features. The existence of the CTS motivates vendors to implement the J2EE specifications faithfully. It increases our confidence in our ability to port standards-compliant applications between servers.

However, the CTS is of limited help in choosing a server and cannot be used as a definitive guide, for the following reasons:

❏   Not all leading contenders appear in the list, as not all vendors have chosen to go through certification. For example, Orion server is not included (as of August 2002), although it's used in production more widely than several of the certified servers. The certification process is expensive, and until recently has discriminated against open source products. For this reason, JBoss has been unable to progress to certification, although it aims to comply with the J2EE specifications (and, in my experience, succeeds).

Remember that the CTS is a mixture of good intentions, politics, and marketing. See http://www.serverworldmagazine.com/opinionw/2002/03/14_j2ee.shtml for a discussion of the JBoss certification issue that concludes that the certification process "is only available to large, well-funded companies" and is therefore "unbalanced".

❏   The tests do not cover server performance or stability.

❏   The tests don't reveal whether all components of the server are ready for use in production. For example, many certified products take some of their functionality from Sun's J2EE Reference Implementation. Much of this code was never intended for use in production.

❏   The J2EE specifications alone do not meet the needs of an enterprise. Value-added features of a server, such as a performant and customizable CMP implementation, are essential to some applications. As more and more servers become compliant to the specifications, these value-added features are likely to become the major determinant of application server choice. Specification compliance alone is not a sufficient basis for choosing an application server.

❏   Some of the most demanding areas of the J2EE specifications – such as CMP entity beans – are of questionable value to real applications. Thus servers that are not fully compliant may deliver efficient, specification-compliant implementation of the most useful features of J2EE.

❏   The tests do not cover ease of server installation and deployment of applications on the server. This is an important issue, as some servers are notoriously difficult to configure, while others can be set up in minutes.

ECPerf

Performance and scalability issues are addressed by ECPerf, another initiative from Sun developed under the JCP. ECPerf is a benchmark application that tries to replicate real-world issues, for which performance results are independently certified. The ECPerf application is based on a relational database and uses CMP entity beans. The main ECPerf home page is at http://java.sun.com/j2ee/ecperf/. ECPerf results are hosted at http://ecperf.theserverside.com/ecperf/. The ECPerf application can be downloaded from the ECPerf home page.

As with the CTS, however, many servers have not submitted ECPerf results. As of August 2002, only five servers – WebLogic, WebSphere, Oracle, Sybase, and Pramati – are represented. ECPerf is useful to a point, but it's geared towards demonstrating performance on particular hardware configuration and with a specific RDBMS.

For example, it's possible to compare the performance of WebLogic on a cluster of HP servers using Oracle 8.1.7 with that of WebSphere on an IBM cluster using DB2. But this is no help if we want to predict the performance of WebLogic and WebSphere on the *same* hardware using the same database (typically hardware availability is largely predetermined and the RDBMS will already have been selected before we select a J2EE application server, so this is what we really need to know in practice). Also, ECPerf results have limited relevance if we use different application architecture such as session beans with JDBC or JDO instead of entity beans.

The Australian **Commonwealth Scientific and Industrial Research Organization (CSIRO)** provides a commercial performance comparison of some leading application servers, available at http://www.cmis.csiro.au/adsat/j2eev2.htm. Unlike ECPerf, this does compare application servers on the same hardware.

> Beyond their use in comparing application servers, ECPerf results are a valuable resource for performance tuning information. ECPerf results must fully document any modifications to default server configuration, such as JVM options, number of EJB containers used, and operating system settings.

Cost

J2EE application servers vary widely in license cost – from zero for JBoss to hundreds of thousands of dollars for a large installation of leading commercial products – and in how license cost are calculated (such as per CPU or per physical server).

In one episode of the wonderful 1980s British TV comedy "Yes, Prime Minister", the scheming civil servant Sir Humphrey Appleby attempts to persuade Prime Minister Jim Hacker to buy a particular type of nuclear missile irrespective of cost (and strategic requirement) because it is simply the best. Sir Humphrey's argument concludes with the stirring phrase "it is the nuclear missile Harrods would sell". In boom times like the dotcom frenzy of the late 1990s, such arguments carry great weight with senior management.

Sir Humphrey as a CTO or CIO (roles in which he would be at home in many companies) will argue that XYZ server is the most expensive, and therefore the best, and that it would reflect lack of confidence for the company not to buy it. He might add, with more justification, that the market expects his company to invest at least as much as its competitors in technology products. The board would probably be more skeptical about an open source solution. This (admittedly cynical) analysis, based on experience, is borne out by industry analysts such as the Gartner Group, who estimated that by late 2001 companies had wasted well over $1 billion on high-end application server technology they didn't really require (see http://www.nwfusion.com/news/2001/0821gartnerapp.html).

In the leaner times of 2001/2, companies are loath to spend money on software products, even to make a strategic investment. There's a tendency to spend as little money as possible initially, while leaving open the possibility of migrating to a more expensive platform, should it become necessary. This can prove even more expensive than overspending up front. Application server costs will only account for a fraction of a project's total budget; development teams cost much more to run. The cost – in customer perception, and staff time and morale – of limping along with an inadequate solution may soon outweigh any initial savings. Also, the uncertainty of a possible migration is a recipe for frustration and paralysis.

> Cost should not be used as the measure of an application server's worth. The true test is whether it meets the organization's needs. Remember to consider total cost of ownership. Outlay on an application server should be only a small proportion of total cost.

Vendor Relationship

Committing to a particular J2EE server means committing to a continuing relationship with the server vendor. The quality of presales advice may indicate the quality of the vendor's experts, but the organization's level of commitment to its customers is important. Some points to consider here are:

❑ Would your organization readily pay for support in addition to the price of the product?

❑ How do other users of the product find the support experience?

Open source products offer a different mix of support positives and negatives from commercial products. On the positive side:

❑ Flourishing open source products offer a wide range of support options, from free mailing lists to commercial consulting. The success of Red Hat demonstrates the viability of a model based on commercial offerings around an open source product.

❑ Developers of open source products are spread around the world and often work on weekends, meaning that you may get a response from the horse's mouth around the clock.

On the other hand, no company can be forced to take responsibility for fixing a problem. Open source developers are normally proud of the product they've contributed to and are often very helpful in fixing bugs and resolving users' problems. If your posting of a problem results in you being flamed rather than helped, you'll have no one to complain to. The archives of the JBoss mailing list display both these positives and negatives.

Open source support also tends to be more democratic than that provided by commercial products. Postings are likely to be given equal attention, whether they come from a single developer, a small or a large organization. Commercial server vendors, on the other hand, are likely to pay more attention to their relationships with key purchasers, meaning that large organizations that have purchased multiple or enterprise-wide licenses are likely to receive priority attention. This is one of the reasons that large enterprises rarely choose open source products.

Vendor Viability

Since its peak in 1999/2000, the application server market has experienced a shakeout due to an excessive number of players and difficult trading conditions. Several smaller players have withdrawn from the application server market to concentrate on their areas of special expertise, and this trend seems set to continue.

Thus, it's important to consider the viability of an application server when making a choice. In the worst case, what would happen if the product were no longer supported? This is especially dangerous if you have relied heavily on a particular capability of that server.

On the positive side, a small company may prove to be more responsive and more concerned about the needs of individual customers, and especially small individual customers.

Development and Deployment

Another important criterion in choosing a server is how easy it will prove to develop and deploy applications on. Ideally the server should not impose onerous proprietary requirements when developing and deploying applications, and should be quick to start up.

It's essential that new releases of software be rolled out without major impact. Ideally, it should be possible to do a release without shutting down the server.

Development and deployment considerations include:

❑ Speed of server startup, speed of application deployment and server memory requirements. These are important issues during development, but matter less in production, so we may need to accept a tradeoff here.

❑ Any additional, proprietary steps required in developing and deploying applications, such as the need to write complex proprietary deployment descriptors and any need to "compile" EJB JAR files before deployment.

❑ The ability to "hot deploy" applications (that is, deploy or redeploy them without shutting down the server).

❑ The sophistication (and reliability) of management tools provided by the server.

❑ Integration with management standards such as **Simple Network Management Protocol (SNMP)** and **Java Management Extensions (JMX)**.

❑ The quality of error reporting at run time. This will influence the server's usability. It's important that stack traces on exceptions can be generated, at least while debugging, and appear reliably in server logs. Servers vary in this regard.

❑ The quality of error reporting at deployment time. This can range from "something went wrong" to helpful messages that enable problems to be tracked down quickly.

Value-added Features

As more servers become J2EE compliant, reliability, scalability, and value-added features increasingly differentiate application servers. As the J2EE specifications don't meet all common requirements, this is inevitable. Value-added features that may prove important include:

❑ The quality of clustering support, including the level of fail-over delivered.

❑ The quality of the JMS solution included with the server. While any compliant server must provide a JMS implementation, some ship with the Sun Reference Implementation, meaning that a third-party messaging solution must be purchased before making mission-critical use of JMS.

❑ Performance. Application performance will be limited by that of the application server.

❑ Support for web services, a major growth area not yet covered by J2EE specifications. However, a third-party product can also deliver web services support. The Apache Axis SOAP package is particularly easy to use, and can add powerful web services capabilities to any server.

❑ Sophisticated support for entity beans with CMP, delivering features like optimistic locking, which are not mandated by the specification. Such features are essential to make CMP entity beans usable, as the specification neglects some important issues.

Quality of Documentation

Most vendors provide excellent free online documentation. This is a valuable resource during server evaluation. It's also a good idea to consider the availability of books and other independently authored resources relevant to the server. This consideration tends to favor the market-leading servers.

Availability of Skills

It's important to ensure that a significant subset of a project team has hands-on experience with the chosen server (rather than just J2EE), and that it's possible to hire more developers with experience using it. It's possible to measure the availability of server-specific skills by checking job sites for requirements from other companies; checking the popularity of any certification program run by the server vendor; and looking for local user groups devoted to the server (however, a developer with a deep understanding of J2EE will soon get up to speed with any server, and will ultimately outperform a developer with knowledge of a particular server but a shallow grasp of J2EE concepts).

Again, this consideration tends to work in favor of the market leading products. Remember that, because agencies and employers tend to look for products (such as WebLogic) rather than technologies (such as EJB) on resumes, many developers are wary about working on projects using obscure products they don't expect to have a big future.

User Experience

It's vital to talk to staff at organizations using each server you evaluate. Vendors should be able to provide reference sites. If possible, it's good to have informal conversation, without any salespeople present. It may be more revealing to talk to individual developers than to organize formal conference calls. Frustrating problems are more likely to be mentioned when talking off the record.

Most server vendors operate newsgroups or mailing lists. These are usually freely accessible, and provide a valuable insight into the experience of working with the products.

❑ Vendors don't usually moderate newsgroups, so newsgroups can be a useful indication of the level of bugs in the product. Are people debating the finer points of extreme applications, or finding basic problems in the product? What prevents them from getting into production? (Ignore the complaints of users who simply seem ignorant about J2EE or the product.)

❑ Newsgroups can be a valuable indication of how difficult it is to install and deploy applications on the product.

❑ How active are the newsgroups? Lack of activity might indicate a product that has proven unusable, or which is failing in the market.

❑ How quickly do people get responses? The more the number of reasonable questions unanswered, the more the likelihood of insufficient knowledge about the product in the community.

❑ Do any of the product's' developers regularly post to newsgroups? Are they helpful? This can happen in both the commercial and open source worlds. For example, many senior WebLogic developers make regular postings, as do JBoss developers.

The following links to newsgroups may prove a useful starting point:

❑ **WebLogic:** BEA hosts many active WebLogic newsgroups. The index is at http://newsgroups.bea.com/cgi-bin/dnewsweb.

❑ **Orion**: Follow the "Mailing List" link from the Orion server home page at http://www.orionserver.com.

❑ **JBoss:** The archives are at http://lists.sourceforge.net/lists/listinfo/jboss-user. There are also a number of forums at http://main.jboss.org/.

Choice Process

I recommend having a semi-formal process for application server choice to ensure that it is transparent and justified by the available evidence. Too much formality will result in endless committee meetings and the production of high-level documents divorced from reality. Too little formality will result in an ad hoc decision and inadequate documentation in case the decision is questioned in future (future deliberations may inadvertently cover the same ground).

The development team should be heavily involved in the final choice. I suggest the following inputs for consideration:

❑   Third-party reports, such as ECPerf and the CSIRO application server comparison.

❑   Commissioned report from a consulting organization or external expert with strong J2EE experience and no vested interests. This should relate to the specific project and enterprise requirements rather than be a standard report.

❑   Discussion of technical issues with presales experts from competing vendors.

❑   Evidence of each server's installed base.

❑   Discussion with other users of short-listed servers. A short list should be drawn up part way through the evaluation process, as the later steps will require significant time to be devoted to each server being evaluated.

❑   Quality of support.

❑   Cost.

❑   An in-house proof of concept, deployed and tested on each short-listed server. This raises many issues and is much more useful than merely running a "standard" application such as Sun's Java Pet Store.

Top Mistakes in Choosing an Application Server

In my experience, the following are some of the commonest (and costliest) mistakes in choosing an application server:

❑   Delusions of grandeur. Spending money and resources on a complex solution to a problem you don't have, even if it's a good solution. A special case of this is the scalability delusion. Although the usage of web applications can increase rapidly, it isn't always vital to be able to support a vast user population, and for many organizations it never will be. This mistake often leads to the waste of money on unnecessarily expensive licenses. An even more harmful result can be increase in costs throughout the project lifecycle because an unnecessarily sophisticated product is unnecessarily complex to administer, given the actual business requirements.

❑   Failure to consider total cost of ownership, and that license costs are only a part of it.

❑   Choosing a server without hands-on experience. No amount of third-party reports, benchmarks, and marketing hype substitutes for hands-on experience in-house by the developers who will build the applications that run on the server.

❑   Decisions handed down by senior management without consulting mere developers and architects. This mistake is sadly prevalent, and usually reflects a fear-based culture that will cripple projects in other ways.

❑ Purchasing a server considering only the requirements of the immediate application if more demanding requirements can reasonably be foreseen in the near future. This mistake is likely to result in an early migration exercise.

The "Neat Technology" Trap

All good developers are excited not only about the technologies they work with, but also about other elegant technologies. Outstanding developers can control this excitement when it's likely to cost their employers money.

Developers have a natural conflict of interest with respect to the use of new and interesting technologies. First, there is the intellectual challenge. Then there is the resume imperative. Since agencies and employers usually begin by scanning a candidate's resume for buzzwords, acquiring new buzzwords (rather than deep new skills) is a priority.

Think hard about the introduction of any new technology, especially if planning to introduce it to solve a single problem. A new technology once introduced may need to be maintained for years, complicating the organization's technology mix. What will be its implications for support? Will it require development skills used nowhere else in the system? Will it have special firewall or other requirements?

> **Avoid using technologies for their own sake. Every new technology added to a project makes it harder to maintain, unless alternative approaches are clearly inadequate. Adding new technologies is a strategic decision, and shouldn't be taken lightly, to solve a particular problem.**

A real case in point: a large dotcom used an EJB server for business logic, with a presentation tier using servlets and JSP. A developer we'll call Joe was asked to develop an in-house administration tool to perform ongoing data migration. Joe's manager was trekking in the Himalayas, and all the senior technical staff was snowed under with a major release, so this was Joe's big opportunity to design and implement a solution.

Joe spent a few minutes thinking about the problem and concluded that EJB wouldn't meet his needs and that a web interface couldn't deliver the functionality (both these assumptions later proved to be wrong). His solution – weeks late – involved RMI, with the interface a hefty Swing applet. Neither RMI nor Swing was used elsewhere in the system, except for the use of RMI under the hood by the J2EE server.

The interface looked beautiful on Joe's machine, but the administration tool was abandoned within three months for the following reasons:

❑ The use of RMI meant that an RMI server needed to be kept running. This was an additional unwelcome job for site management. The use of RMI also required additional firewall rules.

❑ Users of the administration tool proved to use low-spec laptops. The use of Swing meant that the application ran at a painfully slow pace on these systems. It also required installation of the Java Plug-In, requiring the development team to liaise with end users.

❑ The effort put into the attractive interface meant that bug fixing was neglected.

❑ Joe left the company to work with the technologies he preferred. Since the application's architecture was so different from that of the other applications in the system and did not use the frameworks the other developers were familiar with, it was hard to establish what work was required to resolve the bugs. It turned out to be cheaper to scrap the whole thing and start again.

At least in this case, a Swing/RMI solution *could* have been made to work: although misapplied in this case, these technologies are proven. However, "neat technologies" are also often at the bleeding edge, making them inherently risky propositions.

When to Use Alternative Technologies to Supplement J2EE

Just because you've committed to J2EE as a strategic platform doesn't mean that J2EE technology is the best way to solve each and every problem. For example, in the case described above, Joe was facing a database migration problem. He might have done better to begin by surveying database-centric solutions. Other technologies that can often be used for specific tasks are XSLT and database languages such as PL/SQL.

There's a tradeoff to be struck here. The more non-J2EE products incorporated into an application, the harder it is to maintain.

Some indications that we should look beyond J2EE are:

❑ When using a different tool can lead to a dramatic simplification. This may well have happened with Joe's problem.

❑ When it's possible to leverage existing investment. For example, it may be possible to build on existing database stored procedures to solve a particular problem.

❑ When the choice leverages existing skills in the organization, such as DBA or Perl skills.

Many J2EE practitioners take an unduly J2EE-centric view of enterprise software. J2EE is a fine platform, but it can't, and should not attempt to, encompass all the software requirements of an enterprise.

We should remember that J2EE is an excellent integration platform. As such, we shouldn't feel a need to attempt to implement everything using J2EE technologies, but should be prepared to use J2EE to make disparate resources work together as necessary.

Portability Issues

Java's fundamental premise of **Write Once, Run Anywhere (WORA)** ensures that J2EE applications are far more portable than applications written using any comparable platform. We can be sure that Java objects will behave consistently in different environments, while the Sun J2EE Compatibility program helps guarantee that different J2EE servers fulfill the requirements of the J2EE specifications. As J2EE servers tend to be written in Java, servers themselves are usually supported on multiple operating systems.

Unfortunately, the CTS doesn't present the complete picture. It's good that an application written within the bounds of the J2EE specifications can be ported between servers. However, what if a real-world application needs to go beyond the scope of the specifications?

Let's examine what portability actually means in a J2EE context.

What does Portability Mean?

There are several issues around the portability of J2EE applications:

❑ **Portability of applications between application servers**
This is probably the first issue that comes to mind when we think about portability in a J2EE context. Portability of applications between application servers will usually depend on the following factors, most of which are under our control:

   ❑ How faithfully does the target server implement the J2EE specifications?

   ❑ How compliant is the application's code to the J2EE specifications? Unnoticed violations are a hindrance while porting applications, when the target server enforces a different subset of J2EE requirements.

   ❑ How much does the application make use of proprietary features of the original server?

The Sun CTS helps eliminate the first issue. The second can be avoided by a thorough understanding of J2EE, and discipline during application development. This leaves the third: a much harder problem (we should, of course, only use proprietary server features when they deliver real benefit). I'll discuss strategies for ensuring that access to proprietary extensions does not break portability below.

❑ **Portability of applications between server operating systems**
J2EE scores very well here. Java as a language is extremely portable. Virtual machines on all server operating systems are reliable. Leading application servers are tested on multiple platforms, and so it's likely that an application can be ported (for example, from Windows 2000 to Solaris) without any development work being required. The J2EE specifications discourage server-specific implementation features, such as use of the file system in business objects.

❑ **The ability to change important resources that J2EE applications rely on**
The obvious case here is switching database. In fact, this rarely happens after a system is deployed. There is a saying that "Data tends to stick where it lands". In practice, it's much more likely that the J2EE application will be radically altered than that a live database will be migrated. In this case there are two possible scenarios:

   ❑ Change to a comparable, competing resource. Imagine that we need to migrate from a proof of concept with Cloudscape to a deployment on Oracle. JDBC provides a basic level of abstraction here, although it will usually be necessary to modify SQL statements.

   ❑ Change of resource type. This involves a more radical shift: for example, from an RDBMS to an ODBMS. Achieving portability in this case will involve a higher level of abstraction, such as entity beans. However, the likelihood of such change is more remote, and abstraction at such a high level may degrade efficiency and complicate application code.

It's vital to distinguish between these issues. I feel that far too much emphasis is placed on database portability, in particular. This reflects an unrealistic J2EE-centric view of enterprise IT. Organizations invest a lot of money in databases. They don't jump ship often, and expect this investment to be leveraged. Thus, it's unwise to ignore the potential of proprietary database features in simplifying application code and improving performance. Portability between application servers, on the other hand, is more easily achievable and may deliver greater business value.

It's important to remember that we can enjoy some benefit from J2EE's portability even if we never choose to migrate our applications to a different platform. Since J2EE supports such a wide variety of implementations, there is a large community of J2EE developers with experience on a variety of platforms. This makes for a valuable mix of skills in J2EE teams. I'm reminded of this whenever I work with a Microsoft-only organization.

In summary, the J2EE portability news is good, but *complete* portability is neither possible nor desirable. The limits of portability largely reflect performance imperatives and the limits of the J2EE specifications, and the resulting need to use platform-specific technologies. As we shall see, there are techniques we can use to work around these issues.

A Pragmatic Approach to Portability

As we've already discussed, refusing to use *any* vendor-specific functionality is dangerous. Architects and developers are employed to deliver working solutions for real organizations, not produce "pure" J2EE applications.

However, this doesn't mean that it's impossible to *design* for portability. This can be achieved in three ways:

- ❑ Write code that complies with the J2EE specifications. Adopt organization-wide standards for writing J2EE-compliant code, and ensure that all developers understand and follow them. Use the J2EE Reference Implementation verifier tool regularly to check compliance.

- ❑ Know the capabilities of the standard J2EE infrastructure and avoid using platform-specific solutions when a satisfactory standard alternative exists. However, don't just reject proprietary solutions automatically.

- ❑ Use loose coupling to isolate the use of platform-specific features for ensuring that the application's design (if not all its code) remains portable.

Staging Environments and Release Management

Regardless of how well an application is written and the quality of the server it runs on, stability will be disappointing unless there is an efficient release management process and unless there are suitable development and staging environments. It's important to invest time upfront into establishing reliable and repeatable procedures that will be familiar to all involved before the application reaches production.

A typical web project might require three completely separate environments:

❑ **Development environment**
This should closely mirror the Test and Production environments. Developers should be relatively free to make changes.

❑ **Test or Staging environment**
This should mirror the Production environment as closely as possible. In particular, it should contain the same volume of data as the production environment, so that performance testing will be meaningful. Cost may rule out using exactly the same hardware as that in production. However, if deploying on a Production cluster, it's vital that Test should also be clustered, as clustering raises many issues that might otherwise only appear in Production. As load testing will usually be conducted in Test, this is another reason why it should mirror the Production hardware configuration as closely as possible. Releases to Test should require a formal release process. It is vital that Test use the same operating system as Production.

❑ **Production environment**
The environment in which the live site runs. Developers should have no direct access to Production, and deployment into Production should be the culmination of a formal release process, after testing in the Test environment is complete.

In many sites, all developers have their own "pre-development" sandbox on their own workstation. This is often a Windows workstation, while the development and staging servers will often run a flavor of Unix. Although the use of different operating systems introduces some risk, since the JVMs cannot be identical, its benefits in productivity may make it a worthwhile approach, as developers may need to perform other tasks on their local machines that are not best served by the production operating system.

Release management is the task of ensuring that the progress of an application release through Development, Test, and Production is reversible and repeatable. It is vital that every organization develops a release management strategy accepted by all team members before application development begins. The issues addressed by a release management strategy will include:

❑ "Labeling" all sources in a version control system so that it's easy to extract a snapshot of the artifacts included in each release. Thus a release management strategy will be substantially based around the version control system in use.

❑ Deployment onto Test and Production servers. This may include rollout to a cluster of servers. Thus the application server in use – and the deployment tools it provides – is another crucial variable in practical release management.

❑ A rollback strategy, to ensure that if a release causes unexpected problems in Test or Production environments it is possible to roll back to the previous version of the application.

❑ The creation of any database tables required and the provision of data as necessary.

❑ Management of binary dependencies that may change between releases (for example, JAR files shipped with third-party products such as Velocity).

❑ The documentation required with each release.

❑ The sign-off process required for each release.

> Successful J2EE projects depend not only on good application and application server software, but also on sound release management practices and suitable staging environments between developers' local machines and live servers. It's vital to invest sufficient time and involve all project personnel in developing a sound and workable strategy in these areas.

Building a Team

J2EE projects require a wide range of skills and good communication. J2EE developers must not only possess strong Java skills and J2EE knowledge, but must be able to liaise successfully with experts in software they use (such as DBAs and mainframe systems) as well as presentation-tier developers.

Due to the complexity of enterprise (not merely J2EE) projects, attempting to save money on cheap personnel is likely to backfire. It's vital to have at least a core of experienced, highly skilled professionals from the beginning of the project. This allows for mentoring junior developers to supplement investment in training courses.

When it's impossible to obtain first-class skills in-house, it may be worth considering short-term consulting early in the project lifecycle from organizations or individuals with proven expertise – for example, to deliver an architecture document or a proof of concept. This is relatively expensive, but may prove to be a prudent investment if it helps avert future problems.

Again, it's vital that the project begins well. The quality of personnel available in the project's inception and elaboration phase will be especially important. These phases can either establish sound architecture and practices that will see the project through smoothly to successful completion, or result in ongoing problems that cannot be solved by throwing more and more personnel at the project as it begins to miss milestones.

Team Structure

Assuming that your organization has staff with the necessary skills, there remains the problem of organizing them into a team. Again, there is no single right answer, as situations differ. However, there are some common issues that deserve thought.

Who Owns the Architecture?

One of the most important decisions is whether or not to have a "Chief Architect" who will have the final responsibility for design decisions, or whether to do things more democratically.

Having a single chief architect has several advantages:

- Clarity of vision
- Quick decision making
- A single person who can represent the project team when necessary (this may be very important in large, bureaucratic organizations, when liaison with senior management is required)

The success of this strategy will depend largely on the personality and skills of the architect, who must have a deep overall understanding of J2EE and who should be able to command the respect of all project personnel.

However, the following risks must be considered:

❑   Excessive dependency on one individual, who may leave the company (which will mean that others need to be involved in their work anyway).

❑   The likelihood of unilateral decisions that may be resented by developers. This approach isn't based on consensus.

❑   The potential that the architect may become divorced from the coalface. It's essential that an architect is sufficiently hands-on to understand all the practical issues that developers encounter. The architect must be able to focus downwards and upwards in the organization, as a key conduit for project communication.

Another approach is to have a committee with overall responsibility for design. This is more bureaucratic and may slow down decision-making while delivering few advantages. Its success is likely to hinge on an effective chairperson (not necessarily the most senior technical person).

Practitioners of Extreme Programming (XP), a democratic programming model, argue against the notion of a Chief Architect (some argue against the notion of software architecture itself). XP uses **collective code ownership**, where any programmer can change any line of code in the project. This may work in small projects but is not so well suited to large projects since it could be at the mercy of reckless developers. In my experience, a larger project requires a greater level of formality.

> **Regardless of who "owns" the system architecture, it's vital that it's clearly expressed and that the whole team buys into it. It seldom helps to impose a design on developers.**

Vertical or Horizontal Responsibility

Another decision involves allocation of responsibilities to developers. There are two common models here:

The Vertical Approach

This approach gives the responsibility of implementing entire use cases (from markup generation to interaction with databases and legacy systems) to individual developers or small teams. This approach requires all developers to have expertise with the complete J2EE technology stack.

One advantage of this approach is there is no communication overhead between groups of specialists. The vertical approach also works well with an XP-influenced development process, using collective code ownership.

However, the vertical approach may lead to loss of efficiency and uneven code quality. Even a good developer may waste time dealing with issues they are unfamiliar with, compared to a specialist in that area. Lack of experience may result in poor solutions along with wasted time and effort.

The Horizontal Approach

This approach allocates developers to specific areas of expertise such as JSP or EJB.

The horizontal approach is a more traditional and potentially bureaucratic approach to software development. It can foster efficiency, as developers spend all their time honing their skills in a small area. On the other hand, it makes good communication essential between developers working with different technologies, as several developers or small teams will be required to cooperate to implement each use case. However, forcing understanding that would otherwise exist inside the heads of developers to be communicated (and better still, documented) may be a good thing. Using the horizontal approach doesn't force developers in one team (such as JSP) to wait until the work of another team (such as Business Objects) is complete: interfaces should be agreed early, meaning that simple dummy implementations can be used before real integration is possible.

Possible divisions of responsibility in the horizontal approach are:

❑ **Markup developer**
This will encompass HTML/XHTML development and possibly JavaScript.

❑ **Presentation developer**
Responsible for more technical presentation-tier work, rather than designing good-looking HTML. They will deliver JSP pages, XSLT stylesheets, Velocity templates, and other web templates, given the required markup. In an MVC application, JSP pages will contain little Java code, so may even fall into the province of markup developers. In GUI applications such as Swing applications, presentation developers will be true Java developers expert in the windowing library used.

❑ **Web-tier Java developer**
Responsible for MVC framework action classes, JSP tag handlers, and web-tier helper classes.

❑ **Business object developer**
Responsible for implementing application business logic. Business object developers will use EJB where appropriate, and should have a sound understanding of EJB. Web-tier developers and business object developers must work together early in the project lifecycle to define the interfaces that enable communication between their classes to ensure that they can work freely in parallel.

❑ **Data access specialist**
Java developer responsible for efficient DBMS access. Often this role will be taken on by business object developers. Specialist tasks may include configuring and working with O/R mapping products such as TopLink or JDO implementations and making advanced use of an EJB container's entity bean CMP implementation. Such developers are often a bridge between the Java and RDBMS worlds.

❑ **DBA**
Specialist in the underlying database. DBAs can provide valuable assistance to J2EE developers in vital areas such as ensuring good performance and correct locking behavior.

The smaller the team, the more of these roles each developer or group of developers is likely to take on.

It is possible to mix the two team structure models. The following guidelines may prove helpful:

❑ A good design makes it easy to apply either approach, as it results in clean divisions between technologies.

- ❑ Some developers are happiest working with the range of J2EE technologies; others hate leaving their pet areas. Thus which strategy is appropriate may depend on the personality of valued team members.

- ❑ Decoupling markup authoring (or GUI presentation) from middleware coding is one of the areas where it almost always makes sense to use the horizontal approach. Java developers seldom make good HTML coders, and many good HTML coders lack a basic understanding of system architectures. The whole point of designing a web application is to separate presentation from business logic; team structure shouldn't reverse this accomplishment.

- ❑ The larger the team and more formal the development process, the more attractive the horizontal approach is likely to be.

- ❑ In the horizontal approach, it will always be necessary to have a group of senior developers who have a feel for the entire product. These developers will understand the whole architecture and will be able to mentor other developers. Likewise, in the vertical approach it will be necessary to have developers with specialist expertise who can mentor other developers in particular technologies.

- ❑ In the horizontal approach, developers may be rotated through different technologies, while still ensuring a high level of confidence in each group of developers.

Choosing Development Tools

Some aspects of J2EE development require tools. Tools for J2EE development are getting better, but many still fall short of their Microsoft counterparts. However, Java development – and, to a lesser extent, J2EE development – does not usually require heavy dependence on tools.

Generic tools such as a good XML editor can simplify the editing of deployment descriptors and reduce the likelihood of errors.

With EJB – and specifically, CMP entity beans if they are used – J2EE-specific tools become *necessary* rather than merely helpful. Automatic generation and synchronization of the multiple files required for implementing each EJB is helpful, as is generation and maintenance of deployment descriptors. It's possible to handle the Java files and write deployment descriptors manually if you are using only session EJBs and web components. However, EJB 2.0 CMP entity bean deployment descriptors and some server-specific deployment descriptors (again, usually where CMP entities are concerned) are far too complex for manual authoring.

> **Note that tools don't equate to IDEs. Many lower-tech script-based tools are often highly effective in J2EE development.**

Let's survey some of the main types of tools that can be used for J2EE development. This discussion reflects my own experience and opinions; this is an area where there are many alternative approaches.

Visual Modeling Tools

At the slickest end of the tool spectrum are visual modeling tools with the ability to generate J2EE code, such as Together. These products are often expensive. Personally, I don't use them, although this is a matter of preference, and I know some excellent J2EE architects and developers who do. I do sometimes use visual modeling tools for their UML support (including code generation from a visual model), rather than J2EE-specific extensions. As UML modeling tools aren't tied to J2EE, they're not strictly relevant here.

Web-tier components and session EJBs aren't very different from ordinary Java classes, and hence don't require special tools. I tend not to use entity beans. When I do use them, I don't use object-modeling tools to generate code. As we shall discuss in Chapter 7, driving entity bean design from an object model can produce disastrous results as far as relational databases are concerned (the most common case today). Integrated visual modeling and J2EE code generation tools make this design approach dangerously easy. Their very slickness poses the threat that developers are unlikely to question the underlying approach. Inexperienced developers can easily use such tools to generate code quickly without really understanding it – a recipe for future problems.

IDEs

Although many organizations standardize on a single IDE, I feel that individual developers should be left to choose the IDEs they are familiar with. IDEs are a poor repository for project configuration, and developers often have strong likes and dislikes that should be respected. Some developers remain passionately committed to their favorite text editors, although today's Java IDEs are so good that this is hard to justify (I became convinced of this a few years ago, when I said goodbye to vi and TextPad).

In GUI development, a particular IDE may legitimately become critical to the development process: for example if it offers particularly strong "form" building functionality. With server-side development, there tends to be less Java code that's tedious to generate by hand, removing this argument for IDE standardization.

I recommend considering support for refactoring when selecting an IDE. This saves a lot of time and promotes good practice (we'll discuss refactoring in Chapter 4). Eclipse (http://www.eclipse.org), a free open source product, is particularly good in this respect. Eclipse provides automatic support for:

❑   Renaming packages, classes, methods, and variables (including updating all dependencies)

❑   Supporting common refactorings such as "extract method", and promoting a method to a superclass

❑   Searching for references to a class or method throughout a project

Build Utilities

A major problem with IDEs is that their use can't be scripted. Thus, actions can't be placed under version control and can't be repeated predictably. It may be possible to check in project files, but project files are IDE-specific and may use binary formats. Also, some tasks cannot be performed easily by any IDE. This creates a serious problem if a particular IDE is the definitive project repository.

It's impossible to succeed in a J2EE project without an efficient repeatable way of building all project artifacts. Basic tasks include:

❑ Compiling all source code

❑ Compiling test code

❑ Creating J2EE deployment units – WARs, EJB JARs, and EARs

❑ Generating Javadoc for the entire application

❑ Automatically detecting test cases and running tests in a single operation

More advanced tasks include:

❑ Checking code out of a version control system

❑ Tagging all files in the version control system with a specified build identifier

❑ Putting a database in the required state before a test run and cleaning the database after a test run

❑ Deploying onto an application server

All these tasks can be accomplished using **Another Neat Tool (Ant)**, now the de facto standard mechanism for Java build scripts. Ant is an open source tool from the Apache project, available at http://jakarta.apache.org/ant/index.html.

Ant shares many concepts with make, although it is XML based and uses Java, and not shell scripts. An Ant task corresponds to a make target, but Ant is more intuitive, and offers better cross-platform support and much better Java-oriented functionality. Ant's benefits include:

❑ Ant can be used in conjunction with your favorite IDE (in this case, it's a good idea to have Ant compile classes to a location other than where the IDE compiles classes to, to ensure that the IDE doesn't become confused). Most developers will work on code (and compile it in the first instance) in an IDE, but build releases using Ant. Popular IDEs offer Ant integration, allowing Ant tasks to be run from within the IDE.

❑ Ant provides standard "tasks" for many common requirements such as executing system commands, generating Javadocs, copying and moving files, validating XML documents, downloading files from a remote server, and running a SQL script against a database, in addition to compilation of Java source code (which is often considered to be Ant's main role).

❑ Many products offer Ant tasks to simplify their use. For example, WebLogic 6.1 and above use Ant for certain tasks. Many third-party Ant tasks are available to perform a wide range of functionality including packaging and deploying J2EE applications on several application servers.

❑ Ant provides an effective way of scripting deployment to an application server.

❑ Like make, most Ant tasks check dependencies. Thus Ant will automatically recompile only source files that have changed, and skip tasks for which the results are still up to date.

❑ Ant is parameterizable. Ant "properties" can be set to hold values that vary between operating systems and individual machines (such as the absolute location of the root of a classpath), ensuring that the rest of each build script is completely portable. Ant is also capable of performing different sets of tasks depending on criteria such as the operating system or the availability of certain classes.

65

❏   Ant is extensible. It's relatively easy to define custom Ant "tasks" in Java. However, Ant comes with so many tasks to perform common operations – many of them J2EE-related – and so many third-party tasks are available that few developers will need to implement their own Ant tasks.

Ant is used widely in commercial and open source projects, so it's essential for any professional Java developer to understand it.

Ant can be used for many tasks other than simply building source code. Optional tasks (available as an additional download from the main download site) support building WAR, EJB, and EAR deployment units.

I never type in a classpath if there's any likelihood that I will run the command again: I create an Ant `build.xml` file or add a new task to an existing build file for every Java-oriented command, no matter how small. This not only means that I can immediately get something to work if I return to it later, but also that I can comment anything unusual I needed to do, so I won't waste time in future (I even used Ant to back up the source code and documents composing this book).

> If you aren't familiar with it, learn and use Ant. Continue to use your favorite IDE, but ensure that each project action can be accomplished through an Ant target. Spend a little time upfront to write Ant build files and reap the rewards later. See http://jakarta.apache.org/ant/ant_in_anger.html for guidelines on using Ant effectively.

Code Generators

There's little need to auto-generate code for ordinary Java objects and web-tier classes. However, the many artifacts required in EJB development made code generation tools attractive, especially where entity beans are concerned.

EJB code generators are lower tech compared to IDEs, but can be very effective for EJB development.

As discussed, it's impossible to produce and maintain all the required deployment descriptors (both standard and vendor-specific) manually if we are using CMP entity beans. The following free tools use special Javadoc tags in EJB bean implementation classes to drive generation of other Java required source files (home and component interfaces) and deployment descriptors for several servers. Unlike an IDE "EJB Wizard", this is a scriptable approach and is compatible with any IDE or editor.

❏   **EJBGen**
http://www.beust.com/cedric/ejbgen/
This tool, written by BEA developer Cedric Beust, is bundled with WebLogic 7.0.

❏   **XDoclet**
http://xdoclet.sourceforge.net/
This similar, but more ambitious, tool, written by Rickard Oberg, is available in open source, and can be used to perform other tasks as well as EJB generation.

An alternative EJB code generation approach is to define the necessary data in an XML document, enabling use of XSLT to generate the multiple output files required. Again, this is really only necessary for handling the complexity of entity bean CMP. One of several such products is the LowRoad code generator from Tall Software (http://www.tallsoftware.com/lowroad/index.html).

Version Control

It's vital to have a good version control tool; along with a good build tool such as Ant, a version control system is the cornerstone of every successful release-management strategy. CVS is widely used in the open source community and provides a reliable basic level of functionality. Several simple, free GUIs integrate with CVS (the best I've seen is WinCvs, available from www.wincvs.org, although there are also some platform-independent Java GUI clients). Popular IDEs like Forte and Eclipse also provide CVS integration. Any professional organization should already have a version control system in place before undertaking a complex development project such as a J2EE enterprise solution.

Identifying and Mitigating Risks

J2EE is a relatively new technology. Enterprise applications involve a mix of technologies such as J2EE, RDBMS, and mainframes, making interoperability a challenge. For these and other reasons it's vital to tackle risks early.

When Java was less mature, I once worked on a project for a software house that developed mainframe software. My role was to lead the development of a Java web interface for a key mainframe product. As the project unfolded, I was impressed by the professionalism of the mainframe developers. They were an established team and were experts in their technologies, which they'd been working in for many years. It was clear that they assumed that "things always worked as documented".

The project involved Swing applets and needed to run in both, IE and Netscape. We encountered serious rendering problems, and it took days to find workarounds for some of the more serious problems. Initially, my comments such as "this is known not to work in IE" inspired disbelief. Then I remembered my first experience as a C programmer, and the shock of working with early C++ implementations. C worked. If something didn't work, it was the programmer's fault. Yet, early C++ implementations (not compilers, but C++ to C translators) would occasionally produce semantic nonsense from correct statements.

Java has come a long way since then. However, the early years of J2EE brought up many problems that seemed to be ignored by J2EE writers. For example, class loading in web applications had severe problems that required drastic workarounds in several leading products as recently as early 2001.

Most books and articles I've read on J2EE paint too rosy a picture of J2EE development. They fail to convey the pain and suffering that many developers go through. It's important to note that such problems don't afflict just J2EE technology. Having worked in Microsoft shops, I've encountered many irritations and "known issues" with their web technology (Microsoft products no longer have "bugs"). In the last two years, things have improved enormously for J2EE, but there's still some way to go.

Discussing the bugs in particular products isn't helpful, since such a discussion might well be out of date before this book is on the shelves. However, it is important to acknowledge the fact that there probably will be problems and that getting around them will soak up some development time. J2EE specifications are complex and implementations fairly new. Problems may arise from:

❑   Server bugs (in deployment and administration as well as run-time behavior)

❑   Areas in which the J2EE specifications are sketchy (class loading is a rich source of such problems, discussed below)

- ❏ Poorly understood areas of the specification
- ❏ Interaction with other enterprise software applications

In the worst case, such problems may demand a design workaround. For example, the decision to use EJB 2.0 entity beans with CMP may bring to light that the chosen application server's EJB QL implementation cannot cope with the complexity of some of the queries or that EJB QL itself cannot meet the requirements efficiently. These risks can be headed off by a proof of concept early in the development project, which can prompt a decision to avoid EJB QL or choose a different application server.

In less serious cases, such as a problem with a server administration tool, they might involve a server bug that slows down the development process.

Successful risk management depends on early identification of risks, enabling action to be taken before resources have been heavily committed to a given approach. The following general principles are valuable in J2EE project risk management:

- ❏ Attack risks as early as possible. This is one of the key points of the **Unified Software Development Process**. We can adopt this approach without adopting the entire methodology.
- ❏ Ensure that the design is flexible. For example, if we design our application so that we can replace CMP entity beans with another persistence strategy without rewriting large amounts of business logic, problems with EJB QL would have a less severe impact.
- ❏ Allow contingency time in the project plan to handle unexpected problems.
- ❏ Involve more developers when a problem becomes apparent. This promotes lateral thinking, at the cost of a greater total number of developer days.
- ❏ Develop a good relationship with your application server vendor. Once you are sure there is a problem, report it. A fix may be on the way. Other users may also have encountered it, and the vendor may be able to suggest a good workaround even if no fix is available.
- ❏ Learn to distinguish things that are your fault from things that aren't. It's hard to overestimate the importance of this point, which is one of the many reasons why any significant project needs at least one true J2EE expert. Erring either way can dramatically increase the time required to track down a problem.
- ❏ Use the Internet. There is a vast wealth of knowledge online about things that do and don't work. Regular search engines like Yahoo! and Google can uncover it. Benefit from it. No matter how obscure your problem may be, there's a good chance that someone has reported something similar in a newsgroup somewhere.

The following is a list of some of the significant risks encountered in J2EE projects, along with appropriate risk mitigation strategies for each. While we haven't yet discussed the concepts behind some of these problems, they should provide useful practical illustrations of risk management:

Risk	Mitigation strategies
Your development team lacks J2EE skills, threatening to result in poor choices early in the project lifecycle and making it impossible to predict project timescales.	Purchase J2EE consulting services to kick-start the project. Hire a strong J2EE expert on a long-term basis to contribute to the project and mentor other developers. Send key developers on training courses.

Risk	Mitigation strategies
Your application is dependent on a proprietary feature of your application server.	If the feature fills a gap in the J2EE specifications, it's likely that other application servers will offer a similar feature, accessed through a different API. So isolate the proprietary functionality behind a platform-independent abstraction layer, ensuring that you only need to reimplement one or more interfaces to target a different server.
Your application server may no longer be supported, forcing migration to another server.	Use an abstraction layer, as described above, to insulate your application from proprietary features of the server. Consider the viability of the server vendor when selecting a server, and regularly review the market. Regularly check the compliance of your application to the J2EE specifications as described above.
Your application server may not meet your scalability or reliability requirements.	Enlist the help of the server vendor in building a simple proof of concept that can be load tested, before it is too late to switch to a different server.
Your application may not meet your performance or scalability goals.	Build a "vertical slice" of the application early in the development lifecycle to test its performance.
Your application may fail to scale as required, because while it works correctly on a single server, it exhibits incorrect behavior in a cluster.	If clustering is a possibility, consider the implication of session management and session replication in all design decisions. Test your application in a clustered environment long before it is released in a clustered environment. Seek assistance from your server vendor; they (and their documentation) will provide crucial information about their clustering support, which you'll need to understand to achieve good results.
A server bug makes a J2EE feature that your application requires unworkable.	Implement a vertical slice of your application as early as possible to check the implementation of crucial technologies. Report the problem to the server vendor and hope for assistance or a patch. Modify application design to avoid the problem technology. Switch to a superior application server while it is still possible.

Table continued on following page

69

Risk	Mitigation strategies
Your application requires third-party libraries (such as a particular XML library, for example) which may conflict with libraries shipped with your application server.	This risk must be addressed as early as possible through the implementation of a vertical slice. Seek guidance from the server vendor (and their documentation) in ensuring compatibility (for example, it may be possible to configure class loading to avoid the conflict).
An integrated J2EE application using EJBs and web modules encounters class loading issues that reduce productivity. When the same class is loaded by two class loaders the two copies are considered to be different classes if compared; `ClassNotFoundExceptions` may be encountered when one class depends on other classes that have been loaded by a classloader not visible to its classloader. This may happen, for example, when a class used in a web application but actually loaded by the EJB classloader attempts to load classes loaded by the WAR classloader, which the EJB class loader cannot see in most servers. _Class loading is a complex area discussed in more detail in Chapter 14._	Understand the Java class loading hierarchy (documented in the `java.lang.ClassLoader` Javadoc) and the class loading architecture of your target application server. Unfortunately, class loading strategies vary between servers, meaning that this is an area in which portability falls down. Take care in packaging deployment units to ensure that classes are loaded by the correct classloader (WAR or EJB classloader, for example). This requires careful development of build scripts to ensure that classes are included in the correct deployment unit, rather than in all deployment units. Consider especially carefully which classloader loads classes that load other classes by name. Code to interfaces, not concrete classes. This makes it easier to keep groups of implementation classes within the appropriate class loader. Implement a vertical slice as early as possible to verify that class loading poses no risk. In the event of intractable problems, consider whether the use of EJB is really necessary. Class loading issues are much simpler in web applications. As a last resort, consider adding classes required throughout your application to the server's global classpath. This violates the J2EE specification, but can save a lot of time.
Application deployment causes unnecessary downtime.	Master the deployment process on your chosen application server. Develop a release management strategy that meets your needs.

Summary

In this chapter we've considered some of the most important choices to be made in J2EE development projects, other than the architectural decisions we considered in Chapter 1. We've looked at:

- ❑ How to choose an application server. One of the strengths of the J2EE platform is that it allows a choice of competing implementations of the J2EE specifications, each with different strengths and weaknesses. Choosing the appropriate application server will have an important influence on a project's outcome. We've looked at some of the major criteria in choosing an application server, stressing the importance of considering the specific requirements, rather than marketing hype. We've seen the importance of choosing an application server early in the project lifecycle, to avoid wasting resources getting up to speed with multiple servers. We've considered the issue of total cost of ownership, of which license costs are just a part.

- ❑ Managing the technology mix in an enterprise. While an unnecessary proliferation of different technologies will make maintenance more expensive forever, it's important to recognize that J2EE isn't the best solution to all problems in enterprise software development. We should be prepared to use other technologies to supplement J2EE technologies where they simplify implementation.

- ❑ Practical issues surrounding J2EE portability. We've seen how to ensure that we don't unintentionally violate the J2EE specifications, by regularly running the verification tool supplied with Sun's J2EE Reference Implementation, and how to ensure that application design remains portable even if we have good reason to use proprietary features of the target platform.

- ❑ Release management practices. We've seen the importance of having distinct Development, Test, and Production environments, and the importance of having a well-thought-of release management strategy.

- ❑ Issues in building and managing a team for a J2EE project. We've considered the implications of using a "Chief Architect," as opposed to a more democratic approach to architecture, and considered two common team structures: the "vertical" structure, which uses generalists to implement whole use cases, and the "horizontal" structure, which focuses developers on individual areas of expertise. We've considered a possible division of roles in the "horizontal" team structure.

- ❑ Development tools. We've briefly surveyed the types of tools available to J2EE developers. We've stressed the importance of the Ant build tool, which is now a de facto standard for Java development.

- ❑ Risk management. We've seen that successful risk management is based on identifying and attacking risks early in the project lifecycle. We've discussed some overall risk management strategies, and looked at several practical risks to J2EE projects, along with strategies to manage them.

As this is a practically focused book, I haven't discussed choosing a development methodology, or deciding when one is required. However, this is another important choice. We've seen the importance of tackling risks early. I recommend using a methodology for J2EE development that emphasized this. Both the Rational Unified Process and Extreme Programming (XP) meet this requirement. Personally, I prefer "lightweight" or "agile" methodologies (see http://agilealliance.org/principles.html), although the degree of formality appropriate tends to increase the larger the project. I recommend the following resources as starting points for readers unfamiliar with these methodologies: *The Unified Software Development Process* from *Addison-Wesley* (ISBN: 0-201-57169-2), and http://www.extremeprogramming.org ("Extreme Programming: A Gentle Introduction").

In the next chapter we look at testing J2EE applications. Testing is an important concern throughout the software development lifecycle and is accorded particular importance in both these methodologies.

OCEANUS

INSULÆ

PHILIP

PINÆ

Sinoe

I. Ainao

Philippina

Ilocos

Luzon

Moro Hermoso

Pintados

Arcon triste

Luco

G. de Matalcumbert

Pondan

Mandato

Paracalle

Manilha

C. del Spirito Santo de Cobos

Francisco Gomez

Ylhat del Primeiro

Sucridera

Puelhas

A bo comucho Primeiro

Cabusao

Abigo

Passage de S. Clara

I. de Mata Clotes

ARC

I. dos Arecifes

Tunquin

Enseada d

Cauchin d

Sinas

Costa de Praca

Cambo

ia

Cambo

Pulo S. Pelo

Doe Tanquero

Praca

Palo Ciri

Pulo Condor

Pulo Tigao

Mon Pratten

Pulo babe

I. de S. Maria

Calamianes

S. Michael

Praca

Domain

Cavagan

I. de S. Joao

Cantoa

MINDANA

Mindanao

Malagua

A. de Resurreicam

C. Buey

Carangeo

I. de S. Ioannes

I. da Palmeras

S.

Arekma

Borneo

R. de Borneo

Malana

Pucharuru

o Temocorin

Tenardros

BOR
NE
O

Lare devla for
en Manuel de
lima

Palo

Bagnivetam

I. de Sagim

Dameo

Tomon

I. de Tolao

I. de Rao

I. de Dei

Carango

Gilolo

I. dos Greos

le Aguada

Bintan

Banca

Biblikam

Chinabato

Nisagira

Palo

I. Vera Puro

Batua Calapa

N. Sonra

TIbils

Doras

Monmenos

Sues

Memagn

Carioras

Marber

Portugal

Sape

Gome

Sambo

Jucek

Bachian

Batchina

Port Canan CEIRAM

Hic hyberna
de Meneza

Abluas

CELE
BES

Burro

Buoro

Xula

Simeom

Tabe

Chiban

I. de S.
Matheus

Palo Ag

Ruan

Polda

Guiam

AVA, quæ et
IAOA dicitur. Fiderda

Baterlaq

Baindora

Simor

Terra alta
Guliam

Aru

Aqua in berneo Martin
Afonfo de inels

LANT

Baixos

DOL

3

Testing J2EE Applications

In Chapter 2 we saw that decisions made early in the project lifecycle can determine a project's success or failure. Testing is another critical area in which we must develop a strategy and establish good practices from the outset of a project.

Testing is often treated as an uninteresting activity that can be undertaken after development is largely complete. No one seriously believes that this is a good approach, but it's the usual outcome when there's no coherent testing strategy from project commencement. Most developers are aware of the many problems such reluctant testing brings, such as the fact that the cost of rectifying bugs escalates rapidly, the longer they take to emerge.

In this chapter we consider a positive approach to testing. We'll see that testing is something we should do, not just out of fear of the consequences of not doing it, but because it can be used to improve the way we develop code. If we view testing as an integral part of our development process, we can not only raise the quality of our applications and make them much easier to maintain, but also increase productivity.

> **Testing should occur throughout the development lifecycle. Testing should never be an afterthought. Integrating testing into the development process brings many benefits.**

Testing enterprise applications poses many challenges:

- ❏ Enterprise applications usually depend on resources such as databases, which will need to be considered in any testing strategy.
- ❏ Testing web applications can be difficult. They don't expose simple Java interfaces that we can test, and unit testing is complicated by the dependence of web tier components on a web container.

❑ Testing distributed applications is difficult. It may require numerous machines and may be hard to simulate some causes of failure.

❑ J2EE components – especially EJBs – are heavily dependent on server infrastructure.

❑ A J2EE application may involve many architectural layers. We must test that each layer works correctly, as well as perform acceptance testing of the application as a whole.

In this chapter, we discuss these challenges and approaches to meet them. We'll look at:

❑ Testing goals and concepts.

❑ The **Extreme Programming (XP)** approach to testing, which is based on **test-first development**. XP elevates testing into the centerpiece of the development process. Tests are regarded as essential application deliverables. Tests are written *before* code and always kept up to date. Whether or not we consider adopting XP overall, this is a very effective approach. While all good programmers test their code often, there are real advantages from proceeding from an ad hoc approach to a more formal approach, in which tests are documented and easily repeatable.

❑ The JUnit testing framework, which provides a good basis for our testing strategy. JUnit is a simple but highly effective tool, which is very easy to learn, and which enables tests to be written with a minimum of hassle.

❑ The Cactus J2EE testing framework, which builds on JUnit to enable J2EE components such as EJBs to be tested within an application server.

❑ Techniques for testing web interfaces.

❑ The importance of automating tests, so that all tests for an application can be run in a single operation. We'll see how the Ant build tool can be used to automate JUnit tests.

❑ Complementary approaches to testing, such as assertions, which we can use as part of an integrated QA strategy.

What Can Testing Achieve?

It's impossible for testing to guarantee that a program is correct. However, testing can provide a high level of confidence that a program does what we expect of it. Often "bugs" reflect ignorance about what code should really do. As our knowledge of what a program should do grows, we can write tests that tighten its requirements.

It is important to recognize the limitations of testing – testing won't always expose concurrency issues. Here, an ounce of prevention is truly worth a pound of cure (for example, testing may well fail to pick up problems relating to instance data in a servlet being modified concurrently by multiple threads). However, such code will surely fail in production, and no competent J2EE developer should write it in the first place.

> *The longer a bug takes to appear, the more costly it will be. One study found that the cost of eventually fixing a bug multiplied by 10 with each phase of a project – requirements, design, implementation, and post-release – that passed before the bug was spotted. Testing is no substitute for careful thought before writing code; testing can never catch all bugs.*

> While in this chapter we'll focus on testing code, it's important to remember that a sound QA strategy is needed from requirements analysis onwards.

Definitions

Let's briefly define some of the concepts we'll discuss in this chapter:

- **Unit tests**

  Unit tests test a single unit of functionality. In Java, this is often a single class. Unit tests are the finest level of granularity in testing, and should test that each method in a class satisfies its documented contract.

- **Test coverage**

  This refers to the proportion of application code that is tested (usually, by unit tests). For example, we might aim to check that every line of code is executed by at least one test, or that every logical branch in the code is tested.

- **Black-box testing**

  This considers only the public interfaces of classes under test. It is not based on knowledge of implementation details.

- **White-box testing**

  Testing that is aware of the internals of classes under test. In a Java context, white-box testing considers private and protected data and methods. It doesn't merely test whether the class does what is required of it; it also tests how it does it. I don't advocate white-box testing (more of this later). White-box testing is sometimes called "glass-box testing".

- **Regression tests**

  These establish that, following changes or additions, code still does what it did before. Given adequate coverage, unit tests can serve as regression tests.

- **Boundary-value tests**

  These test unusual or extreme situations that code under test should be able to handle (for example, unexpected null arguments to a method).

- **Acceptance tests** (sometimes called **Functional tests**)

  These are tests from a customer's viewpoint. An acceptance test is concerned with how the application meets business requirements. While unit tests test how each part of an application does its job, acceptance tests ignore the implementation details and test the ultimate functionality, using concepts that make sense to a user (or customer, in XP terminology).

- **Load tests**

  These test an application's behavior as load increases (for example, to simulate a greater population of users). The aim of load testing is to prove that the application can cope with the load it is expected to encounter in production and to establish the maximum load it can support. Load tests will often be run over long periods of time, to test stability. Load testing may uncover concurrency issues. Throughput targets are an important part of an application's **non-functional** requirements and should be defined as part of business requirements.

❑ **Stress tests**
 These go beyond load testing to increase load on the application beyond the projected limits. The aim is not to simulate expected load, but to cause the application to fail or exhibit unacceptable response times, thus demonstrating its weak links from the point of view of throughput and stability. This can suggest improvements in design or code and establish whether overloading the application can lead to erroneous behavior such as loss of data or crashing.

Testing Correctness

Let's now examine some issues and techniques around testing the correctness of applications: that is, testing that applications meet their functional requirements.

The XP Approach to Testing

In Chapter 2 I mentioned Extreme Programming (XP), a methodology that emphasizes frequent integration and comprehensive unit testing. The key rules and practices of XP that relate to testing are:

❑ Write tests before code

❑ All code must have unit tests, which can be run automatically in a single operation

❑ When a bug is reported, tests are created to reproduce it before an attempt is made to fix the bug

The pioneers of XP didn't invent test-first development. However, they have popularized it and associated it with XP in common understanding. Among other methodologies, the Unified Software Development Process also emphasizes testing throughout the project lifecycle.

We don't need to adopt XP as a whole in order to benefit from these ideas. Let's look at their benefits and implications.

Writing test cases before writing code – test-first development – has many benefits:

❑ The test cases amount to a specification and provide additional documentation. A working specification, compliance to which can be checked daily or even more often, is much more valuable than a specification in a thick requirements document that no one reads or updates.

❑ It promotes understanding of the requirements. It will uncover, and force the resolution of, uncertainty about the class or component's functionality before any time has been wasted. Other components will never be affected by forced reworking. It's impossible to write a test case without understanding what a component should do; it is possible to waste a lot of coding time on the component itself before the lack of understanding becomes apparent.

 A common example concerns null arguments to methods. It's easy to write a method without considering this possibility, with the result that a call with null arguments can produce unexpected results. A proper test suite will include test cases with null arguments, ensuring that the method is only written after the behavior on null arguments is determined and documented.

❑ Test cases are more likely to be viewed as vital, and updated throughout the project lifecycle.

❑ It's much more difficult to write tests for existing code than to write tests before and while writing code. Developers implementing application code should have complete knowledge of what it should do (and therefore how to test it); tests written afterwards will always play catch-up. Thus test-first development is one of the best ways to maximize test coverage.

A test-first approach doesn't mean that a developer should spend all day writing all possible tests for a class before writing the class. Test cases and code are typically written in the same sitting, but in that order. For example, we might write the tests for a particular method before fully implementing the method. After the method is complete and these tests succeed, we move on to another method.

When we write tests before application code, we should check that they fail before implementing the required functionality. This allows us to test the test case and verifies test coverage. For example, we might write tests for a method, then a trivial implementation of the method that returns null. Now we can run the test case and see it fail (if it doesn't, something is wrong with our test suite).

If we write tests before code, the second rule (that all code should have unit tests) will be honored automatically. Many benefits flow from having tests for all classes:

- ❏ It's possible to automate tests and verify in a single operation that all code is working as we expect. This isn't the same thing as working perfectly. Over the course of a project we'll learn more about how we want our code to work, and add test cases accordingly.

- ❏ We can confidently add new functionality, as we have regression tests that will indicate if we've broken any existing functionality. Thus it's important that we can run all tests quickly and easily.

- ❏ Refactoring is much less stressful to developers and less threatening to overall functionality. This ensures that the quality of the application's code remains high throughout the project lifecycle (for example, there's no need to keep away from that appalling class that sort of works, just because so many other classes depend on it). Similarly, it's possible to optimize a class or subsystem if necessary, with a feeling of security. We have a way of demonstrating that the optimized code does what it did before. With comprehensive unit test coverage, the later stages of the development cycle are likely to become much less stressful.

> **Unit testing will only provide a secure basis for refactoring and bug fixing if we have a comprehensive set of unit tests. A half-hearted approach to unit testing will deliver limited benefit.**

A test-first approach can also be applied to bug fixing. Whenever a bug is reported (or becomes apparent other than through test cases) a failing test case should be written (failing due to the bug) before any code is written to fix the bug. The result is verification that the bug has been fixed without impact on functionality covered by previous tests, and a measure of confidence that that bug won't reappear.

> **Write unit tests before writing code, and update them throughout the project lifecycle. Bug reports and new functionality should first prompt the writing and execution of failing tests demonstrating the mismatch between what the application does and what it should do.**
>
> **Test-first development is the best way to guarantee comprehensive test coverage, as it is much harder to write comprehensive tests for existing code.**
>
> **Remember to use test failures to improve error messages and handling. If a test fails, and it wasn't immediately obvious what went wrong, try first to make the problem obvious (through improved error handling and messages) and then to fix it.**

77

All these rules move much of the responsibility of testing onto the development team. In a traditional large organization approach to software development, a specialized testing team is responsible for testing, while developers produce code to be tested. There is a place for QA specialists; developers aren't always best at writing test cases (although they can learn). However, the distinction between development and technical testing is artificial. On the other hand, acceptance testing is likely to be conducted at least partly outside the development team.

> **There shouldn't be an artificial division between development and testing roles. Developers should be encouraged to value the writing of good test cases as an important skill.**

Writing Test Cases

To enjoy the benefits of comprehensive unit testing, we need to know how to write effective tests. Let's consider some of the key issues, and Java tools to help simplify and automate test authoring.

What Makes a Good Test Case?

Writing good test cases takes practice. Our knowledge of the implementation (or likely implementation, if we're developing test-first) may suggest potential problem areas; however, we must also develop the ability to think outside the developer role. In particular, it's important to view the writing of a failing test as an achievement, not a problem. Common themes of testing will include:

- ❏ Testing the most common execution paths (these should be apparent from the application use cases)
- ❏ Testing what happens on unexpected arguments
- ❏ Testing what happens when components under test encounter errors from components they use

We'll take a practical look at writing test cases shortly.

Recognizing Test Case Authoring and Maintenance as a Core Task

Writing all those test cases does take time, and as they're crucial to the documentation of the system, they must be written carefully. It's vital that the suite of tests continues to reflect the requirements of the application throughout the project lifecycle. Like most code, test suites tend to accrete rubbish over time. This can be dangerous. For example, old tests that are no longer relevant can complicate both test code and application code (which will still be required to pass them). It's essential that test code – like application code – be kept under version control. Changes to test code are as important as changes to application code, so may need to be subject to a formal process. It takes a while to get used to test-first development, but the benefits grow throughout the project lifecycle.

Unit Testing

So we're convinced that unit testing is important. How should we go about it in J2EE projects?

main() Methods

The traditional approach to unit testing in Java is to write a `main()` method in each class to be tested. However, this unnecessarily adds to the length of source files, bloats compiled byte codes and often introduces unnecessary dependencies on other classes, such as implementations of interfaces referenced in the code of the class proper.

A better approach is to use another class, with a name such as `XXXXMain` or `XXXXTest`, which contains only the `main()` method and whatever supporting code it needs, such as code to parse command-line arguments. We can now even put unit test classes in a parallel source tree.

However, using `main()` methods to run tests is still an ad hoc approach. Normally the executable classes will produce console output, which developers must read to establish whether the test succeeded or failed. This is time consuming, and usually means that it's impossible to script `main()` method tests and check the results of several at a time.

Using JUnit

There's a much better approach than `main()` method tests, which permits automation. **JUnit** is a simple open source tool that's now the de facto standard for unit testing Java applications. JUnit is easy to use and easy to set up; there's virtually no learning curve. JUnit was written by Erich Gamma (one of the Gang of Four) and Kent Beck (the pioneer of XP). JUnit can be downloaded from http://www.junit.org/index.htm. This site also contains many add-ons for JUnit and helpful articles about using JUnit.

JUnit is designed to report success or failure in a consistent way, without any need to interpret the results. JUnit executes **test cases** (individual tests) against a **test fixture**: a set of objects under test. JUnit provides easy ways of initializing and (if necessary) releasing test fixtures.

The JUnit framework is customizable, but creating JUnit tests usually involves only the following simple steps:

1. Create a subclass of `junit.framework.TestCase`.

2. Implement a public constructor that accepts a string parameter and invokes the superclass constructor with the string. If necessary this constructor can also load test data used subsequently. It can also perform initialization that should be performed once only for the entire test suite, appropriate when tests do not change the state of the text fixture. This is handy when the fixture is slow to create.

3. Optionally, override the `setUp()` method to initialize the objects and variables (the fixture) used by all test cases. Not all test cases will require this. Individual tests may create and destroy their own fixture. Note that the `setUp()` method is called before every individual test case, and the `tearDown()` method after.

4. Optionally, override the `tearDown()` method to release resources acquired in `setUp()`, or to revert test data into a clean state. This will be necessary if test cases may update persistent data.

5. Add test methods to the class. Note that we don't need to implement an interface, as JUnit uses reflection and automatically detects test methods. Test methods are recognized by their signature, which must be of the form `public test<Description>()`. Test methods may throw any checked or unchecked exception.

79

JUnit's value and elegance lies in the way in which it allows us to combine multiple test cases into a **test suite**. For example, an object of class `junit.framework.TestSuite` can be constructed with a class that contains multiple test methods as an argument. It will automatically recognize test methods and add them to the suite. This illustrates a good use of reflection, to ensure that code keeps itself up to date. We'll discuss the use of reflection in detail in Chapter 4. When we write new tests or delete old tests, we don't need to modify any central list of tests – avoiding the potential for errors. The `TestSuite` class provides an API allowing us to add further tests to a test suite easily, so that multiple tests can be composed.

We can use a number of **test runners** provided by JUnit that execute and display the results of tests. The two most often used are the text runner and the Swing runner, which displays a simple GUI. I recommend running JUnit tests from Ant (we'll discuss this below), which means using the text interface. The Swing test runner does provide the famous green bar when all tests pass, but text output provides a better audit trail.

Test methods invoke operations on the objects being tested and contain **assertions** based on comparing expected results with actual results. Assertions should contain messages explaining what went wrong to facilitate debugging in the case of failures. The JUnit framework provides several convenient assertion methods available to test cases, with signatures such as the following:

```
public void assertTrue(java.lang.String message, boolean condition)
public void assertSame(message, Object expected, Object actual)
```

Failed assertions amount to test failures, as do uncaught exceptions encountered by test methods. This last feature is very handy. We don't want to be forced into a lot of error handling in test cases, as `try/catch` blocks can rapidly produce large amounts of code that may be unnecessarily hard to understand. If an exception simply reflects something going wrong, rather than the expected behavior of the API with a given input, it is simpler not to catch it, but to let it cause a test failure.

Consider the following example of using JUnit, which also illustrates test-first development in action. We require the following method in a `StringUtils` class, which takes a comma-delimited (CSV) list such as "dog,cat,rabbit" and outputs an array of elements as individual strings: for this input, "dog", "cat", "rabbit":

```
public static String[] commaDelimitedListToStringArray(String s)
```

We see that we need to test the following conditions:

- ❑ Ordinary inputs – words and characters separated with commas.

- ❑ Inputs that include other punctuation characters, to ensure that they aren't treated as delimiters.

- ❑ A null string. The method should return the empty array on null input.

- ❑ A single string (without any commas). In this case, the return value should be an array containing a single string equal to the input string.

Using a test-first approach, the first step is to implement a JUnit test case. This will simply extend `junit.framework.TestCase`. As the method we're testing is static, there's no need to initialize a test fixture by overriding the `setUp()` method.

We declare the class, and provide the required constructor, as follows:

```
public class StringUtilsTestSuite extends TestCase {

  public StringUtilsTestSuite(String name) {
    super(name);
  }
```

We now add a test method for each of the four cases described above. The whole test class is shown below, but let's start by looking at the simplest test: the method that checks behavior on a null input string. There are no prizes for short test method names: we use method names of the form test<Method to be tested><Description of test>:

```
public void testCommaDelimitedListToStringArrayNullProducesEmptyArray() {
  String[] sa = StringUtils.commaDelimitedListToStringArray(null);
  assertTrue("String array isn't null with null input", sa != null);
  assertTrue("String array length == 0 with null input", sa.length == 0);
}
```

Note the use of multiple assertions, which will provide the maximum possible information in the event of failure. In fact, the first assertion isn't required as the second assertion will always fail to evaluate (with a NullPointerException, which causes a test failure), if the first assertion would fail. However it's more informative in the event of failure to separate the two.

Having written our tests first, we then implement the commaDelimitedListToStringArray() method to return null.

Next we run JUnit. We'll look at how to run JUnit below. As expected, all the tests fail.

Now we implement the method in the simplest and most obvious way: using the core Java java.util.StringTokenizer class. As it requires no more effort, we've implemented a more general delimitedListToStringArray() method, and treated commas as a special case:

```
public static String[] delimitedListToStringArray(
    String s, String delimiter) {

  if (s == null) {
    return new String[0];
  }

  if (delimiter == null) {
    return new String[] { s };
  }

  StringTokenizer st = new StringTokenizer(s, delimiter);
  String[] tokens = new String[st.countTokens()];
  System.out.println("length is  " + tokens.length);

  for (int i = 0; i < tokens.length; i++) {
    tokens[i] = st.nextToken();
  }
  return tokens;
}

public static String[] commaDelimitedListToStringArray(String s) {
  return delimitedListToStringArray(s, ",");
}
```

All our tests pass, and we believe that we've fully defined and tested the behavior required.

Sometime later it emerges that this method doesn't behave as expected with input strings such as "a,,b". We want this to result in a string array of length 3, containing the strings "a", the empty string, and "b". This is a bug, so we write a new test method that demonstrates it, and fails on the existing code:

```java
public void testCommaDelimitedListToStringArrayEmptyStrings() {

    String[] ss = StringUtils.commaDelimitedListToStringArray("a,,b");
    assertTrue("a,,b produces array length 3, not "
                + ss.length, ss.length == 3);
    assertTrue("components are correct",
                ss[0].equals("a") && ss[1].equals("") && ss[2].equals("b"));
    // Further tests omitted

}
```

Looking at the implementation of the delimitedListToStringArray() method, it is clear that the StringTokenizer library class doesn't deliver the behavior we want. So we reimplement the method, doing the tokenizing ourselves to deliver the expected result. In two test runs, we end up with the following version of the delimitedListToStringArray() method:

```java
public static String[] delimitedListToStringArray(
    String s, String delimiter) {

    if (s == null) {
      return new String[0];
    }

    if (delimiter == null) {
      return new String[] { s };
    }

    List l = new LinkedList();
    int delimCount = 0;
    int pos = 0;
    int delpos = 0;

    while ((delpos = s.indexOf(delimiter, pos)) != -1) {
      l.add(s.substring(pos, delpos));
      pos = delpos + delimiter.length();
    }

    if (pos <= s.length()) {
      // Add remainder of String
      l.add(s.substring(pos));
    }

    return (String[]) l.toArray(new String[l.size()]);
}
```

Although Java has relatively poor string handling, and string manipulation is a common cause of bugs, we can do this refactoring fearlessly, because we have regression tests to verify that the new code performs as did the original version (as well as satisfying the new test that demonstrated the bug).

Here's the complete code for the test cases. Note that this class includes a private method, `testCommaDelimitedListToStringArrayLegalMatch(String[] components)`, which builds a CSV-format string from the string array it is passed and verifies that the output of the `commaDelimitedListToStringArray()` method with this string matches the input array. Most of the public test methods use this method, and are much simpler as a result (although this method name begins with test, because it takes an argument, it won't be invoked directly by JUnit). It's often worth making this kind of investment in infrastructure in test classes:

```
public class StringUtilsTestSuite extends TestCase {

  public StringUtilsTestSuite(String name) {
    super(name);
  }

  public void testCommaDelimitedListToStringArrayNullProducesEmptyArray() {
    String[] sa = StringUtils.commaDelimitedListToStringArray(null);
    assertTrue("String array isn't null with null input", sa != null);
    assertTrue("String array length == 0 with null input", sa.length == 0);
  }

  private void testCommaDelimitedListToStringArrayLegalMatch(
      String[] components) {

    StringBuffer sbuf = new StringBuffer();
    // Build String array
    for (int i = 0; i < components.length; i++) {
    if (i != 0) {
      sbuf.append(",");
      sbuf.append(components[i]);
    }
    System.out.println("STRING IS " + sbuf);

    String[] sa =
      StringUtils.commaDelimitedListToStringArray(sbuf.toString());
    assertTrue("String array isn't null with legal match", sa != null);
    assertTrue("String array length is correct with legal match: returned " +
      sa.length + " when expecting " + components.length + " with String [" +
      sbuf.toString() + "]", sa.length == components.length);
    assertTrue("Output equals input", Arrays.equals(sa, components));
  }

  public void testCommaDelimitedListToStringArrayMatchWords() {
    // Could read these from files
    String[] sa = new String[] { "foo", "bar", "big" };
    testCommaDelimitedListToStringArrayLegalMatch(sa);

    sa = new String[] { "a", "b", "c" };
    testCommaDelimitedListToStringArrayLegalMatch(sa);

    // Test same words
    sa = new String[] { "AA", "AA", "AA", "AA", "AA" };
    testCommaDelimitedListToStringArrayLegalMatch(sa);
  }

  public void testCommaDelimitedListToStringArraySingleString() {
    String s = "woeirqupoiewuropqiewuorpqiwueopriquwopeiurqopwieur";
    String [] sa = StringUtils.commaDelimitedListToStringArray(s);
    assertTrue("Found one String with no delimiters", sa.length == 1);
```

```
      assertTrue("Single array entry matches input String with no delimiters",
         sa[0].equals(s));
   }

   public void testCommaDelimitedListToStringArrayWithOtherPunctuation() {
      String[] sa = new String[] { "xcvwert4456346&*.", "///", ".!", ".", ";" };
      testCommaDelimitedListToStringArrayLegalMatch(sa);
   }

   /** We expect to see the empty Strings in the output */
   public void testCommaDelimitedListToStringArrayEmptyStrings() {
      String[] ss = StringUtils.commaDelimitedListToStringArray("a,,b");
      assertTrue("a,,b produces array length 3, not " + ss.length,
         ss.length == 3);
      assertTrue("components are correct",
         ss[0].equals("a") && ss[1].equals("") && ss[2].equals("b"));
      String[] sa = new String[] { "", "", "a", "" };
      testCommaDelimitedListToStringArrayLegalMatch(sa);
   }

   public static void main(String[] args) {
      junit.textui.TestRunner.run(new TestSuite (StringUtilsTestSuite.class));
   }
}
```

Note the `main()` method, which constructs a new `TestSuite` given the current class, and runs it with the `junit.textui.TestRunner` class. It's handy, although not essential, for each JUnit test case to provide a `main()` method (as such `main()` methods invoke JUnit themselves, they can also use the Swing test runner).

JUnit requires no special configuration. We simply need to ensure that `junit.jar`, which contains all the JUnit binaries, is on the classpath at test time.

We have several choices for running JUnit test suites. JUnit is designed to allow the implementation of multiple "test runners" which are decoupled from actual tests (we'll look at some special test runners that allow execution of test suites within a J2EE server later). Typically we'll use one of the following approaches to run JUnit tests:

❑   Run test classes with a `main()` method from the command line.

❑   Run tests through an IDE that offers JUnit integration. As with invocation via a `main()` method, this also only usually allows us to run one test class at once.

❑   Run multiple tests as part of the application build process. Normally this is achieved with Ant. This is an essential part of the build process, and is discussed under *Automating Tests* towards the end of this chapter.

While automation using Ant is the key to integrating testing into the application build process, integration with an IDE can be very handy as we work on individual classes. The following screenshots show how the JUnit test suite discussed above can be invoked from the Eclipse IDE.

Clicking on the Run icon on the toolbar, we choose JUnit from the list of launchers on the Run With submenu:

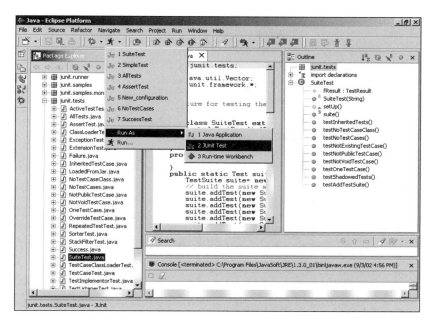

Eclipse brings up a dialog box to display the progress and result of the tests. A green bar indicates success; a red bar, failure. Any errors or failures are listed, with their stack trace appearing in the Failure Trace pane:

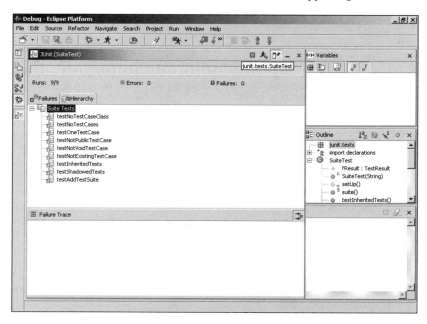

Test Practices

Now that we've seen JUnit in action, let's step back a little and look at some good practices for writing tests. Although we'll discuss implementing them with JUnit, these practices are applicable to whatever test tool we may choose to use.

Write Tests to Interfaces

Wherever possible, write tests to interfaces, rather than classes. It's good OO design practice to program to interfaces, rather than classes, and testing should reflect this. Different test suites can easily be created to run the same tests against implementations of an interface (see *Inheritance and Testing* later).

Don't Bother Testing JavaBean Properties

It's usually unnecessary to test property getters and setters. It's usually a waste of time to develop such tests. Also, bloating test cases with code that isn't really useful makes them harder to read and maintain.

Maximizing Test Coverage

Test-first development is the best strategy for ensuring that we maximize test coverage. However, sometimes tools can help to verify that we have met our goals for test coverage. For example, a profiling tool such as Sitraka's JProbe Profiler (discussed in Chapter 15) can be used to examine the execution path through an application under test and establish what code was (and wasn't) executed.

Specialized tools such as JProbe Coverage (also part of the JProbe Suite) make this much easier. JProbe Coverage can analyze one or more test runs along with the application codebase, to produce a list of methods and even lines of source code that weren't executed.

The modest investment in such a tool is likely to be worthwhile when it's necessary to implement a test suite for code that doesn't already have one.

Don't Rely on the Ordering of Test Cases

When using reflection to identify test methods to execute, JUnit does not guarantee the order in which it runs tests. Thus tests shouldn't rely on other tests having been executed previously. If ordering is vital, it's possible to add tests to a `TestSuite` object programmatically. They will be executed in the order in which they were added. However, it's best to avoid ordering issues by using the `setUp()` method appropriately.

Avoid Side Effects

For the same reasons, it's important to avoid side effects when testing. A side effect occurs when one test changes the state of the system being tested in a way that may affect subsequent tests. Changes to persistent data in a database are also potential side effects.

Read Test Data from the Classpath, Not the File System

It's essential that tests are easy to run. A minimum of configuration should be required. A common cause of problems when running a test suite is for tests to read their configuration from the file system. Using absolute file paths will cause problems when code is checked out to a different location; different file location and path conventions (such as `\home\rodj\tests\foo.dat` or `C:\\Documents and Settings\\rodj\\foo.dat`) can tie tests to a particular operating system. These problems can be avoided by loading test data from the classpath, with the `Class.getResource()` or `Class.getResourceAsStream()` methods. The necessary resources are usually best placed in the same directory as the test classes that use them.

Avoid Code Duplication in Test Cases

Test cases are an important part of the application. As with application code, the more code duplication they contain, the more likely they are to contain errors. The more code test cases contain the more of a chore they are to write and the less likely it is that they will be written. Avoid this problem by a small investment in test infrastructure. We've already seen the use of a private method by several test cases, which greatly simplifies the test methods using it.

When Should We Write "Stub" Classes?

Sometimes classes we wish to test depend on other classes that aren't easy to provide at test time. If we follow good coding practice, any such dependencies will be on interfaces, rather than classes.

In J2EE applications, such dependencies will often be on implementation classes supplied by the application server. However, we often wish to be able to test code outside the server. For example, a class intended for use as a Data Access Object (DAO) in the EJB tier may require a `javax.sql.DataSource` object to provide connections to an RDBMS, but may have no other dependency on an EJB container. We may want to test this class outside a J2EE server.

In such cases, we can write simple stub implementations of interfaces required by classes under test. For example, we can implement a trivial `javax.sql.DataSource` that always returns a connection to a test database (we won't need to implement our own connection pool). Particularly useful stub implementations, such as a test `DataSource` are generic, and can be used in multiple tests cases, making it much easier to write and run tests. We can also use stub implementations of application objects that aren't presently available, or aren't yet written (for example, to enable development on the web tier to progress in parallel with development of the EJB tier).

The `/framework/test` directory in the download with this book includes several useful generic test classes, including the `jdbc.TestDataSource` class that enables us to test DAOs without a J2EE server.

This strategy delivers real value when implementing the stubbed objects doesn't involve too much work. It's best to avoid writing unduly complex stub implementations. If stubbed objects begin to have dependencies on other stubbed objects, we should consider alternative testing strategies.

Inheritance and Testing

We need to consider the implications of the inheritance hierarchy of classes we test. A class should pass all tests associated with its superclasses and the interfaces it implements. This is a corollary of the "Liskov Substitution Principle", which we'll meet in Chapter 4.

When using JUnit, we can use inheritance to our advantage. When one JUnit test case extends another (rather than extending `junit.framework.TestCase` directly), all the tests in the superclass are executed, as well as tests added in the subclass. This means that JUnit test cases can use an inheritance hierarchy paralleling the concrete inheritance hierarchy of the classes being tested.

In another use of inheritance among test cases, when a test case is written against an interface, we can make the test case abstract, and test individual implementations in concrete subclasses. The abstract superclass can declare a protected abstract method returning the actual object to be tested, forcing subclasses to implement it.

> **It's good practice to subclass a more general JUnit test case to add new tests for a subclass of an object or a particular implementation of an interface.**

Let's consider an example, from the code used in our sample application. This code is discussed in detail in Chapter 11. Don't worry about what it does at the moment; we're only interested here in how to test classes and interfaces belonging to an inheritance hierarchy. One of the central interfaces in this supporting code is the BeanFactory interface, which provides methods to return objects it manages:

```
Object getAsSingleton(String name) throws BeansException;
```

A commonly used subinterface is ListableBeanFactory, which adds additional methods to query the names of all managed objects, such as the following:

```
String[] getBeanDefinitionNames();
```

Several classes implement the ListableBeanFactory interface, such as XmlBeanFactory (which takes bean definitions from an XML document). All implementing classes pass all tests against the ListableBeanFactory interface as well as all tests applying to the BeanFactory root interface. The following class diagram illustrates the inheritance hierarchy among these application interfaces and classes:

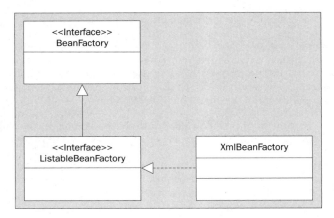

It's natural to mirror this inheritance hierarchy in the related test cases. The root of the JUnit test case hierarchy will be an abstract BeanFactoryTests class. This will include tests against the BeanFactory interface, and define a protected abstract method, getBeanFactory() that subclasses must implement to return the actual BeanFactory. Individual test methods in the BeanFactoryTests class will call this method to obtain the fixture object to run tests against. A subclass, ListableBeanFactoryTests, will include additional tests against the functionality added in the ListableBeanFactory interface and ensure that the BeanFactory returned by the getBeanFactory() method is of the ListableBeanFactory subinterface.

As both these test classes contain tests against interfaces, they will both be abstract. As JUnit is based on concrete inheritance, a test case hierarchy will be wholly concrete. There is little value in test interfaces.

Either one of these abstract test classes can be extended by concrete test classes, such as XmlBeanFactoryTests. Concrete test classes will instantiate and configure the concrete BeanFactory or ListableBeanFactory implementation to be tested and (optionally) add new tests specific to this class (there's often no need for new class-specific tests; the aim is simply to create a fixture object that the superclass tests can be run against). All test cases defined in all superclasses will be inherited and run automatically by JUnit. The following class diagram illustrates the test case hierarchy:

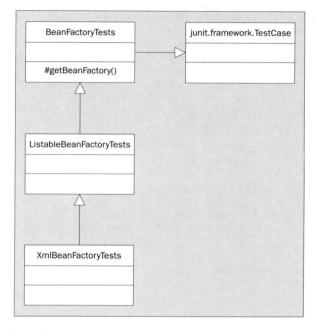

The following excerpt from the BeanFactoryTests abstract base test class shows how it extends junit.framework.TestCase and implements the required constructor:

```
public abstract class BeanFactoryTests
    extends junit.framework.TestCase {

  public BeanFactoryTests(String name) {
    super(name);
  }
```

The following is the definition of the protected abstract method that must be implemented by concrete subclasses:

```
protected abstract BeanFactory getBeanFactory();
```

The following test method from the BeanFactoryTests class illustrates the use of this method:

```
public void testNotThere() throws Exception {
  try {
    Object o = getBeanFactory().getBean("Mr Squiggle");
    fail("Can't find missing bean");
  } catch (NoSuchBeanDefinitionException ex) {
    // Correct behavior
    // Test should fail on any other exception
  }
}
```

The `ListableBeanFactoryTests` class merely adds more test methods. It does not implement the protected abstract method.

The following code fragment from the `XmlBeanFactoryTests` class – a concrete test suite that tests an implementation of the `ListableBeanFactory` interface – shows how the abstract `getBeanFactory()` method is implemented, based on an instance variable initialized in the `setUp()` method:

```
public class XmlBeanFactoryTests
    extends ListableBeanFactoryTests {

  private XmlBeanFactory factory;

  public XmlBeanFactoryTests (String name) {
    super(name);
  }

  protected void setUp() throws Exception {
    InputStream is = getClass().getResourceAsStream("test.xml");
    this.factory = new XmlBeanFactory(is);
  }

  protected BeanFactory getBeanFactory() {
    return factory;
  }

  // XmlBeanFactory specific tests...
}
```

When this test class is executed by JUnit, the test methods defined in it and its two superclasses will all be executed, ensuring that the `XmlBeanFactory` class correctly implements the contract of the `BeanFactory` and `ListableBeanFactory` interfaces, as well as any special requirements that apply only to it.

Where Should Test Cases be Located?

Place tests in a separate source tree from the code to be tested. We don't want to generate Javadoc for test cases for users of the classes, and it should be easy to JAR up application classes without test cases. Both these tasks are harder if tests are in the same source tree as application code.

However, it is important to ensure that tests are compiled with each application build. If tests don't compile, they're out of synch with code and therefore useless. Using Ant, we can build code in a single operation regardless of where it is located.

I follow a common practice in using a parallel package structure for classes to be tested and test cases. This means that the tests for the `com.mycompany.beans` package will also in the `com.mycompany.beans` package, albeit in a separate source tree. This allows access to protected and package-protected methods (which is occasionally useful), but, more importantly, makes it easy to find the test cases for any class.

Should Testing Strategy Affect How We Write Code?

Testing is such an important part of the development process that it is legitimate for the testing strategy we use to affect how we write application code – with certain reservations.

First, the reservations: I don't favor white-box testing and don't advocate increasing the visibility of methods and variables to facilitate testing. The "parallel" source tree structure we've discussed gives test cases access to protected and package-protected methods and variables, but this is not usually necessary. As we've seen, the existence of comprehensive tests promotes refactoring – being able to run existing tests provides reassurance that refactoring hasn't broken anything. White-box testing reduces the value of this important benefit. If test cases depend on implementation details of a class, refactoring the class has the potential to break both class and test case simultaneously – a dangerous state of affairs. If maintaining tests becomes too much of a chore, they won't be maintained, and our testing strategy will break down.

So what implications might a rigorous unit testing strategy have on coding style?

❑ It encourages us to ensure that classes don't have too much responsibility, which makes testing unduly complex. I always use fairly fine-grained objects, so this doesn't tend to affect my coding style. However, many developers do report that adopting test-first development changes their style in this respect.

❑ It prompts us to ensure that class instance variables can only be modified through method calls (otherwise, external changes to instance variables can make tests meaningless; if the state of a class can be changed other than through the methods it declares, tests can't prove very much). Again, this reflects good design practice: public instance variables violate encapsulation.

❑ It encourages us to prompt stricter encapsulation with respect to inheritance. The use of read-write protected instance variables allows subclasses to corrupt the state of a superclass, as does allowing the overriding of concrete methods. In the next chapter, we'll discuss these issues from the perspective of OO design.

❑ It occasionally prompts us to add methods purely intended to facilitate testing. For example, it may be legitimate to add a package-protected method exposing information about a class's state purely to facilitate testing. Consider a class that allows listeners to be registered through a public method, but has no method exposing the listeners registered (because other application code has no interest in this).

Adding a package-protected method returning a Collection (or whatever type is most convenient) of registered listeners won't complicate the class's public interface or allow the class's state to be corrupted, but will be very useful to a test class in the same package. For example, a test class could easily register a number of listeners and then call the package-protected method to check that only these listeners are registered or it could publish an event using the class and check that all registered listeners were notified of it.

By far the biggest effect of having comprehensive unit tests on coding style is the flow-on effect: the refactoring guarantee. This requires that we think of the tests as a central part of the application.

We've already discussed how this allows us to perform optimization if necessary. There are also significant implications for achieving J2EE portability. Consider a session EJB for which we have defined the remote and home interfaces. Our testing strategy dictates that we should have comprehensive tests against the public (component) interface (the container conceals the bean implementation class). These tests amount to a guarantee of the EJB's functionality from the client perspective.

Now, suppose that our present requirement is for a system that uses an Oracle database. We can write a session bean that uses a helper class that runs Oracle-specific SQL. If, in the future, we need to migrate to another database, we can reimplement the bean's implementation class, leaving the component interface alone. The test cases will help ensure that the system behaves as before. This approach isn't "pure" J2EE, but it is effective in practice and it allows us to use the simplest and most efficient implementation at any point.

Of course, we should try to share code between bean implementation classes wherever possible (perhaps in an abstract superclass). If this is not possible – or if the effort involved in achieving it would outweigh the benefit – test cases provide a working specification of what the implementation classes should do, and will make it much easier to provide different implementations if necessary.

Integration and Acceptance Testing

Acceptance testing is testing from a customer perspective. Inevitably this will involve some hands-on testing, in which testers play the role of users, and execute test scenarios. However, we can also automate aspects of acceptance testing.

Integration testing is slightly lower level, and tests how application classes or components work together. The distinction between unit and integration tests blurs in practice; we can often use the same tool (such as JUnit) for both. Integration tests merely involve higher-level classes, that use many other classes (for which there are unit tests) to do their work.

Testing Business Objects

If we follow the design recommendations of Chapter 1, application business logic will be exposed via a layer of business interfaces. Tests written against these interfaces will be the core of application integration testing. Testing application interface layers, such as a web interface, will be simpler because we only need to test whether the interface layer correctly invokes the business interfaces – we know that the implementations of the business interfaces work correctly if invoked correctly.

Typically, we can take the application's use cases and write a number of test cases for each. Often one method on a business interface will correspond to a single use case.

Depending on the architectural choices we discussed in Chapter 1, business objects may be implemented as ordinary Java classes running in the web container (without using EJB, but with access to most of J2EE's container services), or as EJBs. Let's look at the issues in testing each in turn.

Testing Business Objects Implemented Without Using EJB

Testing ordinary Java classes is relatively easy. We can simply use JUnit. The only significant problem is likely to involve configuration required by the class and access to external resources such as databases and container services such as JNDI.

Container services can often be simulated by test objects; for example, we can use a generic test JNDI implementation that enables business objects to perform JNDI lookups when instantiated outside an application server (this is discussed further below).

With business objects, we will always write tests to our business interfaces.

Some business objects depend on other application objects – although such dependencies should be on interfaces, not classes. We have three main choices to address this:

❑   Replace the required objects with test implementations of the relevant interfaces, which return test data. This works well so long as the interfaces aren't complex to implement. It's also essentially a unit testing, rather than integration testing, technique.

❑   Implement tests that can run within the application server, with the application configured as in production. We'll discuss this approach below, as it's often the only option for testing EJBs.

❑   Try to design application infrastructure so that application configuration doesn't depend on the J2EE server. The JavaBeans-based application infrastructure discussed in Chapter 11 facilitates this, enabling the same application-specific configuration files to be read by a test harness as at run time. It ensures that – except where EJBs are concerned – many business objects can be tested outside the EJB container, configured as in production. Business interface implementations that depend on container services can be replaced by test implementations, to allow integration testing without deployment on an application server.

Testing EJBs

Testing EJBs is much harder than testing ordinary Java classes, because EJBs depend on EJB container services.

We will generally focus on testing session beans, rather than entity beans, even if we do choose to use entity beans. Entity beans don't usually contain business logic; their effect on persistent data should be checked by session bean tests.

We can't simply instantiate EJBs and test them like ordinary Java classes. EJBs are managed objects; the EJB container manages their lifecycle at run time and they depend on container services such as connection pools. Furthermore, the container controls access to their functionality, and the behavior added by container interception (such as transaction management and security restrictions) is part of the application itself and needs to be tested.

There are several ways around this problem:

❑   Write a test that is a remote client of the EJB container. This is usually the best approach for testing EJBs with remote interfaces.

❑   Write and deploy a test that executes within the application server. This is a good strategy for testing EJBs with local interfaces. It will require additional infrastructure to supplement JUnit.

❑   Test with stub objects replacing container objects. This will generally only work when EJBs have simple requirements of the EJB container.

The most obvious approach is the remote client approach. This is simple and intuitive. We can write ordinary JUnit test cases, which connect to the EJB server. The test cases run in a separate JVM from the EJB container. We can invoke them as we invoke any JUnit tests, simply needing to take care that we provide the appropriate JNDI properties to allow connection to the EJB container and supply the necessary EJB client binaries. On the negative side, testing through a remote client doesn't enable us to test EJBs via their local interfaces. We are unable to test the effect of local call semantics. Even when we wish to test EJBs with remote interfaces, this may be a problem, as we may wish to allow container optimizations when running EJBs and web applications in the same server instance.

We can get around these problems by writing tests that execute within the application server. Typically, we package tests as web applications, giving them access to EJBs running in the same JVM (this will probably allow local calling, but this isn't presently guaranteed by the J2EE specifications). However, this approach is harder to implement, requires additional infrastructure for JUnit, and complicates application deployment.

Finally, we can simulate our own EJB container to supply the services the EJBs expect at run time. However, this is usually impracticable, because of the complexity of the EJB infrastructure. EJBs don't merely have access to container-provided interfaces such as a `javax.ejb.SessionContext`; they have access to container services other than directly through the API (for example, the ability to access their naming context). Security and transaction management services are also difficult to replicate.

The download for this book includes some useful generic classes in the `/framework/test` directory that can be used with this approach: for example, dummy EJB context objects, and a test JNDI implementation to allow the binding of required objects in a simulated naming context to allow EJBs to perform JNDI lookups as if they are running within a server. However, this approach only works when EJBs have simple requirements of the container. When using this approach we must also ensure that we invoke EJB lifecycle methods such as `setSessionContext()` when creating a test fixture.

The following table summarizes the advantages and disadvantages of the three approaches:

Approach	Advantages	Disadvantages
Testing with a remote client.	Easy to write and run tests. Can use standard JUnit infrastructure. Will ensure that our EJBs support genuine remote semantics. The remote interfaces exposed by the EJB tier in a distributed application usually expose an application's business logic, so this is a natural place to test.	We can't test local interfaces. The application may use call by reference in production, even with remote interfaces.
Testing within the application server (either in the EJB container or web container).	In the case of web applications, this will probably mean that tests will have exactly the same access to the EJB tier as the application code that uses the EJB tier.	Requires additional test framework. More complex implementation, deployment, and invocation of tests.
Testing with stub objects replacing container objects.	We can run tests without an EJB container. We may be able to reuse standard infrastructure components in multiple applications.	We may end up writing a lot of classes simulating container behavior. We haven't tested the application in the application server we will deploy it on.

If we test EJBs using remote interfaces we need no special tools beyond JUnit itself. If we test inside the EJB container, we need a tool that enables test cases to be packaged into a J2EE application.

Cactus

The most sophisticated free tool I'm aware of for testing within the application server is **Cactus** (available at http://jakarta.apache.org/cactus/index.html). It is an open source framework based on JUnit that allows EJBs, servlets, JSP pages, and servlet filters to be tested within the target application server.

Cactus allows test invocation and result reporting on the client side as with ordinary JUnit tests: Cactus takes care of connecting to the server, where the test cases actually run. The test runner in the client JVM connects to a Cactus "redirector" in the server JVM. Although each test class is instantiated in both server and client, the tests are executed within a web application running within the server. Typically this will be the same web application that contains the application's web interface.

Cactus is a complex framework and is relatively complex to set up. However, it's a good approach for testing EJBs, in which case the complexity is unavoidable.

Setting up Cactus involves the following steps:

1. Ensure that the Cactus classpath is set correctly. This area is the most common cause of errors when using Cactus, so please read the documentation on "Setting up Cactus classpaths" included in the Cactus distribution carefully. Most of the Cactus binaries must be included in a WAR distribution, under the /WEB-INF/lib directory.

If more than one application is likely to use Cactus, I recommend including the Cactus binaries at server-wide level, so they will be available to all applications. In JBoss, this simply means copying the JAR files to the /lib directory of the JBoss server to which you deploy applications. When using this approach, there's no need to include Cactus JARs in the /WEB-INF/lib directory of each WAR. When using Cactus to test EJBs, ensure that none of the Cactus servlet test cases is included in the EJB JAR. This will result in class loading problems that will generate mysterious "class not found" errors.

2. Edit the web application's web.xml deployment descriptor to define the Cactus "servlet redirector" servlet that will route requests from the remote tests to the server-side test instances. This definition should look like this:

```
<servlet>
    <servlet-name>ServletRedirector</servlet-name>
    <servlet-class>
        org.apache.cactus.server.ServletTestRedirector
    </servlet-class>
</servlet>
```

We also need to provide a URL mapping to this servlet (note that for some web containers, such as Jetty, it's necessary to drop the trailing / included in the example in Cactus documentation, as I've done in this example):

```
<servlet-mapping>
    <servlet-name>ServletRedirector</servlet-name>
    <url-pattern>/ServletRedirector</url-pattern>
</servlet-mapping>
```

95

3. Include the test classes in the WAR. Cactus test classes must be derived from a Cactus superclass that handles redirection – we'll discuss this below.

4. Configure the Cactus client. We'll need to ensure that all Cactus binaries (those required on the server-side and additional client-side libraries) are available to the client. We must also supply a `cactus.properties` file, to tell Cactus the server URL and port and specify the context path of the web application. For testing the sample application on my local machine, the `cactus.properties` file is as follows. Note that the `servletRedirectorName` property should match the URL mapping we created in `web.xml`:

```
cactus.contextURL = http://localhost:8080/ticket
cactus.servletRedirectorName = ServletRedirector
cactus.jspRedirectorName = JspRedirector
```

Once we've followed all these steps, we can invoke the test cases on the client side like normal JUnit test cases.

Let's look at what's involved in writing a Cactus test case. The principles are the same as for any JUnit test case, but we must extend Cactus's `org.apache.cactus.ServletTestCase`, not `junit.framework.TestCase` directly. The `org.apache.cactus.ServletTestCase` superclass provides the ability to invoke tests and perform reporting in the client, while tests actually run inside the server.

Let's look at a practical example. We begin by extending `org.apache.cactus.ServletTestCase`:

```
public class CactusTest extends ServletTestCase {
```

The remainder of our class uses normal JUnit concepts. We set up a test fixture following normal JUnit conventions, and implement test methods as usual:

```
private BoxOffice boxOffice;

public CactusTest(String arg0) {
  super(arg0);
}

public static Test suite() {
  return new TestSuite (CactusTest.class);
}
```

We can access the server's JNDI context to look up EJBs when creating a test fixture, either in the `setUp()` method, as shown below, or in individual test methods:

```
public void setUp() throws Exception {
  Context ctx = new InitialContext();
  BoxOfficeHome home =
    (BoxOfficeHome) ctx.lookup("java:comp/env/ejb/BoxOffice");
  this.boxOffice = home.create();
}

public void testCounts() throws Exception {
  int all = boxOffice.getSeatCount(1);
  int free = boxOffice.getFreeSeatCount(1);
  assertTrue("all > o", all > 0);
  assertTrue("all > free", all >= free);
}
}
```

The `org.apache.cactus.ServletTestCase` class makes a number of "implicit objects" available to subclass test methods as instance variables, including the `ServletConfig` object, from which we can obtain the web application's global `ServletContext`. This is very useful when we need to access web application attributes.

Cactus also provides the ability to provide test inputs on the client side; through additional methods associated with each test case (this is most relevant for testing servlets, rather than EJBs). Please refer to the detailed Cactus documentation for information about such advanced features.

This is a powerful mechanism of ensuring that we enjoy the benefits offered by JUnit, such as the ability to execute multiple test suites automatically, while actually running tests in the server. However, it complicates application deployment. Typically we'll need distinct build targets to build the application including test cases, Cactus configuration and Cactus binaries for testing, and to build the application without test support for production.

> *JUnitEE (http://junitee.sourceforge.net/) is a simpler framework than Cactus, but is also based on running tests within the J2EE server. Like Cactus, JUnitEE packages tests in WARs. JUnitEE provides a servlet that runs ordinary JUnit test cases within the web container. Instead of using a redirection mechanism with test cases held on both client and server, JUnitEE provides a servlet that allows test cases to be chosen and output generated on the server.*
>
> *It's very easy to implement tests using JUnitEE, because test cases are simply JUnit test cases. All the JUnitEE infrastructure does is to provide a J2EE-aware means of running the test cases. Test cases will simply be implemented with the knowledge that they will run within the J2EE server running the application. The most important implication is that they have access to JNDI, which they can use to look up application EJBs to test.*
>
> *The downside of this simpler approach is that tests can only be invoked from a browser, meaning that it's impossible to automate the test process.*

Cactus didn't support this simpler, more intuitive, approach in the past, but Cactus 1.4 provides a "Servlet test runner" that enables Cactus to use the same approach as JUnitEE. I recommend using Cactus, rather than JUnitEE, even if using this approach, as it's very important to be able to automate tests as part of the build process.

To use the Cactus 1.4 servlet test runner, we need to follow the following steps:

1. Ensure that *all* Cactus binaries – not just the server-side binaries – are distributed in the application WAR (or placed on the server classpath, so as to be available to all applications).

2. Edit `web.xml` to create a servlet definition and URL mapping for the Cactus `ServletTestRunner` servlet. The servlet definition is shown below:

```
<servlet>
    <servlet-name>ServletTestRunner</servlet-name>
    <servlet-class>
        org.apache.cactus.server.runner.ServletTestRunner
    </servlet-class>
</servlet>
```

The URL mapping should look like this:

```
<servlet-mapping>
    <servlet-name>ServletTestRunner</servlet-name>
    <url-pattern>/ServletTestRunner</url-pattern>
</servlet-mapping>
```

3. Ensure that the test cases are included in the WAR. Note that we aren't forced to extend `org.apache.cactus.ServletTestCase` when we use this approach; we can use ordinary JUnit test cases if we prefer (although these won't support Cactus redirection if we want to automate tests).

With this approach, we don't need to worry about client-side configuration, as we can run tests through a browser. All we need to do is to request a URL such as:

http://localhost:8080/mywebapp/ServletTestRunner?suite=com.mycompany.MyTest&xsl=junit-noframes.xsl

The servlet test runner returns the results as an XML document by default; the `xsl` parameter in the above example specifies a stylesheet that can be used to transform the XML results to HTML and render them in a browser (the stylesheet is included with the Cactus distribution, but must be included in each application WAR using the servlet test runner).

Test results will be displayed as in the following example from Cactus documentation:

Unit Test Results

Designed for use with JUnit and Ant.

Summary

Tests	Failures	Errors	Success rate	Time
13	0	0	100.00%	1.331

Note: *failures* are anticipated and checked for with assertions while *errors* are unanticipated.

Packages

Note: package statistics are not computed recursively, they only sum up all of its testsuites numbers.

Name	Tests	Errors	Failures	Time(s)
	0	0	0	0.000

Package

Name	Tests	Errors	Failures	Time(s)
Back to top				

TestCase org.apache.cactus.sample.TestSampleServlet

Name	Status	Type	Time(s)
testReadServletOutputStream	Success		0.360
testPostMethod	Success		0.040
testGetMethod	Success		0.040
testSetAttribute	Success		0.041
testSetRequestAttribute	Success		0.040
testSendParams	Success		0.040
testSendHeader	Success		0.030
testSendCookie	Success		0.220
testSendMultipleCookies	Success		0.020
testReceiveHeader	Success		0.020
testReceiveCookie	Success		0.040
testRequestDispatcherForward	Success		0.220
testRequestDispatcherInclude	Success		0.030

Properties »

Back to top

This has the virtues and disadvantages of the JUnitEE approach to testing within the server. It's relatively simple to configure, but isn't scriptable, and so can't easily be integrated into the application build process.

> **When we use EJBs with remote interfaces, we can write ordinary JUnit test cases that test them from a remote JVM.**
>
> **When we use EJBs with local interfaces, we will usually need to test them within the target application server.**

The disadvantages of testing within the application server are that it complicates application deployment and takes longer to configure and execute than testing ordinary Java classes.

Testing Database Interaction

Business objects, whether they're EJBs or ordinary Java objects, will certainly interact (although not necessary directly) with a database, and will depend on J2EE data sources. Hence we'll have to consider the effect of our tests on data in the database and the data they require. There are several strategies here.

The most radical is to do away with the database at test time and replace actual JDBC classes with mock objects (see http://www.mockobjects.com/papers/jdbc_testfirst.html for more information on this approach). This approach avoids any requirements for or issues relating to modification of persistent data. However, it won't help us test complex queries or updates (which we really want the target database to run as part of our application code), and is difficult to integrate with EJB containers.

Thus normally we will need to access a test database. This means that we'll typically need to write SQL scripts that execute before each test run to put the database into the desired state. These SQL scripts are integral parts of the tests. Using Ant, it's possible to automate the execution of database scripts before we run tests: Ant allows us to execute SQL statements held in a build file or in a separate script.

When testing JDBC helper classes, it may be possible to write a test case that rolls back any changes, meaning that it's not necessary to clean the database afterwards. However, when we test code running in an EJB container this is impossible, as the EJB container should create and commit or rollback the transaction.

Changes to persistent data are central to the functionality of much EJB code. Thus test cases must have the ability to connect to the database and examine data before and after the execution of EJB code. We must also check that rollback occurs when demanded by business logic or if an error is encountered.

To illustrate this, consider testing the following method on an EJB's remote interface:

```
InvoiceVO placeOrder(int customerId, InvoiceItem[] items)
    throws NoSuchCustomerException, RemoteException, SpendingLimitViolation;
```

We need multiple test cases here: one for valid orders, one for orders by non-existent customers to check that the correct exception is thrown, and one for an order of an illegally large amount to check that `SpendingLimitViolation` is thrown. Our test cases should include code to generate orders for random customers and random products.

This level of testing requires that the test cases should be able to access the underlying data. To achieve this, we use a helper object with a connection to the same database as the EJB server to run SQL functions and queries to verify the EJB's behavior. We can also use a helper object to load data from the database to provide a set of customer numbers and item numbers that we can use to generate random orders. We'll discuss suitable JDBC helper classes in Chapter 9.

Consider the following test method that checks that an excessively large order results in a `SpendingLimitViolation` exception being thrown. It's also the responsibility of the EJB to ensure that the transaction is rolled back in this event, and that there are no lasting changes to the database. We should check this as well. This test method requires the existence of two Products (invoice items) in the database, and a Customer with primary key of 1. A test script should ensure that this data is present before the test case runs:

```java
public void testPlaceUnauthorizedOrder() throws Exception {

    int invoicesPre = helper.runSQLFunction("SELECT COUNT(ID) FROM INVOICE");
    int itemsPre = helper.runSQLFunction("SELECT COUNT(*) FROM ITEM");
    InvoiceItem[] items = new InvoiceItem[2];

    // Constructor takes item id and quantity
    // We specify a ridiculously large quantity to ensure failure
    items[0] = new InvoiceItemImpl(1, 10000);
    items[1] = new InvoiceItemImpl(2, 13000);

    try {
        InvoiceVO inv = sales.placeOrder(1, items);
        int id = inv.getId();
        fail ("Shouldn't have created new invoice for excessive amount");
    } catch (SpendingLimitViolation ex) {
        System.out.println("CORRECT: spending limit violation " + ex);
    }

    int invoicesPost = helper.runSQLFunction("SELECT COUNT(ID) FROM INVOICE");
    int itemsPost = helper.runSQLFunction("SELECT COUNT(*) FROM ITEM");
    assertTrue("Must have same number of invoices after rollback",
        invoicesPost == invoicesPre);
    assertTrue("Must have same number of items after rollback",
        itemsPost == itemsPre);
}
```

Thus we need to make a modest investment in infrastructure to support test cases.

Testing Web Interfaces

It's harder to test web interfaces than ordinary Java classes, or even EJBs. Web applications don't provide neat, easily verifiable responses: the dynamic content we need to test exists as islands in a sea of fancy markup. The look and feel of web applications changes frequently; we need to be able to design tests that don't need to be rewritten every time this happens.

There are a host of web-specific issues, some difficult to reproduce in automated testing. For example:

❑   Resubmission of a form (for example, what if the user resubmits a purchase form while the server is still processing the first submission?)

❑   The implications of use of the back button

❑   Security issues, such as resistance to denial of service attacks

❑   Issues if the user opens multiple windows (for example, we may need to synchronize web-tier access to stateful session beans)

❑   The implications of canceled requests

❑   The implications of browser (and possibly ISP) caching

❑   Whether both GET and POST requests should be supported

Like EJBs, web-tier components depend on container services, making unit testing difficult.

JSP pages are particularly hard to unit test. They don't exist as Java classes until they're deployed into a web container, they depend on the Servlet API and they don't offer an easily testable interface. This is one reason why JSP should never implement business logic, which must always be tested. JSP pages are normally tested as part of the application's complete web interface.

Some other view technologies, such as Velocity templates and XSLT stylesheets, are easier to unit test, as they don't depend on the Servlet API. However, in general there's little need to test views in isolation, so this isn't an important consideration.

We'll normally focus on two approaches to testing web interfaces: unit testing of web-tier Java classes; and acceptance testing of the overall web application. Let's discuss each in turn.

Unit Testing Web-Tier Components

We can test web-tier Java classes outside the servlet container using standard JUnit functionality by providing stub objects that emulate the server. The **ServletUnit** project (http://sourceforge.net/projects/servletunit/) provides objects that can be used to invoke servlets and other Servlet API-dependent classes outside a container, such as test `ServletContext`, `HttpServletRequest`, and `HttpServletResponse` implementations. This enables us to invoke any request handling method directly, and make assertions about the response (for example, that it contains appropriate attributes). This approach works well for simple web-tier classes. However, it's less useful if objects require more complex initialization (for example, loading data contained within a WAR's `/WEB-INF` directory).

While the ServletUnit package is an excellent idea, it's a simplistic implementation, which doesn't implement some of the Servlet API methods we will want to work with (such as the status code methods). The `/framework/test/servletapi` directory of the download accompanying this book contains more usable test objects, originally based on the ServletUnit implementations but providing more sophisticated functionality.

It's very simple to use this approach. The test objects not only implement the relevant Servlet API interface, but also provide methods enabling us to provide data to the classes being tested. The commonest requirement is to add request parameters. The following example creates a `GET` request for the URL "`test.html`", with a single "`name`" parameter:

```
TestHttpRequest request = new TestHttpRequest(null, "GET", "test.html");
request.addParameter("name", name);
```

Since it's good practice to implement web applications using an MVC framework, we won't normally need to test servlets directly (MVC frameworks usually provide a single generic controller servlet, which isn't part of our application). Typically we will use test Servlet API objects to test individual request controllers (we can assume that the controller framework has already been tested and that our request controllers will be invoked correctly at run time).

For example, the MVC web application framework used in our sample application (discussed in Chapter 12) requires request controllers to implement the following interface:

```
ModelAndView handleRequest(HttpServletRequest request,
   HttpServletResponse response) throws ServletException, IOException;
```

101

Request controllers don't actually generate response content (this is the role of views), but select the name of a view that should render the response, and provide model data it should display. The ModelAndView object returned by the above method contains both view name and model data. This decoupling of controller and view is not only good design practice, but greatly simplifies unit testing. We can ignore markup generation and simply test that the controller selects the correct view and exposes the necessary model data.

Let's look at a following simple controller implementation, along with a JUnit test class we can use to test it. The controller returns one of three different view names based on the presence and validity of a name request parameter. If a parameter was supplied, it forms the model passed to a view:

```java
public class DemoController implements Controller {

    public static final String ENTER_NAME_VIEW = "enterNameView";
    public static final String INVALID_NAME_VIEW = "invalidNameView";
    public static final String VALID_NAME_VIEW = "validNameView";

    public ModelAndView handleRequest(HttpServletRequest request,
        HttpServletResponse response) throws ServletException {

        String name = request.getParameter("name");
        if (name == null || "".equals(name)) {
            return new ModelAndView(ENTER_NAME_VIEW);
        } else if (name.indexOf("-") != -1) {
            return new ModelAndView(INVALID_NAME_VIEW, "name", name);
        } else {
            return new ModelAndView(VALID_NAME_VIEW, "name",  name);
        }
    }

}
```

The following JUnit test case will check the three cases – name parameter not supplied; name parameter valid; and name parameter invalid:

```java
package com.interface21.web.servlet.mvc;

import javax.servlet.http.HttpServletResponse;

import com.interface21.web.servlet.ModelAndView;

import junit.framework.TestCase;
import servletapi.TestHttpRequest;
import servletapi.TestHttpResponse;

public class DemoControllerTestSuite extends TestCase {

    private Controller testController;

    public DemoControllerTestSuite(String arg0) {
        super(arg0);
    }
```

In the `setUp()` method we will initialize the controller. With real controllers we will usually need to configure the controller by setting bean properties (for example, references to application business objects), but this is not required in this simple example. Any required objects can often be replaced by test implementations that return dummy data. We're not testing the implementation of business logic, but whether it's invoked correctly by web-tier components:

```java
public void setUp() {
    testController = new DemoController();
}
```

Each test method will create a test request and response object and check that the controller selects the appropriate view name and returns any model data required:

```java
public void testNoName() throws Exception {
    TestHttpRequest request =
        new TestHttpRequest(null, "GET", "test.html");
    HttpServletResponse response = new TestHttpResponse();
    ModelAndView mv =
        this.testController.handleRequest(request, response);
    assertTrue("View is correct",
        mv.getViewname().equals(DemoController.ENTER_NAME_VIEW));
    assertTrue("no name parameter", request.getParameter("name") == null);
}

public void testValidName() throws Exception {
    String name = "Tony";
    TestHttpRequest request = new TestHttpRequest(null, "GET", "test.html");
    request.addParameter("name", name);
    HttpServletResponse response = new TestHttpResponse();
    ModelAndView mv = this.testController.handleRequest(request, response);
    assertTrue("View is correct",
        mv.getViewname().equals(DemoController.VALID_NAME_VIEW));
    assertTrue("name parameter matches",
        request.getParameter("name").equals(name));
}

public void testInvalidName() throws Exception {
    String name = "Tony--";
    TestHttpRequest request = new TestHttpRequest(null, "GET", "test.html");
    request.addParameter("name", name);
    HttpServletResponse response = new TestHttpResponse();
    ModelAndView mv = this.testController.handleRequest(request, response);
    assertTrue("View is correct: expected '" +
        DemoController.INVALID_NAME_VIEW + "' not '" + mv.getViewname() + "'",
        mv.getViewname().equals(DemoController.INVALID_NAME_VIEW));
    assertTrue("name parameter matches",
        request.getParameter("name").equals(name));
}

}
```

There are test packages for some common MVC web frameworks, such as Struts, which support the writing of test cases for applications using them. No special support is required for testing request controllers using the framework discussed in Chapter 12, as they don't depend on the controller servlet at run time. Custom support is required for frameworks such as Struts, in which application request handlers depend on the framework's controller servlet.

If we follow the design principles outlined in Chapter 1, we won't need to write many such test classes. The web interface will be such a thin layer that we can rely on web-tier acceptance testing to identify any problems in how it invokes business logic.

We can also unit test web-tier components inside the web container using a tool such as Cactus. In this case we don't need to supply test Servlet API objects. The disadvantage is that test deployment and authoring is more complex. It's so much easier and quicker to perform tests outside the container that I recommend it if it's at all possible.

Acceptance Testing Web Interfaces

Both these approaches amount to unit testing, which is of limited importance in the web tier. As a web interface reflects the user's view of system, we need to be able to implement acceptance testing. The **HttpUnit** project (http://httpunit.sourceforge.net/) allows us to write test cases that run outside the server. (The HttpUnit binaries are also included with Cactus.)

HttpUnit is a set of classes for use in JUnit test cases, enabling us to automate HTTP requests and make assertions about the response. HttpUnit doesn't only work with servlets; it doesn't care what the server-side implementation is, so it's equally applicable to JSP pages and XML-generated content. HttpUnit allows easy access to generated documents: for example, its WebResponse object exposes an array of forms, links, and cookies found on the page. HttpUnit provides an elegant wrapper around screen scraping.

HttpUnit is also a handy library when we need to do HTML screen scraping for any other reason.

The HttpUnit approach is essentially white-box acceptance testing. It has the advantage that we test our application exactly as it will be deployed in production, running on the production server. It's also easy and intuitive to write test cases. The drawback is that screen scraping can be vulnerable to changes in an application's look and feel that don't reflect changes in functionality (a frequent occurrence).

As an example of an HttpUnit test class, consider the following listing. Note that it comes from an ordinary JUnit test case; HttpUnit is a library, not a framework. The highlighted code checks that the page contains no forms and that it contains a nonzero number of links. We could connect to the database in our test case and verify that the links reflected data in the database, if the page was data-driven:

```
public void testGenresPage() throws Exception {

  WebConversation  conversation = new WebConversation();
  WebRequest request = new
    GetMethodWebRequest("http://localhost/ticket/genres.html" );

  WebResponse response = conversation.getResponse( request );
  WebForm forms[] = response.getForms();
  assertEquals( 0, forms.length );

  WebLink[] links = response.getLinks();
  int genreCount = 0;
  for (int i = 0; i < links.length; i++) {
    if (links[i].getURLString().indexOf("genre.html") > 0){
      genreCount++;
    }
  }
  assertTrue(" There are multiple genres", genreCount > 0);
}
```

> In my experience, acceptance testing is more important than unit testing where web interfaces are concerned, as a web interface should be a thin layer on top of the application's business interfaces. The implementation of the application's use cases should be tested against the implementations of the business interfaces.
>
> The HttpUnit class library provides an excellent, intuitive way of implementing web-tier acceptance tests using JUnit.

Design Implications

In summary, we can test EJBs and web-tier components, but it's a lot harder than testing ordinary Java classes. We need to master the testing techniques for J2EE components we've just discussed, but we also need to learn the lesson that our applications will be much easier to test if we design them so that we can test them as far as possible without the need to test J2EE components. The application infrastructure we will discuss in Chapter 11 is designed to facilitate this.

In the EJB tier, we may be able to achieve this by making EJBs a façade for business logic implemented in ordinary Java classes. There will still be problems such as container-managed transaction demarcation, but it's often possible to test key functionality without an EJB container (see http://www.xp2001.org/xp2001/conference/papers/Chapter24-Peeters.pdf for an XP-oriented approach to testing EJBs this way, and discussion of the difficulties of testing EJBs in general).

This approach can't be applied to entity beans, as their functionality is inextricably linked to EJB container services. This is one of the reasons I don't much like entity beans.

In the web tier, it's relatively easy to minimize the need to test servlets. This can be done by ensuring that web-specific controllers (servlets and helper classes) access a well-defined business interface that isn't web-specific. This interface can be tested using ordinary JUnit test cases.

> Where possible, design applications so that their central functionality can be tested against ordinary Java classes, not J2EE components such as EJBs, servlets, or JSP pages.

Testing Performance and Scalability

An application (especially a web application) may pass unit and integration tests, yet perform incorrectly or fail miserably in production. Most of the testing strategies we've considered so far are single-threaded. It is possible to use JUnit to perform multi-threaded tests, but it's not what it was originally designed for.

We usually need to know how an application performs, and especially how it handles increased load. Load and stress testing is an important part of the J2EE development lifecycle. Load tests, like unit tests, are important application artifacts.

We'll look at some practical examples of load testing in Chapter 15. In the following section we'll look at some of the major issues.

> Load (and stress) testing should not be left until an application is substantially complete. We've already considered the importance of tackling risks early. Inadequate performance and scalability is a major risk in enterprise applications, and especially web applications.
>
> It's good practice to implement a proof of concept or "vertical slice" of an application's functionality early in the project lifecycle and run load tests against it. Thus load testing should continue throughout the project lifecycle. Application performance tuning is closely tied to load testing, throughout the project lifecycle.

Load Testing EJBs and Other Business Objects

The load testing of ordinary Java classes doesn't always take a prominent role in J2EE, because the J2EE infrastructure exists partly to take care of issues such as concurrency that may become problems under load. It's usually most important to load test EJBs and the web interface.

However, it may be necessary to load test individual Java classes such as caches directly. Any application code using synchronization is a candidate for load testing in isolation, to ensure that it can't cause deadlocks or seriously limit overall throughput.

Direct load testing of business objects (including EJBs) is a valuable supplement to load testing of the web interface. Comparing the results of load tests of the business objects with those of the entire application (including the interface) will indicate which tiers of the application are taking longest and generating most system load – a vital input into any optimization that might be necessary. As using EJB may add significant overhead – especially in distributed applications – load testing EJBs will also indicate whether EJB is being used appropriately.

As the work of EJBs and other business objects often involves using non-Java resources such as databases, it's important to separate the time consumed by those resources from that taken by the business objects. For example, if it emerges that database access time is a problem, other changes to the EJB tier may not help to improve performance. Instead, we may want to load test our queries and updates so that we can tune them, tune the database, or reconsider our data access strategy. It may also be important to consider the implications of concurrent operations on the database (for example, is a deadlock possible, given the queries the application issues). Such issues can be explored on an ad hoc basis by using concurrent sessions in database tools such as Oracle's SQL*Plus, but it's better to formalize things by writing an automated test.

Where EJBs are concerned, as with functional testing, we must decide where the tests should run. Again it's simplest to run the stress tests in a different virtual machine (possibly a different physical machine), and use remote access to the EJB tier. This prevents the system load generated by the load test client being confused with that of the EJB container itself, but introduces network and serialization overheads (we can also run multiple clients). No special infrastructure is required – we can use any load testing framework and write code that connects to the EJB server. If the application uses local interfaces, or will never be deployed with remote calling, we will need to run the load tests inside the same enterprise applications. However, this will require additional infrastructure.

As a minimum, any Java-based load testing tool should allow us to:

❑ Execute user-defined operations (that is, invocations of ordinary Java objects or EJBs) in multiple threads

❑ Use random sleep times between operations

- ❑ Read data from configuration files to allow easy parameterization
- ❑ Repeat operations as required
- ❑ Produce readable reports

In Chapter 15 we'll look at some tools that meet these requirements, and look at an example of one in action.

Load Testing Web Interfaces

Web interfaces provide an ideal – and very easy – option for load and stress testing. If the results of load testing a web interface (or vertical slice early in the application lifecycle) are satisfactory, we may not need to devote resources to load testing EJBs and other application internals.

Numerous free load testing tools are available for web applications. My preferred tool is **Microsoft's Web Application Stress Tool** (freely available at http://webtool.rte.microsoft.com/), which is particularly easy to use.

Whichever web application stress tool you use, you should aim to simulate a realistic user population. Write scripts that simulate realistic user activity. Depending on your application, this might include the creation and maintenance of user sessions. As with all load tests, the tests must be able to simulate spikes in load.

Automating Tests

The value of an application's test suite is dependent on how easy it is to run. There will be many individual test classes, and it must be possible to run them all in a single operation. While each test run should report success (meaning success of all tests) or failure (meaning failure of one or more test), it should also create a log file detailing any failures, to provide a basis for analysis and debugging.

Fortunately, if we implement all application tests as JUnit test cases, there's an easy way to achieve this level of test automation and to integrate test runs into the application build process. The Ant build tool integrates smoothly with JUnit. It's possible to use Ant to run a set of tests, log the results and provide a simple report indicating whether all tests were passed. The following Ant task, for example, looks under an entire source tree and runs as a test any class with a name matching XXXXTestSuite.java. Success or failure will be displayed to the Ant console, while a detailed log will be created.

```
<target name="fwtests" depends="build-fwtests">
  <tstamp/>

  <mkdir dir="${junit.reports.dir}" />
  <mkdir dir="${junit.reports.dir}/framework-${DSTAMP}-${TSTAMP}" />

  <junit printsummary="yes" haltonfailure="yes">

    <classpath refid="master-classpath" />

    <formatter type="plain" />

    <!-- Convention is that our JUnit test classes have names such as
         XXXXTestSuite.java
```

```
    -->
    <batchtest
         fork="yes"
         todir="${junit.reports.dir}/framework-${DSTAMP}-
    ${TSTAMP}">
       <fileset dir="${framework-test.dir}">
            <include name="**/*TestSuite.java" />
       </fileset>
    </batchtest>
  </junit>
</target>
```

Please refer to the Ant documentation for more details, but the most important Ant task in this example is the <batchtest> task, which runs a number of JUnit test cases. In this example, the <fileset> subelement specifies a wildcard (**/*TestSuite.java) that selects the names of the test classes we wish to run. The todir attribute of the <batchtest> task specifies a directory to which a log should be written.

Using Ant targets such as this to run a test means that we can easily execute all the tests for a set of packages or an entire application with a single command. We can run all the tests after each change or bug fix, or daily.

To ensure that tests are run regularly, it's essential that tests should execute quickly. As a rule of thumb, all tests should be executed within ten minutes: if possible, much quicker. If tests can't be executed within this time scale it may be possible to refactor the test suite to improve its performance. If some tests will inevitably take longer, consider splitting the test suite into tests that provide immediate feedback and tests that can be run overnight.

Complementary Approaches to Testing

While testing is always essential, there are some complementary approaches we can use as part of our overall QA strategy.

J2SE 1.4 introduces **assertions** into the Java language. An assertion is a statement containing a Boolean expression that the programmer believes must be true at that point in the code. An assertion mechanism aborts program execution if a failed assertion is encountered, as this indicates an illegal state. The goal of assertions is to minimize the likelihood of a program containing errors, by identifying erroneous states as soon as possible at run time. See http://java.sun.com/j2se/1.4/docs/guide/lang/assert.html for a description of the Java 1.4 assertion mechanism. The assert keyword is used before assertions, as follows:

```
assert booleanConditionalThatMustBeTrue;
```

The concept of assertions long predates Java: they are, for example, discussed in David Gries' *The Science of Programming* (Springer, 1981), which suggests trying to prove programs correct, rather than debugging.

Unlike test cases, assertions don't necessarily relate to what the code does. Assertions may be based on low-level implementation details, such as the values of private variables, which are not exposed by the object in question. This is one reason that assertions complement, rather than conflict with, the use of unit tests. In my view, assertions are the correct place for checks of how code works, rather than what it does. They are a superior alternative to white-box testing. Assertions should be invisible to users of the code; they have nothing to do with the contracts of the classes involved.

Assertions often concern **invariants**. An invariant is a predicate that is always true. Common examples are **class invariants** (invariants based on a class's member data) and **loop invariants** (invariants that are true before and after each iteration of a loop). If an invariant does not hold, the object or method concerned contains a bug or was improperly used. A common way of using invariants is for each method that changes a class's data to assert a class invariant immediately before returning

Assuming that we allow access to class data only through the class's methods – an essential part of good design – we can be sure that invariants hold at the beginning of each method's execution. Thus an assertion failure at the end of a method indicates a bug in that method, rather than the object being in an illegal state before the method was called – a problem that might be much harder to track down. Multiple class invariants can be gathered into a private Boolean method, allowing them to be updated as a single unit if required, and invoked like this:

```
assert classInvariants();
```

A method asserting the invariants, based on instance data, might look like this:

```
private boolean classInvariants() {
  return this.name != null &&
    this.count >= 0 &&
    this.helper != null;
}
```

It's often worth the effort to identify class invariants. Not only does it enable us to write stronger assertions, it helps to develop understanding of the class itself. Gries argues for developing "a program and its proof hand-in-hand, with the proof ideas leading the way!" Correct use of invariants may also pick up bugs missed by unit tests; occasionally, unit tests for an individual method might work correctly, but miss the fact that the method has corrupted the state of the object that defines it.

Unlike test cases, assertions are integrated into application code. By introducing the new `assert` keyword; Java 1.4 ensures that there should be no performance penalty for liberal use of assertions: it's possible to enable or disable assertions at run time, down to individual class level. It has always been possible to use assertions in Java, using code such as this:

```
if (orderCount < 0)
  throw new RuntimeException("Assertion Failed: Illegal order count of i ("
                      + i + ") when about to process orders");
```

Sometimes a static `Assertions` class is used to provide convenient assertion methods, as does the JUnit testing framework. However, this is relatively verbose, isn't a widely used Java idiom, and has the disadvantage that the assertion condition must always be evaluated. In the simple case above, the performance cost is negligible, but more complex assertion conditions may be slow to compute. A check can be made that assertions are enabled before each assertion is evaluated, but this adds further complexity and is inelegant. Thus the language-level assertion mechanism in Java 1.4 is a big step forward.

Note, however, that where assertions concern the *usage* of a class, the assertion mechanism is inappropriate: the class should simply throw an exception reporting incorrect usage to the erroneous caller. This is a matter of the class's API, not merely internal consistency, so the assertion mechanism, which can be switched off, should not be relied on.

In all versions of Java, **unchecked exceptions** (runtime exceptions that the Java compiler doesn't force us to catch) will have the same effect as assertion failures. This makes them a convenient and correct way of dealing with unrecoverable errors that "shouldn't have happened". We'll talk more about checked and unchecked exceptions in Chapter 4.

> **J2SE 1.4 introduces major enhancements, of which the new assertion mechanism is one of the most important. If using Java 1.4, take advantage of assertions – they're now integrated into the language and offer a performance-neutral way of heading off bugs. Learn to use assertions effectively: this is a skill that takes a little practice to acquire.**

Other practices that complement testing include **code reviews** and XP's more controversial practice of **pair programming**. Such techniques help to ensure that we write good code, which is less likely to contain bugs and is easier to test and debug. In the next chapter, we'll look at design and coding techniques we can use to ensure that we write good code.

Summary

> **Testing should occur throughout the software lifecycle. Testing should be a core activity of software development.**

Test cases should usually be written before code. Instead of considering application code as the sole deliverable, test cases, documentation (Javadoc and other), and application code should be kept in sync, with the test cases being written first. If you can't write a test for a piece of code, you don't know enough to write the code itself. A test that isn't up-to-date is useless.

Unless tests are easy to run, they won't be run. It's vital that unit tests can be run automatically, and that there is no need to interpret the results – there should be a single indication of success or failure. Ant can be used to automate tests written with JUnit. It's important to invest a little time early in the project lifecycle in establishing testing conventions and streamlining the testing process so that all developers can efficiently write and execute tests.

Especially in the case of web applications, stress testing is vital. Unsatisfactory performance is a serious risk in enterprise software development, and should be tackled early, through a proof of concept, while it isn't prohibitively expensive to modify the application's design.

Testing J2EE applications involves many different tests. We've considered the following test strategies:

- Unit testing of classes (from all architectural tiers) with JUnit. As we've seen, the simple, easy-to-use, JUnit testing framework can be used as the basis of our testing strategy. Unit testing is usually the most important type of testing.

- Testing EJBs with remote interfaces using JUnit test suites running in a client JVM.

- Testing EJBs with local interfaces using Cactus (an open source framework built on JUnit that allows tests to be run within the application server).

❑ Unit testing of web-tier classes using JUnit and test implementations of Servlet API interfaces such as `HttpServletRequest` and `HttpServletResponse`. This enables web-tier classes to be tested outside the application server, making testing more convenient.

❑ Acceptance testing of the web interface via "screen scraping" web tools such as HttpUnit.

❑ Load and stress testing of database operations.

❑ Load and stress testing of EJB component interfaces.

❑ Load and stress testing of the web interface.

We've also discussed the desirability of designing applications so that central functionality can be tested against ordinary Java classes, rather than harder-to-test J2EE components.

Testing alone is not enough to ensure that code is bug free. Other useful strategies include using assertions in application code and introducing the practice of regular code reviews. Sound coding and design practices can do much to reduce the likelihood of bugs.

While the concepts discussed in this chapter apply whatever tools we use, I've concentrated on free, simple tools. These are ubiquitous and widely understood, but there are more sophisticated commercial testing tools available, especially for web applications, that are beyond the scope of this chapter.

Design Techniques and Coding Standards for J2EE Projects

As J2EE applications tend to be large and complex, it's vital that we follow sound OO design practice, adopt consistent coding conventions, and leverage existing investment – whether our own or that of third parties. In this chapter we'll look at each of these important areas in turn.

The first two concern code quality, at object-design and code level. What are we trying to achieve? What is good code? These are a few of its characteristics:

- ❑ Good code is extensible without drastic modification. It's easy to add features without tearing it apart.

- ❑ Good code is easy to read and maintain.

- ❑ Good code is well documented.

- ❑ Good code makes it hard to write bad code around it. For example, objects expose clean, easy-to-use interfaces that promote good use. Both good code and bad code breed.

- ❑ Good code is easy to test.

- ❑ Good code is easy to debug. Remember that even if a piece of code works perfectly, it's still a problem if it doesn't favor debugging. What if a developer is trying to track down an error in imperfect code, and the stack trace disappears into perfect but obscure code?

- ❑ Good code contains no code duplication.

- ❑ Good code gets reused.

It's hard to write code that achieves these goals, although Java arguably gives us more help than any other popular language.

I've written and debugged a lot of Java code since I started using the language back in 1996 (and plenty of C and C++ before that) and I'm still learning. I don't pretend that this chapter contains all the answers, and there are many matters of opinion, but hopefully it will provide some guidance and useful food for thought. This is an important area.

We must not only ensure that we write code right, but also that we write the right code, taking advantage of existing solutions wherever appropriate. This means that development teams must work closely to avoid duplication of effort, and that architects and lead developers must maintain up-to-date knowledge of third-party solutions such as open source projects.

This chapter, like this book, is focused on J2EE 1.3, and hence J2SE 1.3. However, language and API improvements in J2SE 1.4 are discussed where relevant, as J2SE 1.4 is already available and can even be used with some J2EE 1.3 application servers.

OO Design Recommendations for J2EE Applications

It's possible to design a J2EE application so badly that, even if it contains beautifully written Java code at an individual object level, it will still be deemed a failure. A J2EE application with an excellent overall design but poor implementation code will be an equally miserable failure. Unfortunately, many developers spend too much time grappling with the J2EE APIs and too little ensuring they adhere to good coding practice. All of Sun's J2EE sample applications seem to reflect this.

In my experience, it *isn't* pedantry to insist on adherence to good OO principles: it brings real benefits.

> **OO design is more important than any particular implementation technology (such as J2EE, or even Java). Good programming practices and sound OO design underpin good J2EE applications. Bad Java code is bad J2EE code.**

Some "coding standards" issues – especially those relating to OO design – are on the borderline between design and implementation: for example, the use of design patterns.

The following section covers some issues that I've seen cause problems in large code bases, especially issues that I haven't seen covered elsewhere. This is a huge area, so this section is by no means complete. Some issues are matters of opinion, although I'll try to convince you of my position.

> **Take every opportunity to learn from the good (and bad) code of others, inside and outside your organization. Useful sources in the public domain include successful open source projects and the code in the core Java libraries. License permitting, it may be possible to decompile interesting parts of commercial products. A professional programmer or architect cares more about learning and discovering the best solution than the buzz of finding their own solution to a particular problem.**

Achieving Loose Coupling with Interfaces

The "first principle of reusable object-oriented design" advocated by the classic Gang of Four design patterns book is: "Program to an interface, not an implementation". Fortunately, Java makes it very easy (and natural) to follow this principle.

> **Program to interfaces, not classes. This decouples interfaces from their implementations. Using loose coupling between objects promotes flexibility. To gain maximum flexibility, declare instance variables and method parameters to be of the least specific type required.**

Using interface-based architecture is particularly important in J2EE applications, because of their scale. Programming to interfaces rather than concrete classes adds a little complexity, but the rewards far outweigh the investment. There is a slight performance penalty for calling an object through an interface, but this is seldom an issue in practice.

A few of the many advantages of an interface-based approach include:

- ❑ The ability to change the implementing class of any application object without affecting calling code. This enables us to parameterize any part of an application without breaking other components.

- ❑ Total freedom in implementing interfaces. There's no need to commit to an inheritance hierarchy. However, it's still possible to achieve code reuse by using concrete inheritance in interface implementations.

- ❑ The ability to provide simple test implementations and stub implementations of application interfaces as necessary, facilitating the testing of other classes and enabling multiple teams to work in parallel after they have agreed on interfaces.

Adopting interface-based architecture is also the best way to ensure that a J2EE application is portable, yet is able to leverage vendor-specific optimizations and enhancements.

Interface-based architecture can be effectively combined with the use of **reflection for configuration** (see below).

Prefer Object Composition to Concrete Inheritance

The second basic principle of object-oriented design emphasized in the GoF book is "Favor object composition over class inheritance". Few developers appreciate this wise advice.

Unlike many older languages, such as C++, Java distinguishes at a language level between **concrete inheritance** (the inheritance of method implementations and member variables from a superclass) and **interface inheritance** (the implementation of interfaces). Java allows concrete inheritance from only a single superclass, but a Java class may implement any number of interfaces (including, of course, those interfaces implemented by its ancestors in a class hierarchy). While there are rare situations in which multiple concrete inheritance (as permitted in C++) is the best design approach, Java is much better off avoiding the complexity that may arise from permitting these rare legitimate uses.

115

Concrete inheritance is enthusiastically embraced by most developers new to OO, but has many disadvantages. Class hierarchies are rigid. It's impossible to change part of a class's implementation; by contrast, if that part is encapsulated in an interface (using delegation and the Strategy design pattern, which we'll discussed below), this problem can be avoided.

Object composition (in which new functionality is obtained by assembling or composing objects) is more flexible than concrete inheritance, and Java interfaces make delegation natural. Object composition allows the behavior of an object to be altered at *run time*, through delegating part of its behavior to an interface and allowing callers to set the implementation of that interface. The Strategy and State design patterns rely on this approach.

To clarify the distinction, let's consider what we want to achieve by inheritance.

Abstract inheritance enables **polymorphism**: the substitutability of objects with the same interface at run time. This delivers much of the value of object-oriented design.

Concrete inheritance enables both polymorphism and more convenient implementation. Code can be inherited from a superclass. Thus concrete inheritance is an implementation, rather than purely a design, issue. Concrete inheritance is a valuable feature of any OO language; but it is easy to overuse. Common mistakes with concrete inheritance include:

❑ Forcing users to extend an abstract or concrete class, when we could require implementation of a simple interface. This means that we deprive the user code of the right to its own inheritance hierarchy. If there's normally no reason that a user class would need it's own custom superclass, we can provide a convenient abstract implementation of the method for subclassing. Thus the interface approach doesn't preclude the provision of convenient superclasses.

❑ Using concrete inheritance to provide helper functionality, by subclasses calling helper methods in superclasses. What if classes outside the inheritance hierarchy need the helper functionality? Use object composition, so that the helper is a separate object and can be shared.

❑ Using abstract classes in place of interfaces. Abstract classes are very useful when used correctly. The Template Method design pattern (discussed below) is usually implemented with an abstract class. However, an abstract class is *not* an alternative to an interface. It is usually a convenient step in the *implementation* of an interface. Don't use an abstract class to define a type. This is a recipe for running into problems with Java's lack of multiple concrete inheritance. Unfortunately, the core Java libraries are poor examples in this respect, often using abstract classes where interfaces would be preferable.

Interfaces are most valuable when kept simple. The more complex an interface is, the less valuable is modeling it as an interface, as developers will be forced to extend an abstract or concrete implementation to avoid writing excessive amounts of code. This is a case where correct interface granularity is vital; interface hierarchies may be separate from class hierarchies, so that a particular class need only implement the exact interface it needs.

> **Interface inheritance (that is, the implementation of interfaces, rather than inheritance of functionality from concrete classes) is much more flexible than concrete inheritance.**

Does this mean that concrete inheritance is a bad thing? Absolutely not; concrete inheritance is a powerful way of achieving code reuse in OO languages. However, it's best considered an implementation approach, rather than a high-level design approach. It's something we should choose to use, rather than be forced to use by an application's overall design.

The Template Method Design Pattern

One good use of concrete inheritance is to implement the **Template Method** design pattern.

The Template Method design pattern (GoF) addresses a common problem: we know the steps of an algorithm and the order in which they should be performed, but don't know how to perform all of the steps. This Template Method pattern solution is to encapsulate the individual steps we don't know how to perform as abstract methods, and provide an abstract superclass that invokes them in the correct order. Concrete subclasses of this abstract superclass implement the abstract methods that perform the individual steps. The key concept is that it is the abstract base class that controls the workflow. Public superclass methods are usually final: the abstract methods deferred to subclasses are protected. This helps to reduce the likelihood of bugs: all subclasses are required to do, is fulfill a clear contract.

The centralization of workflow logic into the abstract superclass is an example of **inversion of control**. Unlike in traditional class libraries, where user code invokes library code, in this approach framework code in the superclass invokes user code. It's also known as the **Hollywood principle**: "Don't call me, I'll call you". Inversion of control is fundamental to **frameworks**, which tend to use the Template Method pattern heavily (we'll discuss frameworks later).

For example, consider a simple order processing system. The business involves calculating the purchase price, based on the price of individual items, checking whether the customer is allowed to spend this amount, and applying any discount if necessary. Some persistent storage such as an RDBMS must be updated to reflect a successful purchase, and queried to obtain price information. However, it's desirable to separate this from the steps of the business logic.

The `AbstractOrderEJB` superclass implements the business logic, which includes checking that the customer isn't trying to exceed their spending limit, and applying a discount to large orders. The public `placeOrder()` method is final, so that this workflow can't be modified (or corrupted) by subclasses:

```
public final Invoice placeOrder(int customerId, InvoiceItem[] items)
    throws NoSuchCustomerException, SpendingLimitViolation {

  int total = 0;
  for (int i = 0; i < items.length; i++) {
    total += getItemPrice(items[i]) * items[i].getQuantity();
  }

  if (total > getSpendingLimit(customerId)) {
    getSessionContext().setRollbackOnly();
    throw new SpendingLimitViolation(total, limit);
  }
  else if (total > DISCOUNT_THRESHOLD) {
    // Apply discount to total...
  }

  int invoiceId = placeOrder(customerId, total, items);
  return new InvoiceImpl(iid, total);
}
```

I've highlighted the three lines of code in this method that invoke protected abstract "template methods" that must be implemented by subclasses. These will be defined in `AbstractOrderEJB` as follows:

```
protected abstract int getItemPrice(InvoiceItem item);

protected abstract int getSpendingLimit(customerId)
  throws NoSuchCustomerException;

protected abstract int placeOrder(int customerId, int total,
                  InvoiceItem[] items);
```

Subclasses of `AbstractOrderEJB` merely need to implement these three methods. They don't need to concern themselves with business logic. For example, one subclass might implement these three methods using JDBC, while another might implement them using SQLJ or JDO.

Such uses of the Template Method pattern offer good separation of concerns. Here, the superclass concentrates on business logic; the subclasses concentrate on implementing primitive operations (for example, using a low-level API such as JDBC). As the template methods are protected, rather than public, callers are spared the details of the class's implementation.

As it's usually better to define types in interfaces rather than classes, the Template Method pattern is often used as a strategy to implement an interface.

Abstract superclasses are also often used to implement some, but not all, methods of an interface. The remaining methods – which vary between concrete implementations – are left unimplemented. This differs from the Template Method pattern in that the abstract superclass doesn't handle workflow.

> **Use the Template Method design pattern to capture an algorithm in an abstract superclass, but defer the implementation of individual steps to subclasses. This has the potential to head off bugs, by getting tricky operations right once and simplifying user code. When implementing the Template Method pattern, the abstract superclass must factor out those methods that may change between subclasses and ensure that the method signatures enable sufficient flexibility in implementation.**
>
> **Always make the abstract parent class implement an interface. The Template Method design pattern is especially valuable in framework design (discussed towards the end of this chapter).**

The Template Method design pattern can be very useful in J2EE applications to help us to achieve as much portability as possible between application servers and databases while still leveraging proprietary features. We've seen how we can sometimes separate business logic from database operations above. We could equally use this pattern to enable efficient support for specific databases. For example, we could have an `OracleOrderEJB` and a `DB2OrderEJB` that implemented the abstract template methods efficiently in the respective databases, while business logic remains free of proprietary code.

The Strategy Design Pattern

An alternative to the Template Method is the **Strategy** design pattern, which factors the variant behavior into an interface. Thus, the class that knows the algorithm is not an abstract base class, but a concrete class that uses a helper that implements an interface defining the individual steps. The Strategy design pattern takes a little more work to implement than the Template Method pattern, but it is more flexible. The advantage of the Strategy pattern is that it need not involve concrete inheritance. The class that implements the individual steps is not forced to inherit from an abstract template superclass.

Let's look at how we could use the Strategy design pattern in the above example. The first step is to move the template methods into an interface, which will look like this:

```
public interface DataHelper {
   int getItemPrice(InvoiceItem item);
   int getSpendingLimit(customerId) throws NoSuchCustomerException;
   int placeOrder(int customerId, int total, InvoiceItem[] items);
}
```

Implementations of this interface don't need to subclass any particular class; we have the maximum possible freedom.

Now we can write a concrete `OrderEJB` class that depends on an instance variable of this interface. We must also provide a means of setting this helper, either in the constructor or through a bean property. In the present example I've opted for a bean property:

```
private DataHelper dataHelper;

public void setDataHelper(DataHelper newDataHelper) {
   this.dataHelper = newDataHelper;
}
```

The implementation of the `placeOrder()` method is almost identical to the version using the Template Method pattern, except that it invokes the operations it doesn't know how to do on the instance of the helper interface, in the highlighted lines:

```
public final Invoice placeOrder(int customerId, InvoiceItem[] items)
    throws NoSuchCustomerException, SpendingLimitViolation {

   int total = 0;
   for (int i = 0; i < items.length; i++) {
     total += this.dataHelper.getItemPrice(items[i]) *
       items[i].getQuantity();
   }

   if (total > this.dataHelper.getSpendingLimit(customerId)) {
     getSessionContext().setRollbackOnly();
     throw new SpendingLimitViolation(total, limit);
   } else if (total > DISCOUNT_THRESHOLD) {
     // Apply discount to total...
   }

   int invoiceId = this.dataHelper.placeOrder(customerId, total, items);
   return new InvoiceImpl(iid, total);
}
```

This is slightly more complex to implement than the version using concrete inheritance with the Template Method pattern, but is more flexible. This is a classic example of the tradeoff between concrete inheritance and delegation to an interface.

I use the Strategy pattern in preference to the Template Method pattern under the following circumstances:

❑ When all steps vary (rather than just a few).

❑ When the class that implements the steps needs an independent inheritance hierarchy.

❑ When the implementation of the steps may be relevant to other classes (this is often the case with J2EE data access).

❑ When the implementation of the steps may need to vary at run time. Concrete inheritance can't accommodate this; delegation can.

❑ When there are many different implementations of the steps, or when it's expected that the number of implementations will continue to increase. In this case, the greater flexibility of the Strategy pattern will almost certainly prove beneficial, as it allows maximum freedom to the implementations.

Using Callbacks to Achieve Extensibility

Let's now consider another use of "inversion of control" to parameterize a single operation, while moving control and error handling into a framework. Strictly speaking, this is a special case of the Strategy design pattern: it appears different because the interfaces involved are so simple.

This pattern is based around the use of one or more callback methods that are invoked by a method that performs a workflow.

I find this pattern useful when working with low-level APIs such as JDBC. The following example is a stripped down form of a JDBC utility class, JdbcTemplate, used in the sample application, and discussed further in Chapter 9.

JdbcTemplate implements a query() method that takes as parameters a SQL query string and an implementation of a callback interface that will be invoked for each row of the result set the query generates. The callback interface is as follows:

```
public interface RowCallbackHandler {
  void processRow(ResultSet rs) throws SQLException;
}
```

The JdbcTemplate.query() method conceals from calling code the details of getting a JDBC connection, creating and using a statement, and correctly freeing resources, even in the event of errors, as follows:

```
public void query(String sql, RowCallbackHandler callbackHandler)
    throws JdbcSqlException {

  Connection con = null;
  PreparedStatement ps = null;
  ResultSet rs = null;
```

```
    try {
      con = <code to get connection>
      ps = con.prepareStatement(sql);
      rs = ps.executeQuery();

      while (rs.next()) {
        callbackHandler.processRow(rs);
      }

      rs.close();
      ps.close();
    } catch (SQLException ex) {
      throw new JdbcSqlException("Couldn't run query [" + sql + "]", ex);
    }
    finally {
      DataSourceUtils.closeConnectionIfNecessary(this.dataSource, con);
    }
  }
```

The DataSourceUtils class contains a helper method that can be used to close connections, catching and logging any SQLExceptions encountered.

In this example, JdbcSqlException extends java.lang.RuntimeException, which means that calling code may choose to catch it, but is not forced to. This makes sense in the present situation. If, for example, a callback handler tries to obtain the value of a column that doesn't exist in the ResultSet, it will do calling code no good to catch it. This is clearly a programming error, and JdbcTemplate's behavior of logging the exception and throwing a runtime exception is logical (see discussion on *Error Handling - Checked or Unchecked Exceptions* later).

In this case, I modeled the RowCallbackHandler interface as an inner interface of the JdbcTemplate class. This interface is only relevant to the JdbcTemplate class, so this is logical. Note that implementations of the RowCallbackHandler interface might be inner classes (in trivial cases, anonymous inner classes are appropriate), or they might be standard, reusable classes, or subclasses of standard convenience classes.

Consider the following implementation of the RowCallbackHandler interface to perform a JDBC query. Note that the implementation isn't forced to catch SQLExceptions that may be thrown in extracting column values from the result set:

```
class StringHandler implements JdbcTemplate.RowCallbackHandler {
  private List l = new LinkedList();

  public void processRow(ResultSet rs) throws SQLException {
    l.add(rs.getString(1));
  }

  public String[] getStrings() {
    return (String[]) l.toArray(new String[l.size()]);
  }
}
```

This class can be used as follows:

```
StringHandler sh = new StringHandler();
jdbcTemplate.query("SELECT FORENAME FROM CUSTMR", sh);
String[] forenames = sh.getStrings();
```

These three lines show how the code that uses the JdbcTemplate is able to focus on the business problem, without concerning itself with the JDBC API. Any SQLExceptions thrown will be handled by JdbcTemplate.

This pattern shouldn't be overused, but can be very useful. The following advantages and disadvantages indicate the tradeoffs involved:

Advantages:

❑   The framework class can perform error handling and the acquisition and release of resources. This means that tricky error handling (as is required using JDBC) can be written once only, and calling code is simpler. The more complex the error handling and cleanup involved, the more attractive this approach is.

❑   Calling code needn't handle the details of low-level APIs such as JDBC. This is desirable, because such code is bug prone and verbose, obscuring the business problem application code should focus on.

❑   The one control flow function (JdbcTemplate.query() in the example) can be used with a wide variety of callback handlers, to perform different tasks. This is a good way of achieving reuse of code that uses low-level APIs.

Disadvantages:

❑   This idiom is less intuitive than having calling code handle execution flow itself, so code may be harder to understand and maintain if there's a reasonable alternative.

❑   We need to create an object for the callback handler.

❑   In rare cases, performance may be impaired by the need to invoke the callback handler via an interface. The overhead of the above example is negligible, compared to the time taken by the JDBC operations themselves.

This pattern is most valuable when the callback interface is very simple. In the example, because the RowCallbackHandler interface contains a single method, it is very easy to implement, meaning that implementation choices such as anonymous inner classes may be used to simplify calling code.

The Observer Design Pattern

Like the use of interfaces, the **Observer** design pattern can be used to decouple components and enable extensibility without modification (observing the Open Closed Principle). It also contributes to achieving **separation of concerns**.

Consider, for example, an object that handles user login. There might be several outcomes from a user's attempt to login: successful login; failed login due to an incorrect password; failed login due to an incorrect username *and* password; system error due to failure to connect to the database that holds login information.

Let's imagine that we have a login implementation working in production, but that further requirements mean that the application should e-mail an administrator in the event of a given number of system errors; and should maintain a list of incorrectly entered passwords, along with the correct passwords for the users concerned, to contribute to developing information to help users avoid common errors. We would also like to know the peak periods for user login activity (as opposed to general activity on the web site).

All this functionality could be added to the object that implements login. We should have unit tests that would verify that this hasn't broken the existing functionality, but this is approach doesn't offer good separation of concerns (why should the object handling login need to know or obtain the administrator's e-mail address, or know how to send an e-mail?). As more features (or **aspects**) are added, the implementation of the login workflow itself – the core responsibility of this component – will be obscured under the volume of code to handle them.

We can address this problem more elegantly using the Observer design pattern. **Observers** (or **listeners**) can be notified of application **events**. The application must provide (or use a framework that provides) an event publisher. Listeners can register to be notified of events: all workflow code must do is **publish** events that might be of interest. Event publication is similar to generating log messages, in that it doesn't affect the working of application code. In the above example, events would include:

❑   Attempted login, containing username and password

❑   System error, including the offending exception

❑   Login result (success or failure and reason)

Events normally include timestamps.

Now we could achieve clean separation of concerns by using distinct listeners to e-mail the administrator on system errors; react to a failed login (added it to a list); and gather performance information about login activity.

The Observer design pattern is used in the core Java libraries: for example, JavaBeans can publish property change events. In our own applications, we will use the Observer pattern at a higher level. Events of interest are likely to relate to application-level operations, not low-level operations such as setting a bean property.

Consider also the need to gather performance information about a web application. We could build sophisticated performance monitoring into the code of the web application framework (for example, any controller servlets), but this would require modification to those classes if we required different performance statistics in future. It's better to publish events such as "request received" and "request fulfilled" (the latter including success or failure status) and leave the implementation of performance monitoring up to listeners that are solely concerned with it. This is an example of how the Observer design pattern can be used to achieve good separation of concerns. This amounts to **Aspect-Oriented Programming**, which we discuss briefly under *Using Reflection* later.

Don't go overboard with the Observer design pattern: it's only necessary when there's a real likelihood that loosely coupled listeners will need to know about a workflow. If we use the Observer design pattern everywhere our business logic will disappear under a morass of event publication code and performance will be significantly reduced. Only important workflows (such as the login process of our example) should generate events.

A warning when using the Observer design pattern: it's vital that listeners return quickly. Rogue listeners can lock an application. Although it is possible for the event publishing system to invoke observers in a different thread, this is wasteful for the majority of listeners that will return quickly. It's a better choice in most situations for the onus to be on listeners to return quickly or spin off long-running tasks into separate threads. Listeners should also avoid synchronization on shared application objects, as this may lead to blocking. Listeners must be threadsafe.

The Observer design pattern is less useful in a clustered deployment than in deployment on a single server, as it only allows us to publish events on a single server. For example, it would be unsafe to use the Observer pattern to update a data cache; as such an update would apply only to a single server. However, the Observer pattern can still be very useful in a cluster. For example, the applications discussed above would all be valid in a clustered environment. JMS can be used for cluster-wide event publication, at the price of greater API complexity and a much greater performance overhead.

In my experience, the Observer design pattern is more useful in the web tier than in the EJB tier. For example, it's impossible to create threads in the EJB tier (again, JMS is the alternative).

In Chapter 11 we look at how to implement the Observer design pattern in an application framework. The application framework infrastructure used in the sample application provides an event publication mechanism, allowing approaches such as those described here to be implemented without the need for an application to implement any "plumbing".

Consider Consolidating Method Parameters

Sometimes it's a good idea to encapsulate multiple parameters to a method into a single object. This may enhance readability and simplify calling code. Consider a method signature like this:

```
public void setOptions(Font f, int lineSpacing, int linesPerPage,
                       int tabSize);
```

We could simplify this signature by rolling the multiple parameters into a single object, like this:

```
public void setOptions(Options options);
```

The main advantage is flexibility. We don't need to break signatures to add further parameters: we can add additional properties to the parameter object. This means that we don't have to break code in existing callers that aren't interested in the added parameters.

As Java, unlike C++, doesn't offer default parameter values, this can be a good way to enable clients to simplify calls. Let's suppose that all (or most) or the parameters have default values. In C++ we could code the default values in the method signature, enabling callers to omit some of them, like this:

```
void SomeClass::setOptions(Font f, int lineSpacing = 1, int linesPerPage = 25,
                           int tabSize = 4);
```

This isn't possible in Java, but we *can* populate the object with default values, allowing subclasses to use syntax like this:

```
Options o = new Options();
o.setLineSpacing(2);
configurable.setOptions(o);
```

Here, the `Options` object's constructor sets all fields to default values, so we need modify only to those that vary from the default. If necessary, we can even make the parameter object an interface, to allow more flexible implementation.

This approach works particularly well with constructors. It's indicated when a class has many constructors, and subclasses may face excessive work just preserving superclass constructor permutations. Instead, subclasses can use a subclass of the superclass constructor's parameter object.

The Command design pattern uses this approach: a command is effectively a consolidated set of parameters, which are much easier to work with together than individually.

The disadvantage of parameter consolidation is the potential creation of many objects, which increases memory usage and the need for garbage collection. Objects consume heap space; primitives don't. Whether this matters depends on how often the method will be called.

> *Consolidating method parameters in a single object can occasionally cause performance degradation in J2EE applications if the method call is potentially remote (a call on the remote interface of an EJB), as marshaling and unmarshaling several primitive parameters will always be faster than marshaling and unmarshaling an object. However, this isn't a concern unless the method is invoked particularly often (which might indicate poor application partitioning – we don't want to make frequent remote calls if we can avoid it).*

Exception Handling – Checked or Unchecked Exceptions

Java distinguishes between two types of exception. **Checked** exceptions extend `java.lang.Exception`, and the compiler insists that they are caught or explicitly rethrown. **Unchecked** or **runtime** exceptions extend `java.lang.RuntimeException`, and need not be caught (although they can be caught and propagate up the call stack in the same way as checked exceptions). Java is the only mainstream language that supports checked exceptions: all C++ and C# exceptions, for example, are equivalent to Java's unchecked exceptions.

First, let's consider received wisdom on exception handling in Java. This is expressed in the section on exception handling in the Java Tutorial (http://java.sun.com/docs/books/tutorial/essential/exceptions/runtime.html), which advises the use of checked exceptions in application code.

> *Because the Java language does not require methods to catch or specify runtime exceptions, it's tempting for programmers to write code that throws only runtime exceptions or to make all of their exception subclasses inherit from `RuntimeException`. Both of these programming shortcuts allow programmers to write Java code without bothering with all of the nagging errors from the compiler and without bothering to specify or catch any exceptions. While this may seem convenient to the programmer, it sidesteps the intent of Java's catch or specify requirement and can cause problems for the programmers using your classes*

> *Checked exceptions represent useful information about the operation of a legally specified request that the caller may have had no control over and that the caller needs to be informed about – for example, the file system is now full, or the remote end has closed the connection, or the access privileges don't allow this action.*

What does it buy you if you throw a RuntimeException or create a subclass of RuntimeException just because you don't want to deal with specifying it? Simply, you get the ability to throw an exception without specifying that you do so. In other words, it is a way to avoid documenting the exceptions that a method can throw. When is this good? Well, when is it ever good to avoid documenting a method's behavior? The answer is "hardly ever".

To summarize Java orthodoxy: checked exceptions should be the norm. Runtime exceptions indicate programming errors.

I used to subscribe to this view. However, after writing and working with thousands of catch blocks, I've come to the conclusion that this appealing theory doesn't always work in practice. I'm not alone. Since developing my own ideas on the subject, I've noticed that Bruce Eckel, author of the classic book *Thinking in Java*, has also changed his mind. Eckel now advocates the use of runtime exceptions as the norm, and wonders whether checked exceptions should be dropped from Java as a failed experiment (http://www.mindview.net/Etc/Discussions/CheckedExceptions).

Eckel cites the observation that, when one looks at small amounts of code, checked exceptions seem a brilliant idea and promise to avoid many bugs. However, experience tends to indicate the reverse for large code bases. See "Exceptional Java" by Alan Griffiths at http://www.octopull.demon.co.uk/java/ExceptionalJava.html for another discussion of the problems with checked exceptions.

Using checked exceptions exclusively leads to several problems:

❑ **Too much code**
Developers will become frustrated by having to catch checked exceptions that they can't reasonably handle (of the "something when horribly wrong" variety) and write code that ignores (swallows) them. Agreed: this is indefensible coding practice, but experience shows that it happens more often than we like to think. Even good programmers may occasionally forget to "nest" exceptions properly (more about this below), meaning that the full stack trace is lost, and the information contained in the exception is of reduced value.

❑ **Unreadable code**
Catching exceptions that can't be appropriately handled and rethrowing them (wrapped in a different exception type) performs little useful function, yet can make it hard to find the code that actually *does* something. The orthodox view is that this bothers only lazy programmers, and that we should simply ignore this problem. However, this ignores reality. For example, this issue was clearly considered by the designers of the core Java libraries. Imagine the nightmare of having to work with collections interfaces such as `java.util.Iterator` if they threw checked, rather than unchecked, exceptions. The JDO API is another example of a Sun API that uses unchecked exceptions. By contrast, JDBC, which uses checked exceptions, is cumbersome to work with directly.

❑ **Endless wrapping of exceptions**
A checked exception must be either caught or declared in the throws clause of a method that encounters it. This leaves a choice between rethrowing a growing number of exceptions, or catching low-level exceptions and rethrowing them wrapped in a new, higher-level exception. This is desirable if we add useful information by doing so. However, if the lower-level exception is unrecoverable, wrapping it achieves nothing. Instead of an automatic unwinding of the call stack, as would have occurred with an unchecked exception, we will have an equivalent, manual unwinding of the call stack, with several lines of additional, pointless, code in each class along the way. It was principally this issue that prompted me to rethink my attitude to exception handling.

❑ **Fragile method signatures**
Once many callers use a method, adding an additional checked exception to the interface will require many code changes.

❑ **Checked exceptions don't always work well with interfaces**
Take the example of the file system being full in the Java Tutorial. This sounds OK if we're talking about a class that we know works with the file system. What if we're dealing with an interface that merely promises to store data somewhere (maybe in a database)? We don't want to hardcode dependence on the Java I/O API into an interface that may have different implementations. Hence if we want to use checked exceptions, we must create a new, storage-agnostic, exception type for the interface and wrap file system exceptions in it. Whether this is appropriate again depends on whether the exception is recoverable. If it isn't, we've created unnecessary work.

Many of these problems can be attributed to the problem of code catching exceptions it can't handle, and being forced to rethrow wrapped exceptions. This is cumbersome, error prone (it's easy to lose the stack trace) and serves no useful purpose. In such cases, it's better to use an unchecked exception. This will automatically unwind the call stack, and is the correct behavior for exceptions of the "something went horribly wrong" variety.

I take a less heterodox view than Eckel in that I believe there's a place for checked exceptions. Where an exception amounts to an alternative return value from a method, it should definitely be checked, and it's good that the language helps enforce this. However, I feel that the conventional Java approach greatly overemphasizes checked exceptions.

> **Checked exceptions are much superior to error return codes (as used in many older languages). Sooner or later (probably sooner) someone will fail to check an error return value; it's good to use the compiler to enforce correct error handling. Such checked exceptions are as integral to an object's API as parameters and return values.**

However, I don't recommend using checked exceptions unless callers are likely to be able to handle them. In particular, checked exceptions shouldn't be used to indicate that something went horribly wrong, which the caller can't be expected to handle.

> **Use a checked exception if calling code can do something sensible with the exception. Use an unchecked exception if the exception is fatal, or if callers won't gain by catching it. Remember that a J2EE container (such as a web container) can be relied on to catch unchecked exceptions and log them.**

I suggest the following guidelines for choosing between checked and unchecked exceptions:

Question	Example	Recommendation if the answer is yes
Should all callers handle this problem? Is the exception essentially a second return value for the method?	Spending limit exceeded in a `processInvoice()` method	Define and used a checked exception and take advantage of Java's compile-time support.

Table continued on following page

Question	Example	Recommendation if the answer is yes
Will only a minority of callers want to handle this problem?	JDO exceptions	Extend `RuntimeException`. This leaves callers the choice of catching the exception, but doesn't force all callers to catch it.
Did something go horribly wrong? Is the problem unrecoverable?	A business method fails because it can't connect to the application database	Extend `RuntimeException`. We know that callers can't do anything useful besides inform the user of the error.
Still not clear?		Extend `RuntimeException`. Document the exceptions that may be thrown and let callers decide which, if any, they wish to catch.

> **Decide at a package level how each package will use checked or unchecked exceptions. Document the decision to use unchecked exceptions, as many developers will not expect it.**
>
> **The only danger in using unchecked exceptions is that the exceptions may be inadequately documented. When using unchecked exceptions, be sure to document all exceptions that may be thrown from each method, allowing calling code to choose to catch even exceptions that you expect will be fatal. Ideally, the compiler should enforce Javdoc-ing of all exceptions, checked and unchecked.**
>
> **If allocating resources such as JDBC connections that must be released under all circumstances, remember to use a finally block to ensure cleanup, whether or not you need to catch checked exceptions. Remember that a finally block can be used even without a catch block.**

One reason sometimes advanced for avoiding runtime exceptions is that an uncaught runtime exception will kill the current thread of execution. This is a valid argument in some situations, but it isn't normally a problem in J2EE applications, as we seldom control threads, but leave this up to the application server. The application server will catch and handle runtime exceptions not caught in application code, rather than let them bubble up to the JVM. An uncaught runtime exception within the EJB container will cause the container to discard the current EJB instance. However, if the error is fatal, this usually makes sense.

> **Ultimately, whether to use checked or unchecked exception is a matter of opinion. Thus it's not only vital to document the approach taken, but to respect the practice of others. While I prefer to use unchecked exceptions in general, when maintaining or enhancing code written by others who favor exclusive use of checked exceptions, I follow their style.**

Good Exception Handling Practices

Whether we used checked or unchecked exceptions, we'll still need to address the issue of "nesting" exceptions. Typically this happens when we're forced to catch a checked exception we can't deal with, but want to rethrow it, respecting the interface of the current method. This means that we must wrap the original, "nested" exception within a new exception.

Some standard library exceptions, such as `javax.servlet.ServletException`, offer such wrapping functionality. But for our own application exceptions, we'll need to define (or use existing) custom exception superclasses that take a "root cause" exception as a constructor argument, expose it to code that requires it, and override the `printStackTrace()` methods to show the full stack trace, including that of the root cause. Typically we need two such base exceptions, one for checked and on for unchecked exceptions.

> *This is no longer necessary in Java 1.4, which supports exception nesting for all exceptions. We'll discuss this important enhancement below.*

In the generic infrastructure code accompanying our sample application, the respective classes are `com.interface21.core.NestedCheckedException` and `com.interface21.core.NestedRuntimeException`. Apart from being derived from `java.lang.Exception` and `java.lang.RuntimeException` respectively, these classes are almost identical. Both these exceptions are abstract classes; only subtypes have meaning to an application. The following is a complete listing of `NestedRuntimeException`:

```java
package com.interface21.core;

import java.io.PrintStream;
import java.io.PrintWriter;

public abstract class NestedRuntimeException extends RuntimeException {

  private Throwable rootCause;

  public NestedRuntimeException(String s) {
    super(s);
  }

  public NestedRuntimeException(String s, Throwable ex) {
    super(s);
    rootCause = ex;
  }

  public Throwable getRootCause() {
    return rootCause;
  }

  public String getMessage() {
    if (rootCause == null) {
      return super.getMessage();
    } else {
    return super.getMessage() + "; nested exception is: \n\t" +
          rootCause.toString();
    }
  }

  public void printStackTrace(PrintStream ps) {
    if (rootCause == null) {
      super.printStackTrace(ps);
    } else {
      ps.println(this);
      rootCause.printStackTrace(ps);
```

```
        }
    }

    public void printStackTrace(PrintWriter pw) {
        if (rootCause == null) {
            super.printStackTrace(pw);
        } else {
            pw.println(this);
            rootCause.printStackTrace(pw);
        }
    }

    public void printStackTrace() {
        printStackTrace(System.err);
    }
}
```

Java 1.4 introduces welcome improvements in the area of exception handling. There is no longer any need for writing chainable exceptions, although existing infrastructure classes like those shown above will continue to work without a problem. New constructors are added to `java.lang.Throwable` and `java.lang.Exception` to support chaining, and a new method `void initCause(Throwable t)` is added to `java.lang.Throwable` to allow a root cause to be specified even after exception construction. This method may be invoked only once, and only if no nested exception is provided in the constructor.

Java 1.4-aware exceptions should implement a constructor taking a throwable nested exception and invoking the new `Exception` constructor. This means that we can always create and throw them in a single line of code as follows:

```
catch (RootCauseException ex) {
    throw new MyJava14Exception("Detailed message", ex);
}
```

If an exception does not provide such a constructor (for example, because it was written for a pre Java 1.4 environment), we are guaranteed to be able to set a nested exception using a little more code, as follows:

```
catch (RootCauseException ex) {
    MyJava13Exception mex = new MyJava13Exception("Detailed message");
    mex.initCause(ex);
    throw mex;
}
```

When using nested exception solutions such as `NestedRuntimeException`, discussed above, follow their own conventions, rather than Java 1.4 conventions, to ensure correct behavior.

Exceptions in J2EE

There are a few special issues to consider in J2EE applications.

Distributed applications will encounter many checked exceptions. This is partly because of the conscious decision made at Sun in the early days of Java to make remote calling explicit. Since all RMI calls – including EJB remote interface invocations – throw `java.rmi.RemoteException`, local-remote transparency is impossible. This decision was probably justified, as local-remote transparency is dangerous, especially to performance. However, it means that we often have to write code to deal with checked exceptions that amount to "something went horribly wrong, and it's probably not worth retrying".

It's important to protect interface code – such as that in servlets and JSP pages – from J2EE "system-level" exceptions such as `java.rmi.RemoteException`. Many developers fail to recognize this issue, with unfortunate consequences, such as creating unnecessary dependency between architectural tiers and preventing any chance of retrying operations that might have been retried had they been caught at a low enough level. Amongst developers who *do* recognize the problem, I've seen two approaches:

❑ Allow interface components to ignore such exceptions, for example by writing code to catch them at a high level, such as a superclass of all classes that will handle incoming web requests that permits subclasses to throw a range of exceptions from a protected abstract method.

❑ Use a client-side façade that conceals communication with the remote system and throws exceptions – checked or unchecked – that are dictated by business need, not the problem of remote method calls. This means that the client-side façade should not mimic the interface of the remote components, which will all throw `java.rmi.RemoteException`. This approach is known as the **Business delegate** J2EE pattern (*Core J2EE Patterns*).

I believe that the second of these approaches is superior. It provides a clean separation of architectural tiers, allows a choice of checked or unchecked exceptions and does not allow the use of EJB and remote invocation to intrude too deeply into application design. We'll discuss this approach in more detail in *Chapter 11*.

Making Exceptions Informative

It's vital to ensure that exceptions are useful both to code and to humans developing, maintaining and administering an application.

Consider the case of exceptions of the same class reflecting different problems, but distinguished only by their message strings. These are unhelpful to Java code catching them. Exception message strings are of limited value: they may be helpful to explain problems when they appear in log files, but they won't enable the calling code to react appropriately, if different reactions are required, and they can't be relied on for display to users. When different problems may require different actions, the corresponding exceptions should be modeled as separate subclasses of a common superclass. Sometimes the superclass should be abstract. Calling code will now be free to catch exceptions at the relevant level of detail.

The second problem – display to users – should be handled by including error codes in exceptions. Error codes may be numeric or strings (string codes have the advantage that they can make sense to readers), which can drive runtime lookup of display messages that are held outside the exception. Unless we are able to use a common base class for all exceptions in an application – something that isn't possible if we mix checked and unchecked exceptions – we will need to make our exceptions implement an `ErrorCoded` or similarly named interface that defines a method such as this:

```
String getErrorCode();
```

The `com.interface21.core.ErrorCoded` interface from the infrastructure code discussed in Chapter 11 includes this single method. With this approach, we are able to distinguish between error messages intended for end users and those intended for developers. Messages inside exceptions (returned by the `getMessage()` method) should be used for logging, and targeted to developers.

> **Separate error messages for display to users from exception code, by including an error code with exceptions. When it's time to display the exception, the code can be resolved: for example, from a properties file.**

If the exception isn't for a user, but for an administrator, it's less likely that we'll need to worry about formatting messages or internationalization (internationalization might, however, still be an issue in some situations: for example, if we are developing a framework that may be used by non-English speaking developers).

As we've already discussed, there's little point in catching an exception and throwing a new exception unless we add value. However, occasionally the need to produce the best possible error message is a good reason for catching and wrapping.

For example, the following error message contains little useful information:

WebApplicationContext failed to load config

Exception messages like this typically indicate developer laziness in writing messages or (worse still) use of a single catch block to catch a wide variety of exceptions (meaning that the code that caught the exception had as little idea what went wrong as the unfortunate reader of the message).

It's better to include details about the operation that failed, as well as preserving the stack trace. For example, the following message is an improvement:

WebApplicationContext failed to load config: cannot instantiate class com.foo.bar.Magic

Better still is a message that gives precise information about what the process was trying to do when it failed, and information about what might be done to correct the problem:

WebApplicationContext failed to load config from file '/WEB-INF/applicationContext.xml': cannot instantiate class 'com.foo.bar.Magic' attempting to load bean element with name 'foo' – check that this class has a public no arg constructor

> Include as much context information as possible with exceptions. If an exception probably results from a programming error, try to include information on how to rectify the problem.

Using Reflection

The Java Reflection API enables Java code to discover information about loaded classes at runtime, and to instantiate and manipulate objects. Many of the coding techniques discussed in this chapter depend on reflection: this section considers some of the pros and cons of reflection.

> Many design patterns can best be expressed by use of reflection. For example, there's no need to hard-code class names into a Factory if classes are JavaBeans, and can be instantiated and configured via reflection. Only the names of classes – for example, different implementations of an interface – need be supplied in configuration data.

Java developers seem divided about the use of reflection. This is a pity, as reflection is an important part of the core API, and forms the basis for many technologies, such as JavaBeans, object serialization (crucial to J2EE) and JSP. Many J2EE servers, such as JBoss and Orion, use reflection (via Java 1.3 dynamic proxies) to simplify J2EE deployment by eliminating the need for container-generated stubs and skeletons. This means that every call to an EJB is likely to involve reflection, whether we're aware of it or not. Reflection is a powerful tool for developing generic solutions.

> Used appropriately, reflection can enable us to write less code. Code using reflection can also minimize maintenance by keeping itself up to date. As an example, consider the implementation of object serialization in the core Java libraries. Since it uses reflection, there's no need to update serialization and deserialization code when fields are added to or removed from an object. At a small cost to efficiency, this greatly reduces the workload on developers using serialization, and eliminates many programming errors.

Two misconceptions are central to reservations about reflection:

❑ Code that uses reflection is slow

❑ Code that uses reflection is unduly complicated

Each of these misconceptions is based on a grain of truth, but amounts to a dangerous oversimplification. Let's look at each in turn.

Code that uses reflection *is* usually slower than code that uses normal Java object creation and method calls. However, this seldom matters in practice, and the gap is narrowing with each generation of JVMs. The performance difference is slight, and the overhead of reflection is usually far outweighed by the time taken by the operations the invoked methods actually do.

Most of the best uses of reflection have no performance implications. For example, it's largely immaterial how long it takes to instantiate and configure objects on system startup. As we'll see in Chapter 15, most optimization is unnecessary. Unnecessary optimization that prevents us from choosing superior design choices is downright harmful. Similarly, the overhead added by the use of reflection to populate a JavaBean when handling a web request (the approach taken by Struts and most other web application frameworks) won't be detectable.

Disregarding whether or not performance matters in a particular situation, reflection also has far from the disastrous impact on performance that many developers imagine, as we'll see in Chapter15. In fact, in some cases, such as its use to replace a length chain of if/else statements, reflection will actually *improve* performance.

The Reflection API *is* relatively difficult to use directly. Exception handling, especially, can be cumbersome. However, similar reservations apply to many important Java APIs, such as JDBC. The solution to avoid using those APIs directly, by using a layer of helper classes at the appropriate level of abstraction, not to avoid the functionality they exist to provide. If we use reflection via an appropriate abstraction layer, using reflection will actually *simplify* application code.

> Used appropriately, reflection won't degrade performance. Using reflection appropriately should actually improve code maintainability. Direct use of reflection should be limited to infrastructure classes, not scattered through application objects.

Reflection Idioms

The following idioms illustrate appropriate use of reflection.

Reflection and Switches

Chains of if/else statements and large switch statements should alarm any developer committed to OO principles. Reflection provides two good ways of avoiding them:

❑ Using the condition to determine a class name, and using reflection to instantiate the class and use it (assuming that the class implements a known interface).

❑ Using the condition to determine a method name, and using reflection to invoke it.

Let's look at the second approach in practice.

Consider the following code fragment from an implementation of the `java.beans.VetoableChangeListener` interface. A `PropertyChangeEvent` received contains the name of the property in question. The obvious implementation will perform a chain of if/else statements to identify the validation method to invoke within the class (the `vetoableChange()` method will become huge if all validation rules are included inline):

```java
public void vetoableChange(PropertyChangeEvent e) throws PropertyVetoException {
  if (e.getPropertyName().equals("email")) {
    String email = (String) e.getNewValue();
    validateEmail(email, e);
  }
  ...
  } else if (e.getPropertyName().equals("age")) {
    int age = ((Integer) e.getNewValue()).intValue();
    validateAge(age, e);

  } else if (e.getPropertyName().equals("surname")) {
    String surname = (String) e.getNewValue();
    validateForename(surname, e);

  } else if (e.getPropertyName().equals("forename")) {
    String forename = (String) e.getNewValue();
    validateForename(forename, e);
  }
}
```

At four lines per bean property, adding another 10 bean properties will add 40 lines of code to this method. This if/else chain will need updating every time we add or remove bean properties.

Consider the following alternative. The individual validator now extends `AbstractVetoableChangeListener`, an abstract superclass that provides a final implementation of the `vetoableChange()` method. The `AbstractVetoableChangeListener`'s constructor examines methods added by subclasses that fit a validation signature:

```java
void validate<bean property name>(<new value>, PropertyChangeEvent)
    throws PropertyVetoException
```

The constructor is the most complex piece of code. It looks at all methods declared in the class that fit the validation signature. When it finds a valid validator method, it places it in a hash table, `validationMethodHash`, keyed by the property name, as indicated by the name of the validator method:

```java
public AbstractVetoableChangeListener() throws SecurityException {

  Method[] methods = getClass().getMethods();
  for (int i = 0; i < methods.length; i++) {
```

```
if (methods[i].getName().startsWith(VALIDATE_METHOD_PREFIX) &&
    methods[i].getParameterTypes().length == 2 &&
      PropertyChangeEvent.class.isAssignableFrom(methods[i].
        getParameterTypes()[1])) {

  // We've found a potential validator
  Class[] exceptions = methods[i].getExceptionTypes();

  // We don't care about the return type, but we must ensure that
  // the method throws only one checked exception, PropertyVetoException
  if (exceptions.length == 1 &&
      PropertyVetoException.class.isAssignableFrom(exceptions[0])) {

    // We have a valid validator method
    // Ensure it's accessible (for example, it might be a method on an
    // inner class)
    methods[i].setAccessible(true);
    String propertyName = Introspector.decapitalize(methods[i].getName().
      substring(VALIDATE_METHOD_PREFIX.length()));

    validationMethodHash.put(propertyName, methods[i]);
    System.out.println(methods[i] + " is validator for property " +
      propertyName);
  }
 }
 }
}
```

The implementation of `vetoableChange()` does a hash table lookup for the relevant validator method for each property changed, and invokes it if one is found:

```
public final void vetoableChange(PropertyChangeEvent e)
    throws PropertyVetoException {

  Method m = (Method) validationMethodHash.get(e.getPropertyName());

  if (m != null) {
    try {
      Object val = e.getNewValue();
      m.invoke(this, new Object[] { val, e });

    } catch (IllegalAccessException ex) {
      System.out.println("WARNING: can't validate. " +
        "Validation method '" + m + "' isn't accessible");

    } catch (InvocationTargetException ex) {
      // We don't need to catch runtime exceptions
      if (ex.getTargetException() instanceof RuntimeException)
        throw (RuntimeException) ex.getTargetException();
      // Must be a PropertyVetoException if it's a checked exception
      PropertyVetoException pex = (PropertyVetoException)
        ex.getTargetException();
      throw pex;
    }
  }
}
```

For a complete listing of this class, or to use it in practice, see the
`com.interface21.bean.AbstractVetoableChangeListener` class under the `/framework/src`
directory of the download accompanying this book.

Now subclasses merely need to implement validation methods with the same signature as in the first example. The
difference is that a subclass's logic will *automatically* be updated when a validation method is added or removed.
Note also that we've used reflection to automatically convert parameter types to validation methods. Clearly it's a
programming error if, say, the `validateAge()` method expects a `String` rather than an `int`. This will be
indicated in a stack trace at runtime. Obvious bugs pose little danger. Most serious problems result from subtle
bugs, that don't occur every time the application runs, and don't result in clear stack traces.

Interestingly, the reflective approach will actually be *faster* on average than the if/else approach if there are
many bean properties. String comparisons are slow, whereas the reflective approach uses a single hash table
lookup to find the validation method to call.

Certainly, the `AbstractVetoableChangeListener` class is more conceptually complex than the if/else
block. However, this is framework code. It will be debugged once, and verified by a comprehensive set of test
cases. What's important is that the *application* code – individual validator classes – is much simpler because of
the use of reflection. Furthermore, the `AbstractVetoableChangeListener` class is still easy to read for
anyone with a sound grasp of Java reflection. The whole of the version of this class I use – including full
Javadoc and implementation comments and logging statements – amounts to a modest 136 lines.

> **Reflection is a core feature of Java, and any serious J2EE developer should have a strong
> grasp of the Reflection API. Although reflective idioms (such as, the ternary operator) may
> seem puzzling at first, they're equally a part of the language's design, and it's vital to be
> able to read and understand them easily.**

Reflection and the Factory Design Pattern

I seldom use the **Factory** design pattern in its simplest form, which requires all classes created by the factory
to be known to the implementation of the factory. This severely limits extensibility: the factory object cannot
create objects (even objects that implement a known interface) unless it knows their concrete class.

The following method (a simplified version of the "bean factory" approach discussed in Chapter 11) shows a
more flexible approach, which is extensible without any code changes. It's based on using reflection to
instantiate classes by name. The class names can come from any configuration source:

```
public Object getObject(String classname, Class requiredType)
    throws FactoryException {

  try {
    Class clazz = Class.forName(classname);
    Object o = clazz.newInstance();
    if (!requiredType.isAssignableFrom(clazz))
      throw new FactoryException("Class '" + classname +
                                  "' not of required type " + requiredType);
    // Configure the object...
    return o;

  } catch (ClassNotFoundException ex) {
```

```
            throw new FactoryException("Couldn't load class '" + classname + "'", ex);

        } catch (IllegalAccessException ex) {
            throw new FactoryException("Couldn't construct class '" + classname +
                                "': is the no arg constructor public?", ex);

        } catch (InstantiationException ex) {
            throw new FactoryException("Couldn't construct class '" + classname +
                                "': does it have a no arg constructor", ex);
        }
    }
```

This method can be invoked like this:

```
MyInterface mo = (MyInterface)
beanFactory.getObject("com.mycompany.mypackage.MyImplementation",
MyInterface.class);
```

Like the other reflection example, this approach conceals complexity in a framework class. It is true that this code cannot be guaranteed to work: the class name may be erroneous, or the class may not have a no arg constructor, preventing it being instantiated. However, such failures will be readily apparent at runtime, especially as the getObject() method produces good error messages (when using reflection to implement low-level operations, be very careful to generate helpful error messages). Deferring operations till runtime does involve trade-offs (such as the need to cast), but the benefits may be substantial.

> *Such use of reflection can best be combined with the use of JavaBeans. If the objects to be instantiated expose JavaBean properties, it's easy to hold initialization information outside Java code.*

This is a very powerful idiom. Performance is unaffected, as it is usually used only at application startup; the difference between loading and initializing, say, ten objects by reflection and creating the same objects using the new operator and initializing them directly is undetectable. On the other hand, the benefit in terms of truly flexible design may be enormous. Once we do have the objects, we invoke them without further use of reflection.

There is a particularly strong synergy between using reflection to load classes by name and set their properties *outside Java code* and the J2EE philosophy of declarative configuration. For example, servlets, filters and web application listeners are instantiated from fully qualified class names specified in the web.xml deployment descriptor. Although they are not bean properties, ServletConfig initialization parameters are set in XML fragments in the same deployment descriptor, allowing the behavior of servlets at runtime to be altered without the need to modify their code.

Using reflection is one of the best ways to parameterize Java code. Using reflection to choose instantiate and configure objects dynamically allows us to exploit the full power of loose coupling using interfaces. Such use of reflection is consistent with the J2EE philosophy of declarative configuration.

Java 1.3 Dynamic Proxies

Java 1.3 introduced **dynamic proxies**: special classes that can implement interfaces at runtime without declaring that they implement them at compile time.

Dynamic proxies can't be used to proxy for a class (rather than an interface). However, this isn't a problem if we use interface-based design. Dynamic proxies are used internally by many application servers, typically to avoid the need to generate and compile stubs and skeletons.

Dynamic proxies are usually used to intercept calls to a delegate that actually implements the interface in question. Such interception can be useful to handle the acquisition and release of resources, add additional logging, and gather performance information (especially about remote calls in a distributed J2EE application). There will, of course, be some performance overhead, but its impact will vary depending on what the delegate actually does. One good use of dynamic proxies is to abstract the complexity of invoking EJBs. We'll see an example of this in Chapter 11.

The `com.interface21.beans.DynamicProxy` class included in the infrastructure code with the sample application is a generic dynamic proxy that fronts a real implementation of the interface in question, designed to be subclassed by dynamic proxies that add custom behavior.

Dynamic proxies can be used to implement **Aspect Oriented Programming (AOP)** concepts in standard Java. AOP is an emerging paradigm that is based on **crosscutting** aspects of a system, based on separation of concerns. For example, the addition of logging capabilities just mentioned is a crosscut that addresses the logging concern in a central place. It remains to be seen whether AOP will generate anything like the interest of OOP, but it's possible that it will at least grow to complement OOP.

For more information on AOP, see the following sites:

❑ http://aosd.net/. AOP home page.

❑ http://aspectj.org/. Home page for AspectJ, an extension to Java that supports AOP.

See the reflection guide with your JDK for detailed information about dynamic proxies.

> **A warning: I feel dangerously good after I've made a clever use of reflection. Excessive cleverness reduces maintainability. Although I'm a firm believer that reflection, used appropriately, is beneficial, don't use reflection if a simpler approach might work equally well.**

Using JavaBeans to Achieve Flexibility

Where possible, application objects – except very fine-grained objects – should be JavaBeans. This maximizes configuration flexibility (as we've seen above), as beans allow easy property discovery and manipulation at runtime. There's little downside to using JavaBeans, as there's no need to implement a special interface to make an object a bean.

When using beans, consider whether the following standard beans machinery can be used to implement functionality:

❑ `PropertyEditor`

❑ `PropertyChangeListener`

❑ `VetoableChangeListener`

❑ `Introspector`

> Designing objects to be JavaBeans has many benefits. Most importantly, it enables objects to be instantiated and configured easily using configuration data outside Java code.

Thanks to Gary Watson, my colleague at FT.com, for convincing me of the many merits of JavaBeans.

Avoid a Proliferation of Singletons by Using an Application Registry

The **Singleton** design pattern is widely useful, but the obvious implementation can be dangerous. The obvious way to implement a singleton is Java is to use a static instance variable containing the singleton instance, a public static method to return the singleton instance, and provide a private constructor to prevent instantiation:

```
public class MySingleton {

   /** Singleton instance */
   private static MySingleton instance;

   // Static block to instantiate the singleton in a threadsafe way
   static {
      instance = new MySingleton();
   }  // static initializer

   /** Enforces singleton method. Returns the instance of this object.
    * @throws DataImportationException if there was an internal error
    * creating the singleton
    * @return the singleton instance of this class
    */
   public static MySingleton getInstance() {
      return instance;
   }

   /** Private constructor to enforce singleton design pattern.
    */
   private MySingleton() {
      ...
   }

   // Business methods on instance
```

Note the use of a static initializer to initialize the singleton instance when the class is loaded. This prevents race conditions possible if the singleton is instantiated in the getInstance() method if it's null (a common cause of errors). It's also possible for the static initializer to catch any exceptions thrown by the singleton's constructor, which can be rethrown in the getInstance() method.

However, this common idiom leads to several problems:

❑   Dependence on the singleton class is hard-coded into many other classes.

❑   The singleton must handle its own configuration. As other classes are locked out of its initialization process, the singleton will be responsible for any properties loading required.

❑   Complex applications can have many singletons. Each might handle its configuration loading differently, meaning there's no central repository for configuration.

❑ Singletons are interface-unfriendly. This is a very bad thing. There's little point in making a singleton implement an interface, because there's then no way of preventing there being other implementations of that interface. The usual implementation of a singleton defines a type in a class, not an interface.

❑ Singletons aren't amenable to inheritance, because we need to code to a specific class, and because Java doesn't permit the overriding of static methods such as getInstance().

❑ It's impossible to update the state of singletons at runtime consistently. Any updates may be performed haphazardly in individual Singleton or factory classes. There's no way to refresh the state of all singletons in an application.

A slightly more sophisticated approach is to use a factory, which may use different implementation classes for the singleton. However, this only solves some of these problems.

> **I don't much like static variables in general. They break OO by introducing dependency on a specific class. The usual implementation of the Singleton design pattern exhibits this problem.**

In my view, it's a much better solution to have one object that can be used to locate other objects. I call this an **application context** object, although I've also seen it termed a "registry" or "application toolbox". Any object in the application needs only to get a reference to the single instance of the context object to retrieve the single instances of any application object. Objects are normally retrieved by name. This context object doesn't even need to be a singleton. For example, it's possible to use the Servlet API to place the context in a web application's ServletContext, or we can bind the context object in JNDI and access it using standard application server functionality. Such approaches don't require code changes to the context object itself, just a little bootstrap code.

The context object itself will be generic framework code, reusable between multiple applications.

The advantages of this approach include:

❑ It works well with interfaces. Objects that need the "singletons" never need to know their implementing class.

❑ All objects are normal Java classes, and can use inheritance normally. There are no static variables.

❑ Configuration is handled *outside* the classes in question, and entirely by framework code. The context object is responsible for instantiating and configuring individual singletons. This means that configuration *outside Java code* (such as an XML document or even RDBMS tables) can be used to source configuration data. Individual objects can be configured using JavaBean properties. Such configuration can include the creation of object graphs amongst managed objects by the application context, without the objects in question needing to do anything except expose bean properties.

❑ The context object will implement an interface. This allows different implementations to take configuration from different sources without any need to change code in managed application objects.

❑ It's possible to support dynamic state changes to "singletons". The context can be refreshed, changing the state of the objects it manages (although of course there are thread safety issues to consider).

❑ Using a context object opens other possibilities. For example, the context may provide other services, such as implementing the Prototype design pattern to serve as a factory for independent object instances. Since many application objects have access to it, the context object may serve as an event publisher, in the Observer design pattern.

❑ While the Singleton design pattern is inflexible, we can choose to have multiple application context objects if this is useful (the infrastructure discussed in Chapter 11 supports hierarchical context objects).

The following code fragments illustrate the use of this approach.

The context object itself will be responsible for loading configuration. The context object may register itself (for example with the `ServletContext` of a web application, or JNDI) or a separate bootstrap class may handle this. Objects needing to use "singletons" must look up the context object in. For example:

```
ApplicationContext application = (ApplicationContext )
servletContext.getAttribute("com.mycompany.context.ApplicationContext");
```

The `ApplicationContext` instance can be used to obtain any "singleton":

```
MySingleton mySingleton = (MySingleton )
applicationContext.getSingleInstance("mysingleton");
```

In Chapter 11 we'll look at how to implement this superior alternative to the Singleton design pattern. Note that it isn't limited to managing "singletons": this is valuable piece of infrastructure that can be used in many ways.

Why not use JNDI – a standard J2EE service – instead of use additional infrastructure to achieve this result? Each "singleton" could be bound to the JNDI context, allowing other components running in the application server to look them up.

Using JNDI adds complexity (JNDI lookups are verbose) and is significantly less powerful than the application context mechanism described above. For example, each "singleton" would be left on its own to handle its configuration, as JNDI offers only a lookup mechanism, not a means of externalizing configuration. Another serious objection is that this approach would be wholly dependent on application server services, making testing outside an application server unnecessarily difficult. Finally, some kind of bootstrap service would be required to bind the objects into JNDI, meaning that we'd probably need to implement most of the code in the application context approach anyway. Using an application context, we can choose to bind individual objects with JNDI if it proves useful.

Avoid a proliferation of singletons, each with a static `getInstance()` method. Using a factory to return each singleton is better, but still inflexible. Instead, use a single "application context" object or registry that returns a single instance of each class. The generic application context implementation will normally
(but not necessarily) be based on the use of reflection, and should take care of configuring the object instances it manages. This has the advantage that application objects need only expose bean properties for configuration, and never need to look up configuration sources such as properties files.

Refactoring

Refactoring, according to Martin Fowler in *Refactoring: Improving the Design of Existing Code* from *Addison-Wesley (ISBN 0-201485-6-72)*, is "the process of changing a software system in such a way that it does not alter the external behavior of the code, yet improves its internal structure. It's a disciplined way to clean up code that minimizes the chances of introducing bugs". See http://www.refactoring.com for more information and resources on refactoring.

Most of the refactoring techniques Fowler describes are second nature to good developers. However, the discussion is useful and Fowler's naming is being widely adopted (For example, the Eclipse IDE uses these names on menus).

> **Be prepared to refactor to eliminate code duplication and ensure that a system is well implemented at each point in time.**

It's helpful to use an IDE that supports refactoring. Eclipse is particularly good in this respect.

I believe that refactoring can be extended beyond functional code. For example, we should continually seek to improve in the following areas:

❑ **Error messages**
   A failure with a confusing error message indicates an opportunity to improve the error message.

❑ **Logging**
   During code maintenance, we can refine logging to help in debugging. We'll discuss logging below.

❑ **Documentation**
   If a bug results from a misunderstanding of what a particular object or method does, documentation should be improved.

Coding Standards

J2EE projects tend to be big projects. Big projects require teamwork, and teamwork depends on consistent programming practices. We know that more effort is spent on software maintenance than initial development, so it's vital to ensure that applications are easy to work on. This makes good Java coding standards – as well as the practice of sound OO design principles – vital across J2EE projects. Coding standards are particularly important if we choose to use XP. Collective code ownership can only work if all code is written to the same standards, and there are no significant discrepancies in style within a team.

Why does a section on Java coding standards (albeit with a J2EE emphasis) belong in a book on J2EE? Because there's a danger in getting lost in the details of J2EE technology, and losing sight of good programming practice. This danger is shown by many J2EE sample applications, which contain sloppy code.

Sun are serious offenders in this respect. For example, the Smart Ticket Demo version 1.1 contains practically no comments, uses meaningless method parameter names such as u, p, zc and cc, and contains serious programming errors such as consistently failing to close JDBC connections correctly in the event of exceptions. Code that isn't good enough to go into a production application is definitely not good enough to serve as an example.

Perhaps the authors of such applications believe that omitting such "refinements" clarifies the architectural patterns they seek to illustrate. This is a mistake. J2EE is often used for large projects in which sloppy practices will wreak havoc. Furthermore, bringing code to production standard may expose inadequacies in the original, naïve implementation.

As with design principles, this is a huge area, so the following discussion is far from comprehensive. However, it tries to address issues that I've found to be of particular importance in practice. Again, there are necessarily matters of opinion, and the discussion is based on my opinions and practical experience.

Start from the Standard

Don't invent your own coding conventions or import those from other languages you've worked in. Java is a relatively simple language, offering only one way to do many things. In contrast, Java's predecessor C++ usually offered several. Partly for this reason, there's a greater degree of standardization in the way developers write in Java, which should be respected.

For example, you may be familiar with "Hungarian notation" or Smalltalk naming conventions. However, Hungarian Notation exists to solve problems (the proliferation of types in the Windows API) that don't exist in Java. A growing proportion of Java developers haven't worked in other languages, and will be baffled by code that imports naming conventions.

Start from Sun's Java coding conventions (available at http://java.sun.com/docs/codeconv/html/CodeConvTOC.doc.html). Introduce refinements and variations if you prefer, but don't stray too far from common Java practice. If you organization already has coding standards, work within them unless they are seriously non-standard or questionable. In that case, don't ignore them: initiate discussion on how to improve them.

Some other coding standards worth a look are:

❑   http://g.oswego.edu/dl/html/javaCodingStd.html
    Java coding standards by Doug Lea, author of *Concurrent Programming in Java* (now somewhat dated).

❑   http://www.chimu.com/publications/javaStandards/part0003.html#E11E4
    Chimu Inc coding standards (partly based on Lea's).

❑   http://www.ambysoft.com/javaCodingStandards.html
    Scott Ambler's coding conventions. A lengthy document, with some of the best discussion I've seen. Ambler, the author of many books on Java and OO design, devotes much more discussion than the Sun conventions to the design end of the coding standards spectrum (issues such as field and method visibility).

It is, however, worth mentioning one common problem that results from adhering to standard Java practice. This concerns the convention of using the instance variable name as a parameter, and resolving ambiguity using `this`. This is often used in property setters. For example:

```
private String name;

public void setName(String name) {
   this.name = name;
}
```

On the positive side, this is a common Java idiom, so it's widely understood. On the negative, it's very easy to forget to use this to distinguish between the two variables with the same name (the parameter will mask the instance variable). The following form of this method will compile:

```
public void setName(String name) {
  name = name;
}
```

As will this, which contains a typo in the name of the method parameter:

```
public void setName(String nme) {
  name = name;
}
```

In both these cases (assuming that the instance variable name started off as null) mysterious null pointer exceptions will occur at runtime. In the first erroneous version, we've assigned the method parameter to itself, accomplishing nothing. In the second, we've assigned the instance variable to itself, leaving it null.

I don't advocate using the C++ convention of prefixing instance or member variables with m_ (for example, m_name), as it's ugly and inconsistent with other Java conventions (underscores are normally only used in constants in Java). However, I recommend the following three practices to avoid the likelihood of the two errors we've just seen:

❑ Consider giving parameters a distinguishing name if ambiguity might be an issue. In the above case, the parameter could be called newName. This correctly reflects the purpose of the parameter, and avoids the problem we've seen.

❑ Always use this when accessing instance variables, whether it's necessary to resolve ambiguity or not. This has the advantage of making explicit each method's dependence on instance data. This can be very useful when considering concurrency issues, for example.

❑ Follow the convention that local variable names should be fairly short, while instance variables names are more verbose. For example, i should be a local variable; userInfo an instance variable. Usually, the instance variable name should be an interface or class name beginning with a lower case letter (for example SystemUserInfo systemUserInfo), while local variable names should convey their meaning in the current context (for example SystemUserInfo newUser).

See http://www.beust.com/cedric/naming/index.html for arguments against standard Java convention in this area, from Cedric Beust, lead developer of the WebLogic EJB container.

Consistent file organization is important, as it enables all developers on a project to grasp a class's structure quickly. I use the following conventions, which supplement Sun's conventions:

❑ Organize methods by function, not accessibility. For example, instead of putting public methods before private methods, put a private method in the same section of a class as the public methods that use it.

❑ Delimit sections of code. For example, I delimit the following sections (in order):

- Any static variables and methods. Note that `main()` methods shouldn't be an issue, as a class that does anything shouldn't include a `main()` method, and code should be tested using JUnit.
- Instance variables. Some developers prefer to group each bean property holder with the related getter and setter method, but I think it is preferable to keep all instance variables together.
- Constructors.
- Implementations of interfaces (each its own section), along with the private implementation methods supporting them.
- Public methods exposed by the class but not belonging to any implemented interface.
- Protected abstract methods.
- Protected methods intended for use by subclasses.
- Implementation methods not related to any one previous group.

I use section delimiters like this:

```
//------------------------------------------------------------------
// Implementation of interface MyInterface
//------------------------------------------------------------------
```

Please refer to the classes in the `/framework/src` directory in the download accompanying this book for examples of use of the layout and conventions described here. The `com.interface21.beans.factory.support.AbstractBeanFactory` class is one good example.

If you need to be convinced of the need for coding standards, and have some time to spare, read http://www.mindprod.com/unmain.html.

Allocation of Responsibilities

Every class should have a clear responsibility. Code that doesn't fit should be refactored, usually into a helper class (inner classes are often a good way to do this in Java). If code at a different conceptual level will be reused by related objects, it may be promoted into a superclass. However, as we've seen, delegation to a helper is often preferable to concrete inheritance.

Applying this rule generally prevents class size blowout. Even with generous Javadoc and internal comments, any class longer than 500 lines of code is a candidate for refactoring, as it probably has too much responsibility. Such refactoring also promotes flexibility. If the helper class's functionality might need to be implemented differently in different situations, an interface can be used to decouple the original class from the helper (in the Strategy design pattern).

The same principle should be applied to methods:

> **A method should have a single clear responsibility, and all operations should be at the same level of abstraction.**

Where this is not the case, the method should be refactored. In practice, I find that this prevents methods becoming too long.

I don't use any hard and fast rules for method lengths. My comfort threshold is largely dictated by how much code I can see at once on screen (given that I normally devote only part of my screen to viewing code, and sometimes work on a laptop). This tends to be 30 to 40 lines (including internal implementation comments, but not Javadoc method comments). I find that methods longer than this can usually be refactored. Even if a unit of several individual tasks within a method is invoked only once, it's a good idea to extract them into a private method. By giving such methods appropriate names (there are no prizes for short method names!) code is made easier to read and self-documenting.

Avoid Code Duplication

It may seem an obvious point, but code duplication is deadly.

A simple example from the Java Pet Store 1.3 illustrates the point. One EJB implementation contains the following two methods:

```
public void ejbCreate() {

  try {
    dao = CatalogDAOFactory.getDAO();
  } catch (CatalogDAOSysException se) {
    Debug.println("Exception getting dao " + se);
    throw new EJBException(se.getMessage());
  }
}
```

and:

```
public void ejbActivate() {

  try {
    dao = CatalogDAOFactory.getDAO();
  } catch (CatalogDAOSysException se) {
    throw new EJBException(se.getMessage());
  }
}
```

This may seem trivial, but such code duplication leads to serious problems, such as:

- ❑ Too much code. In this case, refactoring saves only one line, but in many cases the savings will be much greater.

- ❑ Confusing readers as to the intent. As code duplication is illogical and easy to avoid, the reader is likely to give the developer the benefit of the doubt and assume that the two fragments are not identical, wasting time comparing them.

- ❑ Inconsistent implementation. Even in this trivial example, one method logs the exception, while the other doesn't.

- ❑ The ongoing need to update two pieces of code to modify what is really a single operation.

The following refactoring is simpler and much more maintainable:

```java
public void ejbCreate() {
   initializeDAO();
}

public void ejbActivate() {
  initializeDAO();
}

private void initializeDAO() {

  try {
    dao = CatalogDAOFactory.getDAO();
  } catch (CatalogDAOSysException se) {
    Debug.println("Exception getting dao " + se);
    throw new EJBException(se.getMessage());
  }
}
```

Note that we've consolidated the code; we can make a single line change to improve it to use the new `EJBException` constructor in EJB 2.0 that takes a message along with a nested exception. We'll also include information about what we were trying to do:

```java
throw new EJBException("Error loading data access object: " +
                       se.getMessage(), se);
```

EJB 1.1 allowed `EJBExceptions` to contain nested exceptions, but it was impossible to construct an `EJBException` with both a message and a nested exception, forcing us to choose between including the nested exception or a meaningful message about what the EJB was trying to do when it caught the exception.

Avoid Literal Constants

> **With the exception of the well-known distinguished values 0, null and "" (the empty string) do not use literal constants inside Java classes.**

Consider the following example. A class that contains the following code as part of processing an order:

```java
if (balance > 10000) {
  throw new SpendingLimitExceededException(balance, 10000);
}
```

Unfortunately, we often see this kind of code. However, it leads to many problems:

- ❏ The code isn't self-documenting. Readers are forced to read the code to guess the meaning of the 10000.

- ❏ The code is error prone. Readers will be forced to compare different literals to ensure that they're the same, and it's easy to mistype one of the multiple literals.

- ❏ Changing the one logical "constant" will require multiple code changes.

It's better to use a constant. In Java, this means a static final instance variable. For example:

```java
private static final int SPENDING_LIMIT = 10000;

if (balance > SPENDING_LIMIT) {
   throw new SpendingLimitExceededException(balance, SPENDING_LIMIT);
}
```

This version is much more readable and much less error prone. In many cases, it's good enough. However, it's still problematic in some circumstances. What if the spending limit isn't always the same? Today's constant might be tomorrow's variable. The following alternative allows us more control:

```java
private static final int DEFAULT_SPENDING_LIMIT = 10000;

protected int spendingLimit() {
   return DEFAULT_SPENDING_LIMIT;
}

if (balance > spendingLimit()) {
   throw new SpendingLimitExceededException(balance, spendingLimit());
}
```

At the cost of a little more code, we can now calculate the spending limit at runtime if necessary. Also, a subclass can override the protected `spendingLimit()` method. In contrast, it's impossible to override a static variable. A subclass might even expose a bean property enabling the spending limit to be set outside Java code, by a configuration manager class (see the *Avoiding a proliferation of Singletons by Using an Application Registry* section earlier). Whether the `spendingLimit()` method should be public is a separate issue. Unless other classes are known to need to use it, it's probably better to keep it protected.

I suggest the following criteria to determine how to program a constant:

Requirement	Example	Recommendation
String constant that is effectively part of application code	Simple SQL SELECT statement *used once only* and which won't vary between databases. JDO query *used once only.*	This is a rare exception to the overall rule when there's little benefit in using a named constant or method value instead of a literal string. In this case, it makes sense for the string to appear at the point in the application where it is used, as it's effectively part of application code.
Constant that will never vary	JNDI name – such as the name of an EJB – that will be same in all application servers.	Use a static final variable. Shared constants can be declared in an interface, which can be implemented by multiple classes to simplify syntax.

Requirement	Example	Recommendation
Constant that may vary at compile time	JNDI name – such as the name of the `TransactionManager` – that is likely to vary between application servers.	Use a protected method, which subclasses may override, or which may return a bean property, allowing external configuration,
Constant that may vary at runtime	Spending limit.	Use a protected method.
Constant subject to internationalization	Error message or other string that may need to vary in different locales.	Use a protected method or a `ResourceBundle` lookup. Note that a protected method may return a value that was obtained from a `ResourceBundle` lookup, possibly outside the class.

Visibility and Scoping

The visibility of instance variables and methods is one of the important questions on the boundary between coding standards and OO design principles. As field and method visibility can have a big impact on maintainability, it's important to apply consistent standards in this area.

I recommend the following general rule:

> **Variables and methods should have the least possible visibility (of private, package, protected and public). Variables should be declared as locally as possible.**

Let's consider some of the key issues in turn.

Public Instance Variables

The use of public instance variables is indefensible, except for rare special cases. It usually reflects bad design or programmer laziness. If any caller can manipulate the state of an object without using the object's methods, encapsulation is fatally compromised. We can never maintain any invariants about the object's state.

Core J2EE Patterns suggests the use of public instance variables as an acceptable strategy in the **Value Object** J2EE pattern (value objects are serializable parameters containing data, rather than behavior, exchanged between JVMs in remote method calls). I believe that this is only acceptable if the variables are made final (preventing their values from being changed after object construction and avoiding the potential for callers to manipulate object state directory). However, there are many serious disadvantages that should be considered with any use of public instance variables in value objects, which I believe should rule it out. For example:

❑ If variables aren't made final, the data in value objects can't be protected against modification. Consider the common case in which value objects, once retrieved in a remote invocation, are cached on the client side. A single rogue component that modifies value object state can affect all components using the same value object. Java gives us the tools to avoid such scenarios (such as private variables with accompanying getter methods); we should use them.

149

❏ If variables *are* made final, all variable values must be supplied in the value object constructor, which may make value objects harder to create.

❏ Use of public instance variables is inflexible. Once callers are dependent on public instance variables, they're dependent on the value object's data structure, not just a public interface. For example, we can't use some of the techniques discussed in Chapter 15 for optimizing the serialization of value objects, as they depend on switching to more efficient storage types without changing public method signatures. While we're free to change the implementation of public methods if necessary without affecting callers, changes to value object implementations will require all callers using instance variables first to migrate to using accessor methods, which may prove time-consuming.

❏ Use of public instance variables ties us to coding to concrete classes, not interfaces.

❏ Instance variable access cannot be intercepted. We have no way of telling what data is being accessed.

A value object using public instance variables is really a special case of a **struct**: a group of variables without any behavior. Unlike C++ (which is a superset of C) Java does not have a `struct` type. However, it is easy to define structs in Java, as objects containing only public instance variables. Due to their inflexibility, structs are only suited to local use: for example, as private and protected inner classes. A struct might be used to return multiple values from method, for example, given that Java doesn't support call by reference for primitive types.

I don't see such concealed structs as a gross violation of OO principles. However, structs usually require constructors, bringing them closer to true objects. As IDEs make it easy to generate getter and setter methods for instance variables, using public instance variables is a very marginal time saving during development. In modern JVMs, any performance gain will be microscopic, except for very rare cases. I find that structs are usually elevated into true objects by refactoring, making it wiser to avoid their use in the first place.

> **The advantages in the rare legitimate uses of public instance variables are so marginal, and the consequence of misuse of public instance variables so grave, that I recommend banning the use of public instance variables altogether.**

Protected and Package Protected Instance Variables

Instance variables should be private, with few exceptions. Expose such variables through protected accessor methods if necessary to support subclasses.

I strongly disagree with coding standards (such as Doug Lea's) that advocate making instance variables protected, in order to maximize the freedom for subclasses. This is a questionable approach to concrete inheritance. It means that the integrity and invariants of the superclass can be compromised by buggy subclass code. In practice, I find that subclassing works as perfectly as a "black box" operation.

There are many better ways of allowing class behavior to be modified than by exposing instance variables for subclasses to manipulate as they please, such as using the Template Method and Strategy design patterns (discussed above) and providing protected methods as necessary to allow *controlled* manipulation of superclass state. Allowing subclasses to access protected instance variables produces tight coupling between classes in an inheritance hierarchy, making it difficult to change the implementation of classes within it.

Scott Ambler argues strongly that all instance variables should be private and, further, that "the ONLY member functions that are allowed to directly work with a field are the accessor member functions themselves" (that is, even methods within the declaring class should use getter and setter methods, rather than access the private instance variable directly).

I feel that a protected instance variable is only acceptable if it's final (say, a logger that subclasses will use without initializing or modifying). This has the advantage of avoiding a method call, offering slightly simpler syntax. However, even in this case there are disadvantages. It's impossible to return a different object in different circumstances, and subclasses cannot override a variable as they can a method.

I seldom see a legitimate use for Java's package (default) visibility for instance variables. It's a bit like C++'s `friend` mechanism: the fair-weather friend of lazy programmers.

> **Avoid protected instance variables. They usually reflect bad design: there's nearly always a better solution. The only exception is the rare case when an instance variable can be made final.**

Method Visibility

Although method invocations can never pose the same danger as direct manipulation of instance variables, there are many benefits in reducing method visibility as far as possible. This is another way to reduce the coupling between classes. It's important to distinguish between the requirements of classes that use a class (even subclasses) and the class's internal requirements. This can both prevent accidental corruption of the class's internal state and simplify the task of developers working with the class, by offering them only the choices they need.

> **Hide methods as much as possible. The fewer methods that are public, package protected or protected, the cleaner a class is and the easier it will be to test, use, subclass and refactor. Often, the only public methods that a class exposes will be the methods of the interfaces it implements and methods exposing JavaBean properties.**

It's a common practice to make a class's implementation methods protected rather than private, to allow them to be used by subclasses. This is inadvisable. In my experience, inheritance is best approached as a black box operation, rather than a white box operation. If class `Dog` extends `Animal`, this should mean that a `Dog` can be used where an `Animal` can be used, not that the `Dog` class needs to know the details of `Animal`'s implementation.

The `protected` modifier is best used for abstract methods (as in the Template Method design pattern), or for read-only helper methods required by subclasses. In both these cases, there are real advantages in making methods protected, rather than public.

I find that I seldom need to use package protected (default visibility) methods, although the objections to them are less severe than to protected instance variables. Sometimes package protected methods revealing class state can be helpful to test cases. Package protected *classes* are typically far more useful, enabling an entire class to be concealed within a package.

Variable Scoping

Variables should be declared as close as possible to where they are used. The fewer variables in scope, the easier code is to read and debug. It's a serious mistake to use an instance variable where an automatic method variable and/or additional method parameters can be used. Use C++/Java local declarations, in which variables are declared just before they're used, rather than C-style declarations at the beginning of methods.

151

Inner Classes and Interfaces

Inner classes and interfaces can be used in Java to avoid namespace pollution. Inner classes are often helpers, and can be used to ensure that the outer class has a consistent responsibility.

Understand the difference between static and non-static inner classes. Static inner classes can be instantiated without the creation of an object of the enclosing type; non-static inner classes are linked to an instance of the enclosing type. There's no distinction for interfaces, which are always static.

Inner interfaces are typically used when a class requires a helper that may vary in concrete class, but not in type, and when this helper is of no interest to other classes (we've already seen an example of this).

Anonymous inner classes offer convenient implementation of simple interfaces, or overrides that add a small amount of new behavior. Their most idiomatic use is for action handlers in Swing GUIs, which is of limited relevance to J2EE applications. However, they can be useful when implementing callback methods, which we discussed above.

For example, we could implement a JDBC callback interface with an anonymous inner class as follows:

```
public void anonClass() {
  JdbcTemplate template = new JdbcTemplate(null);
  template.update(new PreparedStatementCreator() {
    public PreparedStatement createPreparedStatement
        (Connection conn) throws SQLException {
      PreparedStatement ps =
        conn.prepareStatement("DELETE FROM TAB WHERE ID=?");
      ps.setInt(1, 1);
      return ps;
    }
  });
}
```

Anonymous inner classes have the disadvantages that they don't promote code reuse, can't have constructors that take arguments and are only accessible in the single method call. In the above example, these restrictions aren't a problem, as the anonymous inner class doesn't need constructor arguments and doesn't need to return data. Any inner class (including anonymous inner classes) can access superclass instance variables, which offers a way to read information from and update the enclosing class, to work around these restrictions. Personally I seldom use anonymous inner classes except when using Swing, as I've found that they're nearly always refactored into named inner classes.

A halfway house between top-level inner classes (usable by all methods and potentially other objects) and anonymous inner classes is a named inner class defined within a method. This avoids polluting the class's namespace, but allows the use of a normal constructor. However, like anonymous inner classes, local classes may lead to code duplication. Named classes defined within methods have the advantages that they can implement constructors that take arguments and can be invoked multiple times. In the following example, the named inner class not only implements a callback interface, but adds a new public method, which we use to obtain data after its work is complete:

```
public void methodClass() {
  JdbcTemplate template = new JdbcTemplate(dataSource);
  class Counter implements RowCallbackHandler {
    private int count = 0;
    public void processRow(ResultSet rs) throws SQLException {
```

```
      count++;
    }
    public int getCount() {
      return count;
    }
  }
}
Counter counter = new Counter();
template.query("SELECT ID FROM MYTABLE", counter);
int count = counter.getCount();
}
```

It would be impossible to implement the above example with an anonymous inner class without making (inappropriate) use of an instance variable in the enclosing class to hold the count value.

Using the final Keyword

The final keyword can be used in several situations to good effect.

Method Overriding and Final Methods

There is a common misconception that making methods final reduces the reusability of a class, because it unduly constrains the implementation of subclasses. In fact, overriding concrete methods is a poor way of achieving extensibility.

I recommend making public and protected non-abstract methods final. This can help to eliminate a common cause of bugs: subclasses corrupting the state of their superclasses. Overriding methods is inherently dangerous. Consider the following problems and questions:

❑ Should the subclass call the superclass's version of the method? If so, at what point should the call happen? At the beginning or end of the subclass method? Whether to invoke the superclass's method can only be determined by reading code or relying on documentation in the superclass. The compiler can't help. This rules out black box inheritance. If the superclass's form of the method is not called, or is called at the wrong point in the subclass method, the superclass's state may be corrupted.

❑ Why is the superclass implementing a method that it does not have enough knowledge to implement on behalf of all subclasses? If it can provide a valid partial implementation it should defer those parts of the operation it doesn't understand to protected abstract methods in the Template Method design pattern; if its implementation is likely to be completely overridden by some subclasses it's best to break out the inheritance tree to provide an additional superclass for those subclasses that share the same behavior (in which the method is final).

❑ If a subclass's overridden implementation of a method does something different to the superclass implementation, the subclass probably violates the **Liskov Substitution Principle**. The Liskov Substitution principle, stated by Barbara Liskov in 1988 *("Data Abstraction and Hierarchy", SIGPLAN Notices, 23 May, 1988)*, states that a subclass should always be usable in place of its superclass without affecting callers. This principle protects the concept of concrete inheritance. For example, a Dog object should be usable wherever an Animal has to be used. Subclasses that violate the Liskov Substitution Principle are also unfriendly to unit testing. A class without concrete method overrides should pass all the unit tests of its superclasses.

153

Another OO principle – the **Open Closed Principle** – states that an object should be open to extension, but closed to modification. By overriding concrete methods, we effectively modify an object, and can no longer guarantee its integrity. Following the Open Closed Principle helps to reduce the likelihood of bugs as new functionality is added to an application, because the new functionality is added in new code, rather than by modifying existing code, potentially breaking it.

Especially in the case of classes that will be overridden by many different subclasses, making superclass methods final when methods cannot be private (for example, if they implement an interface and hence must be public) will simplify the job of programmers developing subclass implementations. For example, most programmers will create subclasses using IDEs offering code helpers: it's much preferable if these present a list of just those non-final methods that can – or, in the case of abstract methods, *must* – be overridden.

Making methods final will produce a slight performance gain, although this is likely to be too marginal to be a consideration in most cases.

Note that there are better ways of extending an object than by overriding concrete methods. For example, the Strategy design pattern (discussed earlier) can be used to parameterize some of the object's behavior by delegating to an interface. Different implementations of the interface can be provided at runtime to alter the behavior (but not compromise the integrity) of the object. I've used final methods as suggested here in several large projects, and the result has been the virtual elimination of bugs relating to corruption of superclass state, with no adverse impact on class reusability.

Final methods are often used in conjunction with protected abstract methods. An idiomatic use of this is what I call "chaining initializers". Consider a hypothetical servlet superclass, AbstractServlet. Suppose that one of the purposes of this convenient superclass is to initialize a number of helper classes required by subclasses. The AbstractServlet class initializes these helper classes in its implementation of the Servlet API init() method.

To preserve the integrity of the superclass, this method should be made final (otherwise, a subclass could override init() without invoking AbstractServlet's implementation of this method, meaning that the superclass state wouldn't be correctly initialized). However, subclasses may need to implement their own initialization, distinct from that of the superclass. The answer is for the superclass to invoke a chained method in a final implementation of init(), like this:

```
public final void init() {
  // init helpers
  //...
  onInit();
}

protected abstract void onInit();
```

The onInit() method is sometimes called a **hook method**. A variation in this situation is to provide an empty implementation of the onInit() method, rather than making it abstract. This prevents subclasses that don't need their own initialization from being forced to implement this method. However, it has the disadvantage that a simple typo could result in the subclass providing a method that is never invoked: for example, by calling it oninit().

This technique can be used in many situations, not just initialization. In my experience, it's particularly important in frameworks, whose classes will often be subclassed, and for which developers of subclasses should have no reason to manipulate (or closely examine) superclass behavior.

I recommend that public or protected non-abstract methods should usually be made final, unless one of the following conditions applies:

❑ A subclass's form of the method won't need to invoke the superclass's form of the method. This commonly arises if the superclass provides a simple default or empty implementation of a method to save all subclass being forced to provide an implementation of an abstract method that is only of interest to a minority of subclasses (as in the variation noted above).

❑ It is logical to call the superclass's form of the method as part of the work of the subclass's form. Overriding the `toString()` method of a Java object is the commonest example of this.

❑ The number of hook methods might otherwise spiral out of control. In this case, we must temper design rigor with practicality. Superclass documentation must scrupulously note at what point subclass methods should call overridden superclass methods.

My views in this area are somewhat controversial. However, experience in several large projects has convinced me of the value of writing code that helps to minimize the potential for errors in code written around it. This position was summarized by the distinguished computer scientist (and inventor of quicksort) C.A.R. Hoare as follows:

> *"I was eventually persuaded of the need to design programming notations so as to maximize the number of errors which cannot be made, or if made, can be reliably detected at compile time" (1980 Turing Award Lecture).*

Final Classes

Final classes are used less frequently than final methods, as they're a more drastic way of curtailing object modification.

The *UML Reference Manual (Addison Wesley; ISBN: 0-20130-998-X)* goes so far as to recommend that only abstract classes should be sub-classed (for the reasons we've discussed when considering final methods). However, I feel that if final methods are used appropriately, there's little need to make classes final to preserve object integrity.

I tend to use final classes only for objects that must be guaranteed to be immutable: for example, value objects that contain data resulting from an insurance quotation.

Final Instance Variables

I've already mentioned the use of final protected instance variables. A final instance variable may be initialized at most once, either at its declaration or in a constructor. Final instance variables are the only way to define constants in Java, which is their normal use. However, they can occasionally be used to allow superclasses to expose protected instance variables without allowing subclasses to manipulate them, or to allow any class to expose public instance variables that cannot be manipulated.

> *Java language gurus will also note that final instance variables can be initialized in a class initializer: a block of code that appears in a class outside a method body, and is evaluated when an object is instantiated. Class initializers are used less often than static initializers, as constructors are usually preferable.*

Implementing toString() Methods Useful for Diagnostics

It's good practice for classes to implement `toString()` methods that summarize their state. This can be especially helpful in generating log messages (we'll discuss logging below).

155

For example, consider the following code, which might be used in a value object representing a user, and which provides a concise, easily readable dump of the object's state which will prove very useful in debugging:

```
public String toString() {
    StringBuffer sb = new StringBuffer(getClass().getName() + ": ");
    sb.append("pk=" + id + "; ");
    sb.append("surname='" + getSurname() + "'; ");
    sb.append("forename='" + getForename() + "'; ");
    sb.append(" systemHashCode=" + System.identityHashCode());
    return sb.toString();
}
```

Note the use of a `StringBuffer`, which is more efficient than concatenating strings with the + operator. Also note that the string forename and surname values are enclosed in single quotes, which will make any white space which may be causing unexpected behavior easy to detect. Note also that the state string includes the object's hash code. This can be very useful to verify if objects are distinct at runtime. The example uses `System.identityHashCode()` instead of the object's `hashCode()` method as the `System.identityHashCode()` method returns the default `Object` hash code, which in most JVMs will be based on an object's location in memory, rather than any override of this method that the object may implement.

Another important use of `toString()` values is to show the type and configuration of an implementation of an interface.

Defensive Coding Practices

`NullPointerExceptions` are a common cause of bugs. Since `NullPointerExceptions` don't carry helpful messages, the problems they cause can be hard to track down. Let's consider some coding standards we can apply to reduce the likelihood of them occurring at runtime.

Handle Nulls Correctly

It's particularly important to consider what will happen when an object is null. I recommend the following guidelines for handling the possibility of nulls:

❑ Document method behavior on null arguments. Often it's a good idea to check parameters for nulls. It's important to document the behavior if null arguments are deemed to indicate erroneous calling code, and a method may legitimately throw a `NullPointerException`.

❑ Write test cases that invoke methods with null arguments to verify the documented behavior, whatever it may be.

❑ Don't assume that an object can never be null at a particular point without good reason. This assumption causes many problems.

Consider the Ordering of Object Comparisons

The following two lines of code will produce the same result in normal operation:

```
if (myStringVariable.equals(MY_STRING_CONSTANT))
```

```
if (MY_STRING_CONSTANT.equals(myStringVariable))
```

However, the second form is more robust. What if `myStringVariable` is null? The second condition will evaluate to false, without error, while the first will throw a `NullPointerException`. It's usually a good idea to perform object comparisons by calling the `equals()` method on the object less likely to be null. If it's an error for the other object to be null, perform an explicit check for null and throw the appropriate exception (which won't be `NullPointerException`).

Use Short-circuit Evaluation

Sometimes we can rely on Java's short-circuit evaluation of Boolean expressions to avoid potential errors: for example, with null objects. Consider the following code fragment:

```
if ( (o != null) && (o.getValue() < 0))
```

This is safe even if the object o is null. In this case, the second test won't be executed, as the condition has already evaluated to false. Of course, this idiom can only be used if it reflects the intention of the code. Something quite different might need to be done (besides evaluating this condition to false) if o is null. However, it's a safe bet that we don't want a `NullPointerException`.

An alternative is to perform the second check in an inner if statement, only after an outer if statement has established that the object is non-null. However, I don't recommend this approach unless there is some other justification for the nested if statements (which, however, there often will be), as statement nesting adds complexity.

Distinguish Whitespace in Debug Statements and Error Messages

Consider the following scenario. A web application fails with the following error:

Error in com.foo.bar.MagicServlet: Cannot load class com.foo.bar.Magic

The developer checks and establishes that the class `com.foo.bar.Magic`, as expected, is in the web application's classpath, in a JAR file in the `/WEB-INF/lib` directory. The problem makes no sense: is it an obscure J2EE classloading issue? The developer writes a JSP that successfully loads the class by name, and is still more puzzled.

Now, consider the alternative error message:

Error in com.foo.bar.MagicServlet: Cannot load class 'com.foo.bar.Magic '

Now the problem is obvious: `com.foo.bar.MagicServlet` is trying to load class `com.foo.bar.Magic` by name, and somehow a trailing space has gotten into the class name. The moral of the story is that white space is important in debug statements and error messages. String literals should be enclosed in delimiters that clearly show what is part of the string and what isn't. Where possible, the delimiters should be illegal in the variable itself.

Prefer Arrays to Collections in Public Method Signatures

Java's lack of generic types mean that whenever we use a collection, we're forced to cast to access its elements, even when – as we usually do – we know that all its elements are of the same type. This longstanding issue may be addressed in Java 1.5 with the introduction of a simpler analog of C++'s template mechanism. Casts are slow, complicate code, and are potentially fragile.

Using collections seldom poses seriously problems within a class's implementation. However, it's more problematic when collections are used as parameters in a class's public interface, as there's a risk that external callers may supply collections containing elements of incorrect types. Public interface methods returning a collection will require callers to cast.

> **Use a typed array in preference to a collection if possible when defining the signatures for public methods.**

Preferring collections to arrays provides a much clearer indication of method purpose and usage, and may eliminate the need to perform casts, which carry a heavy performance cost.

This recommendation shouldn't be applied rigidly. Note that there *are* several situations where a collection is the correct choice:

- ❑ When data may be retrieved only in response to user traversal of the collection (this is often the case in collections returned by JDO and CMP entity beans).

- ❑ In the rare cases when elements may not be of the same type. In this case a collection of Objects correctly models the data.

- ❑ When converting a collection to an array may be inefficient.

- ❑ When the object genuinely is a map of keys to values.

- ❑ When the collection is returned by a superclass that may not know the types of elements handled by subclasses.

Note that it's possible to convert a collection to a typed array in a single line of code, if we know that all the elements are of the required type. For example, if we know that the collection c consists of `Product` objects we can use the following code:

```
Product[] products = (Product[]) c.toArray(new Product[c.size()]);
```

Documenting Code

There is no excuse for inadequate code documentation, in any language. Java goes a step further than most languages in helping developers to document code by standardizing documentation conventions with Javadoc.

> **Code that isn't fully documented is unfinished and potentially useless.**

Remember that documentation should serve to:

- ❑ Provide a contract for objects and methods. Test cases for an object are also valuable specifications, and documentation and test cases should be kept synchronized.

- ❑ Save developers the trouble of needing to read code before they use it. There should be no need to examine a class's code to establish what it does or whether it works. Javadoc exists to establish what it does, and unit tests should establish that it works as documented.

❑ Explain non-obvious features of the implementation. Deciding what is obvious is a tricky issue. Assume that your readers are competent Java and J2EE developers (unless you know otherwise, for example if you are writing a demonstration application for a new deployment). Accordingly, don't document language features, even those that are not universally understood such as the ternary operator. Java is a small, simple language. There is no excuse for developers who aren't familiar with its features and common idioms.

I suggest the following documentation guidelines:

❑ Learn to use the features of Javadoc (such as `@param` and `@throws`). Refer to the documentation with your version of the JDK for detailed information about Javadoc.

❑ Use Javadoc comments on all methods, including private methods. Use an IDE that makes this easy. It's tedious and error prone to generate comments manually, but both Forte and Eclipse, for example, can generate stub Javadoc comments, leaving the developer to fill in the blanks. Add meaningful information in Javadoc comments. Pay particular attention to the way in which methods handle null values.

❑ Always document runtime exceptions that may be thrown by a method *if they're effectively part of the API*. Perhaps the best way to ensure this is to declare these exceptions in the method's throws clauses (which is legal, but not enforced by the compiler). For example, a `NullPointerException` probably indicates a programming error and shouldn't be documented, but if your API, such as JDO, chooses to use runtime exceptions instead of checked exceptions, it's vital to indicate what might go wrong and under what circumstances callers should choose to catch unchecked exceptions.

❑ Javadoc comments on methods and classes should normally indicate *what* the method or class does. It's also usually necessary to implement *how* a class is implemented. Use ordinary // or /* comments for this, within the body of the class or method.

❑ Use /* style comments for implementation comments longer than 3 lines. Use // comments for shorter comments.

❑ Use Javadoc comments on all instance variables.

❑ When a class implements an interface, don't repeat comments about the interface contract (they add nothing to the implementation, and will get out of sync). The comments in classes should focus on the particular implementation; Javadoc method comments in classes should use `@see` tags to refer to the interface documentation for the method (Eclipse automatically generates such comments for implementation classes).

❑ Always document the type of keys and values in a Map, as well as the Map's purpose. I find this a huge help towards understanding classes that use Maps.

❑ Likewise, document the element types permissible in a Collection.

❑ Ensure that all comments add value. High-level languages such as Java are substantially self-documenting. Don't comment something until you are sure you can't make it obvious from the code itself. For example: comments like "loop through the array elements" add no value.

❑ While there's no need to document obvious things, it's essential to document non-obvious things. If you needed to use a tricky workaround for any reason, document it. Otherwise, someone may switch to the "natural" approach in the future and strike the problem you sought to avoid. Such documentation should normally be in implementation comments, not Javadoc comments.

❑ Take every opportunity to improve documentation. Confused as to how to use a method and had to look at the method's implementation? Once you know how it works, take the opportunity to improve the method's documentation. Noticed a non-obvious feature in the code? If you had to figure it out (and realized that it's necessary), add a comment explaining it. Of course, this is no substitute for writing full documentation in the first place.

❑ Include a `package.html` file in each package. This will be picked up by Javadoc (see Javadoc documentation for details).

❑ Document early and always keep documentation up to date. Never plan to add documentation "after coding is complete". Even if you do ever get to write it, you will probably have forgotten some of the vital details. Writing documentation, like writing test cases, helps increase your understanding of your code and design. Consider writing method documentation, then test cases for the method, then the method. Keep all three in sync.

❑ Don't use "endline" (or "trailing") comments. Endline comments are left-justified and appear on the same line as the statement they refer to. Endline comments tend to lead to long lines, and ongoing need to spend time formatting code to keep comments aligned. Endline comments may occasionally be used for variables within a method.

❑ Don't include a change log in class documentation. It's common practice to include a change log (for example, from CVS) in a Javadoc class comment. This information can easily be obtained from the source control system. The change log will become long and no one will read it (they probably won't read the *real* comments either). However, it is a good idea to include the revision id and last committer in the class comment. How to do this will vary with the source control system.

❑ Unless bureaucracy in your organization insists on it, don't use massive comments at the beginning of files containing your company's mission statement, verbose license terms and the like (simply provide a URL if necessary). It's frustrating when one opens a file and can't see any code without scrolling down. Don't bother to include the file path as reported by the version control system: Java's package structure means that we always know the path from the root of the classpath to any file (and that's all we should know).

❑ Generate full Javadoc comments daily and make them available on your intranet. Use Ant or your preferred build tool to integrate the generation of Javadoc comments into the build process. This not only provides essential, up-to-date information for developers, but helps to spot typos such as unterminated formatting tags early, and can serve to shame developers whose code is not adequately documented. Javadoc will also report problems such as incorrect tags, which should be corrected.

Finally, if you don't already, learn to touch type. It's much easier to write comments if you can type fluently. It's surprisingly easy to learn to touch type (and no, non-touch typists never approach the speed of touch typists, even if they seem to have a flurry of activity).

Logging

It's important to **instrument** code: to add logging capabilities that help to trace the application's execution. Adequate instrumentation is so important that it should be a required coding standard.

Logging has many uses, but the most important is probably to facilitate debugging. It's not a fashionable position, but I think that debugging tools are overrated. However, I'm in good company; programming gurus Brian Kernighan and Rob Pike argue this point in *The Practice of Programming,* from *Addison-Wesley (ISBN 0-201-61586-X)*. I find that I seldom need to use debuggers when working in Java.

Writing code to emit log messages is a lower-tech but more lasting solution. Consider the following issues:

❑   Debugging sessions are transient. They help to track down today's bug, but won't make debugging easier tomorrow. There's no record of today's debugging session under version control.

❑   Debugging is time consuming when it becomes necessary to step through code. Searching for a particular pattern in a log file may be much quicker.

❑   Logging encourages thought about a program's structure and activity, regardless of whether bugs are reported.

❑   Debuggers don't always work well in distributed applications (although some IDEs can integrate with J2EE application servers to facilitate debugging distributed applications).

A good logging framework can provide detailed information about program flow. Both Java 1.4 logging and the Log4j logging package offer settings that show the class, method and line number that generated the log output.

As with configuration in general, it's best to configure log output *outside* Java classes. It's common to see "verbose" flags and the like in Java classes themselves, enabling logging to be switched on. This is poor practice. It necessitates recompiling classes to reconfigure logging. Especially when using EJB, this can mean multiple deployments as debugging progresses. If logging options are held outside Java code, they can be changed without the need to change object code itself.

Requirements of a production logging package should include:

❑   A simple API available to application code.

❑   The ability to configure logging *outside Java code*. For example it should be possible to switch logging on or off for one or more packages or classes without modifying their source code.

❑   The division of log messages into several priorities, such as debug, info, and error, and the ability to choose which priority will be the threshold for display.

❑   The ability to query programmatically whether messages with a given priority will be displayed.

❑   The ability to configure message formatting, and the way in which messages are reported (for example, to the file system, as XML documents or to the Windows event log). Ideally this should also be handled declaratively, and divorced from the API.

❑   The ability to buffer output to minimize expensive I/O operations such as file writes or database inserts.

> Never use `System.out` for logging. Console output can't be configured. For example, we can't switch it off for a particular class, or choose to display a subset of messages. Console output may also seriously degrade performance when running in some servers.

Even code that is believed to be "finished" and bug free should be capable of generating log output. There may turn out to be bugs after all, bugs may be introduced by changes, or it may be necessary to switch on logging in a trusted module to see what's going wrong with other classes in development. For this reason, all application servers are capable of generating detailed log messages, if configured to do so. This is not only useful for the server's developers, but can help to track down problems in applications running on them.

161

> Remember that unit tests are valuable in indicating *what* may be wrong with an object, but won't necessarily indicate *where* the problem is. Logging can provide valuable assistance here.

Instrumentation is also vital in performance tuning. By knowing what an application is doing and how it's doing it, it's much easier to establish which operations are unreasonably slow.

> Code isn't ready for production unless it is capable of generating log messages and its log output can easily be configured.

Log messages should be divided into different priorities, and debug messages should indicate the whole workflow through a component. Debug log messages should often show object state (usually by invoking toString() methods).

❑ Use logging heavily in important sections of code.

❑ Modify and improve logging statements during maintenance (for example, if log output seems unclear).

❑ Think carefully when choosing priority (severity) for log messages. It's useless to be able to configure log output if all log messages have the same priority. Log messages with the same priority should expose a consistent level of detail.

Choosing a Logging API

Until the release of Java 1.4, Java had no standard logging functionality. Some APIs such as the Servlet API provided primitive logging functionality, but developers were forced to rely on third-party logging products such as Apache Log4j to achieve an application-wide logging solution. Such products added dependencies, as application code referenced them directly, and were potentially problematic in the EJB tier.

Java 1.4 Logging and a Pre-1.4 Emulation Package

Java 1.4 introduces a new package – java.util.logging – that provides a standard logging API meeting the criteria we've discussed. Since this book is about J2EE 1.3, the following discussion assumes that Java 1.4 isn't available – if it is, simply use standard Java 1.4 logging functionality.

Fortunately, it's possible to benefit from the standard API introduced in Java 1.4 even when running Java 1.3. This approach avoids dependence on proprietary logging APIs and makes eventual migration to Java 1.4 logging trivial. It also eliminates the need to learn a third-party API.

Java 1.4 logging is merely an addition to the core Java class library, rather than a language change like Java 1.4 assertion support. Thus it is possible to provide an API emulating the Java 1.4 API and use it in Java 1.2 and 1.3 applications. Application code can then use the Java 1.4 API. Although the full Java 1.4 logging infrastructure won't be available, actual log output can be generated by another logging package such as Log4j (Log4j is the most powerful and widely used pre-Java 1.4 logging solution). Thus the Java 1.4 emulation package is a fairly simple wrapper, which imposes negligible runtime overhead.

The only catch is that Java 1.4 defines the logging classes in a new java.util.logging package. Packages under java are reserved for Sun. Hence we must import a distinctly named emulation package – I've chosen java14.java.util.logging – in place of the Java 1.4 java.util.logging package. This import can be changed when code is migrated to Java 1.4.

See *Appendix A* for a discussion of the implementation of the Java 1.4 logging emulation package used in the infrastructure code and sample application accompanying this book.

> *Log4j is arguably more powerful than Java 1.4 logging, so why not use Log4j directly? Using Log4j may be problematic in some application servers; there is a clear advantage in using a standard Java API, and it's possible to use the powerful log output features of Log4j while using the Java 1.4 API (which differs comparatively little). However, using Log4j directly may be a good choice when using a third-party product (such as many open source projects) that already uses Log4j.*

We have yet another choice for logging in web applications. The Servlet API provides logging methods available to any web component with access to the application's `ServletContext`. The `javax.servlet.GenericServlet` servlet superclass provided by the Servlet API provides convenient access to the same logging functionality. Don't use Servlet API logging. Most of an application's work should be done in ordinary Java classes, without access to Servlet API objects. Don't end up with components logging to different logs. Use the one solution for all logging, including from servlets.

Java 1.4 Logging Idioms

Once we've imported the emulation package, we can use the Java 1.4 API. Please refer to the Java 1.4 Javadoc for details.

The most important class is the `java.util.logging.Logger` class, used both to obtain a logger and to write log output. The most important methods are:

`Logger.getLogger(String name)`

This obtains a logger object associated with a given component. The convention is that the name for a component should be the class name. For example:

```
Logger logger = Logger.getLogger(getClass().getName());
```

Loggers are threadsafe, so it's significantly more efficient and results in simpler code to obtain and cache a logger to be used throughout the class's lifecycle. I normally use the following instance variable definition:

```
protected final Logger logger = Logger.getLogger(getClass().getName());
```

Often an abstract superclass will include this definition, allowing subclasses to perform logging without importing any logging classes or obtaining a logger. Note that the protected instance variable is final, in accordance with the visibility guidelines discussed earlier. Logging calls will look like this:

```
logger.fine("Found error number element <" +
            ERROR_NUMBER_ELEMENT + ">: checking numeric value");
```

Java 1.4 logging defines the following log level constants in the `java.util.logging.Level` class:

❑ SEVERE: Indicates a serious failure. Often there will be an accompanying Throwable.

❑ CONFIG: Intended for messages generated during application configuration.

❑ INFO: Moderate priority. More likely to indicate what a component is doing (for example, to monitor progress in performing a task) than to be intended to help in debugging the component.

❏ FINE: Tracing information. This and lower priority levels should be used to help debug the class in question, rather than to elucidate the working of the application as a whole.

❏ FINER: Detailed tracing information.

❏ FINEST: Highly detailed tracing information.

Each level has a corresponding convenience method, such as severe() and fine(). Generic methods allow the assigning of a level to a message and logging an exception.

Each message must be assigned one of these logging levels, to ensure that the granularity of logging can be controlled easily at runtime.

Logging and Performance

Correct use of a logging framework should have negligible effect on performance, as a logging framework should consume few resources. Applications should usually be configured to log only errors in production, to avoid excessive overhead and the generation of excessively large log files.

It's important to ensure that generating log messages doesn't slow down the application, even if these messages are never displayed. A common offender in this regard is using toString() methods on complex objects that access many methods and build large strings.

If a log message might be slow to generate, it's important to check whether or not it will be displayed before generating it. A logging framework must provide fast methods that indicate whether messages with a given log priority will be displayed at runtime. Java 1.4 allows the ability to perform checks such as the following:

```
if (logger.isLoggable(Level.FINE)) {
   logger.fine("The state of my complex object is " + complexObject);
}
```

This code will execute very quickly if FINE log output is disabled for the given class, as the toString() method won't be invoked on complexObject. String operations are surprisingly expensive, so this is a very important optimization.

Also remember to take care that logging statements cannot cause failures, by ensuring that objects they will call toString() cannot be null.

An equally important performance issue with logging concerns log output. Both Java 1.4 logging and Log4j offer settings that show the class, method and line number that generated the log output. This setting should be switched off in production, as it's very expensive to generate this information (it can only be done by generating a new exception and parsing its stack trace string as generated by one of its printStackTrace() methods). However, it can be very useful during development. Java 1.4 logging allows the programmer to supply the class and method name through the logging API. At the cost of making logging messages harder to write and slightly more troublesome to read, this guarantees that this information will be available efficiently, even if a JIT makes it impossible to find sufficient detail from a stack trace.

Other logging system configuration options with a significant impact on performance are:

❏ The destination of log messages. Writing log messages to the console or to a database will probably be much slower than writing to a file.

❑ The maximum file size and file rollover configuration. All logging packages should allow automatic rollover to a new log file when the existing log file reaches a certain size. Allowing too large a maximum file size may significantly slow logging, as each write to the file may involve substantial overhead. It's usually necessary to cap the number of log files retained after rollover, as otherwise logging can consume enormous amounts of disk space, which may cause the server and application to fail.

Logging in the EJB Tier

In logging as in many other respects, the EJB tier poses special problems.

❑ The EJB programming restrictions doesn't permit configuration to be loaded from the file system or allow writing (such as of log files) to the file system.

❑ Most logging frameworks technically violate the programming restrictions imposed on application code by the EJB specification (§24.1.2). Several core Log4j classes, for example, use synchronization.

❑ How can objects that may be passed to and from the EJB tier using remote invocation handle logging, as their execution spans distinct virtual machines?

Let's discuss each issue in turn.

Logging configuration isn't a major problem. We can load logging configuration from the classpath, rather than the file system, allowing it be included in EJB JAR files.

What to do with log output is a more serious problem. Two solutions sometimes proposed are to write log output using enterprise resources that EJBs *are* allowed to use, such as databases; or to use JMS to publish log messages, hoping that a JMS message consumer will be able to do something legal with them.

Neither of these solutions is attractive. Using a database will cause logging to have a severe impact on performance, which calls the viability of logging in question. Nor is a database a logical place to look for log messages. Using JMS merely pushes the problem somewhere else, and is also technological overkill (JMS is also likely to have a significant overhead).

Another powerful argument against using enterprise resources such as databases and JMS topics or queues for logging is the real possibility that we will need to log a failure in the enterprise resource being used to generate the log output. Imagine that we need to log the failure of the application server to access its database. If we attempt to write a log message to the same database, we'll produce another failure, and fail to generate a log message.

It's important not to be too doctrinaire about EJB programming restrictions. Remember that EJB should be used to help us achieve our goals; we shouldn't let adopting it make life more difficult. The destination of log messages is best handled in logging system configuration, not Java code. In my view it's best to ignore these restrictions and log to a file, unless your EJB container objects (remember that EJB containers must perform logging internally; JBoss, for example, uses Log4j). Logging configuration can be changed if it is necessary to use a database or other output destination (this may be necessary if the EJB container doesn't necessarily sit on a file system; for example, if it is implemented on a database).

I feel that the synchronization issue calls for a similar tempering of rigid interpretation of the EJB specification with practical considerations. It's impracticable to avoid using libraries that use synchronization in EJB (for example, it would rule out using all pre Java 1.2 collections, such as `java.util.Vector`; while there's seldom good reason to use these legacy classes today, vast amounts of existing code does and it's impossible to exclude it from EJB world). In Chapter 6 we'll discuss the EJB programming restrictions in more detail.

165

Finally, where distributed applications using EJB are concerned, we must consider the issue of remote method invocation. Java 1.4 loggers aren't serializable. Accordingly, we need to take special care when using logging in objects that will be passed between architectural tiers, such as value objects created in the EJB container and subsequently accessed in a remote client JVM. There are three plausible alternative approaches:

❑ Don't use logging in such classes. There is a strong argument that such objects are basically parameters, and should not contain enough intelligence to require log output.

❑ Obtain a logger with each logging statement, ensuring that the object will always obtain a valid logger whatever JVM it runs in.

❑ Obtain a logger by implementing a private `getLogger()` method, which each logging statement uses in place of an instance variable to obtain a logger.

The third method allows caching, and will offer the best performance, although the complexity isn't usually justified. The following code fragment illustrates the approach. Note that the `logger` instance variable is transient. When such an object is passed as a remote parameter, this value will be left null, prompting the `getLogger()` method to cache the logger for the new JVM:

```
private transient Logger logger;

private Logger getLogger() {
   if (this.logger == null) {
     // Need to get logger
     this.logger = Logger.getLogger(getClass().getName());
   }
   return this.logger;
}
```

A race condition is possible at the highlighted line. However, this isn't a problem, as object references (such as the `logger` instance variable) are atomic. The worse that can happen is that heavy concurrent access may result in multiple threads making unnecessary calls to `Logger.getLogger()`. The object's state cannot be corrupted, so there's no reason to synchronize this call (which would be undesirable when the object is used within the EJB container).

Why (and How) Not to Reinvent the Wheel

So far we've considered design and coding standards that help us write quality, maintainable code. Professional enterprise architects and developers not only write good code; they avoid writing code they don't have to write.

Many common problems (beyond those addressed by J2EE application servers) have been solved well by open source or commercial packages and frameworks. In such cases, designing and implementing a proprietary solution may be wasted effort. By adopting an existing solution, we are free to devote all our effort to meeting business requirements.

In this section we'll look at issues in using third-party frameworks to reuse existing investment.

Help! API Overload

Today, there are many API and technology choices for most problems in J2EE.

Even Sun now seems to be at the point where pulling it all together is so complex that we're seeing significant duplication of effort. For example, JDO and EJB 2.0 entity beans with CMP seem to overlap significantly.

Ultimately, we all pay for duplication of effort in increased effort and decreased quality. At least we can do our utmost to control it within our organization. I believe that code reuse *is* possible, and we should do our best to achieve it.

There are many ways to avoid duplication of effort and leverage existing code. I suggest the following practices as a starting point:

- ❑ Adopt existing frameworks where possible. For example, use a standard logging framework and an existing framework for web applications. However, don't force developers to use organization-wide standard frameworks if it seems that they're not proving a good fit to the problem in hand. Where multiple alternative frameworks exist, survey the options. Don't automatically assume that the first product you look at, or the most popular, will best meet your needs.

- ❑ Have zero tolerance for code duplication. This indicates the need for generalization: try to avoid code duplication in the first place, but refactor it out of the way as soon as it appears.

- ❑ Ensure good communication amongst developers. For example, have developers give presentations on modules they've recently completed, so that other developers know what common needs are emerging or have already been met. Encourage developers to encourage other developers to use the infrastructure components they've implemented.

- ❑ Develop and maintain some simple infrastructure packages that implement functionality that's widely used. Document them well and ensure that all developers are aware of them.

- ❑ Adopt standard architectural patterns, even where it's not possible to share code. It's much easier to avoid duplication of effort when working with familiar patterns.

- ❑ Use code reviews. This not only helps to boost quality, but also spurs communication within a team.

Using Frameworks

One particularly valuable way of leveraging existing components, whether third-party or developed in-house, is to build within a **framework**. A framework is a generic architecture that forms the basis for specific applications within a domain or technology area.

A framework differs from a class library in that committing to a framework dictates the architecture of an application. Whereas user code that uses a class library handles control flow itself, using class library objects as helpers, frameworks take responsibility for control flow, calling user code (we've already talked about inversion of control and the Hollywood principle ("Don't call me, I'll call you")). This takes the same approach as the Template Method design pattern, but applies it on a much larger scale.

Frameworks differ from design patterns in that:

- ❑ Frameworks are concrete, not abstract. While design patterns are conceptual, you can take an existing framework and build an application with it by adding additional code. This normally takes the form of implementing framework interfaces or subclassing framework classes.

167

❑ Frameworks are higher-level than design patterns. A framework may use several design patterns.

❑ Frameworks are usually domain-specific or technology-specific, whereas design patterns can be applied to many problems. For example, a framework might handle insurance quotations, or provide a clean separation of logic from presentation for web applications. Most design patterns can be used in just about any application.

Adopting a good framework that is a good fit can slash a project's development time. The toughest design problems may have been solved, based on recognized best practices. Much of the project's implementation will be devoted to filling in the gaps, which shouldn't involve so many difficult design decisions.

On the other hand, trying to shoehorn a project into using a framework that is a poor fit will cause serious problems. The problems will be much worse than choosing an unsuitable class library. In that case, the library can be ignored: application developers will simply have to develop their own, more suitable, library functionality. A poorly fitting framework will impose an unnatural structure on application code.

The performance and reliability of the resulting application can also be no greater than that of the framework. Usually, this is not a problem, as an existing framework is likely to have been widely used in earlier projects and its reliability and performance characteristics are known, but in all cases it justifies a thorough quality check of a framework before making a commitment.

What Makes a Good Framework?

Good frameworks are simple to use, yet powerful.

The Scylla and Charybdis of framework design are excessive flexibility and irritating rigidity.

In Greek mythology, Scylla was a sea monster that lived on one side of the Strait of Messia, opposite the whirlpool Charybdis. Sailors had to chart a course between the two.

Excessive flexibility means that the framework contains code that will probably never be used, and may be confusing to work with (it will also be harder to test, as there are more possibilities to cover). However, if a framework isn't flexible enough to meet a particular requirement, developers will cheerfully implement their own way of doing things, so that the framework delivers little benefit in practice.

Good framework code is a little different to good application code. A good framework may contain complex code: this is justified if it conceals that complexity from code that uses it. A good framework simplifies application code.

Benefits of Using Existing Frameworks

Generally, it's better to avoid building any but simple frameworks in-house. Open source has flowered over the past few years, especially in Java, and there are many existing frameworks. Developing good frameworks is harder than developing applications.

The main benefit of adopting an existing framework is the same as that in adopting J2EE itself: it enables an organization's development team to focus its effort on developing the required product, rather than concerning itself with the underlying infrastructure. If the third-party framework is popular, there is also a potential advantage in the availability of skills working with that framework.

As usual, there's a trade-off: the learning curve in adopting the framework, and a continuing dependency on the framework. The more complex the project, the easier it is to justify the initial investment and ongoing dependency.

Evaluating Existing Frameworks

Adopting a framework is a very important decision. In some cases, it can determine whether a project succeeds or fails; in many cases, it will determine developer productivity. As with choosing an application server, it's important to conduct a thorough evaluation before making a commitment. Remember that even if choosing a framework involves no license costs (in the case of an open source framework) there are many other costs to consider, such as the impact of a learning curve on developer productivity and the likely cost of dealing with any bugs in the framework.

I apply the following criteria to evaluating existing frameworks. Applying them in this order tends to limit the amount of time spent evaluating unsuitable products:

- ❑   What is the quality of the project documentation?
- ❑   What is the project's status?
- ❑   Is the design sound?
- ❑   What is the quality of the code?
- ❑   Does the release include test cases?

Let's look at each criterion in turn.

What is the Quality of the Project Documentation?

Is there a coherent – and persuasive – overview document that explains the framework's rationale and design? Are there Javadocs for all the classes, and do they contain meaningful information?

What is the Project's Status?

If the product is commercial, the main considerations will be the status of the vendor, the place of this product in the vendor's strategy, and the licensing strategy. There is a real danger in adopting a commercial, closed source, product that the vendor will shut shop or abandon it, leaving users unsupported. Clearly this is less likely to happen with a large vendor.

However, large companies such as IBM initiate many projects that don't fit into their longer-term strategy (consider many of the projects on the IBM Alphaworks site). The viability of the vendor is no guarantee that they will continue to resource and support any individual project. Finally, especially if the product is commercial but currently free, does the small print in the license agreement imply that the vendor could begin to charge for it at any time? Is your organization prepared to accept this?

If the product is open source, there are different considerations. How *live* is the project? How many developers are working on it? When was the last release, and how frequently have releases been made? Does the project documentation cite reference sites? If so, how impressive are they? How active are the project mailing lists? Is there anywhere to go for support? Are the project developers helpful? The ideal is to have both helpful developers responding to newsgroup questions and the existence of paid consulting.

Sites such as SourceForge (http://www.sourceforge.net) have statistics on project activity. Other indications are active mailing lists and searching with your favorite search engine for material on the product.

Many managers have reservations about adopting open source products. Although the quality of projects varies widely, such reservations are becoming less and less rational. After all, Apache is now the most widely deployed web server, and has proven very reliable. Several open source Java products are very widely used: for example, the Xerces XML parser and Log4j. We're also seeing interest from major commercial players such as IBM in open source. Xalan and Eclipse, for example, are two significant open source projects that were initially developed at IBM.

Is the Design Sound?

The project's documentation should describe the design used (for example, the design patterns and architectural approach). Does this meet your needs? For example, a framework based entirely on concrete inheritance (such as Struts) may prove inflexible. Not only might this pose a problem for your code, but it might necessitate radical changes in the framework itself to add new functionality in the future. If your classes are forced to extend framework classes, this might require significant migration effort for your organization in future.

What is the Quality of the Code?

This may be time-consuming, but is very important, assuming that the source code is available. Assuming that the product has satisfied the previous criteria, the investment of time is justified.

Spend half a day browsing the code. Apply the same criteria as you would to code written within your organization, and look at some of the core classes to evaluate the cleanliness, efficiency and correctness of the implementation. As an incidental benefit, your team will end up understanding a lot more about the technology in question and, if the framework is well written, may see some useful design and coding techniques.

Does the Release Include Test Cases?

There are challenges developing reliable software with a community of geographically dispersed developers communicating via e-mail and newsgroups. One of the ways to assure quality is to develop a test suite. Successful open source products such as JBoss have large test suites. If an open source product doesn't have a test suite, it's a worrying sign. If you commit to it, you may find that your application breaks with each new release because of the lack of regression tests.

Implementing your own Framework

The first rule of developing frameworks in-house is: *don't*. In general it's better to adopt existing solutions.

However, there are situations where we have unusual needs, or where existing frameworks don't meet our needs. In this case, it will be better to develop a *simple* framework than to use an unsuitable existing product or to code haphazardly without any framework.

Even in this case, it's not a good idea to jump in early. Attempt to design a framework only after you understand the problem, and then try to design the simplest possible framework. Don't expect that your first design will be perfect: let the design evolve before making too big a commitment.

Learn from Existing Frameworks

As writing frameworks is hard, successful frameworks are among the most valuable examples of real world design. Take a close look at successful frameworks in your domain and others, the design patterns they use and how they enable application code to extend them.

Implementing a Framework

When implementing a framework, it's vital to have clear goals up front. It's impossible to foresee every requirement in the framework's future, but, unless you have a vision of what you want to achieve, you'll be disappointed with the results.

Probably the most important lesson of scoping a framework is to deliver maximum value with minimum complexity. Often we find a situation where the framework can solve most, but not all, of the problems in a domain fairly easily, but that providing a complete solution is hard. In this case, it may be preferable to settle for a simple solution to 90% of problems, rather than seek to force a generalization that covers the remaining 10%.

> **Apply the Pareto Principle if designing a framework. If a particular function seems particularly hard to implement, ask whether it's really necessary, or whether the framework can deliver most of its value without tackling this issue.**

Writing a framework differs from writing application code in several ways:

- ❑ *The XP advice of "Writing the simplest thing that could possibly work" isn't always appropriate*
  It's impossible to refactor the interfaces exposed by a framework without breaking code that uses it and severely reducing its usefulness. Even within an organization, the cost of incompatible changes to a framework can be very large (on the other hand, it is possible to refactor the internals of a framework). So the framework must be designed upfront to meet reasonably anticipated needs. However, adding unneeded flexibility increases complexity. This balance calls for fine judgment.

- ❑ *Provide different levels of complexity*
  Successful frameworks provide interfaces on several levels. It's easy for developers to become productive with them without a steep learning curve. Yet it's possible for developers with more complex requirements to use more features if they desire. The goal is that developers should need to handle no more complexity than is required for the task in hand.

- ❑ *Distinguish between framework internals and externals*
  Externals should be simple. Internals may be more complex, but should be encapsulated.

- ❑ *It's even more important than usual to have a comprehensive test suite*
  The cost of framework bugs is usually much higher than the cost of application bugs, as one framework bug may cause many flow-on bugs and necessitate costly workarounds.

An excellent article by Brian Foote and Joseph Yoder of the University of Illinois at Urbana-Champaign entitled "The Selfish Class" uses a biological analogy to characterize successful software artifacts that result in code reuse. It's particularly relevant to framework design (see http://www.joeyoder.com/papers/patterns/Selfish/selfish.html). See http://c2.com/cgi/wiki?CriticalSuccessFactorsOfObjectOrientedFrameworks for a discussion from an XP perspective.

Summary

J2EE projects tend to be complex. This makes good programming practices vital.

In this chapter, we've looked at how good OO practice underpins good J2EE applications.

We've also looked at the importance of consistently applying sound coding standards, to allow efficient teamwork and help to ensure that applications are easy to maintain.

Finally, we've discussed how to avoid writing code, through use of existing frameworks and – in the last resort – the implementation of our own frameworks.

The following table summarizes the OO design principles we've discussed:

Technique	Advantages	Disadvantages	Related design patterns	Impact on performance
Code to interfaces, not concrete classes. The relationship between application components should be in terms of interfaces, not classes.	Promotes design flexibility. Works well when interfaces are implemented by JavaBeans, configured through their bean properties. Doesn't preclude use of concrete inheritance. Implementations can have a parallel but distinct inheritance hierarchy from interfaces.	Marginally more complex to implement than use of concrete inheritance.	Many design patterns are based on interface inheritance.	Negligible
Prefer object composition to concrete inheritance.	Promotes design flexibility. Avoids problems with Java's lack of multiple concrete inheritance. Enables class behavior to be changed at runtime.	May lead to an increased number of classes. May be overkill for simple requirements.	Strategy (GoF)	None
Use the Template Method design pattern when you know how to implement a workflow but not how all individual steps should be implemented.	Ensures that the workflow can be implemented and tested once. Ideal for resolving portability issues in J2EE.	Sometimes delegation is a better model, and the Strategy pattern is preferable.	Template Method (GoF)	None
Use the Strategy design pattern as an alternative to the Template Method pattern when the flexibility of delegation, rather than concrete inheritance, is desirable.	There's greater freedom when implementing the interface than using concrete inheritance. The implementation can vary at runtime. The implementation can be shared with other classes.	Slightly more complex to implement than the Template Method pattern, which is often an alternative.	Strategy (GoF)	None
Use callback methods to achieve extensibility while centralizing workflow.	Can achieve code reuse when other approaches can't deliver it. Allows the centralization of error handling code. Reduces the likelihood of bugs by moving complexity from application code into the framework.	Conceptually complex, although code using it is generally simpler than it would be using other approaches.	A special case of the Strategy design pattern (GoF)	Slight performance degradation if the callback interface is invoked very often

Technique	Advantages	Disadvantages	Related design patterns	Impact on performance
Use the Observer design pattern.	Promotes separation of concerns by decoupling listeners from the execution of business logic that generates events. Enables extensibility without modification of existing code.	Introduces complexity that isn't always warranted. Requires an event publication infrastructure, and event classes. A rogue observer that blocks can lock an application using this pattern. May not always work in a clustered environment.	Observer (GoF)	Having too many observers (listeners) can slow a system down.
Combine multiple method arguments into a single object.	Allows use of the Command design pattern. Makes it easier to extend functionality with breaking interfaces.	Increases the number of objects in a system.	Command (GoF) EJB Command (*EJB Design Patterns*)	Contributes to "object churn." In relatively infrequent calls such as EJB invocation, the cost of the necessary object creation is negligible. In a nested loop, the cost might be severe.
Use unchecked exceptions for unrecoverable errors, and checked exceptions when calling code is likely to be able to handle the problem.	Less code. More readable code; business logic won't be obscured by catching exceptions that can't be handled. Enhanced productivity. No need to catch, wrap and rethrow exceptions; less likelihood of losing stack traces.	Many Java developers are used to using checked exceptions almost exclusively. When using unchecked exceptions be sure to remember to document those that may be thrown the compiler can't assist.	All	None
Use reflection.	A powerful way to parameterize Java code. Superior to implementing the Factory design pattern. Very powerful when combined with JavaBeans. Helps to resolve portability issues in J2EE.	Reflection can be overused. Sometimes a simpler solution is equally effective.	Factory (GoF)	Depends on how often calls are made. Usually there is no significant effect.

Technique	Advantages	Disadvantages	Related design patterns	Impact on performance
Implement application components as JavaBeans.	Makes it easier to configure systems declaratively, consistent with J2EE deployment approach. Allows problems such as input validation to be addressed using the standard JavaBeans API.		All	Usually negligible.
Avoid a proliferation of singletons by using an application context or registry.	Promotes design flexibility. Enables us to implement the "singletons" as normal JavaBeans; they will be configured via their bean properties. In web applications, we can put the context in the ServletContext, avoiding the need even for a getInstance() method on the registry. Anywhere within a J2EE server, we can bind the registry in JNDI. We may be able to use JMX. It's possible to support reloading of "singletons" The application context can provide other services, such as event publication. Provides a central point for configuration management inside the application. Configuration management code will be handled by the application context a generic framework object rather than individual application objects. Application developers will never need to write code to read properties files, for examples. Minimizes dependencies on particular APIs (such as the properties API) in application objects.	Registry will require configuration outside Java, such as an XML document. This is an excellent approach for complex applications, but unnecessary for very simple applications.	Singleton (GoF) Factory (GoF) Prototype (GoF)	None

We discussed the following coding standards:

Technique	Advantages	Disadvantages	Impact on performance
Start from JavaSoft's coding conventions.	Makes it easier for new developers to read your code. Familiarity with Sun's conventions makes it easier for you to read the code of others.	None	
Objects and methods should have clear responsibilities.	Makes code self-documenting. Localizes the impact of changes.	None	
Avoid literal constants in code.	Makes it easier to read and maintain code. Reduces the likelihood of typos causing subtle problems.	None	None
Use only private instance variables. Provide getter and setter methods as necessary.	Favors black-box class reuse and loose coupling. Public instance variables allow object state to be corrupted by any other object. Protected instance variables allow superclass state to be corrupted by subclasses or classes in the same package.	Using private instead of protected instance variables reduces the ability of subclasses to modify superclass behavior. However, this is normally a good thing.	Negligible performance overhead in the use of methods, rather than direct variable access.
Keep a class's public interface to a minimum.	Helps to achieve to loose coupling between classes. Makes classes easier to use.	None	None
Use final methods appropriately.	Final methods can be used to prevent subclasses incorrectly modifying superclass behavior by overriding methods.	Limits the scope of subclasses to customize superclass behavior. However, overriding concrete methods is a poor way to achieve extensibility.	Marginal improvement, as the JVM knows which class the method is defined in.
Implement toString() methods useful during debugging and maintenance.	If all classes have toString() methods debugging is a lot easier, especially when combined with a sound logging strategy.	None	toString() methods can be costly to invoke, so it's important to ensure that they're not invoked unnecessarily (for example, by the generation of logging messages that won't be output).

Technique	Advantages	Disadvantages	Impact on performance
Eliminate code duplication.	Code duplication is disastrous for maintenance and usually reflects time wasted in development. Continually strive to eliminate code duplication.	None	None
Don't publicly expose untyped collections where an array could be used.	Helps make code self-documenting and removes one possibility of incorrect usage. Avoids expensive, error-prone, type casts.	Sometimes converting data to an array type is awkward or slow, or we require a collection (for example, to enable lazy materialization).	Neutral. If it's slower to convert a collection into an array, it's probably not a good idea to use this approach.
Document code thoroughly	Code that isn't thoroughly documented is unfinished and potentially useless. The standard Javadoc tool is the cornerstone of our documentation strategy.	None	None
Instrument code with logging output.	Enormously helpful during debugging and maintenance. Can be helpful to staff administering a running application.	None, if logging is implemented properly.	Careless implementation of logging, or misconfiguration of a logging system, may reduce performance. However, this can be avoided by generating log messages only if we know they'll be displayed.

In the next chapter we'll move from the theoretical to the practical, looking at the business requirements for the sample application that we'll discuss throughout the rest of this book.

Requirements for the Sample Application

In this chapter, we will specify an application realistic enough to provide the basis for worthwhile discussion of J2EE architectural decisions and a meaningful implementation exercise. This application has been designed from the business perspective (with generous input from a business analyst friend) rather than a J2EE technology perspective. Although it is simpler than a real application to avoid introducing irrelevant detail, it is more than an excuse to demonstrate a preconceived set of J2EE technologies.

We will refer back to this chapter throughout the rest of this book to underpin technical decisions, the development of a testing strategy and as we approach implementation.

> *Note: Real application requirements will be more formal than those presented in this chapter. For example, I haven't used any particular methodology (such as the Rational Unified Process) for presenting requirements. The aim here is not to provide an example of how to formulate business requirements, but to convey clear, concise requirements that will provide a basis for discussing the J2EE solution that we'll build throughout the rest of the book.*

Overview

The requirement is for an online seat reservation system for the X Center, an arts and entertainment complex that presents shows in a range of genres such as opera, concert, theater, and comedy. The X Center currently has three performance halls. Each has a default seating plan, used for most performances, but occasionally a particular show may vary this slightly. The seating plan for Mahler's Eighth Symphony might need to remove 20% of seats from sale to accommodate the choir. When Zanetti's circus performs, 6 seats from each row between the stage and the rear of the hall must be withdrawn from sale to make room for the caged walkway through which the lions move. This also affects which seats are considered adjacent.

The X Center is owned by the Z Group, an international entertainment company that owns many other theaters and entertainment venues. The Z Group views the online booking system for the X Center as a pilot, and hopes to use it as a basis for systems for its other venues. Hence from the initial release, this system must allow for rebranding. It must be possible to change the presentation of the site without changing the basic functionality, so that another theatre in the group could allow its customers to book tickets with presentation following that theatre's own branding.

Some of the X Group's other venues are in non-English speaking countries, so although there is no immediate requirement for internationalization, it will be necessary if the system is successful. Some venues are in multi-lingual countries such as Switzerland, so if the system is adopted in these venues it must allow users to choose their own language.

The X Center presently has no online ticketing system. Its 5 to 10 box office employees (more casual staff are employed during peak times) presently use a client-server system based around an Oracle database. No part of this system, except perhaps parts of the database schema, is likely to be reusable for the web interface.

> *The following business requirements do not attempt to describe every functional aspect of a 'real world' ticket reservation system.*

User Populations

The application must support three groups of users: public Internet users (customers); box office users (employees of the X Center who assist customers who have chosen not to purchase online); and administrators (employees of the X Center responsible for posting and updating data).

Public Internet Users

These users are customers, members of the public, accessing the service through a web browser. Most connect using a modem at speeds of up to 56K, and it is important that the system has acceptable response times over a modem connection. Customers wish:

- ❏ To find out what shows are on offer and access information about shows and performances
- ❏ To find out what performance dates still offer seating availability
- ❏ To book seats online, using a credit card

It is possible that premium services, such as the ability to book a larger number of seats in a single transaction, might be offered to a distinct "registered user" community in the future. However, in the initial system, registration is offered only as a convenience to save users re-entering their billing address. The priority is to ensure that the path to purchasing tickets is as straightforward as possible, hence users will not be forced to register, which may risk alienating them.

In order to fulfill these requirements, the system should offer a simple, usable, and fast web interface. It is important that this interface works on as many browsers as possible. Browser-specific functionality should be avoided, and the required browser level should be as low as possible without sacrificing functionality. Applets, Flash animations and the like are considered likely to deter users, and should not be used.

Box Office Users

These are employees of the X Center, who work within the X Center itself, and are on the local network. Some employees may work from home, in which case they will have access to a broadband Internet connection. Box office users perform the following activities:

- ❑ Respond to phone and over-the-counter enquiries by members of the public, principally on the availability of seating. To support this task, box office users must be given powerful query functionality unavailable to public Internet users, to enable them quickly to respond to questions such as, "What is the first date on which I can have 25 adjacent B Reserve seats to Carmen?"

- ❑ Sell tickets to members of the public who wish to see a show.

- ❑ Supply tickets to customers who booked online but chose to collect the tickets from the box office instead of having them delivered by post. This is also necessary for late bookings, when there isn't time to post out tickets.

- ❑ Occasionally, cancel reservations on phone request.

These users are primarily concerned with service reliability and usability. They receive a constant flow of enquiries from customers who expect to be serviced when they call. Thus it is essential that the public Internet interface should not reduce the reliability or performance of the box office interface.

As box office users can be given training on how to use the system, the priority should be functionality, rather than ease of use. Box office users must be given a powerful system that offers a quick way of performing common tasks. As the box office interface is for internal use only, there should be less emphasis on its branding and cosmetics.

The X Center management team wishes to maximize their IT investment and so believe that the same online ticket reservation system should service public Internet users and box office staff. Box office users, like customers, will use a web interface. This interface will be protected from Internet users via role-based security, and will have a separate entry point from the public Internet application. The system will automatically grant the appropriate privileges, based on username and password.

Administrators

These are employees of the X Center in which the ticketing system will be in operation. Admin users must be located within the X Center itself, accessing the local network. They fulfill a variety of clerical, marketing and management functions:

❑   Add new shows and performances

❑   Run management information and financial reports

❑   Configure settings of the ticketing system; such as the maximum number of tickets that can be purchased in one transaction, and the period of time tickets can be reserved before payment is made

The X Center's management wish to use a consistent technology set within their system to minimize the number of skills their IT department requires, hence they would prefer that the same web technology was used for the Admin interface as for the customer and box office interfaces, rather than another technology such as Swing or VB. Management is also keen that the Admin interface should require no installation; authorized staff should be able to access it on any machine within the X Center building, and it should require no rollout process and ongoing updates.

The Admin interface will offer the additional security of running on a port accessible only within the X Center's firewall. This means that the Admin must run in a different web application (although possibly still on the same physical server). The Admin interface will be centered on the Oracle database, which will be its main means of communication with the other interfaces. As the X Center already has some Oracle skills in-house, the development of the Admin interface can be deferred until Phase 2.

Assumptions

Let's now consider the following assumptions:

❑   Internet users will not be required to accept cookies, although it is expected that most will.

❑   Seats for each show will be divided into one or more seat **types**, such as Premium Reserve. Seating plan and the division of seats into types will be associated with shows, not individual performances.

❑   All seats within the same class for the same performance will be the same price. However, different performances of the same show may have different price structures. For example, matinees may be cheaper than evening performances, to attract families.

❑   Users will request a given number of seats of a chosen type for a specified performance, and will not be allowed to request specific seats. Users will not be allowed to provide "hints" for seat allocation such as "towards the front of A Reserve and on the right rather than the left".

❑   Users requesting seats will be assumed to want adjacent seats, although they will be offered whatever is available if sufficient adjacent seats cannot be allocated. Seats are not considered to be adjacent if they are separated by an aisle.

❑   Internet customers will not be able to cancel a booking once payment has been processed. They must call the box office, which will apply the X Center's policies regarding cancellation and refunds, and use the box office interface to cancel bookings when this is allowed.

Scope Limitations

As it is to serve as an example rather than a commercial application, some areas have been ignored. However, these are essentially refinements, and do not affect the system architecture:

❑ No security will be implemented for credit card purchasing. (HTTPs would be used in a real application, but the details of setting this up vary between J2EE servers).

❑ A real system would connect to an external payment processing system to process credit card payments. In the sample application, this is replaced by a dummy component that blocks for a varying period of time and randomly decides whether to approve or reject transactions.

❑ No allowance will be made for special seating requirements such as wheelchair access, although this is an important consideration in most ticketing systems.

Delivery Schedule

The X Center's management has determined that having a true online ticketing solution is a business priority. Thus they have determined a delivery schedule to ensure that the public system comes online as soon as possible. This schedule calls for the application to be delivered in three phases:

❑ Phase 1: Core Internet user interface, as described in the next section, and the box office interface.

❑ Phase 2: Admin interface. In Phase 1, no GUI will be available to Admin users; they will need to work with the database using Oracle tools. Development resources will be available to support Admin users in these tasks during Phase 2 development.

❑ Phase 3: More sophisticated Internet interface. This will offer registered users premium services and add internationalization support.

The sample application will extend only to Phase 1. The whole of the core Internet user interface will be implemented, and part of the box office interface (which won't be fully defined in this chapter). However, the sample application must define an architecture that will provide a basis for the later phases, so their requirements must be considered in the meantime.

Internet User Interface

Let's look in detail at the public Internet user interface. This illustrates many common issues in building J2EE web applications.

Basic Workflow

Although I've used UML state diagram graphics, each box represents a screen presented to a user successfully choosing a performance and purchasing a number of tickets, rather than a state. The following diagram shows an Internet user successfully booking seats:

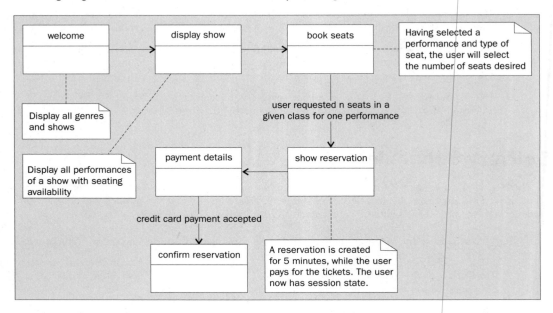

Users are initially presented with the **welcome** screen, a list of all genres (such as Opera) and shows (such as Wagner's *Tristan und Isolde*) playing at the X Center (see *Application Screens* below for screenshots). Users can then proceed to the **display show** screen, which shows all performance dates for a given show, along with the types and prices of seat on sale and the availability of each type of seat. This screen should indicate only whether each type of seat is available or sold out, not the number of seats remaining. This meets the needs of most users while avoiding disclosure of sensitive business information – for example, those tickets to a particular show might be selling poorly. Users can request a number of seats of a given type for a particular performance, in which case these seats are reserved to allow time for online credit card payment.

The system distinguishes between the concepts of **reservation** and **confirmation/purchase** in the booking process. The user can reserve seats for a performance for a period of time (typically 5 minutes), which will be held in system configuration. Reservation protects these seats from being shown as available to other users. Confirmation occurs when the user provides a valid credit card number, at which point a reservation becomes an actual purchase. Reservations are held in the database and in the user's session state. Reservations must either:

❑ Progress to bookings as a result of confirmation.

❑ Expire, if the user fails to proceed to purchase in the given time. These seats will then be available to other users. However, the user who made the reservation may still purchase the seats without seeing an error message if they are still free when (s)he submits the payment form.

❑ Be cleared, as the result of user activity other than continuing on to purchase. For example, if a user makes a reservation but then navigates back to the display show screen, it is assumed that (s)he does not want to proceed to purchase these seats, and that they should be returned to fully available status.

Error Handling

In the event of a system error (such as the J2EE server failing to connect to the database), the user should be shown an internal error screen consistent with the current branding. This should advise the user to try again later. Support staff should be notified by e-mail and through the log file record in the event of serious problems. The user must never see a screen containing a stack trace, "500 Internal Error" or other technology or server-specific error message. A user requesting an invalid URL should see a screen consistent with the current branding advising that the requested page was not found and containing a link to the welcome page.

Application Screens

Let's now take a closer look at workflow in the public Internet interface. The following diagram is a more detailed version of the previous diagram, and shows all screens available to the Internet user, and the transitions between them:

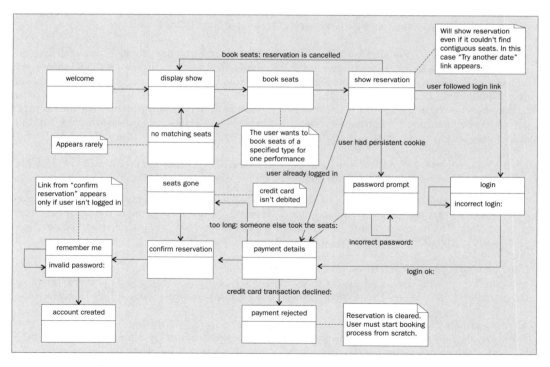

The additional detail concerns failures to complete a booking and the optional user registration process. The user can fail to proceed to reservation or confirmation under the following circumstances:

❑ The user requested the **display show** screen and left a long delay before following one of the links to the **book seats** screen. By the time they proceeded to this screen many more seats had been sold and requested type of seat was no longer available.

❑ The only seats that can be offered to the user are not adjacent. The user does not wish to accept this, and follows the **try another date** link back to the **display show** screen. The unwanted reservation should be cleared and the user must begin the booking process again.

❑ The user made a registration, but failed to submit a credit card number in the lifetime of the reservation. This is not a problem unless the seats have been reserved or purchased by another user. In this case, the problem is explained to the user, who is reassured that their credit card was not debited and offered a link to the **display show** screen.

❑ The user enters a credit card number in a valid format, but the transaction is declined by the credit card processing system. In this case, the user will be informed that the credit card payment was declined and that the reservation has been lost. The reservation is cleared, and the user must begin the reservation progress from scratch.

The registration process is optional. It allows users to enter a password to create an account that will save them entering their billing address and e-mail with each purchase (other premium services may also be offered to registered users in the future). Users should not be forced to register to purchase tickets, as the management feels that this may reduce sales.

Registration will be offered after a user who is not logged in, and who has provided an e-mail address not already associated with a registered user, has made a booking. The user's username will be their e-mail address, which is entered in the course of the booking process. When a user registers and the application detects that the user's browser is configured to accept cookies, their username will be stored in a persistent cookie enabling the application to recognize their registration status on subsequent visits and prompt for a password automatically. This prompt will be introduced into the registration process through a distinct screen between the **reservation** and **payment details** screens. The following rules will apply:

❑ If the user is logged in, billing address and e-mail address (but not credit card details, which are never retained) will be pre-populated on the payment details form.

❑ If a persistent cookie containing the user's e-mail address is found but the user is not logged in, the user will be prompted to enter a password, before proceeding to the payment details form. The user can choose to skip password entry, in which case the persistent cookie will be deleted and the user will see an empty payment details screen.

If the user isn't logged in and doesn't have a persistent cookie, there should be a link on the **show reservation** page to allow the user to try to log in by entering both username and password before seeing the **payment details** screen. In the event of successful login, a persistent cookie will not be created.

The screenshots that follow the table present all the controls and information required on each page. However, they do not fully define the presentation of the application: for example, these screens might be used as the content well, with a custom header and side columns being added. There may be more than one such branding: it is a business requirement that the technical architecture allows this cost-effectively.

The discussion of each screen concludes with a summary of the required handling of some common issues with web interfaces, in the following format:

Screen name	The name of the screen as discussed in this chapter and shown in the diagrams above. The table describes the outcome of a request that will lead to this screen if successful.
Purpose	What the page does (for example, "display user profile").
Alternative screens	Alternative pages that may result from a request that would normally produce this page (for example, the behavior resulting from invalid form input).
URL	URL of the page within the web application, such as /welcome.html. Note that although the chosen extension is html, all pages are dynamic.
Data displayed	The data displayed on this page, and where it comes from (database, user session etc).
Requires existing session state	Yes/No.
Effect on existing session state	What happens to existing session state (such as a seat reservation) following a request to this page?
Effect of refresh/resubmission	What happens if the user refreshes this page?
Effect of the back button	What happens if the user hits the back button?
Parameters required	Lists the names, types, and purpose of the parameters required.
Effect of invalid parameters	What happens if the expected request parameters are missing or invalid?

This summary will be valuable as a basis for testing the web interface.

Welcome Screen

This page provides an index of all shows and performances currently available. It may also include static information and links about the X Center. The aim is to minimize the number of pages the user has to work through to perform common tasks, so this page allows direct progress to information about each show, without making the user browse intervening pages:

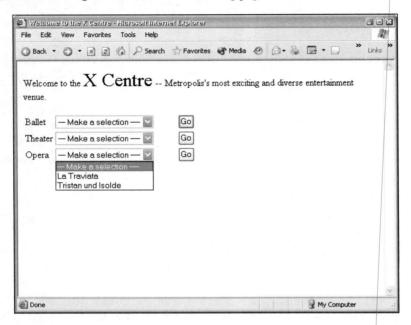

The page must be dynamic: genres and shows must not be hard-coded in HTML. The number of genres will not be so great in the immediate future that having a separate drop-down for each genre is likely to become unworkable. However, the system architecture must support other interfaces, such as splitting this page by having a separate page for each genre, if the number of genres and shows increases significantly. The user's first impression of the system is vital, so this page must load quickly:

Screen name	Welcome
Purpose	Display all genres and shows. If there are no current shows in a genre, that genre should not be displayed.
Alternative screens	None.
URL	/welcome.html. This should be the default page if the user does not specify a URL within the application.
Data displayed	Dynamic genre and show listing from database; static information determined by HTML presentation (such as a photograph of the X Center).

Requires existing session state	No.
Effect on existing session state	None.
Effect of refresh/resubmission	Page should be marked as cacheable by the browser for 1 minute. Requests received by the web server should result in the generation of a page.
Effect of the back button	Irrelevant. The user has no session state for the application.
Parameters required	None.
Effect of invalid parameters	Parameters to this page will be ignored.

Display Show Screen

This screen will allow the user to choose a performance date for a show in which they are interested, and proceed to make a booking. It will also provide information about the show in question such as the history of the work being performed and cast information. It is expected that some users, reluctant to use their credit cards online, will only use the Internet interface to this point, before calling the box office to purchase tickets on a given date; this is an additional reason for providing comprehensive information on this page:

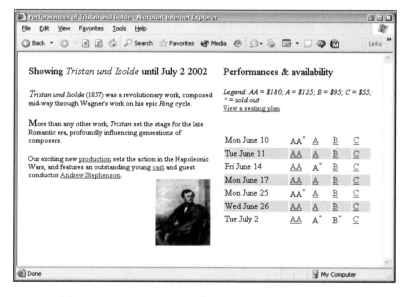

No support is required for pagination in Phase 1 (although this is a potential refinement later); the user may need to scroll down to see all performances. For each performance, there is normally a hyperlink from each type of seat to the booking page. A superscript * is used in place of a hyperlink to indicate that the given class of the given performance is sold out:

Screen name	Display Show
Purpose	Display information about the show. Display a list of all performances of the show, with availability (available/sold out) of each seating type. Include a legend explaining the cost of each type of seat.
Alternative screens	None.
URL	`/show.html`.
Data displayed	Dynamic performance and seat availability information, from database.
	HTML-format information about the show the user is interested in. This must be legal HTML within the content well, and may contain internal and external hyperlinks. This will be maintained by non-programmers with HTML skills. The URL of this document within the web application should be associated with the show in the database. If no URL is specified in the database, the seating plan for the performance should be displayed in place of show information.
Requires existing session state	No.
Effect on existing session state	Any existing reservation will be cleared without notifying the user. However any existing user session will not be destroyed.
Effect of refresh/resubmission	Page should be regenerated by the server.
Effect of the back button	Irrelevant. The user has no session state for the application.
Parameters required	`id` (integer): the unique id of the show.
Effect of invalid parameters	Parameters other than the show id should be ignored. If no show id is supplied or if the show id is non-numeric or out of range, a generic **invalid request** page will be displayed, with a link back to the welcome page. This cannot happen in normal operation, as the user should only arrive at this page as a result of hitting one of the Go buttons on the welcome page.

Book Seats Screen

To arrive at this screen, the user selects a performance date and ticket type by following a seat type link – in the screenshot above, one of the AA, A, B, or C links in the table on the right:

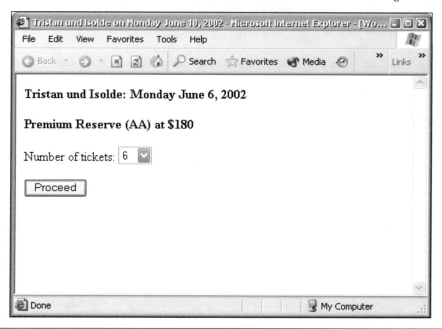

Screen name	Book Seats
Purpose	Provides a form that enabling the user to request a number of seats of a given type for their selected performance.
Alternative screens	If no tickets are available for this performance, a simple screen should say that that type of ticket is sold out and provide a link back to the display show screen.
URL	`/bookseats.html`
Data displayed	The name of the show and the date of the performance.
	The name of the ticket type (such as Premium Reserve) and its unit price.
	A dropdown with a default number of tickets selected. The default value can be set by the Administrator, and should be configured to 6 seats in the application's factory settings. The value initially displayed in the dropdown should be the lower of the default value and the number of tickets of the requested type left (for example, if the default has been set to 8 and only 7 seats are left, the selected value will be 7). The range of the values in the dropdown should be from 1 to the lower of the number of tickets left and a default maximum set by the administrator. A typical value of the default maximum for seats purchased in the same transaction might be 12, to discourage scalpers.

Requires existing session state.	No.
Effect on existing session state.	Any reservation will be cleared. However the session will not be destroyed.
Effect of refresh/resubmission.	Page should be regenerated by the server. It is important that this page always provides up-to-date information on seat availability (implicit in this screen appearing at all, and shown in the values in the dropdown), so no caching is permissible.
Effect of the back button.	Irrelevant. The user has no session state for the application.
Parameters required.	id (integer): the unique id of the show. type (integer): the unique id of the seat type.
Effect of invalid parameters.	Parameters other than the show id and seat type should be ignored. If either parameter is missing, is non-numeric, or is out of range, a generic invalid request page will be displayed, with a link back to the welcome page.

Show Reservation Screen

This screen results from the successful reservation of the number of seats requested. This is the first operation resulting in the creation of session state:

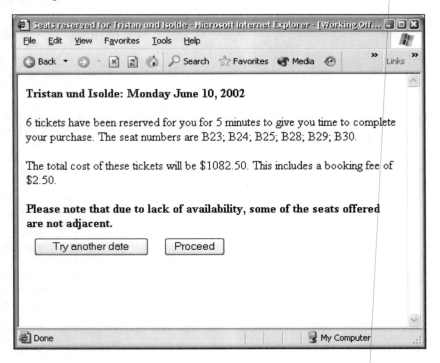

Screen name	Show Reservation
Purpose	Informs the user that (s)he has successfully reserved a number of seats.
Alternative screens	If no seats are available (because the user delayed in submitting the form, and the performance filled up), display a screen explaining the problem and prompting the user to try another date. In this case, no reservation will have been created, and the user will not have session state.
URL	`/reservation.html`
Data displayed	The name of the show and date of the performance selected.
	The number and names of the tickets requested.
	The total cost of the tickets.
	Whether or not the seats are adjacent. If the seats are not adjacent, this should be explained to the user and a link should be provided to allow the user to try another performance date. The seating plan will enable the user to work out how close these seats are (for example, B25 to B28 may be an acceptable gap; A13 to Y40 may not).
	Seating plan (including all seat classes) to enable the user to work out the position of the seats. This seating plan will not be dynamic in Phase 1: there is no need to highlight the position of the reserved seats.
	Remember me link if the user doesn't have a persistent cookie and isn't logged in. This will enable the user to log in before proceeding to the **payment** screen.
Requires existing session state	No. The generation of this page will create session state if none exists.
Effect on existing session state	If the user has an existing reservation, it is cleared before processing the new seat request. It should be impossible for a user to have more than one simultaneous reservation in his/her session state or in the database.
Effect of refresh/resubmission	On resubmission, the application should notice that the reservation held in the user's session matches the request. An identical screen (except that the expiry time of the reservation should be shown rather than the length of the reservation period) should be returned without any updates in the database. The lifetime of the reservation will not be prolonged.
Effect of the back button	
Parameters required	`id` (integer): the unique id of the show.
	`type` (integer): type we wish to reserve seats for.
	`count` (integer): number of seats requested.

Effect of invalid parameters	Parameters other than these should be ignored. A generic invalid request page will be displayed, with a link back to the welcome page if any of the required parameters are missing or invalid, as this should not happen in normal operation.

Payment Details Screen

Note that the password prompt or login page may appear before this page, and may result in pre-population of address and e-mail fields for logged in users. Credit card details will always be blank, as they are not retained under any circumstances:

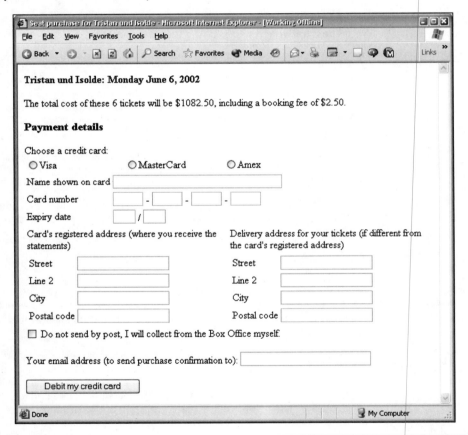

Screen name	Payment Details
Purpose	Allows a user who has successfully reserved seats to pay for tickets and provide an address to which they can be posted.

Alternative screens	A user who isn't logged in but has a persistent cookie will be directed to the password prompt page before arriving here.
	A user who isn't logged in but selected the "login" link from the show reservation page will be directed to the login page before arriving here.
URL	`/payment.html`
Data displayed	Name of show and performance.
	Number of seats reserved.
	Price of seats.
	User profile data if the user is logged in. Otherwise all fields will be empty.
Requires existing session state	Yes. This page should only be shown if the user has a reservation in her session. Requesting this page without a session or without a reservation should result in a generic invalid request page.
Effect on existing session state	None.
Effect of refresh/resubmission	Page should be regenerated by the server. If the reservation held in the user's session has expired, the user should be shown a page indicating this and providing a link back to the "display show" page.
Effect of the back button	
Parameters required	None. This page depends on session state, not request parameters.
Effect of invalid parameters	All parameters will be ignored.

On an invalid submission, this page will be redisplayed, with the missing or invalid field values highlighted and an error message for each field explaining the problem. The exact means of highlighting errors is a detail to be decided later. However, the system should support different styles of highlighting.

All fields are mandatory except line 2 of the address. The following validation rules are to be applied on submission of the form on this page:

❑ Credit card number is 16 digits.

❑ Credit card expiration date is 4 digits.

❑ Postal code is a valid UK postcode format (for example SE10 9AH). However, no attempt will be made to check that this is a real postcode (Submissions that look like UK postcodes may be syntactically correct but semantically meaningless). It is the user's responsibility to enter their address correctly. In subsequent releases, other countries must also be supported, and postal code validation must be implemented based on the country selected from a dropdown. Only a fixed subset of countries will be supported, as the cost and reliability of posting tickets to some countries is considered unacceptable.

❏   E-mail address must pass simple validation checks (that it looks like an e-mail address, with an @ symbol and dots in the right place). However, the transaction can still succeed even if the e-mail address does not prove to work; ticket purchase should not block while a test e-mail is sent.

No attempt will be made to validate the credit card number's checksum. This is a matter for the external credit card processing system.

Confirm Reservation Screen

This screen confirms the user's ticket purchase and provides an electronic receipt:

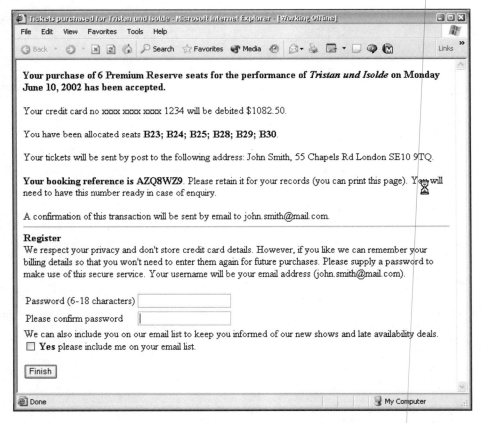

Screen name	Confirm Reservation
Purpose	Confirm the user's credit card payment. Provide a reference number. Allow the user to register if the user isn't logged in (a logged in user will not see the content under the ruled line).

Alternative screens	If the credit card number is in an invalid format or if mandatory fields are missing or invalid, the payment screen is shown again, populated with the rejected values.
	If the credit card is in a valid format but payment is rejected by the credit card processing system, the user should be sent to the **payment rejected** screen and the reservation cleared. This is treated as the end of the reservation process. The attempt to use a questionable credit card number should be prominently logged for the system administrator to see.
	If the user's reservation has expired but the tickets are still available, payment will be processed as normal. If tickets have been sold to another user, the user will be directed to the **seats gone** page, and the expired registration cleared from the user session. The user's credit card will not be debited.
URL	`/confirmation.html`
Data displayed	Seats reserved; booking reference; price paid; user's e-mail address (the e-mail address will not allow modification if the user is logged in). Only the last 4 digits of the credit card number should be displayed. For security reasons, the credit card number should never be held in the users session or in the database.
Requires existing session state	Yes. A seat reservation must be found in the session, and the price must match the payment offered.
Effect on existing session state	The reservation will be removed from the session object, as it will have been converted to a confirmed booking in the database. The user profile object will be retained in the session, which must not be destroyed. A logged in user will remain logged in.
	If a logged in user changed their profile (either of the addresses) the database should be updated automatically with the new information.
Effect of refresh/resubmission	Resubmission must be prevented, to avoid any risk of debiting a user's credit card twice.
Effect of the back button	Resubmission of this form will be impossible, so the back button should cause no problem.
Parameters required	Parameters described under discussion of payment screen.
Effect of invalid parameters	See discussion of payment screen.

Box Office User Interface

The box office interface should enable queries and operations such as the following:

- ❑ For a given show, display the total number of seats of each type available for a given date, as well as the 5 longest runs of adjacent seats (for example, this would enable a box office user to tell a caller that they couldn't have 18 adjacent seats, but could have groups of 16 and 2 or 10 and 8).

- ❑ For a given show, show the first date on which a given number of seats (adjacent or non-adjacent) of a given type are available.

- ❑ Cancel a booking, given the booking reference (the box office user will first be enabled to view the booking data).

The box office interface's welcome page (after mandatory login) should offer immediate access to all common queries.

Each screen in the box office interface should prominently display the time at which it was rendered, and the box office interface must not implement caching of seating availability: box office staff must always have access to up to date information. Each screen in the box office interface relating to a show or performance must display the relevant seating plan. Only those features of the box office interface described above need be implemented for the sample application.

Non-Functional Requirements

Normal activity is fairly modest. However, at peak times (such as when a new performance by a major star is listed), the site may experience sharp peaks of user activity. Such activity will often center on a single show, meaning that the performance requirements for the show page are almost the same as the welcome page. The following table shows the minimum performance requirements for the most performance-critical pages of the public Internet interface:

Page	Hits per second	Time (secs) to render page (discounting network transfer)	Average time (secs) to return page over 56k modem
Welcome	2	1	3
Display Show	2	2	5
Book Seats	2	3	5
Show Reservation	1	3	5
Payment Details	1	3	5
Process payment details (performance will partly depend on the speed of the external credit card processing system)	1	30	30

These are the minimum targets that will meet the immediate business requirements. The aim should be to far exceed them with a single Intel-based server running the application server, demonstrating the potential of the system for wider use within the Z Group (the database will be running on a separate machine).

Special attention must be paid to performance characteristics under concurrent access, and especially to the following scenarios:

❑ Heavy activity for one show or even one performance. This is a realistic possibility – for example, if a movie star makes a guest appearance on a single night during the run of a play.

❑ Supporting concurrent requests for seats when a performance is almost full. This may result in multiple users trying to reserve the same small group of seats. It is vital that this does not seriously impair overall performance, and that the reservation database cannot be corrupted.

❑ Effect on the box office interface of heavy load on the public Internet interface. It is vital that box office staff are able to do their job without being hampered by slow response times.

If necessary to achieve adequate performance, the following trade-offs are acceptable:

❑ A new show or performance added by an Administrator may take up to 1 minute to show up on the web interface. However, the system must not require a restart.

❑ The availability, or lack of availability, of seating for a particular class (as shown to public Internet users on the display show page) may be up to 1 minute out of date, although any time lag should be avoided if possible.

As cancellations are fairly rare, the remote possibility of a user failing to book a seat because the desired class was marked as sold out, when in fact availability reappeared within 1 minute of the user requesting the display show page, is deemed to be acceptable in the interests of performance. The slightly greater possibility that the performance may have sold out after the data was cached is not considered a serious problem: after all, the user could have answered the telephone or discussed the performance dates with friends and family prior to following the link for a given performance date and seat type. Such delays will often be much longer than 1 minute.

Hardware and Software Environment

The target application server will be JBoss 3.0.0, integrated with the Jetty servlet engine. Management is keen to minimize licensing costs, especially as the application may be deployed on a number of sites. The application may need to be ported to another application server in the future, so the design must not be dependent on JBoss. Should such porting be required, a small budget will be allocated for any code changes required and for testing on the new platform. If possible, the application should be verifiable as J2EE-compliant to reassure management that portability is achievable.

The X Center does not presently have its own web-facing hardware. Appropriate hardware will need to be purchased based on performance analysis; management is keen to minimize cost by maximizing performance per cost of hardware.

The application should support clustering if this becomes necessary as demand increases, but management expects that the performance figures described can be exceeded on a single server. All machines in any server cluster would be within the same local network.

The database will be Oracle 8.1.7i, as the X Center already has an Oracle license and Oracle expertise in-house. There is no likelihood of migrating to another database in the foreseeable future. The Oracle database already runs on a Sun server, and this will not change, regardless of the chosen hardware for the web server. The database server and application server(s) will run on the same local network, so rapid connectivity can be assumed.

There are no other constraints regarding technology to be used. Management have made a strategic decision to adopt J2EE because they believe it offers the best chance of successful integration with the legacy booking systems at the other venues with the X Group, but have no preconceptions on how J2EE should be used. Whether to use technologies such as EJB, JSP, and XSLT is a technical decision. As the project will involve building a team, no constraints regarding existing J2EE expertise (such as "strong servlet experience, no EJB experience") need be considered.

A number of the X Center's staff have HTML skills, but are non-programmers. Therefore it is important that HTML content and site presentation can be controlled, as far as possible, without the need for more than a superficial understanding of J2EE technologies.

Summary

In this chapter we've seen the requirements for the sample application. This is the commonest type of J2EE application – a web application using a relational database.

The discussion in the rest of the book will use the process of implementing this application to illustrate the J2EE design and implementation concepts discussed.

In the next chapter we'll take a closer look at options for J2EE architecture, and define a high-level architecture for the sample application.

In *Chapter 7* to *Chapter 9* we'll look at data access options for use in J2EE applications, and how we can efficiently implement the ticketing application's data access requirements.

In *Chapter 11* we'll look at how a generic application infrastructure can be used to solve many common problems, and how it simplifies application-specific code.

In *Chapter 12* and *Chapter 13* we'll look at implementing web interfaces in J2EE applications, using the reservation use case from the sample application to illustrate how to use the MVC architectural pattern.

In *Chapter 14* we'll look at J2EE application deployment, showing how to package the sample application and deploy it on JBoss 3.0.0.

In *Chapter 15* we'll look at meeting the performance targets identified above.

OCEANUS INSULÆ PHILIP PINÆ

ARC

Sinæ

I. Ainan

Tunquin

Enseada de Cauchin China
Costa de Pracel
Cauchin China
Diam el Odia
Champa
Cambo ia
Camboia

Pulo S. Pelo

Doa Tanguero

Philippina

Luco

Moro Hermoso
Pintados
Ancon triste
C. de Matalanbre
Pondan
Mandato
Paraiçalle

C. dd Spirito Santo de Coos
Francisco Gomez
Ylhas del Primeiro
Surgidero
Pueblas
Abo tamucho Primeiro
Caburas
Abejo

Pasage de S. Clara

I. de Matalotes

I. dos Arecifes

Pracel

Pulo Ciri

Pulo Condor

Pulo babe

Calamianes

Pulo Tigao
Men Praton

I. de S. Maria

S. Michael

Pracel

S. Clara

Damaca

Camguin

Bassilan

Malaqua

MINDANA
Mindanao

A. de Resurreicam
C. Bucay
I. da Palmeras
I. de S. Ioannes

S. I

Borneo
R. de Borneo
Malana
Puchauarut
Tanasserim
Tanorabos

BORNEO

Laue lande free in Marsael de Sina

Indian Infideles

S. Clara
I. de S. Joana
Bapariteon

I. de Sagun

Caragua
Carangao
I. de Talao
I. di Rao
I. di Doi
I. dos Graos
Camasu
Batochina
Porte Cacam CEIRAM
Hic hybernauit de Menezes

Bintan

Banca

Bibliotoam
Chinabato

Masao Pero

Batuan
Cadapal
A. Soera

Binaom

Nafsira

Suos
Mamuge
Caricari
Machae
Portugal
Surge
Celona
Marco

Bacham

Absas

Xula

Buono

Sirongo

Caham

CELEBES

Borre

I. de S. Mathees

Timor

Batalia
Baintar

Terra alta
Gusilam

Aru

Agui in bernio Martin
Afonso de mels

AUA, quæ et
AOA dicitur. Fidalda

LANT.

DOL

Baxor

Guaon

Applying J2EE Technologies

In this chapter we'll take a deeper look at some of the key decisions involved in developing a J2EE architecture, especially those we discussed in Chapter 1. We'll discuss:

❑ **Choosing between a collocated and distributed architecture**
   This is a particularly important decision with implications for performance, ease of implementation, scalability, robustness and the type of clients that an application can support. This decision should be made early in the design process, as it has implications for many other design decisions.

❑ **Choosing if and how to use EJB**
   As we saw in Chapter 1, EJB is a powerful technology that can help us solve some complex problems, but which may introduce unwarranted complexity if we don't need its full capabilities. In this chapter, we'll take a closer look at when, and how, to use EJB to enjoy its benefits but avoid its drawbacks.

❑ **Choosing when to use messaging**
   Sometimes business requirements call for asynchronous application behavior or the use of messaging to communicate with other applications. In other cases we may choose to use messaging within an application. We'll consider EJB container services for JMS messaging, and how to decide when to use asynchronous messaging as an implementation strategy.

❑ **Authentication and authorization issues**
   And especially how they relate to web applications.

❑ **Using XML in J2EE applications**
   XML is a core J2EE technology, and XML is becoming increasingly important in web applications and in the enterprise. We'll look at how XML can be used effectively in J2EE applications, and areas in which the use of XML may prove counterproductive.

❑ **Caching issues**
Most applications, and especially web applications, need to cache some data to minimize the expense of querying persistent data sources. We'll consider the potential benefits and challenges of implementing caching.

After we discuss each issue, we'll make the relevant decisions for our sample application. While the sample application is just one – relatively simple – J2EE application, this serves to highlight many common problems and demonstrate the trade-offs called for in real projects.

We won't talk about data access in this chapter. This important topic will be addressed in Chapters 7,8, and 9. We'll also pay relatively little attention to the implementation of the web tier. This will be discussed in detail in Chapters 12 and 13.

When is a Distributed Architecture Appropriate?

Perhaps the most significant architectural decision is whether the application should be distributed, or whether all application components should be collocated on each server running the application.

In some applications, business requirements dictate a distributed architecture. However, we often have a choice (for example, in many web applications).

I believe that J2EE developers too often plump for distributed architectures, without giving this important choice sufficient thought. This is a potentially expensive mistake, as we shouldn't adopt a distributed architecture without good reason. In Chapter 1 we considered the downside of distributed applications in complexity and performance

Let's quickly review the major reasons why we might want to implement a distributed architecture:

❑ To support J2EE technology clients such as Swing applications, providing them with a middle tier. A J2EE web container provides a middle tier for browser-based clients; hence this argument doesn't apply to applications with only a web interface.

❑ When the application must integrate resources distributed throughout an enterprise. Such an application might involve several EJB containers, each accessing an enterprise resource such as a database or legacy application unavailable elsewhere on the network.

❑ To gain control over where each application component is deployed, to improve scalability and reliability.

In rare cases, we might also choose to make an application distributed to introduce an additional firewall between web container and business objects.

If the first or second criterion holds, a distributed architecture, based on EJB with remote interfaces, is the ideal – and simplest – solution.

The issues around the third criterion are far more complex and seldom clear-cut. In the following section we'll look at them in more detail. This discussion assumes we're considering web applications (the commonest type of application in practice), and that RMI access isn't a decisive consideration.

Distributed Applications and Scalability

Is a distributed architecture necessarily more scalable than one in which all components are collocated on each server? J2EE architects and developers tend to assume that distributed applications offer unmatched scalability. However, this assumption is questionable.

Single-JVM solutions are higher-performing than distributed applications, due to the lack of remote invocation overhead, meaning that greater performance can be achieved on comparable hardware. Furthermore, single-JVM solutions can be clustered successfully. Enterprise-quality J2EE web containers provide clustering functionality; this is not the preserve of EJB containers.

Alternatively, incoming HTTP requests can be routed to a server in a cluster by load balancing infrastructure provided to the J2EE server, or by hardware devices such as Cisco Load Balancer. (This looks like a single IP address, but in fact routes requests to any HTTP server behind it; it offers both, round robin and "sticky" routing, for cases when the client will need to go back to the same server to preserve session state). Using hardware load balancing has the advantage of working the same way with any J2EE server.

By adding a tier of remote business objects (such as an EJB tier) we don't necessarily make a web application more scalable. A web application that doesn't require server-side state can scale *linearly* – almost indefinitely – regardless of whether it uses remote calling. When server-side state is required, scalability will be limited, regardless of whether we adopt a distributed model.

If we hold state in the web tier (in the `HttpSession` object), the quality of the web container's clustering support (state replication and routing) will determine scalability. If we hold state in the EJB container, in stateful session beans, the EJB container will have a similarly difficult task. EJB is not a magic bullet that can make the problems of state replication go away. *Plus* we'll normally need to hold state in the web tier as well, unless we resort to the rare approach of serializing the stateful session bean handle into a cookie or hidden form field.

A distributed J2EE application (in which business objects will be implemented as EJBs with remote interfaces) will be intrinsically more scalable than a single-JVM solution only when one or more of the following conditions hold:

❑   **The business objects accessed remotely are stateless, regardless of whether the web tier maintains state**
In J2EE, this means that all business logic will be exposed by stateless session beans. Fortunately, this can often be arranged, as we'll see in *Chapter 10*. We discuss this type of architecture further below.

❑   **There's a marked disparity in load between web tier and business objects**
Unless this condition holds, we can simply run more combined web containers and business object containers. Unless one particular tier of the application is a bottleneck, it doesn't make sense to throw new hardware just at it, rather than the whole application.

Scenarios in which there's a marked load disparity between web tier and business objects include the following:

❑ **Some or all of the business objects consume resources that cannot be allocated to every server in the web tier**
In this rare scenario, collocating web tier and business objects means that we encounter the limitations of scalability of client-server applications. This scenario might arise if the application has an enormous load on the web tier and relatively little on the business objects. In this case, allowing each web container to allocate its own database connection pool, for example, might result in the database needing to support an excessively large number of connections.

❑ **The business objects do a lot more work than the web tier**
In this case we will want to run more EJB containers.

A model with stateless business objects is highly scalable because we can add as many EJB containers as we need, without increasing the number of web containers or increasing the overhead of any state replication that may be required in the web tier. However, only in the event of a disparity in load between web tier and business objects will this approach be significantly *more* scalable than a web application in which all components are collocated on each server.

> A distributed application is not necessarily more scalable than one in which all components are collocated on each server. Only a distributed architecture with a stateful web tier and stateless business objects is inherently more scalable than a web application in which all components are collocated on each server.

Distributed Applications and Reliability

Is a distributed architecture necessarily more robust than one in which all components are collocated on a single server? Again, J2EE architects and developers tend to assume that it is. However, this assumption is also questionable. Any stateful application faces the problem of **server affinity**, in which users become associated with a particular server – a particular threat to robustness. Breaking an application into distributed units doesn't make this problem go away.

If we have a stateless web tier, hardware routing can deliver brilliant uptime. Devices such as Cisco Load Balancer can detect when servers behind them go down and cease sending requests to them. The application's users will be shielded from such failures.

If we maintain server-side state, it will need to be referenced by the web tier, which will become stateful. If we have a stateful web tier, the application, whether distributed or collocated, can only be as reliable as the web tier clustering technology. If a user is associated with one web tier server and it goes down, it won't matter if business objects on another server are still running. The user will encounter problems unless the session data was successfully replicated. By using stateful session beans, we merely move this problem to the EJB container, most often adding the problem of EJB tier replication to that of web tier replication, introducing the potential problem of server affinity (as we'll see in Chapter 10, stateful session beans are likely to be *less*, not more, robust in their handling of session state replication than HttpSession objects).

Only if we have a stateful web tier but stateless business objects (stateless session EJBs in a J2EE application) is a distributed architecture likely to prove more robust (and scalable) than a collocated web application architecture. If the business objects can potentially cause serious failures, getting them "out of process" may deliver greater resilience, especially if the J2EE server offers sophisticated routing of stateless session bean calls. WebLogic, for example, can retry failed calls on stateless session beans to another server running the same EJB, if the failed method is marked as **idempotent** (not causing an update).

> **A distributed architecture is not necessarily more robust than a collocated architecture. An architecture using stateless business objects is the only way to ensure that a distributed architecture is more robust – and more scalable – than a collocated architecture.**

Scalable and Robust Architectures

The key determinant of the scalability and reliability of an architecture is whether it requires server-side state, rather than whether it is distributed. The following three architectures are likely to prove outstandingly robust and scalable (in descending order):

❑ **Stateless architecture, whether distributed or collocated**
This offers unmatched scalability, performance, and reliability. Scalability can be delivered by hardware routing devices, and does not depend on sophisticated application server functionality. New servers can be added at will with no additional performance overhead. Resources outside the J2EE application, such as databases, will usually limit scalability. A surprisingly large proportion of web applications can be made to be stateless, especially if it's possible to use cookies.

❑ **Distributed architecture with stateless business objects**
If the web container doesn't need to maintain session state, adding a stateless, out-of-process, business object layer (such as layer of remote EJBs) usually won't increase scalability, despite impairing performance and complicating design and deployment. The exception is the somewhat artificial scenario of the business objects having largely idempotent methods and being prone to crash the server they run on; as we've seen, WebLogic, at least, can maximize reliability if we use stateless session beans.

However, if the web container does need to maintain session state, it's a different story. By removing the business objects from the servers running the web tier, we may be able to improve web throughput while keeping the overhead of session state replication to a minimum. We can increase overall throughput by adding more EJB containers running stateless session bean business objects. There will be some overhead in scaling up, as the application server will need to manage routing within the cluster, but as no session state replication will be required, such overhead will be modest.

❑ **Web application with all components collocated on each server**
Well-designed web applications offer high performance and excellent scalability and reliability. Only in exceptional cases do we need to look to a distributed architecture with stateless business objects on the grounds of scalability and reliability; a collocated architecture will normally satisfy requirements.

Distributed architectures with stateful business objects (such as stateful session beans) are likely to prove less scalable than any of these, more complex to deploy, and less performant.

207

> When we need to hold session state, distributed architectures with stateless business objects can deliver the ultimate in J2EE scalability and reliability, at the cost of a performance overhead and degree of complexity that is unnecessary in most applications.

The following diagram illustrates such a scalable and robust distributed J2EE architecture. Since business logic is implemented using stateless session beans (SLSB) with remote interfaces, it is possible to run more EJB containers than web containers. In this architecture, adding an EJB container adds lesser overhead than adding a web container, because session state replication is required between web containers:

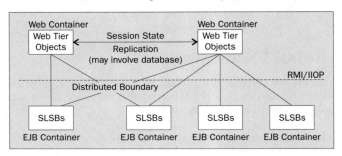

It's important to note that the overhead of adding a new web container to a cluster, where state replication is involved, will differ between servers and with the replication strategy used. I'm assuming the use of **in-memory** replication, in which replicated session data is exchanged between servers in a cluster, but never stored in a database (replication in which a backing store is involved will theoretically scale up almost linearly, but imposes a massive performance overhead, and may encounter problems if a subsequent load-balanced request is received before session data has been stored – a real possibility, as writing to a persistent store is likely to be a slow operation; hence it's usually impracticable).

In servers such as WebLogic, which use a single, randomly selected, **secondary server** to which session state is replicated with every request, the overhead in adding more servers may be modest (at the cost of the possibility of both primary and secondary servers failing at once). In servers such as Tomcat, in which session state is replicated to *all* servers in a cluster, there will be an effective limit on the number of servers that can efficiently function in a cluster without replication overwhelming the LAN and accounting for most of the servers' workload (the benefit being a potential increase in overall resilience).

In my experience, the following principles help to achieve maximum scalability and reliability in web applications:

- ❑ **Avoid holding server-side session state if possible**
- ❑ **If session state must be held, minimize the amount held**
  This will improve the performance of state replication. For example, it's essential that shared data isn't held as part of user session data.
- ❑ **If session state must be held, hold it in the web tier, not the EJB tier**
  As we'll see in *Chapter 10,* HttpSession replication in the web tier is usually more efficient and may be more reliable than stateful session bean replication.
- ❑ **Use several fine grained session objects, not one monolithic session object**
  Hold multiple smaller session objects, rather than one large one, to help the web container to perform state replication efficiently. An efficient web container should then replicate only changes in session state, meaning that the overhead of serialization and replication will be much reduced.

High-level Architecture for the Sample Application

The sample application's requirements do not call for RMI access to business objects. If remote access is required in future, it's more likely to call for an XML-based web services approach. So we have a choice as to whether to use a distributed architecture, and whether EJBs with remote interfaces are required.

The sample application does require server-side session state. Server-side session state, such as a seat reservation held by the user, is so important to the sample application's workflow that trying to evade it by using hidden form fields and the like will prove extremely complex, and a rich source of bugs. We could attempt to hold the user's session state in the database, but this would impact performance even if we weren't running in a cluster (the application initially will run on a single server), and would complicate the application by the need to hold a session key in a cookie or a hidden form field. In this application, it was a business requirement that Internet users were not required to accept cookies (this often isn't the case; if cookies are permissible, there may be alternatives to server-side session state).

We should ensure that the amount of server-side state is kept to the minimum, and that any objects placed in the user's `HttpSession` are serializable efficiently. We should also avoid the temptation to hold all session data in one large object, but put separate objects in the `HttpSession`. For example, seat reservation and user profile objects can be held separately, so that if only one changes, the web container does not need to replicate the data for both. We will take care to ensure that we don't include shared data in individual user sessions.

For example, we will include the numeric primary key of a performance for which a user has reserved, rather than the shared reference data object representing the performance itself. As performance objects are part of a large object graph, which would need to be serialized in its entirety, this is a potentially huge saving if the application ever runs in a cluster. Such replacement of an object with a lookup key is a common and highly effective technique for reducing the volume of session state that must be maintained for each user.

In the sample application, it's unlikely that the business objects will prove to be a bottleneck. We can simply add new servers running the whole application – including the web tier – to scale up. Hence there is no benefit in using a distributed architecture, even with stateless business objects.

Thus we adopt the third architecture discussed above: web application with all components collocated on each server. Not only will this prove scalable and reliable enough to satisfy our requirements, it will also maximize performance and minimize overhead (the business requirements stressed that performance should be maximized per unit hardware).

Deciding When to Use EJB

One of the most important architectural decisions – with implications for deployment, testing, tool requirements and support – is whether to use EJB. In this section we'll examine some of the decisive considerations.

Using EJB to Implement a Distributed Architecture

Use of EJB may be dictated by the choice between a distributed and collocated architecture.

> **If we want a distributed application based on RMI/IIOP, EJB is the perfect J2EE technology to help us implement it.**

By using EJBs with remote interfaces we let the J2EE server handle the details of remote access. The alternative of writing our own RMI infrastructure is far inferior: nonstandard, unnecessarily hard to implement, and likely to prove hard to maintain.

Transaction Management

Even if we don't require EJB to implement a distributed architecture, there may still be reasons to use EJB. In Chapter 1, I noted that **Container-Managed Transactions (CMT)** were probably the most compelling reason for using EJB.

Let's examine J2EE transaction management in general, and how using EJB can help to simplify transactional applications.

Transaction Management in J2EE Applications

A J2EE server must provide the following transaction services:

- ❏ It must be able to coordinate transactions across EIS tier resources. The part of a J2EE server responsible for this is called a transaction manager.
- ❏ It must offer EJBs the option of declarative transaction management, doing away with the need to write code to handle transactions explicitly. The only choice a developer needs to make in this model is whether to roll back a transaction.
- ❏ It must make the standard J2EE Java Transaction API (JTA) and the UserTransaction interface available to objects that wish to manage transactions themselves. These may include both EJBs and objects running in a web container. JTA is a relatively simple transaction management API.

A J2EE server must be able to handle low-level transaction protocols such as X/Open XA that are understood by transactional **resource managers** used by J2EE applications. A resource manager is an EIS tier resource such as a database. Resource managers control persistent state, and are usually transactional.

A J2EE server's transaction manager is responsible for **transaction propagation** between J2EE components, whether collocated or in separate JVMs, and from the J2EE server to transactional resource managers. For example, if a method on an EJB is invoked by a web tier object, any transaction context must be propagated. Transaction contexts are associated with threads within a JVM. A container must be able to use the transactional capabilities of IIOP to handle the transactional requirements of distributed applications by propagating transaction contexts between transaction managers. As IIOP is vendor-independent, this means that transaction propagation works across J2EE servers, even when they are supplied by different vendors.

Part of the J2EE promise is that this low-level detail is completely hidden from developers. Developers can assume that any transactional resource supported by their application server will be managed appropriately if they use standard features of the J2EE platform: declarative transaction management (available in EJBs), or programmatic transaction management using JTA (available in all server-side J2EE components). This is an important boon, as the mechanics of ensuring transaction integrity across disparate resources is complex.

For example, the server should support **two-phase commit** to achieve correct behavior for transactions involving multiple resource managers or multiple EJB containers. Two-phase commit ensures that even in a distributed scenario, all resources enlisted for a transaction either commit or roll back. This is achieved by handling a distributed transaction in two phases. The first issues a **prepare** request to all participating resource managers.

Only when each resource manager has indicated that it is ready to commit its part of the combined operation, will a **commit** request be sent to all resource managers. Two-phase commit can fail in some scenarios. For example, if a resource manager indicates that it is ready to commit, but subsequently fails to commit on a commit request, integrity may be lost. However, two-phase commit is considered a very reliable strategy for distributed transactions. The J2EE specification does not currently require an application server to provide full two-phase commit support. However, it does hint at requiring this in future (refer to documentation supplied with application servers for the degree of two-phase commit support they provide).

Any class running within a J2EE server, but outside the EJB container, can perform programmatic transaction management. This requires obtaining the `UserTransaction` interface from JNDI and using JTA directly.

Any J2EE component may itself manage transactions on a transactional resource such as an RDBMS using an API specific to that resource – in the case of an RDBMS, the JDBC API, or perhaps the JDO API – rather than the integrated JTA. However, this is a poor choice unless J2EE does not offer transactional support for the resource in question. Such transactions are referred to as **local transactions**. They are "local" in being isolated from the integrated transaction management of the J2EE platform.

The J2EE infrastructure, which does not know about local transactions, cannot automatically rollback local transactions if a component marks a J2EE transaction for rollback only. The developer would be left to rollback and commit in code, resulting in unduly complex code and failing to leverage a valuable service of the application server. Local transactions must be created, committed, and rolled back using resource-specific APIs, making applications inconsistent in their approach to transactions.

> **Don't use local transactions (such as JDBC transactions) in J2EE applications, unless the transactional resource in question isn't supported by the server's integrated transaction management. Instead, rely on the transaction management offered by the EJB container, or use JTA to manage transactions. By using local transactions, you deprive the container of the ability to integrate transaction management across transactional resources.**

Transaction Management and EJB

EJBs are the J2EE components best equipped to manage transactions. EJBs benefit from both declarative and programmatic transaction management. In the declarative model, the developer does not need to write any JTA code, ensuring that business logic is not complicated by lower-level transaction management operations. Typically, session EJBs are used to manage transactions, with each method on a session bean delimiting one transaction.

For beans choosing to use **Container-Managed Transactions (CMT)**, the container *declaratively* sets transactional boundaries at method level, eliminating the need to write transaction management code in user applications. Since application developers decide what each method does, this neatly integrates transaction management into the Java language.

With **Bean-Managed Transactions (BMT)**, the developer writes code in the EJB itself to begin, commit or roll back transactions *programmatically* using JTA.

Bean-Managed Transactions

Only session beans and message-driven beans may use BMT. Entity beans *must* use CMT. Using BMT is an all or nothing choice. The choice of BMT or CMT is made at *bean* level, not at method level; so, if only one method of a bean has unusual transactional requirements that seem to require the use of BMT, all methods of the bean will be forced to manage their own transactions (refactoring the design to split the bean may be more appropriate).

BMT has a different meaning for stateless and stateful session beans.

In the case of stateless session beans, the container must detect the situation in which a stateless bean method has returned after starting a transaction, but without committing it or rolling it back. Since a stateless session bean cannot hold state for a particular client between method calls, each method call must complete a unit of work, so this is clearly a programming error. On detecting this situation, the container must react in the same way as to an uncaught throwable from an EJB method, rolling the transaction back and discarding the offending EJB instance. For similar reasons, the same rule applies to message-driven beans, which must conclude any open transaction before the onMessage() method returns.

In the case of stateful session beans, however, the container is not entitled to view a method leaving a transaction open as a programming error. It is possible that several method calls of the stateless bean make up a transaction, and that further method calls are required to complete the unit of work. However, the danger of this scenario is obvious. The client might allow user wait time between calls to the methods in the single transaction. This will waste valuable transactional resources, and potentially lock out other users of resource managers such as relational databases. Worse still, the client might *never* call the method that ends the transaction.

EJBs using BMT must not use the setRollbackOnly() method on the javax.ejb.EJBContext interface. This method is intended to allow easy transaction management for beans using CMT.

> If an EJB is using BMT, it gains little advantage from the EJB container. The same transaction management approach will work without using EJB; the only plus in using EJB is that any transaction will be rolled back automatically in the event of an uncaught throwable. However, a finally block will take care of this situation in cleanly written code; alternatively, a framework class may be used to take care of cleanup in the case of errors.

Container-Managed Transactions

Using CMT is much simpler than using BMT. We don't need to write any transaction management code in our EJBs. We merely need to:

❑ Define method responsibilities so that transaction delimitation at method boundaries is appropriate. EJB methods – especially on remote interfaces – often implement a complete use case, so this often occurs naturally.

❑ Specify the appropriate transaction attribute for each method in the relevant ejb-jar.xml deployment descriptor, from the six recognized by the EJB specification (we'll discuss EJB transaction attributes in detail in Chapter 10).

❑   Call an EJB API method to mark a transaction for rollback if required by business logic.

EJBs with CMT can also normally also use declarative control of **transaction isolation level**, although the EJB specification does not mandate how this should be achieved. Transaction isolation refers to the level of separation between concurrent transactions. We'll discuss this in the next chapter. The J2EE specification doesn't mandate how transaction isolation levels are set. Typically, a container will use an additional proprietary deployment descriptor such as WebLogic's `weblogic-ejb-jar.xml` EJB deployment descriptor to provide this information.

> **EJBs with CMT offer a simple transaction management model that meets most requirements without the need to write any transaction management code. Declarative transaction management with CMT is a strong argument for using EJB.**
>
> **EJBs with BMT offer a poor-value combination of the complexity of EJB and the need to write custom transaction management code. Use EJBs with BMT only in the rare cases when CMT cannot be used to achieve the same result.**

Transaction Management in the Sample Application

The sample application is partly transactional. Therefore, the use of an EJB with a local interface is appropriate for the booking process. This will enable us to use CMT and avoid direct use of JTA.

EJB and Authorization

Most J2EE components have programmatic access to the user's **security principal** to establish which **roles** the user is in. In the web container, this can be obtained from the `javax.servlet.http.HttpServletRequest.getUserPrincipal()` method; in the EJB container, from the `javax.ejb.EJBContext.getCallerPrincipal()` method. The `javax.ejb.EJBContext.isCallerInRole()` method provides a convenient way to check whether a user is in a particular role. Only asynchronous invocations received via JMS are not associated with principal information.

However, EJBs have the alternative of declarative restriction of user principals. We can use the EJB deployment descriptor (`ejb-jar.xml`) to specify which methods are accessible to which user roles without needing to write a line of code. It's also possible to modify these restrictions without changing application code by redeploying the EJB.

The web container offers declarative restriction of application URLs, but this delivers less fine-grained control. It also only protects business objects from unauthorized access via the web interface. In a collocated web application architecture, this is probably all the protection that business objects need, but it's insufficient for distributed applications.

Even if we use EJB authorization, we will also normally implement web tier authorization – we don't want to permit users to attempt operations for which they lack authorization.

Declarative authorization is a valuable service which can indicate the use of EJB. However, it's less critical in collocated web applications, in which there is no risk of unauthorized access to EJBs.

213

EJB and Multi-threading

EJBs are written as though they are single-threaded. The EJB container performs the necessary synchronization behind the scenes. Sometimes this can greatly simplify application code, but, as I observed in Chapter 1, it is probably overrated as an argument for using EJB. Often EJB won't solve all our threading problems. Even in large applications, there is no requirement to write really complex concurrent code. Not to mention that EJB is not the only good solution for multi-threading.

The sample application illustrates this. We don't need to use EJB to simplify threading. Simply by avoiding instance data, we can ensure that servlets and other presentation tier classes are threadsafe. The same approach can easily be extended to our stateless business objects. Threading issues are likely to be encountered in this application only where data caching is concerned.

EJB won't help us with this problem, due to the EJB programming restrictions (discussed later in the chapter) and because we really want to cache data in the web tier, not the EJB tier, to maximize performance. Thus we'll address any threading issues we may encounter using third-party, non-EJB libraries such as Doug Lea's util.concurrent. This means that we don't need to write our own threadsafe caches from scratch, but don't need to rely on EJB for concurrent access.

Of course, where we have already decided to use EJB (in the booking process), we will also take advantage of EJB's concurrency control.

Declarative Configuration Management

Another potential reason to use EJB is the mechanism it offers to manage environment variables and application "wiring" through the standard ejb-jar.xml deployment descriptor, enabling EJBs to be reconfigured without the need to modify Java code.

Such externalization of configuration is good practice. However, it is available to *all* J2EE components to some degree (for example, in the specification of named DataSource objects) and there are simpler ways, such as using ordinary JavaBeans, to separate configuration from code throughout J2EE applications (EJB deployment descriptors are verbose and complex, and only allow XML-based definitions). Hence this is not a strong argument for using EJB.

The Downside of EJB

Before we commit to using EJB, we must consider its negatives as well as positives.

So Much Infrastructure

All EJBs except message-driven beans require at least three Java classes to be implemented by the developer:

❑ The local or remote home interface. This allows the client to create and locate instances of the bean. The EJB container must provide an implementation of this interface at deploy time.

❑ The local or remote interface. This defines the business methods supported by the bean, and is also called the component interface of the bean. The EJB container must provide an implementation of this interface at deployment time, based on the bean implementation class.

❑ The bean implementation class. This implements the relevant interface – javax.ejb.SessionBean or javax.ejb.EntityBean – defining the container callbacks, and provides implementations of the business methods supported by the bean. The bean class should not implement the bean's remote or local interface, although this is legal. However, it is required to implement methods matching the signature of each business method. We'll discuss the "Business Methods Interface" EJB technique, which can be used to formalize this relationship to avoid programming errors, in Chapter 10.

Each group of EJBs deployed in an EJB JAR deployment unit will need one or more XML deployment descriptors, which may be complex. At deployment time, the EJB container is responsible for generating the missing pieces of the EJB jigsaw: stubs and skeletons handling remote invocation, and the implementation of the local or remote home, and the local or remote interface.

Code using EJBs is also more complex than code that uses ordinary Java objects. Callers must perform JNDI lookups to obtain references to EJB component interfaces and must deal with several types of exception.

Why is all this necessary?

To deliver services such as transparent transaction management, the container must have complete control over EJB instances at runtime. The use of container-generated classes enables the container to *intercept* calls to EJBs to manage instance lifecycles, threading, security, transaction demarcation and clustering. When EJB is used appropriately, this is a good tradeoff, enabling the container to take care of issues that would otherwise need to be addressed in user code. In such cases, "simple" non-EJB architectures may turn into a morass of DIY solutions to problems that have already been well addressed by EJB containers.

However, if the payoff introduced by the EJB indirection isn't sufficient, we'll end up with a lot of infrastructure we don't really want. The orthodox J2EE view is that this doesn't matter: tools will synchronize all these classes. However, this is unrealistic. It's better to avoid complexity than to rely on tools to manage it.

> *The introduction of Java 1.3 dynamic proxies – which several EJB containers now use instead of container-generated classes – arguably makes the EJB APIs look dated. Using dynamic proxies, it would be possible to deliver the same container services with fewer special requirements of application code.*

I'll spare you the EJB lifecycle diagrams. However, it *is* important to understand them, and if you're unfamiliar with them, I suggest that you refer to the relevant sections of the EJB 2.0 specification (http://java.sun.com/products/ejb/docs.html).

Programming Restrictions Applying to EJBs

In Chapter 1 we discussed the practical problems that EJBs can produce: essentially, greater complexity in development, deployment, and testing. There's another important problem area that must be considered before using EJB.

Hidden away in section 24.1.2 of the EJB 2.0 Specification (page 494) is a section describing "the programming restrictions that a Bean Provider must follow to ensure that the enterprise bean is *portable* and can be deployed in any compliant EJB 2.0 Container".

This section of the specification is essential reading for all developers working with EJB. Not only does awareness of the restrictions enable us to avoid violating them; it also helps towards understanding the EJB model. Here we discuss some of the most important parts of those restrictions and the rationale behind them.

The individual restrictions can be attributed to three main purposes:

❑ **Clustering**
EJBs must be able to run in a cluster, and the EJB container must be free to manage bean instances across a cluster. This means that we cannot rely on assumptions – such as the behavior of static fields, and the implications of synchronization – that hold true within one JVM.

❑ **Thread management**
The EJB container must be able to manage threads, and EJBs must not be able to hijack such management by creating their own threads or affecting the execution of container-managed threads.

❑ **Security**
The EJB container must be able to manage the security environment of EJBs. Declarative or programmatic security guarantees are worthless if an EJB behaves in an uncontrolled manner.

The following table summarises the most important restrictions and their implications for EJB developers:

Restriction	Restriction category	Notes	Implications for J2EE developers
EJBs should not use read/write static fields.	Clustering	May cause incorrect behavior in a cluster. There is no guarantee that the different JVMs in the cluster will have the same values for the static data.	This restriction makes it difficult to implement the Singleton design pattern in the EJB tier. We discuss this issue later. This restriction does not affect constants.
An EJB must not use thread synchronization.	Thread management Clustering	It is the responsibility of the container, not the bean developer, to perform thread management. Synchronization introduces the risk of deadlock. Synchronization cannot be guaranteed to work as expected if the EJB container distributes instances of a particular EJB across multiple JVMs in a cluster.	This restriction causes few problems in applications that use EJB appropriately, and don't attempt to solve every problem with EJB. One of the main purposes of using EJB is to avoid the need to implement multi-threaded code. The use of synchronization is not necessary, as the container manages concurrent access to the EJB tier.

Restriction	Restriction category	Notes	Implications for J2EE developers
An EJB must not manipulate threads. This includes starting, stopping, suspending or resuming a thread, or changing a thread's priority or name.	Thread management	It is the responsibility of the container to manage threads. If EJB instances manage threads, the container cannot control crucial reliability and performance issues such as the total number of threads in the server instance. Allowing EJB instances to create threads would also make it impossible to guarantee that an EJB method's work is done in a particular transaction context.	Asynchronous activity can be achieved using JMS messaging. The container can ensure efficient load balancing of asynchronous activity initiated using JMS. If JMS is too heavyweight an approach to achieving the required asynchronous functionality, use of EJB may be inappropriate.
An EJB must not attempt to output information to a GUI display or accept keyboard input.	Miscellaneous	EJBs are not presentational components, so there is no reason to violate this restriction. An EJB container may run on a server without a display (in "headless" mode).	None
An EJB must not access the local file system (for example, using the `java.io` package).	Clustering	If EJBs rely on the file system, they may behave unpredictably in a cluster in which different servers may hold the same file with different content. There's no guarantee that an EJB container will even have access to a file system in all servers.	As EJBs are usually transactional components, it doesn't make sense to write data to non-transactional storage such as a file system. If files such as properties files are needed for read-only access, they can be included in an EJB JAR file and loaded via the class loader. Alternatively, read-only data can be placed in the bean's JNDI environment. EJBs are primarily intended to work with enterprise data stores such as databases.

Table continued on following page

217

Restriction	Restriction category	Notes	Implications for J2EE developers
An EJB must not accept connections on a socket or use a socket for multicast.	Miscellaneous	EJBs are intended to serve local or remote clients or consume messages. There is no reason for an EJB to be a network server.	None
An EJB should not attempt to use reflection to subvert Java visibility restrictions.	Security	For example, an EJB should not attempt to access a class or field that is not visible to it because it's private or package visible.	There's no restriction on the use of reflection unless it subverts security. Avoid methods such as `java.lang.class.getDeclaredMethods()` and `java.lang.reflect.setAccessible()`, but there's no problem with using `java.lang.class.getMethods()` (which returns public methods). Anything allowable without granting `java.lang.reflect.ReflectPermission` is acceptable.
An EJB must not attempt to create a classloader or obtain the current classloader.	Security		This prevents use of J2SE 1.3 dynamic proxies in EJB tier application code (as opposed to EJB container implementations), as a dynamic proxy can't be constructed without access to the current classloader. However, there are few other reasons we'd want to obtain the current classloader in an EJB.

Restriction	Restriction category	Notes	Implications for J2EE developers
An EJB must not attempt to load a native library.	Security	If an EJB can load a native library, the sandbox is meaningless, as the EJB container cannot apply security restrictions to the native code. Allowing EJBs to invoke native code may also compromise the stability of the EJB container.	When it's necessary to access native code, EJB is not the correct approach.
An EJB must not attempt to modify security configuration objects (Policy, Security, Provider, Signer and Identity).	Security		When we choose to use EJB, we choose to leave the handling of security to the EJB container, so this restriction isn't a problem if we're using EJB appropriately.
An EJB must not attempt to use the subclass and object substitution features of the Java Serialization protocol.	Security		Doesn't affect normal use of serialization. Only those operations that require the granting of `java.io.Serializab lePermission` are forbidden.
An EJB must not attempt to pass `this` as an argument or method result through its component interface.	Miscellaneous	Returning `this` prevents the container from intercepting EJB method invocations, defeating the purpose of modeling the object as an EJB.	There's a simple workaround to achieve the intended result. Obtain a reference to the EJB's remote or local component interface from the bean's `EJBContext` object.

Most of these restrictions aren't problematic in practice. Remember that we choose to use EJB if it helps to *avoid* the need to write low-level code, such as code that handles concurrent read-write access: it makes little sense to choose to use EJB and then battle against self-imposed restrictions. However, these restrictions do make some common problems hard to solve simply in the EJB tier. Let's consider some of the implications of these restrictions.

How seriously should we take the EJB restriction on synchronization? The EJB specification is clear that EJBs shouldn't use synchronization in their own business methods, and (as we've seen) there is good reason for this. However, the specification doesn't make it clear whether it violates the specification if an EJB uses a helper class that uses synchronization.

I think we need to be pragmatic here. Attempting business operations in EJBs that depend on synchronization (rather than EJB container thread management) reflects use of EJB where it simply doesn't fit, or a lack of understanding of EJB container services. However, some classes that we wish to use as helpers may perform some synchronization – or we may not even have the source code, and be unable to verify that they don't use synchronization. Logging packages and pre-Java 1.2 collection classes such as `java.util.Vector` and `java.util.HashTable` are common examples of packages that use synchronization. If we worry too much about this, we risk spending more time concerned with violating the EJB specification than implementing business logic.

We should satisfy ourselves that such classes don't use synchronization in a way that will break clustering and that their use of synchronization couldn't conflict with EJB container thread management (which might be the case if synchronization is used heavily).

The Singleton Problem in EJB

Developers often find that they want to use the Singleton design pattern – or a more object-oriented alternative that achieves the same ends, such as those we've discussed in *Chapter 4* – in the EJB tier. A common reason is to cache data, especially if it does not come directly from a persistent data store and entity beans are not appropriate. Unfortunately, singleton functionality is a poor fit with the EJB model. In this section, we consider some of the difficulties and potential workarounds.

> *Note that here I assume that the proposed use of a singleton is logical, even in a cluster. If the reason a singleton is inappropriate is because of clustering, EJB isn't imposing any unnecessary restrictions.*

Java Singletons

Ordinary Java singletons – in which the Singleton pattern is enforced by a private constructor and the singleton instance held in a static member variable – can be used in the EJB tier, but are subject to limitations that seriously restrict their use. Since the EJB specification prevents the use of read-write static variables and synchronization, it's impossible to use singletons in many typical ways. This is an instance of the use of synchronization that violates both the spirit and letter of the EJB specification, as it involves application business logic.

It is possible to avoid violating the restriction on read-write static data by initializing the singleton instance in a static initializer, as in the following example, which makes the static member final:

```
public class MySingleton {

  static final MySingleton instance;

  static {
    instance = new MySingleton();
  }

  public static MySingleton getInstance() {
    return instance;
  }

  private MySingleton() {
  }
}
```

Initializing the singleton in a static block is good practice outside the EJB tier, too. The common practice of instantiating the instance only if it's null in the static `getInstance()` method is susceptible to race conditions. Note that the static initializer shouldn't attempt to use JNDI, as there's no guarantee when the EJB container will instantiate the class. In the above example, the singleton instance could have been created when the `instance` variable was declared. However, using a static initializer is the only option if instantiating the singleton can result in an exception. It allows us to catch any exception and rethrow it in the `getInstance()` method.

However, we're still likely to encounter problems, depending on what the singleton does. The likeliest problem is a race condition. As we can't use synchronization in the singleton's business methods and all EJBs running in the container will share the same singleton instance, we have no way of limiting concurrent access. This restricts the use of singletons for data caches: only if race conditions are acceptable can we cache data in a singleton. This may limit caching to read-only data.

Use ordinary Java singletons in the EJB container only under the following circumstances:

- ❑ The singleton instance can be initialized in a static block (or at the point of declaration) to avoid race conditions
- ❑ The singleton isn't prohibitively expensive to initialize
- ❑ The singleton doesn't require JNDI access to initialize
- ❑ The work of the singleton doesn't require synchronization

RMI Objects

Given these restrictions, it seems a good idea to get singletons out of the EJB sandbox. One commonly suggested way of doing this is to make the singletons remote objects, and to access them from EJB code via RMI. However, implementing and accessing singletons as RMI objects is complex and error prone, and I don't recommend it. The singleton isn't managed by the EJB container, and will become a single point of failure. If the RMI server fails, the EJB container will have no way of dealing with the ensuing problems. Remote method invocation between EJBs and RMI object may also limit performance. And we certainly won't want to introduce RMI for this reason if we're using only EJBs with local interfaces.

Stateless Session Bean Pseudo-cache

Sometimes when something is particularly difficult to implement, it's worth taking a step back to look at what we're trying to achieve. What we're trying to achieve with singletons may be achievable with a different implementation strategy.

Stateless session beans are created and destroyed infrequently by an EJB container. Each instance will normally service many clients in its lifetime. Thus a helper object maintained in a stateless session bean can be used to provide some of the caching services of a singleton: data held in it (and built up as an application runs) will be available through ordinary Java method invocation.

The advantages of this approach are that it doesn't violate the EJB programming restrictions and is easy to implement. The issue of synchronization won't arise, as each SLSB instance will behave as if it is single threaded. The disadvantage is that we will end up with one "singleton" instance per session bean instance. In the case of stateless session beans, there will be at most tens of instances, as the stateless session bean lifecycle is independent of any individual client. However, the object duplication will be a problem if it's vital that all session bean instances hold the same cached data (which may be the point of using the singleton pattern).

This approach is of little value when using stateful session beans and of no value to entity beans, as these objects may change identity frequently. However, I can think of few legitimate reasons that an entity bean would need to use a singleton.

"Read-only" Entity Beans

If your EJB container supports "read-only" entity beans, it may be possible to use them as singletons. However, this approach isn't portable, as the EJB specification doesn't currently define read-only entities. The performance implications may be unclear, as locking strategies for read-only entities vary. I don't recommend this approach.

JMX or Startup Class

Another approach is to bind the singleton in JNDI using either proprietary application server functionality (such as WebLogic's "startup classes") or JMX. JBoss provides a particularly elegant way of binding JMX MBeans to a bean's environment. EJBs can then look it up at runtime. However, these approaches arguably remove the singleton from the EJB sandbox in appearance rather than reality. Synchronization, for example, will still violate the EJB programming restrictions.

The Singleton design pattern is a problematic area in EJB. We've considered a number of workarounds, none of which is perfect.

> **When using a collocated architecture, the best solution for singleton functionality is usually to sidestep the EJB-singleton minefield and implement such functionality in the web container. This is consistent with a strategy of using EJB where it provides value; where it makes things *harder*, it is clearly not providing value.**

When using a distributed architecture with remote interfaces exposing core business logic, singleton functionality supporting this business logic will need to stay in the EJB container. In this case we will probably need to choose the lesser of the evils discussed above in the context of the current application.

Timer Functionality

Another piece of commonly required functionality that is problematic to implement in the EJB container is timer or scheduling functionality. Imagine that we want an object in the EJB tier to be prompted regularly to perform a certain operation. Outside the EJB tier, we could simply create a background thread to do this, or use the `java.util.Timer` convenience class introduced in J2SE 1.3. However, both these approaches violate the EJB specification's restrictions on creating threads. There is no satisfactory standard solution to this longstanding problem in EJB 2.0, although EJB 2.1 introduces one. We will usually need to resort to server-specific solutions. JBoss and other servers provide components that address this issue.

EJBs in the Sample Application

The sample application's reservation and booking (confirmation) process is transactional. So by using EJB with CMT we can simplify application code by removing the need to use JTA directly. We don't require EJB thread management services; although we will probably need to implement some multi-threaded code in the web tier (see *Caching* later in the chapter), there's no obvious requirement for really complex multithreaded code.

A choice of not using EJB here would be quite defensible, as the application does not need EJBs to support remote clients – the one service that can not rationally be delivered without using EJB. While using JTA directly might be more error-prone (although not unduly complex), using a framework that offers declarative transaction management without the overhead of EJB would be a reasonable implementation choice.

Deciding How to Use EJB

Assuming that we decide to use EJB to take advantage of the EJB container services we've discussed, there are still many issues to discuss in *how* we use EJB.

What Should EJBs Do?

How we should use EJBs depends largely on whether we're implementing a distributed or collocated application. If the application is distributed, we'll need to use session EJBs to expose as much of the application's business logic as remote clients require. When dealing with a true distributed application, we need to consider interface granularity; remote EJB interfaces must not force clients into "chatty" calling and should ensure that data exchanged is kept to a minimum, or the performance overhead of remoting will become prohibitive.

We can use session EJBs with local interfaces very differently. Although they're heavyweight objects compared to ordinary Java classes, the overhead they impose is far more modest. (They're likely to prove a few times slower to invoke than ordinary Java classes, compared to the hundreds or even thousands of times when using remote invocation, and they may even deliver performance benefits if we use container-managed threading appropriately.) This means that when working with local interfaces, we don't need to distort our object model to ensure that EJBs expose coarse-grained interfaces.

> **EJBs with remote interfaces and EJBs with local interfaces cannot be directly compared; it's not simply a question of exposing different interfaces to the same kind of object. Performance considerations are more important than OO design considerations when designing EJB remote interfaces; they *must* be coarse-grained, the objects exchanged must be serializable, and callers must not be forced into chatty calling. EJBs with local interfaces are much more like true objects; their interfaces will be determined by normal OO design considerations.**

When to Use Local or Remote Interfaces

Local interfaces were introduced into the EJB 2.0 specification primarily to make it more efficient for EJBs to call each other. This makes the **Session Façade** pattern more performant and reduces the overhead associated with entity beans. The Session Façade pattern involves session beans mediating between remote clients and local entity beans running in the same EJB container. In this model, local interfaces are an optimization inside the EJB container, hidden from web components and other objects that use the EJBs behind a remote façade.

I believe that such use of entity beans (which may have relationships with other entity beans) is the one case in which it makes sense for EJBs to call each other. It's best to avoid having EJBs call one another, even through local interfaces. When the invoked EJB is a session bean, a better alternative is to use an ordinary Java helper class, for the following reasons:

❏ **Performance**
Invoking EJBs through local interfaces is much faster than true remote invocation, but it's still slower than calling ordinary Java objects (remember that the overhead of remote invocation is only part of the overhead of invoking an EJB: method interception is quite distinct).

❏ **Complexity**
Using EJBs with local interfaces is more complex than using ordinary Java objects. As with all EJBs with component interfaces, we have at least three source files per bean. Like remote home interfaces, local home interfaces must be looked up in JNDI. Bean instances cannot be obtained directly, but must be obtained through JNDI. And of course deployment is more complex.

We will need to provide some infrastructure to make it easier to configure helper classes in the EJB container. We discuss an approach in Chapter 11.

I believe that in EJB 2.0, the best use of local interfaces is to allow us to use EJB without remote interfaces and without adopting a distributed architecture. In this approach, collocated objects outside the EJB tier, such as business objects running in the web container, invoke EJBs through their local interfaces. This allows us to enjoy many of the advantages EJB offers without much of its complexity.

> **Unless your application is inherently distributed, I recommend against using EJBs with remote interfaces. The introduction of local interfaces in the EJB 2.0 specification justifies a rethink of our approach to EJB, making local interfaces the default choice for EJBs, and remote interfaces a special case.**

Does it Make Sense for a Bean to Have Both Local and Remote Interfaces?

The EJB specification implies that the norm will be for an EJB to have either a local or a remote interface. However, it is legal to provide both. In this case, the two interfaces are independent. They cannot extend a common superclass, as every method on the remote interface must be declared to throw `java.rmi.RemoteException`, while methods on the local interface must not be declared to throw this exception.

While the interfaces are independent, the one method in the bean implementation class may implement a method with the same name and arguments from both the local and the remote interfaces, differing only in that the remote interface signature includes `java.rmi.RemoteException` in the throws clause. The bean implementation may declare the method without `java.rmi.RemoteException` in the throws clause, satisfying both contracts. This is legal Java. However, this convenient approach can be dangerous. Callers using the local interface will be using call-by-reference, and callers using the remote interface, call-by-value. Having the same method invoked with different calling semantics is asking for trouble.

Of course we don't need to double-up with method implementations in this way. It may be wiser to give local and remote interface methods distinguishing names so that the bean implementation is easily understandable.

The following issues should be considered before giving an EJB both a remote and a local interface:

❏ It is potentially confusing to have the same object supporting both call-by-value and call-by-reference, even if this doesn't happen through the same methods.

❑ Remote and local interfaces are likely to vary in level of abstraction and granularity, conflicting with it being good OO practice for all an object's methods to be at a consistent level of abstraction. Remote interfaces should be coarse-grained; the local interfaces may be finer grained.

❑ If the bean is really a remote object, yet provides a local interface to support local callers, it might be better to refactor the functionality used by the local callers into a helper class. Having one EJB call another indicates questionable design.

An alternative approach to giving one EJB both a remote and a local interface is to give the EJB that exposes the underlying business logic only a local interface and add another EJB with a remote interface as a façade to service remote callers. This has the benefit of making explicit the local/remote split. However, we must still be aware that while the local interfaces use call-by-reference, the remote interface uses call-by-value.

Phony Remote Interfaces

Finally, there's the EJB interface approach that most existing EJB deployments end up relying on. In this approach, architects and developers duck the tough decisions of whether the application should be distributed and whether RMI is really appropriate. They implement the application using remote interfaces. However, they then collocate web tier and EJB tier in the same JVM and let the server "optimize" notionally remote calls into calls-by-reference.

The EJB container behaves more or less (but not quite) as it would for local interfaces; it still intercepts EJB calls, allowing it to perform transaction management and other EJB services. However, error handling must follow the remote semantics (returning `java.rmi.RemoteException` and subclasses rather than `javax.ejb.EJBException`) on fatal errors.

Strictly speaking, this subverts the EJB paradigm. However, the reality is that the overhead of remote invocation is so crippling to performance that most servers make this their *default* behavior when EJBs and client code are deployed in the same JVM.

Call-by-reference optimization was a welcome optimization in the days of EJB 1.1; it made EJB usable in many applications where it wouldn't otherwise have performed adequately. However, I think it is a poor solution today, for the following reasons:

❑ I feel uncomfortable with systems that are intended to run in a configuration inconsistent with their declared semantics. Often such applications *cannot* be run with the configuration their declared semantics implies: they won't perform adequately if deployed using RMI.

❑ Applications that depend on this optimization for adequate performance aren't guaranteed to be portable, as this optimization is not part of the J2EE specifications. Although I argue against overemphasis on 100% portability, predicating an application's performance on a single non-standard extension is not something that can easily be modified.

❑ Client code is forced to allow for remote exceptions that will never happen. Client code can still encounter `java.rmi.RemoteException`, but this will indicate a failure within the EJB, not a failure to connect to it.

❑ Vulnerability to hard-to-find bugs due to code being written to RMI semantics failing when called by reference (for example, if callers modify objects passed by reference which are subsequently passed to other callers).

❑   Adverse impact on OO design. Remote object interfaces are usually designed to coarse granularity for performance reasons. This is a very bad thing if those interfaces will never be invoked remotely.

❑   It's no longer necessary. EJB 2.0 gives developers the power to specify the desired call semantics in a standard way.

The one potential advantage is that we can enjoy the performance of call-by-reference without ruling out other deployment options. This can be an important consideration, but it's worth thinking long and hard about whether there *will* be any other deployment options. Usually there won't be. Complicating design just in case is a classic – and potentially costly – example of what XPers call **You Aren't Going to Need It**, and we'll only enjoy a choice of deployment options if we distort OO design to ensure that all business objects have coarse-grained interfaces.

There is one argument in favor of using EJBs with remote interfaces – or giving local EJBs additional remote interfaces – even if an application isn't inherently distributed: EJBs with remote interfaces are easier to test than EJBs with local interfaces. Access via remote interfaces means that test cases don't need to run in the J2EE server, allowing the use of simple tools such as JUnit. However, remote testing will work only if all objects exchanged are serializable, and can be "disconnected" from the J2EE server container. In some cases such as CMP entity bean container-managed collections, this is impossible to achieve.

EJB Interface Summary

Entity beans should *never* be given remote interfaces. Business objects within the same JVM (for example, other EJBs or components in the web container) should access entities through local interfaces. There are such overwhelming performance and design reasons against remote access to entity beans (discussed in Chapter 8) that it's questionable whether the EJB specification should offer it as a design choice. The Session Façade pattern, which mediates entity bean access through session beans, is the appropriate solution for EJB deployments offering remote interfaces that use entity beans.

Session beans should be given remote interfaces only if the application has to be distributed and/or remote clients will access the EJBs using RMI. EJBs that are remote objects should not normally have local interfaces, because they should not be invoked by other objects within the same EJB container. However, there is a special case in which an application that is basically local (such as a web application) also needs to support remote callers using RMI. In this case we can either add remote interfaces to some of the application's EJBs, or implement façade EJBs that invoke them. However, we will need to consider the implications of supporting both call-by-reference and call-by-value.

If an application is not inherently distributed, EJBs should be given local interfaces. I recommend against relying on call-by-reference optimization when EJBs with remote interfaces are collocated with code that calls them.

> **Local interfaces should be the default choice for EJBs. Remote interfaces are a special case, to deliver additional functionality (at a cost in performance, complexity and to OO design) where this is necessary.**
>
> **It is possible for an EJB to expose both a local and remote interface. However, these need to be considered carefully, due to the difference between call-by-reference and call-by-value semantics.**

Using EJBs in the Sample Application

We've already decided that the sample application will not be distributed. Thus we'll use only EJBs with local interfaces. There is no need to expose remote interfaces, although we may be able to in future in the unlikely event that RMI access is required. This means that we don't need to ensure that all EJB invocations are coarse-grained.

Since all application components will be collocated in each server running the application, there's no need for all business objects to be implemented in the EJB container. This means that we can pick and choose where to use EJB: where we want the transaction management, thread management, and other benefits of EJB, but not where the EJB programming restrictions are likely to cause any difficulties. The booking process is the only obvious application for EJB in the sample application.

The following diagram – based on the diagram of the second of the four architectures discussed in Chapter 1 – illustrates the architecture:

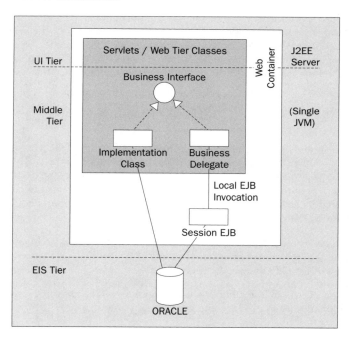

Most of the business interfaces will be implemented by ordinary Java classes running in the web container, while the interface for the booking object will be implemented by a stateless session EJB with a local interface. A business delegate in the web container will front this EJB and ensure that objects running in the web container can access it without having to handle EJB-specific details such as JNDI lookups. Thus, use of EJB is an implementation choice, rather the key to the overall architecture.

Deciding when to Use Asynchronous Calling with JMS

So far we've considered only synchronous functionality, and only remote communication using RMI/IIOP. J2EE also allows us to implement asynchronous functionality, and to use messaging as an alternative form of communication with other applications.

We may need to use messaging to meet some business requirements, or we may choose to use messaging if we believe that an asynchronous model is the best implementation option. In this section we'll consider some of the architectural and implementation choices relating to messaging.

Message-Oriented Middleware (MOM) and JMS

MOM is infrastructure that supports **messaging**: loosely-coupled, standards-based and usually asynchronous communication between components or applications. Messaging involves a message broker that sits between **message producers** (equivalent to method callers in a synchronous model) and **message consumers** (objects that listen for and process messages). There may be multiple message consumers. A message producer can normally continue with its work after publishing a message: unlike a synchronous method invocation, publishing a message does not block. This is sometimes called **fire-and-forget**.

Until recently, MOM has not been widely used in J2EE. However, its value has been proven in many other systems.

Different messaging systems traditionally have proprietary APIs. The **Java Message Service (JMS)** is a standard J2EE API for messaging, which sits on a **Service Provider Interface (SPI)** that can be implemented for different messaging systems. Like JDBC, JMS abstracts the details of low-level access using proprietary conventions. Application code that uses JMS doesn't need to concern itself with the underlying messaging system, or the message transport it uses. JMS supports both **Publish and subscribe (Pub/Sub),** and **Point-to-Point (PTP)** messaging.

The JMS API is available to EJBs, servlets and application clients. J2EE 1.3 integrates the JMS into the EJB model, enabling the EJB container to handle some low-level JMS API issues. Message-driven beans provide special support for JMS message consumers.

We can make full use of JMS in any component managed by a J2EE server. However, EJBs are especially well-equipped both to produce and consume messages.

Producing Messages

Any object running within a J2EE server can produce JMS messages.

EJBs benefit from no special JMS-related services for JMS message publication. Like other objects running within a J2EE server, they must use JNDI and the JMS API to obtain a JMS connection and session before publishing messages.

However, message production – like resource management – can benefit from CMT in the EJB tier. Container-managed transactions can provide transparent transaction management for transacted JMS sessions.

JMS supports the notion of transactions. However, it's important to distinguish between JMS transactions and JTS (that is, ordinary J2EE) transactions. A **transacted JMS session** enables us to batch messages. When creating a JMS session (which we need to do before sending messages in a message producer), we must specify whether or not a session should be transacted. If a session is transacted, either the session's `commit()` or `rollback()` method should be called to let JMS know what to do with any buffered messages. In the event of a commit they will be delivered as a single unit (all delivered atomically); in the event of a rollback, they will all be discarded.

It's possible to work with different JMS session objects if some messages must be transacted while others need not be. Enterprise resources such as databases are *not* enlisted in JMS transactions. Resource enlistment is the business of ordinary JTS transactions. JMS transactions are local transactions with a special meaning. It *is* possible for JTS transactions to enlist JMS resources, so it's usually preferable for message producers to work with JTS transactions (which can, of course, be managed by the container in the EJB tier) than with JMS transactions directly.

If message production is not transactional (for example, if only one message is published per operation, or if each message has to be processed individually), there's no compelling reason to use EJBs as message producers.

Consuming Messages

It is in consuming messages that EJBs really shine.

Consuming Messages without Using EJB

Any component running within an environment managed by the J2EE server can consume JMS messages. However, implementing a message consumer involves using JNDI to look up a JMS destination and registering a listener with it; the JNDI and JMS code involved is fairly complex. While we can use generic infrastructure code to remove these responsibilities from application code, it's better to use standard infrastructure offered by the EJB container, if possible.

We'll discuss generic infrastructure code to simplify the use of JMS in Chapter 11.

Consuming Messages with Message-Driven Beans (MDB)

Consuming messages with MDBs is much easier, as we can specify the message destination and filter declaratively in the `ejb-jar.xml` deployment descriptor, and concentrate on handling messages, not writing low-level JMS or JNDI code. Let's consider some of the capabilities of MDBs, and some important implementation considerations.

MDB Concepts

A MDB is an asynchronous message consumer with access to EJB container services. An MDB is not visible to a client. Unlike session or entity beans, MDBs don't have home or component interfaces; instead, MDB instances are invoked at runtime by an EJB container on receipt of a JMS message. The EJB container knows which MDB to invoke on receipt of a message, based on a declarative mapping in EJB deployment descriptors.

MDBs can consume messages from either topics (in Pub/Sub messaging) or queues (in PTP messaging). The EJB container, not the bean developer, handles JMS message acknowledgment for MDBs; the developer must not use the JMS API to acknowledge messages.

> As the EJB container provides valuable services to MDBs, MDBs are usually the best choice for writing message consumers when using JMS in a J2EE application.

Interfaces

An MDB must implement two interfaces: `javax.ejb.MessageDrivenBean`, and `javax.jms.MessageListener`. The `MessageDrivenBean` interface is analogous to the `SessionBean` and `EntityBean` interfaces, with which it shares the `EnterpriseBean` superinterface. It defines the callback methods the EJB container uses to manage an EJB instance's lifecycle. The `MessageListener` interface is part of the JMS API, rather than the EJB API, and includes a single method, `onMessage()`, which is invoked when the EJB container receives a message relevant to the MDB instance.

Why doesn't the `MessageDriven` interface simply extend the `MessageListener` interface? By keeping the interfaces separate, the EJB specification makes explicit the distinction between message handling infrastructure and the nature of the messages being processed. This reserves the option of future versions of the EJB specification to use the same approach to handling messages from different sources – for example, e-mail messages or Java API for XML-based Messaging (JAXM) messages.

The `onMessage()` method is responsible for all business operations in an MDB. Unlike session bean business methods, this method is weakly typed. The message may be of a type that the MDB doesn't know how to handle, although declarative filtering should reduce the number of unwanted messages.

Like stateless session beans, MDBs must implement a single, no-argument `ejbCreate()` method. Note that as with stateless session beans, this method is *not* required by the relevant interfaces, so failure to provide it will only be evident at deployment time. In *Chapter 11* we'll discuss a convenient, generic superclass we can use for MDBs to help meet the requirements of the EJB specification.

> It is the responsibility of an MDB to ensure that it can handle the messages it "opens". Runtime tests should be performed to avoid class cast exceptions at runtime.

Programming Restrictions Applying to MDBs

The normal EJB programming restrictions apply to MDBs as well. For example, MDBs cannot create threads or use synchronization.

MDBs have most in common with stateless session beans. They can't hold conversational state. They can be pooled in the application server, as all instances of the same MDB are equivalent.

There are a few additional restrictions unique to MDBs.

Exception handling differs from that of other EJB types because MDBs have no client. *Section 15.4.10* of the EJB specification states that MDBs must not throw application exceptions or `java.rmi.RemoteException`. A runtime exception such as an `EJBException` or an uncaught throwable should only be thrown if the bean encounters an unexpected fatal exception. Such an exception will prompt the EJB container to try to redeliver the message, potentially resulting in the same problem being repeated. A message causing this scenario is called a **poison message**, although the problem is more likely to lie in the MDB's implementation than the message itself.

Since an MDB is decoupled from the message sender (or client), it cannot access the security information normally available through the EJB's context at runtime in the `getCallerPrincipal()` and `isCallerInRole()` methods. This limits the use of messaging in practice, as this restriction is sometimes unacceptable (for example, business rules may differ depending on the identity and permissions of the user attempting to perform an operation).

Transactions and MDBs

Like all EJBs, MDBs can use the JTS transaction management services of the EJB container. We've already discussed JMS transactions, which are a distinct issue. However, transactions work differently with MDBs, compared to other types of EJB.

> **MDBs cannot participate in clients' transactions.**

Like session beans, MDBs can be used with either CMT or BMT.

When using CMT, the only legal transaction attributes to specify in the `ejb-jar.xml` deployment descriptor are `Required` and `NotSupported`. If the transaction attribute is `Required`, the EJB container starts a new transaction and invokes the MDB's `onMessage()` method within it. The transaction is committed when this method returns. The message receipt is part of the transaction created by the container. If the transaction aborts (due to a runtime exception or a call to the `MessageDrivenContext`'s `setRollbackOnly()` method) the message remains in the JMS destination and will be redelivered.

This is an important point; it means that if an MDB with CMT and a transaction attribute of `Required` rolls back or aborts a transaction due to an error, subsequent deliveries of the poison message may cause the same problem. Consider the case of sloppy code that fails to check the type of a message before trying to cast it to a `TextMessage`. This will result in a runtime class cast exception – an error that will occur over and over again as the EJB container redelivers the message to the same MDB, although not the same instance. We can avoid this problem by taking extra care that MDBs don't throw runtime exceptions at runtime.

> **MDBs should not indicate an application error by throwing an exception or rolling back the current transaction. This will simply cause the message to be delivered again, in which case the failure will be repeated (and repeated). A better alternative is to publish an error message to a JMS error destination.**
>
> **Only in the case of a fatal (but possibly transient) system-level failure, should a runtime exception be thrown or the current transaction to be rolled back, meaning that the message will be redelivered. The latter behavior might be appropriate, for example, in the event of a failure originating from a database. The database might be temporarily down, in which case it makes sense to have another attempt at processing the message, when the underlying problem may have been resolved.**

When using CMT with a transaction attribute of `NotSupported`, the EJB container will not create a transaction before calling the MDB's `onMessage()` method. In this case, message acknowledgment will still be handled automatically by the container.

When using BMT, transactional boundaries must be set by the bean developer inside the `onMessage()` method. This means that the message receipt is *not* part of the transaction. The message will not automatically be redelivered if the bean-managed transaction rolls back. However, acknowledgment is still handled by the EJB container, rather than the MDB developer. The bean developer should indicate in the `acknowedge-mode ejb-jar.xml` deployment descriptor element whether JMS `AUTO_ACKNOWLEDGE` semantics or `DUPS_OK_ACKNOWLEDGE` semantics should apply (JMS `AUTO_ACKNOWLEDGE` is the default). `DUPS_OK_ACKNOWLEDGE` will incur less JMS overhead.

Subscription Durability

MDBs to be used with a topic (for Pub/Sub messaging) can be marked as using a durable subscription in the optional `<subscription-durability>` element in the `ejb-jar.xml` deployment descriptor. The EJB container will transparently handle the details of the durable subscription (such as subscriber identification to the JMS server). If this element is not supplied, subscription is non-durable.

When to Use Asynchronous Calling

Now that we are familiar with the major issues concerning JMS and MDBs, we can consider when to use messaging.

Indications for Using Messaging

Asynchronous calling can only be used when the caller doesn't need an immediate response. Thus, a method that has a return value isn't a candidate for asynchronous calling. Nor is a method that may throw an application exception. Checked exceptions provide alternative return values for Java methods, and force clients to take action. This isn't possible with asynchronous calling.

Assuming that these essential conditions hold, the following indications suggest the use of JMS. The more of these indications that apply, the more appropriate the use of messaging is likely to be:

❑ **To improve the client's perception of application response**
If a client can be given an immediate response with "fire-and-forget", the system will seem faster than one which blocks on the same action.

❑ **When business logic calls for the result to be delivered to the client other than by a direct method response**
Sending an e-mail is a perfect example of this, and is often a good use of JMS.

❑ **To perform slow operations**
A slow operation that doesn't result in a Java return value and won't throw an exception is a perfect candidate for JMS. Consider, for example, a reporting operation that involves both Java-based calculations and database queries. It might be more appropriate to return such a report in an e-mail, allowing immediate return to the client while the report is generated in the background.

❑ **When the order of processing tasks doesn't matter**
While we can guarantee the ordering of synchronous RMI calls, we can't guarantee the ordering of message processing. It may not be the same as that of message publication. This rules out messaging in some cases.

❑ **To achieve the smoothest possible load balancing**
Stateless session beans offer excellent load balancing, but MDBs are still better. While the EJB container decides which stateless session bean instance should handle a client request, EJB containers that know they have enough spare capacity actually ask for messages to process. Message queuing also allows load balancing over time.

- **To achieve loose coupling between components**
  Note that JMS isn't the only way to achieve loose coupling in J2EE applications: often we can simply use Java interfaces to decouple objects.

- **To integrate distinct applications that expose message-based interfaces**
  In some cases JMS may be the best way to integrate with legacy systems or achieve interoperability with non-J2EE applications.

- **As an alternative to creating threads when this is not an option**
  Remember that it is illegal to create threads in the EJB tier. JMS and MDBs provide an alternative. If a problem could otherwise be solved by creating a background thread and waiting for it to do something, messaging will be a good fit, as an immediate return value is not required.

- **If it's possible to parallelize independent parts of a slow operation**
  This is a special case of the last indication.

- **To escape the EJB sandbox**
  Occasionally we might want to configure a JMS message consumer other than an MDB, to enable an application to perform operations that are illegal within the EJB container, such as call native code. However, messaging isn't the only way to achieve this – we could also use an RMI object, running in a separate process.

Disadvantages of Using Messaging

Using JMS is likely to bring the following disadvantages:

- Although messaging may give the client the perception of faster response, using messaging actually increases the total amount of work the application server will do (although it allows greater freedom in scheduling the work). With durable subscriptions, the amount of work will increase markedly.

- Messaging makes it impossible to take the client's security identity into account when performing work on behalf of the client.

- It's harder to understand and debug an asynchronous system than a synchronous system.

Thus, don't take the decision to adopt JMS lightly (even if the situation suggests that it's appropriate to use messaging).

JMS and Performance

Messaging is often advocated for performance reasons. However, if messaging is to achieve the same degree of reliability as RMI (which at least guarantees that the client knows if something goes wrong on the server), it's unlikely to achieve any performance benefit.

The overhead of JMS varies greatly depending on how it is used: acknowledgment modes, subscription durability etc. Guaranteed delivery (necessary for some operations) is likely to be slow. Imagine a system that queues requests to create user accounts, performing the actual database inserts asynchronously. To be sufficiently reliable, this would have to use guaranteed delivery, meaning that the application server would need to store the messages in a database or other persistent store to ensure that the messages were delivered. Thus the EJB container would probably end up doing a database insert when the message was published anyway, meaning that there would be no performance benefit even in the short term, and increased cost overall.

Only if we can use messaging without guaranteed delivery or if the asynchronous operation is extremely slow is messaging likely to deliver performance gains.

> **Do not use messaging without good reason. Using messaging inappropriately will make a system more complex and error-prone, add no value, and probably reduce performance.**

Alternatives to JMS Messaging

In some situations there may be simpler, lighter-weight alternatives to JMS, using thread creation (allowed outside the EJB container) or the Observer design pattern without JMS (that is, notifying listeners – who may perform actions in the calling thread or in a new thread – using an ordinary Java implementation, and not JMS). The Observer design pattern implemented this way will create much less overhead than JMS. However, whether it works in a clustered environment depends on what listeners must do. The server provides cluster-wide support for JMS; clearly we don't want to build our own cluster-capable Observer implementation, when JMS already delivers this. Situations in which simple implementations of the Observer design pattern are a viable alternative to JMS include:

- ❑ When the application does not run in a cluster and is never likely to.

- ❑ When it doesn't matter if all event processing occurs on the server on which the event was generated. For example, if the event should lead to the sending of an e-mail in the background this condition applies. We only want one e-mail to be sent. On the other hand, if a data cache needs to be invalidated in response to an event, this will normally need to happen on every machine that runs the cache: single-server event processing is insufficient.

JMS in the Sample Application

No part of the sample application's functionality is asynchronous. All user actions must result in synchronous method invocation.

However, it is plausible to use JMS to attempt to improve performance by invalidating cached data in response to events generated when something changes in the system. For example, if a user booked a seat for a particular performance, cached availability details for this performance might be updated across a cluster of servers. This approach would *push* information about data updates to caches, rather than leave them to *pull* new information after a given timeout. Messages might also be sent on other events including cancellation of a booking or the entry of a new performance or show. This would use JMS as a cluster-capable implementation of the Observer design pattern.

Whether this will improve performance will depend on how significant the JMS overhead proves and whether a synchronous alternative (such as refreshing cached data on request if it is deemed to have timed out) will prove adequate. The asynchronous approach has the disadvantage of making the application harder to deploy and test.

Such questions, which have significant architectural implications, should be resolved as early as possible: usually by implementing a vertical slice of the application's functionality early in the project lifecycle. In this case, a vertical slice will enable us to run benchmarks to establish whether a simple cache will meet our performance requirements (it's best to test the simpler approach first, as if it proves satisfactory we will never need to implement the more complex approach). This benchmark is discussed in Chapter 15.

The conclusion is that, where seat availability data is concerned, a cache can produce very good performance results, even if set to time data out at 10 seconds. Thus incurring the overhead of JMS messaging every time a booking is made is unnecessary. The fact that reservations can time out in the database if the user doesn't proceed to purchase is also problematic for a JMS approach to availability updates.

It's a different matter with reference data about genres, shows and performances. This data takes much longer to retrieve from the database, and changes rarely. Thus publishing a JMS message is a very good approach. We will use JMS in the sample application only to broadcast reference data updates.

Authentication and Authorization

J2EE provides both declarative and programmatic support for authentication and authorization, analogous to its declarative and programmatic support for transaction management.

Authentication is the task of ascertaining a user's identity. Users present **credentials** to the server – most often, a password – to prove their identity. **Authorization** is the problem of determining what resources within the application a particular identity should be allowed to access.

J2EE integrates authentication and authorization across all architectural tiers and components. Typically, users will identify themselves to the application interface (for example, a web interface, or a Swing GUI). The J2EE server is responsible for propagating this identification to all application components that the user's actions cause to be invoked. This will be done by associating a user identity with a thread of execution.

The container's transparent management of authorization frees developers to devote more resources to implementing application functionality.

The Standard Security Infrastructure

J2EE security is **role-based**. Each user of a system can have a number of roles. Different access privileges can be associated with different roles.

Each synchronous call to a J2EE component carries the following security information, obtained through the component APIs:

❑ A java.security.Principal object. This can be used to find the authenticated username.

❑ Whether the user is in a particular role. This can be used for programmatic restriction of user permissions.

> **If the username obtained from the security principal is the primary key to the user's persistent data, the standard security infrastructure can be used to avoid the need to pass primary key parameters with method invocations for authenticated users. This is particularly helpful in the case of stateless session beans. This is a good example of how standard infrastructure provided by the server can be used to simplify the programming model.**

Access to protected resources may be limited declaratively to users in certain roles. This is done in the web.xml and ejb-jar.xml deployment descriptors. It's up to the server how users are mapped onto these roles, as we'll see. The EJB specification (§21.2.4) recommends the use of declarative, rather than programmatic, security, "The Bean Provider should neither implement security mechanisms nor hard-code security policies in the enterprise beans' business methods".

If a user is forbidden access to a protected resource because of declarative restrictions, the result varies based on the type of request. A web request will be given a standard HTTP return code indicating unauthorized access, or a page defined by the web application for display in this event. A method invocation on an EJB will throw a java.rmi.RemoteException if the client is remote or a javax.ejb.EJBException if the client is local.

Web containers are most likely to process users' security credentials. The servlet specification requires J2EE-compliant web containers to support **HTTP basic authentication** and **form-based** authentication. Basic authentication is defined in the HTTP specification and authenticates a user in a **realm** (a security protection space) based on a username and password. Basic authentication is not secure and it's impossible to customize its appearance in the browser, so it shouldn't be used in enterprise applications.

Form-based authentication is much more useful, and the servlet specification describes a standard mechanism for managing it. A web container must implement a POST action with the distinguished pseudo-URL j_security_check, which takes username and password parameters with the defined names j_username and j_password. The container must implement the action to establish the user's identity and the roles. The login form submitted for invoking the security check action is part of the web application. This allows it to be given any desired branding. Servers should allow the login form to be submitted using HTTPS, to ensure that user credentials are not compromised in transport.

The container will force the user to authenticate by submitting the login form only when required (for example, when an unauthenticated user tries to access a protected resource). This is termed **lazy authentication**, and means that users who never attempt to access protected resources will never be forced to authenticate. Once authenticated, a user will not be challenged again within a session. The user identity will be carried through to calls to other components of the application. Thus there is no need for user code behind protected resources to check that authentication has occurred. It's also possible to change the set of resources that are protected – perhaps to reflect changing business rules – without modifying the underlying code.

The choice between basic and form authentication is made declaratively in the web application's deployment descriptor. There is no need to modify application code.

There is presently no similar standard approach to authenticating users of application clients (non-web remote GUIs using EJBs).

> **Both declarative and programmatic authorization techniques are simple to use. However, the declarative model is preferable, as it simplifies the programming model and enhances deployment flexibility.**

The Server Implementation

Although it defines how a J2EE server should challenge users to enter their credentials and how it must propagate security identities with calls within an application, J2EE does not mandate how a server should implement authentication. For example, if a user presents a username and password to a web application when challenged as a result of requesting a restricted URL, how should the container determine whether the credentials are valid, and what roles the user is in? J2EE does not specify how user information should be stored, and how it should be checked.

There is also no standard API to make a user authenticated without submitting the application's login form – a problematic omission. We might need this functionality, for example, when we create a new user account. Obviously we don't want to make the user login using the username and password they just provided. We need to resort to proprietary server extensions to achieve this.

Authentication has traditionally been server-specific. Typically, each server will define a security management interface that must be implemented to perform custom authentication against a database, directory server or other store of user information. For example, WebLogic uses pluggable security realms that implement the `weblogic.security.acl.BasicRealm` interface.

It's important to ensure that custom security managers are efficient. The container may call them frequently to check user permissions; even after a user session has been established (WebLogic provides a caching realm to reduce the workload of any underlying security manager).

Unfortunately, custom security managers will not normally have access to components within user applications such as entity beans or JDOs exposing user data. This is because security checks are likely to be made at a server-wide level, rather than an application level (although this varies between application servers). So there is a potential problem of duplication of data access logic, and possibly the update of the underlying data store by the user manager and application components.

Refer carefully to your application server's documentation when addressing authentication requirements.

A potential standard alternative interface for checking supplied credentials is **Java Authentication and Authorization API (JAAS)**, defined in the `javax.security.auth` package and sub-packages. JAAS provides for pluggable authentication and authorization implementation. How easy it is to integrate with a J2EE server varies between servers. Please refer to the following resources for further information about JAAS:

- ❑ http://www.pramati.com/docstore/1270002/
  Documentation from Pramati on integrating JAAS with a J2EE server.

- ❑ http://www.theserverside.com/resources/article.jsp?l=JAAS
  Article on integrating JAAS authentication with Struts or any other MVC web framework, which also contains many useful references.

- ❑ http://java.sun.com/products/jaas/
  The JAAS home page.

- ❑ Security documentation with your application server.

The catch to using the standard J2EE security infrastructure is that it will probably
be necessary to write custom code to check user credentials and establish user
permissions. However, similar code would be necessary as part of any homegrown
security system. Application servers provide documented interfaces for user
management. These interfaces can be implemented for each application server an
application is deployed on without affecting the application codebase, ensuring that
the design remains portable. Application servers may also provide support (such as
abstract superclasses for implementing custom user managers).

JAAS provides a newer, standard alternative for authentication, although custom
configuration will still be required. Please refer to documentation with your server on
how JAAS may be integrated with it.

Deciding When to Use XML

XML is a core J2EE technology. Due to its use for the standard J2EE deployment descriptors
(`application.xml`, `web.xml` and `ejb-jar.xml`) and the proprietary deployment descriptors
required by most servers, it's impossible for J2EE developers to avoid using XML. XML technologies
can also be used by choice to provide a valuable complement to Java-based J2EE technologies. One of
the important enhancements in J2EE 1.3 is that it guarantees that the JAXP 1.1 API is available to J2EE
applications (JAXP makes a further move into the core Java libraries in J2SE 1.4). JAXP provides
standard support for XML parsing and XSL transformations in J2EE applications.

J2EE applications may need to generate and parse XML documents to achieve interoperability with
non-J2EE platforms. (However, web services style interoperability can largely conceal the use of XML
under the hood; XML may also be used to support client devices and user agents.)

Using XSLT in J2EE Applications

Another strong reason to use XML technologies, which applies even *within* J2EE applications, is to
enable the use of XSLT to transform XML data into a wide variety of output formats. This is most
valuable in web applications when generating HTML, XHTML or WML, which means that XSLT may
be an alternative to web tier view technologies such as JSP.

XSLT guru Michael Kay (author of the excellent *XSLT Programmer's Reference*, Wrox Press) writes that
"When I first saw the XSL transformation language, XSLT, I realized that this was going to be the SQL
of the web, the high-level data manipulation language that would turn XML from being merely a
storage and transmission format for data into an active information source that could be queried and
manipulated in a flexible, declarative way".

If data is held in the form of XML documents, or can easily be converted to an XML representation,
XSLT provides powerful functionality that is superior to Java-based technologies such as JSP in the
following areas:

❑ Transforming tree-structured data. XSLT provides powerful functionality for navigating and
selecting tree nodes, using XPath expressions.

❑ Sorting and filtering data elements.

- ❑ XML and XSLT skills are not Java specific. For example, many Microsoft technology projects use XSLT for the presentation tier and use XSLT specialists. This may mean that we can call on valuable domain-specific, rather than J2EE-specific, skills.

- ❑ The XML/XSLT paradigm cleanly separates data model (XML document) from presentation (XSLT stylesheet). We can achieve this using JSP, but there's a greater temptation to ignore the need for such separation.

However, XSLT is weaker than Java-based technologies such as JSP in the following areas:

- ❑ XSLT is integrated with J2EE at API, rather than specification, level. Using XML and XSLT requires some custom coding, and may require the use of third party libraries or frameworks.

- ❑ Performance. XSLT transforms are usually significantly slower than rendering output using JSP, especially if the data first has to be converted from Java objects to XML documents. However, this performance overhead may not matter in many applications and may be outweighed by other positives of using XML and XSLT.

- ❑ String manipulation. XSLT isn't a true programming language, and string manipulation using it is awkward and unintuitive.

- ❑ Tool support. XSLT is very powerful but harder to edit without tools than JSP. XSLT tools are still relatively disappointing. When strong XSLT skills are available, this may not matter. However, a JSP solution may be simpler for many organizations to implement.

"Deep" Use of XML

To use XSLT, we need XML documents to transform. These don't need to exist as strings or on the file system: they can exist as W3C `org.w3c.dom.Node` objects before transformation.

There is no problem when data naturally exists as XML: for example, if it comes from an XML database, XML content management system or external system that the J2EE application communicates with using XML. While XML databases are not commonly used, the last two of these scenarios are often seen in practice.

However, if the data doesn't already exist as XML, but we wish to use XSLT for presentation, we need to decide at what point in our J2EE architecture we will convert data to XML form. We must choose between "deep" use of XML (where data is passed around the application in the form of XML rather than Java objects) and superficial use of XML (in which case XML documents are created only at the boundary of the system; for example immediately before performing an XSLT transform).

J2EE and XML Development from *Manning (ISBN 1-930110-30-8)* advocates "deep" use of XML. In this approach, XML documents replace Java value objects within the J2EE system, making it easy to use XSLT at the boundaries.

Often this data will come from an RDBMS, so we can try to convert query results to XML form. Ronald Bourret maintains an excellent site on this issue at http://www.rpbourret.com/xml/XMLDBLinks.htm. Bourret has also published an article on the subject, at http://www.xml.com/pub/a/2001/05/09/dtdtodbs.html?page=1, which is a useful starting point.

There's a choice between doing the mapping work in Java code, inside the J2EE server, and performing it in the database. RDBMS vendors are rushing to provide XML support, and some relational databases, such as Oracle 9i, even allow us to store XML directly in the database. We may also be able to obtain query results in XML. Such approaches aren't portable, as no relevant standards exist yet.

Unfortunately, wherever we do the conversion, it will be a non-trivial task. In the next few chapters we'll discuss the "impedance mismatch" between RDBMS schema and Java object model. There is a comparable impedance mismatch between RDBMS schema and XML document, and a similar degree of complexity in trying to bridge it. The trivial examples of RDBMS result set to XML mappings shown in books such as *J2EE and XML Development* are insufficient for real applications: queries can become extremely complex (and expensive to run) if we try to build a deep XML hierarchy from one or more relational queries.

The relational model for data is not hierarchical, and it's difficult to build hierarchies using it. We can run multiple RDBMS queries to produce separate shallow XML documents, hoping to use XSLT to "join" the data on the client-side (XSLT allows nodes to be looked up – in the same or in another document – by ID in an approach analogous to an RDMBS JOIN). However, this is relatively complex to implement in XSLT, and ignores the capabilities of the RDBMS itself. It's only appropriate where a small amount of reference data is concerned. For example, it might be a valid approach where a table of countries is concerned, but inappropriate where a table of invoices is concerned.

The difficulty in extracting relational data directly into XML documents is just one of several major problems with "deep" use of XML, which I believe should preclude its use in general:

- ❑ We shouldn't modify overall application architecture to support a particular view strategy. What if we need to present data in a format that XSLT won't help us to generate? For example, XSLT is poor at generating binary formats.

- ❑ If the application is distributed and uses EJBs with remote interfaces, passing XML documents from the EJB tier to EJB clients may be slower than passing Java objects, and we may run into serialization difficulties. W3C Node objects are not necessarily serializable; this depends on the implementation.

- ❑ Java components inside the application will find it harder to work with XML documents than with Java objects. One exception is the case of tree-structured data, for which the XPath API may be used effectively. Working with XML APIs is far more cumbersome than working with Java objects.

- ❑ XML does not support object-oriented principles such as encapsulation, polymorphism and inheritance. We lose even Java's strong typing – wholly, in the case of XML with DTDs, and partially, if we use the more complex XML Schema.

- ❑ Working with XML is likely to prove much slower than working with Java objects. Applications that make "deep" use of XML are often slow and may waste server resources in XML and string processing.

- ❑ Applications are likely to be harder to test. It's easier to test Java objects returned by an application than XML documents.

> I don't advocate "deep" use of XML within J2EE applications. While superficially attractive applications – especially if we wish to use XSLT for presentation – built on internal communication using XSLT are likely to be slower, harder to understand, maintain, and test than applications based on Java objects and sound OO design principles.

Converting Between JavaBeans and XML

When we need to convert data to XML, it's usually a better idea to do so closer to the boundary of the system. If we do so in the web tier itself, immediately before the XSL transform, we can achieve interchangeability of view technology, allowing us to choose between using XSLT and JSP and other solutions, without modifying the entire architecture (we'll talk about how to achieve this important design goal in Chapters 12 and 13).

In J2EE applications, data normally exists as JavaBeans before rendering to a client such as a web browser. If we use Java-based technologies such as JSP, we can work with JavaBeans directly. If we need to expose data using XML (for example, to transform it using XSLT) we need to convert the JavaBeans to an XML representation. Fortunately, there is a fairly natural mapping from JavaBeans to XML documents, making this a far less complex problem than converting relational data to XML.

There are several approaches to generating XML from a graph of Java objects:

- ❑ **Code a `toElement()` method in each class that we'll want to represent as XML**
  This obvious but naïve approach has severe disadvantages. It adds complexity, and the need to understand XML, to every class in an object graph. It hard-codes the XML document structure and element and attribute names into each class. What if we need to generate a slightly different type of document? What if we're really interested in generating XML from an interface which has multiple implementations that don't share a superclass?

- ❑ **Use the GoF Visitor design pattern to facilitate XML generation**
  In this approach, each class in an object graph implements a `Visitable` interface. An XML visitor is responsible for traversing the graph and generating an XML document. This is a much superior approach to hard-coding element generation in application objects. The XML knowledge is concentrated in the visitor implementation. It's easy to generate different types of XML document. It works well with interfaces. Making each class in the graph implement the `Visitable` interface may prove useful for other tasks; the Visitor design pattern is very powerful.

- ❑ **Write a custom XML generator that knows about a particular object graph and can generate XML for it**
  This is similar to the Visitor approach, but less general. It also has the advantage of localizing XML generation code in one or more specialized classes, rather than littering it through the application's object model.

- ❑ **Generate XML nodes from Java objects using reflection, without requiring application-specific XML generation code**
  This approach uses generic XML generation infrastructure to generate XML from application objects, which need not know anything about XML. XML generation may either occur as the result of a complete traversal of the object graph, or objects may be converted to nodes on the fly, when required by XPath expressions. This approach will require a third-party library. It will be slightly slower than using custom XML generation, but the performance overhead will usually be less than that of transforming the generated XML. I'll refer to this approach as **domification**: the generation of XML DOM nodes from Java objects.

The second and fourth approaches are usually best. I've used the last three approaches successfully in several projects. The fourth approach – "domification" using reflection – is most attractive, as it minimizes the amount and complexity of code written by application developers. While the use of reflection will incur a small performance overhead, it will probably be smaller than the overhead of transforming the XML.

One major benefit of the use of reflection is that it will ensure that XML-generation code is always up to date; there will be no need to modify bloated XML-generation classes when objects change. We won't need to write verbose XML-generation code either; the domification library will hide the details of XML document creation. If domification is done on the fly, only the object properties actually needed by a stylesheet will be invoked at runtime, meaning that some of the overhead can be avoided.

There are a few things we need to consider before relying on domification:

❑ Although different libraries have different capabilities, the objects exposed will probably need to be JavaBeans. Bean property getters don't require arguments; ordinary methods often do, and therefore can't be invoked automatically. Although JSP and template languages such as WebMacro (http://www.webmacro.org) provide means of calling methods as well as getting bean property values, most presentation technologies work best when exposing JavaBeans. As it's good design practice (encouraged in the JSP specification) to make models JavaBeans, this shouldn't be a major problem.

❑ We may need to customize XML generation for some types, although we can rely on the domification library to handle primitive types. A sophisticated domification library could allow pluggable handling for individual object types.

❑ Cyclic references may pose a problem. These are legal in Java object graphs, but don't make sense in XML trees.

❑ Unexpected errors may result if any bean property getters throw exceptions. It's unlikely that a domification library will be able to handle such errors usefully. As all data retrieval should be complete before models are passed to views, this shouldn't be a problem.

There are several published libraries for converting Java objects to XML. My favorite is the **Domify** open source project (http://domify.sourceforge.net/). Domify was originally part of the Maverick MVC web framework but was split into a separate project in December 2001. It's a tiny library (only eight classes) and is very easy to use. Other, more sophisticated, but more complex, products include Castor (http://castor.exolab.org/xml-framework.html), which "can marshal almost any 'bean-like' Java Object to and from XML". See http://www.rpbourret.com/xml/XMLDataBinding.htm for a directory of several XML-Java conversion products.

Domify uses the on-the-fly approach to XML node creation, with lazy loading. Nodes in the logical DOM tree that are never accessed, by XSLT or other user code are never created. Once created, nodes are cached, so subsequent accesses will be faster.

To use Domify, it's first necessary to create an object of class `org.infohazard.domify.DOMAdapter`. Once a `DOMAdapter` has been created, its `adapt(Object, String)` method can be used to domify objects. A `DOMAdapter` object is thread-safe, hence can be used repeatedly (however, `DOMAdapter` objects are cheap to instantiate so there's no problem in creating many objects). The entire process looks like this:

```
DOMAdapter domAdapter = new DOMAdapter();
Node node = domAdapter.adapt(javaBean, "nameOfRootElement");
```

The `adapt()` method throws an unchecked exception if the transformation fails: most likely, because an invoked getter method threw an exception. As this is not recoverable, and should not happen when traversing a web tier model, this is a reasonable approach (as discussed in Chapter 4).

Domify doesn't check for cyclic references, so we must ensure that beans to be domified don't have any (again, this is not usually a problem with Java bean models in web applications).

To illustrate how Domify works, let's take a simple bean and look at the XML document Domify generates from it. The following simple bean has four properties, of `String`, `int`, `Collection`, and `Map` type respectively, which are highlighted in the listing below, along with methods allowing data to be added:

```
public class Person {
  private int age;
  private String name;
  private List hobbies = new LinkedList();
  private Map family = new HashMap();

  public Person(String name, int age) {
    this.age = age;
    this.name = name;
  }

  public void addHobby(String name) {
    hobbies.add(name);
  }

  public void addFamilyMember(String relation, String name) {
    family.put(relation, name);
  }

  public int getAge() {
    return age;
  }
  public String getName() {
    return name;
  }
  public Collection getHobbies() {
    return hobbies;
  }
  public Map getFamily() {
    return family;
  }
}
```

I've omitted the no-arg constructor and property setters for brevity. Let's construct a simple bean:

```
Person p = new Person("Kerry", 35);
p.addHobby("skiing");
p.addHobby("cycling");
p.addFamilyMember("husband", "Rod");
p.addFamilyMember("son", "Tristan");
```

Domify will automatically expose the four bean properties. Each node is created only on demand, and cached thereafter in case it is required again in the same XML operation. The following illustrates the complete XML document. Note the treatment of the `Collection` and `Map` properties (highlighted):

```
<?xml version="1.0" encoding="UTF-8"?>
<person>
  <name>Kerry</name>
  <age>35</age>
  <hobbies>
    <item type="java.lang.String">skiing</item>
    <item type="java.lang.String">cycling</item>
  </hobbies>
  <family>
    <item key="son" type="java.lang.String">Tristan</item>
    <item key="husband" type="java.lang.String">Rod</item>
  </family>
</person>
```

It's easy to write an XSLT stylesheet to format this data as desired. This approach is very simple, yet powerful. The Maverick MVC web application framework demonstrates its effectiveness.

Converting in the opposite direction – from XML representation to JavaBean – is also relatively straightforward, and is a widely used approach for getting application configuration out of Java code.

Many applications and frameworks use XML documents to provide long-term persistence for JavaBeans, such as JBoss's `jboss.jcml` XML configuration file, which uses XML to configure JMX MBeans. Each bean property is usually represented as an XML element, with an attribute value holding the property name. The generic framework we'll describe in this book and use for our sample application also uses this approach. Most application objects will be JavaBeans, their properties and relationships held outside Java code in XML documents. This is discussed in detail in Chapter 11.

J2SE 1.4 introduces "Long Term JavaBeans Persistence" to standardize such functionality, although it is too early to tell how widely this standardization will be accepted. In Java 1.4, the `java.beans` API is extended to read and write a bean as an XML representation of its property values. As this book is concerned with the J2EE 1.3 platform, which is based on J2SE 1.3, it's assumed that this new API isn't available. However, its introduction indicates the importance of Java beans to XML mapping.

J2EE and XML in the Future

J2EE will become still more closely integrated with XML – even besides web services support. Important forthcoming enhancements include **Java Architecture for XML Binding (JAXB)**, which automates the mapping between Java objects and XML documents by providing tools to generate Java classes from XML DTDs or schemas. The generated classes can efficiently handle XML parsing and formatting, simplifying code that uses them and offering the potential of much better performance than is available with traditional XML parsing or Java-to-XML converters such as Domify. The JAXB homepage is at http://java.sun.com/xml/jaxb/index.html. The JAXB specification is presently in draft, and should be complete by the end of 2002.

> **XML is a core J2EE technology. XSLT is a viable alternative to JSP as a view technology in J2EE applications if it simplifies presentation logic, and when data already exists as XML or can efficiently be converted to XML form.**
>
> **I don't favor "deep" use of XML within a J2EE architecture. XML documents are loosely typed and cumbersome to access and manipulate in J2EE applications.**

XML in the Sample Application

There's no reason to use XML deep within the sample application's architecture. However, it is reasonable to consider the option of using XSLT as a view technology. A key business requirement is the ability to "rebrand" the application by modifying the presentation without revising the workflow. XML and XSLT provides an excellent way of doing this, although we can also achieve it with JSP and other view technologies, so long as we use an MVC approach in the web tier.

We may want to retain the option of using XML and XSLT to generate web content, but have no reason to tie ourselves to using XML. This suggests that we should create our data models as JavaBeans, and use a package such as Domify to convert them to XML documents if needed. The volume of user-specific data to be converted and styled (in reservation objects, for example) is modest, so the performance overhead of this approach should not be a problem. Where reference data (such as performance dates) is concerned, we may want to cache converted documents, as more data is involved and more pages are concerned.

It would be difficult to justify using XML and XSLT in Phase 1 except as a strategic choice, or unless practical considerations suggested it (such as the availability of strong XSLT skills but no JSP skills). JSP, will prove simpler and quicker to generate the screens described in the initial requirements. However, XSLT might well come into its own in the future (for example, it would be well suited to sort reference data in the web tier). In Chapter 13 we will discuss XSLT as a view technology in detail, along with a demonstration of how it could be used in the sample application without changing the application's overall architecture.

Caching to Improve Performance

Data caching is an important architectural issue in many J2EE applications, especially as web applications tend to read data much more often than they update it.

Caching is especially important in distributed applications, as without it the overhead of remote invocation is likely to prove far more of a problem. However, it's valuable even in collocated web applications such as our sample application, especially when we need to access data from persistent stores.

Thus, caching is more than just an optimization; it can be vital to making an architecture work.

Caching can offer quick performance wins and significantly improve throughput by reducing server load. This will benefit the entire application, not just those use cases that use cached data.

However, caching can also lead to complex issues of concurrent code and cluster-wide synchronization. Do not implement caching (especially if such implementation is non-trivial) without evidence that it is required to deliver adequate performance; it's easy to waste development resources and create unwarranted complexity by implementing caching that delivers no real business value.

Caching Options

The sample application requires a moderate amount of heavily-accessed reference data. We will definitely want to cache this data, rather than run new Oracle queries every time any of it is used. Let's consider the caching options available to this type of application, and some common issues surrounding caching.

Caching will deliver greater performance benefit the closer the cache is to the user. We have the following choices in the sample application (moving from the RDBMS, from which data is obtained, towards the client):

❑ **Rely on RDBMS caching**
Databases such as Oracle cache data if configured correctly, and hence can respond to queries for reference data very fast. However, this will not produce the desired performance or reduction in server load. There is still a network hop between the J2EE server and the database; there is still the overhead of talking to the database through a database connection; the application server must allocate a pooled connection and we must go through all layers of our J2EE application.

❑ **Rely on entity bean caching implemented by the J2EE server**
This requires that we use entity beans to implement data access, and that we choose to access reference data through the EJB container. It also caches data relatively far down the application call path: we'll still need to call into the EJB server (which involves overhead, even if we don't use RMI) to bring the cached data back to the web tier. Furthermore, the effectiveness of entity bean caching will vary between J2EE servers. Most implement some kind of "read-only" entity support, but this is not guaranteed by the EJB specification.

❑ **Use another O/R mapping solution such as JDO, that can cache read-only data**
This doesn't tie us to data access in the EJB tier and offers a simpler programming model than entity beans. However, it's only an option if we choose to adopt an O/R mapping approach to data access.

❑ **Cache data in the form of Java objects in the web tier**
This is a high-performance option, as it enables requests to be satisfied without calling far down the J2EE stack. However, it requires more implementation work than the strategies already discussed. The biggest challenge is the need to accommodate concurrent access if the data is ever invalidated and updated. Presently there is no standard Java or J2EE infrastructure to help in cache implementation, although we can use packages such as Doug Lea's util.concurrent that simplify the concurrency issues involved. JSR 107 (JCache – Java Temporary Caching API) may deliver standard support in this area (see http://www.jcp.org/jsr/detail/107.jsp).

❑ **Use JSP caching tags**
We could use a JSP tag library that offers caching tags that we can use to cache fragments of JSP pages. Several such libraries are freely available; we'll discuss some of them in Chapter 13. This is a high-performance option, as many requests will be able to be satisfied with a minimum of activity within the J2EE server. However, this approach presupposes that we present data using JSP. If we rely on the use of caching tags for acceptable performance, we're predicating the viability of our architecture on one view technology, subverting our MVC approach.

❑ **Use a caching filter**
Another high performance option is to use a caching Servlet 2.3 filter to intercept requests before they even reach the application's web tier components. Again, there are a variety of free implementations to choose from. If a whole page is known to consist of reference data, the filter can return a cached version. (This approach could be used for the first two screens of the sample application – the most heavily accessed – which can be cached for varying periods of time). Filter-based caching offers less finely grained caching than JSP tags; we can only cache whole pages, unless we restructure our application's view layer to enable a filter to compose responses from multiple cached components. If even a small part of the page is truly dynamic, filtering isn't usually viable.

❏ **Use HTTP headers to minimize requests to unaltered pages**
We can't rely solely on this approach, as we can't control the configuration of proxy caches and browser caches. However, it can significantly reduce load on web applications and we should combine it with those of the above approaches we choose.

JSP tags and caching filters have the disadvantage that caching will benefit only a web interface. Both these types of caches don't "understand" the data they cache, only that they may hold the information necessary to respond to an incoming request for content. This won't be a problem for the sample application's initial requirements, as no other interfaces are called for. However, another caching strategy, such as cached Java objects in the web tier, might be required if we need to expose a web services interface. On the positive side, "front caching" doesn't care about the origin of data it caches, and will benefit all view technologies. It doesn't matter whether data was generated using XML/XSLT, Velocity, or JSP, for example. It will also work for binary data such as images and PDF.

Whatever caching strategy we use, it's important that we can disable caching to verify that we aren't covering up appalling inefficiency. Architectures that rely on caching to conceal severe bottlenecks are likely to encounter other problems.

A Caching Strategy for the Sample Application

To implement a successful caching strategy in our sample application, we need to distinguish between reference data (which doesn't change, or changes rarely) and dynamic data, which must always be up-to-date. In this application, reference data, which changes rarely, but should be no more than one minute out of date, includes:

❏ Genres.

❏ Shows.

❏ Performance dates.

❏ Information about the types of seats, their name and price for each show.

❏ The seating plan for each performance: which seats are adjacent, how many seats there are in total, etc.

The most heavily requested dynamic data will be the availability of seating for each type of seat for each performance of a show. This is displayed on the "Display Show" screen. The business requirements mandate that this availability information can be no more than one minute out of date, meaning that we can only cache it briefly. However, if we don't cache it at all, the display show screen will require many database queries, leading to heavy load on the system and poor performance. Thus we need to implement a cache that is capable of accommodating relatively frequent updates.

We *could* handle caching entirely by using "front caching". The "Welcome" and "Display Show" screens could be protected by a caching filter set to a one minute timeout. This approach is simple to implement (we don't need to write any code) and would work whatever view strategy (such as JSP or XSLT) we use. However, it has serious drawbacks:

❏ While the requirements state that data should be no more than one minute out of date, there is business value in ensuring that it is more up to date if possible. If we use a filter approach, we can't do this; all data will need to be updated at once regardless of what has changed. If we use a finer-grained caching strategy, we may be able to ensure that if we do hold more recent data as part of this page (for example, if a booking attempt reveals that a performance is sold out) this information appears immediately on the display show screen.

❏ A web services interface is a real possibility in the future. A filter approach won't benefit it.

These problems can be addressed by implementing caching in Java objects in the web tier.

There are two more issues to consider before finalizing a decision: updates from other applications and behavior in a cluster. We know from the requirements that no other processes can modify the database (The one exception is when an administrator updates the database directly; we can provide a special internal URL that administrators must request to invalidate application caches after making such a change). Thus, we can assume that unless our application creates a booking, any availability data it holds is valid. Thus, if we are running the application on a single server and caching data in Java objects, we *never* need to requery cached data: we merely need to refresh the cached data for a performance when a booking is made.

If the application runs in a cluster, this optimization is impossible, unless the cache is cluster-wide; the server that made the booking will immediately reflect the change, but other servers will not see it until their cached data times out. We considered the idea of sending a JMS message that will be processed by all servers when a booking is made, getting round this problem. However, we decided that caching with a timeout offered sufficiently good performance that the overhead of JMS message publication was hard to justify.

Such data synchronization issues in a cluster of servers are a common problem (they apply to many data access technologies, such as entity beans and JDO). Ideally we should try to design our sample application so that it can achieve optimum performance on a single server (there is no requirement that it ever will run in a cluster if it's fast enough) yet be configurable to work correctly in a cluster. Thus we should support both "never requery" and "requery on timeout" options, and allow them to be specified on deployment, without the need to modify Java code. As the one minute timeout value may change, we should also parameterize this.

Summary

Let's finish by reviewing some of the key issues we've covered in this chapter and the decisions we've taken for our sample application.

We've decided that there's no justification for making the application distributed. The requirements are purely for a web application, so we don't need to enable remote access via RMI. If this application ever needed to support remote access, it would be much more likely to involve XML-based web services. A collocated web application architecture can provide excellent web services support, so this would prove no problem to add. Enabling web tier components and EJBs to be run on separate servers wouldn't make the application more robust, as it depends on web tier state. However, it would make things a lot more complicated.

Since the booking process is transactional, we've decided to use EJB to implement it. As we don't want a distributed model, we'll be using EJBs with local interfaces, meaning that we don't need to worry about the performance overhead of remote calling, or the requirement for coarse-grained EJB interfaces.

Using local interfaces means that we don't need to put all business logic (or necessarily all data access) inside the EJB container. Due to the complexity of working with EJB, we won't be using EJB unless it delivers clear value; hence, we won't be using EJB for the non-transactional parts of the application. This enables us to avoid problems with EJB programming restrictions (for example, relating to singleton functionality).

Choosing not to implement business logic inside the EJB container doesn't mean that we tie business logic intimately to the web interface. Web interfaces change, and it's important to retain a distinct layer of business interfaces that we could expose as web services. These will be ordinary Java interfaces, implemented in either the web tier or by EJBs accessed locally.

None of the application's functionality is asynchronous, so we will use JMS in Phase 1 of this project only to publish reference data update events, enabling caches holding genre, show and performance data to requery the database only when a change is known to have occurred. The Observer design pattern would provide a simple solution were the application to run on only a single server. However, using JMS will ensure that the application will continue to behave correctly if it is ever deployed in a cluster of servers.

There is no reason to use XML in the application's internals (for example, to hold data from database queries and pass it around the application until it can be displayed by XSLT). However, XSLT may be a valid choice as a web tier view technology.

This is the second architecture (*Web application accessing local EJBs*) of the four we discussed in Chapter 1.

Data Access in J2EE Applications

Data access is vital to enterprise applications. Often the performance of the data source and the strategies used to access it will dictate the performance and scalability of a J2EE application. One of the key tasks of a J2EE architect is to achieve a clean and efficient interface between J2EE business objects and data source.

As we shall see, it's important to decouple business logic components from the details of data access. The EJB specification provides entity beans to achieve the necessary abstraction. However, the entity bean model isn't always appropriate, and there are other techniques we can use to achieve this objective without committing to it.

This chapter takes a high-level view of the practical data modeling and data access choices facing J2EE architects and developers, paying special attention to the common problem of **Object-Relational (O/R)** mapping when using a relational database. It concludes by developing a data access strategy for our sample application.

In the following two chapters, we'll look more closely at specific data access strategies. These strategies are the subject of religious debate among J2EE developers. We'll take a pragmatic approach, looking at how best to achieve results in real applications.

> **A disclaimer – I can't tell you everything you need to know about data access in J2EE applications. This requires expert knowledge of the underlying data sources you work with. For example, is the aim efficient and reliable access to an ODBMS or an RDBMS? Access to Oracle, DB2, or Sybase? There is no satisfactory "one size fits all" solution unless data access requirements are trivial.**

By the end of this chapter you should be convinced that J2EE developers need a strong understanding of database technology, and should be prepared to seek specialist advice when necessary.

Data Access Goals

I assume the following goals for data access:

- ❑ It should be efficient.

- ❑ It should ensure data integrity.

- ❑ It should ensure correct behavior on concurrent attempts to access and manipulate the same data. This usually means preventing concurrent updates from compromising data integrity, while minimizing the impact of the necessary locking on application throughput.

- ❑ Data access strategy shouldn't determine how we implement business logic. Business logic should be implemented in object-oriented Java code running in the J2EE server, however we choose to access data.

- ❑ It should be possible to change an application's persistence strategy without rewriting its business logic, in the same way as we should be able to change an application's user interface without affecting business logic. Usually, this means using an abstraction layer such as ordinary Java interfaces or entity EJBs between business objects and persistent store.

- ❑ Data access code should be maintainable. Without due care, data access can account for much of an application's complexity. In this chapter and the following two chapters, we'll look at strategies for minimizing complexity in data access, including using O/R mapping frameworks, using an abstraction library to simplify the use of JDBC and concealing some data access operations inside the target database.

Business Logic and Persistence Logic

The second and third of the above goals imply a distinction between business logic and data access, which it is important to clarify.

Business logic is concerned with the application's core workflow. It's independent of the application's user interface, and where persistent data is stored.

In contrast to business logic, **persistence logic** concerns the application's access to and manipulation of persistent data. Persistence logic normally has the following characteristics:

- ❑ It doesn't require the application of business rules. As in the above example, persistence logic handles the details of a task that has already been decided on. If deleting a user involved cascading deletes only under certain circumstances, a business logic component would be used to make the decision and request operations as necessary.

- ❑ It is unlikely to change on updates to business rules.

- ❑ It doesn't need to handle security issues.

- ❑ It may involve preserving data integrity.

- ❑ It requires knowledge of the target persistence store to implement (although not to define) operations.

> Persistence logic is not only distinct from business logic; it's a good idea to remove it entirely from business logic components. The business rules captured in Java business objects will be much more clearly expressed and easier to maintain if the nuts and bolts of persistence management are moved into helper classes.

While business logic should be handled by Java objects – often, but not necessarily, session EJBs – there are many choices for implementing persistence logic in a J2EE application. Important choices that we'll consider in this chapter and the next two chapters include:

- ❏ JDBC and SQL (for accessing relational databases)
- ❏ Entity beans
- ❏ Java Data Objects (JDO)
- ❏ Third-party persistence frameworks such as TopLink
- ❏ Stored procedures, which can sometimes be used appropriately to move persistence logic inside a database

Object-Driven and Database-Driven Modeling: A Philosophical Debate

Whether to use a relational database (RDBMS) or an object database (ODBMS) for a project is beyond the scope of this book. The following discussion is oriented more towards relational databases, as these are used by most real J2EE systems.

There are two basic approaches to data modeling in J2EE applications:

- ❏ **Object-driven modeling, in which data modeling is driven from an object layer (often a layer of entity beans) reflecting the J2EE application's concept of persistent domain objects**
  An example is using a modeling tool such as Rational Rose to generate entity beans from a UML model and to generate RDBMS tables from these entity beans. Several application servers, including Orion and WebLogic, offer the option of creating database tables themselves from a set of entity beans.

- ❏ **Database-driven modeling, in which data modeling is driven from the database schema**
  In this approach, a database schema is created that efficiently represents the data to be persisted, based on the characteristics of the target database. The design of this schema will be largely independent of the fact that a J2EE application will work with it. For example, a relational schema will structure data based on relational concepts such as normalization. An example is designing an RDBMS schema appropriate to the data to be persisted (possibly using a data modeling tool such as Erwin), and then writing Java code to access and update it.

These two approaches may produce very different results.

Object-driven modeling is seductive ("We know objects are good, so let's use them everywhere"), and is usually advocated by books on EJB. Its advantages include:

❑ Greater potential for automation: We'll probably be able to use a modeling tool to generate Java code, rather than code data access objects manually. We'll also be freed from the requirement to write SQL or use other database-specific technologies in application code. The use of automation can deliver significant productivity gains in development.

❑ Greater portability: As an abstraction layer is necessary between object model and database, it should be possible to target the application to different databases without changing the object model.

When working with an ODBMS, object-driven modeling will occur naturally. When working with relational databases, on the other hand, the arguments for database-driven modeling are compelling:

❑ Object-driven modeling often isn't an option. The database may already be established.

❑ The database may prove more durable than the object model. One of the key assumptions of J2EE is that presentation changes more often than the data structures behind it. This is an argument for achieving an efficient database representation, rather than one that serves the needs of a particular J2EE application.

❑ Object-driven modeling usually means rejecting many of the capabilities of the database, such as stored procedures and the potential for efficient custom queries. A large company may have paid a lot of money for an RDBMS with highly sophisticated functionality. Relational databases are proven in practice unlike entity beans

❑ Object-driven modeling reduces architectural flexibility. It closely couples Java code and RDBMS schema. This schema can probably be created in a different database if the application is ported, but what if there are other business reasons to modify the database schema (a likelier scenario in practice)?

❑ Database-driven modeling will usually deliver better performance. This is often a decisive issue. In the rest of this chapter we'll see a number of areas in which object-driven modeling makes it difficult to achieve satisfactory performance when accessing an RDBMS.

❑ Portability between databases may not be the advantage it seems, and may not even be achievable in practice. We'll discuss this issue further below.

❑ Communication may be impaired within a term. Object-driven modeling disregards the input of experts in the underlying database technology. A good DBA has valuable experience in developing enterprise applications. DBAs will need to maintain and tune the system in production.

❑ By creating a database in the idiom natural to the database product, rather than to your object model, you are more likely to be able to leverage existing reporting tools. For example, Oracle Forms or Microsoft Access might be used to minimize the amount of work involved in implementing a simple in-house administration and reporting system.

J2EE experts disagree on whether to favor object-driven or database-driven modeling. For example, Richard Monson-Haefel, author of several books on EJB and J2EE, strongly favors database-driven modeling (http://java.oreilly.com/news/ejbtips_0500.html), while Ed Roman (author of *Mastering Enterprise JavaBeans* from *Wiley (ISBN: 0-471-41711-4)* recommends using the EJB object model to drive the data model.

> I recommend database-driven modeling. Object-driven modeling is seductive, but has real dangers. Its fundamental problem is that it ignores the facts that relational databases are (a) very complex applications; and (b) proven to work very well. It's naïve and arrogant (a dangerous combination!) to assume that J2EE, in a few years of evolution, has delivered a superior solution to decades of database theory and practice.

I find it helpful to think of J2EE as playing the role of the conductor of an orchestra with respect to the other component technologies of an enterprise system. Without the conductor to lead it, the orchestra exists only as a group of individuals and cannot function usefully, but this doesn't mean that the conductor attempts to play individual instruments.

Database-driven modeling may require us to write more Java code, although there will probably be much less code in total. However, it gives us greater control of both data and J2EE implementation. It leaves more scope to tackle any performance problems. Done well, it does not reduce portability.

O/R Mapping and the "Impedance Mismatch"

The fact that most J2EE applications access data from relational databases has both positive and negative implications for J2EE architects and developers.

On the positive side, RDBMS have over twenty years of experience behind them, and the best are proven to work very well. On the negative side, mapping between an object model and an RDBMS schema is difficult. Much effort has been put into **Object-Relational (O/R)** mapping in Java and other OO languages, with mixed results.

> O/R mapping is the attempt to map the state of Java objects onto data in an RDBMS, providing transparent persistence.

The relational database and object-oriented models of the world differ markedly. Relational databases are based on mathematical concepts for storing and retrieving data. The goal of relational database design is to **normalize** data (eliminate data redundancy). The goal of OO design is to model a business process by breaking it into objects with identity, state, and behavior. Relational databases do not support object concepts such as classes, inheritance, encapsulation or polymorphism. A modern RDBMS is not merely a bucket of data, but can also hold rules guaranteeing data integrity and operations acting on data. However, this does not amount to the OO inclusion of behavior as part of object definition.

The challenges these different models pose for O/R mapping are often collectively termed the **Object-Relational impedance mismatch**. Some of the key problems are:

❑ How do we convert between column values in a SQL query result and Java objects?

❑ How do we efficiently issue SQL updates when the state of mapped Java objects changes?

❑ How do we model object relationships?

❑ How do we model inheritance in Java objects mapped to the database?

❑ How do we model Java objects whose data spans multiple tables in the RDBMS?

❑   What caching strategies should we use in the object layer to try to reduce the number of calls to the RDBMS?

❑   How do we perform aggregate functions?

Few solutions meet all – or even most – of these challenges. O/R mapping solutions typically map each object onto a single row of data, usually in one table, but occasionally resulting from a join. (It may be possible to use a view to simplify the mapping if the RDBMS supports updateable views. Typically, O/R mapping solutions allow this mapping to be done without custom coding, hiding the low-level data access from the programmer. The mapping is normally held in metadata outside the mapped classes.

O/R mapping works very well in some situations, but is probably oversold. The assumption that O/R mapping is the solution for all J2EE applications that access relational databases goes largely unchallenged. I believe that this assumption is questionable. O/R mapping has drawbacks as well as advantages, which mean that we should think carefully before using it.

The central value propositions of O/R mapping are that it removes the need for developers to write low-level data access code (which can deliver large productivity gains in some applications); ensures that application code deals exclusively with objects; and can lead to the creation of a **domain object model** that can support multiple use cases.

However, there is a risk that O/R mapping doesn't so much reduce total complexity as move it elsewhere. The result may be complex deployment descriptors, such as those necessary for entity bean CMP, and the price for transparent data access is reduced control over that access.

Efficiency is also questionable. O/R mapping solutions typically assume that RDBMSs are intended to operate on individual rows and columns. This is a fallacy: RDBMSs operate best on sets of tuples. For example, we can update many rows in a single SQL operation much faster than each row individually. O/R mapping solutions deliver excellent performance if it's feasible to cache data in the object layer; if this is impossible or when aggregate updates are required, O/R mapping usually adds significant overhead.

Really sophisticated O/R mapping solutions allow us to enjoy O/R mapping benefits without some of these drawbacks.

> **Don't assume that O/R mapping is the best solution to all data access problems. It works very well in some situations; but sometimes adds little value.**

The following are indications that an O/R mapping solution is not fulfilling a useful role:

❑   In the case of object-driven modeling, it results in an unnatural RDBMS schema, which limits performance and is useless to other processes. Indications of an unnatural RDBMS schema include the need for complex joins in common data retrieval operations; inability of the RDBMS to enforce referential integrity; and the need to issue many individual updates where a better schema could have permitted efficient use of an aggregate operation.

❑   In the case of data-driven modeling, it produces a layer of objects with a one-to-one relationship to the tables in the RDBMS. Unless the tables were produced from the object model, these are probably not true objects, and working with them is likely to prove unnatural and inefficient. Should the schema ever change, all the code that works with those objects will also need to change?

❑   It results in inefficient queries or updates. (It's a good idea to examine the queries running in the database as a result of using any O/R mapping layer.)

❑   Some tasks that could be performed easily and efficiently inside the database using relational operations may require substantial Java coding to accomplish in the J2EE server, or may lead to the unnecessary creation of many Java objects.

In such cases, there are legitimate alternatives to O/R mapping, as we'll see.

O/R mapping solutions are often a good choice in OLTP (On-Line Transaction Processing) systems, in which users typically perform operations on a small dataset, and which are often based on simple queries. However, they are seldom a good choice where there are OLAP (On-Line Analytic Processing) or data warehousing requirements. OLAP involves the manipulation of very large data sets and the execution of complex queries. These are best handled using relational operations.

The Data Access Object (DAO) Pattern

It's possible to be less ambitious in accessing an RDBMS, and not attempt to map objects directly onto data – or at least, not design business objects that require such a mapping. When we distinguish between business logic and persistence logic, we can decouple business logic from persistent storage by defining a persistence interface that business logic components can use. The Data Access Object pattern (shown in detail in Chapter 9) uses an abstraction layer of ordinary Java interfaces between business logic and persistence logic components. The implementations of these interfaces handle persistence logic. The DAO pattern is described in *Core J2EE Patterns*, although it's really just a special case of the Strategy GoF pattern, which we discussed in Chapter 4.

In Sun Java Center's examples, the DAO pattern is usually associated with entity beans with **Bean-Managed Persistence (BMP)**. However, it can be used anywhere in a J2EE application. Entity beans provide a similar abstraction between business logic and persistence storage, but they lock us into one way of accessing data and one particular O/R mapping solution: the DAO pattern leaves us a choice. For example, we can use JDBC, JDO or entity beans to implement DAO interfaces. The DAO pattern also has the important advantage of working inside or outside an EJB container: often we can use the same DAO implementations in either location, which increases the flexibility of our architecture.

The DAO pattern differs from entity beans or O/R mapping approach in that:

❑   It isn't necessarily based around O/R mapping. Whereas O/R mapping is concerned with nouns, such as a Customer or an Invoice, persistence facades can also deal with verbs, such as "total the amounts of all invoices for a given customer". Yet a DAO implementation may use an O/R mapping approach. DAO interfaces will use domain objects (such as Customer or Invoice) as necessary as method arguments and return values, to allow database-agnostic invocation from business objects.

❑   It's a lightweight approach, based on good OO design principles. It uses ordinary Java interfaces, rather than special infrastructure such as that associated with entity beans.

❑   It does not aim to handle transactions or security, but leaves this to business logic components.

❑   It works with any underlying persistence technology.

With the DAO pattern the business logic determines the data access interfaces. With O/R mapping there is a risk that the data layer will dictate the working of the business logic layer. This is one of the reasons I'm skeptical about object-driven modeling. I have often seen situations where the modeling of one entity bean per RDBMS table dictates the nature of session bean code and results in excessive complexity. This is the tail wagging the dog: the point of an application is to express business rules, not work with a predetermined and possibly artificial data structure.

The following two diagrams illustrate how the DAO pattern can be used to conceal very different data access strategies from a business object. Both illustrate the use of a DAO implementing a `MyDAO` interface. The left hand diagram (Scenario 1) illustrates use of an implementation of this interface that uses JDBC. The right hand diagram (Scenario 2) illustrates use of an implementation that uses a layer of entity beans to abstract access to the RDBMS. Although the resulting architectures look very different, because the business object accesses the DAO through a fixed interface there is no need for changes in business logic to accommodate these two data access strategies.

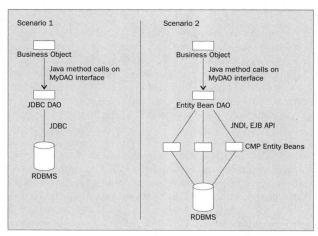

DAOs, like business objects, are part of an application's middle tier.

In Chapter 9, we'll look at how to implement the DAO pattern to cleanly decouple business logic from persistence logic. We'll also use this pattern in our sample application.

> It's important to recognize that there are times when it isn't practicable or beneficial to try to decouple business logic from persistence logic, whatever abstraction we use and however desirable such separation is. For example, sometimes we are unable to separate the two without fatally compromising performances; sometimes it's inappropriate to force every implementation to use a certain O/R mapping or even certain value objects.
>
> In such cases, we should apply good OO design principles – there's nothing special about data access. We should try to minimize the amount of code that requires a mix of business and persistence logic and decouple it from other business objects by isolating it behind Java interfaces. We can then reimplement these interfaces as necessary. By writing unit tests to the interfaces, rather than concrete classes, we will be able to start with comprehensive unit tests if we ever need to port the application to another persistent store.

Working with Relational Databases

As relational databases are used in most J2EE applications, let's examine some important RDBMS characteristics and capabilities, which we should take into account when formulating a data access strategy.

Referential Integrity

All RDBMSs offer sophisticated mechanisms for enforcing referential integrity, such as **constraints** (which prevent the addition of data that does not honor existing relationships) and **cascade delete** (in which related data is automatically deleted when its "parent" row is deleted).

In my experience, it's unusual for a J2EE application to have a database to itself in an enterprise system. As databases are a good means of communication between different applications, rather than extensions of J2EE applications, this makes sense. Hence RDBMS-based referential integrity mechanisms are essential in most enterprise applications, and we should not rely on our application's Java code as the sole guardian of data integrity.

> *EJB 2.0 offers a referential integrity mechanism for entity beans with CMP, as do many other O/R mappings. This is useful, but it's only a supplement to referential integrity enforced by the RDBMS.*

Stored Procedures, Triggers, and Views

Most RDBMSs offer **stored procedures**: operations on stored data that run within the database. Unfortunately, the language used differs between databases, although stored procedure languages tend to be SQL-oriented, such as Oracle's PL/SQL.

Many RDBMSs offer **triggers**: stored procedures associated with a particular table that is automatically invoked on an event such as insertion, and don't need to be called by application code.

Clearly, stored procedures and triggers can be abused. While an obvious use is to ensure referential integrity, what about the use of a trigger to enforce a business logic constraint? For example, what if a trigger was to veto an attempt to add a row to a order table based on the business rule that orders over $700 can only be accepted from Albania if the customer has previously made (and paid for) at least three orders over $50? This is business logic, and shouldn't be in the database in a J2EE application. Such business rules should be enforced by business objects.

Views – virtual tables, usually based on a query executed transparently as the view is accessed – can be useful to simplify queries and enable O/R mappings to joins. However, the level of support depends on the underlying database (for example, join views are partially updateable in Oracle 7.3 and later, but not in Cloudscape 3.6.). Usually, views are suitable only for backing read-only objects.

These implementation-specific features of RDBMSs have a place in J2EE applications, so long as the following criteria are satisfied:

- They produce a real benefit, by reducing the amount and complexity of code or producing a worthwhile performance gain
- They leave business logic in Java business objects
- They are hidden behind a portable abstraction layer

Stored procedures are particularly important, and deserve more detailed discussion.

J2EE developers (and Java developers in general) tend to hate stored procedures. There is some justification for this:

❑ Stored procedures aren't object-oriented. Readers familiar with Oracle will counter that Oracle 8.1.5 introduced Java stored procedures. However, they don't solve the O/R impedance mismatch as much as move it inside the database, and they don't foster truly object-oriented use of Java.

❑ Stored procedures aren't portable. Support for stored procedures varies much more than SQL dialects between RDBMSs. Nevertheless, it would be rare to lose the entire investment in a set of stored procedures on migrating from one RDBMS to another.

❑ If stored procedures grow complex, they may reduce an application's maintainability.

Some other common objections have less validity:

❑ *"Using stored procedures puts business logic in the wrong place"*
If we distinguish between persistence logic and business logic, the idea of putting persistence logic in a relational database makes perfect sense.

❑ *"Using stored procedures means that J2EE security may be compromised"*
Security is a matter of business logic, not persistence logic: if we keep our business logic in J2EE, there is no need to restrict access to data.

❑ *"The database will become a performance bottleneck"*
Especially, if a single database instance is serving a cluster of J2EE servers, the processing of stored procedures may limit overall performance. However, there are trade-offs to consider:

❑ In my experience, it's *much* commoner to see network performance between application server and database limit the overall performance of a J2EE application than the performance of a well-designed database.

❑ There's no reason to perform an operation in a stored procedure rather than a J2EE component unless the operation can be done more naturally and efficiently inside the database server than in Java. Thus if we've implemented an operation efficiently inside the RDBMS and it still eats the server's CPU, it probably indicates that the RDBMS is badly tuned or needs to run on better hardware. Performing the same heavily-requested operation less efficiently in the application server will probably result in a more severe problem, and the need for more additional hardware.

The use of stored procedures from J2EE applications is an area where we should be pragmatic, and avoid rigid positions. I feel that many J2EE developers' blanket rejection of stored procedures is a mistake. There are clear benefits in using stored procedures to implement persistence logic in some situations:

❑ Stored procedures can handle updates spanning multiple database tables. Such updates are problematic with O/R mapping.

❑ (A more general form of the first point) Stored procedures can be used to hide the details of the RDBMS schema from Java code. Often there's no reason that Java business objects should know the structure of the database.

- ❏ Round trips between the J2EE server and the database are likely to be slow. Using stored procedures can consolidate them in the same way in which we strive to consolidate remote calls in distributed J2EE applications to avoid network and invocation protocol overhead.

- ❏ Stored procedures allow use of efficient RDBMS constructs. In some cases, this will lead to significantly higher performance and reduce load on the RDBMS.

- ❏ Many data management problems can be solved much more easily using a database language such as PL/SQL than by issuing database commands from Java. It's a case of choosing the right tool for the job. I wouldn't consider using Perl in preference to Java to build a large application; neither would I waste my time and my employer's money by writing a text manipulation utility in Java if I could write it in Perl with a fraction of the effort.

- ❏ There may be an investment in existing stored procedures that can be leveraged.

- ❏ Stored procedures are easy to call from Java code, so using them tends to reduce, rather than increase, the complexity of J2EE applications.

- ❏ Very few enterprises with existing IT shops have ported all their applications to J2EE, or are soon likely to. Hence persistence logic may be more useful in the RDBMS than in the J2EE server, if it can be used by other non-J2EE applications (for example, custom reporting applications or in-house VB clients).

The danger in using stored procedures is the temptation to use them to implement business logic. This has many negative consequences, for example:

- ❏ There is no single architectural tier that implements the application's business logic. Updates to business rules may involve changing both Java and database code.

- ❏ The application's portability will reduce as stored procedures grow in complexity.

- ❏ Two separate teams (J2EE and DBA) will share responsibility for business logic, raising the possibility of communication problems.

If we distinguish between persistence logic and business logic, using stored procedures will not break our architecture. Using a stored procedure is a good choice if it meets the following criteria:

- ❏ The task cannot be accomplished simply using SQL (without a stored procedure). There is a higher overhead in invoking a stored procedure using JDBC than in running ordinary SQL, as well as greater complexity in the database.

- ❏ The stored procedure can be viewed as a database-specific implementation of a simple Java interface.

- ❏ It is concerned with persistence logic and not business logic and does not contain business rules that change frequently.

- ❏ It produces a performance benefit.

- ❏ The code of the stored procedure is not unduly complex. If a stored procedure is appropriate, part of the payoff will be a simpler implementation than could have been achieved in a Java object running within the J2EE server. Especially in an organization with DBA resources, 10 lines of PL/SQL will prove easier to maintain than 100 lines of Java, as such a size discrepancy would prove that PL/SQL was the right tool for the job.

> Do not use stored procedures to implement business logic. This should be done in Java business objects. However, stored procedures are a legitimate choice to implement some of the functionality of a DAO. There is no reason to reject use of stored procedures on design grounds.

A case in point: In late 2001, Microsoft released a .NET version of Sun's Java Pet Store which they claimed to be 28 times faster. This performance gain appeared largely due to Microsoft's data access approach, which replaced entity beans with SQL Server stored procedures.

I found reaction to Microsoft's announcement in the J2EE community disappointing and worrying (see, for example http://www.theserverside.com/discussion/thread.jsp?thread_id=9797). J2EE purists reacted in horror at Microsoft's use of stored procedures, arguing that the Java Pet Store reflected a far superior design, with the benefits of "an object oriented domain model" and portability between databases. Most of all, the purists were concerned about the likely corrupting effect of the Microsoft benchmark on managers, who should clearly never be allowed to determine how fast an application should run.

I'm an enthusiastic advocate of OO design principles, as you know after digesting Chapter 4, but I read such responses with incredulity. Design is a tool to an end. Real applications must meet performance requirements, and design that impedes this is bad design.

Also, the panic and denial was unnecessary. The benchmark did not prove that J2EE is inherently less performant than .NET. The architectural approach Microsoft used could equally be implemented in J2EE (more easily than Sun's original Pet Shop example, in fact), but it did prove that J2EE orthodoxy can be dangerous.

> Isn't the use of stored procedures going back to the bad old days of two-tiered applications? No, it's not; two-tiered solutions went to the database to perform business logic. Stored procedures should only be used in a J2EE system to perform operations that will always use the database heavily, whether they're implemented in the database or in Java code that exchanges a lot of data with the database.

RDBMS Performance Issues

The heavier a J2EE application's use of an RDBMS, the more important it will be to ensure that the schema is efficient and the database is tuned.

RDBMS Performance Tuning

RDBMSs, like J2EE application servers, are complex pieces of software: much more complex than the vast majority of user applications. As with J2EE servers, application performance can be significantly affected by a host of tuning options that require expert knowledge. Hire a DBA.

Clearly, performance tuning is a losing battle if:

❑ The schema cannot efficiently support common access requirements.

❑ The queries used are inefficient.

❑ The queries or the way in which they are run cause excessive locking in the database. Unfortunately, queries that are efficient in one RDBMS may prove to create contention in others: SQL is neither syntactically nor semantically anywhere near as portable as Java.

One potential quick win is the creation of **indexes**. Indexes, as the name implies, enable the RDBMS to locate a row very quickly, and based on values in one or more columns. These are automatically created on primary keys in most databases, but may need to be created to support some use cases regardless of what data access strategy we use in our Java code. For example, if we have several million users in our user table. Data for each user includes a numeric primary key (indexed by default), an e-mail address, and password. If the e-mail address is the user's login, we'll need to locate rows quickly by e-mail address and password when a user attempts to login. Without an index on these columns, this will require a **full table scan**. On a table this size this will take many seconds, and heavy disk access. With an index on e-mail and password, locating a user's row will be almost instant, and load on the RDBMS minimal.

Denormalization

Occasionally, certain queries remain slow regardless of query optimization and performance tuning, usually because they involve multi-table joins. In such cases, there is a last resort: **denormalization**, or the holding of redundant data in the database for performance reasons. Typically, this greatly reduces the complexity of joins required. I assume that the reader is familiar with the relational concept of normalization. This is essential knowledge for any J2EE developer, so please refer to a relational database primer if necessary.

Denormalization carries serious risks. It increases the size of the database, which may prove a problem if there is a lot of data. Most importantly, it can impair data integrity. Whenever something is stored more than once, there's the potential for the copies to get out of sync.

Sometimes it's possible to denormalize in Java, rather than in the database. This creates non-permanent redundancy, so is preferable in principle. This is usually only an option when we can cache a manageable amount of reference data in a partially read-only data structure: Java code may be able to navigate this structure more efficiently than it could be in the database.

Occasionally, denormalization is attempted simply to enable J2EE applications to work more easily with an RDBMS. This is seldom a good idea, because of the risk involved.

> Don't denormalize a relational database purely to support a J2EE application. The database schema may well outlive the J2EE application, in which case so will the costs of denormalization.

Portability Versus Performance

It's important to consider whether there is any real likelihood of changing your database technology. This isn't the same thing as changing database vendor. For example, changing from a Microsoft SQL Server relational database to an Oracle database should have a far smaller impact than changing from a relational database to an object database. Nor is it the same thing as changing a database schema within the same database. This is likely enough to happen that we should be able to cope with it.

Organizations make a heavy investment in databases, both in license costs and staffing. Then they fill them with valuable data. They aren't going to simply throw this investment away. In practice, it's rare for J2EE applications to be ported between fundamentally different databases. In fact, it's more likely that an organization would move from one application server to another (even one application server *platform*, such as J2EE, to another, such as .NET, or vice versa), than move from an RDBMS to an ODBMS. Even a switch between RDBMS vendors is uncommon in practice, due to the investment involved.

Why is this question important? Because it has implications for the way in which we approach persistence. The unfortunate results of the assumption that database portability is paramount are (a) a lukewarm interest in an application's target database; and (b) effort being wasted achieving what for most application is a non-goal: complete portability between databases. The assumption that organizations will view J2EE as the center of their data access strategy flaws much thinking on persistence in J2EE.

Consider a realistic scenario. A company has spent hundreds of thousands of dollars on an Oracle installation. The company employs several Oracle DBAs, as several applications in its software suite besides J2EE applications use the database. The J2EE team doesn't liaise with the DBAs, and insists on developing "portable" applications that don't take advantage of any of Oracle's features. Clearly, this is a poor strategy in terms of the company's strategic investment in Oracle and actual business need.

If it's clear that your organization is committed to a particular database technology (and very likely a particular vendor), the next question is whether to take advantage of vendor-specific functionality.

The answer is yes, *if that functionality can deliver real benefits*, such as improved performance. We should never reject such a possibility because we aim to achieve an application with 100% code portability; instead, we should ensure that we have a portable design that isolates any non-portable features behind Java interfaces (remember that good J2EE practice is based on good OO practice). Total portability of code often indicates a design that cannot be optimized for any platform.

We need abstraction to achieve portability. The question is at what level we should achieve that abstraction.

Let's consider an example, with two alternative implementation approaches illustrating different levels of abstraction.

❑ **Abstraction using a DAO**
We can decouple business logic from data access code and achieve a portable design by deciding that "the `AccountManager` session bean will use an implementation of a data access interface that can return value objects for all accounts with a balance over a specified amount and transactions of last month totaling more than a specified amount". We've deferred the implementation of data access to the DAO without imposing any constraints on how it should go about it.

❑ **Abstraction using CMP entity beans**
An attempt at complete code portability is to say, The `Account` entity bean will use CMP. Its local home interface will have a `findByAccountBalanceAndTransactionTotal()` method to return entities meeting these criteria. This method will rely on an `ejbSelectByAccountBalance()` method that returns entities meeting the balance criteria, which is backed by an EJB QL query that's not RDBMS-specific. The `findByAccountBalanceAndTransactionTotal()` method will iterate over the collection of entities returned by the `ejbSelectByAccountBalance()` method, navigating the associated collection of Transaction entities for each to add their values.

This roundabout approach is necessary because EJB QL (as of EJB 2.0) does not support aggregate functions: probably because these are considered a relational concept. I think I got that algorithm right, but I'd definitely be writing unit tests to check the implementation (of course this would be relatively difficult, as the code would run only inside an EJB container)!

Let's assume that we're developing the application in question to work with an RDBMS.

The first of these two approaches can be implemented using the capabilities of the database. The data access interface offers a high level of abstraction. Its implementation will most likely use JDBC, and the logic in the query can efficiently be implemented in a single SQL query. Porting the application to another database would at most involve reimplementing the same simple DAO interface using another persistence API (in fact, the SQL query would probably be portable between RDBMSs).

The second approach adds significant overhead because it forces us to perform the abstraction at too low a level. As a result, we can't use the RDBMS efficiently. We must use an EJB QL query that is much less powerful than the SQL query, and are forced to pull too much data out of the database and perform data operations in Java in the J2EE server. The result is greater complexity and much poorer performance.

In the business situation I've described, the fact that the second approach delivers total code portability is of no real benefit. The first approach gives us an optimal solution now, and we've neatly isolated the little code we'd need to reimplement if the back-end ever changes significantly.

There are many things that we can do in EJB QL without this kind of pain, so this example shows the EJB QL abstraction in its worst light. It illustrates the fact that inflexible pursuit of code portability can result in highly inefficient data access.

> **If it's impossible for an application to take advantage of worthwhile database-specific functionality, the application has a poor architecture.**

Exchanging Data in Distributed Applications

We've previously noted how much more complex distributed applications are, in comparison to collocated applications. This complexity also affects data access. However we implement the nuts and bolts of persistence in a distributed application, we're going to need to send data back to the remote client. This data needs to be disconnected from the backing data store. Of course, we could send the client remote references to entity beans, but that guarantees dreadful performance and scalability.

The Value Object J2EE Pattern

A **value object** is a serializable Java object that can be passed across the network efficiently and contains the data necessary in the context of the current use case. Value objects are usually JavaBeans on which the server invokes setter methods and the client getter methods. However, a client might modify the state of a value object and pass it back to the server to update persistent data. There are many possible refinements; for example, the client may be presented with an object having an immutable interface, while the server implementation adds getter methods.

Value objects are sometimes referred to as Data Transfer Objects (DTOs).

The **Value Object** J2EE pattern describes the use of value objects to avoid chatty remote calling. In EJB 1.1, this was commonly used between session beans and entity beans. EJB 1.1 entity beans needed methods to perform bulk data retrieval and update, so that session beans could update data in a single remote call, rather than by invoking individual setter methods. As EJB 2.0 entities should be given local interfaces, there is no longer any need for entity beans to implement methods that work with value objects.

265

This is a good thing, as value objects are artifacts of a business process, not data storage. One entity may in fact require multiple value objects in different circumstances. (Although the following discussion uses an entity bean as an example, the issues it raises are common to many persistence strategies.)

Consider a Car entity (not a realistic attempt at modeling!) containing the following data: year of manufacture, model name, manufacturer (one-to-one relationship), color, registration plate, and the car's owners (one-to-many relationship). In our simple model, each owner may only own one car, and must have one associated insurance policy object. Each insurance policy object is associated with one insurer.

The following UML class diagram illustrates these relationships among persistent objects:

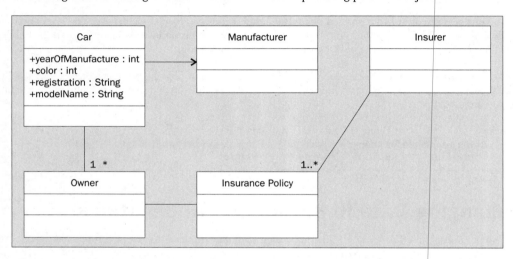

No single `Car` value object will be universally useful: it will contain too little or too much data. For example, if we take just the information held directly in the Car entity, we're left with year, model name, color, and registration plate. This may be useful in some cases, but what if we're interested in the car's ownership history? If we decide that our single value object should traverse relationships, we are left with the problem of where to stop, or will end up performing too many lookups and sending back too much data, seriously reducing performance (for example, should we stop at a Car's associated `Owner` objects, or should we go on to materialize the transitive closure, including `InsurancePolicy` and `Insurer` objects?).

The best, but fairly complex, solution is to use multiple value objects: for example, we might have a `CarOwnership` value object, containing the primary key of the car and an array of value objects holding information about its owners. Collocated applications do not usually face this problem, as there's no need to "disconnect" data.

A component that creates value objects in response to business need implements the **Value Object Assembler** pattern (*Core J2EE Patterns*). Value object assemblers may be session beans or persistence façades.

> **Create value objects as needed to support use cases. Don't automatically use one value object per entity bean or RDBMS table (although there are times when this is appropriate).**

"Generic" Value Objects

The Value Object pattern requires a lot of effort to implement. We may need multiple value objects per persistent object, and will need to write custom code to create and return value objects. It's often possible to auto-generate a value object for an entity bean or other mapped object, but this will produce a "one size fits all" value object which, as we've seen, won't satisfy all requirements.

Especially when many value objects are necessary for one persistent object, a `HashMap` can be considered as an alternative to send data to the client. This doesn't have the advantage of strong typing, but may be worthwhile if it eliminates excessive amounts of code in value objects.

Another untyped approach is to use XML documents as generic value objects. However, we concluded in Chapter 6 that this approach had serious disadvantages that make it inappropriate in most cases.

"Disconnected" Data Access Using JDBC Rowsets

Another alternative to the Value Object pattern uses standard JDBC infrastructure.

The `javax.sql.RowSet` interface is a subinterface of the `java.sql.ResultSet` interface that can be disconnected from the database. It's a resultset that is also a set of value objects. *EJB Design Patterns* suggests using rowsets to marshal read-only data back to the client in the so-called **Data Transfer Rowset** J2EE pattern.

This is efficient and generic, with the potential to save code in custom value objects. However, I don't feel it deserves to be regarded as a pattern, and don't recommend it. There are serious drawbacks to using JDBC rowsets in this way from an architectural perspective:

❑   It sacrifices type safety.

❑   It's not object-oriented. While we may store objects in a hashmap (admittedly forcing clients to perform type cases), data exists in relational (not object) form in a rowset.

❑   All the rowset `getXXXX()` methods are inherited from the `ResultSet` interface, meaning that they throw `java.sql.SQLException`. Clients are forced to catch these exceptions; in fact they should be able to rely on data successfully extracted from the database by the EJB tier, without worrying about potential problems. This reflects the fact that rowset objects are at too low a level of abstraction to be manipulated by clients.

❑   Column names and structures from the database will be built into client code. This will create severe problems if the database schema changes. Perhaps the biggest drawback.

❑   Even though porting from an RDBMS to an ODBMS may be unlikely, there's no justification for exposing the database technology to the UI tier. One of the purposes of the middle tier is to provide an abstraction concealing such low-level details.

❑   The `RowSet` interface contains many methods that are irrelevant to clients.

❑   Given that a major factor in the performance of J2EE applications is network bandwidth between application tiers, it's unwise to send large chunks of unprocessed data to clients straight from the database. The chances are that processing this data in the middle tier would reveal that the UI tier only required a subset of it.

If the number of value objects in a distributed application is becoming problematic, sending hashmaps back to the client is preferable to using rowsets, and not much more difficult to implement. However, the hashmap approach is little help when we face complex issues of how far to traverse associations. For example, we can conditionally include associated fields of an object in a hashmap, but will strike problems if we want to traverse the associations of these fields only to a certain depth. We will normally need to resort to coding custom value objects in such cases, and may end up needing to implement and maintain a large number of value objects.

Common Data Access Issues

Regardless of which data access strategy – and type of database – we use, we will encounter some common issues. Those discussed below will have a crucial impact on scalability and performance.

Transaction Isolation

Transaction isolation levels determine database behavior, but are managed by the J2EE server, which is responsible for overall transaction co-ordination. Transaction isolation levels control the degree of isolation between concurrent transactions accessing the same database. SQL92 defines four transaction isolation levels, which are supported in the JDBC API. In decreasing order of isolation, these are:

- ❏ TRANSACTION_SERIALIZABLE
- ❏ TRANSACTION_REPEATABLE_READ
- ❏ TRANSACTION_READ_COMMITTED
- ❏ TRANSACTION_READ_UNCOMMITTED

The higher the level of isolation for a transaction, the greater the guarantee that its work will not be corrupted by other concurrent transactions, but the greater its impact will be on the total throughput of the resource. In the case of a relational database, the transaction isolation level will control the locking of rows or tables (see http://www.onjava.com/pub/a/onjava/2001/05/23/j2ee.html?page=2 for a good, concise, summary of SQL92 transaction isolation levels).

> **Transaction isolation levels can have a dramatic effect on data integrity and performance. However, their exact meaning differs between databases. This is one reason that transparent persistence is elusive.**

Most databases don't support all four transaction isolation levels, meaning that a J2EE server may be unable to guarantee the expected behavior. For example, Oracle does not support the TRANSACTION_READ_UNCOMMITTED isolation level. However, Oracle does guarantee non-blocking reads, which preserve the intent of the READ_UNCOMMITTED isolation level.

Outside the EJB container, we will need to use API-specific, programmatic control over transaction isolation, such as the setTransactionIsolation() method on the java.sql.Connection interface.

Although the EJB specification doesn't specify the way in which EJB containers should control transaction, we should be able to set it declaratively for EJBs using CMT. This is a further advantage of using EJBs with CMT to co-ordinate data access. We can use the standard ejb-jar.xml deployment descriptor to tell any container when to begin and how to propagate transactions, but there is no standard way of telling the container exactly what a transaction should mean.

Usually this is specified in a container-specific deployment descriptor. For example, in WebLogic there's an element in the `weblogic-ejb-jar.xml` file that looks like this:

```
<transaction-isolation>
  <isolation-level>TRANSACTION_SERIALIZABLE</isolation-level>
  <method>
    <ejb-name>Booking</ejb-name>
    <method-name>*</method-name>
  </method>
</transaction-isolation>
```

> **Always specify the transaction isolation level for EJB methods, if your EJB container allows it. Otherwise you're relying on the default transaction isolation level of the target server, and have compromised portability unnecessarily.**

Pessimistic and Optimistic Locking

There are two basic strategies to database concurrency: **pessimistic** and **optimistic** locking. Pessimistic locking takes the "pessimistic" view that users are highly likely to corrupt each other's data, and that the only safe option is to serialize data access, so at most one user has control of any piece of data at one time. This ensures data integrity, but can severely reduce the amount of concurrent activity the system can support.

Optimistic locking takes the "optimistic" view that such data collisions will occur rarely, so it's more important to allow concurrent access than to lock out concurrent updates. The catch is that we can't allow users to corrupt each other's data, so we have a problem if concurrent updates are attempted. We must be able to detect competing updates, and cause some updates to fail to preserve data integrity. An update must be rejected if the data to be updated has changed since the prospective updater read it. This means that we require a strategy for detecting such changes; often an **optimistic locking attribute** is used: a version number in the object or row that's incremented each time it is modified.

Transaction isolation levels can be used to enforce pessimistic locking. However, the EJB specification provides no support for optimistic locking, although particular implementations of entity bean CMP may, and many O/R mapping products do. To implement optimistic locking, we typically need to write code to check optimistic locking attributes and to roll back transactions if an inconsistency is detected.

Whether to choose pessimistic or optimistic locking for a particular scenario depends on business requirements and even the underlying database.

> **Locking, like transaction isolation levels, works very differently in different databases. I strongly recommend reading a good reference on the database(s) you work with. For example, *Expert One-on-One Oracle* from *Wrox Press (ISBN: 1-86100-4-826)* explains these issues clearly where Oracle is concerned.**

Primary Key Generation Strategies

Persistence stores require objects to have unique keys (primary keys, in RDBMS terminology). We may need to generate a new primary key each time we insert data.

The following discussion assumes the use of **surrogate keys**: primary keys without business meaning. If a primary key is a field with business meaning, such as e-mail, or a combination of fields with business meaning, it is called an **intelligent** or **natural** key, and there is no need to generate new keys – they're created as part of new data.

Surrogate keys are common in enterprise systems, although there are arguments for each type of key. These keys are easier to work with using entity beans, may lead to better performance and offer protection against changes in business rules (for example, if e-mail is used as a natural primary key for a User table, the table will need a new key if users are ever allowed to share e-mail addresses). Surrogate keys must never be exposed to manipulation; if they acquire business meaning they share the drawbacks of natural keys. See http://www.bcarter.com/intsurr1.htm for discussion of the pros and cons of intelligent and surrogate keys.

The problem of surrogate key generation is not unique to J2EE. It's often solved by **auto-increment columns** or other database-specific approaches. These aren't portable, and hence are distrusted by many J2EE developers. They can also be difficult to use from entity beans and JDBC.

EJB containers often provide a way to generate primary keys for CMP entity beans; although no standard approach is defined in the EJB specification (a disappointing omission). When such a mechanism is available, it's best to use it, if using entity beans. Check your server's documentation on entity bean CMP.

The key generation problem is encountered when using entity beans with BMP, or when implementing persistence with JDBC or another low-level API. The contract for entity bean BMP requires the ejbCreate() method to return the new primary key on entity creation. This means that we can't rely on database functionality such as auto-increment key columns. The problem is that we have no way of knowing which row we just inserted. We can try to do a SELECT based on the data values we've just inserted, but this is inelegant and not guaranteed to work. There might just be a valid reason why there could be duplicate data besides the primary key in logically distinct rows. The only alternative is to generate a unique primary key before the insert, and include the new primary key in the insert.

> Note that the problem of primary key generation doesn't always apply unless we are using entity beans. It isn't always necessary to know the primary key of a newly inserted row.

There is much discussion on J2EE forums such as TheServerSide.com about how to generate primary keys in a way that's portable between databases and application servers. I feel that this is misguided: the value of simplicity outweighs portability.

Don't battle with increased complexity trying to generate unique primary keys in a way that's portable between databases. Instead, use the relevant features of your target database, isolating implementation-specific features so that the design remains portable.

It's better to face a simple reimplementation task if an application is ported to another database than to add additional complexity to ensure total code portability from the outset. The first alternative means there's always a simple, understandable, code base.

Three strategies are often suggested for primary key generation:

❑ An entity bean that represents a sequence from the database

❑ Generating a unique ID from within Java

❑ Using a stored procedure or other database-specific means of generating primary keys

The first two solutions are portable. Let's consider each of these in turn.

Sequence Entity Bean

This approach uses numeric keys. An entity bean stores a single number in the database and increments it whenever a client requests a new key. For example, we might have an RDBMS table like this:

KEYS	
NAME	CURRENT_VALUE
USER	109

Entity bean instances could wrap primary keys for each entity bean. The value in the CURRENT_VALUE column would be updated each time a key was requested.

This approach illustrates the dangers of rating a portable solution above a good solution. It can only be made to perform adequately by interposing a session bean that periodically requests a block of keys from the entity. If the entity is used every time a new key is requested, key generation will create a point of contention, as generating a key requires the CURRENT_VALUE column to be updating, serializing access to the KEYS table. This means that we need to deploy two EJBs purely to handle primary key generation: they contribute nothing towards implementing the application's business logic. This approach is unworkable.

Unique ID Generation in Java

In this approach, surrogate key generation is done entirely outside the database. We use an algorithm that guarantees that each time a key is generated, it must be unique. Such algorithms are normally based on a combination of a random number, the system time, and the IP address of the server. The challenges here are that we may be running in a cluster, so we must make sure that individual servers can never generate the same key; and that Java only enables us to find the system time to a millisecond (for this reason, Java isn't a great language in which to generate unique IDs).

Unique ID generation involves an algorithm, rather than state, so it doesn't run into the problems of using singletons in the EJB tier, and hence we don't need to use additional EJBs to implement it.

Unique ID generation in Java is fast and portable. However, it has the following disadvantages:

- ❑ It generates lengthy keys, regardless of the number of rows that the table will hold

- ❑ Keys are strings, not numbers, which may complicate indexing in the database

- ❑ Keys are not sequential

This approach ignores RDBMS capabilities and insists on using Java where it is weak.

Database-Specific ID Generation

In my opinion, the best way to generate primary keys is using database-specific functionality. As primary key creation is a fundamental database problem, each database offers a fast solution that minimizes contentions when multiple users create rows. Usually this will involve performing the update through calling a stored procedure, rather than running a SQL INSERT. Remember, that since we need to know the ID of the new row, we can't simply rely on an auto-increment column or an insert trigger to create a new primary key as the INSERT runs.

The stored procedure must take input parameters for all the data values for the new row, and an output parameter that will enable it to return the generated primary key to the JDBC caller. It must insert the new data, returning the new primary key. Depending on the database, the primary key may be created automatically when the INSERT occurs (for example, if the primary key column is an auto-increment column), or the primary key may be created before the insert. This approach will give us portable JDBC code, but will require database-specific coding for the stored procedure.

The following example shows this approach with Oracle (Simply type the code into SQL*Plus to try it). Let's look at generating keys as we add rows to the following simple table, with only a single data value besides the primary key:

```
CREATE TABLE person (
  id NUMERIC PRIMARY KEY,
  name VARCHAR(32)
);
```

Oracle uses sequences instead of auto-increment columns, so we need to define a sequence that we can use with this table:

```
CREATE SEQUENCE person_seq
  start WITH 1
  increment BY 1
  nomaxvalue;
```

Now we need to write a stored procedure to do the INSERT; for Oracle, I used PL/SQL. Note that this stored procedure has an output parameter, which we use to return the new id to calling JDBC code:

```
CREATE OR REPLACE
PROCEDURE person_add(p_name in varchar, p_id out number)
AS
BEGIN
  SELECT person_seq.nextval INTO p_id FROM dual;
  INSERT INTO person(id, name) VALUES(p_id, p_name);
END;
/
```

We've dealt with Oracle-specific code inside the database, but the JDBC code we use to call this is portable. Whatever RDBMS we use, all we need is to ensure that we have a stored procedure with the name person_add and the same parameters. In a real-world situation there would be many more input parameters, but always only one output parameter.

First, we must call the stored procedure. This is very similar to invoking a PreparedStatement:

```
Connection con = cf.getConnection();
CallableStatement call = con.prepareCall("{call person_add(?, ?)}");
call.setString(1, "Frodo");
call.registerOutParameter(2, java.sql.Types.INTEGER);
call.execute();
```

Now we can extract the value of the output parameter:

```
int pk = call.getInt(2);
System.out.println("The primary key for the new row was " + pk);
call.close();
```

This approach gives us simple, portable, Java code, but will require us to implement a new stored procedure if we ever switch database. However, as the stored procedure is so simple, this is not likely to be a problem. The stored procedure is effectively the implementation of an interface defined in our Java code.

JDBC 3.0

Another option is available when using a database driver that supports JDBC 3.0. The JDBC 3.0 `Statement` interface allows us to obtain the keys created by an insert. The following is a simple example of using this functionality:

```
Statement stmt = connection.createStatement();
stmt.executeUpdate("INSERT INTO USERS (FIRST_NAME, LAST_NAME) " +
                "VALUES ('Rod', 'Johnson')", Statement.RETURN_GENERATED_KEYS);
ResultSet rs = stmt.getGeneratedKeys();

if ( rs.next() ) {
  int key = rs.getInt(1);
}
```

This solves the primary key generation problem if the database has a trigger to create a new primary key or if the primary key is an auto-increment column. However, JDBC 3.0 support is not yet widely available, so this strategy is usually not an option. To use this in a J2EE application, both your database vendor and application server will need to support JDBC 3.0, as application code is likely to be given server-specific wrapper connections for the underlying database connections.

JDBC 3.0 is a required API in J2EE 1.4, so J2EE 1.4 applications using JDBC will be guaranteed the ability to learn the primary keys of newly inserted rows, allowing primary key generation to be concealed within the RDBMS.

Where to Perform Data Access

Now that we've considered some major data access issues, let's consider the key architectural decision of where to perform data access in a J2EE application.

Let's survey the options for accessing data sources in J2EE. We'll look at the recommended options in more detail in later chapters.

Data Access in the EJB Tier

Most books on J2EE recommend performing data access from EJBs. In a distributed J2EE application this is sound advice; in this case, code in the distributed web containers should depend only on the architectural tier directly beneath them (the remote EJBs), and not communicate independently with data sources. However, in collocated applications there is a less compelling case of performing data access from EJB.

The advantages of performing data access from EJBs are:

❑   We have the option of using entity beans

❑   We can benefit from CMT. Transaction management is essential to most data access, so this is a major plus

❑   All data access will occur through a single tier

273

The disadvantages are all the drawbacks of EJB (such as complexity) we've previously discussed, plus the serious consideration that data access code is likely to be hard to test, as it depends on an EJB container. Let's look at the options for data access in the EJB tier.

Entity EJBs

An entity bean is a standard J2EE component intended to support access to persistent data. An entity bean layer formalizes the good design practice of decoupling business logic from persistence logic. It is (at least theoretically) independent of the underlying data source. Whatever data source we use, a layer of entity beans objectifies it. In this model, entity beans will expose local interfaces, while the business objects will normally be session beans. However, any objects collocated in the same JVM can work with the entity beans through their local interfaces.

Entity beans are a very basic O/R mapping solution. While they are guaranteed to be available by the EJB specification, they neglect most of the O/R mapping challenges we listed earlier. Object inheritance is forbidden. Data can only come from a single table. Entity beans don't allow us to access aggregate functions in the database without writing custom code, effectively subverting the abstraction they exist to provide. However, EJB 2.0 CMP does support object relationships (EJB 1.1 did not).

> **Entity beans in EJB 1.1 have limited functionality, and inferior performance, compared with entity beans written with the EJB 2.0 CMP contract. As the CMP 2.0 contract differs from the CMP 1.0 contract, CMP entities require code changes to migrate from EJB 1.1 to EJB 2.0. When using an EJB container that does not support EJB 2.0, don't use entity beans.**

Although given the special blessing of the EJB specification for data access, entity beans are perhaps the most controversial technology in J2EE. We'll discuss the pros and cons of using entity beans in more detail in the next chapter, but the following disadvantages rule out their use to solve many J2EE data access problems (some of these disadvantages apply to any simple O/R mapping):

- ❑ Using entity beans reflects sound design principles by separating business logic from data access, but it locks us into a particular implementation of this approach that will affect code in business objects. Working with any type of EJB is more complex than working with ordinary Java objects.

- ❑ They are the only persistence strategy that is only available to EJBs. We're forced to use EJB, whether it's appropriate on other grounds or not.

- ❑ Entity beans with BMP have serious and intractable performance problems, which we'll discuss in the next chapter and which preclude their use in many cases.

- ❑ The entity bean lifecycle is rigid. This makes it difficult to implement coarse-grained entity beans.

- ❑ Using entity beans may tie us to an RDBMS schema. If we use a one-to-one mapping from entity beans to RDBMS tables, we'll have a lot of work to do if the schema ever changes.

- ❑ Using fine-grained entity beans makes it difficult to use relational databases efficiently; for example, it will be difficult to update multiple rows in one statement, as entity beans push us in the direction of mapping to individual rows.

- ❑ Compared with more established O/R mapping solutions, entity beans (even with EJB 2.0 CMP) offer very basic functionality.

- ❑ There are serious questions regarding the performance of entity beans in most EJB containers.

❑ The portability advantages of an entity bean solution are debatable. Locking and concurrency behavior is very different between leading databases. Given that EJB containers normally delegate these problems to the underlying database to achieve higher throughput, the abstraction provided by entity beans may actually prove misleading if we port it.

❑ Compared with the payoff for using session beans (transparent thread, security, and transaction management for limited deployment complexity), adopting entity beans delivers a more questionable payoff, for significantly greater deployment complexity.

The essential contradiction in using entity beans for data access is arguably that EJBs – due to the complexity of accessing them and their relatively heavyweight nature – are best considered as *components*, rather than ordinary objects. Data access usually requires much finer granularity than EJBs can efficiently deliver.

> **Entity beans can be effective in some J2EE architectures, but they're not the ideal abstraction between business logic and physical data store. If session beans access entity beans directly, session beans risk becoming tied to a particular schema. It's also hard to replace the entity bean layer with another approach if performance proves to be a problem.**

Session EJBs and Helper Classes

Even if we choose to use EJB and implement business logic in session EJBs, we're not forced to use entity beans for data access. Session EJBs are business logic components. This means that they shouldn't deal with the details of data access.

However, this leaves the option of using session beans to control data access, and using the DAO pattern to abstract the details of that access. This is a very flexible approach. Unlike using entity beans, which commits us to one approach, we retain control of how persistence is handled. DAOs can use any persistence API, such as JDO, JDBC, a proprietary mapping framework, or even entity beans. This flexibility (and the reduced overhead compared with the entity bean infrastructure) often leads to better performance than using entity beans.

The only difference between using the DAO pattern from session beans and from other types of business object is the availability of declarative transaction management. Often the same DAOs will work inside or outside an EJB container.

> *This approach is sometimes referred to as **Session Managed Persistence (SMP)**, in contrast to entity bean CMP and BMP. I don't much like this term, as it implies that the persistence code is actually contained in session beans – a poor implementation choice. Also, the DAO approach isn't tied to the use of EJB.*

Data Access in the Middle Tier without Using EJB

As we've seen, J2EE web applications can have a distinct middle tier of business objects without using EJB (EJBs are the only choice for the middle tier in distributed applications with remote clients). This means that we can have middle tier business objects running inside a J2EE web container, but which are not web-specific (in fact they can also support remote access via web services). Such objects have access to programmatic global transaction management with JTA, and connection pooling (J2EE web containers, like EJB servers, provide connection pools, accessible to user code with JNDI lookup. This means that we don't need to use an EJB container to access enterprise data).

Such business objects can use any data access strategy available to J2EE applications. Typically, they will use an O/R mapping framework, such as JDO or TopLink, or a resource-specific API, such as JDBC. They lack the option of declarative transaction management, but this approach offers good performance (as it avoids the overhead of EJB) and is easy to test. Typically, data access objects used in the web container depends only on the ability to access a JDBC datasource via JNDI or an O/R mapping framework. Such requirements can easily be met by test harnesses, unlike EJB container services.

Such data access without EJB is a good option for collocated applications when:

❑   We don't want to use EJB. As we've seen, the data access benefits of EJB do not usually justify using EJB where it would not otherwise be considered.

❑   Data access is non-transactional. In this case, EJB CMT delivers no benefit.

❑   Some functionality related to data access (such as data caching requirements) conflicts with the programming restrictions applying to EJBs. In this case, it may be simpler to combine the data access implementation with the caching functionality, rather than access data in the EJB tier and cache it in the web container.

In a collocated application, there's no need to perform all data access in the same place. For example, it's legitimate to perform transactional data access from EJBs (to leverage CMT) and non-transactional data access from objects in the web container (because it's simpler and faster). We'll adopt this mixed approach in the sample application.

Data Access in the Web Tier

In contrast, data access in the web tier (the logical architectural layer concerned with presenting a web interface) is a poor design choice. Business objects running in the web container should be distinct from web tier components, will depend on the Servlet API.

Servlets and Web-Specific Classes

There is no justification for performing data access from web-specific classes. There's no reason that data access objects should be tied to the Servlet API. This will prevent their use in an EJB container if required. UI code should also be shielded from data source implementation issues: changing a table or column name in an RDBMS, for example, should never break a web interface. Data access from web-specific classes is unnecessary, as there should be a layer of business objects available to them.

Data Access from JSP Pages

However, there is still one worse option for performing data access. The least attractive data access option in J2EE systems is data access from JSP pages. It tends to lead to problems with error handling and loss of the distinction between business logic, data access and presentation. Yet it is surprisingly widespread, so we can't ignore it.

In the early days of JSP, JSP "Model 1" systems were common. Many developers attempted to replace servlets altogether with JSP pages, partly for the enhanced authoring convenience. JSP pages often contained data access code, along with much of the rest of the application. The results were appalling.

Today there's wide awareness of the value of MVC concepts in Java web applications (we'll discuss this issue in detail in Chapters 12 and 13). However, with the introduction of custom tags in JSP 1.1, welcome though they were in other ways, data access from JSP pages has once more raised its ugly head.

JDBC access from custom tags is superficially appealing, because it's efficient and convenient. Consider the following JSP fragment from the JSP Standard Tag Library 1.0 specification, which transfers an amount from one account to another using two SQL updates. We'll discuss the JSP STL Expression Language in Chapter 13. The ${} syntax is used to access variables already defined on the page:

```
<sql:transaction dataSource="${dataSource}">
  <sql:update>
    UPDATE account
    SET Balance = Balance - ?
    WHERE accountNo = ?
    <sql:param value="${transferAmount}"/>
    <sql:param value="${accountFrom}"/>
  </sql:update>
  <sql:update>
    UPDATE account
    SET Balance = Balance + ?
    WHERE accountNo = ?
    <sql:param value="${transferAmount}"/>
    <sql:param value="${accountTo}"/>
  </sql:update>
</sql:transaction>
```

Now let's consider some of the design principles such a JSP violates and the problems that it is likely to produce:

❑ The JSP source fails to reflect the structure of the dynamic page it will generate. The 16 lines of code shown above are certain to be the most important part of a JSP that contains them, yet they generate no content.

❑ (Distributed applications only) Reduced deployment flexibility. Now that the web tier is dependent on the database, it needs to be able to communicate with the database, not just the EJB tier of the application.

❑ Broken error handling. By the time we encounter any errors (such as failure to communicate with the database); we're committed to rendering one particular view. At best we'll end up on a generic error page; at worst, the buffer will have been flushed before the error was encountered, and we'll get a broken page.

❑ The need to perform transaction management in a JSP, to ensure that updates occur together or not at all. Transaction management should be the responsibility of middle tier objects.

❑ Subversion of the principle that business logic belongs in the middle tier. There's no supporting layer of middle tier objects. There's no way to expose the business logic contained in this page to non-web clients or even web services clients.

❑ Inability to perform unit testing, as the JSP exposes no business interface.

❑ Tight coupling between page generation and data structure. If an application uses this approach and the database schema changes, many JSP pages are likely to need updating.

❑ Confusion of presentation with content. What if we wanted to expose the data this page presents in PDF (a binary format that JSP can't generate)? What if we wanted to convert the data to XML and transform it with an XSLT stylesheet? We'd need to duplicate the data access code. The business functionality encapsulated in the database update is tied to JSP, a particular view strategy.

277

If there is any place for data access from JSP pages using tag libraries, it is in trivial systems or prototypes (the authors of the JSP standard tag library share this view).

> **Never perform data access from JSP pages, even when it is given the apparent respectability of a packaged tag library. JSP pages are view components.**

Summary

In this chapter we've looked at some of the key issues in data access in J2EE systems. We've discussed:

❑ The distinction between business logic and persistence logic. While business logic should be handled by Java business objects, persistence logic can legitimately be performed in a range of J2EE components, or even in the database.

❑ The choice between object-driven and database-driven data modeling, and why database-driven modeling is often preferable.

❑ The challenges of working with relational databases.

❑ O/R mapping concepts.

❑ The use of Data Access Objects – ordinary Java interfaces – to provide an abstraction of data access for use by business objects. A DAO approach differs from an O/R mapping approach in that it is made up of verbs ("disable the accounts of all users in Chile") rather than nouns ("this is a User object; if I set a property the database will be transparently updated"). However, it does not preclude use of O/R mapping.

❑ Exchanging data in distributed applications. We discussed the Value Object J2EE pattern, which consolidates multiple data values in a single serializable object to minimize the number of expensive remote calls required. We considered the possible need for multiple value objects to meet the requirements of different use cases, and considered generic alternatives to typed value objects which may be appropriate when remote callers have a wide variety of data requirements.

❑ Strategies for generating primary keys.

❑ Where to implement data access in J2EE systems. We concluded that data access should be performed in EJBs or middle-tier business objects, and that entity beans are just one approach. Although middle-tier business objects may actually run in a web container, we saw that data access from web-specific components such as servlets and JSP pages is poor practice.

I have argued that portability is often unduly prioritized in data access. Portability of design matters greatly; trying to achieve portability of code is often harmful. An efficient, simple solution that requires a modest amount of persistence code to be reimplemented if the database changes creates more business value than an inefficient, less natural but 100% portable solution. One of the lessons of XP is that it's often a mistake to try to solve tomorrow's problems today, if this adds complexity in the first instance.

Data Modeling in the Sample Application

Following this discussion, let's consider data access in our sample application.

The Unicorn Group already uses Oracle 8.1.7i. It's likely that other reporting tools will use the database and, in Phase 1, some administration tasks will be performed with database-specific tools. Thus database-driven (rather than object-driven) modeling is appropriate (some of the existing box office application's schema might even be reusable).

This book isn't about database design, and I don't claim to be an expert, so we'll cover the data schema quickly. In a real project, DBAs would play an important role in developing it. The schema will reflect the following data requirements:

- ❑ There will be a number of **genres**, such as Musical, Opera, Ballet, and Circus.

- ❑ There will be a number of **shows** in each genre. It must be possible to associate an HTML document with each show, containing information about the work to be performed, the cast and so on.

- ❑ Each show has a **seating plan**. A seating plan describes a fixed number of seats for sale, divided into one or more **seat types**, each associated with a name (such as Premium Reserve) and code (such as AA) that can be displayed to customers.

- ❑ There are multiple performances of each show. Each performance will have a **price structure**, which will assign a price to each type of seat.

- ❑ Although it is possible for each show to have an individual seating plan, and for each performance to have an individual price structure, it is likely that shows will use the default seating plan for the relevant hall, and that all performances of a show will use the same price structure.

- ❑ Users can create booking **reservations** that hold a number of seats for a performance. These reservations can progress to confirmations (seat purchases) on submission of valid credit card details.

First we must decide what to hold in the database. The database should be the central data repository, but it's not a good place to store HTML content. This is reference data, with no transactional requirements, so it can be viewed as part of the web application and kept inside its directory structure. It can then be modified by HTML coders without the need to access or modify the database. When rendering the web interface, we can easily look up the relevant resources (seating plan images and show information) from the primary key of the related record in the database. For example, the seating plan corresponding to the primary key 1 might be held within the web application at `/images/seatingplans/1.jpg`.

An O/R modeling approach, such as entity EJBs will produce little benefit in this situation. O/R modeling approaches are usually designed for a **read-modify-write** scenario. In the sample application, we have some reference data (such as genre and show data) that is never modified through the Internet User or Box Office User interfaces. Such read-only reference data can be easily and efficiently obtained using JDBC; O/R approaches are likely to add unnecessary overhead. Along with accessing reference data, the application needs to create booking records to represent users' seat reservations and purchase records when users confirm their reservation.

This dynamic data is not well suited to O/R modeling either, as there is no value in caching it. For example, the details of a booking record will be displayed once, when a user completes the booking process. There is little likelihood of it being needed again, except as part of a periodic reporting process, which might print and mail tickets.

As we know that the organization is committed to using Oracle, we want to leverage any useful Oracle features. For example, we can use Oracle **Index Organized Tables (IOTs)** to improve performance. We can use PL/SQL stored procedures. We can use Oracle data types, such as the Oracle date type, a combined date/time value which is easy to work with in Java (standard SQL and most other databases use separate date and type objects).

Both these considerations suggest the use of the DAO pattern, with JDBC as the first implementation choice (we'll discuss how to use JDBC without reducing maintainability in Chapter 8). JDBC produces excellent performance in situations where read-only data is concerned and where caching in an O/R mapping layer will produce no benefit. Using JDBC will also allow us to make use of proprietary Oracle features, without tying our design to Oracle. The DAOs could be implemented using an alternative strategy if the application ever needs to work with another database.

The following E-R diagram shows a suitable schema:

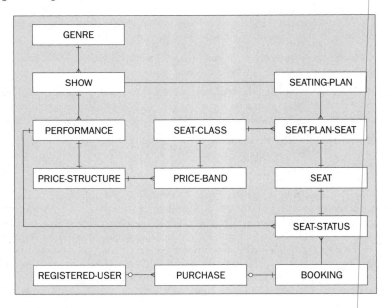

The DDL file (`create_ticket.ddl`) is included in the download accompanying this book, in the /db directory. Please refer to it as necessary during the following brief discussion.

The tables can be divided into reference data and dynamic data. All tables except the SEAT_STATUS, BOOKING, PURCHASE, and REGISTERED_USER tables are essentially reference tables, updated only by Admin role functionality. Much of the complexity in this schema will not directly affect the web application. Each show is associated with a seating plan, which may be either a standard seating plan for the relevant hall or a custom seating plan. The SEAT_PLAN_SEAT table associates a seating plan with the seats it contains. Different seating plans may include some of the same seats; for example, one seating plan may remove a number of seats or change which seats are deemed to be adjacent. Seating plan information can be loaded once and cached in Java code. Then there will be no need to run further queries to establish which seats are adjacent etc.

Of the dynamic data, rows in the BOOKING table may represent either a seat reservation (which will live for a fixed time) or a seat purchase (in which case it has a reference to the PURCHASE table).

The SEAT_STATUS table is the most interesting, reflecting a slight denormalization of the data model. While if we only created a new seat reservation record for each seat reserved or purchased, we could query to establish which seats were still free (based on the seats for this performance, obtained through the relevant seating plan), this would require a complex, potentially slow query. Instead, the SEAT_STATUS table is pre-populated with one row for each seat in each performance. Each row has a nullable reference to the BOOKING table; this will be set when a reservation or booking is made. The population of the SEAT_STATUS table is hidden within the database; a trigger (not shown here) is used to add or remove rows when a row are added or removed from the PERFORMANCE table.

The SEAT_STATUS table is defined as follows:

```
CREATE TABLE seat_status (
  performance_id NUMERIC NOT NULL REFERENCES performance,
  seat_id NUMERIC NOT NULL REFERENCES seat,
  price_band_id NUMERIC NOT NULL REFERENCES price_band,
  booking_id NUMERIC REFERENCES booking,
  PRIMARY KEY(performance_id, seat_id)
)
organization index;
```

The price_band_id is also the id of the seat type. Note the use of an Oracle IOT, specified in the final organization index clause.

Denormalization is justified here on the following grounds:

❑   It is easy to achieve in the database, but simplifies queries and stored procedures.

❑   It boosts performance by avoiding complex joins.

❑   The resulting data duplication is not a serious problem in this case. The extent of the duplication is known in advance. The data being duplicated is immutable, so cannot get out of sync.

❑   It will avoid inserts and deletes in the SEAT_STATUS table, replacing them with updates. Inserts and deletes are likely to be more expensive than updates, so this will boost performance.

❑   It makes it easy to add functionality that may be required in the future. For example, it would be easy to take remove some seats from sale by adding a new column in the SEAT_STATUS table.

It is still necessary to examine the BOOKING table, as well as the SEAT_STATUS table, to check whether a seat is available, but there is no need to navigate reference data tables. A SEAT_STATUS row without a booking reference always indicates an available seat, but one with a booking reference may also indicate an available seat if the booking has expired without being confirmed. We need to perform an **outer join** with the BOOKING table to establish this; a query which includes rows in which the foreign key to the BOOKING table is null, as well as rows in which the related row in the BOOKING table indicates an expired reservation.

There is no reason that Java code – even in DAOs – should be aware of all the details of this schema. I have made several decisions to conceal some of the schema's complexity from Java code and hide some of the data management inside the database. For example:

❑ I've used a sequence and a stored procedure to handle reservations (the approach we discussed earlier this chapter). This inserts into the BOOKING table, updates the SEAT_STATUS table and returns the primary key for the new booking object as an out parameter. Java code that uses it need not be aware that making a reservation involves updating two tables.

❑ I've used a trigger to set the purchase_date column in the PURCHASE table to the system date, so that Java code inserting into this table need not set the date. This ensures data integrity and potentially simplifies Java code.

❑ I've used a view to expose seating availability and hide the outer join required with the BOOKING table. This view doesn't need to be updateable; we're merely treating it as a stored query. (However, Java code that only queries needn't distinguish between a view and a table.) Although the rows in the view come only from the SEAT_STATUS table, seats that are unavailable will be excluded. The Oracle view definition is:

```
CREATE OR REPLACE
  VIEW available_seats AS
  SELECT seat_status.seat_id, seat_status.performance_id,
  seat_status.price_band_id
    FROM seat_status, booking
    WHERE
      booking.authorization_code is NULL
      AND (booking.reserved_until is NULL or
        booking.reserved_until < sysdate)
    AND seat_status.booking_id = booking.id(+) ;
```

Using this view enables us to query for available seats of a given type very simply:

```
SELECT seat_id
FROM available_seats
WHERE performance_id = ? AND price_band_id = ?
```

The advantages of this approach are that the Oracle-specific outer join syntax is hidden from Java code (we could implement the same view in another database with different syntax); Java code is simpler; and persistence logic is handled by the database. There is no need for the Java code to know how bookings are represented. Although it's unlikely that the database schema would be changed once it contained real user data, with this approach it could be without necessarily impacting Java code.

Oracle 9i also supports the standard SQL syntax for outer joins. However, the requirement was for the application to work with Oracle 8.1.7i.

In all these cases, the database contains only persistence logic. Changes to business rules cannot affect code contained in the database. Databases are good at handling persistence logic, with triggers, stored procedures, views, and the like, so this results in a simpler application. Essentially, we have two contracts decoupling business objects from the database: the DAO interfaces in Java code; and the stored procedure signatures and those table and views used by the DAOs. These amount to the database's public interface as exposed to the J2EE application.

Before moving onto implementing the rest of the application, it's important to test the performance of this schema (for example, how quickly common queries will run) and behavior under concurrent usage. As this is database-specific, I won't show this here. However, it's a part of the integrated testing strategy of the whole application.

Finally, we need to consider the locking strategy we want to apply – pessimistic or optimistic locking. Locking will be an issue when users try to reserve seats of the same type for the same performance. The actual allocation of seats (which will involve the algorithm for finding suitable adjacent seats) is a business logic issue, so we will want to handle it in Java code. This means that we will need to query the AVAILABLE_SEATS view for a performance and seat type. Java code, which will have cached and analyzed the relevant seating plan reference data, will then examine the available seat ids and choose a number of seats to reserve. It will then invoke the reserve_seats stored procedure to reserve seats with the relevant ids.

All this will occur in the same transaction. Transactions will be managed by the J2EE server, not the database. Pessimistic locking will mean forcing all users trying to reserve seats for the same performance and seat type to wait until the transaction completes. Pessimistic locking can be enforced easily by adding FOR UPDATE to the SELECT from the AVAILABLE_SEATS view shown above. The next queued user would then be given and have locked until their transaction completed the seat ids still available.

Optimistic locking might boost performance by eliminating blocking, but raises the risk of multiple users trying to reserve the same seats. In this case we'd have to check that the SEAT_STATUS rows associated with the selected seat ids hadn't been changed by a concurrent transaction, and would need to fail the reservation in this case (the Java component trying to make the reservation could retry the reservation request without reporting the optimistic locking failure to the user). Thus using optimistic locking might improve performance, but would complicate application code. Using pessimistic locking would pass the work onto the database and guarantee data integrity.

> *We wouldn't face the same locking issue if we did the seat allocation in the database. In Oracle we could even do this in a Java stored procedure. However, this would reduce maintainability and make it difficult to implement a true OO solution. In accordance with the goal of keeping business logic in Java code running within the J2EE server, as well as ensuring that design remains portable, we should avoid this approach unless it proves to be the only way to ensure satisfactory performance.*

The locking strategy will be hidden behind a DAO interface, so we can change it if necessary without needing to modify business objects. Pessimistic locking works well in Oracle, as queries without a FOR UPDATE clause will never block on locked data. This means that using pessimistic locking won't affect queries to count the number of seats still available (required rendering the **Display performance** screen). In other databases, such queries may block – a good example of the danger that the same database access code will work differently in different databases.

Thus we'll decide to use the simpler pessimistic locking strategy if possible. However, as there is scope to change it without trashing the application's design, we can implement optimistic locking if performance testing indicates a problem supporting concurrent use or if need to work with another RDBMS.

Finally, the issue of where to perform data access. In this chapter, we decided to use EJB only to handle the transactional booking process. This means that data access for the booking process will be performed in the EJB tier; other (non-transactional) data access will be performed in business objects running in the web container.

Data Access Using Entity Beans

Entity beans are the data access components described in the EJB specification. While they have a disappointing track record in practice (which has prompted a major overhaul in the EJB 2.0 specification), their privileged status in the J2EE core means that we must understand them, even if we choose not to use them.

In this chapter we'll discuss:

- ❏   What entity beans aim to achieve, and the experience of using them in practice
- ❏   The pros and cons of the entity bean model, especially when entity beans are used with relational databases
- ❏   Deciding when to use entity beans, and how to use them effectively
- ❏   How to choose between entity beans with container-managed persistence and bean-managed persistence
- ❏   The significant enhancements in the EJB 2.0 entity bean model, and their implications for using entity beans
- ❏   Entity bean locking and caching support in leading application servers
- ❏   Entity bean performance

> **I confess. I don't much like entity beans. I don't believe that they should be considered the default choice for data access in J2EE applications.**

If you choose to use entity beans, hopefully this chapter will help you to avoid many common pitfalls. However, I recommend alternative approaches for data access in most applications. In the next chapter we'll consider effective alternatives, and look at how to implement the Data-Access Object pattern. This pattern is usually more effective than entity beans at separating business logic from data-access implementation.

Entity Bean Concepts

Entity beans are intended to free session beans from the low-level task of working with persistent data, thus formalizing good design practice. They became a core part of the EJB specification in version 1.1; version 2.0 introduced major entity bean enhancements. EJB 2.1 brings further, incremental, enhancements, which I discuss when they may affect future strategy, although they are unavailable in J2EE 1.3 development.

Entity beans offer an attractive programming model, making it possible to use object concepts to access a relational database. Although entity beans are designed to work with any data store, this is by far the most common case in reality, and the one I'll focus on in this chapter. The entity bean promise is that the nuts and bolts of data access will be handled transparently by the container, leaving application developers to concentrate on implementing business logic. In this vision, container providers are expected to provide highly efficient data access implementations.

Unfortunately, the reality is somewhat different. Entity beans are heavyweight objects and often don't perform adequately. O/R mapping is a complex problem, and entity beans (even in EJB 2.0) fail to address many of its facets. Blithely using object concepts such as the traversal of associations with entity beans may produce disastrous performance. Entity beans don't remove the complexity of data access; they do reduce it, but largely move it into another layer. Entity bean deployment descriptors (both standard J2EE and container-specific) are very complex, and we simply can't afford to ignore many issues of the underlying data store.

There are serious questions about the whole concept of entity beans, which so far haven't been settled reassuringly by experience. Most importantly:

❑　Why do entity beans need remote interfaces, when a prime goal of EJB is to gather business logic into session beans? Although EJB 2.0 allows local access to entity beans, the entity bean model and the relatively cumbersome way of obtaining entity bean references reflects the heritage of entity beans as remote objects.

❑　If entity beans are accessed by reference, why do they need to be looked up using JNDI?

❑　Why do entity beans need infrastructure to handle transaction delimitation and security? Aren't these business logic issues that can best be handled by session beans?

❑　Do entity beans allow us to work with relational databases naturally and efficiently? The entity bean model tends to enforce row-level (rather than set-oriented) access to RDBMS tables. This is not what relational databases are designed to do, and may prove inefficient.

❑　Due to their high overhead, EJBs are best used as *components*, not fine-grained objects. This makes them poorly suited to modeling fine-grained data objects, which is arguably the only cost-effective way to use entity beans. (We'll discuss entity bean granularity in detail shortly.)

❑　Is entity bean portability achievable or desirable, as databases behave in different ways? There's real danger in assuming that entity beans allow us to forget about basic persistence issues such as locking.

Alternatives such as JDO avoid many of these problems and much of the complexity that entity beans introduce as a result.

It's important to remember that entity beans are only one choice for data access in J2EE applications. Application design should not be based around the use of entity beans.

> **Entity beans are one implementation choice in the EJB tier. Entity beans should not be exposed to clients. The web tier and other EJB clients should never access entity beans directly. They should work only with a layer of session beans implementing the application's business logic. This not only preserves flexibility in the application's design and implementation, but also usually improves performance.**

This principal, which underpins the **Session Façade** pattern, is universally agreed: I can't recall the last time I saw anyone advocate using remote access to entity beans. However, I feel that an additional layer of abstraction is desirable to decouple session beans from entity beans. This is because entity beans are inflexible; they provide an abstraction from the persistence store, but make code that uses it dependent on that somewhat awkward abstraction.

> **Session beans should preferably access entity beans only through a persistence façade of ordinary Java data access interfaces. While entity beans impose a particular way of working with data, a standard Java interface does not. This approach not only preserves flexibility, but also future-proofs an application. I have grave doubts about the future of entity beans, as JDO has the potential to provide a simpler, more general and higher-performing solution wherever entity beans are appropriate. By using DAO, we retain the ability to switch to the use of JDO or any other persistence strategy, even after an application has been initially implemented using entity beans.**

We'll look at examples of this approach in the next chapter.

> **Due to the significant changes in entity beans introduced in EJB 2.0, much advice on using entity beans from the days of EJB 1.1 is outdated, as we'll see.**

Definition

Entity beans are a slippery subject, so let's start with some definitions and reflection on entity beans in practice.

The EJB 2.0 specification defines an entity bean as, "a component that represents an object-oriented view of some entities stored in a persistent storage, such as a database, or entities that are implemented by an existing enterprise application". This conveys the aim of entity beans to "objectify" persistent data. However, it doesn't explain why this has to be achieved by EJBs rather than ordinary Java objects.

Core J2EE Patterns describes an entity bean as, "a distributed, shared, transactional and persistent object". This does explain why an entity bean needs to be an EJB, although the EJB 2.0 emphasis on local interfaces has moved the goalposts and rendered the "distributed" characteristic obsolete.

All definitions agree that entity beans are data-access components, and not primarily concerned with business logic.

Another key aim of entity beans is to be independent of the persistence store. The entity bean abstraction can work with any persistent object or service: for example, an RDBMS, an ODBMS, or a legacy system.

I feel that this persistence store independence is overrated in practice:

❑   First, the abstraction may prove very expensive. The entity bean abstraction is pretty inflexible, as abstractions go, and dictates *how* we perform data access, so entity beans may end up working equally inefficiently with any persistence store.

❑   Second, I'm not sure that using the same heavyweight abstraction for different persistence stores adds real business value.

❑   Third, most enterprises use relational databases, and this isn't likely to change soon (in fact, there's still no clear case that it *should* change).

In practice, entity beans usually amount to a basic form of O/R mapping (when working with object databases, there is little need for the basic O/R mapping provided by entity beans). Real-world implementations of entity beans tend to provide a view of one row of a relational database table.

> **Entity beans are usually a thin layer objectifying a non-object-based data store. If using an object-oriented data store such as an ODBMS, this layer is not needed, as the data store can be accessed using helper classes from session beans.**

The EJB specification describes two types of entity beans: entity beans with **Container Managed Persistence (CMP)**, and entity beans with **Bean Managed Persistence (BMP)**. The EJB container handles persistence for entities with CMP, requiring the developer only to implement any logic and define the bean properties to be persisted. In the case of entities with BMP, the developer is responsible for handling persistence, by implementing callback methods invoked by the container.

How Should We Use Entity Beans?

Surprisingly, given that entity beans are a key part of the EJB specification, there is much debate over how to use entity beans, and even what they should model. That this is still true as the EJB specification is in its third version, is an indication that experience with entity beans has done little to settle the underlying issues. No approach to using entity beans has clearly shone in real applications.

There are two major areas of contention: the granularity of entity beans; and whether or not entity beans should perform business logic.

The Granularity Debate

There are two major alternatives for the object granularity entity beans should model: **fine-grained** and **coarse-grained** entity beans. If we're working with an RDBMS, a fine-grained entity might map to a row of data in a single table. A coarse-grained entity might model a logical record, which may be spread across multiple tables, such as a User and associated Invoice items.

EJB 2.0 CMP makes it much easier to work with fine-grained entities by adding support for container-managed relationships and introducing entity home methods, which facilitate operation on multiple fine-grained entities. The introduction of local interfaces also reduces the overhead of fine-grained entities. None of these optimizations was available in EJB 1.1, which meant that coarse-grained entities were usually the only choice to deliver adequate performance. Floyd Marinescu, the author of *EJB Design Patterns*, believes that the EJB 2.0 contract justifies deprecating the coarse-grained entity approach.

Coarse-grained **Composite Entities** are entity beans that offer a single entry point to a network of related **dependent objects**. Dependent objects are also persistent objects, but cannot exist apart from the composite entity, which controls their lifecycles. In the above example, a User might be modeled as a composite entity, with Invoice and Address as dependent objects. The User composite entity would create Invoice and Address objects as needed and populate them with the results of data loading operations it manages. In contrast to a fine-grained entity model, dependent objects are not EJBs, but ordinary Java objects.

Coarse-grained entities are arguably more object-oriented than fine-grained entities. They need not slavishly follow the RDBMS schema, meaning that they don't force code using them to work with RDBMS, rather than object, concepts. They reduce the overhead of using entity beans, because not all persistent objects are modeled as EJBs.

The major motivation for the Composite Entity pattern is to eliminate the overhead of remote access to fine-grained entities. This problem is largely eliminated by the introduction of local interfaces. Besides the remote access argument (which is no longer relevant), the key arguments in favor of the Composite Entity pattern are:

- ❑ Greater manageability. Using fine-grained entity beans can produce a profusion of classes and interfaces that may bear little relationship to an application's use cases. We will have a minimum of three classes per table (local or remote interface, home interface, and bean class), and possibly four or five (adding a business methods interface and a primary key class). The complexity of the deployment descriptor will also be increased markedly.

- ❑ Avoiding data schema dependency. Fine-grained entity beans risk coupling code that uses them too closely to the underlying database.

Both of these remain strong arguments against using fine-grained entities, even with EJB 2.0.

Several sources discuss composite entity beans in detail (for example, the discussion of the **Composite Entity** pattern in *Core J2EE Patterns*). However, Craig Larman provides the most coherent discussion I've seen about how to model coarse-grained entities (which he calls **Aggregate Entities**). See http://www.craiglarman.com/articles/Aggregate%20Entity%20Bean%20Pattern.htm. Larman suggests the following criteria that distinguish an entity bean from a dependent object:

- ❑ Multiple clients will directly reference the object
- ❑ The object has an independent lifecycle not managed by another object
- ❑ The object needs a unique identity

The first of these criteria can have an important effect on performance. It's essential that dependent objects are of no interest to other entities. Otherwise, concurrent access may be impaired by the EJB container's locking strategy. Unless the third criterion is satisfied, it will be preferable to use a stateless session bean rather than an entity; stateless session beans allow greater flexibility in data access.

The fatal drawback to using the Composite Entity pattern is that implementing coarse-grained entities usually requires BMP. This not only means more work for developers, but there are serious problems with the BMP entity bean contract, which we'll discuss below. We're not talking about simple BMP code, either – we must face some tricky issues:

❑ It's unacceptably expensive to materialize all the data in a coarse-grained entity whenever it's accessed. This means that we must implement a **lazy loading** strategy, in which data is only retrieved when it is required. If we're using BMP, we'll end up writing a lot of code.

❑ The implementation of the ejbStore() method needs to be smart enough to avoid issuing all the updates required to persist the entire state of the object, unless the data has changed in all the persistent objects.

Core J2EE Patterns goes into lengthy discussions on the "Lazy Loading Strategy", "Store Optimization (Dirty Marker) Strategy" and "Composite Value Object Strategy" to address these issues, illustrating the implementation complexity the composite entity pattern creates. The complexity involved begins to approach writing an O/R mapping framework for every Composite Entity.

The Composite Entity pattern reflects sound design principles, but the limitations of entity bean BMP don't allow it to work effectively. Essentially, the Composite Entity pattern uses a coarse-grained entity as a persistence façade to take care of persistence logic, while session beans handle business logic. This often works better if, instead of an entity bean, the persistence façade is a helper Java class implementing an ordinary interface.

In early drafts released in mid-to-late 2000, the EJB 2.0 specification appeared to be moving in the direction of coarse-grained entities, formalizing the use of "dependent objects". However, dependent objects remained contentious on the specification committee, and the late introduction of local interfaces showed a complete change of direction. This appears to have settled the entity granularity debate.

> **Don't use the Composite Entity pattern. In EJB 2.0, entity beans are best used for relatively fine-grained objects, using CMP.**

The Composite Entity pattern can only be implemented using BMP or by adding significant hand-coded persistence logic to CMP beans. Both these approaches reduce maintainability. If the prospective Composite Entity has no natural primary key, persistence is better handled by a helper class from a session bean than through modeling an entity.

The Business Logic Debate

There is also debate about whether entity beans should contain business logic. This is another area in which much EJB 1.1 advice has been rendered obsolete, and even harmful, by the entity bean overhaul in EJB 2.0.

It's generally agreed that one of the purposes of entity beans is to separate business logic from access to persistence storage. However, the overhead of remote calling meant that chatty access to entity beans from session beans in EJB 1.1 performed poorly. One way of avoiding this overhead was to place business logic in entity beans. This is no longer necessary.

There are arguments for placing two types of behavior in entity beans:

- ❏ Validation of input data
- ❏ Processing to ensure data integrity

Personally, I feel that validation code shouldn't go in entity beans. We'll talk more about validation in Chapter 12. Validation often requires business logic, and – in distributed applications – may even need to run on the client to reduce network traffic to and from the EJB container.

Ensuring data integrity is a tricky issue, and there's more of a case for doing some of the work in entity beans. Type conversion is a common requirement. For example, an entity bean might add value by exposing a character column in an RDBMS as a value from a set of constants, While a user's registration status might be represented in the database as one of the character values I, A, or P, an entity bean can ensure that clients see this data and set it as one of the constant values `Status.INACTIVE`, `Status.ACTIVE`, or `Status.PENDING`. However, such low-level data integrity checks must also be done in the database if other processes will update it.

In general, if we distinguish between business logic and persistence logic, it's much easier to determine whether specific behavior should be placed in entity beans. Entity beans are one way of implementing persistence logic, and should have no special privilege to implement business logic.

> **Implement only persistence logic, not business logic, in entity beans.**

Session Beans as Mediators

There's little debate that clients of the EJB tier should not work with entity beans directly, but should work exclusively with a layer of session beans. This is more an architectural issue than an issue of entity bean design, so we'll examine the reasons for it in the next chapter.

One of the many arguments for using session beans to mediate access to entity beans is to allow session beans to handle transaction management, which is more of a business logic issue than a persistence logic issue. Even with local invocation, if every entity bean getter and setter method runs in its own transaction, data integrity may be compromised and performance will be severely reduced (due to the overhead of establishing and completing a transaction).

Note that entity beans *must* use CMT. To ensure portability between containers, entity beans using EJB 2.0 CMP should use only the `Required`, `RequiresNew`, or `Mandatory` transaction attributes.

> It's good practice to set the transaction attribute on entity bean business methods to `Mandatory` in the `ejb-jar.xml` deployment descriptor. This helps to ensure that entity beans are used correctly, by causing calls without a transaction context to fail with a `javax.transaction.TransactionRequiredException`. Transaction contexts should be supplied by session beans.

CMP Versus BMP

The EJB container handles persistence for entities with CMP, requiring the developer only to implement any logic and define the bean properties to be persisted. In EJB 2.0, the container can also manage relationships and finders (specified in a special query language – EJB QL – used in the deployment descriptor). The developer is required only to write abstract methods defining persistent properties and relationships, and provide the necessary information in the deployment descriptor to allow the container to generate the implementing code.

The developer doesn't need to write any code specific to the data store using APIs such as JDBC. On the negative side, the developer usually can't control the persistence code generated. The container may generate less efficient SQL queries than the developer would write (although some containers allow generated SQL queries to be tuned).

> *The following discussion refers to a relational database as an example. However, the points made about how data must be loaded apply to all types of persistence store.*

In the case of entities with BMP, the developer is completely responsible for handling persistence, usually by implementing the `ejbLoad()` and `ejbStore()` callback methods to load state and write state to persistent storage. The developer must also implement all finder methods to return a Collection of primary key objects for the matching entities, as well as `ejbCreate()` and `ejbRemove()` methods. This is a lot more work, but gives the developer greater control over how the persistence is managed. As no container can offer CMP implementations for all conceivable data sources, BMP may be the only choice for entity beans when there are unusual persistence requirements.

The CMP versus BMP issue is another quasi-religious debate in the J2EE community. Many developers believe that BMP will prove more performant than CMP, because of the greater control it promises. However, the opposite is usually true in practice.

The BMP entity bean lifecycle – in which data must either be loaded in the `ejbLoad()` method and updated in the `ejbStore()` method, or loaded in individual property getters and updated in individual property setters – makes it very difficult to generate SQL statements that efficiently meet the application's data usage patterns. For example, if we want to implement lazy loading, or want to retrieve and update a subset of the bean's persistent fields as a group to reflect usage patterns, we'll need to put in a lot of effort. An EJB container's CMP implementation, on the other hand, can easily generate the code necessary to support such optimizations (WebLogic, for example, supports both). It is much easier to write efficient SQL when implementing a DAO used by a session bean or ordinary Java object than when implementing BMP entity beans.

The "control" promised by BMP is completely illusory in one crucial area. The developer can choose *how* to extract and write data from the persistent store, but not *when* to do so. The result is a very serious performance problem: the **n+1 query finder problem**. This problem arises because the contract for BMP entities requires developers to implement finders to return entity bean *primary keys*, not entities.

Consider the following example, based on a real case from a leading UK web site. A User entity ran against a table like this, which contained three million users:

```
USERS
PK          NAME          MORE COLUMNS...
1           Rod           ...
2           Gary          ...
3           Portia        ...
```

This entity was used both when users accessed their accounts (when one entity was loaded at a time) and by workers on the site's helpdesk. Helpdesk users frequently needed to access multiple user accounts (for example, when looking up forgotten passwords). Occasionally, they needed to perform queries that resulted in very large resultsets. For example, querying all users with certain post codes, such as North London's N1, returned thousands of entities, which caused BMP finder methods to time out.

Let's look at why this occurred. The finder method implemented by the developer of the User entity returned 5,000 primary keys from the following perfectly reasonably SQL query:

```
SELECT PK FROM USERS WHERE POSTCODE LIKE 'N1%'
```

Even though there was no index on the POSTCODE column, because such searches didn't happen frequently enough to justify it, this didn't take too long to run in the Oracle database. The catch was in what happened next. The EJB container created or reused 5,000 User entities, populating them with data from 5,000 separate queries based on each primary key:

```
SELECT PK, NAME, <other required columns> FROM USERS WHERE PK = <first match>
...
SELECT PK, NAME, <other required columns> FROM USERS WHERE PK = <5000th match>
```

This meant a total of n+1 SELECT statements, where n is the number of entities returned by a finder. In this (admittedly extreme) case, n is 5,000. Long before this part of the site reached production, the development team realized that BMP entity beans wouldn't solve this problem.

Clearly this is appallingly inefficient SQL, and being forced to use it demonstrates the limits of the "control" BMP actually gives us. Any decent CMP implementation, on the other hand, will offer the option of preloading the rows, using a single, efficient query such as:

```
SELECT PK, NAME, <other required columns> FROM USERS WHERE POSTCODE LIKE 'N1%'
```

This is still overkill if we only want the first few rows, but it will run far quicker than the BMP example. In WebLogic's CMP implementation, for example, preloading happens by default and this finder will execute in a reasonable time.

> *Although CMP performance will be much better with large resultsets, entity beans are usually a poor choice in such situations, because of the high overhead of creating and populating this number of entity beans.*

There is no satisfactory solution to the n + 1 finder problem in BMP entities. Using coarse-grained entities doesn't avoid it, as there won't necessarily be fewer instances of a coarse-grained entity than a fine-grained entity. The coarse-grained entity is just used as a gateway to associated objects that would otherwise be modeled as entities in their own right. This application used fine-grained entities related to the User entity, such as Address and SavedSearch, but making the User entity coarse-grained wouldn't have produced any improvement in this situation.

The so-called "Fat Key" pattern has been proposed to evade the problem. This works by holding the entire bean's data in the primary key object. This allows finders to perform a normal SELECT, which populates the "fat" objects with all entity data, while the bean implementation's ejbLoad() method simply obtains data from the "fat" key. This strategy does work, and doesn't violate the entity bean contract, but is basically a hack. There's something wrong with any technology that requires such a devious approach to deliver adequate performance. See http://www.theserverside.com/patterns/thread.jsp?thread_id=4540 for a discussion of the "Fat Key" pattern.

Why does the BMP contract force the finders to return primary keys and not entities when it leads to this problem? The specification requires this to allow containers to implement entity bean caches. The container can choose to look in its cache to see if it already has an up-to-date instance of the entity bean with the given primary key before loading all the data from the persistent store. We'll discuss caching later. However, permitting the container to perform caching is no consolation in the large result set situation we've just described. Caching entities for all users for a populous London postcode following such a search would simply waste server resources, as hardly any of these entities would be accessed before they were evicted from the cache.

One of the few valid arguments in favor of using BMP is that BMP entities are more portable than CMP entities; there is less reliance on the container, so behavior and performance can be expected to be similar across different application servers. This is a consideration in rare applications that are required to run on multiple servers.

BMP entities are usually much less maintainable than CMP entities. While it's possible to write efficient and maintainable data-access code using JDBC in a helper class used by a session bean, the rigidity of the BMP contract is likely to make data-access code less maintainable.

There are few valid reasons to use BMP with a relational database. If BMP entity beans have any legitimate use, it's to work with legacy data stores. Using BMP against a relational database makes it impossible to use the batch functionality that relational databases are designed for.

> **Don't use entity beans with BMP. Use persistence from stateless session beans instead. This is discussed in the next chapter. Using BMP entity beans adds little value and much complexity, compared with performing data access in a layer of DAO.**

Entity Beans in EJB 2.0

The EJB 2.0 specification, released in September 2001, introduced significant enhancements relating to entity beans, especially those using CMP. As these enhancements force a reevaluation of strategies established for EJB 1.1 entity beans, it's important to examine them.

Local Interfaces

The introduction of local interfaces for EJBs (discussed in Chapter 6) greatly reduces the overhead of using entity beans from session beans or other objects within the same JVM (However, entity beans will always have a greater overhead than ordinary Java objects, because the EJB container performs method interception on all calls to EJBs).

The introduction of local interfaces makes entity beans much more workable, but throws out a basic assumption about entity beans (that they should be remote objects), and renders much advice on using entity beans obsolete. It's arguable that EJB 2.0 entities no longer have a philosophical basis, or justification for being part of the EJB specification. If an object is given only a local interface, the case for making it an EJB is greatly weakened. This leaves as the only argument for modeling objects as entity beans the data access capabilities that entity beans deliver, such as CMP; this must then be compared on equal terms with alternatives such as JDO.

> In EJB 2.0 applications, **never give entity beans remote interfaces**. This ensures that remote clients access entities through a layer of session beans implementing the application's use cases, minimizes the performance overhead of entity beans, and means that we don't need to get and set properties on entities using a value object.

Home Interface Business Methods

Another important EJB 2.0 enhancement is the addition of business methods on entity bean home interfaces: methods whose work is not specific to a single entity instance. Like the introduction of local interfaces, the introduction of home methods benefits both CMP and BMP entity beans.

Home interface business methods are methods other than finders, create, or remove methods defined on an entity's local or remote home interface. Home business methods are executed on any entity instance of the container's choosing, *without access to a primary key*, as the work of a home method is not restricted to any one entity. Home method implementations have the same run-time context as finders. The implementation of a home interface can perform JNDI access, find out the caller's role, access resource managers and other entity beans, or mark the current transaction for rollback.

The only restriction on home interface method signatures is that, to avoid confusion, the method name must not begin with `create`, `find`, or `remove`. For example, an EJB home method on a local interface might look like this:

```
int getNumberOfAccountsWithBalanceOver(double balance);
```

The corresponding method on the bean implementation class must have a name beginning with `ejbHome`, in the same way that create methods must have names beginning `ejbCreate()`:

```
public int ejbHomeGetNumberOfAccountsWithBalanceOver(double balance);
```

Home interface methods do more than anything in the history of entity beans to allow efficient access to relational databases. They provide an escape from the row-oriented approach that fine-grained entities enforce, allowing efficient operations on multiple entities using RDBMS aggregate operations.

In the case of CMP entities, home methods are often backed by another new kind of method defined in a bean implementation class: an `ejbSelect()` method. An `ejbSelect()` method is a query method. However, it's unlike a finder in that it is not exposed to clients through the bean's home or component interface. Like finders in EJB 2.0 CMP, `ejbSelect()` methods return the results of EJB QL queries defined in the `ejb-jar.xml` deployment descriptor. An `ejbSelect()` method must be abstract. It's impossible to implement an `ejbSelect()` method in an entity bean implementation class and avoid the use of an EJB QL query. Unlike finders, `ejbSelect()` methods need not return entity beans. They may return entity beans or fields with container-managed persistence. Unlike finders, `ejbSelect()` methods can be invoked on either an entity in the pooled state (without an identity) or an entity in the ready state (with an identity).

Home business methods may call `ejbSelect()` methods to return data relating to multiple entities. Business methods on an individual entity may also invoke `ejbSelect()` methods if they need to obtain or operate on multiple entities.

There are many situations in which the addition of home interface methods allows efficient use of entity beans where this would have proven impossible under the EJB 1.1 contract. The catch is that EJB QL, the portable EJB query language, which we'll discuss below, isn't mature enough to deliver the power many entity home interface methods need. We must write our own persistence code to use efficient RDBMS operations, using JDBC or another low-level API. Home interface methods can even be used to call stored procedures if necessary.

Note that business logic – as opposed to persistence logic – is still better placed in session beans than in home interface methods.

EJB 2.0 CMP

The most talked about entity bean enhancement in EJB 2.0 is the addition of support for container-managed relationships between entity beans, which builds on the introduction of local interfaces.

Support for CMP entities in EJB 1.1 is rudimentary and capable only of meeting simple requirements. Although the EJB 2.0 specification requires that containers honor the EJB 1.1 contract for CMP entities, the EJB 2.0 specification introduces a new and quite different contract for CMP entities.

Basic Concepts

In practice, EJB 1.1 CMP was limited to a means of mapping the instance variables of a Java object to columns in a single database table. It supported only primitive types and simple objects with a corresponding SQL type (such as dates). The contract was inelegant; entity bean fields with container-managed persistence needed to be public. An entity bean was a concrete class, and included fields like the following, which would be mapped onto the database by the container:

```
public String firstName;
public String lastName;
```

Since EJB 1.1 CMP was severely under-specified, applications using it became heavily dependent on the CMP implementation of their target server, severely compromising the portability that entity beans supposedly offered. For example, as CMP finder methods are not written by bean developers, but generated by the container, each container used its own custom query language in deployment descriptors.

EJB 2.0 is a big advance, although it's still essentially based on mapping object fields to columns in a single database table. The EJB 2.0 contract for CMP is based on abstract *methods*, rather than public instance *variables*. CMP entities are abstract classes, with the container responsible for implementing the setting and retrieval of persistent properties. Simple persistent properties are known as **CMP fields**. The EJB 2.0 way of defining `firstName` and `lastName` CMP fields would be:

```
public abstract String getFirstName();
public abstract void setFirstName(String fname);
public abstract String getLastName();
public abstract void setLastName(String lname);
```

As in EJB 1.1 CMP, the mapping is defined outside Java code, in deployment descriptors. EJB 2.0 CMP introduces many more elements to handle its more complex capabilities. The `ejb-jar.xml` describes the persistent properties and the relationship between CMP entities. Additional proprietary deployment descriptors, such as WebLogic's `weblogic-cmp-rdbms-jar.xml`, define the mapping to an actual data source.

The use of abstract methods is a much superior approach to the use of public instance variables (for example, it allows the container to tell when fields have been modified, making optimization easier). The only disadvantage is that, as the concrete entity classes are generated by the container, an incomplete (abstract) CMP entity class will compile successfully, but fail to deploy.

Container-Managed Relationships (CMR)

EJB 2.0 CMP offers more than persistence of properties. It introduces the notion of **CMRs** (relationships between entity beans running in the same EJB container). This enables fine-grained entities to be used to model individual tables in an RDBMS.

Relationships involve local, not remote, interfaces. An entity bean with a remote interface may have relationships, but these cannot be exposed through its remote interface. EJB 2.0 supports one-to-one, one-to-many and many-to-many relationships. (Many-to-many relationships will need to be backed by a **join table** in the RDBMS. This will be concealed from users of the entity beans.) CMRs may be unidirectional (navigable in one direction only) or bidirectional (navigable in both directions).

Like CMP fields, CMRs are expressed in the bean's local interface by abstract methods. In a one-to-one relationship, the CMR will be expressed as a property with a value being the related entity's local interface:

```
AddressLocal getAddress();
void setAddress(AddressLocal p);
```

In the case of a one-to-many or many-to-many relationship, the CMR will be expressed as a Collection:

```
Collection getInvoices();
void setInvoices(Collection c);
```

It is possible for users of the bean's local interface to manipulate exposed Collections, subject to certain restrictions (for example, a Collection must never be set to `null`: the empty Collection must be used to indicate that no objects are in the specified role). The EJB 2.0 specification requires that containers preserve referential integrity – for example, by supporting cascading deletion.

While abstract methods in the local interface determine how callers use CMR relationships, deployment descriptors are used to tell the EJB container how to map the relationships. The standard `ejb-jar.xml` file contains elements that describe relationships and navigability. The details of mapping to a database (such as the use of join tables) will be container-specific. For example, WebLogic defines several elements to configure relationships in the `weblogic-cmp-rdbms-jar.xml` file. In JBoss 3.0, the `jbosscmp-jdbc.xml` file performs the same role.

> Don't rely on using EJB 2.0 CMP to guarantee referential integrity of your data unless you're positive that no other processes will access the database. Use database constraints.

It *is* possible to use the coarse-grained entity concept of "dependent objects" in EJB 2.0. The specification (§10.3.3) terms them **dependent value classes**. Dependent objects are simply CMP fields defined through abstract get and set methods that are of Java object types with no corresponding SQL type. They must be serializable concrete classes, and will usually be persisted to the underlying data store as a binary object.

Using dependent value objects is usually a bad idea. The problem is that it treats the underlying data source as a dumb storage facility. The database probably won't understand serialized Java objects. Thus the data will only be of use to the J2EE application that created it: for example, it will be impossible to run reports over the data. Aggregate operations won't be able to use it if the data store is an RDBMS. Dependent object serialization and deserialization will prove expensive. In my experience, long-term persistence of serialized objects is vulnerable to versioning problems, if the serialized object changes. The EJB specification suggests that dependent objects be used only for persisting legacy data.

EJB QL

The EJB 2.0 specification introduces a new portable query language for use by entities with CMP. This is a key element of the portability promise of entity beans, intended to free developers from the need to use database-specific query languages such as SQL or proprietary query languages as used in EJB 1.1 CMP.

I have grave reservations about EJB QL. I don't believe that the result it seeks to achieve – total code portability for CMP entity beans – justifies the invention (and learning) of a new query language. Reinventing the wheel is an equally bad idea, whether done by specification committees and application server vendors, or by application developers.

I see the following conceptual problems with EJB QL (we'll talk about some of the practical problems shortly):

❑ It introduces a relatively low-level abstraction that isn't necessary in the vast majority of cases, and which makes it difficult to accomplish some tasks efficiently.

❑ It's not particularly easy to use. SQL, on the other hand, is widely understood. EJB QL will need to become even more complex to be able to meet real-world requirements.

❑ It's purely a query language. It's impossible to use it to perform updates. The only option is to obtain multiple entities that result from an `ejbSelect()` method and to modify them individually. This wastes bandwidth between J2EE server and RDBMS, requires the traversal of a Collection (with the necessary casts) and the issuing of many individual updates. This preserves the object-based concepts behind entity beans, but is likely to prove inefficient in many cases. It's more complex and much slower than using SQL to perform such an update in an RDBMS.

❑ There's no support for subqueries, which can be used in SQL as an intuitive way of composing complex queries.

❑ It doesn't support dynamic queries. Queries must be coded into deployment descriptors at deployment time.

❑ It's tied to entity beans with CMP. JDO, on the other hand, provides a query language that can be used in any type of object.

❑ EJB QL is hard to test. We can only establish that an EJB QL query doesn't behave as expected by testing the behavior of entities running in an EJB container. We may only be able to establish *why* an EJB QL query doesn't work by looking at the SQL that the EJB container is generating. Modifying the EJB QL and retesting will involve redeploying the EJBs (how big a deal this is, will vary between application servers). In contrast, SQL can be tested without any J2EE, by issuing SQL commands or running scripts in a database tool such as SQL*Plus when using Oracle.

❑ EJB QL does not have an ORDER BY clause, meaning that sorting must take place after data is retrieved.

❑ EJB QL seems torn in two directions, in neither of which it can succeed. If it's frankly intended to be translated to SQL (which seems to be the reality in practice), it's redundant, as SQL is already familiar and much more powerful. If it's to stay aloof from RDBMS concepts – for example, to allow implementation over legacy mainframe data sources – it's doomed to offer only a lowest common denominator of data operations and to be inadequate to solve real problems.

To redress some of these problems, EJB containers such as WebLogic implement extensions to EJB QL. However, given that the entire justification for EJB QL is its portability, the necessity for proprietary extensions severely reduces its value (although SQL dialects differ, the subset of SQL that will work across most RDBMSs is far more powerful than EJB QL).

EJB 2.1 addresses some of the problems with EJB QL by introducing support for aggregate functions such as AVG, MAX, and SUM, and introducing an ORDER BY clause. However, it still does not support updates, and is never likely to. Other important features such as subqueries and dynamic queries are still deferred to future releases of the EJB specification.

Limitations of O/R Modeling with EJB 2.0 Entities

Despite the significant enhancements, CMP entity beans *as specified* remain a basic form of O/R mapping. The EJB specification ignores some of the toughest problems of O/R mapping, and makes it impossible to take advantage of some of the capabilities of relational databases. For example:

❑ There is no support for optimistic locking.

❑ There is poor support for batch updates (EJB 2.0 home methods at least make them possible, but the container – and EJB QL – provide no assistance in implementing them).

❑ The concept of a mapping from an object to a single table is limiting, and the EJB 2.0 specification does not suggest how EJB containers should address this.

❑ There is no support for inheritance in mapped objects. Some EJB containers such as WebSphere implement this as a proprietary extension. See http://www.transarc.ibm.com/Library/documentation/websphere/appserv/atswfg/atswfg12.ht m#HDREJB_ENTITY_BEANS.

Custom Entity Behavior with CMP/BMP Hybrids

I previously mentioned the use of custom code to implement persistence operations that cannot be achieved using CMP, CMR, and EJB QL.

This results in CMP/BMP hybrids. These are entities whose lifecycle is managed by the EJB container's CMP implementation, and which use CMP to persist their fields and simple relationships, but database-specific BMP code to handle more complex queries and updates.

299

In general, home interface methods are the likeliest candidates to benefit from such BMP code. Home interface methods can also be implemented using JDBC when generated EJB QL proves slow and inefficient because the container does not permit the tuning of SQL generated from EJB QL.

Unlike ejbSelect() methods and finders on CMP entities, the bean developer – not the EJB container – implements home interface business methods. If ejbSelect() methods cannot provide the necessary persistence operations, the developer is free to take control of database access. An entity bean with CMP is not restricted from performing resource manager access; it has merely chosen to leave most persistence operations to the container. It will need a datasource to be made available in the ejb-jar.xml deployment descriptor as for an entity with BMP. Datasource objects are not automatically exposed to entities with CMP.

It's also possible to write custom extensions to data loading and storage, as the EJB container invokes the ejbLoad() and ejbStore() methods on entities with CMP. Section 10.3.9 of the EJB 2.0 Specification describes the contract for these methods.

CMP/BMP hybrid beans are inelegant, but they are sometimes necessary given the present limitations of EJB QL.

The only serious complication with CMP/BMP hybrids is the potential effect on an EJB container's ability to cache entity beans if custom code updates the database. The EJB container has no way of knowing what the custom code is doing to the underlying data source, so it must treat such changes in the same way as changes made by separate processes. Whether or not this will impair performance will depend on the locking strategy in use (see discussion on locking and caching later). Some containers (such as WebLogic) allow users to flush cached entities whose underlying data has changed as a result of aggregate operations.

> **When using entity beans, if a CMP entity bean fails to accommodate a subset of the necessary operations, it's usually better to add custom data access code to the CMP entity than to switch to BMP. CMP/BMP hybrids are inelegant. However, they're sometimes the only way to use entity beans effectively.**

When using CMP/BMP hybrids, remember that:

❑ Updating data may break entity bean caching. Make sure you understand how any caching works in your container, and the implications of any updates performed by custom data access code.

❑ The portability of such beans may improve as the EJB specification matures – if the BMP code queries, rather than updates. For example, EJB home methods that need to be implemented with BMP because EJB 2.0 doesn't offer aggregate functions may be able to be implemented in EJB QL in EJB 2.1.

❑ If possible, isolate database-specific code in a helper class that implements a database-agnostic interface.

Entity Bean Caching

Entity bean performance hinges largely on the EJB container's entity bean caching strategy. Caching in turn depends on the locking strategy the container applies.

> In my opinion, the value of entity beans hinges on effective caching. Unfortunately, this differs widely between application scenarios and different EJB containers.

If it is possible to get heavy cache hits, using read-only entity beans or because your container has an efficient cache, entity beans are a good choice and will perform well.

Entity Bean Locking Strategies

There are two main locking strategies for entity beans, both foreshadowed in the EJB specification (§10.5.9 and §10.5.10). The terminology used to describe them varies between containers, but I have chosen to use the WebLogic terminology, as it's clear and concise.

It's essential to understand how locking strategies are implemented by your EJB container before developing applications using entity beans. Entity beans do not allow us to ignore basic persistence issues.

Exclusive Locking

Exclusive locking was the default strategy used by WebLogic 5.1 and earlier generations of the WebLogic container. Many other EJB containers at least initially used this caching strategy. Exclusive locking is described as "Commit Option A" in the EJB specification (§10.5.9), and JBoss 3.0 documentation uses this name for it.

With this locking strategy, the container will maintain a single instance of each entity in use. The state of the entity will usually be cached between transactions, which may minimize calls to the underlying database. The catch (and the reason for terming this "exclusive" locking) is that the container must serialize accesses to the entity, locking out users waiting to use it.

Exclusive locking has the following advantages:

❑ Concurrent access will be handled in the same way across different underlying data stores. We won't be reliant on the behavior of the data store.

❑ Genuinely serial access to a single entity (when successive accesses, perhaps resulting from actions from the same user, do not get locked out) will perform very well. This situation does occur in practice: for example if entities relate to individual users, and are accessed only by the users concerned.

❑ If we're not running in a cluster and no other processes are updating the database, it's easy to cache data by holding the state of entity beans between transactions. The container can skip calls to the `ejbLoad()` method if it knows that entity state is up to date.

Exclusive locking has the following disadvantages:

❑ Throughput will be limited if multiple users need to work with the same data.

❑ Exclusive locking is unnecessary if multiple users merely need to *read* the same data, without updating it.

Database Locking

With the database locking strategy, the responsibility for resolving concurrency issues lies with the database. If multiple clients access the same logical entity, the EJB container simply instantiates multiple entity objects with the same primary key. The locking strategy is up to the database, and will be determined by the transaction isolation level on entity bean methods. Database locking is described in "*Commit Options B and C*" in the EJB specification (§10.5.9), and JBoss documentation follows this terminology.

Database locking has the following advantages:

❑　It can support much greater concurrency if multiple users access the same entity. Concurrency control can be much smarter. The database may be able to tell which users are reading, and which are updating.

❑　There is no duplication of locking infrastructure. Most database vendors have spent a decade or more working on their locking strategies, and have done a pretty good job.

❑　The database is more likely to provide tools to help detect deadlocks than the EJB container vendor.

❑　The database can preserve data integrity, even if processes other than the J2EE server are accessing and manipulating data.

❑　We are allowed the choice of implementing optimistic locking in entity bean code. Exclusive locking is pessimistic locking enforced by the EJB container.

Database locking has the following disadvantages:

❑　Portability between databases cannot be guaranteed. Concurrent access may be handled very differently by different databases, even when the same SQL is issued. While I'm skeptical of the achievability of portability across databases, it is one of the major promises of entity beans. Code that can run against different databases, but with varying behavior, is dangerous and worse than code that requires explicit porting.

❑　The `ejbLoad()` method must *always* be invoked when a transaction begins. The state of an entity cannot be cached between transactions. This can reduce performance, in comparison to exclusive locking.

❑　We are left with two caching options: A very smart cache; and no cache, whether or not we're running in a cluster.

WebLogic versions 6.0 and later support both exclusive and database locking, but default to using database locking. Other servers supporting database locking include JBoss, Sybase EAServer and Inprise Application Server.

> *WebLogic 7.0 adds an "Optimistic Concurrency" strategy, in which no locks are held in EJB container or database, but a check for competing updates is made by the EJB container before committing a transaction. We discussed the advantages and disadvantages of optimistic locking in Chapter 7.*

Read-only and "Read-mostly" Entities

How data is accessed affects the locking strategy we should use. Accordingly, some containers offer special locking strategies for read-only data. Again, the following discussion reflects WebLogic terminology, although the concepts aren't unique to WebLogic.

WeLogic 6.0 and above provides a special locking strategy called **read-only locking**. A read-only entity bean is never updated by a client, but may periodically be updated (for example, to respond to changes in the underlying database). WebLogic never invokes the `ejbStore()` method of an entity bean with read-only locking. However, it invokes the `ejbLoad()` method at a regular interval set in the deployment descriptor. The deployment descriptor distinguishes between normal (read/write) and read-only entities. JBoss 3.0 provides similar functionality, terming this "Commit Option D".

WebLogic allows user control over the cache by making the container-generated home interface implementations implement a special `CachingHome` interface. This interface provides the ability to invalidate individual entities, or all entities (the home interface of a read-only bean can be cast to WebLogic's proprietary `CachingHome` subinterface). In WebLogic 6.1 and above, invalidation works in a cluster.

Read-only beans provide good performance if we know that data won't be modified by clients. They also make it possible to implement a "read mostly" pattern. This is achieved by mapping a read-only *and* a normal read-write entity to the same data. The two beans will have different JNDI names. Reads are performed through the read-only bean, while updates use the read/write bean. Updates can also use the `CachingHome` to invalidate the read-only entity.

Dmitri Rakitine has proposed the "Seppuku" pattern, which achieves the same thing more portably. Seppuku requires only read-only beans (not proprietary invalidation support) to work. It invalidates read-only beans by relying on the container's obligation to discard a bean instance if a non-application exception is encountered (we'll discuss this mechanism in Chapter 10). One catch is that the EJB container is also obliged to log the error, meaning that server logs will soon fill with error messages resulting from "normal" activity. The Seppuku pattern, like the Fat Key pattern, is an inspired flight of invention, but one that suggests that it is preferable to find a workaround for the entire problem. See http://dima.dhs.org/misc/readOnlyUpdates.html for details.

> *The name Seppuku was suggested by Cedric Beust of BEA, and refers to Japanese ritual disembowelment. It's certainly more memorable than prosaic names such as "Service-to-Worker"!*

Tyler Jewell of BEA hails read mostly entities as the savior of EJB performance (see his article in defense of entity beans at http://www.onjava.com/lpt/a//onjava/2001/12/19/eejbs.html). He argues that a "develop once, deploy n times" model for entity beans is necessary to unleash their "true power", and proposes criteria to determine how entity beans should be deployed based on usage patterns. He advocates a separate deployment for each entity for each usage pattern.

The multiple deployment approach has the potential to deliver significant performance improvements compared to traditional entity bean deployment. However, it has many disadvantages:

❑ Relying on read-only beans to deliver adequate performance isn't portable. (Even in EJB 2.1, read-only entities with CMP are merely listed as possible addition in future releases of the EJB specification, meaning that they will be non-standard until at least 2004.)

❑ There's potential to waste memory on multiple copies of an entity.

❑ Developer intervention is required to deploy and use the multiple entities. Users of the entity are responsible for supplying the correct JNDI name for their usage pattern (a session façade can conceal this from EJB clients, partially negating this objection).

❑ Entity bean deployment is already complicated enough; adding multiple deployments of the same bean further complicates deployment descriptors and session bean code, and is unlikely to be supported by tools. Where container-managed relationships are involved, the size and complexity of deployment descriptors will skyrocket. There are also some tough design issues. For example, which of the several deployments of a related entity bean should a read-only bean link to in the deployment descriptor?

The performance benefits of multiple deployment apply only if data is read often and updated occasionally. Where static reference data is concerned, it will be better to cache closer to the user (such as in the web tier). Multiple deployment won't help in situations where we need aggregate operations, and the simple O/R mapping provided by EJB CMP is inadequate.

Even disregarding these problems, the multiple deployment approach would only demonstrate the "true power" of entity beans if it weren't possible to achieve its goals in any other way. In fact, entity beans are not the only way to deliver such multiple caches. JDO and other O/R mapping solutions also enable us to maintain several caches to support different usage patterns.

Transactional Entity Caching

Using read-only entity beans and multiple deployment is a cumbersome form of caching that requires substantial developer effort to configure. It's unsatisfactory because it's not truly portable and requires the developer to resort to devious tricks, based on the assumption that out-of-the-box entity bean performance is inadequate. What if entity bean caching was good enough to work without the developers' help?

Persistence PowerTier (http://www.persistence.com/products/powertier/index.php) is an established product with a transactional and distributed entity bean cache. Persistence built its J2EE server around its C++ caching solution, rather than adding caching support to an EJB container.

PowerTier's support for entity beans is very different from that of most other vendors. PowerTier effectively creates an in-memory object database to lessen the load on the underlying RDBMS. PowerTier uses a shared transactional cache, which allows in-memory data access and relationship navigation. (Relationships are cached in memory as pointers, avoiding the need to run SQL joins whenever relationships are traversed).

Each transaction is also given its own private cache. Committed changes to cached data are replicated to the shared cache and transparently synchronized to the underlying database to maintain data integrity. Persistence claims that this can boost performance up to 50 times for applications (such as many web applications) that are biased in favor of reads. PowerTier's performance optimizations include support for optimistic locking. Persistence promotes a fine-grained entity bean model, and provides tools to generate entities (including finder methods) from RDBMS tables. PowerTier also supports the generation of RDBMS tables from an entity bean model.

Third-party EJB 2.0 persistence providers such as TopLink also claim to implement distributed caching. (Note that TopLink provide similar caching services without the need to use entity beans, through its proprietary O/R mapping APIs.)

I haven't worked with either of these products in production, so I can't verify the claims of their sales teams. However, Persistence boasts some very high volume, mission-critical, J2EE installations, such as the Reuters Instinet online trading system and FedEx's logistics system.

> **A really good entity bean cache will greatly improve the performance of entity beans. However, remember that entity beans are not the only way to deliver caching. The JDO architecture allows JDO persistence managers to offer caching that's at least as sophisticated as any entity bean cache.**

Entity Bean Performance

Using entity beans will probably produce worse performance than leading alternative approaches to persistence, unless your application server has an efficient distributed and transactional entity bean cache, or substantial developer effort is put into multiple deployments. In the latter case, performance will be determined by the nature of the application; applications with largely read-only access to data will perform well, while those with many writes will gain little benefit from caching.

Why does this matter? Because entity bean performance, without effective caching, may be very bad indeed.

Efficient performance from the entity bean model rests on the following conditions:

❑ Data is likely to be modified (and not simply read) when it is accessed. Excepting proprietary support for read-only entities, entity beans assume a read-modify-write model.

❑ Modification occurs at the individual mapped object level, not as an aggregate operation (that is, updates can efficiently be done with individual objects in Java rather than to multiple tuples in an RDBMS).

Why do entity beans have performance problems in many cases?

❑ Entity beans use a one-size fits-all approach. The entity bean abstraction may make it impossible to access persistent data efficiently, as we've seen with RDBMSs.

❑ The entity bean contract is rigid, making it impossible to write efficient BMP code.

❑ It's hard to tune entity bean data access, whether we use BMP or CMP.

❑ Entity beans have considerable run-time overhead, even with the use of local, rather than remote, interfaces. (If no security roles or container transactions are defined for an EJB in its deployment descriptor element, many application servers may skip transaction and security checks when instances of the bean are invoked at run time. When combined with local calling, this can remove much of the overhead of entity beans. However, this is not guaranteed to happen in all servers, and an entity bean will always have a much higher overhead than an ordinary Java class.)

❑ Entity bean performance in practice often comes down to O/R mapping performance, and there's no guarantee that a J2EE application server vendor has strong expertise in this area.

Entity beans perform particularly badly, and consume excessive resources, with large resultsets, especially if the resultsets (like search results) are not modified by users. Entity beans perform best with data that's always modified at the individual record level.

Tool Support for Entity Beans

Entity beans don't usually contain business logic, so they're good candidates for auto-generation. This is just as well, as entity beans tend to contain a lot of code – for example in getter and setter methods. The deployment descriptors for EJB 2.0 CMP entities are also far too complex to hand-author reliably.

Good tool support is vital to productivity if using entity beans. Several types of tools are available, from third parties and application server vendors. For example:

❑ Object modeling tools such as Rational Rose and Together. These use the object-driven modeling approach we discussed in Chapter 7, enabling us to design entities graphically using UML and generate RDBMS tables. This is convenient, but object-driven modeling can create problems.

❑ Tools to generate entity beans from RDBMSs. For example, Persistence PowerTier supports this kind of modeling.

❑ Tools to generate entity bean artifacts from a simpler, easier-to-author, representation. For example, both EJBGen and XDoclet can generate local and home interfaces, J2EE standard and application-server-specific deployment descriptors from special Javadoc tags in an entity bean implementation class. Such simple tools are powerful and extensible, and far preferable to hand-coding.

> There is a strong case that entity beans should never be hand authored. One argument in favor of using entity beans is the relatively good level of tool support for entity bean authoring.

Summary

In practice, entity beans provide a basic O/R mapping described in the EJB specification. This mapping has the virtue of standardization. However, it doesn't presently approach the power of leading proprietary O/R mapping products. Nor is O/R mapping always the best solution when using an RDBMS.

Entity beans were foreshadowed in EJB 1.0 and have been a core part of the EJB specification since EJB 1.1. The EJB 2.0 specification introduces important enhancements in entity bean support, with more sophisticated container-managed persistence and the introduction of local interfaces. EJB 2.1 makes incremental enhancements.

The EJB 2.0 specification helps to settle some of the uncertainties regarding how to use entity beans. For example, the debate as to the granularity of entity beans seems to have been settled in favor of fine-grained entities. Such entities can be given local interfaces allowing session beans to work with them efficiently. EJB 2.0 CMP supports the navigation of relationships between fine-grained entities. EJB 2.0 entities can also use methods on their home interfaces to perform persistence logic affecting multiple entities.

However, entity beans have a checkered record in practice. In particular, their performance is often disappointing.

The future of entity beans as a technology probably depends on the quality of available CMP implementations. The EJB 2.0 specification requires application servers to ship with CMP implementations; we are also seeing the emergence of third-party implementations from companies with a strong track record in O/R mapping solutions. Such implementations may go beyond the specification to include features such as high-performance caching, optimistic locking, and EJB QL enhancements.

Entity beans can be valuable in J2EE solutions. However, it's best to treat the use of entity beans as one implementation choice rather than a key ingredient in application architecture. This can be achieved by using an abstraction layer of ordinary Java interfaces between session beans and entity beans.

I feel that a strategy of data access exclusively using entity beans is unworkable, largely for performance reasons. On the other hand, a strategy of data access from session beans (using helper classes) *is* workable, and is likely to perform better.

It's vital that components outside the EJB tier don't work directly with entity beans, but work with session beans that mediate access to entity beans. This design principle ensures correct decoupling between data and client-side components, and maximizes flexibility. EJB 2.0 allows us to give entity beans only local interfaces, to ensure that this design principle is followed.

There's also a strong argument for avoiding direct entity bean access in session beans themselves; this avoids tying the application architecture to entity beans, allowing flexibility if required to address performance issues or to take advantage of the capabilities of the data source in use.

If using entity beans, I recommend the following overall guidelines:

- **Don't use entity beans if your EJB container supports only EJB 1.1**
  Entity beans as specified in EJB 1.1 were inadequate to meet most real-world requirements.

- **Use CMP, not BMP**
  The greater control over the management of persistence offered by BMP is largely illusory. BMP entity beans are much harder to develop and maintain than CMP entity beans, and usually deliver worse performance.

- **Use ejbHome() methods to perform any aggregate operations required on your data**
  ejbHome() methods, which can act on multiple entities, help to escape the row-level access imposed by the entity bean model, which can otherwise prevent efficient RDBMS usage.

- **Use fine-grained entity beans**
  The "Composite Entity" pattern, often recommended for EJB 1.1 development, is obsolete in EJB 2.0. Implementing coarse-grained entities requires a lot of work, and is likely to deliver a poor return on investment. If fine-grained, EJB 2.0 style, entity beans don't meet your requirements, it's likely that use of entity beans is inappropriate.

- **Don't put business logic in entity beans**
  Entity beans should contain only persistence logic. When using EJB, business logic should normally go in session beans.

- **Investigate your EJB container's locking and caching options for entity beans**
  Whether or not entity beans are a viable option depends on the sophistication of your EJB container's support for them. How you structure your entity bean deployment may have a big effect on your application's performance.

The following guidelines apply primarily to distributed applications:

- **Never allow remote clients to access entity beans directly; mediate entity bean access through session beans, using the Session Façade pattern**
  If remote clients access entities directly, the result is usually excessive network traffic and unacceptable performance. When any components outside the EJB tier access entity beans directly (even within the same JVM), they arguably become too closely coupled to the data access strategy in use.

307

❑ **Give entity beans local interfaces, not remote interfaces**
Accessing entity beans through remote interfaces has proven too slow to be practical. Remote clients should use a session façade.

❑ **Create Value Objects in session beans, not entity beans**
As we discussed in Chapter 7, value objects are often related to use cases, and hence to business logic. Business logic should be in session beans, not entity beans.

*A **personal note**: I was enthusiastic about the idea of entity beans when they were first described as an optional feature of EJB 1.0. As recently as the first draft release of EJB 2.0 in June 2000, I was hopeful that the limitations that I and other architects had encountered working with entity beans in EJB 1.1 would be overcome, and that entity beans would become a strong feature of EJB. However, I have become progressively disillusioned.*

Entity bean performance has proven a problem in most systems I have seen that use entity beans. I have become convinced that remote access to entity beans and the transaction and security management infrastructure for entity beans is architecturally gratuitous and an unnecessary overhead. These are issues to be handled by session beans. The introduction of local interfaces still leaves entity beans as unnecessarily heavyweight components. Entity beans still fail to address the hardest problems of O/R mapping.

My feeling is that JDO will supplant entity beans as the standard-based persistence technology in J2EE. I think that there's a strong case for downgrading the status of entity beans to an optional part of the EJB specification. Entity bean support accounts for well over a third of the EJB 2.0 specification (as opposed to slightly more than a fifth of the much shorter EJB 1.1 specification), and much of the complexity of EJB containers. Removing the requirement to implement entity beans would foster competition and innovation in the application server market and would help JDO become a single strong J2EE standard for accessing persistent data. But that's just my opinion!

> **I prefer to manage persistence from session beans, using an abstraction layer of DAOs comprising a persistence facade. This approach decouples business logic code from the details of any particular persistence model.**

We will use this approach in our sample application as shown in practice in the next chapter.

OCEANUS

INSULÆ

PHILIP

PINÆ

ARC

I. Ainan

I. de Matalotes

I. dos Arecifes

Pulo S. Pelo

Siley

Ilocos

Luzon

Philippina

Pintados

Ancon triste

G. de Matalhambre

Pontan

Mandato Paragalle

C. del Spirito Santo

Calos

Francisco Gomez

Ylhas del Primeiro

Suzridera

Puelhos

Abo camucho Primeiro

Caburas

Abro

Manilha

Luco

los Lunados

Praćel

Calamianes

Lucu Iradora

Lucu S. Mora

S. Michael

S. Clara

I. Semuilu

MINDANA

Mindanao

Malaqua

Passage de S. Clara

A. de Resurreicam

C. Bicoy

I. da Palmeras

I. de S. Ioannes

I. de Mata

Corigao

I. de Talau

I. de Rao

I. de Dos

I. dos Graos

As Aguada

Sinoe

Tunquin

Enseada de Cauchin

Sinoa

Costa de Palo Cambo

Camboia

Cambo ia

Palo Ciri

Pulo Condor

Palo babe

Pulo Tigao

Mon Praten

Arch

Malanu

Borneo

Mala Canal

R. de Canal

Melana

Puttam ará

Tanasserim

Tamaraton

BOR NE O

Lar donde fue Manuel de Lima

Cauas Piru

Bintan

Banca

Bibilham

Chinabato

Nusasira

Porto CaciamCEIRAM

Hic hybernavit de Menezes

Aru

Agua in berzerain Martin Afonso de mels

I. de S. Juan

I. de Sagin

Raguenam

Damea

Corigao

Canala

Pulo

Tidore

Motir

CELEBES

Ablas

Buorus

Cabian

Buro

I. de S. Matheus

Batula Bandara

Terra alta Guaban

AVA, quæ et AOA dicitur. Fidelda.

LANT

DOL

Timor

Guaon

Baixos

9

Practical Data Access

In this chapter, we survey some leading data-access technologies and choose one for use in our sample application.

The data access technologies discussed in this chapter can be used anywhere in a J2EE application. Unlike entity beans, they are not tied to use in an EJB container. This has significant advantages for testing and architectural flexibility. However, we may still make good use of session EJB CMT, when we implement data access within the EJB container.

This chapter focuses on accessing relational databases, as we've previously noted that most J2EE applications work with them.

We consider SQL-based technologies and O/R mapping technologies other than entity beans. We will see the potential importance of Java Data Objects, a new API for persisting Java objects, which may standardize the use of O/R mapping in Java.

We focus on JDBC, which best fulfils the data access requirements of the sample application.

We look at the JDBC API in detail, showing how to avoid common JDBC errors and discussing some subtle points that are often neglected.

As the JDBC API is relatively low-level, and using it is error-prone and requires an unacceptable volume of code, it's important for application code to work with higher-level APIs built on it. We'll look at the design, implementation, and usage of a JDBC abstraction framework that greatly simplifies the use of JDBC. This framework is used in the sample application, and can be used in any application using JDBC.

As we discussed in Chapter 7, it's desirable to separate data access from business logic. We can achieve this separation by concealing the details of data access behind an abstraction layer such as an O/R mapping framework or the **Data-Access Objects (DAO)** pattern.

We conclude by looking at the DAO pattern in action, as we implement some of the core data-access code of the sample application using the DAO pattern and the JDBC abstraction framework discussed in this chapter.

Data Access Technology Choices

Let's begin by reviewing some of the leading data-access technologies available to J2EE applications. These technologies can be divided into two major categories: SQL-based data access that works with relational concepts; and data access based on O/R mapping.

SQL-Based Technologies

The following technologies are purely intended to work with relational databases. Thus they use SQL as the means of retrieving and manipulating data. While this requires Java code to work with relational, rather than purely object, concepts, it enables the use of efficient RDBMS constructs.

Note that using RDBMS concepts in data-access code doesn't mean that business logic will depend on SQL and RDBMS. We will use the Data-Access Object pattern, discussed in Chapter 7, to decouple business logic from data access implementation.

JDBC

Most communication with relational databases, whether handled by an EJB container, a third-party O/R mapping product or the application developer, is likely to be based on JDBC. Much of the appeal of entity beans – and O/R mapping frameworks – is based on the assumption that using JDBC is error-prone and too complicated for application developers. In fact, this is a dubious contention so long as we use appropriate helper classes.

JDBC is based around SQL, which is no bad thing. SQL is not an arcane technology, but a proven, practical language that simplifies many data operations. There may be an "impedance mismatch" between RDBMSs and Java applications, but SQL is a good language for querying and manipulating data. Many data operations can be done with far fewer lines of code in SQL than in Java classes working with mapped objects. The professional J2EE developer needs to have a sound knowledge of SQL and cannot afford to be ignorant of RDBMS fundamentals.

JDBC is also an ideal technology when we need to call stored procedures, execute unusual custom queries, or use proprietary RDBMS features.

The key is how we use JDBC. A naïve approach, littering JDBC code and SQL statements through application code, is a recipe for disaster. It ties the entire application to a particular persistence strategy, guarantees problems if the database schema changes, and leaves application code containing an inappropriate mix of abstraction levels. However, JDBC can be used effectively in application code, so long as we follow a few golden rules:

❑ Decouple business logic from JDBC access wherever possible. JDBC code should normally be found only in data-access objects.

❑ Avoid raw JDBC code that works directly with the JDBC API. JDBC error handling is so cumbersome as to seriously reduce productivity (requiring a `finally` block to achieve anything, for example). Low-level details such as error handling are best left to helper classes that expose a higher-level API to application code. This is possible without sacrificing control over the SQL executed.

The J2EE orthodoxy that it's always better to let the container handle persistence than to write SQL is questionable. For example, while it can be difficult or impossible to tune container-generated statements, it's possible to test and tune SQL queries in a tool such as SQL*Plus, checking performance and behavior when different sessions access the same data. Only where significant object caching in an O/R mapping layer is feasible is coding using an O/R mapping likely to equal or exceed the performance of JDBC.

> There's nothing wrong with managing persistence using JDBC. In many cases, if we know we are dealing with an RDBMS, only through JDBC can we leverage the full capability of the RDMBS.
>
> However, don't use JDBC directly from business objects such as a session EJBs or even DAOs. Use an abstraction layer to decouple your business component from the low-level JDBC API. If possible, make this abstract layer's API non-JDBC-specific (for example, try to avoid exposing SQL). We'll consider the implementation and usage of such an abstraction layer later in this chapter.

SQLJ

SQLJ is an alternative to JDBC that offers closer integration between Java code and RDBMS. It offers the same basic model as JDBC, but simplifies application code and may improve efficiency. It was developed by a group of companies including Oracle, IBM, Informix, Sun, and Sybase. SQLJ consists of three parts:

❑ **Part 0 – Embedded SQL**
This provides the ability to embed static SQL statements in Java code by escaping into SQL. In contrast, JDBC uses dynamic SQL, and is based on API calls rather than an escape mechanism. SQLJ Part 0 has been adopted as an ANSI standard.

❑ **Part 1 – SQL Routines**
This defines a mechanism for calling Java static methods as stored procedures.

❑ **Part 2 – SQL Types**
This consists of specifications for using Java classes as SQL user-defined data types.

SQLJ Part 0, Embedded SQL, is comparable in functionality to JDBC. The syntax enables SQL statements to be expressed more concisely than with JDBC and facilitates getting Java variable values to and from the database. A SQLJ **precompiler** translates the SQLJ syntax (Java code with embedded SQL) into regular Java source code. The concept of embedded SQL is nothing new: Oracle's Pro*C and other products take the same approach to C and C++, and there are even similar solutions for COBOL.

SQLJ provides convenient escaping in SQL and binding of Java variables to SQL parameters. The following example illustrates both features, the use of #sql escape syntax and binding to Java variables using the : syntax in the embedded SQL. The example inserts a new row into a table, taking the values from Java variables, and then selects the new data back into the variables:

```
int age = 32;
String forename = "Rod";
String surname = "Rod";
String email = "rod.johnson@interface21.com";
#sql {
INSERT INTO
  people (forename, surname, email)
VALUES
  (:forename, :surname, :email)
};
```

```
#sql {
SELECT
  forename, surname, email
INTO
  :forename, :surname, :email
FROM
  people
WHERE
  email='rod.johnson@interface21.com'
};
```

Note that I've omitted error handling: we must catch java.sql.SQLExceptions in SQLJ as in JDBC, and must ensure that we close the connection in the event of errors. However, we don't need to work with JDBC Statement and PreparedStatement objects, making this code less verbose than the JDBC equivalent. SQLJ Parts 1 and 2 attempt to standardize database-specific functionality such as stored procedures.

SQLJ can be used in J2EE architecture in the same way as JDBC: for example, in implementations of data-access interfaces. So choosing between SQLJ and JDBC is an issue of only local significance within an application. The advantages of SQLJ over JDBC include:

❑ SQLJ offers compile-time rather than run-time checking of SQL. While with JDBC we will only learn that a SQL statement is nonsense at run time, SQLJ will pick this up at compile time.

❑ Performance may be enhanced through the use of static, rather than dynamic SQL.

❑ SQLJ code is simpler to write and understand than JDBC code.

The disadvantages of SQLJ include:

❑ The development-deployment cycle is more complex, requiring the use of the SQLJ precompiler.

❑ SQLJ doesn't simplify JDBC's cumbersome error handling requirements.

❑ SQLJ syntax is less elegant than Java syntax. On the other hand, SQLJ may achieve some tasks in far fewer lines of code than Java using JDBC.

❑ Although SQLJ is a standard, a SQLJ solution is less portable than a JDBC solution as not all RDBMS vendors support SQLJ. (This needn't be an objection if SQLJ is used to implement a DAO targeted at a particular database.)

Despite its potential, and despite the fact that it is now several years old, SQLJ doesn't appear to be used widely, and is still strongly identified with Oracle.

> *For more information on SQLJ see* www.sqlj.org, *and* Java Programming with Oracle SQLJ from *O'Reilly (ISBN: 0-596-00087-1) – http://www.oreilly.com/catalog/orasqlj/).*

O/R Mapping Technologies

O/R mapping frameworks offer a completely different programming model to APIs such as JDBC or SQLJ. They can also be used to implement data access anywhere in a J2EE application. Some products provide a pluggable CMP persistence manager for EJB 2.0, which offers richer functionality than implementations shipped with application servers.

The best O/R mapping frameworks have far more real-world experience behind them than entity beans. However, they have traditionally been expensive products (although this seems to be changing in 2002), and have required commitment to proprietary APIs. To my knowledge, no open source product currently offers an enterprise-ready O/R mapping solution (although I'd be very glad to hear that I'm wrong).

A new entrant on the scene is Sun's JDO specification. Like J2EE, this is a specification – essentially an API – rather than a product. However, many companies already support or are implementing the JDO specification. Importantly, some of the major existing O/R mapping frameworks now support JDO, using their existing mapping infrastructure. Some ODBMS vendors are also supporting JDO. JDO may bring comparable standardization to use of O/R mapping in Java to that which JDBC delivered for RDBMS access in Java.

Established Commercial Products

Let's consider commercial O/R mapping products first, as they have been around longest and are proven in production. There are many products competing in this space, but we'll discuss only the two that are most widely used: TopLink and CocoBase. Many of the points made in relation to these two products apply to all O/R mapping products.

TopLink

TopLink is probably the market leader, and predates the EJB specification. It has experienced several changes of ownership and is now part of Oracle 9i Application Server, although it can be downloaded separately and used with other application servers. It offers a pluggable EJB 2.0 CMP solution, although its documentation suggests that TopLink's developers do not favor the entity bean approach. TopLink allows entity beans to be mixed with lightweight persistent Java objects.

TopLink's feature list shows how far entity beans have to go beyond standard EJB 2.0 CMP to become a mature O/R mapping framework. The following are some of the TopLink features missing in the EJB specification:

- ❑ The ability to map a Java object to more than one table.
- ❑ Support for Java object inheritance.
- ❑ Optimistic locking support.
- ❑ Support for nested transactions ("units of work" in TopLink parlance). *This isn't supported by J2EE, not merely EJB.*

- ❑ Customizable transformation of data between database and object. As well as simply mapping a column value onto an object property, TopLink allows the programmer to customize the mapping.

- ❑ The ability to customize SQL instead of relying on generated SQL.

- ❑ Support for stored procedures.

- ❑ Caching to reduce the number of accesses to the underlying database. Caching is synchronized between nodes.

Like most O/R mapping frameworks, TopLink can be used with either database-driven or object-driven modeling. If a database exists, TopLink's mapping tool can be used to generate Java objects to use it. Alternatively, TopLink can be used to create a database schema from mapped Java objects. Mappings are defined in TopLink's GUI Mapping Workbench. Mapped objects generally don't need to contain TopLink-specific code (unlike CMP entity beans, which must implement a special API); however, code that uses mapped objects is heavily dependent on proprietary APIs.

TopLink offers its own object-based query language. The following example from the TopLink 4.6 demos uses an `Expression` object to filter for objects of a given class with a budget property greater than equal to a given value:

```
Expression exp = new ExpressionBuilder().get("budget").greaterThanEqual(4000);
Vector projects = session.readAllObjects(LargeProject.class, exp);
```

TopLink 4.6 additionally supports JDO as a query API.

TopLink has traditionally been expensive (comparable in price to leading J2EE application servers). Following its acquisition by Oracle in June 2002 it is free for development use and its production pricing is likely to be more attractive.

TopLink's strength is that it is a proven product with powerful and configurable O/R mapping capabilities. Its main weakness is that code that uses it is dependent on proprietary libraries. However, its support for JDO may remove this objection.

See http://otn.oracle.com/products/ias/toplink/content.html for more information on TopLink.

CocoBase

CocoBase, from Thought Inc, is another established O/R mapping product. Like TopLink, CocoBase includes an EJB 2.0 CMP persistence manager and offers a distributed cache. It also offers transparent persistence: objects to be persisted don't need to implement special interfaces. Mappings are held outside classes to be persisted.

CocoBase supports sophisticated O/R mapping: for example, the ability to map a Java object to more than one table. As with TopLink, it is possible to tune generated SQL queries. CocoBase is more closely integrated with the underlying RDBMS than many O/R mapping solutions: it's easy to call stored procedures, and queries are written in SQL, rather than in a proprietary query language.

See http://www.thoughtinc.com/ for more information on CocoBase.

Java Data Objects (JDO)

JDO is a recent specification developed under the Java Community Process (1.0 release, March 2002) that describes persistence-store-neutral persistence of Java objects. While it's beyond the scope of the present book to discuss JDO in detail, I feel that JDO is a very important API to J2EE developers, and hope that the following section will serve to whet your appetite.

JDO is most likely to be used as an O/R mapping, but it is not tied to RDBMSs. For example, JDO may become the standard API for Java access to ODBMSs.

In contrast to the entity bean model, JDO does not require objects to be persisted to implement a special interface. Most ordinary Java objects can be persisted, so long as their persistent state is held in their instance data. While objects used in a JDO **persistence manager** must implement the `javax.jdo.PersistenceCapable` interface, developers do not normally write code that implements this interface. The additional methods required by the `PersistenceCapable` interface are usually added to compiled class files by a **byte code enhancer** provided by the JDO vendor: a tool that can take ordinary class files and "enhance" them for use with a JDO persistence engine.

JDO is more lightweight than entity beans, partly because objects being persisted are much closer to ordinary Java classes. JDO is likely to have much lower overhead in creating new objects: an important consideration when queries return large result sets.

Application code works with a JDO `PersistenceManager`, which handles one transaction at a time. `PersistenceManager` instances must be obtained from a `PersistenceManagerFactory` provided by the JDO vendor. This allows for a range of caching approaches, leaving the choice to the JDO vendor.

Caching can occur at `PersistenceManagerFactory` level as well as within transactions. Several JDO implementations support caching in a clustered environment. JDO also allows for programmatic application control over caching. Entity beans don't provide similar control. JDO also explicitly supports optimistic locking and inheritance of persistent Java objects; again, this can be controlled programmatically.

JDO mappings are defined in XML documents that are simpler and easier to understand than CMP entity bean deployment descriptors. However, mappings are not fully portable between JDO implementations, as they are dependent on vendor-specific extensions.

JDO is not currently part of J2EE. However, it seems likely that JDO will eventually become a required API, in the same way as JDBC and JNDI.

Despite Sun's denials, there is a definite overlap between JDO and entity beans. They both amount to a object-relational mapping and define a query language for operating on persistent data. It's hard to see the justification for two quite different O/R mapping standards and, especially, two different query languages, within J2EE.

However, JDO complements J2EE and EJB (in contrast to entity beans), rather than competes with them.

The JDO query language is called JDOQL. A JDO **query** is a reusable, threadsafe object that defines a result class and a JDOQL **filter**. JDOQL filter expressions are Java expressions, although they are held in string literals or variables and cannot be validated against the persistence store at compile time. Unlike EJB QL, JDOQL is used in Java code, meaning that queries are dynamic, rather than static. The following example shows the construction of a query that looks for `Customer` objects with a given `email` address and `password` (both instance variables):

```
Query loginQuery = persistenceManager.newQuery(Customer.class);
loginQuery.setFilter("email == pEmail && password == pPassword");
loginQuery.declareParameters("String pEmail,String pPassword");
loginQuery.compile();
```

This query can be executed as follows:

```
Collection c = (Collection) loginQuery().execute("rod.johnson@interface21.com",
"rj");
Customer cust = (Customer) c.iterator().next();
```

Changes made to objects resulting from queries, such as the `Customer` object above, will normally cause the backing data store to be updated transparently. However, JDO allows objects to be explicitly disconnected from the data store if desired. Once JDOs are retrieved, it is possible to navigate associations (joins in an RDBMS) transparently.

The most important of the several `execute()` methods on the JDO `Query` interface takes an array of `Object` as a parameter; the above example uses the convenience method that takes two strings and invokes the generic method.

JDO has been criticized for its use of string query filters, rather than an object-based query API such as TopLink's proprietary API. The loss of compile-time checking is unfortunate, but the approach works and is convenient to use. It is easy, for example, to use Java syntax to build complex combinations of `OR`s and `AND`s that are easily understandable by Java developers.

Although JDO, like JDBC, provides a transaction management API that can be used without a global transaction infrastructure, this is inappropriate in J2EE. JDO implementations can detect and work within JTA transactions, whether created by user code or resulting from EJB CMT.

Chapter 16 of the JDO specification details the way in which JDO can be used from EJBs to handle persistence. Integration with session beans is particularly attractive, as JDO operations can use declarative transaction delimitation provided by session beans. Although it is sometimes advocated, it's hard to see the point of using JDO from entity beans with BMP. JDO already provides an object view of the database, rendering the additional abstraction layer of entity beans unnecessary and even harmful. (The result is likely to be a lowest common denominator of the functionality supported by both JDO and EJB.)

As all JDO exceptions are runtime exceptions, any code using JDO isn't forced to catch them (although it can where exceptions are likely to be recoverable). This leads to a significant reduction in the volume of code and improvement in readability compared with APIs such as JDBC that use checked exceptions.

For more information about JDO, see the following resources:

- ❏ http://access1.sun.com/jdo/
  Index page maintained by Craig Russell, JDO specification lead. Links to other useful resources.

- ❏ http://www.jdocentral.com/index.html
  JDO Portal. The forums are particularly interesting, featuring discussion of many practical issues in JDO development.

- ❏ http://www.onjava.com/pub/a/onjava/2002/02/06/jdo1.html
  Simple introduction to JDO, including a complete example.

- ❏ http://theserverside.com/discussion/thread.jsp?thread_id=771#23527
  ServerSide.com discussion comparing JDO to entity beans.

- ❏ http://www.ogilviepartners.com/JdoFaq.html
  JDO FAQ, maintained by a private consulting organization.

- ❏ http://www.solarmetric.com/
  Home page of Kodo, one of the first JDO implementations. Kodo is easy to use and supports caching across a cluster. *Kodo is well documented, and a good choice for getting to grips with JDO.*

- ❏ http://www.prismtechnologies.com/English/Products/JDO/index.html
  Home of OpenFusion, a JDO implementation from PrismTech.

JDO is likely to prove a very important technology for J2EE. However, at the time of writing (mid 2002), JDO is yet to prove mature enough for use in mission-critical enterprise applications.

When JDO matures, I suspect it may render entity beans obsolete. JDO preserves the good qualities of entity beans (such as hiding data access detail from application code, an O/R mapping solution, use within transactions delimited by session beans, and the potential for object caching to reduce requests to the database) and eliminates many of their problems (such as the inability to use ordinary Java classes as persistent objects, gratuitous remote access to data objects, and the heavyweight run-time infrastructure).

Choosing a Data Access Strategy for the Sample Application

We noted in Chapter 7 that the sample application can benefit little from an O/R mapping layer. There's little opportunity for caching, for example. We also saw that use of stored procedures could efficiently conceal some of the data management complexity inside the RDBMS. This means that JDBC is the obvious data access strategy.

As it's important to ensure that our design remains portable, we will conceal the use of JDBC behind an abstraction layer of data-access interfaces, using the DAO pattern discussed in Chapter 7. These interfaces will be database-agnostic. They won't depend on JDBC or RDBMS concepts, allowing the potential for very different implementations.

In the remainder of this chapter we will:

❑ Take a closer look at JDBC, considering some subtle points that we must understand in order to write robust, efficient code.

❑ Examine the implementation and usage of an abstraction layer of generic infrastructure classes that simplifies working with JDBC and minimizes the likelihood of JDBC-related errors.

❑ Look at the implementation of some of the sample application's data-access requirements using JDBC and our generic abstraction layer.

JDBC Subtleties

Since we'll be working with JDBC in the sample application, let's consider the major challenges of using JDBC in practice, and examine some subtle points of the JDBC API that are often neglected. This is an important topic; in my experience, J2EE applications often contain sloppy JDBC code, which can cause major problems.

Correct Exception Handling

The main challenge in writing robust JDBC code is ensuring correct exception handling. Most JDBC API methods can throw the checked `java.sql.SQLException`. Not only must we ensure that we catch this exception, we must ensure that cleanup occurs even if an exception is thrown.

The following code listing, which performs a trivial SELECT, shows a common JDBC error, with serious consequences:

```
public String getPassword(String forename) throws ApplicationException {

    String sql = "SELECT password FROM customer WHERE forename='" +
                    forename + "'";

    String password = null;
    Connection con = null;
    Statement s = null;
    ResultSet rs = null;
    try {
        con = <get connection from DataSource>;
        s = con.createStatement();
        rs = s.executeQuery(sql);

        while (rs.next()) {
            password = rs.getString(1);
        }
        rs.close();
        s.close();
        con.close();

    } catch (SQLException ex) {
        throw new ApplicationException("Couldn't run query [" + sql + "]", ex);
    }
    return password;
}
```

Code like this can crash a whole application, and even bring down a database. The problem is that each of the highlighted lines can throw a SQLException. If this happens, we will fail to close the Connection, as the connection is closed only if we reach the last line of the try block. The result will be a "leaked" connection, stolen from the application server's connection pool. Although the server may eventually detect the problem and release the stolen connection, the impact on other users of the connection pool may be severe. Each connection costs the RDBMS resources to maintain, and pooled connections are a valuable resource. Eventually all connections in the pool may become unavailable, bringing the application server to a halt, and the application server may be unable to increase the size of the pool because the database can support no more concurrent connections.

The following, correct, version of this method adds a finally block (highlighted) to ensure that the connection is always closed. Note that in this version, as in the first version, we need to throw an application-specific exception (ApplicationException) wrapping any SQLExceptions encountered:

```java
public String getPassword(String forename) throws ApplicationException {

    String sql = "SELECT password FROM customer WHERE forename='" +
                forename + "'";

    String password = null;
    Connection con = null;
    Statement s = null;
    ResultSet rs = null;
    try {
      con = <get connection from DataSource>;
      s = con.createStatement();
      rs = s.executeQuery(sql);

      while (rs.next()) {
        password = rs.getString(1);
      }
      rs.close();
      s.close();
    }
    catch (SQLException ex) {
      throw new ApplicationException("Couldn't run query [" + sql + "]", ex);
    }
    finally {
      try {
        if (con != null) {
          con.close();
        }
      }
      catch (SQLException ex) {
        throw new ApplicationException("Failed to close connection", ex);
      }
    }
    return password;
  }
```

This is much more robust, but it's also much more verbose. It's absurd to have to write 39 lines of code to accomplish just about the simplest possible JDBC operation. It's clear that we need a better solution than using the JDBC API directly.

321

> When using JDBC directly, it's essential to use a `finally` block to ensure that the connection is closed, even in the event of an exception.

Extracting Information from SQLExceptions

Another important facet of JDBC exception handling is extracting the maximum possible information from SQLExceptions. Unfortunately, JDBC makes this rather cumbersome.

`java.sql.SQLExceptions` can be chained. The `getNextException()` method on SQLException returns the next SQLException associated with the failure, (or null, if there is no further information. Whether or not checking for further exceptions is necessary seems to depend on the RDBMS and driver (for example, I've found it very useful in Cloudscape 3.6, but generally unnecessary in Oracle).

Although JDBC uses the one exception class (SQLException) for almost all problems, it is possible to extract useful details from a SQLException. SQLExceptions also include two potentially useful error codes: the **vendor code** and the **SQLState** code.

The vendor code is an `int` returned by the `getErrorCode()` method. As the name implies, the vendor code may differ between vendors, even for common error conditions such as deadlocks. Thus, code that relies on it won't be portable. For example, in the case of Oracle, the vendor code will be the numeric code that Oracle reports in all its error messages (not just to JDBC), such as "ORA-00060: deadlock detected while waiting for resource". Occasionally this non-portable functionality is vital, as it's otherwise impossible to ascertain exactly what went wrong with a SQL statement.

We can even use an error code ourselves for custom application exceptions. Consider an Oracle stored procedure that includes the following line:

```
raise_application_error(-20100, 'My special error condition');
```

This error code will appear to JDBC like a standard error code: the message with the SQLException will be `ORA-20100: My special error condition` and the vendor code will be `20100`.

The `SQLException.getSQLState()` method returns a 5-character string that is at least theoretically a portable error code. The first two characters contain high-level information in a **class code**; the next three more specific (often vendor-specific) information. The SQLState codes aren't documented in the JDBC API. The only free online documentation I have been able to find is at http://developer.mimer.se/documentation/html_91/Mimer_SQL_Mobile_DocSet/App_return_status2.html#1110406.

Unfortunately, the SQLState codes are not guaranteed to be supported by all databases, and may not carry enough information to establish the nature of a problem. Sometimes the vendor code is the only way to obtain the detail we need. Most databases have many more vendor codes than SQLState codes, and better documentation describing them. Sometimes there is no standard SQLState code to represent a problem, such as Oracle's 8177 ("can't serialize access for this transaction"), which may carry crucial information to a J2EE application but which is unique to the implementation of a particular RDBMS.

We must understand the `java.sql.SQLWarning` exception as well as `SQLExceptions`. Like `SQLException`, this is a checked exception (it's actually a subclass of `SQLException`), but it's never actually thrown by the JDBC API. Non-fatal SQL errors, such as data truncation on reading, can be reported as SQL warnings, which are attached to `ResultSets`, `Statements`, or `Connections` after the execution of offending statements. Each of these JDBC API objects has a `getWarnings()` method that returns `null` if there are no warnings, or the first in a chain of `SQLWarnings` analogous to a chain of `SQLExceptions` if warnings were raised. Warnings are reset when a new operation is undertaken.

Warnings are another reason that using JDBC directly isn't a viable option. In a framework implemented to simplify JDBC, it's easy to throw an exception on warnings if desired, or save warnings for future reference. In code that uses the JDBC API directly, the process of checking for warnings adds still further code bloat; it's simply too much trouble to do in practice, unless we resort to a massive cut and paste exercise that will produce many other problems.

The PreparedStatement Question

It's important to understand the distinction between the `java.sql.PreparedStatement` interface and the `java.sql.Statement` interface. With a **prepared statement**, we provide the necessary SQL containing ? place holders for **bind variables** and set a parameter for each placeholder. With an ordinary statement, we provide the entire SQL string, including a string representation of each parameter value.

Prepared statements should generally be preferred.

First, they significantly simplify the handling of strings and other objects. If we don't use prepared statements, we will need to escape illegal characters in strings. For example, the following query will fail:

```
SELECT id FROM customers WHERE surname='d'Artagnan'
```

The surname d'Artagnan contains an illegal `'` character, which the database will view as the terminator of a string literal. In Oracle we'll get error ORA-01756 with the message `quoted string not properly terminated`. We'll need to amend the query as follows to get it to work:

```
SELECT id FROM customers WHERE surname='d''Artagnan'
```

We will also have problems with DATEs and other standard object types, for which we'll need to use an RDMBS-specific string format. With prepared statements we don't need to worry about escaping or object conversion. If we call the correct `setXXXX()` methods or know the appropriate JDBC type (one of the constants defined in the `java.sql.Types` class) corresponding to the RDBMS type, the JDBC driver will transparently take care of the conversion and any escaping. Our JDBC code will also be more portable, as the driver will know how to convert standard Java objects to and from the SQL types appropriate for the target database.

Second, prepared statements are also potentially more efficient than string statements, although the extent of any performance gain will vary between platforms. Prepared statements are more expensive to create than ordinary string statements, yet may reduce the amount of work the JDBC driver, and perhaps even the database, has to do if they are reused. The first time a prepared statement is executed, it can be parsed and compiled by the database, and is likely to be placed in a statement cache. The database is thus able to store the execution path for the statement, which is likely to reduce the amount of work it needs to do to execute the statement in future. In contrast, regular SQL string statements cannot be cached in this way if they have variable parameters, because statements with different literal parameter values appear different to the database. Not only does this prevent useful caching, it may also significantly increase overall load on the database by breaking the caching of other statements. The database's statement cache may fill up with the apparently different statements, leaving no room for genuinely cacheable statements from the same or other applications.

Unfortunately it's impossible to be certain of this behavior with all databases, JDBC drivers, and application servers, as the JDBC 2.0 API (the version guaranteed with J2EE 1.3) and J2EE specifications do not require prepared statement caching. Nor can we ensure caching ourselves: we're forced to close prepared statements after we create them if we want to close the connection we obtained (which we usually do in a J2EE environment). This means that we're reliant on the application server's JDBC connection pool, rather than our code, for any reuse of `PreparedStatements`. Fortunately, most modern servers appear to pool `PreparedStatements`. The performance benefit this brings will depend on the underlying JDBC driver and the database.

JDBC 3.0 introduces `PreparedStatement` caching as standard. This is largely transparent to developers: it's assumed that a connection pool implementation may provide support for prepared statement caching. Thus `PreparedStatements` will become still more attractive in the future.

> Prefer JDBC `PreparedStatements` to `Statements`. They lessen the likelihood of type errors and may improve efficiency.

A Generic JDBC Abstraction Framework

It's not enough to understand the JDBC API and the issues in using it correctly. Using JDBC directly is simply too much effort, and too error-prone. We need not just understanding, but a code framework that makes JDBC easier to use.

In this section we'll look at one such solution: a generic JDBC abstraction framework, which we'll use in the sample application, and which can significantly simplify application code and minimize the likelihood of making errors.

> The JDBC API is too low-level for using it directly to be a viable option. When using JDBC, always use helper classes to simplify application code. However, don't try to write your own O/R mapping layer. If you need O/R mapping, use an existing solution.
>
> In this section, we'll examine the implementation and usage of the JDBC abstraction framework used in the sample application, which is included in the framework code in the download accompanying this book. This is a generic framework, which you can use in your own applications to simplify use of JDBC and lessen the likelihood of JDBC-related errors.

Motivation

Writing low-level JDBC code is painful. The problem is not the SQL, which is usually easy to author and understand, and accounts for little of the total code volume, but the incidentals of using JDBC. The JDBC API is not particularly elegant and is too low-level for use in application code.

As we've seen, using the JDBC API even to perform very simple tasks is relatively complex and error-prone. Take the following example, which queries the IDs of available seats in our ticketing system:

```java
public List getAvailableSeatIds(DataSource ds, int performanceId,
        int seatType) throws ApplicationException {

  String sql = "SELECT seat_id AS id FROM available_seats " +
               "WHERE performance_id = ? AND price_band_id = ?";
  List seatIds = new LinkedList();

  Connection con = null;
  PreparedStatement ps = null;
  ResultSet rs = null;
  try {
    con = ds.getConnection();
    ps = con.prepareStatement(sql);
    ps.setInt(1, performanceId);
    ps.setInt(2, seatType);
    rs = ps.executeQuery();

    while (rs.next()) {
      int seatId = rs.getInt(1);
      seatIds.add(new Integer(seatId));
    }
    rs.close();
    ps.close();
  }
  catch (SQLException ex) {
    throw new ApplicationException("Couldn't run query [" + sql + "]", ex);
  }
  finally {
    try {
      if (con != null)
        con.close();
    }
    catch (SQLException ex) {
      // Log and ignore
    }
  }
  return seatIds;
}
```

Although the SQL is trivial, because of the use of a view in the database to conceal the outer join required, executing this query requires 30-odd lines of JDBC code, few of which actually do anything. (I've highlighted the functional lines of code.) Such a predominance of "plumbing" code that doesn't deliver functionality indicates a poor implementation approach. An approach that makes very simple things so hard is unworkable. If we use this approach every time we need to perform a query, we'll end up with reams of code and the potential for many errors. Important operations like closing the connection, which are incidental to the data retrieval operation, dominate the listing. Note that closing the connection requires a second try...catch block in the finally block of the outer try...catch. Whenever I see a nested try...catch, I feel a powerful desire to refactor that code into a framework class.

I haven't included code to obtain the DataSource, *which would use JNDI in a J2EE application.
I assume that this is accomplished elsewhere using a suitable helper class to avoid JNDI access
further bloating the code.*

A simple abstraction framework can make this query much simpler, while still using the JDBC API
under the covers. The following code defines a reusable, threadsafe query object extending a framework
class, which we'll look at in detail later:

```
class AvailabilityQuery extends
    com.interface21.jdbc.object.ManualExtractionSqlQuery {

  public AvailabilityQuery(DataSource ds) {
    super(ds, "SELECT seat_id AS id FROM available_seats WHERE " +
              "performance_id = ? AND price_band_id = ?");
    declareParameter(new SqlParameter(Types.NUMERIC));
    declareParameter(new SqlParameter(Types.NUMERIC));
    compile();
  }

  protected Object extract(ResultSet rs, int rownum) throws SQLException {
    return new Integer(rs.getInt("id"));
  }
}
```

This takes one third of the code of the first version, and every line does something. The troublesome
error handling is left to the superclass. We need only to write code to provide the SQL query, provide
the bind parameters (after specifying their JDBC types) and extract the results. In other words, we only
need to implement application functionality, not plumbing. The framework superclass provides a
number of execute methods, one of which we can run like this:

```
AvailabilityQuery availabilityQuery = new AvailabilityQuery(ds);
List l = availabilityQuery.execute(1, 1);
```

Once constructed, we can reuse this query object. The execute() method throws a runtime exception,
not a checked exception, meaning that we need only catch it if it's recoverable. The resemblance to the
JDO Query interface, which we've just discussed, is intentional. The JDO API is easy to use and already
familiar to a growing number of developers, hence it makes sense to apply the same principles to JDBC.
The key difference, of course, is that our JDBC query doesn't return mapped objects; changes to the
returned objects will have no effect on the database.

In the remainder of this section we'll look at how this abstraction framework is implemented and how it
can be used to simplify application code.

Aims

Remember the Pareto Principle (the 80:20 rule)? The best results can be achieved with JDBC
abstraction by not trying to achieve too much.

The following areas account for most developer effort using the JDBC API directly and are most error-
prone. Our abstraction should try to address each:

❑ Too much code – Queries, for example, must acquire a `Connection`, a `Statement` and a `ResultSet`, and iterate over the `ResultSet`.

❑ Correct cleanup in the event of errors (ensuring that connections and statements are closed, as we discussed above). Most competent Java developers have cleaned up a lot of broken `try...catch` blocks around JDBC code, after seeing the number of open connections gradually mount in server-side applications.

❑ Dealing with `SQLExceptions` – These are checked exceptions, which application code shouldn't really be forced to catch, as catching them requires knowledge of JDBC.

❑ Making it easier for user code to establish the cause of exceptions, without needing to examine SQLState or vendor codes.

Surprisingly, there don't seem to be many libraries or frameworks that address these problems. Most are much more ambitious (aiming at some form of O/R mapping, for example), meaning they become complex to implement and to use. Hence, I've developed a framework for the sample application, which we'll talk about now and which can be used in any application using JDBC (these classes are actually the most recent in a line of such classes I've developed for various clients).

This isn't the only way to address the challenges of working with JDBC, but it's simple and highly effective.

Another key problem – the danger of SQL being sprinkled around the application – is best addressed with the DAO pattern, which we've already discussed. In this section, we'll talk about implementing data access objects, not their place in overall application architecture.

Exception Handling

Exception handling is such an important issue that we should develop a consistent strategy for it before we begin to implement our framework proper.

The JDBC API is an object lesson in how *not* to use exceptions. As well as ensuring that we release resources even if we encounter errors, our abstraction layer should provide a better exception handling model for application code than JDBC does.

JDBC uses a single exception class – `java.lang.SQLException` – for all problems except data truncation. Catching a `SQLException` in itself provides no more information than "something went wrong". As we've seen, it's only possible to distinguish between problems by examining potentially vendor-specific codes included in SQL exceptions.

JDBC could in fact have offered more sophisticated error handling while retaining portability between databases. The following are just a few of the errors that are meaningful in any RDBMS:

❑ Grammatical error in SQL statement issued using JDBC

❑ Data integrity constraint violation

❑ Attempt to set the value of a SQL bind variable to an incorrect type

Such standard problems could – and should – have been modeled as individual subclasses of `java.lang.SQLException`. In our abstraction framework, we will provide a richer exception hierarchy that does use individual exception classes.

We'll also address two other issues with JDBC exception handling.

- ❑ We don't want to tie code using our abstraction layer to JDBC. Our abstraction layer is primarily intended for use to implement the Data-Access Object pattern. If code using DAOs ever needs to catch resource-specific exceptions, such as SQLExceptions, the decoupling of business logic and data access implementation that the DAO pattern exists to provide is lost. (Exceptions thrown are an integral part of method signatures.) So while the JDBC API, reasonably enough, uses JDBC-specific exceptions, we won't tie our exceptions to JDBC.

- ❑ Following our discussion of checked and runtime exceptions in Chapter 4, we will make our API much easier to use by making all exceptions runtime, rather than checked exceptions. JDO takes this approach with good results. Using runtime exceptions, callers need catch only those exceptions (if any) that they may be able to recover from. This models JDBC (and other data-access) usage well: JDBC exceptions are often unrecoverable. For example, if a SQL query contained an invalid column name, there's no point catching it and retrying. We want the fatal error logged, but need to correct the offending application code.

- ❑ If we're running the query from an EJB, we can simply let the EJB container catch the runtime exception and roll back the current transaction. If we caught a checked exception in the EJB implementation we'd need to roll back the transaction ourselves, or throw a runtime exception that would cause the container to do so. In this example, using a checked exception would allow more scope for application code to cause incorrect behavior. Likewise, failure to connect to a database is probably fatal. In contrast, a recoverable error that we might want to catch would be an optimistic locking violation.

A Generic Data-Access Exception Hierarchy

We can meet all our exception handling goals by creating a generic data-access exception hierarchy. This won't be limited to use with JDBC, although some JDBC-specific exceptions will be derived from generic exceptions within it. This exception hierarchy will enable code using DAOs to handle exceptions in a database-agnostic way.

The root of all data-access exceptions is the abstract DataAccessException class, which extends the NestedRuntimeException class discussed in Chapter 4. Using the NestedRuntimeException superclass enables us to preserve the stack trace of any exceptions (such as SQLExceptions) we may need to wrap.

Unlike SQLException, DataAccessException has several subclasses that indicate specific data-access problems. The direct subclasses are:

- ❑ DataAccessResourceFailureException
  Complete failure to access the resource in question. In a JDBC implementation, this would result from failure to get a connection from a datasource. However, such errors are meaningful for any persistence strategy.

- ❑ CleanupFailureDataAccessException
  Failure to clean up (for example, by closing a JDBC Connection) after successfully completing an operation. In some cases we might want to treat this as a recoverable error, preventing the current transaction from being rolled back (for example, we know that any update succeeded).

❑ DataIntegrityViolationException
Thrown when an attempted update is rejected by the database because it would have violated data integrity.

❑ InvalidDataAccessApiUsageException
This exception indicates not a problem from the underlying resource (such as a SQLException), but incorrect usage of the data-access API. The JDBC abstraction layer discussed below throws this exception when it is used incorrectly.

❑ InvalidDataAccessResourceUsageException
This exception indicates that the data-access resource (such as an RDBMS) was used incorrectly. For example, our JDBC abstraction layer will throw a subclass of this exception on an attempt to execute invalid SQL.

❑ OptimisticLockingViolationException
This indicates an optimistic locking violation and is thrown when a competing update is detected. This exception will normally be thrown by a Data-Access Object, rather than an underlying API like JDBC.

❑ DeadlockLoserDataAccessException
Indicates that the current operation was a deadlock loser, causing it to be rejected by the database.

❑ UncategorizedDataAccessException
An exception that doesn't fit within the recognized categories listed above. This exception is abstract, so resource-specific exceptions will extend it carrying additional information. Our JDBC abstraction layer will throw this exception when it catches a SQLException it cannot classify.

All these concepts are meaningful for any persistence strategy, not just JDBC. Generic exceptions will include nested root causes, such as SQLExceptions, ensuring that no information is lost and ensuring that all available information can be logged.

The following UML class diagram illustrates our exception hierarchy, contained in the com.interface21.dao package. Note how some JDBC-specific exceptions in the com.interface21.jdbc.core package (shown below the horizontal line) extend generic exceptions, enabling the maximum information to be included about a problem without making calling code dependent on JDBC. Calling code will normally catch generic exceptions, although JDBC-specific DAO implementations can catch JDBC-specific subclasses they understand, while letting fatal errors propagate to business objects that use them.

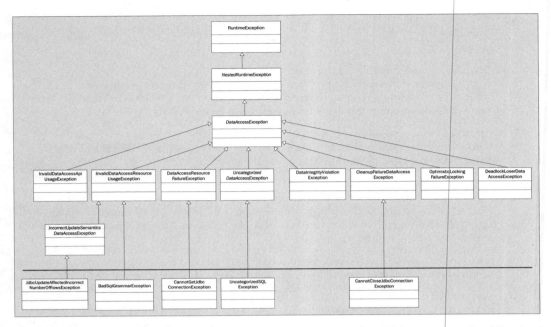

Although this exception hierarchy may appear complex, it can help to deliver a great simplification in application code. All these exception classes will be thrown by our framework; application code need only catch those it considers recoverable. Most application code won't catch any of these exceptions.

This hierarchy automatically gives us much more useful information than a SQLException and makes application code that needs to work with exceptions much more readable. While we can choose to catch the base DataAccessException if we want to know if *anything* went wrong (in the same way as we catch a SQLException), it will be more useful in most cases to catch only a particular subclass.

Consider a plausible requirement to perform an update operation and apply a recovery strategy if the operation resulted in a data integrity violation. In an RDBMS context, the operation might have attempted to set a non-nullable column's value to null. Using the exception hierarchy we've just examined, all we need to do is catch com.interface21.dao.DataIntegrityViolationException. All other exceptions can be ignored, as they're unchecked. The following code clearly conveys the recovery requirement just described. As a bonus, it isn't dependent on JDBC:

```
try {
    // do data operation using JDBC abstraction layer
}
catch (DataIntegrityViolationException ex) {
    // Apply recovery strategy
}
```

Now consider how we would need to do this using JDBC, without an abstraction layer. As SQLExceptions are checked, we can't let exceptions we're not interested in through. The only way to establish whether we *are* interested in the exception is to examine its SQLState string or vendor code. In the following example we check the SQLState string. As this may be null, we need to check it's non-null before examining it:

```
try {
  // do data operation using JDBC
}
catch (SQLException ex) {
  boolean recovered = false;
  String sqlstate = sqlex.getSQLState();
  if (sqlstate != null) {
    String classCode = sqlstate.substring(0, 2);
    if ("23".equals(classCode) ||
        "27".equals(classCode) ||
        "44".equals(classCode)) {
      // Apply recovery strategy
      recovered = true;
    }
  }
  if (!recovered)
    throw new ApplicationSpecificException("Other SQL exception", ex);
}
// Finally block omitted
```

There's no doubt which is the simpler, more readable, and more maintainable approach. Not only is the second approach far more complex, it makes the calling code dependent on intimate details of the JDBC API.

Converting JDBC Exceptions to Generic Exceptions

In the class diagram above, all the classes above the horizontal line are generic. These are the exceptions that calling code will work with.

The exceptions below the line are JDBC-specific subclasses of generic data access exceptions. Most callers won't use these exceptions directly (because such use would tie them to JDBC), but they provide more specific information if necessary. The BadSqlGrammarException, for example, extends the generic InvalidDataAccessResourceUsageException, and is thrown when the specified SQL is invalid.

So far we haven't considered how to convert between SQL exceptions and our generic exceptions. To do this we'll need to examine SQLState or vendor codes. However, as SQLState codes aren't sufficient to diagnose all problems, we must retain the option of RDBMS-specific implementation.

We do this by creating an interface that defines the translation functionality required, enabling us to use any implementation without affecting the working of our abstraction framework. (As usual, interface-based design is the best way to achieve portability). Our JDBC abstraction layer will use an implementation of the com.interface21.jdbc.core.SQLExceptionTranslater interface, which knows how to translate SQLExceptions encountered during JDBC operations to exceptions in our generic hierarchy:

```
public interface SQLExceptionTranslater {

  DataAccessException translate(String task,
                                String sql,
                                SQLException sqlex);

}
```

The default implementation is
com.interface21.jdbc.core.SQLStateSQLExceptionTranslater, which uses the portable
SQLState code. This implementation avoids the need for chains of if/else statements by building a
static data structure of SQLState class codes. The following is a partial listing:

```java
public class SQLStateSQLExceptionTranslater
    implements SQLExceptionTranslater {

  private static Set BAD_SQL_CODES = new HashSet();

  private static Set INTEGRITY_VIOLATION_CODES = new HashSet();

  static {
    BAD_SQL_CODES.add("42");
    BAD_SQL_CODES.add("65");

    INTEGRITY_VIOLATION_CODES.add("23");
    INTEGRITY_VIOLATION_CODES.add("27");
    INTEGRITY_VIOLATION_CODES.add("44");
  }

  public DataAccessException translate(String task, String sql,
      SQLException sqlex) {

    String sqlstate = sqlex.getSQLState();
    if (sqlstate != null) {
      String classCode = sqlstate.substring(0, 2);
      if (BAD_SQL_CODES.contains(classCode))
        throw new BadSqlGrammarException("(" + task +
              "): SQL grammatical error '" + sql + "'", sql, sqlex);
      if (INTEGRITY_VIOLATION_CODES.contains(classCode))
        throw new DataIntegrityViolationException("(" + task +
              "): data integrity violated by SQL '" + sql + "'", sqlex);
    }

    // We couldn't categorize the problem
    return new UncategorizedSQLException("(" + task +
          "): encountered SQLException [" + sqlex.getMessage() +
          "]", sql, sqlex);
  }
}
```

The following partial listing illustrates an Oracle-specific implementation,
com.interface21.jdbc.core.oracle.OracleSQLExceptionTranslater, which uses the
vendor code to identify the same range of problems. Note that vendor codes are far more expressive
than SQLState codes:

```java
public class OracleSQLExceptionTranslater
    implements SQLExceptionTranslater {

  public DataAccessException translate(String task, String sql,
      SQLException sqlex) {

    switch (sqlex.getErrorCode()) {
      case 1 :
        // Unique constraint violated
```

```
            return new DataIntegrityViolationException(
                    task + ": " + sqlex.getMessage(), sqlex);

        case 1400:
            // Can't insert null into non-nullable column
            return new DataIntegrityViolationException(
                    task + ": " + sqlex.getMessage(), sqlex);

        case 936 :
            // Missing expression
                return new BadSqlGrammarException(task, sql, sqlex);

        case 942 :
            // Table or view does not exist
                return new BadSqlGrammarException(task, sql, sqlex);
    }

    // We couldn't identify the problem more precisely
    return new UncategorizedSQLException("(" + task +
            "): encountered SQLException [" +
            sqlex.getMessage() + "]", sql, sqlex);
    }
}
```

Two Levels of Abstraction

Now that we have a powerful, database-agnostic approach to exception handling, let's look at implementing an abstraction framework that will make JDBC much easier to use.

The JDBC framework used in the sample application involves two levels of abstraction. (In Chapter 4 we discussed how frameworks are often layered, enabling developers using them to work with the appropriate level of abstraction for the task in hand.)

The lower level of abstraction, in the `com.interface21.jdbc.core` package, takes care of JDBC workflow and exception handling. It achieves this using a callback approach, requiring application code to implement simple callback interfaces.

The higher level of abstraction, in the `com.interface21.jdbc.object` package (which we've seen in use), builds on this to provide a more object-oriented, JDO-like interface that models RDBMS operations as Java objects. This completely hides the details of JDBC from application code that initiates these operations.

Let's look at each level of abstraction in turn.

A Framework to Control JDBC Workflow and Error Handling

The lower level of abstraction handles the issuing of JDBC queries and updates, taking care of resource cleanup and translating `SQLExceptions` into generic exceptions using the `SQLExceptionTranslator` discussed above.

"Inversion of Control" Revisited

Remember our discussion of the Strategy design pattern and "inversion of control" in Chapter 4? We saw that sometimes the only way to ensure that complex error handling is concealed by generic infrastructure code is for infrastructure code to invoke application code (an approach termed "inversion of control"), rather than for application code to invoke infrastructure code as in a traditional class library. We saw that infrastructure packages that apply this approach are usually termed **frameworks**, rather than class libraries.

The complexity of JDBC error handling demands this approach. We want a framework class to use the JDBC API to execute queries and updates and handle any errors, while we supply the SQL and any parameter values. To achieve this, the framework class must invoke our code, rather than the reverse.

The com.interface21.jdbc.core package

All JDBC-specific classes comprising the lower level of abstraction are in the com.interface21.jdbc.core package.

The most important class in the com.interface21.jdbc.core package is JdbcTemplate, which implements core workflow and invokes application code as necessary. The methods in JdbcTemplate run queries while delegating the creation of PreparedStatements and the extraction of the results from JDBC ResultSets to two callback interfaces: the PreparedStatementCreator interface and the RowCallbackHandler interface. Application developers will need to provide implementations of these interfaces, not execute JDBC statements directly or implement JDBC exception handling.

The following UML class diagram illustrates the relationship of the JdbcTemplate class to the helper classes it uses and the application-specific classes that enable it to be parameterized:

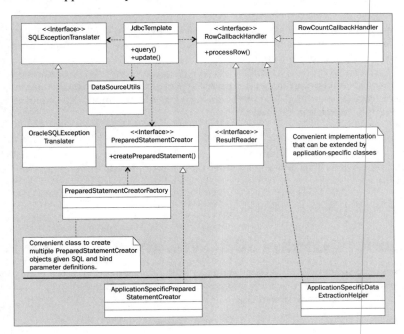

Let's consider each class and interface in turn. The classes above the horizontal line belong to the framework; those below the line indicate how application-specific classes implement framework interfaces.

The PreparedStatementCreator Interface and Related Classes

The `PreparedStatementCreator` interface must be implemented by application-specific classes to create a `java.sql.PreparedStatement`, given a `java.sql.Connection`. This means specifying the SQL and setting bind parameters for an application-specific query or update, which will be run by the `JdbcTemplate` class. Note that an implementation of this interface doesn't need to worry about obtaining a connection or catching any `SQLExceptions` that may result from its work. The `PreparedStatement` it creates will be executed by the `JdbcTemplate` class. The interface is as follows:

```
public interface PreparedStatementCreator {
  PreparedStatement createPreparedStatement(Connection conn)
    throws SQLException;
}
```

The following shows a typical implementation, which uses standard JDBC methods to construct a `PreparedStatement` with the desired SQL and set bind variable values. Like many implementations of such simple interfaces, this is an anonymous inner class:

```
PreparedStatementCreator psc = new PreparedStatementCreator() {

  public PreparedStatement createPreparedStatement(Connection conn)
      throws SQLException {
    PreparedStatement ps = conn.prepareStatement(
      "SELECT seat_id AS id FROM available_seats WHERE " +
      "performance_id = ? AND price_band_id = ?");
    ps.setInt(1, performanceId);
    ps.setInt(2, seatType);
    return ps;
  }
};
```

The `PreparedStatementCreatorFactory` class is a generic helper that can be used repeatedly to create `PreparedStatementCreator` objects with different parameter values, based on the same SQL statement and bind variable declarations. This class is largely used by the higher-level, object-abstraction framework described below; application code will normally define `PreparedStatementCreator` classes as shown above.

The RowCallbackHandler Interface and Related Classes

The `RowCallbackHandler` interface must be implemented by application-specific classes to extract column values from each row of the `ResultSet` returned by a query. The `JdbcTemplate` class handles iteration over the `ResultSet`. The implementation of this interface may also leave `SQLExceptions` uncaught: the `JdbcTemplate` will handle them. The interface is as follows:

```
public interface RowCallbackHandler {
  void processRow(ResultSet rs) throws SQLException;
}
```

Implementations should know the number of columns and data types to expect in the `ResultSet`. The following shows a typical implementation, which extracts an `int` value from each row and adds it to a list defined in the enclosing method:

```
RowCallbackHandler rch = new RowCallbackHandler() {
  public void processRow(ResultSet rs) throws SQLException {
    int seatId = rs.getInt(1);
    list.add(new Integer(seatId));
  }
};
```

The `RowCountCallbackHandler` class is a convenient framework implementation of this interface that stores metadata about column names and types and counts the rows in the `ResultSet`. Although it's a concrete class, its main use is as a superclass of application-specific classes.

The `ResultReader` interface extends `RowCallbackHandler` to save the retrieved results in a `java.util.List`:

```
public interface ResultReader extends RowCallbackHandler {
  List getResults();
}
```

The conversion of each row of the `ResultSet` to an object is likely to vary widely between implementations, so there is no standard implementation of this interface.

Miscellaneous Classes

We've already examined the `SQLExceptionTranslater` interface and two implementations. The `JdbcTemplate` class uses an object of type `SQLExceptionTranslater` to convert `SQLExceptions` into our generic exception hierarchy, ensuring that this important part of the `JdbcTemplate` class's behavior can be parameterized.

The `DataSourceUtils` class contains a static method to obtain a `Connection` from a `javax.sql.DataSource`, converting any `SQLException` to an exception from our generic hierarchy, a method to close a `Connection` (again with appropriate error handling) and a method to obtain a `DataSource` from JNDI. The `JdbcTemplate` class uses the `DataSourceUtils` class to simplify obtaining and closing connections.

The JdbcTemplateClass: The Central Workflow

Now let's look at the implementation of the `JdbcTemplate` class itself. This is the only class that runs JDBC statements and catches `SQLExceptions`. It contains methods that can perform *any* query or update: the JDBC statement executed is parameterized by static SQL or a `PreparedStatementCreator` implementation supplied as a method argument.

The following is a complete listing of the `JdbcTemplate` class:

```
package com.interface21.jdbc.core;

import java.sql.Connection;
import java.sql.PreparedStatement;
import java.sql.ResultSet;
import java.sql.SQLException;
import java.sql.SQLWarning;
import java.sql.Statement;
```

```
import java14.java.util.logging.Level;
import java14.java.util.logging.Logger;
import javax.sql.DataSource;
import com.interface21.dao.DataAccessException;

public class JdbcTemplate {
```

The instance data consists of a Logger object, used to log info messages about SQL operations, a DataSource object, a boolean indicating whether SQLWarnings should be ignored or treated as errors, and the SQLExceptionTranslater helper object. All these instance variables are read-only after the JdbcTemplate has been configured, meaning that JdbcTemplate objects are threadsafe:

```
protected final Logger logger = Logger.getLogger(getClass().getName());
private DataSource dataSource;
private boolean ignoreWarnings = true;
private SQLExceptionTranslater exceptionTranslater;
```

The constructor takes a DataSource, which will be used throughout the JdbcTemplate's lifecycle, and instantiates a default SQLExceptionTranslater object:

```
public JdbcTemplate(DataSource dataSource) {
  this.dataSource = dataSource;
  this.exceptionTranslater = new SQLStateSQLExceptionTranslater();
}
```

The following methods can be optionally used to modify default configuration before using the JdbcTemplate. They enable behavior on warnings and exception translation to be parameterized:

```
public void setIgnoreWarnings(boolean ignoreWarnings) {
  this.ignoreWarnings = ignoreWarnings;
}

public boolean getIgnoreWarnings() {
  return ignoreWarnings;
}

public void setExceptionTranslater(
  SQLExceptionTranslater exceptionTranslater) {
  this.exceptionTranslater = exceptionTranslater;
}

public DataSource getDataSource() {
  return dataSource;
}
```

The remainder of the JdbcTemplate class consists of methods that perform JDBC workflow using the callback interfaces discussed above.

The simplest query() method, which takes a static SQL string and a RowCallbackHandler to extract results from the query ResultSet, illustrates how the use of callbacks centralizes control flow and error handling in the JdbcTemplate class. Note that this method throws our generic com.interface21.dao.DataAccessException, allowing callers to find the cause of any error without using JDBC:

337

```
public void query(String sql, RowCallbackHandler callbackHandler)
    throws DataAccessException {

  Connection con = null;
  PreparedStatement ps = null;
  ResultSet rs = null;
  try {
    con = DataSourceUtils.getConnection(this.dataSource);
    ps = con.prepareStatement(sql);
    rs = ps.executeQuery();
    if (logger.isLoggable(Level.INFO))
      logger.info("Executing static SQL query '" + sql +"'");

    while (rs.next()) {
      callbackHandler.processRow(rs);
    }

    SQLWarning warning = ps.getWarnings();
    rs.close();
    ps.close();

    throwExceptionOnWarningIfNotIgnoringWarnings(warning);
  }
  catch (SQLException ex) {
    throw this.exceptionTranslater.translate("JdbcTemplate.query(sql)",
                                  sql, ex);

  }
  finally {
    DataSourceUtils.closeConnectionIfNecessary(this.dataSource, con);
  }
} // query
```

The throwExceptionOnWarningIfNotIgnoringWarnings() method is a private helper used in several public workflow methods. If the warning it is passed is non-null and the JdbcTemplate is configured not to ignore exceptions, it throws an exception. If a warning was encountered, but the JdbcTemplate is configured to ignore warnings, it logs the warning:

```
private void throwExceptionOnWarningIfNotIgnoringWarnings(
    SQLWarning warning) throws SQLWarningException {

  if (warning != null) {
    if (this.ignoreWarnings) {
      logger.warning("SQLWarning ignored: " + warning);
    } else {
      throw new SQLWarningException("Warning not ignored", warning);
    }
  }

}
```

A more general query() method issues a PreparedStatement, which must be created by a PreparedStatementCreator implementation. I've highlighted the major difference from the query() method listed above:

```
public void query(PreparedStatementCreator psc,
    RowCallbackHandler callbackHandler) throws DataAccessException {

  Connection con = null;
  Statement s = null;
  ResultSet rs = null;
  try {
    con = DataSourceUtils.getConnection(this.dataSource);
    PreparedStatement ps = psc.createPreparedStatement(con);
    if (logger.isLoggable(Level.INFO))
      logger.info("Executing SQL query using PreparedStatement: ["
                  + psc + "]");
    rs = ps.executeQuery();

    while (rs.next()) {
      if (logger.isLoggable(Level.FINEST))
        logger.finest("Processing row of ResultSet");
        callbackHandler.processRow(rs);
    }

    SQLWarning warning = ps.getWarnings();
    rs.close();
    ps.close();
    throwExceptionOnWarningIfNotIgnoringWarnings(warning);
  }
  catch (SQLException ex) {
    throw this.exceptionTranslater.translate(
        "JdbcTemplate.query(psc) with PreparedStatementCreator [" +
        psc + "]", null, ex);
  }
  finally {
    DataSourceUtils.closeConnectionIfNecessary(this.dataSource, con);
  }
}
```

We apply the same approach to updates. The following method allows the execution of multiple updates using a single JDBC Connection. An array of PreparedStatementCreator objects supplies the SQL and bind parameters to use. This method returns an array containing the number of rows affected by each update:

```
public int[] update(PreparedStatementCreator[] pscs)
    throws DataAccessException {

  Connection con = null;
  Statement s = null;
  int index = 0;
  try {
    con = DataSourceUtils.getConnection(this.dataSource);
    int[] retvals = new int[pscs.length];
    for (index = 0; index < retvals.length; index++) {
      PreparedStatement ps = pscs[index].createPreparedStatement(con);
      retvals[index] = ps.executeUpdate();
      if (logger.isLoggable(Level.INFO))
```

```
                logger.info("JDBCTemplate: update affected " + retvals[index] +
                            " rows");
            ps.close();
        }

        return retvals;
    }
    catch (SQLException ex) {
        throw this.exceptionTranslater.translate("processing update " +
            (index + 1) + " of " + pscs.length + "; update was [" +
            pscs[index] + "]", null, ex);
    }
    finally {
        DataSourceUtils.closeConnectionIfNecessary(this.dataSource, con);
    }
}
```

The following convenience methods use the above method to execute a single update, given static SQL or a single `PreparedStatementCreator` parameter:

```
public int update(final String sql) throws DataAccessException {

    if (logger.isLoggable(Level.INFO))
        logger.info("Running SQL update '" + sql + "'");
    return update(PreparedStatementCreatorFactory.
        getPreparedStatementCreator(sql));
}

public int update(PreparedStatementCreator psc)
    throws DataAccessException {
    return update(new PreparedStatementCreator[] { psc })[0];
}
```

Note that the `JdbcTemplate` object maintains a `javax.sql.DataSource` instance variable, from which it obtains connections for each operation. It's important that the API should work with `DataSource` objects rather than `java.sql.Connection` objects, because otherwise:

❑ We'd have to obtain the connections elsewhere, meaning more complexity in application code and the need to catch `SQLExceptions` if using the `DataSource.getConnection()` method.

❑ It's important that `JdbcTemplate` closes the connections it works with, as closing a connection can result in an exception, and we want our framework to take care of all JDBC exception handling. Obtaining the connections elsewhere and closing them in the `JdbcTemplate` class wouldn't make sense and would introduce the risk of attempts to use closed connections.

Using a `DataSource` doesn't limit the `JdbcTemplate` class to use within a J2EE container: the `DataSource` interface is fairly simple, making it easy to implement for testing purposes or in standalone applications.

Using the JdbcTemplate Class

Now that we've looked at the implementation, let's see the `com.interface21.jdbc.core` package in action.

Performing Queries

Using the `JdbcTemplate` class, we can accomplish the JDBC query for seat IDs, shown under *Motivation* above, as follows, using anonymous inner classes to implement the `RowCallbackHandler` and `PreparedStatementCreator` interfaces. This implementation of `RowCallbackHandler` saves data in a list of `Integers` defined in the enclosing method:

```java
public List getAvailableSeatIdsWithJdbcTemplate(
    DataSource ds, final int performanceId, final int seatType)
    throws DataAccessException {
JdbcTemplate t = new JdbcTemplate(ds);
final List l = new LinkedList();

PreparedStatementCreator psc = new PreparedStatementCreator() {
    public PreparedStatement createPreparedStatement(Connection conn)
        throws SQLException {
      PreparedStatement ps = conn.prepareStatement(
        "SELECT seat_id AS id FROM available_seats WHERE " +
        "performance_id = ? AND price_band_id = ?");
      ps.setInt(1, performanceId);
      ps.setInt(2, seatType);
      return ps;
    }
};
RowCallbackHandler rch = new RowCallbackHandler() {
    public void processRow(ResultSet rs) throws SQLException {
      int seatId = rs.getInt(1);
      l.add(new Integer(seatId));
    }
};
t.query(psc, rch);
return l;
}
```

This halves the amount of code required and addresses most of the problems we identified in using the JDBC API directly. We can work with `PreparedStatement` and `ResultSet` objects with a minimum of irrelevant code. Most importantly, using the `JdbcTemplate` class eliminates the major causes of errors. There is no risk that the connection won't be closed: the `JdbcTemplate` class ensures this. Application code doesn't need to catch checked, uninformative `SQLExceptions`: our generic data access exception hierarchy offers a richer classification of exceptions but, since data access exceptions are unchecked, application code can typically leave exceptions to be dealt with by the application server.

Performing Updates

If we use the JDBC API directly, updates call for a similar amount of code to queries. Again error handling is dominant and the SQL we want to execute is obscured. Again the `JdbcTemplate` class can deliver real benefits. The `JdbcTemplate` `update()` method is capable of running updates using the `PreparedStatementCreator` callback interface we've already seen. The following example (not part of our sample application!) would delete all seat reservations and bookings for a particular seat type in a given performance. The example assumes we already have a `JdbcTemplate` object in scope. As `JdbcTemplate` objects are threadsafe, we will normally keep one as an instance variable in DAO implementations using JDBC:

```
class PerformanceCleanerPSC implements PreparedStatementCreator {
  private int pid;
  private int pb;

  public PerformanceCleanerPSC(int pid, int pb) {
    this.pid = pid;
    this.pb = pb;
  }

  public PreparedStatement createPreparedStatement(Connection conn)
      throws SQLException {
    PreparedStatement ps = conn.prepareStatement("UPDATE seat_status " +
      "SET booking_id = null WHERE performance_id = ? AND " +
      "price_band_id = ?");
    ps.setInt(1, pid);
    ps.setInt(2, pb);
    return ps;
  }
};
PreparedStatementCreator psc = new PerformanceCleanerPSC (1, 1);
int rowsAffected = jdbcTemplate.update(psc);
```

Updates using static SQL are even easier. The following example would mark all seats in our ticketing application as available, without any need to implement callback interfaces:

```
template.update("UPDATE SEAT_STATUS SET BOOKING_ID = NULL");
```

A Higher Level of Abstraction: Modeling RDBMS Operations as Java Objects

Using the JdbcTemplate class solves most of the problems we saw with use of raw JDBC, but it's still arguably too low-level. Application code using the JdbcTemplate class still requires knowledge of JDBC Statements and ResultSets. The use of callbacks, although essential to move workflow within the framework, is conceptually complex (although the implementations of callback interfaces are usually very simple).

The com.interface21.jdbc.core package solves the most complex problems of using JDBC, but we want to present the solution more simply to application code. We need a higher level of abstraction, building on the functionality provided by the com.interface21.jdbc.core package.

Implementation of the com.interface21.jdbc.object Package

The com.interface21.jdbc.object package conceals the com.interface21.jdbc.core package (on which it is built), offering a higher-level, JDO-like object abstraction. Application code doesn't need to implement callback methods. Instead, each query, or other RDBMS operation, is modeled as a reusable, threadsafe object. Once configured, each object can be run repeatedly, with different parameters, mapped onto SQL bind variables, supplied each time.

An important difference from JDO is that because our RDBMS operation objects are classes, not interfaces, it is possible for application queries to subclass them. (Application code using JDO has to obtain instances of the Query interface from a PersistenceManager.) By using an individual subclass for each RDBMS operation we can completely conceal SQL from calling code. Objects representing RDBMS operations may implement interfaces that aren't tied to relational databases.

This approach can be used consistently for queries, updates, and stored procedures. The following UML class diagram illustrates the inheritance hierarchy among the framework classes, and the place of a hypothetical ApplicationSpecificQuery class in it. It also shows how these classes relate to the lower-level JDBC abstraction classes discussed above:

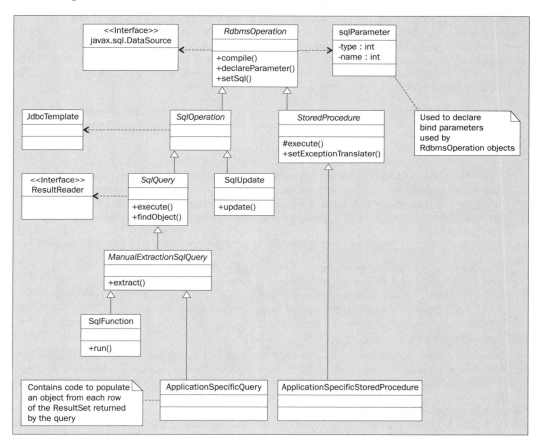

Let's look at each class in this inheritance hierarchy in detail. Due to the number of classes involved, it's impossible to provide a complete listing here. Please refer to the com.interface21.jdbc.object package under the /framework/src directory of the download as necessary while reading the description below.

The RdbmsOperation Base Class

RdbmsOperation is an abstract class and is the root of the class hierarchy. It holds a javax.sql.DataSource and SQL string as instance variables and allows bind parameters to be declared. (Queries, updates and stored procedures share the concept of bind variables.) Once it has been configured, an RdbmsOperation must be "compiled" – another idea borrowed from the JDO Query interface. The meaning of compilation will vary between subclasses, but it will at least validate that a DataSource and SQL have been supplied. After compilation, no more parameters can be added, but the operation can be executed repeatedly.

RDBMS operations are JavaBeans. The SQL to execute and the `DataSource` to use are exposed as bean properties, and subclasses will normally expose their own configuration properties as bean properties.

Parameters are declared using the `declareParameter(SqlParameter)` method. The `SqlParameter` class is defined in the `com.interface21.jdbc.core` package, but is used principally by this package. The main purpose of parameter declaration is to specify each parameter's JDBC type, as enumerated in the `java.sql.Types` class. This ensures that the framework code can use the JDBC `PreparedStatement set<Type>()` methods rather than `setObject()` to set bind variables, which is necessary to ensure correct handling of `null` values and is potentially more efficient. Parameters to queries and updates don't require names (merely the correct ordering and types); stored procedures support output as well as input parameters, and thus require parameter names.

Although the `RdbmsOperation` class ensures consistent concepts for queries, updates, and stored procedures, it doesn't know how to perform database operations. Subclasses must add methods to perform these.

> An **RdbmsOperation** is a reusable Java object representing a SQL query, update, or stored procedure. **RdbmsOperations** may have parameters, declared before they are used, which correspond to SQL bind variables. Once configured and "compiled", an **RdbmsOperation** object can be executed repeatedly, with different parameter values each time.

The class hierarchy described here is a good example of appropriate use of concrete inheritance. In this case we want to inherit instance variables and implementation, as well as enable polymorphism. As parameterization is largely handled by the `com.interface21.jdbc.core` *package, there is no need to use interface-based design to allow greater flexibility.*

The SqlOperation Class

`SqlOperation` is an abstract class that extends `RdbmsOperation` to serve as a superclass for SQL-based queries and updates (as opposed to stored procedures). Its compilation implementation checks that the number of bind variables expected in the SQL statement (that is, the number of ? characters) matches the number of `SqlParameters` declared, and configures a `PreparedStatementCreatorFactory` that can efficiently create `PreparedStatementCreator` objects for the SQL and parameters specified at configuration time. The `SqlOperation` class creates a `JdbcTemplate` that subclasses can use to perform database operations.

The SqlQuery Class

This is the superclass for all query objects, and uses the `JdbcTemplate` instance variable inherited from `SqlOperation` to execute queries given SQL and bind variables.

`SqlQuery` is abstract, using the **Template Method** design pattern to defer the extraction of results to subclasses, which are required to implement the following protected abstract method:

```
protected abstract ResultReader newResultReader(
        int rowsExpected, Object[] parameters);
```

We discussed the `ResultReader` interface earlier: this is defined in the `com.interface21.jdbc.core` package and saves results from `RowCallbackHandler` callbacks in a `List` of objects, each representing the data from one row.

Like the JDO `Query` interface, the `SqlQuery` class provides a number of convenient `execute()` methods with different arguments, such as `execute(int)`, `execute(int, int)` and `execute(String)`. As with the JDO `Query`, the `execute(Object[])` method – which all other `execute()` methods invoke – takes an array of `Object` as an argument. The arguments to `execute()` methods represent the dynamic values of the bind variables declared in the `SqlQuery` object. All `execute()` methods return a list of results, produced by the `SqlQuery`'s `ResultReader` implementation.

The `SqlQuery` class also exposes a number of convenient `findObject()` methods. These are analogous to single-object entity bean finders, such as `findByPrimaryKey()`; they raise an error if more than one object matches.

Subclasses can either rely on the inherited `execute()` or `findObject()` methods, or implement their own query methods with meaningful names. For example, a subclass method that required four parameters might take an object argument and conceal the work of invoking the generic superclass method:

```
public List purchasesByAddress(Address a) {
  return execute(new Object[] {
    a.getStreet(), a.getLine2(), a.getCity(), a.getPostCode()
  });
}
```

A subclass finder that returned a single `Seat` object might be implemented as follows, concealing the necessary type cast from code using it:

```
public Seat findSeat(int seatId) {
  return (Seat) super.findObject(seatId);
}
```

A subclass method might also convert a `List` returned by an inherited `execute()` method to a typed array, as the subclass would know what application object represented each row of the query's result.

The ManualExtractionSqlQuery Class

Application queries don't usually extend `SqlQuery` directly, but instead subclass the abstract `ManualExtractionSqlQuery` subclass of `SqlQuery`. The `ManualExtractionSqlQuery` class uses the Template Method design pattern to force subclasses to implement the following abstract method, which is invoked for each row of the `ResultSet` resulting from the query. However, this is much simpler for subclasses to implement than the `SqlQuery` `newResultReader()` method:

```
protected abstract Object extract(ResultSet rs, int rownum)
  throws SQLException;
```

The implementation will look like that of the `RowCallbackHandler` interface we looked at above. The `ManualExtractionSqlQuery` class takes care of building a `List` from each returned object. The following implementation of the `extract()` method creates a hypothetical, application-specific `Customer` object from each row of a returned `ResultSet`:

```
protected Object extract(ResultSet rs, int rownum) throws SQLException {
  Customer cust = new Customer();
  cust.setForename(rs.getString("forename"));
  cust.setId(rs.getInt("id"));
  return cust;
}
```

Note that subclasses of RdbmsOperation don't need to catch SQLExceptions. Any SQLException thrown will be handled by the JdbcTemplate class, as discussed above, causing a generic data access exception to be thrown. Note also that subclass code can easily set multiple property values based on a single column value. We'll look at several complete subclasses of the ManualExtractionSqlQuery class below, when we look at using this framework.

You may be wondering why I didn't go the extra mile and do away with the "manual extraction" of an object from each row of the ResultSet. It would be possible to implement a ReflectionExtractionSqlQuery that used reflection to create a JavaBean and set bean properties from column values from each row of the ResultSet. This is appealing as it further reduces the amount of application code required.

I'm normally optimistic about use of reflection and I've implemented this approach several times. However, I'm not convinced that it adds any real value. It has the following disadvantages:

- ❑ It makes the framework significantly more complex.

- ❑ It arguably *moves* complexity, rather than eliminating it. For example, it will be necessary to use mappings controlling conversion from RDBMS column values to JavaBean properties. Even if mappings are held outside Java code, they will need to be created and maintained.

- ❑ It doesn't allow for computed properties such as properties based on the value of several columns, without the introduction of great complexity in the framework.

- ❑ It doesn't allow different object types to be used for different rows (for example, if a subclass is sometimes indicated).

This decision shows the Pareto Principle in action. The saving of a relatively few lines of code to extract values from a single row of a ResultSet (which are no longer very complex because there is no need to catch SQLExceptions) doesn't add sufficient value to justify the complexity involved.

The SqlFunction Class

SQL functions can be viewed as special cases of SQL queries, returning a single row. Thus, we can easily apply the same approach. The com.interface21.jdbc.object.SqlFunction class is a simple concrete class that extends ManualExtractionSqlQuery to enable queries whose results can be held in a Java int to be run simply by providing SQL and declaring parameters. A SqlFunction object can be constructed as follows:

```
SqlFunction freeSeatsFunction = new SqlFunction(dataSource,
    "SELECT count(seat_id) FROM available_seats WHERE performance_id = ?");
freeSeatsFunction.declareParameter(new SqlParameter(Types.NUMERIC));
freeSeatsFunction.compile();
```

This SqlFunction can then be used like this:

```
freeSeatsFunction.run(performanceId);
```

As with the SqlQuery class, the SqlFunction class provides a number of convenient run() methods with different arguments, as well as a generic form that takes an array of Object.

The SqlUpdate Class

Updates share many concepts with queries, such as SQL, bind variable declarations, and the use of a JdbcTemplate class to help implementation. Hence the SqlUpdate class extends SqlOperation, inheriting the JdbcTemplate helper and the validation logic that checks that bind variable declarations tally with the supplied SQL.

The SqlUpdate class is concrete, as there are no results to extract and no need for subclasses to implement custom extraction. It exposes a number of update() methods, each returning the number of rows affected by the update. As with query methods, all update() methods invoke a generic update method that takes an array of Object parameter values:

```
public int update(Object[] args)
    throws InvalidDataAccessApiUsageException
```

The StoredProcedure Class

Our modeling naturally supports stored procedures as well as ordinary SQL queries and updates. The abstract StoredProcedure class extends RdbmsOperation, as it doesn't require a JdbcTemplate helper and, as the supplied SQL is merely the name of the stored procedure, it is impossible to validate it against bind variable declarations. (Only when the stored procedure is invoked at run time will an incorrect number of parameters cause a failure.)

Calling a stored procedure using JDBC directly involves creating an object of the java.sql.CallableStatement interface and providing a **call string**. Call strings include placeholders like the ones used for JDBC prepared statements, and look like the following example, used in the sample application:

```
{call reserve_seats(?, ?, ?, ?)}
```

Once a CallableStatement object is created, invoking the stored procedure requires similar error handling to queries and updates. Stored procedures can return ResultSets, but more often we use **output parameters**. (The mechanics of getting stored procedures to return ResultSets varies between RDBMSs. It's quite complex in Oracle.)

The StoredProcedure class must be subclassed by application-specific classes. Each subclass effectively becomes a Java proxy for the stored procedure. The only major difference from the queries and updates we've seen is that a stored procedure can have input/output as well as input parameters. The StoredProcedure class automatically builds the call string and conceals the use of a CallableStatement and the necessary error handling. Input parameters are supplied and output parameters returned in java.util.Map objects.

Using the JDBC Object Abstraction

Now that we've taken a look at the implementation of this object-based JDBC abstraction, let's look at using it to perform common tasks.

Performing Queries

JDBC is very efficient at performing queries, although we cannot transparently update objects created from JDBC queries. We can, however, perform queries with many parameters and involving complex joins that cannot easily be accomplished using O/R mapping. The objects resulting from JDBC queries are ideal value objects, as they're disconnected from the database and have no dependencies on persistence APIs.

The following three code examples illustrate three idioms that can be used with RdbmsOperations and subclasses.

Application-specific queries will normally subclass ManualExtractionSqlQuery. As a minimum, we will need to implement the protected abstract extract() method. The following anonymous inner class implements just this method. Note that the query is configured using the configuration methods inherited from RdbmsOperation:

```
SqlQuery customerQuery = new ManualExtractionSqlQuery() {
  protected Object extract(ResultSet rs, int rownum) throws SQLException {
    Customer cust = new Customer();
    cust.setForename(rs.getString("forename"));
    cust.setId(rs.getInt("id"));
    return cust;
  }
};
customerQuery.setDataSource(ds);
customerQuery.setSql("SELECT id AS id, forename AS forename FROM " +
                "customer WHERE id=?");
customerQuery.declareParameter(new SqlParameter(Types.NUMERIC));
customerQuery.compile();
```

This query can be executed with one of the convenient execute() methods from SqlQuery as follows:

```
List l = customerQuery.execute(1);
```

The following query implementation is slightly more sophisticated. It hides the SQL, parameter declaration, and compilation process into the constructor, providing better encapsulation. The implementation of the extract() method is the same as in our first example:

```
private class CustomerQuery extends ManualExtractionSqlQuery {

  public CustomerQuery (DataSource ds) {
    super(ds, "SELECT forename, id FROM customer WHERE id=?");
    declareParameter(new SqlParameter(Types.NUMERIC));
    compile();
  }

  protected Object extract(ResultSet rs, int rownum) throws SQLException {
    Customer cust = new Customer();
    cust.setForename(rs.getString("forename"));
    cust.setId(rs.getInt("id"));
    return cust;
  }

}
```

It is simpler to create objects of this type, but we must still rely on the inherited `execute()` methods. This query object can be used as follows:

```
SqlQuery customerQuery = new CustomerQuery(dataSource);
List customers = customerQuery.execute(6);
```

As `RdbmsOperation` objects are threadsafe, we will typically construct such objects once, and hold them as instance variables in Data-Access Objects.

The following version is a more sophisticated query that not only hides SQL, parameter declaration and compilation inside its constructor, but implements a new query method, which enables it to take a combination of parameters for which there is no convenient `execute()` method in the `SqlQuery` class:

```
class CustomerQuery extends ManualExtractionSqlQuery {

  public CustomerQuery(DataSource ds) {
     super(ds, "SELECT id AS id, forename AS forename FROM customer " +
            "WHERE mystring=? AND myint=? AND string3=?");
     declareParameter(new SqlParameter(Types.VARCHAR));
     declareParameter(new SqlParameter(Types.NUMERIC));
     declareParameter(new SqlParameter(Types.VARCHAR));
     compile();
  }

  protected Object extract(ResultSet rs, int rownum) throws SQLException {
    Customer cust = new Customer();
    cust.setForename(rs.getString("forename"));
    cust.setId(rs.getInt("id"));
    return cust;
  }
}
```

The new query method can take strongly typed parameters, and can be given a meaningful name:

```
public List findWithMeaningfulName(
    String myString, int id, String string3) {
  return execute(new Object[] {
    myString, new Integer(id), string3 } );
  }
};
```

We can use this as shown below. Note that this code is self-documenting:

```
CustomerQuery customerQuery = new CustomerQuery(ds);
List l = customerQuery.findWithMeaningfulName("foo", 1, "bar");
```

It's easy to avoid code duplication in practice by the use of inheritance among query objects. For example, the implementation of the `extract()` method can be provided in a base class, while subclasses provide different SQL and variable declarations. When only the SQL WHERE clause varies, multiple query objects of the same class can be created, each configured to execute different SQL.

Performing Updates

Using a SQL-based JDBC approach we can't have true O/R mapping, which typically results in transparent updates when object properties change. However, we can achieve efficient updates where O/R mapping is inappropriate, such as updates affecting multiple rows and updates using stored procedures.

The following update object performs the same update as the `JdbcTemplate` update shown above, but conceals the SQL used and the parameter declarations in its constructor:

```
class PerformanceCleaner extends com.interface21.jdbc.object.SqlUpdate {

    public PerformanceCleaner(DataSource dataSource) {
        setSql("UPDATE seat_status SET booking_id = null " +
                "WHERE performance_id = ? AND price_band_id = ?");
        setDataSource(dataSource);
        declareParameter(new SqlParameter(Types.NUMERIC));
        declareParameter(new SqlParameter(Types.NUMERIC));
        compile();
    }

    public int clearBookings(int performanceId, int type) {
        return update(new Object[] {
        new Integer(performanceId), new Integer(type) });
    }
}
```

The `clearBookings()` method invokes the superclass `update(Object[])` method to execute with the given parameters, simplifying the API for callers – the same approach we've previously seen for query `execute()` methods.

This update object can be used as follows:

```
PerformanceCleaner pc = new PerformanceCleaner(dataSource);
pc.clearBookings(1, 1);
```

Calling Stored Procedures

As the stored procedure invocations in our sample application are fairly complex and use proprietary Oracle features, let's consider an example outside the sample application of calling a stored procedure that has two numeric input parameters and one output parameter.

The constructor is very similar to those of the queries and updates we've seen, declaring parameters and invoking the `compile()` method. Note that the SQL is the name of the stored procedure:

```
class AddInvoice extends com.interface21.jdbc.object.StoredProcedure {

    public AddInvoice(DataSource ds) {
        setDataSource(ds);
        setSql("add_invoice");
        declareParameter(new SqlParameter("amount", Types.INTEGER));
        declareParameter(new SqlParameter("custid", Types.INTEGER));
        declareParameter(new OutputParameter("newid", Types.INTEGER));
        compile();
    }
```

We must implement a method to execute the stored procedure. (Although I've used the name execute(), we could give this method any name.) The highlighted line is a call to the StoredProcedure class's protected execute(Map) method. We invoke this with a Map of input parameters built from the new method's arguments. We build a return value from a Map of output parameters returned by the execute() method. This means that code using our stored procedure object can use strong typing. For more complex stored procedures, arguments and return values could be of application object types:

```java
public int execute(int amount, int custid) {
  Map in = new HashMap();
  in.put("amount", new Integer(amount));
  in.put("custid", new Integer(custid));
  Map out = execute(in);
  Number Id = (Number) out.get("newid");
  return Id.intValue();
 }
}
```

Just 20 lines of Java code, and we have an object that could implement an interface that's not stored procedure or JDBC-specific.

An improvement in JDBC 3.0 makes it possible to use named parameters, instead of indexed parameters, with the CallableStatement interface. This brings into the JDBC API one of the features of the StoredProcedure class I've presented. However, it still makes sense to use a higher level of abstraction than the JDBC API, as the error handling issue remains.

JDBC Abstraction Summary

The abstractions we've just described aren't the only valid approach to making JDBC easier to work with. However, they are much preferable to using JDBC directly and can drastically reduce the amount of code in applications and the likelihood of errors.

The biggest gains concern error handling. We've seen how a generic hierarchy of data-access exceptions can give application code the ability to react to specific problems, while allowing it to ignore the majority of unrecoverable problems. This also ensures that business objects don't require any knowledge of the persistence strategy (such as JDBC) used by the application.

We've looked at two levels of abstraction. The com.interface21.jdbc.core package, which uses callback interfaces to enable JDBC workflow and error handling to be managed by the framework, makes JDBC easier to use, but leaves application code to work with JDBC PreparedStatements and ResultSets.

The com.interface21.jdbc.object package builds on the com.interface21.jdbc.core package to offer a higher level of abstraction in which RDBMS operations (queries, updates, and stored procedures) are modeled as reusable objects. This is usually a better approach, as it localizes SQL operations within RdbmsOperation objects and makes code using them simple and largely self-documenting.

Unlike most O/R mapping approaches, these abstractions don't sacrifice any control over use of the RDBMS. We can execute any SQL we like; we can easily execute stored procedures. We've simply made JDBC easier to use.

The alert reader will have spotted that I've ignored my own advice (in Chapter 4) about externalizing strings. The classes shown above include SQL string literals – not even constants. The desirability of separating SQL from Java code is questionable. While we should always externalize configuration strings, SQL is not really configuration data, but code. If the SQL changes, the behavior of the Java code that uses it may also change, so externalizing SQL strings may be unwise. For example, imagine that we have two versions of the same query, one with FOR UPDATE suffixed. These are not the same query – they'll behave very differently. As making it easy to change the SQL without changing the Java code can be dangerous, the SQL belongs in DAOs. (In contrast, making it easy to change configuration without changing code is wholly beneficial.)

Note that while we may not want to separate SQL from Java, we definitely do want to localize all SQL in DAO implementations. Not only does this make it easy to change the SQL if necessary, but it hides SQL from the rest of the application.

Application code using these JDBC abstraction packages is easy to test. As all framework classes take connections from a datasource, we can easily provide a test datasource, enabling data access code to be tested without an application server. As any code running within a J2EE server can obtain a managed DataSource from JNDI, we can use such DAOs inside or outside an EJB container, boosting architectural flexibility.

The framework code itself is relatively simple. It doesn't attempt to solve really complex problems: it just removes the obstacles that make working with JDBC awkward and error-prone. Hence, it doesn't have a steep learning curve. For example, this approach doesn't provide any special handling for locking or concurrency. Essentially, it lets us use SQL with a minimum of hassle. It's up to us to ensure proper behavior for our target RDBMS.

Similarly, the JDBC abstraction interface doesn't make any effort at transaction management. The "global" JTA API or EJB CMT should be used for managing transactions. If we use the JDBC API to manage transactions we deprive the J2EE server of the ability to enlist multiple resources in the same transaction and to roll back all operations automatically if necessary.

Floyd Marinescu describes the "Data Access Command Bean" pattern in EJB Design Patterns, giving examples and common superclasses for JDBC. This approach has similar goals to the approach described here, but differs in that data-access objects are commands (intended for single use), the API is based on the javax.sql.RowSet *interface, and application code is forced to catch exceptions when extracting each column value from the result set. When working with many database columns, this will prove extremely verbose. (Nor is there any concept of data store-agnostic exception handling: application code is left to use JDBC error handling directly.) The "Data Access Command Bean" approach is preferable to using JDBC directly, but I believe that the approach described in this chapter is superior.*

An RdbmsOperation *is not a command. While commands are typically created per use case, an* RdbmsOperation *is created once and reused. However, the* RdbmsOperation *model is compatible with the Command design pattern. Once created and configured, an* RdbmsOperation *can execute commands repeatedly.*

Implementing the DAO Pattern in the Sample Application

Armed with our generic JDBC infrastructure, let's look at implementing data access in our sample application.

Let's focus on the booking process. To use the DAO pattern, we need to separate persistence logic operations from business logic operations. The first step is to try to create a technology-agnostic DAO interface, which we can then implement with whatever persistence technology we choose.

We'll look at the implementation of business logic in the next chapter. For now, let's look at the most important methods on the BoxOffice interface – the public interface of the ticket reservation system:

```
public interface BoxOffice {

  int getSeatCount(int performanceId);

  int getFreeSeatCount(int performanceId);

  SeatQuote allocateSeats(SeatQuoteRequest request)
    throws NotEnoughSeatsException;

  // Additional methods omitted
}
```

For now, we can ignore the details of the SeatQuote and SeatQuoteRequest parameter classes. The PriceBand class is a read-only object that we'll examine below.

We want to keep the seat allocation algorithm in Java. In this case, it's a simple exercise to separate out the persistence operations required into a DAO interface. (Often this separation is harder to accomplish; occasionally it is impossible.) We must try to ensure that the interface, while not dictating a persistence strategy, allows for efficient implementation. A suitable DAO interface will look like this:

```
public interface BoxOfficeDAO {

  /**
   * @return collection of Seat objects
   */
  List getAllSeats(int performanceId) throws DataAccessException;

  /**
   * @return list of PriceBand objects for this performance
   */
  List getPriceBands(int performanceId) throws DataAccessException;

  /**
   * @return list of Integer ids of free seats
   * @param lock guarantees that these seats will be available
   * to the current transaction
   */
```

```
    List getFreeSeats(int performanceId, int classId, boolean lock)
      throws DataAccessException;

    int getFreeSeatCount(int performanceId) throws DataAccessException;

    String reserve(SeatQuote quote);

    // Purchase operation omitted
}
```

Nothing in this interface ties us to using JDBC, Oracle, or even an RDBMS. Each of these methods throws our generic `com.interface21.dao.DataAccessException`, ensuring that even in the event of error, business objects using it don't need to work with RDBMS concepts.

The third, `lock` parameter to the `getFreeSeats()` method allows us to choose programmatically whether to lock the seats returned. If this parameter is `true`, the DAO must ensure that the seats with the returned IDs are locked against reservation by other users, and are guaranteed to be able to be reserved in the current transaction. The lock will be relinquished once the current transaction completes. If this parameter is `false`, we want to query current availability without impacting on other users, to display information, rather than as part of the reservation process.

This interface doesn't encompass transaction management, which should be accomplished using JTA. We plan to use a stateless session EJB with CMT to handle this declaratively, but don't need to worry about transaction management to implement and test the DAO.

Now we've defined a DAO interface, we should write tests against it. Tests involving persistent data tend to be verbose, so we won't show the test classes here, but this step is very important. Once we have a test harness, we can use it to test any DAO implementation; this will prove invaluable if we ever need to migrate to another persistence technology or database. To create effective tests, we must:

❑ Ensure that we create test data before each test run. We must never run such tests against a production database. We may create test data in the `setUp()` method of a JUnit test case, or using Ant's SQL capability before the test case is run.

❑ Write test methods that verify database work. For each test, we will write code that checks the results of the operation in question, connecting directly to the database. Using our JDBC abstraction API (which we can assume has already been tested) we can issue queries without writing too much code.

❑ Ensure that we return the database to its old state. We will have committed many transactions during the test run, so we won't be able to roll back, so this step may be complex. We can use the `tearDown()` method of a JUnit test case or Ant or a similar tool.

We can write and run tests before we attempt a real implementation of our DAO interface, by using a dummy implementation in which all tests should fail. (The dummy implementation's methods should do nothing, return `null`, or throw `java.lang.UnsupportedOperationException` to check the test harness. Any IDE will help us create such a dummy implementation of an interface without manual coding.)

Now that we have a complete test harness, let's look at implementing our DAO interface using JDBC. (We could use SQLJ, but with our JDBC abstraction layer it's hardly necessary.) See the `com.wrox.expertj2ee.ticket.boxoffice.support.jdbc.OracleJdbcSeatingPlanDAO` class for a full listing of the implementation.

Using the object-based JDBC abstraction described above, we will create an `RdbmsOperation` object for each query, update, and stored procedure invocation required. All the `RdbmsOperation` objects used will be modeled as inner classes, as they should only be visible inside the `OracleJdbcSeatingPlanDAO` class. This also has the advantage that the enclosing class's `DataSource` member variable `ds` is visible, simplifying object construction.

First, let's consider the implementation of the `PriceBand` query, which returns lightweight read-only objects (an ideal application for JDBC):

```
private class PriceBandQuery extends ManualExtractionSqlQuery {

  public PriceBandQuery() {
    super(ds, "SELECT id AS class_id, price AS price " +
          "FROM price_band WHERE price_band.price_structure_id = " +
          "(SELECT price_structure_id FROM performance WHERE id = ?) "+
          "ORDER BY price DESC");
    declareParameter(new SqlParameter("price_structure_id",
                     Types.NUMERIC));
    compile();
  }

  protected Object extract(ResultSet rs, int rownum) throws SQLException {
    int id = rs.getInt("class_id");
    double price = rs.getDouble("price");
    return new PriceBand(id, price);
  }
}
```

This shows a slightly more complex query than we've seen so far. The fact that the SQL accounts for much of the object's code shows that we have a concise Java API! The query behind the `getAllSeats()` method will be similar.

We declare a `PriceBandQuery` object as an instance variable in the `OracleJdbcSeatingPlanDAO` class, and initialize it in the constructor as shown below:

```
private PriceBandQuery priceBandQuery;
...

this.priceBandQuery = new PriceBandQuery();
```

Using the `PriceBandQuery` instance, the implementation of the `getPriceBands()` method from the `BoxOfficeDAO` interface is trivial:

```
public List getPriceBands(int performanceId) {
  return (List) priceBandQuery.execute(performanceId);
}
```

Now let's consider the queries for available seats. Remember that the database schema simplifies our task in two important respects: it provides the AVAILABLE_SEATS view to prevent us needing to perform an outer join to find available seats, and it provides the reserve_seats stored procedure that conceals the generation of a new primary key for the BOOKING table and the associated updates and inserts. This makes the queries straightforward. To get the ids of the free seats of a given type for a performance, we can run a query like the following against our view:

```
SELECT seat_id AS id FROM available_seats
        WHERE performance_id = ? AND price_band_id = ?
```

To ensure that we honor the contract of the getFreeSeats() method when the lock parameter is true, we need a query that appends FOR UPDATE to the select shown above. These two queries are quite distinct, so I've modeled them as separate objects.

Two points to consider here: Oracle, reasonably enough, permits SELECT...FOR UPDATE only in a transaction. We must remember this, and ensure that we have a transaction, when testing this code; and the FOR UPDATE clause used against a view will correctly lock the underlying tables.

Both queries share the same parameters and extraction logic, which can be gathered in a common base class. The usage in which an abstract superclass implements the extraction of each row of data, while subclasses vary the query's WHERE clause and parameters is very powerful; this is merely a trivial example. The two queries, and their superclass, will look like this:

```java
private static final String FREE_SEATS_IN_CLASS_QUERY_SQL =
    "SELECT seat_id AS id FROM available_seats " +
    "WHERE performance_id = ? AND price_band_id = ?";

private abstract class AbstractFreeSeatsInPerformanceOfTypeQuery
    extends ManualExtractionSqlQuery {

  public AbstractFreeSeatsInPerformanceOfTypeQuery(String sql) {
    super(ds, sql);
    declareParameter(new SqlParameter("performance_id", Types.NUMERIC));
    declareParameter(new SqlParameter("price_band_id", Types.NUMERIC));
    compile();
  }

  protected Object extract(ResultSet rs, int rownum) throws SQLException {
    return new Integer(rs.getInt("id"));
  }
}

private class FreeSeatsInPerformanceOfTypeQuery
    extends AbstractFreeSeatsInPerformanceOfTypeQuery {

  public FreeSeatsInPerformanceOfTypeQuery() {
    super(FREE_SEATS_IN_CLASS_QUERY_SQL);
  }
}

private class LockingFreeSeatsInPerformanceOfTypeQuery
    extends AbstractFreeSeatsInPerformanceOfTypeQuery {

  public LockingFreeSeatsInPerformanceOfTypeQuery() {
    super(FREE_SEATS_IN_CLASS_QUERY_SQL + " for update");
  }
}
```

The OracleJdbcSeatingPlanDAO constructor (after a DataSource is available) can create new objects of each of these two concrete classes like this:

```java
freeSeatsQuery = new FreeSeatsInPerformanceOfTypeQuery();
freeSeatsLockingQuery = new LockingFreeSeatsInPerformanceOfTypeQuery();
```

We can now query for free seats with either of these queries by calling the `execute(int, int)` method from the `SqlQuery` superclass. We use the lock parameter to the `getFreeSeats()` method from the `SeatingPlanDAO` interface to choose which query to execute. The complete implementation of this method is:

```
public List getFreeSeats(int performanceId, int classId, boolean lock) {
  if (lock) {
    return freeSeatsLockingQuery.execute(performanceId, classId);
  } else {
    return freeSeatsQuery.execute(performanceId, classId);
  }
}
```

Calling the stored procedure to make a reservation is a little more complicated. Although we've implicitly coded to Oracle by relying on our knowledge of Oracle's locking behavior, so far we haven't done anything proprietary. As the PL/SQL stored procedure takes a table parameter, enabling the IDs of the seats to be reserved to be passed in a single database call, we need to jump through some Oracle-specific hoops.

First, let's consider what we need to do in the database. We need to define the following custom types:

```
CREATE or REPLACE TYPE seatobj AS object(id NUMERIC);
/

CREATE or REPLACE TYPE seat_range AS table OF seatobj;
/
```

Now we can use the `seat_range` type as a table parameter to the following PL/SQL stored procedure:

```
CREATE or REPLACE
PROCEDURE reserve_seats(
                perf_id IN NUMERIC,
                seats IN seat_range,
                hold_till DATE,
                new_booking_id OUT NUMBER)
AS
BEGIN
     -- Get a new pk for the booking table
     SELECT booking_seq.nextval INTO new_booking_id FROM dual;

     -- Create a new booking
     INSERT INTO booking(id, date_made, reserved_until)
         VALUES (new_booking_id, sysdate, hold_till);

     -- Associate each seat with the booking
     FOR i in 1..seats.count LOOP
       UPDATE seat_status
                SET booking_id = new_booking_id
                WHERE seat_id = seats(i).id
                AND performance_id = perf_id;
       END LOOP;
END;
/
```

To pass a Java array as the table parameter to the stored procedure, we need to perform some Oracle-specific operations in our JDBC as well.

The `StoredProcedure` superclass allows us not merely to pass in a `Map` to the `execute()` method, but also to pass in a callback interface that creates a parameter map given a `Connection`:

```
protected interface ParameterMapper {
   Map createMap(Connection con) throws SQLException;
}
```

This is necessary when we need the `Connection` to construct the appropriate parameters, as we do in this case. The `reserve_seats` stored procedure object needs to make the database types `seat` and `seat_range` available to JDBC, before executing the stored procedure. These types can only be made available using an Oracle connection. Apart from this, the process of creating an input parameter `Map` and extracting output parameters is as in the simple `StoredProcedure` example we looked at earlier:

```
private class SeatReserver extends StoredProcedure {

   public SeatReserver(DataSource ds) {
      super(ds, "reserve_seats");
      declareParameter(new SqlParameter("perf_id", Types.INTEGER));
      declareParameter(new SqlParameter("seats", Types.ARRAY));
      declareParameter(new SqlParameter("hold_till", Types.TIMESTAMP));
      declareParameter(new OutputParameter("new_booking_id", Types.INTEGER));
      compile();
   }

   public int execute(final int performanceId, final int[] seats) {
      Map out = execute(new StoredProcedure.ParameterMapper() {
         public Map createMap(Connection con) throws SQLException {

            con = getOracleConnection(con);

            // Types MUST be upper case
            StructDescriptor sd = StructDescriptor.createDescriptor(
               "SEATOBJ", con);
            ArrayDescriptor ad = ArrayDescriptor.createDescriptor(
               "SEAT_RANGE", con);

            Object[] arrayObj = new Object[seats.length];
               for (int i = 0; i < arrayObj.length; i++) {
                  arrayObj[i] = new Object[] { new Integer(seats[i])};
                  //System.out.println("Will reserve seat with id " +
                  //  new Integer(seats[i]));
            }

            // Need Con to create object (association with Map)
            ARRAY seatIds = new ARRAY(ad, con, arrayObj);

            Map in = new HashMap();
            in.put("perf_id", new Integer(performanceId));
            in.put("seats", seatIds);
            Timestamp holdTill = new Timestamp(System.currentTimeMillis()
                                             + millisToHold);
            in.put("hold_till", holdTill);
            return in;
```

```
      }
   });
   Number Id = (Number) out.get("new_booking_id");
   return Id.intValue();
  }
 }
```

Working with a custom type in the database increases the complexity of JDBC code, whatever abstraction layer we use. (Type descriptors can be used to take advantage of object-relational features in Oracle and other databases, although there are simpler approaches such as Oracle's JPublisher that should be considered in more complex cases.) As this isn't a book on advanced JDBC or Oracle JDBC, we won't dwell on the details of this listing: the point is to show how we can use proprietary RDBMS features without ill effect to our architecture, as they are gathered in a single class that implements a common interface.

> *Note that we use a* `java.sql.Timestamp` *to hold the Oracle* `DATE` *type. If we use a* `java.sql.Date` *we will lose precision.*

The highlighted line shows that this `StoredProcedure` requires the ability to obtain an Oracle-specific connection from the connection it is given by its datasource. In most application servers, datasources will return wrapped connections rather than an RDBMS vendor-specific connection. (Connection wrapping is used to implement connection pooling and transaction control.) However, we can always obtain the underlying connection if necessary. We need to override the `OracleJdbcSeatingPlanDAO` `getOracleConnection()` method, which takes a pooled `Connection` and returns the underlying Oracle-specific connection, for each application server. The following override, in the `JBoss30OracleJdbcSeatingPlanDAO` class, will work for JBoss 3.0:

```
protected Connection getOracleConnection(Connection con) {
  org.jboss.resource.adapter.jdbc.local.ConnectionInPool cp =
    (org.jboss.resource.adapter.jdbc.local.ConnectionInPool) con;
  con = cp.getUnderlyingConnection();
  return con;
}
```

> *For the complete listing of the* `OracleJdbcSeatingPlanDAO` *and* `JBoss30OracleJdbcSeatingPlanDAO` *classes, see the download.*

By using the DAO pattern, we have been able to use Oracle-specific features without affecting the portability of our architecture. We have a simple interface that we can implement for any other database, relational, or otherwise. By using a JDBC abstraction library, we have greatly simplified application code, and made it more readable and less error-prone.

Summary

In this chapter we've surveyed some of the most effective data-access approaches for J2EE applications. We've considered:

❑ SQL-based approaches, such as JDBC and SQLJ. These can deliver very high performance, with minimal overhead, when we are working with relational databases and when O/R mapping is inappropriate. (We discussed the criteria for deciding whether to use O/R mapping in Chapter 7.) As most J2EE applications use relational databases, SQL-based approaches are very important in practice.

❑ Approaches based on O/R mapping, such as proprietary O/R mapping frameworks and JDO. JDO is particularly worthy of attention, as it may emerge as the standard J2EE API for accessing persistent data, whether in RDBMSs or ODBMSs.

All the approaches discussed in this chapter can be used in either the EJB container or web container of a J2EE application server. They can also easily be tested outside a J2EE application server: an important consideration, as we saw in Chapter 3. We can use any of these strategies in entity beans with BMP, but, as we have seen, BMP is unusable in many cases and imposes a complex, prescriptive model that delivers little or no benefit.

We concluded that a SQL-based approach using JDBC was most appropriate for our sample application, as it could not benefit significantly from caching in an O/R mapping layer, and because we saw in Chapter 7 that we can make effective use of stored procedures to move some of its persistence logic into the RDBMS. However, as we don't want our application's design to be dependent on use of an RDBMS, we chose to use the DAO pattern to conceal the use of JDBC behind an abstraction layer of persistent-store-independent interfaces.

As the sample application will use JDBC, we took a closer look at the JDBC API. We saw the importance (and difficulty) of correct error handling, how to extract information about the cause of a problem from a `javax.sql.SQLException,` and the pros and cons of JDBC `PreparedStatements` and `Statements`.

We concluded that using the JDBC API directly isn't a viable option, as it requires too much code to be written to accomplish each task in the database. Thus we need a higher level of abstraction than the JDBC API provides, even if we don't want to use an O/R mapping framework.

We examined the implementation of a generic JDBC abstraction framework, which delivers such a higher level of abstraction. We use this framework in the sample application, and it can be used in any application working with JDBC. This framework offers two levels of abstraction:

❑ The `com.interface21.jdbc.core` package, which uses callback methods to enable the framework `JdbcTemplate` class to handle the execution of JDBC queries and updates and JDBC error handling, relieving application code of the commonest causes of errors when using JDBC.

❑ The `com.interface21.jdbc.object` package, which builds on the `com.interface21.jdbc.core` package to model each RDBMS query, update, or stored procedure invocation as a reusable, threadsafe Java object, entirely concealing SQL and JDBC usage from application code. Using this package, we can greatly reduce the complexity of code using JDBC.

Another important benefit of our abstraction framework is that it enables code using it to work with a generic hierarchy of data-access exceptions, rather than JDBC SQLExceptions. This ensures that business objects never depend on JDBC-specific concepts. As all data access exceptions are runtime, rather than checked exceptions, application code is greatly simplified by being able to ignore unrecoverable exceptions. (JDO illustrates the effectiveness of this approach.)

We looked at how the sample application implements the DAO pattern using our JDBC abstraction framework. Using the abstraction framework enables us to write much simpler code than would have been required making direct use of JDBC. Using the DAO pattern enables us to use proprietary features of the Oracle target database without making our application's overall design dependent on Oracle, or even relational concepts. In this case the use of proprietary features is justified as it enables us to use efficient RDBMS constructs, and use PL/SQL stored procedures to handle persistence logic that would be much harder to implement in Java code.

This concludes our examination of data access in J2EE applications.

In the next chapter we'll look at effective use of session EJBs.

Sinae ... Alta ...

I. Ainan

O CEANUS

Siluy Illocos Luzon

Moro Hermoso

Pintados Ancon triste

INSULÆ

Doa Tanquero

Philipyna

G. de Matalobambre

Pondan

Mandato

Paragalle

Cd. Spirito Santo de Cobos

PHILIP

Luco

Tanquen

Enseada de Cauchin ... Sinoa

Cauchin Costa de Prasel

Cambai

Chantila

Franceiseo Gomez

Ylhas del Primeiro

Succidere

Pudlas

Abo comucho Primeiro

Caburae

PINÆ

AR

Man.

Camboia

Prael

Abejo

Manilha

Palo Cir

Calamianes

Damau

Castigar

Passage de S. Clara

I. de Mata lotes

Palo Condor

I. de S. Mora

Michael Prael Terende

MINDANA

Malagua

Pulo bahe

Mindanao

I. los Arecifes

Palo Tigao

Mon Pratan

S. Clara

A. de Resurreicam

C. Butay

I. de S. Ioanne

Carangao

I. da Palmeras

I. de S. Ioana

I. de la Mata

Bagueiram

I. de Sugim

I. de Talaa

I. de Rao

S.

BOR
NE
O

I. de Dei

I. dos Graos

As Aquada

Tamasa Sonda

R. de Borneo

Molans

Puchavarai

Tomacaurem

Tavordos

Ladem depde fez a Manuel de Lima

Thiols Duras de Macasar

Moo

Lucu

Hic hybernavit de Menes

Bintan

Cajoa Pura

Batinai Calapobi A Sorra

Jaus Monago Coricari Harboes Portuga Soga Coma Salor

Bachian

Batachina

Porto Cavam CEIRAM

Banca

CELE
BES

Ablas

Buxho

Simeno

Cabora

Bibliam Chinabato

Xula

Burre

I. Cupel

Nixabra

Beaures

P. Aga

Tobo

Arc

I. de S. Matheus

Agua in bernen Martin Afonso de mels

JAVA, quæ et IAOA dicitur. Fideida

Batolga Batatura

Terra alta Guilaan

Timor

Guaon

C LANT

Buxos

DOI

10
Session Beans

In our discussion of overall design in Chapter 1 and Chapter 6, we've considered how to decide when to use EJB, and the key services provided by the EJB container, such as container-managed transactions. In Chapter 8 we examined entity beans and concluded that they are a questionable choice for data access in most cases; hence it is session beans that provide most of the value of EJB.

In this chapter we'll take a deeper look at issues relating to implementing business logic with session beans.

We'll begin by discussing the choice between stateless and stateful session beans. As we'll see, stateful session beans have significant disadvantages (principally concerning reliability and scalability in a clustered environment), meaning that stateless session beans should normally be preferred.

We'll look at two important J2EE design patterns relating to session bean usage: the **Session Façade** pattern and the **EJB Command** pattern.

The Session Façade pattern makes a session bean (usually a stateless session bean) the entry point to the EJB tier. This pattern is most important in distributed applications, for which session beans should provide the remote interface. Implementation details such as entity beans or Data Access Objects are concealed behind the session façade. Session beans may also be used to implement a web services interface. Some application servers already support this, and EJB 2.1 adds standard support for web services endpoints. In collocated applications, session beans are used to implement business interfaces where EJB container services simplify application code.

In contrast, the EJB Command design pattern is based on moving *code* (rather than merely data) from client to EJB container. Although this pattern differs significantly from the more common use of session beans as façades, it is also implemented using a stateless session bean.

We'll look in detail at container services affecting session beans, such as how an EJB container reacts when an EJB throws an exception, and the implications for implementing session beans; and how declarative transaction attributes can be used to ensure that CMT delivers the required behavior.

We'll conclude by examining some good implementation practices when writing session beans.

> In distributed J2EE application, use session beans to implement your application's use cases. In collocated applications, use session beans to implement business logic that can benefit from EJB container services. Stateless session beans should generally be used in preference to stateful session beans if there is a choice.

Using Stateless Session Beans

Stateless session beans are the staples of EJB systems. They offer the key benefits of J2EE – container-managed lifecycle, remote access, automatic thread safety, and transparent transaction management – with minimal overhead in performance and deployment complexity.

Benefits of Stateless Session Beans

Stateless session beans (SLSBs) are the most scalable and reliable of J2EE components for distributed applications. As we saw in Chapter 6, only distributed applications using stateless business objects such as SLSBs are likely to prove more scalable and robust than collocated applications. In collocated applications, SLSBs offer fewer advantages over ordinary Java classes.

SLSBs are particularly well adapted to running in a cluster, as all instances are identical from the client's viewpoint. This means that incoming calls can always be routed to the best performing server. In contrast, stateful session beans are likely to encounter the problem of **server affinity**, where a client becomes bound to a particular server, regardless of other demand for that server. Thus stateless session bean deployments are highly reliable, even in the event of the failure of one or more server instances. WebLogic takes this to the extreme of being able to recover even in the event of a stateless session instance failing *during* a method invocation. Such recovery is performed by the client-side `EJBObject` stub if the method is identified in a WebLogic deployment descriptor as being **idempotent**: that is, if repeated calls to the method cannot result in duplicate updates.

Since all instances are identical, an EJB container can manage a **pool** of stateless session beans, ensuring that thread safety can be guaranteed for each bean's business methods without blocking client access to the stateless session bean. The scalability of such stateless components with managed lifecycles has been demonstrated in platforms other than J2EE, such as Microsoft Transaction Server (MTS), which predates EJB.

The disadvantage of using stateless session beans is that they are not true objects from the client perspective (they lack identity). This poses difficulties for OO design, but unfortunately the realities of scalable enterprise architecture demand some sacrifices. As stateless session beans are often only *façade* objects, they can sit atop an object-oriented architecture inside the EJB tier.

Stateless Session Beans and Internal State

> **There's a common misconception that stateless session beans cannot hold state. They are stateless because they do not hold state between method invocations *on behalf of any single client*. They are free to maintain internal state – for example, to cache resources and data used on behalf of *all* the clients they serve.**

This distinction is important, because it allows us to optimize stateless session beans by performing certain slow operations – such as the retrieval of read-only data – once and caching the results. Such data can be cached when a bean instance is created and the container invokes its `ejbCreate()` method, or when it is first required by a business method. EJB containers allow us to control the number of stateless session beans in the pool, meaning that we can be sure in practice that session bean instances will be reused. The size of a stateless session pool should always be less than the maximum number of threads the server is configured to permit. Maintaining a pool of more SLSB instances than the maximum number of threads wastes server resources, as it will be impossible for all the instances to be used simultaneously (this can only happen if there is one thread of execution using each SLSB instance). The point of pooling is to minimize contention for individual SLSB instances; there is no point in maintaining instances beyond the maximum number that can be used simultaneously.

Implications of Stateless Session Bean Pooling

It is through SLSB pooling that an EJB container allows us to write SLSB code as though it is single-threaded. Such pooling is efficiently implemented in J2EE application servers (although whether or not an ordinary Java object would be preferable depends on the particular case) and normally we don't need to worry about it.

Occasionally, however, it is important to consider usage patterns and the implications for SLSB instance pooling when assigning operations to SLSBs. For example, suppose that grouping by use case means that a `CustomerServices` stateless session EJB offers a `login()` method as well as a `performWeirdAndWonderful()` method. The `login()` method is used heavily and requires no state to be held in the stateless session bean. On the other hand, the `performWeirdAndWonderful()` method is rarely invoked, but requires a lot of state to be held in the stateless session bean (that is, internal state; not state exposed to any individual client). In this case it would be better to split the `CustomerServices` bean into two: one would contain the frequently used `login()` method. As it would consume little memory, there could be a large pool of these beans. The other would contain the `performWeirdAndWonderful()` method. Only a single instance, or a very small pool, might be required to support the bean's usage pattern, saving memory.

Occasionally it is important to understand how your EJB container performs pool management at run time for a particular class of EJB. Some servers, such as WebLogic, provide GUI tools that enable monitoring of the number of pooled instances for each deployed EJB. However, I have also found the following strategies helpful:

- ❑ Use logging messages in the `ejbCreate()` method to show when instances are created and initialized.

- ❑ Maintain a static instance variable in the EJB implementation class as a counter, incrementing it each time the `ejbCreate()` method is invoked. Note that this violates the restriction on EJBs holding read/write instance data, and won't work in a cluster. It's merely a useful, if hacky, technique for showing pooling behavior in a single server deployment.

Needless to say, both these strategies should only be used during development.

Using Stateful Session Beans

Stateful Session Beans (SFSBs) have their uses, but are far from being the staple of EJB that their stateless counterparts are. It's questionable whether they deserve the prominence they are accorded in the EJB specification, which implies that stateful session beans are the norm, and stateless session beans a special case.

Unlike stateless session beans, stateful session beans add significant memory and performance overhead. Stateful session beans are not shared between clients, meaning that the server must manage one SFSB instance for each client. In contrast, a few SLSB instances may service the requests of many clients.

Applications can often be designed to accomplish their work using stateless methods. Where this is possible, it will usually produce superior scalability. Even when server-side state must be maintained, stateful session beans are not the only, and may not be the best, option.

Why Not to Use Stateful Session Beans

There are strong arguments for avoiding the use of stateful session beans. Let's look at the most important.

Performance and Scalability Issues

The number of SFSB instances maintained on a server is proportional to the number of distinct active clients at any time. As SFSBs are relatively heavyweight objects, this limits the number of clients an application can serve concurrently in a given deployment configuration. It also places an onus on clients to free server-side resources when they are finished with them that does not apply to clients of stateless session or entity beans.

> If using SFSBs, ensure that your client code removes them when they are no longer required, by invoking the `remove()` method on the bean's component or home interface.

To help manage the overhead imposed by maintaining stateful session bean instances, the EJB specification allows containers to **passivate** and re-**activate** stateful session bean instances using a policy of their choosing. This means that the least recently used instances may be swapped out of memory into a persistent store. (The choice of store is left to the container.) Passivation and re-activation are usually implemented using Java language serialization to a database Binary Large Object (BLOB) or disk file, although the EJB specification allows EJB containers to use other strategies.

The subset of the stateful session bean's conversation state that survives passivation and re-activation is described in section 7.4 of the EJB 2.0 specification. It follows the rules for Java language serialization, with the addition that enterprise resources such as EJB local and remote home interfaces, EJB local and remote interfaces, `SessionContext` references, JNDI contexts, and resource manager connection factory references are preserved. It is the bean provider's responsibility to implement the `ejbPassivate()` method (invoked by the container to notify an instance of impending passivation) to ensure that instance methods are left with legal values.

> When coding stateful session beans, ensure that your beans can be passivated according to the rules outlined in section 7.4 of the EJB specification, and will have the correct behavior when re-activated after passivation. This means that you should use the `ejbPassivate()` method to ensure that instance variables have legal values before bean passivation.

For example, any JDBC connections must be closed, with the referencing instance variables set to `null`. The `ejbActivate()` method must ensure that any necessary resources that couldn't be preserved are reset to valid values.

The following code example shows a correct partial implementation of a hypothetical stateful session bean that uses a helper instance variable, `MyHelper`, which is not serializable, and thus is not a legal value for an instance variable at passivation:

```
public class MySessionBean implements javax.ejb.SessionBean {

    private MyHelper myHelper;
```

The `ejbCreate()` method initializes this instance variable when the SFSB is first used. Note that the `ejbActivate()` method is called only when a bean is re-activated after being passivated; it is not part of the bean's initialization by the container (see the lifecycle diagram in section 7.6 of the EJB specification):

```
public void ejbCreate() {
   this.myHelper = new MyHelper();
}
```

The implementation of the `ejbPassivate()` method sets the instance variable to `null`, which is an acceptable value:

```
public void ejbPassivate() {
   this.myHelper = null;
}
```

The implementation of the `ejbActivate()` method re-initializes the helper if the bean instance is re-activated:

```
public void ejbActivate() throws CreateException {
   this.myHelper = new MyHelper();
}
```

Note that the `myHelper` instance variable could be marked as transient, in which case it would be unnecessary to set it to `null` in `ejbPassivate()`, but it would still be necessary to re-initialize it in the `ejbActivate()` method.

Remember the discussion of Java 1.4 assertions in Chapter 4? A check that the `ejbPassivate()` method leaves instance data in a legal state would be a good use of an assertion.

Also remember that the container can time out passivated stateful session instances. This means that they can no longer be used by clients, who will receive a `java.remote.NoSuchObjectException` (a subclass of `java.remote.RemoteException`) when trying to access them.

On the other hand, using stateful session beans may improve performance in a distributed environment (in comparison with stateless session beans) by reducing the amount of context that needs to be passed up to the server with each method call: a stateful session bean holds state on behalf of its client, and therefore usually only needs to be told *what* to do, not what to do on what data.

Reliability Issues

Given that EJB is intended to help build robust, scalable applications, it may come as a surprise that stateful session beans are little help on either count. The central problem is that stateful session beans pose difficulties for efficient **replication** of state between clustered servers – an essential requirement if they are to prove reliable as the application deployment scales up.

The EJB specification makes no guarantees about the failover of stateful session beans. This means, for example, that implementing an online store with a stateful session bean to hold each user's shopping cart (as suggested in the EJB specification) is risky. The chances are that if the server hosting any particular shopping cart instance goes down, that user (along with many others) will lose their shopping cart. For truly reliable EJB state management, there is no alternative to using database persistence, managed through either entity beans or session beans using another persistence strategy.

To understand the limitations of stateful session failover, let's consider how stateful session beans behave in a cluster in WebLogic 7.0, probably the current market leading server. WebLogic has only supported replication of the conversational state of stateful session beans since version 6.0, and that replication is limited, because of its potential effect on performance. Each stateful session bean has a **primary** and a **secondary** WebLogic server instance in the cluster.

> Note that failover support and the necessary replication is not the same thing as load balancing of the creation of stateful session instances across a cluster, which WebLogic has long supported.

Normally, the EJBObject stub (that is, the implementation of the bean's remote interface supplied by WebLogic) routes all calls to the instance of a given bean on the primary server. Whenever a transaction is committed on the stateful session bean, WebLogic replicates the bean's state to the secondary server using **in-memory replication** (the alternative is no replication at all, WebLogic's default). Should the primary server instance fail, subsequent client method calls will be routed to the EJB instance on the secondary server, which will become the new primary server. A new secondary server will be assigned to restore failover capabilities. This approach has the following consequences:

- ❑ Stateful session bean instances are bound to one server in normal operation, resulting in server affinity.

- ❑ We cannot guarantee that state will be preserved in the event of failure, because replication occurs in memory, without a backing persistent store. As the replication involves only two servers, both may fail, wiping out the bean's state altogether.

- ❑ We cannot guarantee that clients will always see the committed state of persistent resources updated by the stateful session bean. Although the scenario is unlikely, it is possible that a transaction is successfully committed against the stateful session bean instance on the primary WebLogic server, but that server fails before the stateful session bean's state is replicated to the secondary server. When the client next invokes a method against the stateful session bean, the call will go to the old secondary server (now the primary), which will have out-of-date conversational state, which may conflict with the results of any committed persistent updates.

❑ It's impossible to recover gracefully from a failure on the primary server while a client is waiting for a return from a call on a stateful session bean. Such recovery may be possible with stateless session beans.

❑ Even in-memory replication will have an impact on performance. By contrast, there is no need to replicate state between stateless session bean instances in a cluster.

❑ Regardless of the replication strategy adopted by a container, correctly reverting the conversational state on a stateful session bean in the event of a transaction rollback is entirely the responsibility of the bean provider. Even if the stateful session bean implements the `SessionSynchronization` interface (discussed below), causing it to receive notifications on transaction boundaries, potentially complex code must be written to handle rollbacks.

In contrast, the handling of data set in a Servlet API `HttpSession` is typically more robust. WebLogic and other products offer the option to back `HttpSession` state persistence with a database, rather than merely offering in-memory replication (of course, database-backed persistence is a severe performance hit).

Perhaps the biggest problem for both reliability and scalability is that an SFSB's state is likely to be replicated *as a whole*, in its serialized representation, regardless of the extent of changes since it was last replicated. The EJB specification provides no way of identifying which part of a SFSB's state has changed after each method invocation, and it is very difficult for a container to work this out at run time.

The need to replicate each SFSB's entire state typically imposes greater overhead than is necessary for `HttpSession` objects, to which multiple fine-grained attributes can be bound and replicated only when rebound following changes. Oracle 9iAS, which offers highly configurable state management, provides a non-portable way of using a proprietary `StatefulSessionContext` to mark which parts of an SFSB's state have changed and need to be replicated, imitating `HttpSession` behavior (see http://otn.oracle.com/tech/java/oc4j/doc_library/902/ejb/cluster.htm#1005738 for details). The use of a proprietary class indicates how difficult it is to implement fine-grained SFSB replication within the EJB specification.

Often the use of stateful session beans leads to state being held in two locations. Client code can only benefit from the use of a stateful session bean if it holds a reference or handle to it. For example, in a web application, an `HttpSession` object might hold a reference to the user's stateless session bean. This means that we must manage not one, but *two*, session state objects for the one client. If we'll need an `HttpSession` object anyway, we may be able to avoid this by holding *all* the required session state in the `HttpSession` object, rather than having an additional stateful session bean in the EJB tier.

One potential way around this is to hold a representation of the session object's handle in a cookie or hidden form field. However, this is more complex than using an `HttpSession` object and not guaranteed to work in all servers (we don't know how large a handle might be).

Proponents of stateful session beans will argue that this problem of duplication doesn't apply to clients without a web front end. However, such clients are likely to be more sophisticated and interactive than web clients and are more likely to want to hold their own state – a Swing standalone application, for example, has no need for its state to be managed on the server.

> **Advocacy of using stateful session beans as the norm for session beans indicates an unrealistic view of J2EE: the view that sees J2EE as it *should* work. The fact is that SFSBs do not work as developers might expect, even in the most sophisticated application server on the market. This severely reduces their value.**

When to Use Stateful Session Beans

I feel that the circumstances under which SFSBs should be used are relatively rare. For example:

❑ **When a stateless interface would be unduly complex and would require the transport of excessive amounts of user data across the network**
Sometimes attempting to model the EJB tier in terms of stateless interfaces results in excessive complexity: for example, SLSB methods that require an unacceptable amount of session state to be passed with each invocation.

❑ **When multiple client types require state to be handled in the same location, or even shared**
For example, a SFSB might validly hold state on behalf of an applet and a servlet application. (However, such sharing normally occurs in persistent storage.)

❑ **To handle clients that frequently connect and disconnect**
In this, a typical scenario, if reliable preservation of state is vital, it must be held in the database. However, if an SFSB offers adequate reliability, the client may be able to store an SFSB handle and efficiently reconnect to the server at will.

❑ **When scalability is not a major priority**
Sometimes we don't need to consider the performance implications of clustering with stateful session beans – for example, if we're sure that an application will never run on more than one server. In this case, there's no need to complicate design by considering the impact of state replication (however, an HttpSession object is likely to be a simpler alternative in a web application).

The first three of these four criteria apply only to distributed applications.

> Note that none of these criteria justifying the use of SFSBs applies to web applications – the most common use of J2EE.

Session Synchronization

Stateful session beans have one unique property: a stateful session bean can implement the javax.ejb.SessionSynchronization interface to receive callbacks about the progress of transactions they are enlisted in but do not control (EJB §7.5.3, §17.4.1). This interface contains three methods:

```
public void afterBegin();
public void beforeCompletion();
public void afterCompletion(boolean success);
```

The most important method is afterCompletion(). The success parameter is true if the transaction is committed, false if it is rolled back.

The SessionSynchronization interface allows SFSBs to reset conversational state on transaction rollback, indicated by an afterCompletion() callback with a parameter value of false. We can also use this interface to control data caching: while the bean's state indicates that we're still within a transaction, we can treat cached data as up-to-date. We might also choose to cache resources, such as database connections.

A stateful session bean may only implement the `javax.ejb.SessionSynchronization` interface if it uses CMT (it wouldn't make sense for a bean with BMT to implement this interface, as it handles transaction delimitation itself and doesn't need to be informed about it). Only three transaction attributes are allowed: `Required`, `RequiresNew`, or `Mandatory`. Stateful session beans implementing the `SessionSynchronization` interface are passive users of CMT, being informed of the progress of transactions delimited elsewhere (we've so far considered the use of CMT to delimit transactions).

Session synchronization raises serious design concerns. If the stateful session bean doesn't control its own transactions, who does? Stateless session beans don't normally call stateful session beans. Clearly, we don't want entity beans to call stateful session beans. So the likelihood is that the transactions will be managed outside the EJB tier.

Allowing transactions to be managed by remote clients is very dangerous. For example, we must trust the remote caller to end the transaction before it times out – if it doesn't, any resources the stateful bean keeps open may be locked until the container eventually cleans up. Imagine, for example, that the remote client experiences a connection failure after beginning a transaction. The transaction will be left to time out, probably locking valuable resources from other components.

This last danger doesn't apply to transactions managed by objects in the web tier of the same server instance in an integrated application deployment. However, this indicates a likely design mistake: if we are using EJB, why are we using JTA to manage transactions, rather than EJB CMT, which is arguably the biggest benefit that EJB provides?

> Don't use the `javax.ejb.SessionSynchronization` interface for stateful session beans. This promotes poor application design, with remote clients of the EJB tier delimiting transactions, or the use of JTA for transaction management when EJB CMT would be a better option.

Protecting Stateful Session Beans from Concurrent Calls

It's illegal to make concurrent calls to stateful session beans. When using SFSBs, we need to take care to ensure that this cannot happen.

This situation can easily arise in practice. Imagine that a user has brought up two browser windows on a web site, and is browsing simultaneously in both. In this situation, if user state is held in an SFSB, it's possible that it may experience illegal concurrent invocations. The result will be that some calls will fail.

This problem isn't unique to SFSBs. However we handle user state in web applications, we will need to address it. However, it does show that even when we use SFSBs, we'll need to solve some tricky problems ourselves (in this case, probably by synchronization in web-tier code).

Patterns for Achieving Stateful Functionality with SLSBs

Since SLSBs offer superior scalability and are more robust in a cluster, it's a good idea to tweak design to replace SFSBs with SLSBs if possible. Let's consider some approaches.

Object Parameter

The usual way of mimicking stateful behavior is to pass state from client to SLSB as necessary with each method call. Often, instead of a number of parameters, we pass a single, larger object. In web applications, the state will be held in the web tier in `HttpSession` objects. Passing state objects with each SLSB call isn't usually a problem in collocated applications, but may affect performance in distributed applications.

If the volume of state is very large, we may need to pass a lot of state with each method call. In such cases we may need to re-examine the design. Often holding an excessive amount of user state indicates poor design, which should be questioned. As we've seen in Chapter 6, however we go about implementing our application, holding a large amount of state per user will limit its scalability.

The need for large amounts of state per user may be an indication to use an SFSB. However, if we can implement each use case in a single SLSB method call, the system will still probably be more scalable if we pass state up with each method call. Often state is limited (for example, a primary key that will drive a database lookup).

Using a "Required Workflow Exception" to Mimic an SFSB State Machine

With a little inventiveness, we can sometimes make stateless session beans do the work of stateful session beans. The following example illustrates the use of stateless beans to manage client-side workflow.

I once had to design a registration system for a web portal that enforced new username, password, and profile requirements. Most existing users could simply log in and be marked as active on the new system. Others, whose logins were illegal in the new system, were forced to perform one or more steps to update their account before successful login. For example, some users might be required to change invalid usernames and supply additional profile information in separate operations before logging in. This migration process needed to be managed in the EJB tier, as it was possible that other client types would be added to the initial web application.

My initial design used a stateful session bean – essentially a state machine – to represent the login process. Each user's state largely consisted of the point in the process they had reached. Unfortunately, it emerged that the application had to run on a geographically dispersed cluster and that SFSB replication wasn't a viable option.

I was forced to design a system using stateless session beans. By using exceptions as alternative return values, I succeeded in directing client-side workflow from the EJB tier. No state was required in the web application or EJB tier, and the application proved to scale very well.

The login workflow began with the client (a web-tier controller accessing the `UserManager` SLSB via a business delegate) invoking the following method on the `UserManager` SLSB:

```
UserProperties login(String login, String password)
    throws NoSuchUserException, RequiredWorkflowException, RemoteException;
```

A successful return meant that login was complete, and the client had valid user data. The client was forced to catch the two application exceptions. The `NoSuchUserException` meant that the login process was over; the user's credentials had been rejected. If a `RequiredWorkflowException` was encountered, the client checked a code in the exception. For example, in the case of duplicate logins, the code was the constant value `MUST_IDENTIFY_FURTHER`. In this case, the controller forwarded the user to a form prompting them to enter their e-mail address. On submission of this form, the client issued another login request, to the following method on the stateless `UserManager`:

```
void identifyUserFromEmail(String login, String password, String email)
    throws NoSuchUserException, RequiredWorkflowException, RemoteException;
```

This method also threw a `NoSuchUserException` (if the user could not be identified), or a `RequiredWorkflowException` with a code indicating whether the user should be forced to change their username or password. One or other change was always required, but the `UserManager` implemented rules for determining which.

This method succeeded in concealing the details of account migration in the EJB tier, in a stateless session bean. State was effectively held in the client's browser – the URL of each form submission and attached data prompted calling of the correct EJB method.

Using a Stateful Session Bean as Controller

It's generally agreed that the **Model View Controller** architectural pattern is most appropriate for web interfaces and many other GUIs. In typical web application architectures, the controller component is a servlet or MVC framework-specific class.

A plausible alternative implementation for web or other GUI applications using EJB – advocated by Sun Java Center – moves the controller inside the EJB container, as a stateful session bean. This gathers controller code in the EJB tier (although some will inevitably remain in the UI tier). This means that the same controller may be usable by different client types, if the SFSB exposes a remote interface.

I feel that this approach illustrates the wishful thinking that characterizes a lot of J2EE literature. It *should* work. If it did work, the world would be a better place, but I don't know of any real, heavily used, application that adopts it, because of its performance implications. (The Java Pet Store, which does, performs very poorly.)

Performance issues are a key consideration in J2EE design tradeoffs. It's important to minimize the depth of calling down the layers of J2EE architecture to service each client request. If we force each request to call down into the EJB tier, performance and scalability will be seriously affected.

> **Use a stateful session bean only after considering reasonable alternatives. Usually, the indications for using a stateful session bean are that: (a) trying to solve the problem with a stateless interface leads to excessive complexity; and (b) the requisite state cannot be held in an `HttpSession` object in the web tier (perhaps because the application has no web tier).**

The value of stateful session beans is hotly debated among EJB experts. Many share my skepticism. See, for example, http://www.onjava.com/pub/a/onjava/2001/10/02/ejb.html for a highly polemical article criticizing stateful session beans by Tyler Jewell, a Principal Technology Evangelist for BEA Systems. On the other hand, Sun Java Center architects favor the use of stateful session beans.

J2EE Design Patterns Applicable to Session Beans

Let's now look at two J2EE design patterns applicable to session beans. The **Session Façade** pattern is a proven staple for applications using entity beans, while the **EJB Command** pattern offers an interesting alternative that is sometimes appropriate.

Both these patterns are most relevant to distributed applications. Both are typically implemented using stateless session beans.

The Session Façade Pattern in Distributed J2EE Applications

In distributed J2EE applications, remote clients should communicate with the EJB tier exclusively via session beans, regardless of whether entity beans are used. In a distributed application, session beans will implement the application's use cases, handle transaction management, and mediate access to lower-level components such as entity beans, other data access components, and helper objects. This approach is known as the Session Façade design pattern and can significantly improve performance, compared to having clients use entity beans directly.

The performance gain in using a session façade comes in the reduction of the number of expensive network round trips needed to implement a given use case. Such network round trips result from remote method calls and client-side JNDI lookups. Thus, even when clients really want to work with underlying components such as entity beans, adding the extra layer of a session façade improves performance. The session beans can communicate efficiently *within the EJB container* to lower-level components.

Consider a use case implementation that calls on three entity beans. If the client were to implement this use case, it would potentially require three JNDI lookups for remote objects and would need to make a minimum of three remote calls to the entities required. The client would also need to perform transaction management, to ensure that all three calls occurred in the same transaction (normally the intended behavior). Using a session façade, on the other hand, a client would need only one remote JNDI lookup and one remote call. This will lead to a large performance gain.

Remote method calls are often *hundreds* of times slower than local calls. By definition, a client will have to make at least *one* remote call to access any EJB method (often, two will be required, as it will be necessary to call the EJB home to obtain an EJB reference before invoking a business method). The more we can accomplish with each remote call, the better our distributed application will perform, even if this means that the amount of data exchanged in any one call is greater. By invoking a session façade to implement our use case, we can usually avoid even this tradeoff, as most of the data required for the business logic will never leave the server. For example, objects created during the work of the method may never be exposed to the client and never pass down the wire.

Finally, if remote clients are able to invoke low-level components such as entity beans directly, they are tightly coupled to the architecture of the EJB tier. This makes refactoring within the EJB tier unnecessarily difficult. For example, it's impossible to replace entity beans with another persistence strategy if performance requirements dictate.

In collocated applications, these performance considerations don't apply. Interface granularity is no longer a decisive factor in designing EJB interfaces, but there is still an argument for hiding the implementation of the EJB tier – for example, whether it uses entity beans – from code outside the EJB container.

The EJB Command Design Pattern

An alternative to the Session Façade pattern is the EJB Command pattern – a special case of the GoF **Command** design pattern. This pattern was used heavily in IBM's San Francisco business framework, which predated EJB. It's particularly suited for use in distributed applications, but can also be useful in collocated applications.

Implementing the EJB Command Design Pattern

This pattern is an object-oriented form of a callback method (we discussed callback methods in Chapter 4, and used them in the JDBC abstraction framework discussed in Chapter 9).

Application functionality is encapsulated in serializable **command** objects. In distributed applications, commands are created by remote clients and passed over the wire to the EJB container. Typically commands are JavaBeans, with input and output properties. All commands implement a common interface that includes an `execute()` method. For example:

```
public interface Command extends java.io.Serializable {
  void execute() throws CommandException;
}
```

A command is constructed on the client, which sets its input properties (for example, HTTP request parameters might be bound to a command's bean properties). The command is then passed to the EJB server, where its `execute()` method is invoked by a generic stateless session bean. Thus the code in the `execute()` method can access the EJB's run-time environment, via the JNDI environment (for example, to access EJBs or resource managers). The `execute()` method either throws an exception, which will be returned to the client, or sets the output properties of the command object. The command object is then returned to the client, which uses the value of the output properties.

Note that as the signature of the `Command execute()` method is fixed, command implementations may only throw a checked `CommandException`, constraining their method signatures. Typically they will throw a generic command exception that nests another exception within it, or a custom subclass of `CommandException`.

Here we're focusing on the use of an SLSB as command executor, but the command pattern isn't tied to use of EJB. There must be a `CommandExecutor` interface, which can be implemented by an SLSB. A typical `CommandExecutor` interface might have a single method:

```
public interface CommandExecutor {
  Command executeCommand(Command command)
    throws RemoteException, CommandException;
}
```

An SFSB remote interface might extend this (the `executeCommand()` method has to throw `java.rmi.RemoteException` to allow this).

The following is a complete implementation of a simple command executor SLSB:

```
import java.rmi.RemoteException;
import javax.ejb.EJBException;
import javax.ejb.SessionBean;
import javax.ejb.SessionContext;

public class CommandExecutorEJB implements SessionBean, CommandExecutor {

  private SessionContext sessionContext;

  public void setSessionContext(SessionContext sessionContext)
```

375

```
      throws EJBException, RemoteException {
    this.sessionContext = sessionContext;
  }

  public void ejbRemove() throws EJBException, RemoteException {
  }

  public void ejbActivate() throws EJBException, RemoteException {
  }

  public void ejbPassivate() throws EJBException, RemoteException {
  }

  public void ejbCreate() {
  }
}
```

The implementation of the executeCommand() method is completely generic, as the command itself contains all the application-specific code. Note that if an exception is encountered executing the command, the CommandExecutorEJB ensures that the current transaction is rolled back. The command executor session bean uses CMT, so the executeCommand() method runs in its own transaction:

```
public Command executeCommand(Command command) throws CommandException {
  try {
    command.execute();
  } catch (CommandException ex) {
    sessionContext.setRollbackOnly();
    throw ex;
  }
  return command;
}
```

A typical command object might look like this:

```
public class CustomerDataCommand implements Command {

  private int custid;
  private String name;
  private int invoices;

  public void setCustomerId(int id) {
    this.custid = id;
  }

  public void execute() throws CommandException {
    try {
      Context ctx = new InitialContext();
      SalesHome home = (SalesHome) ctx.lookup("java:comp/env/ejb/sales");
      Sales sales = home.create();
      Customer cust = sales.findCustomer(this.custid);
      this.name = cust.getForename();
```

```
      this.invoices = <code to count invoices omitted>
    } catch (Exception ex) {
      throw new CommandException("Failed to execute command in EJB container",
                                ex);
    }
  }

  public String getName() {
    return name;
  }

  public int getInvoices() {
    return invoices;
  }
}
```

This command has one input property (`customerId`) and two output properties: `name` and `invoices`. The highlighted `execute()` method runs within the EJB container, where it is able to connect to another EJB to look up this data. Thus a complete use case – find customer data – executes in a single network round trip, and in a single transaction.

> *Note that a real command would probably used the Service Locator pattern – discussed in the next chapter – to reduce the amount of code needed to look up the EJBs it references.*

The following code fragment shows how, with a reference to a `CommandExecutor` EJB, we could execute this command from the clientside. Note that the `tc` variable, which holds the command sent to the EJB tier, is set to the command returned from the EJB on successful execution of the command. This ensures that client code can access any output properties of the command, such as the `name` and `invoices` properties:

```
TestCommand tc = new TestCommand();
tc.setCustomerId(customerId);
try {
   tc = (TestCommand) commandExecutor.executeCommand(tc);
   System.out.println("Customer name is " + tc.getName());
   System.out.println("Customer has " + tc.getInvoices() + " invoices");

} catch (CommandException ex) {

} catch (RemoteException ex) {

}
```

This code could be held in a client-side command executor that would hide the details of EJB access from other client-side code.

Advantages and Disadvantages of the EJB Command Design Pattern

The EJB Command design pattern has the following advantages:

❑ It delivers the usual benefits of the GoF Command design pattern, allowing queuing and logging of commands.

❑ It promotes the execution of an entire use case in a single round trip, minimizing network overhead.

❑ It makes the EJB tier extensible without modifying EJBs.

- ❏ It allows multiple return values from the EJB tier.

- ❏ It's relatively robust against distributed failures, as it only requires only one remote call for each operation.

- ❏ It's not tied to an EJB implementation. Clients work with command objects, rather than with EJBs. In the above example, the `CommandExecutor` interface could be implemented without using EJB.

The disadvantages are not all so obvious:

- ❏ We need to include all command classes in the EJB container, so we need to redeploy the command executor EJB whenever we add a new command. It's possible for the EJB container to "export" classes to clients, but it's impossible to "import" additional classes into the EJB container, for security and other reasons.

- ❏ It makes the client dependent on libraries used in the EJB tier. For example, if some commands use JDO, the client needs access to the JDO libraries.

- ❏ Sometimes efficiency may dictate that what goes up to the EJB server shouldn't come back down. Using a typical implementation of the command design pattern like that shown above, the input data is returned redundantly to the client with the response.

- ❏ Clumsy error handling. All exceptions must be wrapped in a generic `CommandException`. Client code must extract further details as necessary.

- ❏ While a session bean can normally cache resources and data, a command can't, as new commands are constantly being created and all command data has to be serialized and deserialized twice. For example, we will need to do a JNDI lookup with each `execute()` call to obtain EJB references that could have been cached if the operation were implemented in a normal SLSB. However, JNDI lookups should be fast within the EJB container.

- ❏ A command can only rollback the current transaction by throwing a `CommandException`, as it doesn't have access to the command executor EJB's `SessionContext`. Although it would be possible to pass the `SessionContext` as a parameter to the `execute()` method, this increases the client's dependency on an EJB implementation.

- ❏ The EJB Command design pattern introduces a real risk of code duplication. As using the EJB Command pattern tends to alter the way in which teams work, it is easier for developers to implement the same functionality without refactoring common code. Close teamwork can help to minimize this risk, but there is also a serious danger of the Command pattern making it hard to share common code.

> **Due to these disadvantages, I don't tend to use the EJB Command design pattern. However, it's a viable option, and worth discussing as it demonstrates one approach to ensuring that an entire use case executes in one remote call in distributed applications.**

Using Commands without Adopting the Command Design Pattern

The idea of encapsulating a request to the EJB tier – or any business interface – as a single object, rather than individual parameters, can be used without shipping executable code from client to server.

We can simply provide a method on our business interfaces, which may or may not be implemented using EJB, to handle each command. In this approach, the command does not contain the necessary business logic, just one request to the application. In this approach, we don't always need to return the command (we can return a distinct output object), and such business methods can throw any exceptions we choose.

This approach, which we'll use in the sample application, promotes good practice in web applications by formalizing the role of web tier code to convert user gestures into commands and command responses to views to display to the user. It also facilitates testing. Many web applications use this approach, and the design of most MVC web application frameworks encourages it.

The following example from the sample application illustrates this approach. Some of the methods on the `com.wrox.expertj2ee.ticket.boxoffice.BoxOffice` interface take object (command) arguments rather than multiple primitive or object parameters. For example, the `allocateSeats()` method, which initiates the booking process, has the following signature:

```
public interface BoxOffice {

  // Other methods omitted

  Reservation allocateSeats(ReservationRequest request)
      throws NotEnoughSeatsException, NoSuchPerformanceException,
          InvalidSeatingRequestException;
}
```

The `ReservationRequest` parameter is a command. Its properties are automatically populated from `HttpRequest` parameter values by infrastructure code invoked by `com.wrox.expertj2ee.ticket.web.TicketController`, the application's web-tier controller class. This use of a single object, instead of multiple parameters, means that the `BoxOffice` interface does not need to change if more information needs to be carried with each reservation request, and that it's easy to queue and log commands or publish events (using the Observer design pattern) when a command is issued or processed.

The implementation of the `BoxOffice` interface, not the `ReservationRequest` command object, contains the business logic necessary to process this command.

Session Bean Implementation issues

Now that we've considered which type of session bean to use and some idioms frequently used with session beans, let's take a look at some important implementation issues concerning session beans. In this section we'll consider the EJB error handling model and how it affects bean developers; transaction propagation using EJB CMT and its implications for implementing session beans; and an EJB implementation pattern that can help us to avoid a common cause of deployment errors.

Error Handling in EJBs

As EJBs are managed objects, the EJB container steps in to handle some types of exceptions they throw. This section discusses the rules defined in the EJB specification, and how developers can use them to advantage. These considerations are important as we implement business logic in session beans and define session bean local and remote interfaces.

379

The EJB Container's Behavior on Exceptions

The EJB specification's approach to exceptions thrown by EJBs is simple and elegant. The specification distinguishes between **application exceptions** and all other exceptions, referred to as **system exceptions**.

An application exception is a checked exception defined in the throws clause of a method of an EJB's local or remote home or local or remote interface, other than java.remote.RemoteException. (Remember that Java RMI requires that all remote methods declare this exception in their throws clause.)

A system exception is an unchecked exception or throwable thrown by an EJB implementation class method at run time, or an uncaught java.remote.RemoteException resulting from a call on another EJB within the application. (It's up to the bean developer to decide whether or not a method in a bean class catches RemoteExceptions resulting from calling other EJBs. It will usually only make sense to do so if the error is recoverable, or to add context information to the nested exception.)

It is assumed that the EJB client understands application exceptions, and how they might be recovered from. It is up to the client to decide that a particular exception is unrecoverable. Consequently, the container does not step in when an application exception is thrown. It simply causes the EJB client to catch the same application exception. The container will not normally log application exceptions, and the status of the current transaction will be unaffected.

System exceptions are handled very differently. The container assumes that the client didn't expect such an exception, and that it's likely to prove fatal for the current use case. This is a reasonable assumption. In contrast to application exceptions, which are checked and which the client *must* know about because it is forced by the Java compiler to catch them, system exceptions may be meaningless to the client. Take, for example, a runtime exception from a JDO persistence manager. The client should not even know the EJB tier's persistence mechanism, and can't be expected to recover from a problem it doesn't understand.

Accordingly, the container takes drastic action. It marks the current transaction *irreversibly* for rollback. It discards the EJB instance so that it can service no further calls. The fact that the EJB instance will be discarded means that the developer need not make any effort to clean up any conversational or internal state maintained in the bean. This reduces developer workload and removes a potential source of bugs. The EJB container must log the offending system exception. If the client is remote, the EJB container throws a java.remote.RemoteException (or a subclass) to the client. If the client is local, the EJB container throws a javax.ejb.EJBException to the client.

A bean that has encountered an unrecoverable checked exception that it cannot rethrow should throw a javax.ejb.EJBException or subclass wrapping the checked exception. This will be treated as an unexpected exception by the container. This container behavior on unexpected exceptions should not be used as a substitute for explicitly rolling back transactions using the setRollbackOnly() method. It is a convenient cleanup facility offered by the container when a bean instance encounters an unrecoverable error. Since it results in the bean instance being discarded, it will reduce performance if this situation occurs frequently at run time.

Let's now consider some of the implications when designing and implementing session beans:

- ❑ **We must never allow an EJB method to throw a runtime exception in normal operation**
  An uncaught throwable will cause not only the call stack to unwind as usual, but also the container to roll back the current transaction.

❑ **We should consider whether or not to catch `RemoteExceptions` thrown by EJBs whose remote interfaces we use in EJB methods**
We do have the simpler choice of declaring our EJB implementation to throw the `RemoteException`, but this will be treated as fatal error, and the bean instance will be discarded. If the exception is recoverable, it must be caught.

❑ **If a runtime exception is fatal, we needn't catch it, but may leave the EJB container to handle it**
A good example is a runtime exception from a JDO persistence manager. Unless we believe we can retry the operation, there's no point in catching such exceptions.

❑ **If an EJB method catches a checked exception that it cannot recover from, it should throw a `javax.ejb.EJBException` wrapping the original exception.**

❑ **An application exception on an EJB local or remote interface must be a checked exception**
The container treats all runtime exceptions as fatal system errors. This means that we don't have the choice of using unchecked exceptions on the signatures of EJB methods *or on any interfaces that are likely to be implemented by EJBs*. This is perhaps the only unfortunate result of the EJB approach to error handling, as client code doesn't have the option of dealing with runtime exceptions only in unusual cases – an approach discussed in Chapter 4, which can prove very useful.

> The guarantee that the EJB container will step in to handle an unchecked exception and ensure transaction rollback makes it particularly attractive to define fatal exceptions thrown by helper classes likely to be used by EJBs to be unchecked exceptions. For example, the JDBC abstraction framework discussed in Chapter 9 throws the unchecked `DataAccessException`, which EJBs that use it can simply ignore, on encountering an unrecoverable `java.sql.SQLException`. In the unlikely event that an EJB needs to intercept this exception, it still can implement a `catch` block.

Understanding EJB API Exceptions

The `javax.ejb` package defines eleven exceptions. Those of most interest to J2EE developers are:

❑ `javax.ejb.EJBException`
This is a convenient runtime wrapper exception intended for wrapping unrecoverable checked exceptions. We may use it to wrap fatal exceptions such as JDBC exceptions that must be caught. However, there's a strong case that any exception that we define ourselves that must be wrapped in an `EJBException` and rethrown should simply be an unchecked (runtime) exception. This will simplify EJB code. As the `catch` block that throws an `EJBException` doesn't need to perform any cleanup (the EJB container will roll back the transaction and discard the bean instance), catching and rethrowing the exception adds no value.

The following are standard EJB application exceptions. They are reported to clients:

❑ `javax.ejb.CreateException` and subclasses
This should be thrown from an `ejbCreate()` method if the failure to create the bean should be viewed as an application error. For example, a stateful session bean `ejbCreate()` method might throw this exception if it was passed invalid arguments by a client. If the failure to create a bean reflects a system exception, a runtime exception should be used (the `EJBException` wrapper exception if necessary). For example, there's no point in telling a remote client that a table is missing in a relational database. The remote client shouldn't even know that the EJB tier uses a relational database.

381

❏   `javax.ejb.RemoveException` and subclasses
Analogous to `CreateException`.

❏   `javax.ejb.FinderException` and subclasses (entity beans only, but often encountered by session bean implementations)
Finder exception must be included in the `throws` clause of every finder method on an entity bean's home interface. A finder should throw this exception on failure to locate a requested object, or encountering inconsistent results from the persistent store (for example, if a single object finder finds multiple matching records). Note that an empty Collection returned from a multi-object finder does not indicate an error. In the case of entity beans with CMP, finder methods will be generated by the EJB container.

Transaction Attributes for EJBs using CMT

EJBs are normally transactional components. As we saw in Chapter 6, one of the strongest arguments for using session EJBs to implement business logic is the option of using declarative Container Managed Transactions (CMT). We specify CMT behavior in EJB deployment descriptors, causing the container to create transactions if necessary for EJB method invocations, freeing the developer from the need to use JTA directly. This is an important productivity gain. However, it's important to understand exactly how CMT works.

There is an overhead associated with creating a transaction, so we don't want to create transactions unnecessarily. Yet, transactions are vital to the integrity of business logic that involves multiple updates of transactional resources.

Focusing on session beans with CMT, let's consider the transaction attributes allowed by the deployment descriptor and how they affect the behavior of our code. (As we saw in Chapter 6 we should always prefer CMT to BMT if we have a choice.) The EJB specification recognizes six transaction attributes, which are associated with EJB methods in the `ejb-jar.xml` deployment descriptor. The following table summarizes the behavior each confers:

Transaction attribute as specified in deployment descriptor	Meaning for the method so marked (referred to as method m) and other resources m invokes	Effect if a caller already has a transaction	Notes	Recommended use
Required	The method is guaranteed to run in a JTA transaction. If the caller has a transaction, it will be used. If not, a new transaction will be created.	Method m will run in the caller's transaction.	If the caller's transaction is rolled back, the work of method m will be rolled back automatically. This is the most flexible option. It allows the caller to use method m as a piece of a larger, reversible, unit of work. Yet method m can still be used independently. For example, it is able to support calls from clients outside the EJB tier.	This should be the default transaction attribute for session bean methods, which define the public interface of the EJB tier.
RequiresNew	The method is guaranteed to run in a *new* transaction, whether or not the caller has a transaction.	The caller's transaction is suspended during execution of the method.	This can be dangerous. If method m succeeds and commits changes, but the caller's transaction is rolled back, the changes made by method m will not be reversed. This means that the caller does not have overall control of the business operation. *Note that the creation of a new transaction when the client already has a transaction context does not amount to a nested transaction.* With nested transactions, rollback of the parent transaction will cause rollback of all child transactions. In the RequiresNew case we have two separate flat transactions, with no relationship and no effect on each other's rollback status.	Only useful in the unusual case that method m implements a distinct piece of work that must commit regardless of the success of any higher-level operation in progress. An example might be an auditing action, where a persistent record must be made of the fact that a user *attempted* a certain action, regardless of its success.

Table continued on following page

383

Transaction attribute as specified in deployment descriptor	Meaning for the method so marked (referred to as method m) and other resources m invokes	Effect if a caller already has a transaction	Notes	Recommended use
NotSupported	The method is assumed not to be interested in JTA transactions, and will execute without a transaction context. If the method invokes other EJBs or resource managers, no transaction context will be propagated.	The caller's transaction is suspended during execution of the method.	Rollback of the caller's transaction will have no effect on any changes made by method m. Not available to entity beans.	Appropriate if the method's implementation is non-transactional. Don't use if the method updates persistent data. Can be useful for read-only methods. For example, Oracle SELECTs do not need to run in a transaction, and Oracle won't create a transaction if none exists. Therefore query methods will be most efficient with a NotSupported transaction attribute.
Supports	If the caller has a transaction, it will be propagated to the method, and execution will occur as in the Required case. If the caller does not have a transaction, the container will not create one, and the method will execute without one, as in the NotSupported case.	Method m will run in the caller's transaction, as in the Required case.	Potentially dangerous. The semantics of method m will vary depending on whether the client has a transaction context. Not available to entity beans.	Don't use this transaction attribute for updates. In the case of read-only operations, it can be used safely and will behave the same way as NotSupported.

Transaction attribute as specified in deployment descriptor	Meaning for the method so marked (referred to as method m) and other resources m invokes	Effect if a caller already has a transaction	Notes	Recommended use
Mandatory	The method requires a JTA transaction, which *must be provided by the client.* If the client does not have a transaction context when calling the method, the container throws a javax.transaction.Transact ionRequiredException.	This is the only valid case.	Often an alternative to Requires. Limits the situations in which the method may be called. However, this may be a good thing.	Useful for entity bean methods when using a session façade. In this case, we want the client to work through the façade, rather than manipulate low-level components such as entity beans, possibly coming in under the radar of our business logic and breaking system integrity. Of course, a client could still obtain the UserTransaction object and create a transaction before invoking method m. Do not use for session bean methods, as this would prevent their use by clients without transactions (the ideal client scenario).
Never	The opposite of Mandatory. The method *must not* be called by a client with a transaction context. If it is, the container throws a java.rmi.RemoteException. Within the method, behavior will be the same as in the NotSupported case.	Not permitted.	An alternative to NotSupported if it is considered essential to prevent a client with a transaction context calling the method. Not available to entity beans.	

> The safest EJB transaction attributes are `Required` (for session beans) and `Mandatory` (for entity beans). These attributes ensure the expected transaction behavior, regardless of the caller's transaction context. A transaction attribute of `NotSupported` can be used to boost the performance of read-only methods, for which transactions are not required. This situation arises often, as web applications frequently use read-only data.

The EJB specification suggests that an "Application Assembler", distinct from the EJB developer, may set transaction attributes. This is potentially dangerous. As we've seen, changing the transaction attributes of an EJB method can change the method's semantics. Only if the bean developer defines the transaction attributes can they develop meaningful unit tests for EJBs. While the removal of the specification of EJB transaction attributes from Java code is desirable, their removal from the control of the bean developer is misguided.

Although the details of transaction management are best left to the EJB container, deciding whether a transaction should be rolled back is usually a matter of business logic (remember that if there's a runtime exception, the EJB container will automatically ensure rollback, whether a bean uses BMT or CMT). Accordingly, it's easy to ensure rollback in a bean using CMT.

All EJBs have access to an instance of the EJB context interface, supplied at run time by the container. There are three subinterfaces of `javax.ejb.EJBContext`, available at run time to the three kinds of EJB: `javax.ejb.SessionContext`, `javax.ejb.EntityContext`, and `javax.ejb.MessageDrivenContext`. The `EJBContext` superinterface offers a `setRollbackOnly()` method that allows CMT beans to mark the current transaction *irreversibly* for rollback.

The Business Methods Interface "Pattern"

As the EJB container, not the bean developer, provides the implementation of an EJB's component interface (the local or remote interface), how do we ensure that the component interface and bean implementation class remain in synch? Lack of such synchronization is a common cause of problems at deployment time, so this is an important issue, unless we are prepared to become dependent on tool support for EJB development.

We can choose to make the bean implementation class implement the component interface, but this has the following disadvantages:

❑   As the component interface must extend either `javax.ejb.EJBObject` or `javax.ejb.EJBLocalObject`, the bean implementation will be forced to provide empty implementations of methods from these interfaces that will never be invoked by the container. This is confusing to readers.

❑   It will be possible to return `this` to remote or local clients, in place of the container-generated implementation of the component interface. This is a serious programming error that probably won't be detected by the EJB container and may cause subtle problems at run time.

Fortunately, there is a simple and effective solution, which is widely recognized: to have both component interface and bean implementation class implement a common "business methods" interface. The business methods interface does not extend any EJB infrastructure interfaces, although it may extend other application business interfaces.

If we're dealing with an EJB with a remote interface, each method in the business methods interface must be declared to throw `javax.remote.RemoteException`. In the case of EJBs with remote interfaces, the business methods interface is normally an EJB-tier implementation detail: clients will work with the bean's remote interface, not the business methods interface.

In the case of EJBs with a local interface, the business method interface's methods may not throw `RemoteException`, which means that the business methods interface need not be EJB-specific. Often the business methods interface, rather than the EJB's local interface, is of most interest to clients of the EJB. In the sample application, for example, the `com.wrox.expertj2ee.ticket.boxoffice.BoxOffice` interface is an ordinary Java interface, which could be implemented without using EJB. Clients invoke methods on this interface, rather than the EJB's local interface, which extends it.

Use of a "**Business Methods Interface**" isn't really a design pattern – it's more a workaround for an inelegant feature of the EJB specification. But as it's often referred to as a pattern, I'm following established terminology.

Let's look at how we use this pattern for the sample application's `BoxOffice` EJB, and the naming conventions used. Using this pattern involves the following four classes for the EJB:

❑ `BoxOffice`
The interface that defines the business methods on the EJB, extended by the component interface and implemented by the bean implementation. In the sample application, this interface is defined apart from the EJB implementation and is used by clients. Even if clients will work only with the EJB's local or remote interface, such an interface can be introduced purely as an EJB tier implementation choice to synchronize the classes required to implement the bean.

❑ `BoxOfficeLocal`
The EJB component interface. The component interface should be empty. It will extend both the business methods interface and one or other of `javax.ejb.EJBObject` (in the case of a remote interface) or `EJBLocalObject` (in the case of a local interface), inheriting all its methods. In the sample application, we use a local interface. Note that I have suffixed `Local` to the end of the business interface name; a suffix of `Remote` should be used for remote interfaces.

❑ `BoxOfficeHome`
The bean's home interface. Unless a bean has both a local and remote interface (a relatively rare case), I don't consider it necessary to distinguish between `BoxOfficeLocalHome` and `BoxOfficeRemoteHome`.

❑ `BoxOfficeEJB`
The bean implementation class. This will implement both `javax.ejb.SessionBean` and the business methods interface. Some sources recommend names of the form `BoxOfficeBean`, but I avoid this as I tend to use the suffix "Bean" for implementations of a particular interface that are ordinary JavaBeans (as opposed to EJBs). If the bean implementation is tied to a particular technology, indicate that in the name: for example, `JdbcBoxOfficeEJB`. As with any implementation of an interface, the name should indicate what characterizes that implementation, not merely repeat the interface name as closely as possible.

The following UML class diagram illustrates the relationship between these classes and interfaces and those required by the EJB specification. The business methods interface is circled. Note that the bean implementation class, `BoxOfficeEJB`, extends a generic superclass, `com.interface21.ejb.support.AbstractionStatelessSessionBean`, that helps to meet the requirements of the EJB specification. We'll discuss this and other EJB support classes when we look at application infrastructure in the next chapter:

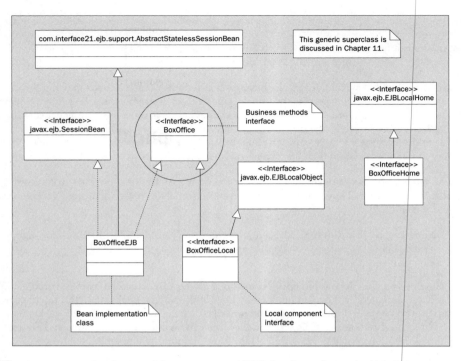

The following is a complete listing of the `BoxOffice` EJB's local interface, which defines no new methods:

```
public interface BoxOfficeLocal extends javax.ejb.EJBObject,
      com.wrox.expertj2ee.ticket.boxoffice.BoxOffice {
}
```

The following shows how the bean's implementation class implements the business interface as well as the `javax.ejb.SessionBean` interface required by the EJB specification:

```
public class BoxOfficeEJB extends AbstractStatelessSessionBean
      implements SessionBean, BoxOffice {
  // Implementation omitted
}
```

Although the EJB Business Methods Interface is widely advocated, not everyone agrees on naming conventions. Some sources advocating using a `BusinessMethods` suffix for the name of the business methods interface. Whatever naming convention you decide to adopt, use it consistently in all your EJB implementations to avoid confusion.

The Business Methods Interface pattern is a simple technique that can save a lot of time. However, it can't detect problems in synchronization between an EJB's home interface and implementation class. For example, home interface `create()` methods must correspond to `ejbCreate()` methods. Problems synchronizing between home interface and bean implementation class may produce mysterious "abstract method errors" in some servers. The generic superclasses discussed in the next chapter help to avoid such errors, where stateless session beans and message-driven beans are concerned.

> Use the Business Methods Interface pattern to help avoid problems with keeping
> component interface and business methods in sync. Errors will be picked up at compile
> time, rather than when the beans are deployed to an EJB container. Although it may be
> possible to synchronize these classes with an IDE, the business methods interface uses the
> compiler, and is thus guaranteed to work whatever the development environment.

Session Beans in the Sample Application

The sample application requires us to hold server-side state on behalf of users executing some use cases. Ticket reservations must be held during the booking process; user profiles may be held during the booking process. However, pages outside the booking process do not require session state to be maintained.

We could hold this session state in SFSBs. However, there are good reasons to prefer web container state management:

❑   Using SFSBs would tie us to using EJB. There's no other reason to predicate our architecture on using EJB; we've merely chosen to use EJB where it simplifies transaction management.

❑   This is a web application. There's no need to hold session state on behalf of remote RMI clients.

❑   Web container state management is likely to outperform SFSB state management. We won't need to invoke EJBs to access user state, and there may be a reduced overhead of state replication in a cluster.

❑   Holding state in the web container is simpler. We'll probably need to use `HttpSession` objects regardless of whether we use SFSBs. The added complexity of JNDI lookups for SFSBs would produce no benefit.

Thus we'll hold user state for the ticketing application in the web container, using `HttpSession` objects, and use SLSBs. As the amount of session state involved is modest (once we ensure that reference data is shared between users) and we are invoking our single EJB through a local interface, there is no problem passing user state to the EJB container with each method invocation.

We'll be using CMT, as the major reason we have chosen to use an EJB to implement the booking process is to simplify transaction management.

Summary

This chapter has covered some of the major issues of session-bean design and implementation. We have seen that:

❑   Stateless session beans are usually the best way to implement business logic when we choose to use EJBs.

❑   Stateful session beans should only be used when there is no alternative to a stateful model in the EJB tier, as they consume more resources in the EJB container than SLSBs and do not provide truly robust state management. (In particular, application servers are likely to find it more difficult to replicate changes to SFSBs in a cluster than to replicate changes to `HttpSession` state.) We've looked at some techniques that may allow us to use stateless session beans in place of stateful session beans.

- ❑ The **Session Façade** design pattern can be used to enhance performance, simplify implementation, and maximize design flexibility, especially in distributed applications. It is usually the best way for remote clients to access the EJB tier.

- ❑ The **EJB Command** design pattern is an alternative to the Session Façade pattern, based on moving *code* from client to server and executing it on the server.

We've built on our knowledge of EJB container services by considering:

- ❑ The EJB container's behavior when an EJB throws an exception. While **application exceptions** (checked exceptions other than `java.rmi.RemoteException`) are thrown to the EJB client as in ordinary Java method invocation, without any intervention by the EJB container, **system exceptions** (`java.rmi.RemoteException` and unchecked exceptions) cause the EJB container to mark the current transaction for rollback and discard the offending EJB instance. This behavior can be used to simplify error handling, meaning that we don't need to catch fatal runtime exceptions, but can simply leave the EJB container to deal with them. It also means that if we want the current transaction rolled back in the event of an application exception, we must use the `setRollbackOnly()` method in application code, as the EJB container will take no action.

- ❑ The meaning of the six **transaction attributes** for EJB CMT and how they affect the behavior of session bean methods.

We've looked at the "Business Methods Interface" pattern, a simple coding technique that can prevent errors by ensuring that an EJB's component interface and implementation class are always in sync. This involves making both component interface and bean implementation class implement a "business methods interface", enabling the compiler to check that method signatures match.

We've discussed the following good session bean implementation practices:

- ❑ Use session beans to delimit transactions.

- ❑ In distributed applications, execute a complete use case in each method on a remote interface if possible.

- ❑ When implementing session beans, cache the results of JNDI lookups, such as EJB home references and `DataSource` objects. When implementing SLSBs, cache resources and data on behalf of *all* clients.

The following recommendations apply to stateful session beans:

- ❑ If deploying applications using SFSBs in a clustered environment, read your application server documentation regarding stateful session bean behavior in a cluster closely. Different servers have different behavior that can affect the performance and even the viability of using SFSBs. (For example, is session state replicated after completed transactions, or after each method call? Is there any way of ensuring fine-grained replication, rather than replication of the whole of an SFSB's state every time?)

- ❑ Keep transactions short, as SFSB conversational state is likely to be most vulnerable during transactions (although this will depend on your EJB container).

- ❑ Don't use the `javax.ejb.SessionSynchronization` interface. Try to manage transactions in individual methods, relying on EJB CMT.

❑ Remember to leave instance data in a legal state after the `ejbPassivate()` method and in a usable state after the `ejbActivate()` method.

❑ Synchronize client code if necessary to protect SFSBs against illegal concurrent calls.

In the next chapter we'll move on to overall application infrastructure, including some generic EJB superclasses that can simplify development and reduce the likelihood of errors when implementing session beans and message-driven beans.

11

Infrastructure and Application Implementation

In this chapter, we'll look at implementing business logic in J2EE applications. However, first we'll consider infrastructure that enables us to limit application code *to* implementing business logic. This is a key goal of the J2EE specifications, but unfortunately the complexity of the J2EE APIs means that it isn't delivered out of the box.

In this chapter, we'll look at how additional infrastructure can be used to solve common problems and simplify the use of J2EE. We'll consider:

❑   The goals that a strong application infrastructure should deliver, and why it's important that applications should use one.

❑   The motivation behind and implementation of some generic packages included with the sample application, including:

❑   Packages that enable a consistent approach to application configuration via JavaBeans and facilitate interface-based design, as discussed in Chapter 4.

❑   Packages that simplify the use of complex J2EE APIs such as EJB and JMS.

Finally, we'll look at implementation of some of the key functionality of the sample application using the generic infrastructure described in this chapter, illustrating how it simplifies application code, benefiting both productivity and maintainability.

Infrastructure

It's essential for an application to have a strong infrastructure that enables application code to concentrate on addressing business problems without the distraction of handling "plumbing". This is why we choose to use J2EE; why we may choose to use EJB if we would otherwise need to write unduly complex code; and why adequate infrastructure classes are almost as important as an application server.

We usually need to build some infrastructure ourselves, but it's generally best to use existing infrastructure where it's an option.

Unfortunately there are no standards relating to infrastructure that simplifies the use of J2EE. Thus the choice will vary between projects. Possible sources of infrastructure include:

❑ Existing in-house infrastructure. Most large organizations will have developed many common packages, though their quality varies highly. Often there is a lack of a coherent strategy and potential for reuse across projects is lost. This is an expensive lost opportunity; in this chapter we'll see a number of areas in which code can be reused and consistent practices adopted across projects, with significant benefits.

❑ MVC web application frameworks. Some products, such as Struts, can provide a framework for web applications, rather than just an MVC implementation. However, MVC web frameworks are, naturally enough, intended only for use in web applications; thus predicating an application's overall infrastructure on one may make testing difficult and reduce the potential for reuse.

❑ Open source application frameworks. No product in this space is anywhere near as well-known or widely adopted as leading MVC web application frameworks, and many products are highly complex. Consequently, I can't recommend one here.

❑ Commercial products, such as a framework supplied with an application server or a framework promising to simplify J2EE development. Again, no product in this space has achieved wide usage. Offerings from application server vendors typically lock users into the application server in question, ruling out portability between application servers.

❑ The infrastructure code described in this chapter, which addresses many common problems. This infrastructure is relatively simple, and makes extensive use of JavaBeans to minimize the dependence of application code on it, avoiding lock-in as far as possible.

In this chapter we'll look at the issue of infrastructure primarily through examining the support packages used in the sample application. This code – which is based on my experience of successful approaches in several real projects – illustrates some of the major issues and provides a simple solution to problems that I haven't seen well-addressed elsewhere. The source code of all the classes discussed and the supporting classes is included in the download with this book, so it can be used as a basis for your applications.

> **Emphasis on supporting infrastructure is a major difference between my approach in this book and much J2EE literature. Most J2EE books concentrate on J2EE APIs, rather than the reality of using them. Hence they tend to show quick and dirty approaches (for example, compromising correct error handling), or neglect productivity and maintainability considerations.**
>
> **In this book, I'm trying to demonstrate the use of J2EE to meet business requirements, rather than as an end in itself. As a bonus, this means that the download accompanying this book includes much code that you can either use directly in your applications or use as the basis for your own code.**

The approach discussed in this chapter is just one of many approaches for structuring J2EE applications. However, I've found the principles behind it to deliver high productivity and quality solutions in several real projects. The problems this infrastructure addresses and serves to illustrate are relevant to all J2EE applications.

Goals of a Strong Infrastructure

Using a strong standard infrastructure can deliver better applications, faster. A strong infrastructure makes this possible by achieving the following goals:

❏ Allowing application code to concentrate on implementing business logic and other application functionality with a minimum of distraction. This reduces time to market by reducing development effort, and reduces costs throughout the project lifecycle by making application code more maintainable (because it is simpler and focused on the problem domain). This is the ultimate goal, which many of the following goals help us to achieve.

❏ Separating configuration from Java code.

❏ Facilitating the use of OO design by eliminating the need for common compromises.

❏ Eliminating code duplication, by solving each problem only once. Once we have a good solution for a problem such as a complex API we should *always* use that solution, in whatever components or classes that encounter the problem

❏ Concealing the complexity of J2EE APIs. We've already seen this with JDBC; other APIs that are candidates for a higher level of abstraction include JNDI and EJB access.

❏ Ensuring correct error handling. We saw the importance of this when working with JDBC in Chapter 9.

❏ Facilitating internationalization if required.

❏ Enhancing productivity without compromising architectural principles. Without adequate infrastructure it is tempting to cut corners by adopting quick, hacky solutions that will cause ongoing problems. Appropriate infrastructure should encourage and facilitate the application of sound design principles.

❏ Achieving consistency between applications within an organization. If all applications use the same infrastructure as well as the same application server and underlying technologies, productivity will be maximized, teamwork more effective, and risk reduced.

❏ Ensuring that applications are easy to test. Where possible, a framework should allow application code to be tested without deployment on an application server.

Essentially we're going to use standard infrastructure to help achieve the goals that we identified in Chapter 4.

It's important that infrastructure isn't web-centric, even if we're developing a web application. This makes applications unnecessarily hard to test and dependent on one particular user interface. Thus infrastructure should not be limited to a web framework such as Struts (although such web frameworks are valuable, if used correctly). It's not enough to get business logic out of presentation layer artifacts such as JSP pages: business logic shouldn't be in web-specific classes at all. For examples, a Struts `Action` class is tied to the Servlet API. This makes Struts actions a poor place for business logic, which doesn't depend on the Servlet API. Thus while it *is* important to use a web application framework, the web-tier should remain a thin layer over a distinct business logic layer.

Infrastructure will often take the form of frameworks, rather than class libraries. Often inversion of control is essential to conceal complexity from application code. We saw the benefits of this approach with JDBC in Chapter 9.

A framework should be extensible. Although a well-designed framework will meet most requirements out of the box, it will fail unless it can be extended to meet unforeseen requirements. Use of interfaces within the framework will help to achieve this goal.

A framework should be easy to use. Unduly complex frameworks will be ignored by developers, and create problems of their own. Irrelevant, or seldom-used, capabilities are a key danger. The Pareto Principle is particularly relevant to framework design. Often it's best to settle for a simple solution to most problems than a comprehensive, but complex solution that makes many tasks harder than they should be (J2EE itself arguably falls into the latter category).

Let's consider the core infrastructure used in the sample application. Like most successful infrastructures, the infrastructure described here is layered. When using it we can choose from different levels of abstraction, each building on lower-level components.

Using a Framework to Configure Application Components

Let's begin by addressing the goals of externalizing configuration and facilitating the use of OO design.

The Problem

It's vital to adopt consistent practices in application configuration. While externalizing configuration (getting it out of Java code) is essential to parameterize applications, it's difficult to achieve without supporting infrastructure.

Without such infrastructure, configuration management is usually haphazard. J2EE applications often hold configuration in a variety of formats, such as properties files, XML documents (an increasingly popular choice), EJB JAR and WAR development descriptors, and database tables. In large applications there is often little consistency in how configuration is managed. For example, property naming conventions (if there are any) may differ between developers and for different classes.

More seriously, application classes are bloated by configuration management code irrelevant to their business responsibilities. Many application objects may read properties files or parse XML documents. Even if they use helper classes to simplify use of the underlying API, their business purpose is still obscured and they remain tied to the configuration format initially envisaged.

Equally harmfully, without a central infrastructure for configuration management, application code is likely to use a variety of approaches to locating application objects. The Singleton design pattern is often overused, resulting in problems we'll discuss below. Alternatively, some application objects may be bound to JNDI or attached to the global `ServletContext` (in web applications), both of which approaches may complicate testing outside a JNDI server. Each application object is usually configured independently.

> **Generic, reusable infrastructures should be used to centralize configuration management and "wire up" applications in a consistent way. In this section we'll look at how the infrastructure used by the sample application uses JavaBean-based configuration, ensuring consistency throughout applications.**

In this section we'll look at an application framework that centralizes configuration management and solves the problems we've just discussed.

Using JavaBeans

We discussed the benefits of JavaBeans in Chapter 4. For example, bean-based manipulation is excellent for applying configuration data held outside Java code, and performing "data binding", such as from HTTP requests onto Java object state.

> **If we make all application components JavaBeans, we maximize our ability to separate configuration data from application code. We also ensure that application components can be configured in a consistent way, wherever configuration data is held. Even if we don't know an application's class at run time (as opposed to the interfaces it implements), we know how to configure it if it is a JavaBean.**

An object doesn't need to implement any special interfaces or extend a special superclass to be a simple JavaBean, exposing bean **properties** but not supporting bean **events**. All that is required is a no-argument constructor and property methods following a simple naming convention. Unlike EJBs, JavaBeans impose no run-time overhead. However, *manipulating* beans is more complex, and requires the use of reflection to instantiate objects and invoke methods by name. The core JavaBeans API does not provide the ability to perform some useful operations on beans, such as:

❑ Setting multiple properties in a single operation, throwing a single combined exception if one or more property setters fail.

❑ Getting or setting **nested** properties – properties of properties, such as `getSpouse().getAge()`. Java 1.4 introduces support for this, through the new `java.beans.Statement` and `java.beans.Expression` classes.

❑ Supporting bean event propagation without complicating the implementation of JavaBeans. With only the standard beans API, bean classes will need to do their own plumbing by calling API classes such as `java.beans.PropertyChangeSupport`.

❑ Providing a standard method to perform initialization on a bean after all bean properties have been set.

Since invoking methods by name and instantiating beans means handling exceptions from the core reflection package, error handling can also become cumbersome unless we use a higher level of abstraction.

> **The lowest layer of the framework used in the sample application is the com.interface21.beans package. This provides the ability to manipulate beans easily and adds the enhanced functionality described above, while respecting and avoiding duplicating the standard JavaBeans infrastructure.**

The center of this package is the `BeanWrapper` interface and the default implementation, `BeanWrapperImpl`. A `BeanWrapper` object can be created given any JavaBean, and provides the ability to manipulate properties individually or in bulk and add listeners that will be notified when the bean is manipulated using the `BeanWrapper`. The most important methods in the `BeanWrapper` interface include:

```
Object getPropertyValue(String propertyName) throws BeansException;
```

This returns a property value, given a string name following JavaBeans conventions. The string "age" would return a property exposed via a `getAge()` accessor method. However, all `BeanWrapper` methods also support nested properties to arbitrary depth: the string "spouse.age" would try to get the age property on the object value of the `spouse` property. This would even work if the declared type of the spouse property didn't expose an `age` property, but the current value did.

The `setPropertyValue()` method is a parallel setter method with the following signature:

```
void setPropertyValue(String propertyName, Object value)
     throws PropertyVetoException, BeansException;
```

This method throws the `java.beans.PropertyVetoException` to allow the use of event listeners to "veto" property changes, as described in the JavaBeans specification. The new value parameter can be converted from a string if necessary using the standard beans API `PropertyEditor` support (discussed below). Another setter method has the following signature:

```
void setPropertyValue(PropertyValue pv)
     throws PropertyVetoException, BeansException;
```

This method is similar to the previous `setPropertyValue()` method, but takes a simple object holding the property name and value. This is necessary to allow combined property updates, performed by the following method:

```
void setPropertyValues(PropertyValues pvs) throws BeansException;
```

This sets a number of properties in a single bulk update. The `PropertyValues` parameter contains multiple `PropertyValue` objects. Property setting continues on exceptions encountered attempting to set individual properties. Any exceptions are saved in a single exception, `PropertyVetoExceptionsException`, which is thrown once the entire operation is complete. Properties set successfully remain updated. Bulk property updates are useful in many situations, such as when populating JavaBeans from HTTP request parameters.

The `BeanWrapper` interface includes convenience methods to find whether properties exist, such as:

```
boolean isReadableProperty(String propertyName);
```

It is possible to obtain the object wrapped by a `BeanWrapper` using the following method:

```
Object getWrappedInstance();
```

This enables us to move to ordinary Java invocation once bean manipulation is complete – for example, after initialization.

It is possible to add and remove event listeners that implement standard JavaBeans interfaces using methods such as the following:

```
void addPropertyChangeListener(PropertyChangeListener l);
void addVetoableChangeListener(VetoableChangeListener l);
```

This means that, if a `BeanWrapper` is used to manipulate its bean properties, property change events will be fired even if a JavaBean being manipulated does not implement property change support.

I took the important design decision to make the root of the beans package exception hierarchy, `com.interface21.beans.BeansException`, unchecked. As we usually use beans manipulation in initialization code, this is appropriate; failure to manipulate a named property will usually be fatal. However, it is still possible for application code to catch `BeanExceptions` if we choose. Several subclasses of `BeanException` are defined in the `com.interface21.beans` package, including:

❑   `TypeMismatchException`, thrown when it is impossible to convert a property value to the required type

❑   `NotWritablePropertyException`, thrown when an attempt is made to set a property that isn't writable

❑   `MethodInvocationException`, thrown when a property getter or setter method throws an exception

Let's look at a simple example of using the `BeanWrapper` interface. `TestBean` is a concrete class that implements the interface `ITestBean`, which contains three properties: age (`int`), name (`String`), and spouse (`Person`), defined using normal JavaBeans naming conventions as follows:

```
public interface ITestBean {
    int getAge();
    void setAge(int age);
    String getName();
    void setName(String name);
    ITestBean getSpouse();
    void setSpouse(ITestBean spouse);
}
```

By creating a new `BeanWrapper` object we can easily set and get property values:

```
TestBean rod = new TestBean();
BeanWrapper bw = new BeanWrapperImpl(rod);
bw.setPropertyValue("age", new Integer(32));
bw.setPropertyValue("name", "rod");
bw.setPropertyValue("spouse", new TestBean ());
bw.setPropertyValue("spouse.name", "kerry");
bw.setPropertyValue("spouse.spouse", rod);

Integer age = (Integer) bw.getPropertyValue("age");
String name = (String) bw.getPropertyValue("name");
String spousesName = (String) bw.getPropertyValue("spouse.name");
```

Information obtained via reflection is cached for efficiency, so using a BeanWrapper imposes relatively little overhead.

Sometimes values to be set must be provided as strings (for example, the values of HTTP request parameters). The BeanWrapperImpl class can automatically convert a string representation to any primitive type. However, sometimes a string representation must be used to create a custom object. The com.interface21.beans package supports the standard JavaBeans API approach to this problem. We can register a java.beans.PropertyEditor implementation for the class in question, implementing the setAsText() method, and the BeanWrapper class and all classes that use it will automatically gain the ability to create the class from strings.

The JavaBeans API provides the java.beans.PropertyEditorSupport convenience class, which we can extend to implement property editors very easily. Consider the following class that can create TestBean objects from strings of the form <name>_<age>:

```
class TestBeanEditor extends PropertyEditorSupport {
  public void setAsText(String text) {
    TestBean tb = new TestBean();
    StringTokenizer st = new StringTokenizer(text, "_");
    tb.setName(st.nextToken());
    tb.setAge(Integer.parseInt(st.nextToken()));
    setValue(tb);
  }
}
```

We ignore the GUI-oriented methods of the java.beans.PropertyEditor interface, inheriting the default implementations provided by the PropertyEditorSupport class. The setValue() method, highlighted in the above listing, sets the object value that will be returned by the PropertyEditor for the given input string.

We can register this PropertyEditor using standard JavaBeans machinery as follows:

```
PropertyEditorManager.registerEditor(ITestBean.class, TestBeanEditor.class);
```

Now we can set properties of type ITestBean as follows:

```
TestBean rod = new TestBean();
BeanWrapper bw = new BeanWrapperImpl(rod);
bw.setPropertyValue("spouse", "Kerry_34");
```

The BeanWrapperImpl class registers a number of property editors (defined in the com.interface21.beans.propertyeditors package) by default. These include support for java.util.Property objects (specified in any format supported by the java.util.Property class) and string arrays (specifying in CSV format).

Using a "Bean Factory"

The com.interface21.beans package provides powerful functionality, but it's too low-level for direct use in most cases. It's essentially a building block, on which we can base a higher level of abstraction that conceals the low-level details.

However easy we make bean-based "late binding", we usually want to use ordinary Java invocation in application code. It's simpler, faster (although the performance overhead of reflection is often exaggerated) and, unless we want to do something unusual, good design will normally mean that we know which interfaces (but *not* which concrete classes) we are working with.

At application startup, however, it's a different matter. The complexity can be managed by framework code; performance overhead is negligible, as initialization operations will account for a tiny proportion of total application activity; and, most importantly, there are very good reasons to use late binding in this situation.

> The **com.interface21.beans.factory** package defines a way of obtaining beans by name from a central configuration repository using a "bean factory". The goal of a bean factory is to remove any need for individual Java objects to read configuration properties or instantiate objects. Instead, configuration is read by a central component, the bean factory, and the bean properties exposed by each application object are set to reflect configuration data. The factory then makes available instances of beans, each with a unique name. Sophisticated object graphs can be created within the bean factory, as managed beans may reference other beans within the same factory.

Our implementation of a bean factory uses the com.interface21.beans package, concealing its low-level concepts from application code.

To illustrate the power of this approach, consider the business objects in our sample application. Most of our business objects need access to two fundamental business objects: the Calendar object, which returns information about genres, shows, and performances, and the BoxOffice object, which implements the booking process. A single instance of each of the Calendar and BoxOffice should be shared across the whole application.

An obvious approach would be to make the Calendar and BoxOffice singletons, and for business objects requiring them to obtain references using their getInstance() methods. Such an approach is used in many applications, but it has the following disadvantages:

❑ Using singletons makes it hard to work with interfaces. In the example, we would have hard-coded dependence on concrete classes Calendar and BoxOffice throughout our application. It would be impossible to switch to a different implementation.

❑ Each singleton will need to look up its own configuration data – perhaps using properties, JNDI, or JDBC. It's likely that configuration management will be inconsistent, and singleton code will be cluttered with configuration management code that isn't relevant to its business purpose.

❑ The inherent problems with the Singleton design pattern, such as inflexibility. What if we ever want more than one `BoxOffice` object?

These problems could be slightly relieved by separating object creation (in a traditional factory) from object implementation, but the major objections would remain.

The "bean factory" described here differs from a traditional factory in that it is generic. It can create objects of any type, based on configuration information supplied at run time. In my experience, the loss of type safety – an issue only on application initialization, and which is largely concealed within infrastructure code – is far more than made up by the enormous gain in flexibility.

Using the bean factory approach described below, `Calendar` and `BoxOffice` would be interfaces, not concrete classes. Implementations of each of these interfaces would expose JavaBean properties allowing a bean factory to configure them. Bean properties might be primitives, or might be objects, resolved by references to other beans in the bean factory. The work of configuration would be moved entirely out of application code into infrastructure.

Each business object requiring these objects would also be a JavaBean, and would expose `calendar` and `boxOffice` properties enabling the bean factory to "wire up" the application on initialization. Application classes would contain no irrelevant configuration management code, configuration management would be consistent, and application code would be wholly written to interfaces, rather than concrete classes. This would ensure that the application was totally "pluggable": the implementation of any interface could be switched in configuration without changing a line of Java code.

> If the `Calendar` and `BoxOffice` objects were EJBs, client code could look them up via JNDI, which would also avoid dependence on a concrete class. However, an EJB container is a very heavyweight "bean factory" if it delivers no other value, and client code would be considerably complicated by EJB access code.

There's widespread awareness of the serious disadvantages of singletons. However, no superior alternative seems to be in widespread use. The core Java `java.beans.beancontext` package uses a similar approach to that discussed here, although it's complex, GUI-oriented, and appears to be rarely used. The Apache Avalon server framework is also somewhat similar, but more complex, and with a greater requirement on application code to implement framework interfaces (see http://jakarta.apache.org/avalon/index.html). JMX offers the potential for a widely adopted, standards-based solution, but is far more heavyweight and complex.

Perhaps the package that comes closest to the goals we've set is the Digester, formerly part of Struts and now a distinct open source project in Apache Commons. This uses a rule-based approach for configuring Java objects (usually, but not necessarily, JavaBeans) from an XML representation, which also relies on the use of reflection. The Digester is more flexible for XML-based mapping than the XML bean factory implementation described in this chapter, but is tied to XML, and cannot support mapping definitions held in other representations. The Digester is also arguably less intuitive, and typically requires the application developer to write more code (see http://jakarta.apache.org/commons/digester.html for more information).

The `com.interface21.beans.factory.BeanFactory` interface contains only two methods:

```
public interface BeanFactory {

  Object getBean(String name) throws BeansException;

  Object getBean(String name, Class requiredType) throws BeansException;
}
```

The first method enables beans to be obtained by name as follows:

```
MyInterface mi = (MyInterface) getBean("myInterface");
```

The second method is a convenience method that throws an exception if the object found is not of the required type. The following line of code is the same as the above, with this added check:

```
MyInterface mi = (MyInterface) getBean("myInterface", MyInterface.class);
```

Depending on the implementation, the `getBean()` method may return a singleton (a shared instance returned by all `getBean()` calls with the same `name` argument in the current bean factory) or a prototype (an independent instance based on configuration managed by the bean factory). The shared instance approach is the more valuable, and is used most often. By maintaining a single bean factory, an application can avoid the need for individual application classes to be implemented as singletons: the "singleton" functionality is enforced by the bean factory. Should requirements change, we can choose how many bean factories we want to use in our application.

Once we've separated configuration management (handled by a framework bean factory implementation) from application code (in application-specific JavaBeans), we can easily hold configuration in any format we choose.

The bean definition format used most in the sample application is an XML document as used by the `com.interface21.beans.factory.xml.XmlBeanFactory` implementation of the `BeanFactory` interface.

Consider the same simple bean class (`TestBean`) we discussed above. Using the XML format, we can achieve the same object graph without any Java coding, as follows. The XML format is largely self-describing, with `name` attributes identifying property names and element values containing string representations of property values. Note the references to other beans within the bean factory, which I've highlighted:

```
<bean name="rod"
  singleton="true"
  class="com.interface21.beans.TestBean">
  <property name="name">Rod</property>
  <property name="age">31</property>
  <property name="spouse" beanRef="true">kerry</property>
</bean>

<bean name="kerry" class="com.interface21.beans.TestBean">
  <property name="name">Kerry</property>
  <property name="age">34</property>
  <property name="spouse" beanRef="true">rod</property>
</bean>
```

With this definition we could obtain a reference to the shared instance of the first bean as follows:

```
TestBean rod = (TestBean) beanFactory.getBean("rod");
```

Another implementation of the `BeanFactory` interface,
`com.interface21.beans.factory.support.ListableBeanFactoryImpl`, can read definitions
from properties files. This is a simpler way of defining beans than XML documents, which can tie in
with the core Java internationalization support provided by the `java.util.ResourceBundle` class.
The above beans could be defined as follows using the properties syntax, which specifies the class of
each bean and again sets property values as strings:

```
rod.class=com.interface21.beans.TestBean
rod.name=Rod
rod.age=32
rod.spouse(ref)=kerry

kerry.class=com.interface21.beans.TestBean
kerry.name=Kerry
kerry.age=35
kerry.spouse(ref)=rod
```

Note the special `(ref)` suffix used to indicate which properties are references to other beans defined in
the same bean factory.

Another framework implementation used in the sample application,
`com.interface21.jndi.JndiBeanFactory`, takes bean definitions from EJB environment
variables, defined in `ejb-jar.xml`. This is a more verbose format (the way in which environment
variables must be defined), so I'll show only the start of the above definitions using this syntax:

```
<env-entry>
  <env-entry-name>beans.rod.class</env-entry-name>
  <env-entry-type>java.lang.String</env-entry-type>
  <env-entry-value>com.interface21.beans.TestBean</env-entry-value>
</env-entry>
<env-entry>
  <env-entry-name>beans.rod.name</env-entry-name>
  <env-entry-type>java.lang.String</env-entry-type>
  <env-entry-value>Rod</env-entry-value>
</env-entry>
 ...
```

The `com.interface21.jndi.JndiBeanFactory` implementation enables EJBs to use the same
configuration management as other Java classes, and avoids the need to write verbose JNDI lookup
code to retrieve environment variables in application EJBs.

There is no limit to potential implementations of the `BeanFactory` interface: for example, they could read
data from a database, or deserialize persistent objects or create new objects without using reflection at all.

A useful subinterface of `BeanFactory`, `ListableBeanFactory`, adds the ability to query all
definitions (while a `BeanFactory` implementation might load bean definitions only on request, a
`ListableBeanFactory` must know about *all* possible bean definitions). Our `XmlBeanFactory` is
actually a `ListableBeanFactory`, as it parses the XML input as a DOM document. The
`ListableBeanFactory` interface is defined as follows:

```
public interface ListableBeanFactory extends BeanFactory {

    String[] getBeanDefinitionNames();
    int getBeanDefinitionCount();
    String[] getBeanDefinitionNames(Class type);

}
```

The ability to find all bean definitions of a given class or interface can be very useful during initialization: for example, it allows the web application framework described in the next chapter to obtain references to all classes that can handle HTTP requests.

Often a bean needs to know when all its properties have been set, so that it can validate its state and/or perform initialization. Our bean factory defines an approach for this. If a bean created by a bean factory implements the com.interface21.beans.factory.InitializingBean interface, it will receive a callback after all properties have been set. The InitializingBean interface includes a single method:

```
public interface InitializingBean {

    void afterPropertiesSet() throws Exception;

}
```

A typical implementation of this method might check that one or more properties have been set to valid values, before performing initialization. The following example checks that a jndiName property has been set before trying to perform a JNDI lookup:

```
public final void afterPropertiesSet() throws Exception {
    if (this.jndiName == null || this.jndiName.equals(""))
        throw new Exception("Property 'jndiName' must be set on " +
                            getClass().getName());
    Object o = lookup(jndiName);
    initialize(o);
}
```

As all application objects will be created by a bean factory, we can use this in any application class that does not have its own lifecycle management solution.

Sometimes we may want to create a bean definition that performs custom processing before returning a bean instance. For example, we might need a bean definition that registers the returned bean as a JMS listener; creates an object of a specified class and returns a dynamic proxy wrapping it; or returns a bean resulting from a method invocation on another object. The bean factory concept supports "custom bean definitions", in which a custom bean definition class can perform any action before returning a bean.

A custom bean definition works as follows:

❑   The bean factory loads the custom definition class, which must be specified. The custom definition class must be a JavaBean.

❑   The bean factory sets properties on the custom definition class, which must be distinguished with a special syntax.

405

❑ The configured custom bean definition class returns a BeanWrapper wrapping the returned bean. Before returning a BeanWrapper, the custom definition class can perform any processing it likes.

❑ The bean factory sets properties on the returned BeanWrapper as if it were a normal bean definition.

The following custom bean definition illustrates this:

```
<bean name="referenceDataListener"
      definitionClass="com.interface21.jms.JmsListenerBeanDefinition"
>
   <customDefinition property="listenerBean">
    com.wrox.expertj2ee.ticket.referencedata.support.DataUpdateJmsListener
   </customDefinition>

   <customDefinition property="topicConnectionFactoryName">
      jms/TopicFactory
   </customDefinition>

   <customDefinition property="topicName">
      jms/topic/referencedata
   </customDefinition>

   <property name="cachingCalendar" beanRef="true">calendar</property>
</bean>
```

The definitionClass attribute of the <bean> element indicates that this is a custom bean definition, and supplies the custom definition class.

The <customDefinition> elements set properties on the custom definition. The meaning of properties will vary with custom definition class. In this example, the listenerBean property specifies the class of the actual returned bean. In the above list, the custom definition will create an instance of DataUpdateJmsListener and register it as a JMS listener.

The <property> element sets the cachingCalendar property of the actual returned bean. This mechanism makes the bean factory interface indefinitely extensible. It's particularly valuable for concealing the complexity of J2EE API usage.

The Application Context

The bean factory concept solves many problems, such those resulting from overuse of the Singleton design pattern. However, we can move to a higher level of abstraction to help to pull applications together.

Application Context Goals

Building on the bean factory, an **application context** provides a namespace for the JavaBeans that compose an application or subsystem, and the ability to share working objects at run time. The com.interface21.context.ApplicationContext interface extends the ListableBeanFactory interface, adding the ability to:

❑ Publish events using the Observer design pattern. As we discussed in Chapter 4, the Observer design pattern provides the ability to decouple application components and achieve clean separation of concerns.

❑ Participate in a hierarchy of application contexts. Application contexts can have parent contexts, allowing developers to choose the amount of configuration shared between subsystems.

❑ Share working objects between application components at run time.

❑ Look up messages by string name, allowing support for internationalization.

❑ Facilitate testing. With an application context, as well as a bean factory, it's often possible to provide a test implementation that enables application code to be tested outside an application server.

❑ Provide consistent configuration management in different types of applications. Application contexts behave the same way in different kinds of applications, such as Swing GUI applications or web applications, and inside and outside a J2EE application server.

The most important added methods in the `ApplicationContext` interface are:

```
ApplicationContext getParent();
void publishEvent(ApplicationEvent e);
void shareObject(String key, Object o);
```

An application context is a directory of cooperating beans that offers some additional services. The sample application uses the `com.interface21.web.context.support.XmlWebApplicationContext` `ApplicationContext` implementation, which is associated with a `javax.servlet.ServletContext` object provided by the web container, and which uses the XML bean definition format we've already seen. However other implementations do not require a web container, and allow testing (or the building of applications) without a web interface.

Each bean in the application context is given access to the application context if it requires. It simply needs to implement the optional `com.interface21.framework.context.ApplicationContextAware` callback interface, enabling it to access other beans, publish events, or look up messages. This interface contains only two methods, making it very simple to implement:

```
public interface ApplicationContextAware {

    void setApplicationContext(ApplicationContext ctx)
      throws ApplicationContextException;

    ApplicationContext getApplicationContext();

}
```

However, this capability shouldn't be used without good reason. One of the strengths of the framework described here is that application code can benefit from it without depending on it. This minimizes lock-in to the framework and retains the option of configuring the application differently.

407

> Although it is possible for beans to register for notification of the application context they operate within by implementing an optional interface, there are no special requirements for beans used within a bean factory of application context.

Each application context has a parent context. If the parent context is `null`, it is the root of the application context hierarchy. If the parent context is non-null, the current context will pass to the parent requests for beans it cannot find, and requests for messages it cannot resolve. This enables us to determine precisely how much application state should be shared between different components.

The Observer support provided by an `ApplicationContext` is limited to the current server; it makes no effort to broadcast messages in a cluster (JMS Pub/Sub messaging should be used for this). However, a lightweight event publication framework limited to the current server is still very useful. Often there's no need for messages to be broadcast more widely. Consider, for example, a message that should result in the sending of an e-mail. Using the Observer design pattern, we are able to add listeners that perform such tasks without complicating the code of business objects that generate such events.

Web Application Context

An application of type `com.interface21.web.context.WebApplicationContext` integrates with the `javax.servlet.ServletContext`.

In a web application, the application context hierarchy works as follows:

- ❑ The `/WEB-INF/applicationContext.xml` file defines the root context of the application. Definitions here are available to all objects managed by the `WebApplicationContext`. The root context is added to the `ServletContext` as an attribute, making it available to all web tier objects, including servlet filters and custom tags, which often fall outside the domain of application configuration management.

- ❑ Each servlet using the framework has its own application context, a child of the root context, defined by a file with a name of the form `/WEB-INF/<servletName>-servlet.xml`. The servlet name is the value of the `<servlet-name>` subelement of the relevant `<servlet>` element in the web application's `web.xml` file. This allows us, for example, to have multiple controller servlets, each with a distinct namespace, but able to access global objects.

Our sample application uses only one servlet, with the name `ticket`, and requires no custom global configuration. Hence all bean definitions are placed in the `/WEB-INF/ticket-servlet.xml` file.

Testing Implications

The infrastructure I've described here is test-friendly: an important consideration.

Although it's possible to integrate an application context with the Servlet API and use a bean factory in an EJB, the core interfaces do not depend on J2EE APIs. Thus it is possible create a test application context enabling tests to be run against application objects without the need for a J2EE server. For example, a JUnit test case could create an `XmlApplicationContext` from the application context definition documents in a web application, and use it to get beans by name and test their behavior.

Summary of Application Configuration Infrastructure

The following UML diagram illustrates the relationship between the framework classes and interfaces we've described:

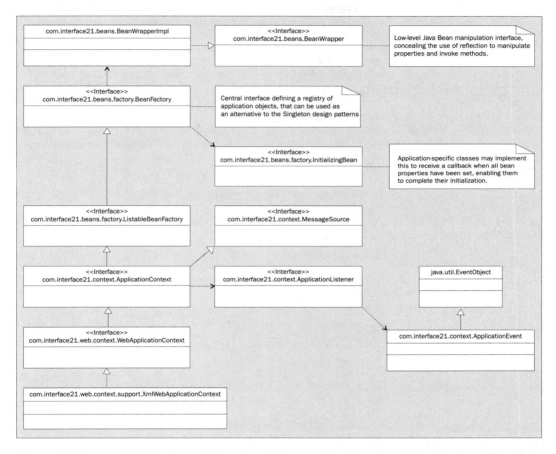

I've omitted some of the implementation classes; the aim is to show the public interfaces. Note that application code doesn't need to work with these classes; it's possible to write an application that is "wired up" by an application context but doesn't depend on any framework classes.

The version of the framework used in the sample application doesn't support dynamic reconfiguration. I concluded that the value of such functionality did not justify the complexity it would introduce. However, it could be added if necessary; this approach is much more flexible than using singletons and other "hard-coded" approaches to configuration.

Later in this chapter we'll look in more detail at how the sample application's code is simplified by use of this framework.

> **The infrastructure described above enables us to code to interfaces and never concrete classes, relying on a central configuration manager (an "application context") to "wire up" the application on initialization. This completely removes configuration data and plumbing code from application objects, which merely need to expose JavaBean properties. This also has the advantage that the application code is not dependent on the supporting infrastructure – a problem that affects many frameworks.**

Managing API Complexity

Now that we have a strong infrastructure for pulling our application together, let's move on to how infrastructure can be used to tackle the problem of J2EE API complexity. In the following section we'll look at how several of the key J2EE APIs can be made much easier to use and their use less error-prone.

Implementing EJBs

So long as we avoid using infrastructure components that violate the EJB specification (for example, by obtaining the current classloader, which rules out dynamic proxy solutions), there's nothing special about EJB code. However, by deriving application EJB implementation classes from generic superclasses we can greatly simplify EJB code.

Abstract Superclasses for EJBs

We should derive our EJBs from common superclasses that achieve the following goals:

❑ Implement lifecycle methods that are irrelevant to bean implementation classes.

❑ Where possible, force EJBs to implement methods from the home interface, which aren't required by the interfaces EJBs must implement.

❑ Provide a consistent logging solution.

❑ Avoid the need for EJBs to use JNDI to look up environment variables, simplifying configuration management.

The following UML class diagram shows the hierarchy of EJB superclasses offered by our generic infrastructure, and how they relate to the interfaces required by the EJB specification. All infrastructure classes are in the `com.interface21.ejb.support` package. We'll look at a complete code listing for each below.

Note that we don't attempt to provide superclasses for entity beans. Entity beans should use CMP, and shouldn't normally contain business logic, placing the onus on the container to provide infrastructure code.

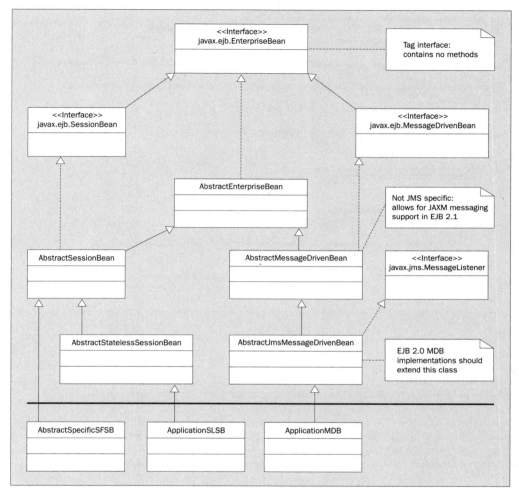

Although there are quite a few classes here, each class is simple and the inheritance hierarchy enables us to support stateless and stateful session beans and message-driven beans without code duplication. The classes above the horizontal line belong to the framework; those below the line show how application EJB implementation classes can extend these framework classes.

The root of the inheritance hierarchy – not used directly as a superclass by any application EJBs – is the AbstractEnterpriseBean class. This implements the javax.ejb.EnterpriseBean tag interface and provides standard logging and configuration management. The following is a complete listing:

```
package com.interface21.ejb.support;

import java14.java.util.logging.Logger;
import javax.ejb.EJBException;
import javax.ejb.EnterpriseBean;
```

```
import com.interface21.beans.BeansException;
import com.interface21.beans.factory.ListableBeanFactory;
import com.interface21.jndi.JndiBeanFactory;

public abstract class AbstractEnterpriseBean implements EnterpriseBean {

  protected final Logger logger = Logger.getLogger(getClass().getName());

  private ListableBeanFactory beanFactory;

  protected final ListableBeanFactory getBeanFactory() {
    if (this.beanFactory == null) {
      loadBeanFactory();
    }
    return this.beanFactory;
  }

  private void loadBeanFactory() {
    logger.info("Loading bean factory");
    try {
      this.beanFactory = new JndiBeanFactory("java:comp/env");
    }
    catch (BeansException ex) {
      throw new EJBException("Cannot create bean factory", ex);
    }
  }
}
```

The protected `logger` instance variable uses the Java 1.4 logging emulation package discussed in Chapter 4, or standard Java 1.4 logging if available. The `getBeanFactory()` method lazily loads a bean factory from environment variables. This is very useful, as it avoids the need to use JNDI to look up environment variables, yet allows parameterization at EJB deployment time. We can instantiate and configure helper objects such as DAOs, and put configuration variables in a simple bean.

We've replaced a low-level API with the same high-level API we use throughout our applications. By facilitating factoring functionality into helper classes (rather than EJB code) we promote good practice and improve testability. We can often test helper classes used in EJBs without an EJB container. For example, the following environment variables define a DAO for the sample application's `BoxOffice` EJB:

```
<env-entry>
  <env-entry-name>beans.dao.class</env-entry-name>
  <env-entry-type>java.lang.String</env-entry-type>
  <env-entry-value>
      com.wrox.expertj2ee.ticket.boxoffice.support.jdbc.
      JBoss30OracleJdbcBoxOfficeDao
  </env-entry-value>
</env-entry>
```

This particular DAO doesn't require any properties, but these can be set using our bean factory conventions. Simply by editing the `ejb-jar.xml` deployment descriptor we can change the class of the DAO helper to any other object that implements the `com.wrox.expertj2ee.ticket.boxoffice.support.BoxOfficeDao` interface, without needing to change EJB code.

The EJB specification requires all session beans to implement the `javax.ejb.SessionBean` interface, shown below. This includes the `setSessionContext()` method and other lifecycle methods:

```
package javax.ejb;

import java.rmi.RemoteException;

public interface SessionBean extends EnterpriseBean {
   void ejbActivate() throws EJBException, RemoteException;
   void ejbPassivate() throws EJBException, RemoteException;
   void ejbRemove() throws EJBException, RemoteException;
void setSessionContext(SessionContext ctx)
        throws EJBException, RemoteException;
}
```

Thus all session beans can be derived from a simple subclass of our `AbstractEnterpriseBean` base class that implements the `setSessionContext()` to store the `SessionContext` in an instance variable, and exposes the saved context via a protected `getSessionContext()` method. We also add an empty implementation of the required `ejbRemove()` lifecycle method, which can be overridden if necessary:

```
package com.interface21.ejb.support;

import javax.ejb.SessionBean;
import javax.ejb.SessionContext;

public abstract class AbstractSessionBean extends AbstractEnterpriseBean
    implements SessionBean {

  private SessionContext  sessionContext;

  protected final SessionContext getSessionContext() {
    return sessionContext;
  }

  public void setSessionContext(SessionContext sessionContext) {
    logger.info("setSessionContext");
    this.sessionContext = sessionContext;
  }

  public void ejbRemove() {
    logger.info("AbstractSessionBean NOP ejbRemove");
  }
}
```

Stateful session beans can subclass this class directly. Stateful session beans often don't need to implement the `ejbRemove()` method, but they always need to ensure correct behavior on the `ejbPassivate()` and `ejbActivate()` lifecycle methods. We discussed how to implement these methods correctly in Chapter 10. Hence we leave these methods unimplemented in `AbstractSessionBean`.

413

By contrast, it is illegal for an EJB container to invoke the `ejbPassivate()` and `ejbActivate()` lifecycle methods on stateless session beans, although stateless session bean implementation classes are (illogically) required to implement them. Thus stateless session beans can be derived from a simple subclass of `AbstractSessionBean`, which implements these two lifecycle methods to throw an exception. There is no reason for any subclass to override this implementation, although we can't make these methods final, as it violates the EJB specification.

Our superclass for stateless session beans also forces subclasses to implement a no-argument `ejbCreate()` method – matching the required `create()` method on the home interface – by defining this as an abstract method. This moves to compile time a check that would otherwise only take place on EJB deployment, as this method isn't required by the EJB API. Here is the complete listing of the `AbstractStatelessSessionBean` class, which should be used as a superclass by SLSB implementation classes:

```
package com.interface21.ejb.support;

import javax.ejb.CreateException;
import javax.ejb.EJBException;

public abstract class AbstractStatelessSessionBean
    extends AbstractSessionBean {

  public abstract void ejbCreate() throws CreateException;

  public void ejbActivate() throws EJBException {
    throw new IllegalStateException(
      "ejbActivate must not be invoked on a stateless session bean");
  }

  public void ejbPassivate() throws EJBException {
    throw new IllegalStateException(
      "ejbPassivate must not be invoked on a stateless session bean");
  }
}
```

This leaves SLSB subclasses to implement an `ejbCreate()` method and their business methods. Remember that application EJBs will usually implement a "business methods" interface, ensuring that they match the methods defined on their component interface. In rare situations, an SLSB may override the `ejbRemove()` method defined in `AbstractSessionBean`. The implementation of the `ejbCreate()` method may use the bean factory available from the `AbstractEnterpriseBean` superclass to create helper objects such as DAOs. These superclasses can be used by EJBs with local or remote interfaces or both.

Let's look at an example, showing how the business methods interface pattern can be combined with our generic superclass to ensure that the compiler, not just deployment tools, enforces that an SLSB implementation class is valid. The following business methods interface defines the remote methods of a hypothetical EJB:

```
import java.rmi.RemoteException;

public interface Calculator {
  int getUncacheableValue() throws RemoteException;
  int getCacheableValue() throws RemoteException;
}
```

Following the business methods pattern described in the last chapter, the EJB's remote interface will contain no methods of its own, but will extend both this interface and `javax.ejb.EJBObject`:

```
import javax.ejb.EJBObject;

public interface CalculatorRemote extends EJBObject, Calculator {
}
```

The bean implementation class will implement the business methods interface and extend `AbstractStatelessSessionBean`. This means that the compiler will force us to implement all the methods required for a valid EJB. I've highlighted the lines in the following listing showing how the `ejbCreate()` method can be implemented to load a helper object from the bean factory exposed by the `AbstractEnterpriseBean` base class:

```
import java.rmi.RemoteException;

import javax.ejb.CreateException;
import com.interface21.ejb.support.AbstractStatelessSessionBean;

public class CalculatorEJB extends AbstractStatelessSessionBean
    implements Calculator {

  private MyHelper myHelper;

  public void ejbCreate() {
    this.myHelper = (MyHelper) getBeanFactory().getBean("myHelper");
  }

  public int getUncacheableValue() {
  return 0;
  }

  public int getCacheableValue() {
    return 0;
  }
}
```

Our superclasses have delivered real value. This EJB implementation class contains no code irrelevant to its business purpose, and is easily able to load helper objects whose configuration is held entirely outside Java code.

Let's finish by considering message-driven beans (MDB). MDB implementation classes must also meet some requirements beyond implementing the `javax.ejb.MessageDrivenBean` interface: they must also implement an `ejbCreate()` method without arguments; and they must implement the `javax.jms.MessageListener` interface to handle JMS messages. We can extend `AbstractEnterpriseBean` to save the `MessageDrivenContext` and force subclasses to implement an `ejbCreate()` method as follows:

```
package com.interface21.ejb.support;

import javax.ejb.MessageDrivenBean;
import javax.ejb.MessageDrivenContext;

public abstract class AbstractMessageDrivenBean extends AbstractEnterpriseBean
    implements MessageDrivenBean {
```

```
    private MessageDrivenContext messageDrivenContext;

    protected final MessageDrivenContext getMessageDrivenContext() {
      return messageDrivenContext;
    }

    public void setMessageDrivenContext(
        MessageDrivenContext messageDrivenContext) {
      logger.fine("setMessageContext");
      this.messageDrivenContext = messageDrivenContext;
    }

    public abstract void ejbCreate();

    public void ejbRemove() {
      logger.info("ejbRemove");
    }
  }
```

Although EJB 2.0 supports only JMS messaging, EJB 2.1 supports JAXM messaging as well, meaning that the `javax.jms.MessageListener` is only one of three alternative messaging interfaces that an EJB 2.1 MDB might implement. Thus, rather than tie the `AbstractMessageDrivenBean` class to use of JMS, we ensure forward compatibility with EJB 2.1 by putting the requirement to implement `javax.jms.MessageListener` in a JMS-specific subclass:

```
package com.interface21.ejb.support;

import javax.jms.MessageListener;

public abstract class AbstractJmsMessageDrivenBean
    extends AbstractMessageDrivenBean implements MessageListener {

  // Empty

}
```

An application MDB that subclasses this class is guaranteed to meet the requirements of an EJB 2.0 JMS MDB. A trivial subclass automatically stubbed by an IDE will look like this:

```
public class SimpleMDB extends AbstractJmsMessageDrivenBean {

  public void ejbCreate() {
  }

  public void onMessage(Message message) {
  }
}
```

As with session beans, the `ejbCreate()` method can access the bean factory provided by the `AbstractEnterpriseBean` superclass.

Of course we don't *need* to use these (or similar) superclasses when implementing EJBs, but as they simplify application code and reduce the likelihood of errors resulting in wasted development-deploy cycles, they provide very good value. There's seldom any problem in the use of concrete inheritance depriving application EJBs of their own inheritance hierarchy. Due to the EJB programming restrictions, making an object an EJB by subclassing it to implement the required lifecycle methods is rarely a good idea. Our solution, however, makes it easy for a new EJB to use existing code, through using existing classes as helper objects instantiated through its bean factory. Custom application EJB superclasses can simply subclass one of the above framework superclasses to add additional application-specific behavior.

Accessing EJBs

It's important to achieve loose coupling between EJBs and code that uses them. There are many disadvantages in EJB client code accessing EJBs directly:

❑ Client code must deal with JNDI lookups in multiple places. Obtaining and using EJB references is cumbersome. We need to do a JNDI lookup for the EJB home interface and invoke a create method on the home interface.

❑ EJB JNDI names will be held in multiple places, making it difficult to modify client code.

❑ Clients are too closely coupled to the EJB tier, making it difficult to change the interfaces it exposes.

❑ It's impossible to introduce a consistent caching strategy for application data returned by the EJB tier or server resources such as naming contexts and EJB home interface references. Especially in distributed applications, caching the result of invoking EJBs may be essential to meet performance requirements.

❑ Client code must deal with low-level checked exceptions from the EJB tier. For both local and remote EJBs there are JNDI `NamingExceptions` and `EJBCreate` exceptions. For remote EJBs every call on home or EJB may throw `java.rmi.RemoteException`. Except for remote exceptions (which we'll consider below) this is a lot of exception handling to achieve very little. In a local application, failure to look up an EJB home or create an stateless session EJB using a `create()` method that has no arguments that could be invalid almost certainly indicates serious application failure. Most likely we'll want to log this and gracefully inform the user that their action cannot be processed at this time due to an internal error.

Most importantly, if we allow code to work with EJB access APIs directly, we tie code unnecessarily to a particular implementation strategy.

> **Abstract inter-tier communication with Java interfaces, not on J2EE technologies such as EJB. Technologies are features of *implementations*.**

Two well-known J2EE patterns – the **Service Locator** and **Business Delegate** patterns – address these problems. In this section, we'll discuss their benefits and how to implement them. As with implementing EJBs, generic infrastructure classes can be used to simplify application code. We can integrate EJB access with our overall application infrastructure by making service locators and business delegates JavaBeans, configured by an application bean factory.

Local versus Remote Access

There's a profound difference between accessing EJBs through local and remote interfaces.

Invoking an EJB through a local interface isn't radically different from invoking an ordinary Java object. The EJB container will intercept each method call, but both caller and EJB are running in the same JVM, meaning that there is no possibility of distributed failures and no serialization issues.

Remote invocation is a completely different problem. We may encounter distributed failures, and we must consider efficiency: "chatty" calling, or exchanging an excessive amount of parameter data, will prove disastrous for performance.

We can choose between two fundamental strategies for remote invocation: we can try to achieve **local-remote transparency**, concealing from callers the issue of remote invocation; or we can use a client-side façade to provide a locally accessible point of contact for the EJB invocation.

I don't advocate local-remote transparency. As the designers of Java RMI didn't either, it's relatively hard to achieve when invoking EJBs. Secondly, it's an invitation to gross inefficiency.

It's much better to provide a local façade through which all communication with the EJB tier passes. This is an excellent application for the Business Delegate pattern, which is discussed below.

The Service Locator and Business Delegate J2EE Patterns

The first step in decoupling calling code from an EJB implementation is to ensure that all EJB references are obtained through a common factory. This avoids the duplication of JNDI lookup code, and enables the caching of the results of JNDI lookups to boost performance (although the overhead varies between servers, obtaining a naming context and looking up a home interface are potentially expensive operations). Such an object is called a **service locator** (*Core J2EE Patterns*).

The disadvantage is that clients will still need to work directly with the EJBs. They must still handle remote exceptions in a distributed application and may need to catch exceptions thrown when creating EJBs. However, a service locator can return references to SLSB EJB instances, rather than merely home interfaces (the service locator can invoke the no argument `create()` method as necessary). This frees clients of the need to handle the checked exceptions that may be thrown by attempting to create an EJB from a home interface.

When this is possible, clients needn't know that EJB is being used to implement business interfaces. This is clearly desirable; unless we use EJB to implement a distributed model, there's no reason to view EJB as more than a helpful framework for particular implementations of business interfaces. The Service Locator pattern works well with local EJB access.

Let's consider two approaches to service location where SLSBs are concerned.

Using a Typed Service Locator to Access EJBs

In the first approach, we use a dedicated, thread-safe service locator for each SLSB. Each service locator implements a factory interface that isn't EJB-specific: a method that can be implemented to return any implementation of the relevant business interface. When an EJB is used to implement this interface, the object returned will be an EJB reference, and the EJB's component interface will extend the business interface.

In my preferred implementation of this approach, the factory method throws a runtime exception, not a checked exception, as failure to create a business object is likely to be fatal. If it's possible to retry, the service locator can retry before throwing an exception to callers.

Each service locator implementation will need to perform a JNDI lookup to cache the home interface for the relevant EJB. This suggests the use of generic infrastructure classes to conceal the use of JNDI. Our framework includes convenient support for this; application service locators need merely to subclass the `com.interface21.ejb.access.AbstractLocalStatelessSessionServiceLocator` class and implement the abstract `setEjbHome()` method as well as the relevant factory interface.

The `com.interface21.ejb.access.AbstractLocalStatelessSessionServiceLocator` class extends the `com.interface21.jndi.AbstractJndiLocator` class, which can be used to perform any JNDI lookup and cache the result. This allows the Service Locator pattern to be used not only for EJB access, but also to look up and cache any resource obtained through JNDI. The `AbstractJndiLocator` class is designed for use as a Java bean in our application framework. The following is a complete listing:

```
package com.interface21.jndi;

import java14.java.util.logging.Logger;
import javax.naming.NamingException;

import com.interface21.beans.factory.InitializingBean;

public abstract class AbstractJndiLocator implements InitializingBean {

  protected final Logger logger = Logger.getLogger(getClass().getName());

  private static String PREFIX = "java:comp/env/";

  private String jndiName;

  public AbstractJndiLocator() {
  }
```

The `JndiName` property setter enables the JNDI name of the EJB or other resource to be held outside Java code:

```
public final void setJndiName(String jndiName) {
  if (!jndiName.startsWith(PREFIX))
    jndiName = PREFIX + jndiName;
  this.jndiName = jndiName;
}

public final String getJndiName() {
  return jndiName;
}
```

The implementation of the `afterPropertiesSet()` method, which is invoked by the bean factory after all properties have been set, performs the JNDI lookup. If the object is successfully located, the `afterPropertiesSet()` method invokes the abstract template method `located()` with the object. Subclasses must implement this to perform their own initialization, based on the type of object. If the lookup fails, the resulting `javax.Naming.NamingException` is thrown to be handled by the application framework (this will be considered a fatal initialization exception):

```
    public final void afterPropertiesSet() throws Exception {
      if (this.jndiName == null || this.jndiName.equals(""))
        throw new Exception("Property 'jndiName' must be set on " +
                            getClass().getName());
      Object o = lookup(jndiName);
      located(o);
    }

    protected abstract void located(Object o);

    private Object lookup(String jndiName) throws NamingException {
      logger.info("Looking up object with jndiName '" + jndiName + "'");

      // This helper will close JNDI context
      Object o = new JndiServices().lookup(jndiName);

      logger.fine("Looked up objet with jndiName '" + jndiName +
                  "' OK: [" + o + "]");
      return o;
    }
  }
```

The `AbstractLocalStatelessSessionServiceLocator` subclass implements the `located()` `template` method to check that that the object is actually an EJB local home, and to invoke an abstract `setEjbHome()` method that must be implemented by subclasses that know the application-specific type of the EJB home, enabling them to obtain EJB references from it:

```
    package com.interface21.ejb.access;

    import javax.ejb.EJBLocalHome;

    import com.interface21.beans.FatalBeanException;
    import com.interface21.jndi.AbstractJndiLocator;

    public abstract class AbstractLocalStatelessSessionServiceLocator
        extends AbstractJndiLocator {

      public AbstractLocalStatelessSessionServiceLocator() {
      }

      public AbstractLocalStatelessSessionServiceLocator(String jndiName) {
        super(jndiName);
      }

      protected abstract void setEjbHome(EJBLocalHome home);

      protected final void located(Object o) {
        if (!(o instanceof EJBLocalHome))
          throw new FatalBeanException("Located object with JNDI name '" +
                  getJndiName() + "' must be an EJBLocalHome object", null);
        setEjbHome((EJBLocalHome) o);
      }
    }
```

It's always safe to cache a reference to a local EJB home interface. Although the EJB specification (§6.2.1) implies that it's safe to cache a remote home, there is a slight chance that a cached remote home reference may become "stale" in some servers (for example, if the remote server hosting the EJB was restarted during the client's lifetime).

The following UML class diagram illustrates the superclasses for both local and remote SLSB service locators, and how a `LocalSLSBBoxOfficeFactory` class might be used in the sample application to create `BoxOffice` objects (actually EJBs) as required:

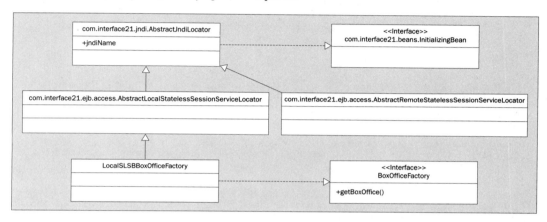

Let's look at how these superclasses can be used to simplify the implementation of a real service locator. The `BoxOfficeFactory` interface is the public interface of our application-specific typed service locator:

```
public interface BoxOfficeFactory {
   BoxOffice getBoxOffice() throws FatalException;
}
```

Extending the `com.interface21.ejb.access.AbstractionLocalStatelessSessionServiceLocator` superclass makes it trivial to implement this interface:

```
public class LocalSLSBBoxOfficeFactory
      extends AbstractLocalStatelessSessionServiceLocator
      implements BoxOfficeFactory {
```

The implementation of the protected abstraction `setEjbHome()` method caches the home interface, after casting it to the appropriate type. This method will be invoked once, when the service locator is initialized:

```
private BoxOfficeHomehome;

protected void setEjbHome(EJBLocalHome home) {
   this.home = (BoxOfficeHome) home;
}
```

The implementation of the getBoxOffice() method from the BoxOfficeFactory interface, which will be invoked by code using the EJB, creates a new SLSB reference as required. EJBCreate exceptions are caught and an unchecked exception, FatalException, is rethrown:

```
public BoxOffice getBoxOffice() throws FatalException {
  try {
    return home.create();
  }
  catch (CreateException ex) {
    throw new EjbConnectionFailure(
      "Cannot create BoxOffice EJB from home", ex);
  }
}
```

The following bean definition shows how such a service locator could be defined in the sample application's bean factory. The only property that must be set is jndiName, inherited from the AbstractJndiLocator superclass:

```
<bean name="boxOfficeFactory"
  class="com.wrox.expertj2ee.ticket.framework.ejb.LocalSLSBBoxOfficeFactory" >
  <property name="jndiName">ejb/BoxOffice</property>
</bean>
```

This is a simple approach that works very well with local EJBs. It hides EJB access from code that uses the business interface. One disadvantage is that it requires a factory interface and an implementing class for each EJB. This isn't usually a major problem, as with sensible design few systems need a vast number of EJBs. Slightly more seriously, all code that uses the EJB must work with the factory object: it's impossible to hold on to a reference to the business interface.

Transparent Dynamic Proxy: An Alternative to the Typed Service Locator for Local EJB Access

An alternative to the Service Locator pattern that achieves the same end is to conceal the factory in a custom bean definition, as described when we discussed our "bean factory" approach above. The custom bean definition looks up and caches the bean's home interface before returning an object of the required interface, which is actually a dynamic proxy wrapping a new instance of the SLSB. Before each method invocation, the dynamic proxy – which is threadsafe – transparently creates a new instance of the SLSB. Although the custom bean definition doesn't know the type of the EJB, it knows that an SLSB local interface must expose a create() method without arguments, which it can use a BeanWrapper object to invoke by name. Benchmarks show that this approach has only a small performance overhead.

This use of dynamic proxies and reflective method invocation sounds complex, but the complexity is hidden within framework code; it enables us to write less application code. Applications need only define a bean using the custom bean definition, as follows. Note the specification of the JNDI name and business interface:

```
<bean name="boxOffice"
      definitionClass=
      "com.interface21.ejb.access.LocalStatelessSessionProxyBeanDefinition">

  <customDefinition property="businessInterface">
     com.wrox.expertj2ee.ticket.boxoffice.BoxOffice
  </customDefinition>
```

```
<customDefinition property="jndiName">
    ejb/BoxOffice
</customDefinition>

</bean>
```

That's it: calling code can simply obtain a `BoxOffice` object like this, and cache it:

```
BoxOffice boxOffice = (BoxOffice) beanFactory.getBean("boxOffice");
```

Most likely, this won't even be necessary: objects that need to use the `BoxOffice` interface can simply expose a bean property and have the application context set it to the `boxOffice` reference at run time.

This approach has the advantage of requiring *no* custom code to access an EJB. We need only define a bean using the custom definition.

This is the approach used in the sample application, although it would be simple to switch to the Typed Service Locator approach, code for which is included in the download.

> *See the code in the* `com.interface21.ejb.access.`
> `LocalStatelessSessionProxyBeanDefinition` *class for the implementation of this approach.*

Using the Business Delegate Pattern for Remote EJB Access

A higher level of decoupling is achieved by the **Business Delegate** pattern, in which a client-side object exposes business methods that are implemented by calls to the EJB. This is more of a façade than a proxy approach, as the business delegate may change method signatures – for example, changing exception types or combining method calls, or even invoking multiple EJBs.

As the Business Delegate pattern requires more work to implement than the Service Locator, I'll focus on its use with remote interfaces, with which it delivers real value (its benefits are reduced with local EJB access). The benefits of a business delegate approach include:

- ❑ The business delegate may be able to retry failed transactions if this is indicated, without calling code being complicated.

- ❑ It's possible to handle exceptions from the server in a consistent way without every client needing to catch J2EE infrastructure-related exceptions such as `java.rmi.RemoteException` and `javax.naming.NamingException`. The business delegate can catch such low-level exceptions, log them and throw an application-specific exception that makes more sense to client code. Or it may be appropriate to wrap EJB-tier exceptions as unchecked exceptions to simplify client code. This makes sense when exceptions are fatal – for example, if we've established that there's no point retrying after encountering a remote exception that prevents execution of a use case.

- ❑ It may be possible to implement operations at a higher level of abstraction. For example, if a particular use case requires multiple EJB invocations, these may be able to be performed in the business delegate.

- ❑ It may be possible to introduce caching by providing a caching implementation of the business delegate interface. This will benefit all clients.

The drawback of using a business delegate is the potential duplication of the business interface exposed by the EJB tier on the client-side. However, using a business delegate offers an opportunity to provide an interface that best fits the needs of clients. For example, we can simplify the interface exposed by the EJB tier by omitting irrelevant operations. We can simplify client code by only throwing checked exceptions if they're part of the API, and the client can be expected to handle them.

It's superficially attractive for the business delegate to implement the session bean's business methods interface. However, this fails to decouple EJB tier and client tier, and cannot deliver some of the benefits we've identified, such as concealing remote exceptions and simplifying the client API. Hence, I don't recommend copying method signatures in the business delegate (the approach recommended in *EJB Design Patterns*). If this is appropriate, the Service Locator pattern is simpler and should be preferred.

Our framework provides easy support for implementing business delegates. The same superclass we used for the typed service locator, `AbstractLocalStatelessSessionServiceLocator`, can be used as a superclass for a business delegate. Instead of merely returning an instance of the EJB on demand, a subclass would implement business operations, calling the EJB as necessary.

As the sample application uses EJBs with local interfaces, there is no need to use the Business Delegate pattern, which requires more work to implement than a service locator.

The following example illustrates the use of a business delegate to access a remote EJB. It uses a hypothetical EJB with a remote interface that exposes two `int` values: one of which can be cached, and one of which cannot. We saw this EJB's business methods interface and component interface under *Implementing EJBs* above. The remote interface exposes the following business methods:

```
int getUncacheableValue() throws RemoteException;
int getCacheableValue() throws RemoteException;
```

By using the Business Delegate pattern, we can simplify calling code by hiding remote exceptions and rethrowing unchecked fatal exceptions, and improve performance by caching the cacheable data value for a given period.

When using the Business Delegate pattern, it is good practice to define a business delegate interface, which application code will work with. This enables a caching implementation to be substituted without impact on client code, for example. The interface might look as follows for this EJB:

```
public interface MyBusinessDelegate {
   int getUncacheableValue() throws FatalException;
   int getCacheableValue() throws FatalException;
}
```

The following implementation extends the `AbstractRemoteStatelessSessionServiceLocator` framework superclass, which performs the necessary JNDI lookup and provides it with an EJB home it can cache in the `setEjbHome()` method:

```
public class MyBusinessDelegateImpl
    extends AbstractRemoteStatelessSessionServiceLocator
    implements MyBusinessDelegate {

   private static long MAX_DATA_AGE = 10000L;
   private CalculatorHome  home;
```

```
    private long lastUpdate = 0L;

    protected void setEjbHome(EJBHome home) {
        this.home = (MyHome) home;
    }

    private CalculatorRemote create() throws FatalException {
        try {
            return home.create();
        }
        catch (CreateException ex) {
            throw new EjbConnectionFailure(
                "Cannot create BoxOffice EJB from home", ex);
        }
        catch (CreateException ex) {
            throw new EjbConnectionFailure(
                    "Cannot create BoxOffice EJB from home", ex);
        }
    }

    public int getUncacheableValue() throws FatalException {
        try {
            return create().getUncacheableValue();
        }
        catch (RemoteException ex) {
            throw new EjbConnectionException("Can't connect to EJB", ex);
        }
    }

    public synchronized int getCacheableValue() throws FatalException {
        if (System.currentTimeMillis() - lastUpdate > MAX_DATA_AGE) {
            try {
                this.cachedValue = create().getCacheableValue();
                lastUpdate = System.currentTimeMillis();
            }
            catch (RemoteException ex) {
                throw new EjbConnectionException("Can't connect to EJB", ex);
            }
        }
        return this.cachedValue;
    }
}
```

> **It's important to abstract access to EJBs. With EJBs with local interfaces, use the
> Service Locator pattern, or the Business Delegate if there is a good reason that calling
> code shouldn't work with the EJB interface. With EJBs with remote interfaces, use the
> Business Delegate pattern, and conceal remote access details from clients.**

Using JMS

Like JDBC, JMS is a complex API. Working with it directly can obscure the purpose of application code. Thus an abstraction layer is appropriate. The com.interface21.jms.JmsTemplate class applies the same approach as the JdbcTemplate we examined in Chapter 9. We should try to conceal in framework code the complexity of the necessary JNDI lookups and the requirement to work with multiple JMS API objects.

Let's consider com.interface21.jms.JmsTemplate class's support for Pub/Sub messaging. On startup, a JmsTemplate instance does a JNDI lookup for the TopicConnectionFactory. The JNDI name is passed into the constructor, as it may differ between application servers. The following method uses the cached TopicConnectionFactory to invoke a callback interface to create a message given a TopicSession, which it then publishes:

```
private static String PREFIX = "java:comp/env/";

public void publish(String topicName, PubSubMessageCreator
    pubSubMessageCreator) throws JmsException {

  if (!topicName.startsWith(PREFIX))
    topicName = PREFIX + topicName;

  TopicConnection topicConnection = null;

  try {
    topicConnection = topicConnectionFactory.createTopicConnection();
    TopicSession session = topicConnection.createTopicSession(
      false, Session.AUTO_ACKNOWLEDGE);
    Topic topic = (Topic) jndiServices.lookup( topicName);
    TopicPublisher publisher = session.createPublisher(topic);

    Message message = pubSubMessageCreator.createMessage(session);
    logger.info("Message created was [" + message + "]");
    publisher.publish(message);

    logger.info("Message published OK");
  }
  catch (NamingException ex) {
    throw new JmsException("Couldn't get topic name [" + topicName + "]", ex);
  }
  catch (JMSException ex) {
    throw new JmsException("Couldn't get connection factory or topic", ex);
  }
  finally {
    if (topicConnection != null) {
      try {
        topicConnection.close();
      }
      catch (JMSException ex) {
        logger.logp(Level.WARNING, "com.interface21.jms.JmsTemplate",
          "publish", "Failed to close topic", ex);
      }
    }
  }
}
```

The com.interface21.jms.JmsException exception is unchecked, meaning that we have a choice as to whether to catch it. Calling code can implement the PubSubMessageCreator inner interface of JmsTemplate (shown below) without deep knowledge of JNDI:

```
public interface PubSubMessageCreator {
  Message createMessage(TopicSession topicSession) throws JMSException;
}
```

Thus a message can be published with the following code:

```
JmsTemplate jmsTemplate = new JmsTemplate("jms/TopicFactory");
jmsTemplate.publish("jms/topic/referencedata",
  new JmsTemplate.PubSubMessageCreator() {
  public Message createMessage(TopicSession session) throws JMSException {
    TextMessage msg = session.createTextMessage();
    msg.setText("This is a test message");
    return msg;
  }
});
```

Message consumers can also benefit from a simplifying infrastructure. Note that it's often best to use MDBs as message consumers, as the EJB container provides valuable infrastructure for JMS message consumption; however, we can't always use EJB. We always need to implement the `MessageListener` interface. However, we don't want to have to deal with the complexity of registering a listener with a topic, which also involves multiple JNDI lookups. The `JmsTemplate` class provides a convenience method for this, with the following signature:

```
public TopicConnection subscribeToTopicNonDurable(String topicName,
    MessageListener listener, String messageSelector)
    throws JmsException;
```

A custom bean definition of class `com.interface21.jms.JmsListenerBeanDefinition` can automatically register any JMS listener to a given topic. The following example is from the sample application, in which the `com.wrox.expertj2ee.ticket.referencedata.support.DataUpdateJmsListener` JMS listener notifies caching objects of a data update:

```
<bean name="referenceDataListener"
    definitionClass="com.interface21.jms.JmsListenerBeanDefinition">

  <customDefinition property="listenerBean">
      com.wrox.expertj2ee.ticket.referencedata.support.DataUpdateJmsListener
  </customDefinition>

  <customDefinition property="topicConnectionFactoryName">
      jms/TopicFactory
  </customDefinition>

  <customDefinition property="topicName">
      jms/topic/referencedata
  </customDefinition>

  <property name="cachingCalendar" beanRef="true">
      calendar
  </property>
</bean>
```

This enables us to implement a simple JMS listener that responds to events and refreshes data cached in another application component without the need to write any low-level JMS code, as shown in the following listing:

```
public class DataUpdateJmsListener implements MessageListener {

  protected final Logger logger = Logger.getLogger(getClass().getName());
  private CachingCalendar calendar;

  public void setCachingCalendar(CachingCalendar calendar) {
    this.calendar = calendar;
  }

  public void onMessage(Message m) {
    try {
      logger.info("Refresing calendar in response to JMS message ["
                  + m + "]");
      calendar.refresh();
    }
    catch (Exception ex) {
      logger.logp(Level.SEVERE, getClass().getName(), "onMessage",
                  "Failed to refresh calendar", ex);
    }
  }
}
```

This simple abstraction doesn't take care of all JMS requirements – the JMS API includes many features such as transacted sessions, which pose more problems for abstraction. However, it provides a simple infrastructure for the commonest needs.

Implementing Business Logic

As a professional developer, you know how to program in Java. What I want to discuss here is how to put an application together and how to focus your programming skills on your application's domain. Thus the following discussion of the sample application does not address low-level details such as the implementation of the adjacent seating algorithm, but focuses on how the sample application's components are configured and work together.

We'll look both at how the sample application uses standard J2EE infrastructure and how it uses the infrastructure we've discussed so far in this chapter.

The sample application's code is available in the download accompanying this book. Please refer to it as necessary during the following discussion, as it's impractical to provide a complete listing of all the classes mentioned.

Implementing the Sample Application

Let's now consider some of the key business logic of the sample application. Let's focus on two key issues: how we obtain reference data about genres, shows, and performances; and how we obtain information about seat availability and implement the booking process.

These use cases are described in detail in Chapter 5, so I'll just provide a quick summary of the requirements here, along with the high-level design decisions taken in the last few chapters concerning them.

Genre, show, and performance data changes rarely and can be shared between all users of the application. The retrieval of this data need not be transactional.

The booking process requires transactional data access, and involves the holding of user session state. We have chosen to hold user session state in an `HttpSession` object in the web container.

Defining Business Interfaces

The first step is to define the necessary business interfaces. These will not be web-specific; however, they will run in the web container in a collocated application.

These interfaces should be able to be implemented with or without EJB without affecting code that uses them. In a collocated application such as our sample application, we'll use the Service Locator pattern, discussed above, to hide the details of EJB access completely.

There is only one area in which retaining the option of using EJB affects our design: exception handling. As EJBs handle unchecked exceptions as fatal system exceptions, as we saw in Chapter 10, we are unable to use unchecked exceptions in a business interface that might be implemented by an EJB. Occasionally this calls for compromises.

Consider the case of a request to find the number of seats free for a performance, given a performance ID that doesn't match any performance. Such a request cannot occur in our application, as the user can only request availability using links from pages that will provide valid performance IDs. Thus it makes no sense to complicate application code by catching a checked `NoSuchPerformanceException`.

However, given that we would like the ability to implement our `BoxOffice` interface using EJB, we must choose the lesser of the following two evils: make all our application exceptions (including `NoSuchPerformanceException`) checked and cope with the overhead of catching checked exceptions where this serves no useful purpose; or lose the ability to switch between EJBs and other business object implementations transparently. In the present application we opt for the use of checked exceptions. We could use the Business Delegate pattern, to catch checked exceptions from EJBs and rethrow unchecked exceptions. However, this requires more work to implement.

In the sample application, we will want two separate interfaces to handle the functionality we're considering here: one to deal with reference data, and one to deal with availability and the booking process. Let's consider each in turn.

The `com.wrox.expertj2ee.ticket.referencedata.Calendar` interface handles reference data requirements:

```
public interface Calendar {
    List getCurrentGenres();
    Show getShow(int id) throws ReferenceDataException;
    Performance getPerformance(int id) throws ReferenceDataException;
}
```

The `Genre`, `Show`, and `Performance` objects are lightweight value objects, disconnected from the data source. They expose a tree structure, navigable downwards: from a genre we can find shows, and from each show we can get a list of performances. The entire tree can be cacheable for up to one minute, or as long as we know that there has been no change to reference data (the complexity of caching objects individually is unwarranted, as it would deliver little benefit).

429

The `com.expertj2ee.ticket.boxoffice.BoxOffice` interface exposes information about seating availability and exposes the booking process. It includes the following methods:

```
public interface BoxOffice {

    int getSeatCount(int performanceId) throws NoSuchPerformanceException;

    int getFreeSeatCount(int performanceId)
      throws NoSuchPerformanceException;

    Reservation allocateSeats(ReservationRequest request)
      throws NotEnoughSeatsException, NoSuchPerformanceException
      InvalidSeatingRequestException;

    Booking confirmReservation(PurchaseRequest purchaseRequest)
      throws ExpiredReservationTakenException,
      CreditCardAuthorizationException,
      InvalidSeatingRequestException,
      BoxOfficeInternalException;
}
```

The first two methods expose seat availability. The `allocateSeats()` method creates a reservation, while the `confirmReservation()` method turns an existing reservation into a purchase. There is little opportunity for caching here, and the two booking methods are transactional.

The `ReservationRequest` object, used as a parameter to the `allocateSeats()` method, is a command, as is the `PurchaseRequest` parameter to the `confirmReservation()` method. The use of command objects has the following advantages, where multiple individual parameters would otherwise be required:

❑   It's possible to add parameter data without breaking method signatures.

❑   Commands provide an excellent basis for event publication if necessary, using JMS or a simple Observer implementation. For example, we could easily publish an event with a command attached to enable an e-mail to be sent when a user makes a successful reservation.

❑   It may be possible to bind HTTP request parameters values onto a command. Most MVC web application frameworks can automatically populate JavaBean properties of command objects from HTTP request parameters. This can greatly simplify application request processing code in the web tier.

A listing of the `ReservationRequest` command shows that such commands are merely simple data holders. This object is serializable not to enable remote invocation, but to allow it to be stored in an `HttpSession`, which may need to be replicated across a cluster or written to a persistent store if swapped out of application server RAM:

```
public class ReservationRequest implements Serializable {

    private static final long MILLIS_PER_MINUTE = 1000L * 60L;

    private int performanceID;
    private int seatsRequested;
```

```java
private double bookingFee;
private int classID;
private boolean reserve;
private Date holdTill;
private boolean mustBeAdjacent;

public ReservationRequest() {
}

public ReservationRequest(int performanceID, int classID,
    int seatsRequested, boolean reserve, double bookingFee,
    int minutesToHold)
    throws InvalidSeatingRequestException  {

  this.performanceID = performanceID;
  this.classID = classID;
  this.seatsRequested = seatsRequested;
  this.reserve = reserve;
  this.bookingFee = bookingFee;
  holdFor(minutesToHold);
}

public int getPerformanceID() {
  return performanceID;
}

public void setPerformanceID(int performanceID) {
  this.performanceID = performanceID;
}

public int getSeatsRequested() {
  return seatsRequested;
}

public void setSeatsRequested(int seatsRequested) {
  this.seatsRequested = seatsRequested;
}

public boolean getSeatsMustBeAdjacent() {
  return mustBeAdjacent;
}

public void setSeatsMustBeAdjacent(boolean mustBeAdjacent) {
  this.mustBeAdjacent = mustBeAdjacent;
}

public double getBookingFee() {
  return bookingFee;
}

public void setBookingFee(double bookingFee) {
  this.bookingFee = bookingFee;
}
```

```
    public void holdFor(int minutes)
        throws InvalidSeatingRequestException {

      if (holdTill != null)
        throw new InvalidSeatingRequestException(
          "holdFor is immutable: cannot reset");
      holdTill = new Date(System.currentTimeMillis() +
                          minutes * MILLIS_PER_MINUTE);
    }

    public Date getHoldTill() {
      return holdTill;
    }

    public int getClassID() {
      return classID;
    }

    public void setClassID(int classID) {
      this.classID = classID;
    }

    public boolean isReserve() {
      return reserve;
    }

    public void setReserve(boolean reserve) {
      this.reserve = reserve;
    }
  }
```

Business interface return values, such as the Reservation object, are coded to interfaces. This enables implementations to return an immutable implementation, to prevent manipulation – inadvertent or malicious – by calling code.

Determining Implementation Strategy

The Calendar interface involves non-transactional data access. Thus there is no need to implement it using an EJB; we can use DAOs in the web container.

The BoxOffice interface involves transactional data manipulation. Thus a stateless session bean with a local interface is an obvious implementation choice, because using CMT can simplify application code.

These decisions will not affect code that uses these objects. Thus if we wish to increase or decrease use of EJB in the future, or use a different data-access strategy, there will be limited impact on the codebase.

Let's consider the implementation of the Calendar interface first. The com.wrox.expertj2ee.ticket.referencedata.jdbc.JdbcCalendar class provides a threadsafe implementation using the JDBC abstraction packages discussed in Chapter 9. The source code is similar to that shown in Chapter 9. The JdbcCalendar class implements the com.interface21.beans.factory.InitializingBean interface, enabling it to load data in its initialization of the afterPropertiesSet() method.

As all other application objects are coded to use the `Calendar` interface, rather than the `JdbcCalendar` implementation, caching can be handled by the `com.wrox.expertj2ee.ticket.referencedata.support.CachingCalendar` class, which proxies any underlying `Calendar` implementation (such as a `JdbcCalendar`) and uses copy-on-write to construct a new `Calendar` implementation when its `refresh()` method is invoked. Such use of a caching proxy is a natural idiom for interface-based design, which can significantly benefit performance while keeping caching logic separate from application implementation.

Implementing the BoxOffice

The `BoxOfficeEJB` uses two helper objects: the `BoxOfficeDAO` interface, which hides the details of data access behind an abstraction layer and which we looked at in Chapter 9; and the `CreditCardProcessor` interface, which provides the ability to process credit card payments. The sample application uses a dummy implementation of this interface; in a real application, an implementation would probably contact an external payment processing system.

The `com.wrox.expertj2ee.boxoffice.ejb.BoxOfficeEJBLocal` EJB component interface extends the `BoxOffice` interface (its "business methods" interface) as well as `javax.ejb.EJBLocalObject`, as required by the EJB specification:

```
public interface BoxOfficeLocal extends BoxOffice, EJBLocalObject {
}
```

The local home interface, `com.wrox.expertj2ee.boxoffice.ejb.BoxOfficeHome`, specifies the single create method required of all stateless session beans:

```
public interface BoxOfficeHome extends EJBLocalHome {
  BoxOfficeLocal create() throws CreateException;
}
```

The bean implementation class will extend our `com.interface21.ejb.support.AbstractStatelessSessionBean` framework class and implement the `BoxOffice` business interface:

```
public class BoxOfficeEJB extends AbstractStatelessSessionBean
    implements BoxOffice {
```

Extending `AbstractStatelessSessionBean` forces us to implement a method with the signature `ejbCreate()`, matching the `create()` method on the home interface, which we use to obtain and cache in instance variables helper objects defined in the bean factory:

```
public void ejbCreate() {
  logger.config("Trying to load data source bean");
  this.dao = (BoxOfficeDAO)
    getBeanFactory().getBean("dao");
  logger.config("Data source loaded OK: [" + this.dao + "]");
  this.creditCardProcessor = (CreditCardProcessor)
    getBeanFactory().getBean("creditCardProcessor");
  logger.config("Credit card processing loaded OK: [" +
            this.creditCardProcessor + "]");
}
```

The corresponding bean definitions in the `ejb-jar.xml` deployment descriptor use the JNDI bean factory syntax described earlier in this chapter, as follows:

```
<env-entry>
  <env-entry-name>beans.dao.class</env-entry-name>
  <env-entry-type>java.lang.String</env-entry-type>
  <env-entry-value>
     com.wrox.expertj2ee.ticket.boxoffice.support.jdbc.
     JBoss30OracleJdbcBoxOfficeDao
  </env-entry-value>
</env-entry>

<env-entry>
  <env-entry-name>beans.creditCardProcessor.class</env-entry-name>
  <env-entry-type>java.lang.String</env-entry-type>
  <env-entry-value>
     com.wrox.expertj2ee.ticket.boxoffice.support.DummyCreditCardProcessor
  </env-entry-value>
</env-entry>
```

Please see the download for a complete listing of this EJB. However, let's look at the implementation of the `confirmReservation()` method, which illustrates use of CMT. This method is marked in the deployment descriptor to run in a transaction. We use programmatic rollback via the `setRollbackOnly()` method of the `SessionContext` if we fail to authorize a credit card transaction. Before we attempt credit card authorization we attempt to create a booking. This makes it very unlikely that the user can be debited for a purchase, yet fail to be given a booking.

This method will throw only checked exceptions, as we want to preserve exceptions for clients:

```
public Booking confirmReservation(PurchaseRequest purchase)
   throws ExpiredReservationTakenException,
          CreditCardAuthorizationException,
          BoxOfficeInternalException,
          InvalidSeatingRequestException {
```

Before we attempt to authorize payment, we create a purchase record that will create a permanent record in the event of a later, unexpected failure:

```
int purchaseId = dao.createPurchaseRecord(purchase.getReservation());
String authorization = null;
```

We use CMT to roll this data update back if the credit card transaction is declined (in the highlighted code below). In the unlikely event that payment is accepted, but we fail to update the purchase record with the authorization code (a fatal internal error), we create a log record but throw a checked exception. Throwing a runtime exception would result in the transaction being rolled back, which would lose the new purchase record, which should remain in the database:

```
try {
   authorization = creditCardProcessor.process(
     purchase.getReservation().getTotalPrice(),
     purchase.getCardNumber(), purchase.getExpiry());

   // Complete data update for purchase
```

```
            dao.setAuthorizationCode(purchaseId, authorization);

            Booking booking = new ImmutableBooking(
                authorization, new Date(), purchase.getReservation());
            logger.info("Booking successful [" + booking + "]");
            return booking;
        }
        catch (CreditCardAuthorizationException ex) {
            logger.severe("Failed to authorize credit card number");
            getSessionContext().setRollbackOnly();
            throw ex;
        }
        catch (DataAccessException ex) {
            // Failed to authorize: we know we've created pending purchase record
            // DO NOT ROLLBACK: this will lose PENDING record
            // This is unusual: of course the tx may not commit, so we want to log
            // as much information as possible as well
            String mesg ="**** Database problem: failed to set authorization code '"
                + authorization + "' for purchase id " + purchaseId
                + "; payment WAS accepted for reservation ["
                + purchase.getReservation() + "] ****";
            logger.severe(mesg);
            // Must throw a checked exception to avoid automatic rollback
            throw new BoxOfficeInternalException(mesg);
        }
    }
```

By using EJB with CMT, we've simplified our application code: transaction management adds minimal complexity.

Note that we can catch the generic com.interface21.dao.DataAccessException described in Chapter 9 without introducing dependency on the use of JDBC to implement the BoxOfficeDAO data access interface.

Using JMS to Propagate Data Updates

For efficiency we choose to cache reference data until we know that it has been updated. However, such updates must work across a cluster of servers, so we cannot use the support for the Observer design pattern built into our application framework – we must use JMS. A JMS listener will cause cached data to be refreshed on messages to a data update topic. When the Admin interface is available, it will publish JMS messages on changes to reference data; before the Admin interface is completed, administrators will need to access a restricted URL that will cause a reference data update event to be published after updating the database.

> Note that as the cached data isn't held in the EJB container, we cannot use an MDB as a message consumer.

We saw the implementation of the com.wrox.expertj2ee.ticket.referencedata.support.DataUpdateJmsListener class, which consumes JMS messages, in our discussion of JMS infrastructure above. This invokes the refresh() method of the CachingCalendar object, causing all reference data to be reread from the database.

Pulling It All Together

Now we have our interfaces and implementations, we can use our application framework to hook them up. The following excerpts from the `ticket-servlet.xml` application context XML definition file illustrate how the application components we've discussed are wired up as JavaBeans.

The following two bean definitions define a `Calendar` implementation that uses JDBC, and a "caching calendar" that creates new objects using the `realCalendar` definition when it receives update events. Note that the `singleton` attribute of the `realCalendar` definition is set to `false`, so a new object will be returned each time the `cachingCalendar` asks for an instance of this bean definition:

```
<bean name="realCalendar"
  singleton="false"
  class="com.wrox.expertj2ee.ticket.referencedata.jdbc.JdbcCalendar" >
</bean>

<bean name="calendar"
  class="com.wrox.expertj2ee.ticket.referencedata.support.CachingCalendar" >
</bean>
```

The following custom bean definition, discussed earlier, registers a JMS listener that notifies the `CachingCalendar` object when reference data is updated:

```
<bean name="referenceDataListener"
  definitionClass="com.interface21.jms.JmsListenerBeanDefinition">

  <customDefinition property="listenerBean">
      com.wrox.expertj2ee.ticket.referencedata.support.DataUpdateJmsListener
  </customDefinition>

  <customDefinition property="topicConnectionFactoryName">
      jms/TopicFactory
  </customDefinition>

  <customDefinition property="topicName">
      jms/topic/referencedata
  </customDefinition>

  <property name="cachingCalendar" beanRef="true">
      calendar
  </property>

</bean>
```

The `BoxOffice` bean definition uses the dynamic proxy bean definition discussed above to hide the complexity of EJB access. We specify the business interface the EJB implements and the bean's JNDI name:

```
<bean name="boxOffice"
      definitionClass="
        com.interface21.ejb.access.LocalStatelessSessionProxyBeanDefinition">

  <customDefinition property="businessInterface">
      com.wrox.expertj2ee.ticket.boxoffice.BoxOffice
  </customDefinition>

  <customDefinition property="jndiName">
```

```
       ejb/BoxOffice
    </customDefinition>

  </bean>
```

There is no need for any application objects to perform JNDI lookups or use the EJB API directly: they can simply use the object created by this bean definition as an implementation of the `com.wrox.expertj2ee.ticket.boxoffice.BoxOffice` business interface.

Using the infrastructure discussed in this chapter, application components that use these interfaces need simply expose bean properties that can be set by the framework appropriately: they don't need to depend on framework code and they don't need to look up objects managed by the framework. For example, the application's main web-tier controller exposes `calendar` and `boxOffice` properties, which the framework sets automatically based on the following bean definition:

```
<bean name="ticketController"
  class="com.wrox.expertj2ee.ticket.web.TicketController" >

  // Other properties omitted

  <property name="calendar" beanRef="true">calendar</property>
  <property name="boxOffice" beanRef="true">boxOffice</property>

</bean>
```

The controller doesn't need to do any configuration lookup, but merely has to implement the following methods to save references to instance variables:

```
public void setBoxOffice(BoxOffice boxOffice) {
  this.boxOffice = boxOffice;
}

public void setCalendar(Calendar calendar) {
  this.calendar = calendar;
}
```

We will discuss the web tier in detail in the next chapter. As this example indicates, it is very closely integrated with the overall infrastructure we've examined.

Summary

In this chapter we've discussed the importance and benefits of a strong generic infrastructure backing application implementation. While a J2EE application server provides powerful standard infrastructure for J2EE applications, we need to use additional infrastructure components to make the J2EE APIs easier to use, ensure that application code focuses on addressing business problems, and solve problems that the J2EE specifications do not.

To illustrate these points, and to provide a potential basis for your own applications, we've examined some of the key infrastructure packages used by the sample application, and the problems they exist to solve.

437

We've considered the importance of infrastructure that enables central configuration management. We've seen how making application components JavaBeans can allow them to be configured by a generic application framework, removing the need for application code to implement configuration management such as property file lookups. In combination with interface-based design – in which code is always written to interfaces, rather than classes – the use of JavaBeans is an incredibly powerful means of assembling and parameterizing applications without modifying Java code.

Once configuration management is centralized, it is possible to read configuration from any source – such as XML documents, properties files, or JNDI – without any need to change application code. Configuration via JavaBean properties ensures consistency across applications and between architectural tiers. For example, EJBs can use the same approach to configuration management as ordinary Java classes.

We've looked at several layers of infrastructure that enable us to achieve central configuration management:

❏ A package that abstracts the use of reflection to manipulate JavaBeans. This is valuable basic infrastructure that can be used not only in configuration management, but also for other tasks such as initializing JavaBean objects from HTTP requests (as discussed in the next chapter), simplifying request processing in web applications. This functionality is so useful that several open source projects, such as Apache Commons, provide their own implementations; however, I am yet to see a really good one, and the com.interface21.beans package described in this chapter is the most sophisticated I know of.

❏ A "bean factory" that uses this lower-level functionality to maintain a registry of application objects. When application objects are defined as JavaBeans, they need not depend on this infrastructure; infrastructure can work behind the scenes to set bean properties to configure objects, including setting relationships between objects, based on definitions held outside Java code.

With the combination of built-in support for primitive properties, the ability to set relationships between managed objects, and the availability of the standard JavaBeans PropertyEditor functionality to represent object types as strings, concise bean factory syntax can define complex application configurations. We looked at standard bean factory implementations based on XML documents, properties files, and environment variables defined in EJB JAR deployment descriptors.

❏ An "application context" that builds on the bean factory concept to implement the Observer design pattern, provides a standard way to look up messages to meet internationalization requirements, and allows application components to communicate as necessary at run time.

The standard J2EE infrastructure makes some simple things difficult, which has caused widespread frustration with J2EE in practice. This can be addressed by a simplifying infrastructure that makes J2EE APIs and services easier to work with. We've seen how infrastructure can be used to simplify working with complex J2EE APIs, including:

❏ Support classes that make it easier to implement EJBs and reduce the likelihood of common errors.

❏ Infrastructure classes that help to implement the Service Locator and Business Delegate J2EE patterns, decoupling code that uses EJBs from dependence on JNDI and EJB APIs. We saw that the Service Locator pattern is usually simplest and most appropriate for accessing EJBs through local interfaces, while the Business Delegate is the better choice to access EJBs through remote interfaces. In this case the Business Delegate can be used to conceal the details of remote access from client code.

❑ Classes that make it easier to send and consume JMS messages, concealing the necessary JNDI lookup, simplifying error handling and the need to work with multiple JNDI API objects.

Whether or not you choose to use the specific infrastructure described in this chapter, all these issues should be addressed outside application code, which should concentrate on the problem domain and implementing business logic.

Finally, we looked at some of the core implementation of the sample application, illustrating how it is simplified through use of appropriate infrastructure.

Web-Tier MVC Design

In this chapter we'll look at web-tier design and how to ensure that a web interface is a simple and maintainable layer built on business objects and overall application infrastructure.

This is a very important topic. A poorly designed web interface is one of the quickest paths to an unmaintainable application and overall project failure. Experience with poorly designed web interfaces that proved hugely expensive in development effort and business opportunity first made me passionate about J2EE design.

After surveying the problems we seek to avoid in web application design, we'll focus on the MVC architectural pattern, which has proven the key to writing successful web interfaces.

After examining MVC theory and the concepts shared between successful implementations of the MVC pattern, we'll look at three open source MVC web application frameworks: Struts, Maverick, and WebWork. We'll then look at the design and use of a simple but powerful web application framework integrated with the infrastructure that I introduced in the last chapter, and which we'll use for the sample application. Like the infrastructure components we've seen so far, this framework is intended for use in real applications, and not merely as a demo.

I chose to implement this framework rather than use an existing framework for several reasons:

- ❑ To demonstrate the potential to integrate an MVC web application framework into an overall application infrastructure, and the benefits that this brings.

- ❑ To formalize the relationship between web-tier components and business objects, which are independent of the web interface. I feel that the relationship between web-tier components and business objects is often neglected in MVC applications, with too much application code being web-specific.

❑ Because I have considerable experience in this area and have implemented previous production frameworks, from which this is a natural evolution.

❑ Because no existing MVC web framework meets all the design goals we will discuss.

❑ Because the design of this framework clearly illustrates the MVC concepts central to this chapter, and especially the complete decoupling of views from controllers. We'll see the benefits of this when we look at alternative view technologies in the next chapter.

Naturally, this framework builds not only on my experience, but also on the concepts used in existing frameworks. It borrows some concepts from Struts and Maverick, in particular.

We'll also look at the issue of session state management and data validation in web applications.

Finally, we'll look at implementing the web tier of the sample application using the MVC framework discussed in this chapter, paying special attention to how web components access business objects.

The Challenges of Web Development

Why is designing web interfaces so hard and why are the consequences of getting it wrong so dire? Some of the many reasons include the following:

❑ **Web interfaces change frequently**
For example, re-branding may change the look and feel, but not necessarily the workflow, of a web application. A successful application can accommodate such change without the need to change business objects or even web-tier control code.

❑ **Web interfaces involve complex markup**
Typical web sites contain nested tables and lengthy JavaScripts; pages may even be designed using GUI tools that produce hard-to-read markup. Usually only a small proportion of the content is dynamic. It's vital that the generation of complex markup doesn't obscure the generation of dynamic content. Getting this markup right is the business of specialists; Java developers are seldom good at it and their skills are better employed elsewhere. Thus separation of the roles of markup developer and Java developer is crucial.

❑ **Web interfaces use a very different model compared to traditional UIs in languages such as Java**
The web programming model is punctuated by requests and responses; it's impossible to update GUI components dynamically when an underlying model changes, as in a traditional MVC approach such as Java Swing.

❑ **HTTP requests can carry only string parameters**
Thus we frequently need to convert string values to and from Java objects. This can be difficult and error-prone.

❑ **Web interfaces make it difficult to validate user input, as we have limited control over the client browser**
We must be prepared to reject invalid user input and make users resubmit it. In contrast, we can use custom controls to prevent users entering invalid data in Swing or VB interfaces, as we have complete control over UI presentation.

❑ **HTML offers a limited choice of UI controls**
Again, this is in sharp contrast to traditional GUI applications, which offer a rich range of controls and the ability to implement custom controls.

❑ **Ensuring that a web site looks right and works correctly in all common browsers can be difficult**
This can significantly complicate markup and add to the challenge of separating presentation issues from Java programming issues.

❑ **There are many efficiency considerations**
Often we cannot restrict or predict the number of users using a web application. Both performance and concurrency are likely to be particularly important in web applications.

❑ **Web interfaces are relatively hard to test**
This is one of many reasons that we should ensure that as little application functionality as possible is web-specific.

Lessons Learned in Java Web Development

Designing web interfaces to achieve maintainable and extensible applications requires discipline. The best motivation for achieving this discipline is awareness of the consequences of failing to achieve it. The following brief discussion of the history of Java web development serves to illustrate the dangers that we must avoid.

The Shortcomings of Servlet-only Solutions

The first Java web technology was servlets. The first release of the Servlet API back in 1997 was an improvement on the dominant existing technology, the primitive **Common Gateway Interface (CGI)** standard for server-side script invocation. Instead of scripts written in languages such as C or Perl, which usually caused a new process to be created to handle each request, servlets allowed dynamic content to be generated by reusable Java objects. Servlets had full access to the power of the Java language, including JDBC and the Java object model, and so elevated web development to true OO development.

At least in theory – the Servlet specification was a big step forward, but developers soon ran into problems building real applications. Servlets proved very good at invoking business objects. However, generating complex markup from Java code is awkward. If markup strings are embedded in servlet and helper classes, changes to the presentation of web content always require modification of Java code and recompilation; Java developers must always be involved. Furthermore, it can be very difficult to see how a complete page is assembled from markup littered throughout Java objects, making sites very difficult to maintain. Servlets proved much more effective at generating binary content. However, this is a rarer requirement.

> **Generating markup from Java objects such as servlets is clumsy and leads to unmaintainable web applications. The servlet specification alone is not enough to meet the challenges of most web applications.**

It was clear that additional infrastructure was needed. Many developers used **templating** approaches, in which markup was held outside Java code, with servlets responsible for generating only the dynamic content. However, there was no widely adopted standard.

JSP: Promise and Temptation

Thus the release of the JSP 0.92 specification in 1998 created widespread excitement. JSP was a standard templating solution, endorsed by Sun. Although JSP pages are transparently compiled into servlets by a web container, JSP pages use a very different approach from servlets. While servlets are Java objects capable of generating markup, JSP pages are markup components that permit escaping into Java as necessary to initiate processing.

JSP was soon in wide use, and overenthusiastic adoption led to a host of new problems. Experience quickly demonstrated that a model based on escaping into Java as necessary to generate dynamic content was a new evil in place of the old need to generate markup from Java code. The release of JSP 1.0 in 1999 was a significant improvement on JSP 0.92, but did not change the underlying model or address these problems.

"JSP Model 1" Architecture

To understand these problems, let's consider the simplest and most obvious architecture for a J2EE web application's interface. Imagine that we use JSP pages to implement the entire web interface. Each JSP handles incoming requests, creating domain objects from request parameters and using them to invoke business objects. Each JSP then renders the result of the business processing. The JSP infrastructure makes it easy to implement this approach, using JSP pages with a mix of markup and embedded Java code. The standard JSP infrastructure allows JSP pages:

❑ To automatically populate JavaBeans declared on them with request parameter values, using the <jsp:useBean> standard action

❑ To access and manipulate session attributes and application-wide ServletContext attributes

❑ To perform any kind of logic using **scriptlets** (blocks of Java code embedded in JSP pages)

This kind of web application architecture is often termed the **JSP Model 1** architecture. *Core J2EE Patterns* uses the more meaningful, but rather overblown, term, **Physical Resource Mapping Strategy**. I'll use the older term, JSP Model 1, in this chapter.

This approach is simple to implement. All we need to do is write the JSP pages and provide the support classes. There is no need to write servlets or define URL-to-servlet mappings in the web.xml deployment descriptor. Development-deployment cycles are often short, as JSP pages can be recompiled automatically by the web container as they are modified.

However, this approach mostly produces very poor results in practice. Applications built using this approach (and far too many are, even today), face the following severe problems:

❑ Each JSP must either know how to handle all possible paths resulting from a request (for example, the path on invalid or missing parameters), resulting in complex conditionals; or must forward to another JSP as necessary, making application workflow hard to follow. It's a mistake to commit to one JSP when it's too early to predict what content we'll need to display.

❑ Broken error handling. What if, halfway down the JSP, after the buffer has been flushed so it's too late to forward to another page, we encounter an exception? Although the standard JSP error page mechanism works well enough for trivial Model 1 systems, it won't help us in this plausible scenario.

❑ The web interface is tied to JSP. In fact, JSP is just one view technology available to J2EE applications. JSP pages are unsuited to presenting binary data, and other technologies such as XSLT are superior at tackling some problems.

❑ Java code in JSP scriptlets is hard to test and cannot be reused. Not only is this approach not object-oriented, it fails to deliver even the code reuse we would achieve in a well-written procedural application.

❑ JSP pages will contain a mish-mash of markup and Java code, making them hard for either Java developers or markup experts to maintain.

❑ JSP pages will bear little resemblance to the markup they generate. This defeats the point of using JSP pages, which are essentially markup components.

> **The JSP Model 1 architecture, in which JSP pages handle incoming requests, results in non-maintainable applications. JSP Model 1 should never be used in real applications: its only use is in prototyping.**

The Temptation of the JSP Standard Infrastructure

Hopefully you're already convinced that JSP pages are not the ultimate answer to J2EE web interfaces. In case you aren't, let's consider some of the shortcomings of the JSP standard infrastructure, which makes it easy to attempt many things that subvert good design, and makes the JSP Model 1 architecture plausible on first impression.

Request parameters can be mapped onto JSP beans in two ways. Individual request parameters can be mapped onto a bean property using a `<jsp:setProperty>` action like this:

```
<jsp:setProperty name="bean" property="propertyName" param="paramName" />
```

Alternatively, all request properties can be mapped onto a bean in a single `<jsp:setProperty>` action like this:

```
<jsp:setProperty name="bean" property="*" />
```

The JSP mechanism for mapping request parameters onto bean properties is an unrealistically naïve approach to **data binding** (a problem we'll discuss in detail later). Problems include the following:

❑ There is no mechanism for handling type mismatches. For example, if the value of a parameter corresponding to an `int` property is non-numeric, the mapping will fail *silently*. The `int` property on the bean will be left with its default value. The bean isn't capable of holding the invalid value the user supplied on any resubmission page. Without checking the request parameter directly, we can't distinguish between a missing parameter and a type mismatch.

❑ The only way to establish whether a parameter was supplied is to set the default to an out-of-band value. This may not always be possible.

❑ There's no mechanism for handling any exceptions thrown by the bean's property setters.

❑ There's no way to specify which properties are required and which are optional.

❑ We can't resolve these problems by intercepting the handling of the fields: we have no control over how the mapping is performed.

We'll end up needing to write our own request handling code in the JSP to address these shortcomings, which defeats the purpose of the property mapping infrastructure.

> **The standard JSP infrastructure for mapping request parameters onto JSP beans is primitive and next to useless in real applications.**

Another tempting feature of the JSP standard architecture, which encourages Model 1 architectures, but shouldn't be used in real applications, is the ability to define methods and even classes in JSP pages. Normally code in scriptlets ends up in the JSP's `_jspService()` method. By using `<%!` syntax instead of `<%` we can ensure that embedded Java code goes outside this method, defining methods, variables, and classes in the generated class itself.

JSP is very powerful, but its power creates as much danger as benefit. JSP lets us do anything we might legitimately want to do in a view, and a lot of things that we're best not to attempt. Since its initial release, JSP has gained new capabilities: most significantly, the addition of **custom tags**, which enable Java helper code to be concealed behind markup. However, the basic model hasn't changed, and nor has the fact that JSP pages are excellent at displaying data, and ill-suited to request processing and initiating business logic.

Striking a Balance

Both the approaches discussed so far – servlet-only and JSP Model 1 – have severe disadvantages and make it impossible to achieve separation of responsibility between Java developer and markup developer roles. Such separation is essential on complex web sites.

However, by using the two technologies together – servlets to handle control flow, and JSP pages or another view technology to render content – we can avoid the problems I've described.

A so-called JSP **Model 2** architecture introduces a controller servlet as the central entry point, rather than individual JSP pages. The controller is responsible for request processing, and chooses a JSP to render content depending on request parameters and the result of the necessary business operations. In fact, as we'll see, there are many refinements to this model: it's important to avoid having a single "God" servlet, but ensure that the servlet works with a number of sub-controllers.

I won't refer to this as JSP Model 2 architecture, as in fact this architecture isn't dependent on JSP: it works with any templating technology. Its basis is servlets – by far the more important of J2EE web technologies. I'll use the term **Front Controller** pattern, which is used by *Core J2EE Patterns*. This is an attempt to apply the MVC architectural pattern (which we'll discuss further below) to web applications.

This pattern, which we'll discuss in detail below, is the key to designing maintainable J2EE web applications, and the central point of this chapter.

> **Both servlets and view technologies (such as JSP) are required for building maintainable J2EE web applications. Servlets and helper classes should be used to handle control flow and initiate business operations; JSP should only be used to render content.**

Web-Tier Design Goals

Enough negatives: what features should a *good* web interface have? The following two goals are central to maintainability and extensibility.

A Clean Web Tier

As JSP Model 1 experience shows, a web application is doomed to failure if markup generation is inextricably mixed with control flow and business object invocations.

> **A clean web tier separates control flow and the invocation of business objects (handled by Java objects) from presentation (handled by view components such as JSP pages).**

Java classes should be used to control flow and initiate business logic. Java classes *should not* be used to generate markup. It should be possible to change presentation markup without modifying Java classes. JSP pages – or whatever templates are used – will contain only markup and simple presentation logic. This permits an almost complete separation of Java developer and markup author roles.

A Thin Web Tier

However, achieving a clean web tier is not enough. It's also vital to ensure that the web tier is as *thin* as possible. This means that the web tier should contain no more Java code than is necessary to initiate business processing from user actions, and display the results. It means that the web tier should contain only web-specific control logic (such as the choice of the layout data should be displayed in) and not business logic (such as data retrieval).

Why is this so important? Applications in which business logic is tied to the webtier – even web tier Java objects such as servlets, rather than JSP pages – fail to meet the goals we identified in Chapter 1. Such applications:

❑ Are hard to test – a very important consideration. Testing web interfaces is much harder than testing ordinary Java objects. If we expose business objects as JavaBeans implementing well-defined interfaces, we can easily write test harnesses that test business logic in isolation from any user interface. In applications in which business objects expose well-defined interfaces, testing the web interface is a comparatively simple problem of checking that the interface correctly translates user actions into the correct business requests and correctly displays the results. If an application's web tier *contains* business logic, we can only test the business logic through testing the web interface as a whole, which is likely to be much harder.

❑ Reduce potential to reuse business logic code, even within the same web application. Code in a servlet's `service()` method, for example, won't be available even to other servlets.

❑ Are likely to prove vulnerable to changes in web interface workflow (although not necessarily to changes in presentation). If we have a distinct layer of business interfaces, we can easily run regression tests at any time. If some of our business logic is in the web tier, it's likely that changing the workflow will introduce bugs. Tests against the web interface will need to be rewritten to reflect the changed workflow, making testing the new workflow problematic.

❑ Aren't pluggable. If we expose business operations in a layer of business interfaces, we can easily change the implementing class of one or more business objects without affecting calling code (assuming we have a framework that facilitates interface-based design, like the one I discussed last chapter). If business operations are tied to the web tier, there's unlikely to be such a straightforward way to change implementation.

❑ Make it hard to expose an interface other than a web GUI, such as a web services interface.

> **In a well-designed J2EE application, the web tier should be a thin layer built on well-defined business interfaces. It should be responsible only for translating user actions into application events, and the results of processing user input into results displayable by the web interface.**
>
> **This point deserves to be emphasized. Although a thin web tier is as important as a clean web tier, the relationship between web tier and business objects seems to get far less attention than the MVC approach to ensuring a clean web tier.**

MVC Concepts and the Front Controller J2EE Pattern

Let's look in more detail at what it means to adopt an MVC approach to web applications. In this section we'll consider theory and general principles. In the next section we'll look at some real MVC web frameworks that simplify the implementation of applications using an MVC approach.

Concepts

Let's start by looking at basic MVC concepts.

The MVC Triad

The MVC approach divides components into three kinds of object: **model** data objects; **view** objects that present model data on screen; and **controller** objects that react to user input, updating models appropriately.

In a true MVC architecture, such as that of Java's Swing GUI libraries, each view registers with a model, which publishes events when its data is updated. Consider the Swing `JList` component. This simple view component displays items in a list and allows item selection. The list data is defined in an object implementing the `ListModel` interface, which publishes `ListDataEvents` when the data changes. The `JList` view component provides a `ListDataListener` implementation that registers with the `ListModel` and updates the display as events are received. This is a **push** model: the model *pushes* notifications to any number of listeners, which are typically (but not necessarily) views.

As changes in a web application are usually only displayed to the user when a request is received and a new page is generated, the push model doesn't work. Hence a web application view will only render once. It won't help to register it to receive ongoing notifications. The solution is to use a **pull** model, in which a view is given access to the models required to render a dynamic page, and the view pulls data from the model as necessary. Since a web page may contain different controls and sections of dynamic data, more than one model may be required to back it.

Whether we use a push or pull model, the MVC architecture still delivers its key benefits. Each component type has a clear responsibility. Models contain no view-specific code. Views contain no control code or data-access code and concentrate on displaying data. Controllers create and update models; they do not depend on particular view implementations.

Although the MVC approach has the potential to improve web-tier code tremendously, it is a little complex to set up. Thus we will generally use a generic MVC web application framework, rather than implement the pattern ourselves.

Controller

As the controller is central to MVC in a web application, let's consider the controller first.

The key responsibilities of a web application controller are:

❑ **To examine and extract request parameters**
This may lead to the creation of command domain objects, which will be passed to business objects. An MVC framework usually provides infrastructure that simplifies working with request parameters: for example, by populating JavaBeans with parameter values.

❑ **To invoke business objects, passing the data extracted from the request**
Controllers will usually catch application exceptions resulting from business method invocations, modifying model creation, and view selection accordingly. (However, some fatal exceptions can simply be left to be handled by the web container, as web applications have a standard "error page" mechanism.)

❏ **To create the model that views will display based on the results of invoking business methods and any session state**

❏ **In applications with server-side state, to create and manipulate session state**

❏ **To choose a view and cause it to render, making the model data available to it**

Other responsibilities may include generating web-tier log output and enforcing security restrictions (although security can also be handled declaratively in J2EE, as we saw in Chapter 6).

As these responsibilities are a mixture of application functionality (such as invoking application-specific business objects) and plumbing (such as passing model data to a named view and causing it to render content), they are usually split between application-specific and generic framework classes when using an MVC web application framework.

It's vital that controller objects have easy access to application business objects. Neither model nor view objects should require such access.

Model

A model contains data displayed by a view. In the J2EE web application, the model normally consists of JavaBeans. Many view technologies, including JSP, work best if models are JavaBeans. Models in web applications (as opposed to "true," traditional MVC) are usually dumb storage objects, such as value objects, that represent the result of a complete business operation. Once a controller completes its processing and selects a view to generate content, the model should contain all the data to display. The model itself should not perform any further data access, and it should not contact business objects. There is no reason for a model to depend on the Servlet API or a web application framework; JavaBeans used as part of a model need not be web-specific. They will often be domain objects, usable outside the web tier.

In the JSP paradigm, models are added to the request as attributes using the `request.setAttribute()` method. However, this isn't the only way to communicate a model to a view; not all views may find request attributes useful.

View

A view displays the information contained in a model, taking entire responsibility for markup or other content generation. A view needn't know anything about the implementation of the controller or the underlying business objects.

JSP is the most used view technology for J2EE applications, although, as we'll see in the next chapter, there are several valid alternatives. We've noted that JSP gives us the power to do things that are inappropriate in views. The following guidelines indicate what operations *are* appropriate in views:

❏ A view should be wholly responsible for generating web content, given data models.

❏ A view should not work directly with request parameters. A controller should intercept incoming requests, and provide the view with models.

❑ A view should not perform data retrieval (for example, by running SQL queries). The view should merely display data, which will be exposed by one or more models. The **Dispatcher View** J2EE Pattern (*Core J2EE Patterns*) in which a JSP view retrieves data using a helper as it renders, is fundamentally broken, as it is vulnerable to unexpected errors during rendering. *Core J2EE Patterns* terms the controller-managed data retrieval described here the **Service-to-Worker** pattern. (No, I don't understand how they thought up these names, either.)

❑ A view may need to perform **display logic**, as distinct from control logic or business logic. Examples of display logic include displaying the rows of a table in alternate colors, or displaying additional information on a generated page if the model contains optional data. Such logic does not belong in controllers, as it's unique to a particular presentation.

❑ A view should not have to deal with data-retrieval failures. In practice, this means that properties and methods exposed by models should not throw exceptions; data retrieval should be complete before a view begins to render

Last, and most importantly:

> It should be possible to replace any view in a web application with another that displays the same data without modifying model or controller code. A view should be thought of as meeting a contract: "Display this kind of data." It should be possible to substitute any view for another without affecting the working of the application. This is *the* key to ensuring that presentation can be updated without affecting workflow.
>
> It should be possible even to replace a view with another that uses a different view technology without affecting controller or model code. For example, it should be possible to replace a JSP view with an XSLT view.
>
> Many think that view substitutability is impossible – or prohibitively difficult – to achieve in practice. I believe otherwise, and in this chapter and the next chapter will demonstrate how it can be achieved, and the benefits it brings.

Of course, unless a view contains the correct links or form fields, it may be impossible to continue using the application. But this is a question of displaying available information, not control logic.

Giving view components such limited and clearly defined responsibilities is the best way to ensure the separation between the roles of Java developers and markup (presentation) developers that is essential on large web sites.

It also has great benefits for testing. If we know that our views merely pull data from a model supplied by a controller, we can change presentation by modifying views without any risk of breaking the behavior of our application. Testing can be limited to checking that the modified view contains no syntax errors, and displays the correct content.

Unit and regression tests will be written for controller components, to check that they initiate the correct business logic operations and expose the correct models. It's much easier to write unit tests and regression tests for Java classes than for JSP pages or other rendering technologies, so this works well. If, on the other hand, our "views" perform data retrieval, we will need to perform regression testing when we change presentation.

Control Flow

To illustrate these concepts in action, let's consider a possible flow of control in a simple MVC implementation. (Real MVC web application frameworks are a bit more refined, as we'll see.) Imagine that the request is to book several seats of a particular type for a performance of a show. Our sample application uses a more sophisticated workflow for this – the following is a stripped down example:

1. A controller servlet receives a request. There is a mapping from the request URL to controller servlet in the application's web.xml deployment descriptor.

2. The controller servlet examines the request parameters. The performanceId, seatTypeId, and count parameters are required. If any of these is missing or non-numeric, the user should be sent back to the welcome view, welcome.jsp.

3. With valid data from request parameters, the servlet invokes an allocateSeats() method on a business object that it obtains and stores as an instance variable on application startup.

4. If the attempted booking succeeds, the servlet adds the returned array of Seat objects (the model) to the HttpServletRequest as an attribute and forwards the request to the view displayReservation.jsp. If there aren't enough seats, the servlet adds the exception containing this information to the HttpServletRequest and forwards the request to the view retryBooking.jsp.

This simplified workflow indicates how one type of request (usually a request to a particular URL) can lead to multiple views, and how views need only render content after data retrieval is complete.

The following diagram illustrates the workflow described in the text:

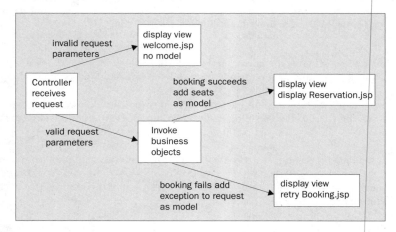

Pattern Variants

There are many variants of front controller implementation. Let's consider some of them before we move on to discuss real MVC frameworks.

Template Selection Servlet

The simplest front controller approach is to use what I'll call a **template selection servlet** to handle incoming requests. Each template selection servlet will process request parameters, invoke the appropriate business objects and conclude by choosing a template and making model data available to it (pretty much the same workflow as in our simple walkthrough above).

As an illustration of this approach, let's look at a popular implementation. The WebMacro template solution, which we'll discuss in more detail in the next chapter, provides a convenient generic superclass, `org.webmacro.servlet.WMServlet`, for template selection servlets using WebMacro templates as views.

Application-specific subclasses of `WMServlet` need to implement the following method to process the request, initiate the necessary business operations, make model data available to WebMacro, and return the selected WebMacro Template to generate content. The request and response objects are available via the `WebContext` argument:

```
public Template handle(WebContext context) throws HandlerException
```

To use this approach, each request URL in our application must be mapped to a separate template servlet in `web.xml`. On the positive side, this means there's no need for a framework-specific approach to map request URLs to handlers. On the negative side, mapping in `web.xml` is verbose, and we'll need to define a new template servlet instance for each URL.

> *Note that we can apply this approach very easily using JSP as the templating technology; each servlet can simply use a `RequestDispatcher` object to dispatch to the appropriate JSP. There is no need for the kind of infrastructure provided by the `WMServlet` class.*

This is a simple, effective approach, and a big advance on a servlet-only or JSP Model 1 strategy. However, it fails to deliver all of the goals we have set ourselves, and I don't recommend it. In particular:

- ❑ Controllers (in this approach, implemented as template selection servlets) are dependent on a particular view technology. We're out of luck if we decide, for example, to change from WebMacro to XSLT or PDF views. This may prove a serious problem, for example, if we need to generate binary output.

- ❑ We must work with request parameters directly. There's no overall framework providing a higher-level workflow than the Servlet API.

- ❑ There's no application framework to help us achieve a thin web tier.

How Many Controller Servlets?

There is a debate among MVC proponents about how many controller servlets an application should have. Should we use one servlet for each type of request (as in the template selection servlet approach), or a single front controller that handles all requests to an application or subsystem? *Core J2EE Patterns* terms the latter approach the **Multiplexed Resource Mapping Strategy**. If we use a single front controller, it should be generic, and should forward requests to a number of sub-controllers.

Many of the arguments against using a single controller servlet are unsound – such as the idea that it introduces a single point of failure (threads can die, not objects); or that it means that the controller will be too large (we can use a generic controller with many application-specific delegates, rather than one huge, all-knowing controller). One valid criticism is the need to duplicate the standard mapping of URL to request-handling class. While we can map URLs directly onto servlets in web.xml, when we use one controller to front many URLs we will usually map all URLs onto the controller, which must then use its own mapping format to route URLs among its sub-controllers. However, this isn't a real problem in practice.

The advantages of using a single controller include that it ensures consistency of control flow – for example, ensuring that necessary resources are available to all sub-controllers. It also means that each sub-controller doesn't have to be a servlet; an important point as we can allow sub-controllers to implement a less complex interface.

It's natural to ask what the performance implications are of the additional overhead in funneling requests through a single controller. A typical controller servlet implementation will need to do hash table lookups based on the URL of each request. Some frameworks use reflection (although an efficient framework should cache the results of reflection). Fortunately, the performance impact is negligible. Pretty much anything we do *once per request* will have no measurable effect on the overall performance of a web application. In profiling applications running in MVC frameworks, I've consistently found the framework overhead to be insignificant – even undetectable.

All the real frameworks I know of use a single controller servlet for a whole application or a set of related use cases. The controller servlet then delegates work to helper classes that implement a framework-specific interface or extend a base class provided by the framework.

JSP or Servlet Controller?

Another key question is whether the controller should be a servlet or JSP. *Core J2EE Patterns* terms these the **Servlet Front** and **JSP Front** strategies respectively, and some Sun examples show the use of a JSP as a controller. (I was guilty of such a sample application myself in my first publication on JSP.)

The JSP Front approach is naïve and misguided, and does not deserve to be dignified as a "strategy". JSP pages are poorly suited for use as controllers, for many reasons. For example, they are not first rate Java classes. (We can't subclass a JSP if we want to customize its behavior, for example.) They also don't foster code reuse.

The only argument in favor of using JSP controllers is that they're a little easier to implement, as we sidestep web.xml servlet mappings: a tiny saving that isn't worth compromising an architecture for.

Servlets are essential in J2EE web applications; JSP is one option for views. It's illogical to try to use JSP pages to perform a role that uses none of their strengths and displays many of their weaknesses, especially as Java classes are very good at this type of control flow.

> **Do not use JSP pages as controllers. The purpose of JSP is to generate markup, not handle control flow.**

Should a Request Cause the Creation of a Command?

A common approach is for a request to result in the generation of a **Command object**: a business object containing data associated with the request, but not dependent on the Servlet API. This approach has the following advantages:

- ❏ We can enjoy the advantages of the Command design pattern, such as the ability to queue, log, and possibly undo commands.

- ❏ We may be able to use transparent data binding from request to command bean properties. This may free application code from the need to handle request parameters.

- ❏ The command is not dependent on the Servlet API, so can be passed to business objects. This promotes clean interaction between servlets and business objects.

- ❏ The command approach works well with the Observer design pattern; it's easy to publish events on receipt of commands.

The disadvantages are that a command approach may be overkill in simple cases. For example, if a request has no parameters associated with it, creating an "empty" command to represent it doesn't make sense.

> **A command should be generated on receipt of a request if data binding (discussed later in this chapter) will prove useful – for example, if there are many request parameters – or if there's a real business value in using the Command design pattern. In the latter case, the use of the Command design pattern should be driven by the relevant business interfaces; it is for business objects, not web interface, to determine the design patterns that will be used in intra-application communication.**

Implementation Goals

Using a web application framework should simplify application code and promote clean interaction between web interface components and business objects.

A web application framework should allow the use of any view technology, without the need to modify controller code. For example, it should be possible to use XSLT stylesheets instead of JSP pages without changing any Java code.

> **There's a lot of fear about MVC. In particular, developers often think that MVC approaches add complexity, compared with JSP-centric solutions, and that MVC solutions run slower. The first fear is plain wrong; the second is irrelevant in real applications.**

Using an MVC framework, the result should be *simpler* code that's easier to write and debug, in all but trivial applications. A good MVC framework should reduce the amount of code you need to write, and simplify application code. Even if you write your own framework (which you shouldn't need to), MVC frameworks aren't particularly complex to implement.

MVC applications do a little more work than JSP-centric solutions, but this is usually limited to a couple of hash table lookups, concealed within the framework, which won't produce any detectable change in application performance. Any successful MVC framework will be efficient.

> *Using an MVC framework may even improve performance, by giving us the opportunity to use view technologies that may perform better than JSP in a particular situation. In Chapter 15 we'll see that JSP isn't necessarily the fastest way to render content.*

Web Application Frameworks

As the MVC Front Controller pattern is almost universally advocated, there are several implementations available.

> *Although it's by far the most popular, MVC isn't the only way to structure web applications. Some products, such as the Tapestry framework (see the overview at http://tapestry.sourceforge.net/doc/api/overview-summary.html), take a different approach to solving the problems that the MVC patterns addresses. However, none has been widely adopted, so I won't discuss them here.*

Although it's not particularly difficult to implement a controller framework, you're unlikely to have any reason to. Let's move from pattern theory to practice, looking first at what real frameworks do and then at some implementations.

Common Concepts

Most MVC web application frameworks use the following concepts:

❑   A single generic controller servlet for a whole application or part of an application. All application URLs are mapped in the standard web.xml deployment descriptor onto the framework's controller servlet.

❑ Proprietary mappings (often defined in an XML file) that enable the controller servlet to choose a delegate to handle each request. Such mappings are also usually based on request URL. Delegates will implement a framework-specific API. I'll refer to such delegates as **request controllers** below: the controller servlet is effectively a meta-controller.

❑ What I call the **named view** strategy. Views are identified by name, enabling request controllers to specify view names, rather than view implementations when selecting a view. Framework infrastructure will resolve view names. This decouples view implementation and controller. The implementation of a view with a particular name can change without affecting controller code.

Many frameworks add the role of **command** (discussed above) to those of model, view, and controller. However, these four roles are not necessarily played by separate objects. In Struts and the application framework used for the sample application, the four roles are usually separate, with controllers reused throughout the application lifecycle. In WebWork and Maverick, command, controller, and model are normally the same object, created to handle a single request.

> **Choosing a web application framework is a second order issue, compared with committing to an MVC approach: even a poor MVC implementation will do a much better job of separating presentation and business logic than a clever JSP Model 1 implementation. Alternative frameworks share so many common concepts that, having learned one, it's fairly easy to work with others.**
>
> **Remember that the web tier should be thin. The code that uses a framework shouldn't be complex. If much application code depends on a particular framework, the framework is poorly designed or is being used incorrectly.**

Available Frameworks

In this section, I'll briefly survey some leading MVC frameworks.

Struts

The most widely adopted MVC framework is the open source Apache Struts (http://jakarta.apache.org/struts/). Struts was originally written by Craig McClanahan, the main developer of the Tomcat servlet engine, and was released in mid 2000, making it the longest-established open source web application framework. Partly because of its relatively long history, Struts has achieved remarkable buy-in by developers, with many add-ons now available around it. At the time of writing, Struts version 1.1 is in late beta. Hence I'll discuss the capabilities of both version 1.0 and 1.1, but concentrate on 1.1, which contains significant enhancements and should be used in any new projects using Struts.

There are several books and many online articles devoted to Struts, for example *Java Web Development With Struts* from Manning (ISBN: 1-930110-50-2) so I won't describe it in detail here, but will merely survey how it approaches the concepts we've discussed.

Struts uses a single controller servlet for a whole web application or subset of a web application. Struts 1.0 only allows one controller servlet per application – a serious limitation as it means that the single controller's configuration file will become unmanageably large. Struts 1.1 allows multiple controllers, each with its own configuration file. A Struts controller is of the concrete framework class org.apache.struts.action.ActionServlet. The standard controller servlet is responsible for handling all incoming requests, and is configured by the /WEB-INF/struts-config.xml file. (As I noted above, many frameworks use XML for their configuration.)

As in most frameworks, the controller servlet is generic. It doesn't contain application-specific code, and it isn't usually necessary to subclass it (at least in Struts 1.1; subclassing was often necessary in Struts 1.0). The controller uses its mapping information to choose an **action** that can handle each request. A Struts action extends the org.apache.struts.action.Action class. The most important method is the following, invoked on each request:

```
public ActionForward execute(ActionMapping mapping,
        ActionForm form,
        HttpServletRequest request,
        HttpServletResponse response)
    throws Exception;
```

> *This method was named* perform() *in Struts 1.0;* perform() *is deprecated as of Struts 1.1.*

A Struts action must be threadsafe: as actions essentially extend the functionality of the controller servlet, the threading issues are exactly the same as in coding a servlet.

Struts documentation advises that actions shouldn't include business logic but "should invoke another object, usually a JavaBean, to perform the actual business logic. This lets the action focus on error handling and control flow, rather than business logic." However, Struts does not provide infrastructure for managing business objects and exposing them to web-tier actions.

The two Struts-specific parameters to the action execute() method (the ActionMapping and ActionForm parameters) convey the core Struts functionality, so let's look at them in more detail.

The ActionMapping parameter contains information about the mapping from the request to the ActionForm instance: most importantly, the definition of "forwards" which enables the ActionForm to return a named view at run time.

The ActionForm parameter is a bean that extends the org.apache.struts.action.ActionForm class to expose bean properties corresponding to request parameters. ActionForm beans are automatically populated by Struts from request parameters. Struts uses the Apache Commons beans manipulation package, which has similar goals to the com.interface21.beans package I discussed in the last chapter. However, the Commons bean package is less sophisticated and, in particular, lacks good error handling.

Struts `ActionForms` have several peculiarities that we must consider. As all `ActionForms` must extend the Struts superclass, they all depend on Struts and the Servlet API. This means that they can't be passed to business objects, as business objects shouldn't depend on a particular web application framework or the Servlet API. Secondly, any request parameters that may contain invalid data (such as numeric inputs, for which the user might enter non-numeric data) must be matched by `ActionForm` properties of type `String`. The bean manipulation code behind the scenes will attempt to convert string request parameters to the appropriate type, but any exceptions in attempting to set properties will result in the `org.apache.struts.util.RequestUtils` class failing the request by throwing a `ServletException`.

Thus a Struts `ActionForm` is not a true domain object. It's a place to hold user data until it can be validated and transferred into domain objects such as commands. The advantage of this approach is that invalid data can be re-displayed easily; the disadvantage is that we will need to get this data into true domain objects at some point, so Struts has only taken us part of the way towards true data binding.

The need to derive `ApplicationForms` from a single superclass has always seemed to me a design flaw. Not only does it tie commands to the Struts framework and Servlet API, it incorrectly exposes inherited framework properties to update via data binding from request parameters. For example, adding a `servlet` parameter with a string value will break just about any page generated by a Struts 1.0 application (with a failure to set a property of type `ActionServlet` to a string). Struts 1.1 introduces a workaround for this particular problem, but the root of the problem is the whole `ActionForm` concept.

The `ActionForm` class also defines a `validate()` method with the following signature:

```
public ActionErrors validate(ActionMapping mapping,
                             HttpServletRequest request);
```

Subclasses may override this method to validate the state of an action form after population from request parameters. Struts also offers alternative approaches to validation. We'll discuss validation in general, and the Struts approach to validation, in detail later in this chapter.

> In the Struts model a standard controller servlet (the Struts **ActionServlet**) delegates to a number of **Action** objects. Each **Action** object is given as a parameter an **ActionForm** object, which contains JavaBean properties pre-populated from the request using reflection. As **ActionForm** objects are tied the Struts framework, they cannot be used as commands in an application. Each **Action** object is responsible for initiating the business operations required to handle the request. After processing is complete, each action should return a mapped view or "action forward".

Struts also comes with several JSP tag libraries to handle data binding and other operations. Note that some of these tag libraries are superseded by the new **JSP Standard Tag Library (JSTL)**, discussed in the next chapter.

The key Struts tag libraries are:

❑ **Bean**

Miscellaneous tags that perform tasks such as: exposing a cookie value as a request variable; defining scripting variables based on header values, request parameters, and bean properties; and invoking another resource within the application and saving the generated output to a string.

❑ **HTML**

Tags that help build forms for submission to Struts actions. These tags can use a backing bean value to populate form fields, simplifying JSP code. The tags in this library, such as `<html:text>`, are used in place of HTML input tags: the custom tags expose all the necessary attributes and generate the required HTML. While custom tags are essential to populate some HTML controls such as dropdowns and radio buttons, using Struts controls in place of normal HTML controls can make the HTML harder to understand and more difficult to edit with a GUI tool. I prefer an approach in which tags provide data values, but don't generate markup.

❑ **Logic**

Conditional tags enabling comparisons and iteration without using scriptlets. JSTL tags are likely to supersede some of these tags.

❑ **Template**

Tags to establish a common layout that can be parameterized by specifying the content in each section.

*Note that all Struts tags enable access to **nested properties**. For example, the property path* `spouse.age` *passed to a tag will cause an evaluation of* `getSpouse().getAge()`. *The JSTL Expression Language, discussed in the next chapter, removes the need for such support in web application frameworks.*

There are also various add-on tag libraries available, although not all the tags depend on the Struts framework itself. The availability of a range of associated tag libraries is a major reason for Struts' success.

Despite its popularity, I'm not a big fan of Struts. It's good enough, but far from an ideal J2EE web application framework:

❑ The `ActionForm` approach – central to the Struts request processing model – is poor. Bean binding is primitive, meaning that only string properties are really useful. This adds little value over simply querying request parameters. The idea of copying properties from an action form to a business command is inelegant and there's no support for type checking.

❑ Struts is too JSP-oriented, although it is possible to use Struts with other templating technologies.

❑ Struts is based almost entirely on concrete classes. This makes it hard to customize Struts' behavior.

❑ Although things have improved significantly with version 1.1, the Struts codebase is poor. Not surprisingly, there have been numerous deprecations in moving to 1.1.

Struts 1.1 corrects many (but not all) of the shortcomings of Struts 1.0: for example, by allowing the use of multiple controller servlets in an application. (The mechanism for this isn't very elegant, however – it's clear that it was an afterthought.) Other enhancements in Struts 1.1 include the introduction of the `org.apache.struts.actions.DispatchAction` superclass, allowing several actions to be performed by the same class. This is very useful in cases where many request types call for simple handling; it avoids the proliferation of many trivial action classes. We'll discuss this concept further below. Struts 1.1 also introduces **declarative exception handling**: another concept discussed later.

Maverick

Another open source framework is Maverick (http://mav.sourceforge.net), which concentrates on delivering MVC workflow, and doesn't provide presentation support such as tag libraries (the name is a play on MVC). One of the two main Maverick developers, Jeff Schnitzer, is also the author of the JUnitEE test framework, which we discussed in Chapter 3. Maverick is presently in version 2.1, which is discussed here. Version 2.0 was a major revision of the original model. Maverick version 1.0 was released in mid 2001.

Like Struts and most other frameworks, Maverick uses a single controller servlet as the entry point. A Maverick controller servlet is of class `org.infohazard.maverick.Dispatcher`. All application URLs are mapped onto this servlet in `web.xml`. The controller servlet takes its configuration from the Maverick-specific `/WEB-INF/maverick.xml` config file. Maverick currently allows only a single controller servlet – and hence, configuration file – per web application. As with Struts 1.0, this can make configuration hard to manage in large applications.

> *It's difficult to provide a brief overview of Maverick, as Maverick is highly configurable (much more so than Struts). The basic workflow can be customized by the user, and Maverick provides several standard classes that web-tier application classes can extend to provide different workflows. The following discussion describes the model offered by Maverick 1.0, and which still appears to be advocated in Maverick 2.0, judging by its use in the "FriendBook" sample application. This model is based on the use of "throwaway" controllers.*

Maverick differs from Struts in that a Maverick request controller is usually a JavaBean. In this model, a new "throwaway" controller instance is created to handle each request. (However, Maverick 2.x also supports reusable controllers, as used by Struts.) In this model, Maverick does not separate between controller (analogous to a Struts action) and command (analogous to a Struts `ActionForm`). This has the advantage that each new controller doesn't need to be threadsafe – it doesn't need to support concurrent invocation. However, it creates a proliferation of controller instances.

A request is handled as follows:

❑ A new `org.infohazard.maverick.flow.Controller` object is created using reflection (the controller must have a no-arg constructor). An application controller normally extends the `org.infohazard.maverick.ctl.ThrowawayBean2` superclass provided by the Maverick framework.

❑ Bean properties are set on the controller from request parameters using reflection, by the `org.infohazard.maverick.ctl.ThrowawayBean2` superclass. The controller bean itself can validate properties that are successfully set; a fatal `ServletException` will result on any type mismatches (meaning that we need to stick with string properties as with Struts `ActionForms` to guarantee a chance to validate all input). Bean properties population is performed using the same Apache Commons `BeanUtil` package used by Struts, although it is possible to use Maverick with alternative bean population strategies.

❑ The protected `perform()` method defined by the `org.infohazard.maverick.ctl.ThrowawayBean2` superclass is invoked, and should return the string name of a view defined in the Maverick configuration file after invoking business objects. Each controller has access to an `org.infohazard.maverick.flow.ControllerContext` object, from which it can obtain the servlet request and response, `ServletContext` and `ServletConfig`. However, a controller's populated bean properties should normally contain most of the data needed by the controller to do its work.

When its processing is complete, a controller must set the model object to be displayed by views by invoking the `setModel()` method on the `ControllerContext` object. Thus the model is restricted to a single object. To return multiple objects, it's necessary to define a container object that includes all necessary data. The `org.infohazard.maverick.ctl.ThrowawayBean2` superclass returns itself as the model, combining two more of the four object roles we discussed earlier.

Each named view must implement the `org.infohazard.maverick.flow.View` interface, which provides a view technology-agnostic way of passing model data to any view in a consistent way. View resolution is handled by the `org.infohazard.maverick.flow.Command` class, which invokes controllers. The `View` interface contains the following single method, which must be implemented to render output given model data:

```
public void go(ViewContext vctx) throws ServletException, IOException;
```

The `ViewContext` interface exposes model data via the `getModel()` method (which returns the model object exposed via the controller), and exposes request and response objects.

Standard implementations of the `View` interface provided with Maverick include an implementation that adds the model to the request as an attribute before forwarding to a JSP, and a redirect view that passes model data (converted to string form) to an external URL in a GET query string. There is also support for the WebMacro and Velocity template engines. As the view interface is so simple, custom views can easily be implemented.

Maverick's approach to view substitution is simple and elegant, and I've borrowed the concept in my framework, discussed below. The explicit separation of the model promotes good practice: it discourages the haphazard setting of request attributes to provide a messy, JSP-only model.

Probably Maverick's most interesting concept is the transparent "domification" or conversion of JavaBean data to XML on the fly to support the use of XSLT stylesheets. (Jeff Schnitzer is a vigorous advocate of XSLT, rather than JSP, views). Maverick's domification library is now a separate open source offering. We've already discussed the concept of domification in Chapter 10; this approach is surprisingly effective in practice. Maverick also supports a configurable "pipeline" of transformations, which can be useful with XSLT but is less relevant to other view technologies.

Another interesting feature is the use of simple basic dispatcher functionality, on which different workflows can be grafted by extending a variety of superclasses provided with the framework. This allows Maverick to support a wide range of idioms without the need to subclass the controller servlet.

On the negative side, the lack of separation between command and controller in the "throwaway controller" model is a different approach leading to the same problem that Struts action forms encounter: the command is dependent on the Servlet and Maverick APIs. This means that it's difficult to achieve a clean separation between web tier and business interface. For example, we can't validate command data without depending on the Maverick API, making it hard to implement validation that isn't web-specific. The creation of a new controller instance to handle each request also makes it hard to parameterize controllers; a single reusable object can expose as many configuration properties as required to be set *once* only.

> **Maverick is a capable alternative to Struts. Maverick is typically used to create a new controller to handle each request (although Maverick supports other models). Controllers are JavaBeans, and the framework transparently sets bean properties behind the scenes. Maverick is relatively easy to use (although the Maverick 2.x model is much more complex than Maverick 1.0), and has built-in support for transparent generation of XML nodes from JavaBean model.**

WebWork

A more recent framework is WebWork, another open source offering, designed by distinguished J2EE developer Rickard Oberg, who has contributed to JBoss and other projects. WebWork 1.0 (the version discussed here) was released in mid 2002 (http://opensymphony.com/webwork/)

WebWork, despite its name, isn't purely a web application framework. It adopts a clever approach that minimizes the dependency of application code on web concepts.

WebWork is based on the Command design pattern. Unlike a Struts action, which is a reusable, threadsafe object analogous to a servlet, a WebWork action is a command, created to handle a specific request (the same basic approach as in Maverick). An action is a JavaBean, enabling its properties to be set automatically. A WebWork action must implement the `webwork.action.Action` interface, which contains the following method:

```
public String execute() throws Exception;
```

The implicit inputs are the state of the action's bean properties. The return value is a string representing the result – usually the name of the view that should be used to render output. The data outputs (the model) are the state of action bean properties after the `execute()` method has been called. Thus WebWork combines the role of command, controller, and model in each action object.

Control flow works as follows:

❑ Incoming requests are handled by the main dispatcher servlet, `webwork.dispatcher.ServletDispatcher` (note that this isn't the only way of invoking WebWork actions: different control flows are possible).

❑ A new action instance is created. It's possible to implement and set a custom "action factory" to create actions. The default factory uses `Class.newInstance()`.

❑ The command's bean properties are populated. In a web application, this population will occur from request parameters; however, the basic approach should work with any interface. (The way in which this is done is rather complicated, through a chain of `ActionFactory` implementations. The `webwork.action.factory.ParametersActionFactoryProxy` handles bean property setting.) Type mismatches during property setting can be recorded by WebWork for redisplay; this ability to save such exceptions is a significant improvement on the relatively primitive bean property population of Struts and Maverick.

❑ The command's "context" is set. A WebWork context – of type `webwork.action.ActionContext` – is associated with the current thread. In a web interface, an action can access request parameters and `ServletContext` through its context. However, this is discouraged as it means that such actions can only be used in a web interface. Thus WebWork actions are not necessarily dependent on the Servlet API (although the `ActionContext` class is – it would have been better to make only a web-specific subclass of `ActionContext` dependent on the Servlet API). An action doesn't need to know its context, although it can find it by invoking the static `webwork.action.ActionContext.getContext()` method. The way in which a context is provided at invocation time is analogous to the provision of context objects to EJB instances.

❑ The action's `execute()` method is invoked. Any exception thrown will be treated as a system exception (resulting in a `ServletException`), except for the special case of `webwork.action.ResultException`, which seems intended to provide an alternative return value.

❑ The return value of the `execute()` method is the name of a view that will render the result. The action is made available to the view, for which it provides the model.

Like Struts, WebWork comes with its own JSP tag libraries. However, it's less closely tied to JSP than Struts. There's also support for the Velocity template engine (discussed in the next chapter), and WebWork offers an equivalent to Maverick's XML domification functionality.

WebWork is more elegantly designed and implemented than Struts. Its workflow is more similar to that of Maverick. The `ActionContext` idea is original and clever. WebWork helps to minimize dependence of application code on the Servlet API and provides more incentive towards good design. However, its negatives include:

❑ The creation of an action on *every* request may be overkill, when there isn't a lot of request data. As with Maverick, it's harder to configure many new actions than one reusable action. It also may be harder for new objects to access business objects.

❑ WebWork imposes the Command design pattern on every user interaction, whether or not it's appropriate.

❑ Exception handling faces one of the classic problems of the Command design pattern: we don't know what types of exception a particular command may throw. Thus the `execute()` method is forced to throw `Exception`.

❑ The separation of action from web-tier concepts may not always be realistic or worthwhile. Imposing an abstraction based on the request-response web paradigm unduly constrains the more sophisticated interaction possible with traditional GUIs such as Swing.

The WebWork framework is based on the Command design pattern, resulting in a basic model more similar to that of Maverick than Struts. WebWork tries to model user actions as interface-agnostic commands, without dependency on the Servlet API.

Integrating a Web Application Framework into Overall Application Architecture

Any good web application framework will help us achieve our first goal – a clean web tier. However, this doesn't guarantee that we achieve the second goal – a *thin* web tier.

All three frameworks we've discussed enable us to clean up the web tier, separating presentation and content. However, none gives us much help in integrating our web tier with well-designed architecture.

WebWork helps us to create interface-agnostic commands; however, it doesn't provide an infrastructure to enable these commands to invoke business objects in a standard way.

Struts enables custom "plug-ins" to be defined in `struts-config.xml` files, as a way of enabling Struts web components to access other application objects. Plug-ins are configuration wrappers for user-specific application components, and must implement the `org.apache.struts.action.PlugIn` interface. Struts plug-ins can expose simple bean properties, which can be populated from elements in the `struts-config.xml` file, as in the following example from the Struts 1.1 sample application:

```
<plug-in
  className="org.apache.struts.webapp.example.memory.MemoryDatabasePlugIn"
>
  <set-property
    property="pathname"
    value="/WEB-INF/database.xml"/>
</plug-in>
```

Population is performed by the Struts Digester. Plug-ins normally set themselves as attributes on the global `ServletContext` to allow action implementations to access them. However, this is a much less capable and less general approach than the bean-based configuration approach we discussed in the last chapter:

❑ It's impossible to build a graph of application objects that depend on each other, as only primitive properties, not object references, are supported

❑ The only way to define business objects is in the Struts XML configuration file

❑ Plug-in implementations are tied to the Struts API

❑ The configuration of business objects is dependent on the web framework – a problem if we want to implement a different kind of interface

The Java Pet Store sample application (version 1.3), which includes its own web application framework, makes one of the most determined attempts I've seen at achieving a thin web tier, by formalizing the creation of events and the invocation of a centralized event processor (which must implement the `com.sun.j2ee.blueprints.waf.controller.web.WebClientController` interface).

This has the significant advantage that web-tier application code only creates events or commands representing user actions, and displays the result of business processing; framework code (not web -ier application code) invokes business objects to process the events. Unfortunately, this approach, while interesting in theory, isn't workable for real applications. There's a reason successful web application frameworks don't attempt to enforce such prescriptive workflow: it's inflexible and is inappropriate in many cases.

Thus we need to use a web application framework in conjunction with an overarching application infrastructure, and the more easily the two integrate, the better off we are.

> **Since the web interface should be thin, a web application framework should not provide the center of gravity for an application, imposing overall structure. This is the role of the application's business interfaces. A web application framework should merely make it easy to process user input and display the results, and offer easy – interface-based – integration with business objects.**

It's possible to integrate the bean-based infrastructure I discussed in the last chapter with any web application framework. The root `com.interface21.web.context.WebApplicationContext` object, which defines JavaBeans and their relationships without the need to use the Singleton design pattern, is added to a web application's `ServletContext` by the `com.interface21.web.context.ContextLoaderServlet`, and can thus be accessed by any object with access to the `ServletContext`, which includes controllers in any framework. This will provide a superior alternative to using Singleton business objects, or simple factory objects, in any framework. It's achieves as close integration with the web application framework as do Struts plug-ins, despite the fact that they are defined in the Struts configuration file.

Close integration with Struts could easily be achieved by implementing a generic Struts plug-in that created an `ApplicationContext` object – for example, based on a string parameter specifying the location of an XML bean definition file – and added it to the `ServletContext`. This would enable a Struts configuration file to specify the location of business object bean definitions via a `<plug-in>` element, and Struts actions to access business objects by looking up the `ApplicationContext` in the `ServletContext`.

However, with a powerful JavaBeans-based infrastructure, it's not only possible to achieve closer integration of application objects with web application components: it's possible to configure most of the framework itself within the overall application context, meaning that framework components can be transparently configured in exactly the same way as application objects. Such a beans-based infrastructure simplifies both the implementation and the use of a framework.

The Web Application Framework Used in the Sample Application

Hence, for the sample application, I've chosen to use my own web application framework – more precisely, the most recent of several web application frameworks I have written.

I considered carefully whether to use an existing framework such as Struts or Maverick. However, I decided that integrated application architecture I wanted to demonstrate could not be achieved so successfully with any existing framework and that no existing framework met all the goals I wanted to achieve. However, the beauty of open source is that I was able to borrow some of the best concepts from these products for my own framework.

My experience in developing web application frameworks goes back a long way. I developed my first production web application framework in early 2000 – before Struts or any alternatives were available – and have since refined the concepts. This has given me the freedom, unavailable to the Struts developers, to develop a clean-room implementation based on this experience without concern for backward compatibility. However, it should be noted that my first framework is still in production on several high-volume web sites after two years, and has proven to support maintainable, quality applications.

> **The framework described here is not intended merely as a demo, and is not limited to the sample application. It's ready for production use; feel free to use it in real applications.**

All the source code, some of which is discussed here, is included in the download with this book, in the `/framework` subdirectory.

Design Goals

Starting from the basis of the JavaBeans-based infrastructure we discussed in Chapter 11, implementing a web application framework was surprisingly easy.

I adopted the following design goals:

❑ The framework should be JavaBeans-based and closely integrated with the infrastructure I've described in the previous chapters:

   ❑ All framework objects, such as controllers and views, should themselves be JavaBeans, allowing for easy and consistent configuration (including the configuration of relationships with application objects).

   ❑ All application objects, whether web processing components or business objects, should be JavaBeans, configurable in the same way by the application context, and with access to all other objects in the same application context. This means that framework definitions can be held in a variety of formats if necessary, not just XML.

This approach makes it much easier to implement a thin web tier, and makes it easy to test business objects outside a J2EE server.

❑ The framework should explicitly separate the roles of controller, model, and view and – where applicable – command.

❑ Application code built using the framework should have as little dependence as possible on the Servlet API. For example, while controllers will normally depend on the Servlet API, models should not.

❑ The framework should be extensible, through loose coupling throughout the framework based on the use of interfaces, rather than concrete or abstract classes, and consistent use of JavaBeans. For example:

   ❑ The framework should work easily with any view technology. It should not be JSP-centric.

   ❑ The framework should support any mapping strategy from request to logical resource (including custom mappings). This makes it possible to adopt mapping strategies other than the URL-based mapping strategies most frameworks enforce.

❑ The framework should completely decouple controllers from views, achieving complete view substitutability (the ability to swap one view for another without affecting any application code).

❑ The framework should provide standard view implementations for JSP, XSLT, Velocity, and WebMacro templating technologies, and XMLC (these and other view technologies are discussed in the next chapter). It should be possible to implement support for any view technology easily.

❑ The framework should have a clean, maintainable implementation, meeting the code quality, and OO design standards we discussed in Chapter 4.

❑ The size of the codebase should be kept small by avoiding irrelevant capabilities. Struts, for example, provides a JDBC connection pool. As a connection pool must be provided by a J2EE application server, this is redundant.

❑ The framework should provide a simple MVC implementation, on which different workflows can be layered.

❑ The framework should support internationalization.

❑ The framework should allow the generation of HTTP cache-control headers at an individual page level, to allow for an important performance optimization. None of the frameworks we've discussed allows this. *This important topic is discussed in Chapter 15.*

❑ The framework should provide custom superclasses to simplify the implementation of typical usage patterns.

Basic MVC Control Flow

Let's look at how this framework supports basic MVC control flow.

The control flow is more similar to that of Struts than the other frameworks I've described, although the view management approach is closer to that of Maverick. Incoming requests are handled by a single generic controller servlet, to which all application URLs are mapped in web.xml. This controller servlet uses its own mappings from incoming requests (not necessarily URL-based, although the default mapping is URL-based) to request controller beans defined in the application context. It's possible to have multiple controller servlets, each with a separate configuration file. These will share a root WebApplicationContext, but be otherwise independent. Each application-specific request controller bean is a threadsafe, reusable object like a Struts action.

The following sequence diagram illustrates the flow of control (it's actually slightly simplified, but it illustrates the basic concepts). I'll discuss each of the four messages in more detail below, and we'll look at each class and interface in detail later:

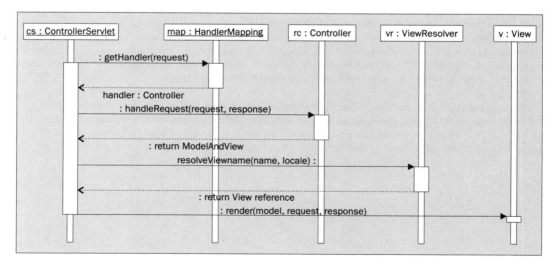

1. On receiving an incoming HTTP request, the controller servlet asks an implementation of the `com.interface21.web.servlet.HandlerMapping` interface for an application request controller to handle this request. The default implementation of the `HandlerMapping` interface chooses a controller (implementing the `com.interface21.web.servlet.mvc.Controller` interface) based on request URL; however a custom implementation could use any approach (actually the controller maintains a list of `HandlerMapping` objects that are applied in a fixed order until one matches, allowing for more sophisticated mapping than any of the frameworks we've discussed).

2. The controller servlet calls the request controller's `handleRequest()` method. This must return an object of type `com.interface21.web.servlet.ModelAndView` that contains the name of a view and model data to display.

3. The controller servlet invokes an object of type `com.interface21.web.servlet.ViewResolver` to obtain a reference to the View object with the name returned by the request controller. A `ViewResolver` should be able to support internationalization, and so may return a different view instance depending on the request locale.

4. The controller servlet calls the `render()` method of the view to generate content. As with Maverick, there's no dependence on any particular view technology.

The core framework workflow doesn't involve the creation of command objects. This is often, but not always, desirable functionality. Including it in the basic MVC workflow would unnecessarily complicate simple interactions where it's overkill to create a command. Such workflow refinements can be implemented by abstract implementations of the `com.interface21.web.servlet.mvc.Controller` interface, which application-specific controllers can extend, without adding complexity to the basic workflow described above. A variety of different superclasses are included with the framework. The core workflow leaves as much choice as possible: custom controller superclasses can support different kinds of command flow, including the use of command objects as in Struts. Alternatively, adapters can be implemented to allow the use of different workflows without concrete inheritance from framework classes.

The following class diagram shows the relationships between the classes and interfaces involved, and how this web application framework integrates with the application framework discussed in the last chapter. It also shows how the `ControllerServlet` is derived from framework superclasses that provide integration with the root `WebApplicationContext`.

This diagram is a lot to take in one go. It's best used as a reference as you read the following discussion:

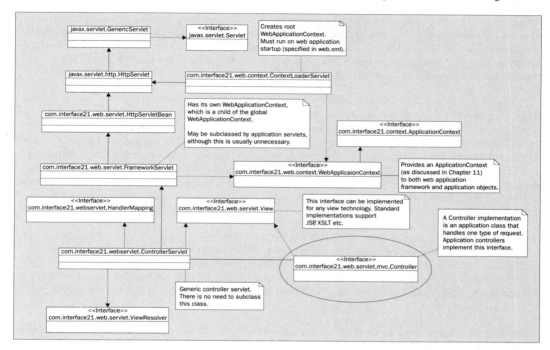

The `com.interface21.web.servlet.mvc.Controller` interface, circled in the diagram, is implemented by application-specific controllers. In most applications, there is no need to implement any of the other interfaces or extend any of the classes shown in the diagram, as the default implementations meet common requirements.

Let's now consider each important class and interface in turn.

Controller Servlet

The entry point of an MVC web application with any framework is a generic controller servlet. In the Interface21 framework, the controller is a servlet of class `com.interface21.web.servet.ControllerServlet`. This is a concrete class; there is no need to subclass, as it is parameterized through the application context it runs in.

A controller servlet does not itself perform control logic. It is a controller of controllers: its role is to choose an application-specific **request controller** to handle each request and to delegate request processing to it.

A web application may have multiple controller servlets, each associated with a `WebApplicationContext` (an extension of `ApplicationContext` specific to web applications), although the sample application uses a single controller. All controller servlets in a web application share a common parent application context, enabling them to share as much or as little configuration as they wish. This allows large applications to use one controller servlet for a group of related use cases, keeping the size of each configuration file manageable (as Struts 1.1 allows), while providing a formal mechanism for sharing business objects (as opposed to more haphazard sharing via the `ServletContext`).

The `com.interface21.web.servlet.HttpServletBean` base servlet class extends `javax.servlet.HttpServlet` to enable servlet bean properties to be transparently set at initialization time from `web.xml` servlet `<init-param>` elements. This superclass can be extended by any servlet, regardless of whether the framework described here is used – it doesn't depend on the MVC implementation. As with our `BeanFactory` configured by EJB environment variables, this ensures that servlets need only expose bean properties to be configured. There's no need to look up servlet configuration parameters in servlet code, and type conversion is automatic, using a `PropertyEditor` if necessary.

The immediate superclass of `ControllerServlet` is `com.interface21.web.servlet.FrameworkServlet`, which extends `HttpServletBean` to obtain the root `WebApplicationContext` (which must have been set as an attribute in the `ServletContext` by the `ContextLoaderServlet`, which we'll discuss shortly) and create its own independent child context, defining its own beans. It will also have access to beans defined in the parent, global, context.

By default each framework servlet's child context will be defined by an XML document (although a bean property can be used to set a custom context class name) with the URL within the WAR `/WEB-INF/<servlet-name>-servlet.xml`, where the servlet name is set by the `<servlet-name>` element in `web.xml`. Thus for the sample application, the context for the single controller servlet instance must be located at `/WEB-INF/ticket-servlet.xml`.

The controller servlet for the sample application is configured in `web.xml` as follows:

```
<servlet>
    <servlet-name>ticket</servlet-name>
    <servlet-class>
        com.interface21.web.servlet.ControllerServlet
    </servlet-class>

    <init-param>
        <param-name>debug</param-name>
        <param-value>false</param-value>
    </init-param>

    <load-on-startup>2</load-on-startup>
</servlet>
```

We also need to define a `<servlet-mapping>` element in `web.xml`. In this case we want to ensure that this controller servlet handles all requests for `.html` resources. I prefer this approach to the usual practice with Struts and Maverick, of using `.do` and `.m` as the respective default mapping extension. When using virtual URLs, we don't need to expose the technology we use to users:

```
<servlet-mapping>
        <servlet-name>ticket</servlet-name>
        <url-pattern>*.html</url-pattern>
</servlet-mapping>
```

Note that when we map `.html` *URLs onto the controller servlet, any static HTML files that may be included in request processing must have an* `.htm` *or another extension other than* `.html`, *or requests for them will be intercepted by the controller.*

In an application using multiple controller servlets, we would probably map individual URLs onto each controller, unless it was logical for each server to handle requests with a different extension or virtual directory. See section 11.1 of the Servlet 2.3 specification for an explanation of the rules for defining mappings in the `web.xml` deployment descriptor.

All further configuration of the controller servlet is held in the beans defined in `/WEB-INF/ticket-servlet.xml`. This has the added advantage that there's no need to learn complex DTDs such as the Struts config format: the same property configuration syntax is used for all configuration, web-specific and otherwise, so we simply need to know which properties of which classes we need to configure.

Request to Controller Mapping (com.interface21.web.servlet.HandlerMapping)

The controller servlet chooses which request controller to invoke to handle incoming requests using implementations of the `com.interface21.web.servlet.HandlerMapping` interface defined in the current bean factory, or attempting to match the request URL to a controller bean name if no `HandlerMapping` implementation is defined.

The sample application uses a standard mapping from request to controller, based on request URL. The framework class `com.interface21.web.servlet.UrlHandlerMapping` supports a simple mapping syntax from the incoming URL to the name of a controller bean in the same bean definition, as shown here:

```
<bean name="a.urlMap"
      class="com.interface21.web.servlet.UrlHandlerMapping">
      <property name="mappings">
            /welcome.html=ticketController
            /show.html=ticketController

            /foo/bar.html=otherControllerBeanName
            *=defaultControllerBeanName
      </property>
</bean>
```

The highlighted line specifies a default controller, if no other controller matches. If no default controller is specified, URLs that don't match will result in the controller servlet sending an HTTP 404 Not Found response code.

Note that the `mappings` property of the `com.interface21.web.servlet.UrlHandlerMapping` class is set to a string value in a format supported by the `java.util.Properties` class. This is achieved because the `com.interface21.beans.BeanWrapperImpl` class, discussed in Chapter 11, registers a standard property editor for class `java.util.Properties`; conversion from `String` to `Properties` is automatically performed by the framework.

It's not necessary to understand the workings of handler mappings to use the framework. The standard mapping syntax shown above is sufficient for most purposes and does as much as is possible with many frameworks. However, the framework allows custom mappings to be defined simply by implementing the simple `HandlerMapping` interface, which might choose a controller based on any aspect of the request, such as URL, cookies, user authentication status, or request parameters.

It's possible to define any number of mappings as desired for each controller servlet. The controller servlet will find all beans in its application context that implement the `HandlerMapping` interface, and *apply them in alphabetical order by bean name* until one finds a match, throwing an exception if none does. Thus the bean name given to mappings is significant, although they are never retrieved by name by application code.

This approach to mapping requests to controllers is more powerful and easier to customize than the approach used in any other framework I'm aware of.

Request Controller (com.interface21.web.servlet.mvc.Controller)

> The `com.interface21.web.servlet.mvc.Controller` interface defines the contract that application controllers must extend. Implementations of this interface are multithreaded, reusable objects analogous to Struts actions.

A request controller is essentially an extension of the controller servlet's functionality. By delegating to one of a number of controller objects, the controller servlet remains generic and application code is freed from the need for chains of `if...else` statements.

Request controllers normally handle requests to a single URL. Request controllers implement the `com.interface21.framework.web.servlet.mvc.Controller` interface, which contains a single method:

```
ModelAndView handleRequest(HttpServletRequest request,
                           HttpServletResponse response)
     throws ServletException, IOException;
```

The returned `ModelAndView` object contains a data **model** (a single object or a `java.util.Map`) and the name of a view that can render the model. This doesn't introduce a dependency on any view technology: the name is resolved by a `ViewResolver` object. A `null` return from a controller's `handleRequest()` method indicates that the controller generated the response itself by writing to the `HttpServletResponse`.

Controllers, like servlets and Struts actions, are multithreaded components. Therefore any instance data should normally be read-only, lest its state becomes corrupted or the need to synchronize access degrades performance.

Controllers, like all applications, objects in this framework, are JavaBeans. This enables their properties to be set in the application context definition associated with the relevant servlet. Bean properties are all set at initialization time, so will be read-only at run time.

The following XML element defines the main controller used in the sample application. Note that this controller exposes bean properties that enable the framework to make business objects available to it (in the highlighted lines), as well as configuration properties that enable its behavior to be changed without modifying Java code:

```
<bean name="ticketController"
      class="com.wrox.expertj2ee.ticket.web.TicketController" >
      <property name="calendar" beanRef="true">
            calendar
      </property>
      <property name="boxOffice" beanRef="true">
            boxOffice
      </property>
      <property name="availabilityCheck" beanRef="true">
            availabilityCheck
      </property>
      <property name="userValidator" beanRef="true">
            userValidator
      </property>
      <property name="bookingFee">3.50</property>
      <property name="minutesToHoldReservations">1</property>
</bean>
```

We'll look at controller implementations shortly. Although the Controller interface is very simple, the framework provides several abstract implementations offering different workflows, which application controllers can extend.

The framework can also work with any other controller interface for which a "HandlerAdapter" SPI implementation is provided. This is beyond the scope of the present discussion, but delivers great flexibility.

Models

A controller returns both a model and a view name. The `com.interface21.web.servlet.ModelAndView` class contains model data and the string name of the view that should render the model. Unlike in Maverick and WebWork, the model data isn't tied to a single object, but is a map. A convenience constructor for the `ModelAndView` class enables us to return a single, named object like this:

```
ModelAndView mv = new ModelAndView("viewName", "modelName", modelObject);
```

This is analogous to the Maverick single-model approach.

The name parameter may be used to add model values to an `HttpServletRequest` if necessary.

> *Why return model data as a Map, instead of simply exposing model data as request attributes? By setting model data as request attributes, we constrain view implementations. For example, an XSLT view would require model data in the form of JavaBeans, not request parameters. A view that forwarded to another system might try to render model values as string parameters. Thus there is a real value in exposing the model without dependence on the Servlet API.*

> **A model consists of one or more Java objects (usually, JavaBeans). Each model object has an associated name; hence the complete model is returned as a Map. Often this map will have a single entry.**

Views

A view is an object that can render a model. The purpose of the `View` interface is to decouple controller code from view technology by hiding view technology specifics behind a standard interface. Thus this framework achieves the goal of view substitutability that we considered earlier this chapter.

A view does not perform any request processing or initiate any business logic: it merely takes the model data it is given and renders it to the response. This formalizes use of the "Service-to-Worker" early data retrieval strategy discussed above.

Like controllers, views must be threadsafe, as they execute on behalf of multiple clients. Views are also normally JavaBeans, enabling them to be defined using our consistent property management approach.

A view must implement the `com.interface21.web.servlet.View` interface. The most important method is:

```
void render(Map model,
            HttpServletRequest request,
            HttpServletResponse response)
```

This writes output to the response object, based on model data.

A view may use any one of a number of strategies to implement this method. For example:

❑ Forwarding to a resource such as a JSP, as in the standard `com.interface21.web.servlet.view.InternalResourceView` implementation.

❑ Performing an XSL transform. The standard `com.interface21.web.servlet.view.xslt.XsltView` implementation performs an XSL Transform, using a precompiled stylesheet.

❑ Using a custom output generation library to generate PDF or a graphics format.

To understand how this works, let's consider the implementation of the `com.interface21.web.servlet.view.InternalResourceView` implementation used to forward JSP pages. This takes the JSP's path within the WAR as a bean property. In the `render()` method, it:

❑ Creates a request attribute for each "static value" defined in the view. Views can expose static attributes that are configured at view definition time, and don't vary at run time, although they can be overridden by dynamic model attributes.

❑ Creates a request attribute for each value in the dynamic model supplied by the controller. The attribute name is the map key in each case.

❑ Forwards to the JSP view, using a request dispatcher. In this model, the JSP will consist largely of template data, but can generate dynamic content if necessary.

Custom views can easily implement the `View` interface, or extend the `com.interface21.web.servlet.view.AbstractView` convenience superclass. For example, in one recent project I implemented a custom view that extracted embedded HTML from a fixed XPath within a model that was guaranteed to be XML, and wrote it to the response. In this situation, this was a simpler and more efficient approach than using a JSP or even an XSLT view.

It's also easy to provide view implementations that use just about any output technology to expose model data. For example, views provided with the framework support radically different output technologies such as XMLC and PDF generation.

ViewResolver

Controllers normally return `ModelAndView` objects including view *names* rather than view *references*, thus decoupling controller from view technology. Unlike Struts view definitions, which may be global but are normally associated with actions, all view definitions are global.

> *In my opinion, the notion of view scope adds less value than complexity. View names can include qualifiers such as package paths if necessary to identify them uniquely in an application with many views.*

It is possible to construct a `ModelAndView` object containing an actual view reference in rare cases where it's appropriate to return an anonymous inner class or other instantiated view, rather than a shared view object used by the entire application. A controller could do this as follows:

```
View myView = new MySpecialView(params);
ModelAndView mv = new ModelAndView(myView, "modelName", modelObject);
```

The way in which the framework resolves view names is configurable through a controller servlet's application context. An implementation of the `com.interface21.web.servlet.ViewResolver` interface can be set in a controller servlet's context with the predefined bean name `viewResolver`. If none is specified, a standard implementation, `com.interface21.web.servlet.view.ResourceBundleViewResolver`, looks *on the classpath* (that is, under `/WEB-INF/classes`) for a resource bundle with the default name `views.properties`, containing definitions of views as beans.

This enables transparent support for internationalization using the standard Java ResourceBundle functionality. For example, we could define another file, views_fr.properties or views_fr_ca.properties to provide separate view definitions (perhaps using different JSP pages) for French and French Canadian locales. (The ease of harnessing standard implementation support is the main reason I've chosen to use a properties format, rather than XML, for default view configuration.)

It's easy to write a custom view resolver if necessary (it's free to create and return view objects any way it pleases), but the standard implementation meets all normal requirements. Often we want to ensure that each of several controller servlets uses a unique name for its views definition file, by setting the basename parameter of the ResourceBundleViewResolver class as follows:

```
<bean name="viewResolver"
      class="com.interface21.web.servlet.view.ResourceBundleViewResolver">
      <property name="cache">true</property>
      <property name="basename">ticketServlet</property>
</bean>
```

View definitions for the ResourceBundleViewResolver follow the properties bean definition syntax we've already seen. The following view from the sample application uses a default view class suitable for exposing JSP pages within the WAR (this file is found within the sample application's WAR at /WEB-INF/classes/views.properties):

```
welcomeView.class=com.interface21.web.servlet.view.InternalResourceView
welcomeView.url=/welcome.jsp
```

The following view uses a standard View implementation that provides XML data on the fly for an XSLT stylesheet. (This is implemented using the same Domify package as used by Maverick.) The root property sets the name of the root element domification should create for the model:

```
xView.class=com.interface21.web.servlet.view.xslt.XsltView
xView.root=myDocument
xView.stylesheet=/xsl/default.xsl
```

> As **ResourceBundles** and properties files are normally loaded from the classpath, they're normally found under **/WEB-INF/classes** in a WAR. XML-based configuration files are loaded by URL by framework code, and are normally located in the **/WEB-INF** directory, which is not itself of the classpath. This is true of most web application frameworks.

ContextLoaderServlet

We've covered all the moving parts of the framework. However, there's one vital piece of plumbing left to consider.

Before any controller servlet works a root WebApplicationContext object must be attached to the ServletContext. This contains read-only data, so it won't matter that each server in a cluster will have its own instance.

The root `WebApplicationContext` is created and set as a `ServletContext` attribute by the `com.interface21.web.context.ContextLoaderServlet`, which must be set to load on startup before any other servlet, using the `<load-on-startup>` web.xml element.

Note that the global `WebApplicationContext` object isn't merely available to classes in our web application framework; it can be accessed by servlet filters, JSP custom tags, or components implemented using other web frameworks, allowing them to access business objects exposed as JavaBeans.

In the sample application, the following element in web.xml defines the `ContextLoaderServlet`:

```
<servlet>
      <servlet-name>config</servlet-name>
      <servlet-class>
            com.interface21.web.context.ContextLoaderServlet
      </servlet-class>
      <init-param>
            <param-name>contextClass</param-name>
            <param-value>
                  com.interface21.web.context.support.XmlWebApplicationContext
            </param-value>
      </init-param>
      <load-on-startup>1</load-on-startup>
</servlet>
```

Note that there are no URL mappings onto this servlet: its purpose is to load configuration and make it available to other web components. I could have modeled this object as a Servlet 2.3 application listener. However, there was no reason to break compatibility with Servlet 2.2 merely to do this. Furthermore, should the `ContextLoaderServlet` ever need to present a web interface – for example, to return information about the root `WebApplicationContext` – the decision to model it as a servlet will pay off.

Custom Tags

Finally, there are a number of custom tags, used to perform data binding, expose messages with internationalization support, and iterate over models. These are useful bonuses, not central functionality, as JSP is only intended to be one of the view technologies supported by this framework. We'll discuss some of these custom tags later in this chapter.

Workflow Refinements

Now we understand how the basic MVC workflow is implemented, let's look at the framework's abstract implementations of `com.interface21.servlet.mvc.Controller` to deliver various different workflows.

The following UML class diagram shows the relationship between these implementations, and how application-specific controllers can extend them. The classes above the line are generic framework classes; those below the line are application-specific examples we'll consider shortly.

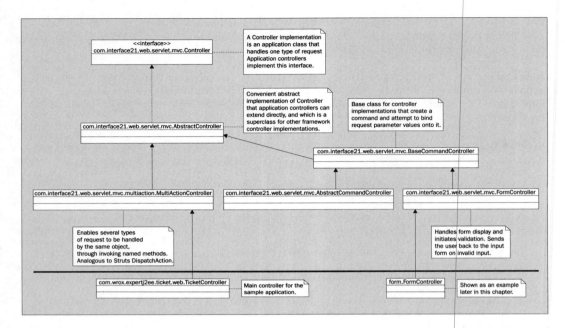

The classes most likely to be extended by application controllers are the following. All use the Template Method design pattern:

❑ com.interface21.web.servlet.mvc.AbstractController
Simple implementation of a controller that provides a logger object and other helper functionality.

❑ com.interface21.web.servlet.mvc.AbstractCommandController
Controller that automatically creates a new instance of a command class and tries to populate it with request parameters, passing command, and any errors, to a protected template method to be implemented by subclasses. This is similar to the Struts Action contract, although it can use a domain object that does not depend on the web framework as a command.

❑ com.interface21.web.servlet.mvc.FormController
Controller that displays a form bound to a Java object, and can automatically redisplay the form in the event of validation errors. We'll discuss this class under *Processing User Input* below.

❑ com.interface21.web.servlet.mvc.multiaction.MultiActionController
Controller that allows subclasses to handle multiple request types by mapping each request type to a method, rather than an object.

We'll see these classes in action in the examples in the next section.

Examples

Let's now look at some simple code examples. Later we'll look at more realistic examples from the sample application.

The examples discussed in this section are included in a separate download from the sample application, called i21-web-demo. This download, which includes an Ant build script, can also be used as a skeleton for web applications using this framework.

A Basic Controller Implementation

The following is a complete listing of a simple implementation of the Controller interface, which chooses a view depending on the presence and validity of a "name" request parameter. If the name parameter is present, it attempts to validate it (for demonstration purposes, validation merely checks whether the name contains a hyphen character, which is deemed to be illegal). This controller can forward to any of three views, in the following three scenarios:

- ❑ No name supplied (enterNameView)

- ❑ Name present but invalid (invalidNameView)

- ❑ Name present and valid (validNameView)

```
package simple;

import javax.servlet.ServletException;
import javax.servlet.http.HttpServletRequest;
import javax.servlet.http.HttpServletResponse;

import com.interface21.web.servlet.ModelAndView;
import com.interface21.web.servlet.mvc.Controller;

public class SimpleController implements Controller {

    public ModelAndView handleRequest(HttpServletRequest request,
        HttpServletResponse response) throws ServletException {

      String name = request.getParameter("name");
      if (name == null || "".equals(name)) {
        return new ModelAndView("enterNameView");
      } else if (name.indexOf("-") != -1) {
        return new ModelAndView("invalidNameView", "name", name);
      } else {
        return new ModelAndView("validNameView", "name",  name);
      }
    }

}
```

Often we'll want to extend the com.interface21.web.servlet.mvc.AbstractController class, which provides the following support:

- ❑ Creating a protected Logger instance variable, available to subclasses.

- ❑ Implementing the com.interface21.context.ApplicationContextAware interface to ensure that it is given a reference to the current servlet's WebApplicationContext object, which it saves to expose to subclasses.

❑ Exposing a bean property that specifies which request methods are allowed. For example, this makes it possible to disallow GET requests.

❑ Exposing a bean property that specifies whether the invocation of the controller should only succeed if the user already has session state.

The AbstractController class uses the Template Method design pattern, providing a final implementation of the handleRequest() method that enforces the request method and session checks and forcing subclasses to implement the following method, which is invoked if they succeed:

```
protected abstract ModelAndView handleRequestInternal(
    HttpServletRequest request,
    HttpServletResponse response)
  throws ServletException, IOException;
```

The contract for this method is identical to that for the handleRequest() method from the Controller interface.

A Controller Exposing Bean Properties

Controllers are very easy to parameterize as they're JavaBeans, obtained by the controller from the application bean factory. All we need to do to be able to externalize configuration is to add bean properties to a controller. Note that these bean properties are set once at configuration time, so are read-only when the application services requests, and don't pose threading issues.

> *This ability to configure controller instances at startup is a major advantage of using multi-threaded, reusable controllers, as opposed to the Maverick and WebWork new controller per request model. Struts, which also uses reusable controllers, also provides the ability to set properties on controllers (actions) in its configuration file, through <set-property> elements nested within <action> elements. However, Struts only supports simple properties; it cannot handle relationships to other framework objects, limiting the ability to "wire up" action objects as part of an integrated application.*

Let's consider the following simple controller. It uses a bean property, name (highlighted), which can be set outside Java code to modify the model data output by the controller. I've made this controller extend AbstractController so that it can override the init() lifecycle method to check that its name parameter has been set.

This controller sends the user to the enterNameView if they haven't supplied a name parameter. If a name parameter is supplied, the user is sent to a greetingView for which the model is a greeting string greeting the user by name and showing the value of the name property of the controller instance:

```
package simple;

import java.io.IOException;

import javax.servlet.ServletException;
import javax.servlet.http.HttpServletRequest;
import javax.servlet.http.HttpServletResponse;
```

```
import com.interface21.context.ApplicationContextException;
import com.interface21.web.servlet.ModelAndView;
import com.interface21.web.servlet.mvc.AbstractController;

public class HelloController extends AbstractController {

  private String name;

  public void setName(String name) {
    this.name = name;
  }

  protected ModelAndView handleRequestInternal(
      HttpServletRequest request, HttpServletResponse response)
      throws ServletException, IOException {

    String pname = request.getParameter("name");
    if (pname == null) {
      return new ModelAndView("enterNameView");
    } else {
      return new ModelAndView("greetingView", "greeting",
                       "Hello " + pname + ", my name is " + this.name);
    }
  }

  protected void init() throws ApplicationContextException {
    if (this.name ==  null)
      throw new ApplicationContextException(
        "name property must be set on beans of class " +
        getClass().getName());
    }
}
```

We can configure this object as follows:

```
<bean name="helloController"
      class="simple.HelloController" >
      <property name="name">The Bean Controller</property>
</bean>
```

Bean properties are often of business interface types, enabling them to be set to other beans in the same application context. We'll see this usage pattern in the sample application.

The ability to parameterize controllers so easily, and in a standard way, has many advantages. For example:

❑   We never need to write code in web tier controllers to look up configuration.

❑   We never need to use the Singleton design pattern or call factory methods: we can simply expose a property of a business interface type and rely on external configuration to initialize it.

❑   We can often use different object instances of the same controller class to meet different requirements.

❑   It's easy to test controller beans outside a web container. We can simply set their bean properties and invoke their `handleRequest()` methods with test request and response objects, as discussed in Chapter 3. Such a simple testing strategy won't work if controllers need to perform complex lookups (such as JNDI lookups) at run time.

A Multi-Action Controller

While using a single controller per request type is often a good model, and has advantages such as the ability to use a common superclass for all controllers, it isn't always appropriate. Sometimes many application controllers end up being trivial, and there's a confusing proliferation of tiny classes. Sometimes many controllers share many configuration properties, and, although concrete inheritance can be used to allow the common properties to be inherited, modeling the controllers as distinct objects is illogical. In such cases, it's more natural for a *method,* rather than a *class,* to process an incoming request. This is a pragmatic approach that can improve productivity, but isn't always the best design decision.

Struts 1.1 introduces support for method-based mapping with the `org.apache.struts.actions.DispatchAction` superclass, and I have borrowed the idea in the present framework in the `com.interface21.web.servlet.mvc.multiaction.MultiActionController` superclass, which implements the `Controller` interface to invoke methods on subclasses by name for each request. None of the other frameworks I know of supports this feature. Multiple request URLs can be mapped onto a `DispatchAction` or `MultiActionController` controller.

The only way to achieve method-based functionality is to use reflection to invoke methods by name. This will have a negligible performance overhead if done once per incoming request, and is a good example of the benefits of reflection concealed by a framework. Both the Struts `DispatchAction` and my `MultiActionController` cache methods, meaning that the overhead of reflection is minimized.

The main challenge is to decide which named method to invoke. The framework superclass can analyze concrete subclasses at startup to identify and cache request handling methods. In the present framework, request handling methods must accept at least `HttpServletRequest` and `HttpServletResponse` objects as parameters and must always return a `ModelAndView` object. Request handling methods can have any name, but must be public, as otherwise it's more difficult to use them reflectively. A typical signature for a request handling method is:

```
public ModelAndView meaningfulMethodName(
    HttpServletRequest request, HttpServletResponse response);
```

The Struts `DispatchAction` determines the name of the request handling method to use from the value of a request parameter, although the abstract `LookupDispatchAction` subclass defers this choice to concrete subclasses. My `MultiActionController` is more flexible in that it uses the Strategy design pattern to factor this choice into the following simple interface, an instance of which can be set on any controller that extends `MultiActionController` as a bean property:

```
public interface MethodNameResolver {
    String getHandlerMethodName(HttpServletRequest request)
    throws NoSuchRequestHandlingMethodException;
}
```

The Struts `LookupDispatchAction` *overrides* `DispatchAction` *to look up a method name matching a special request parameter in application properties. It seems that the designers of Struts don't believe in interfaces. Putting the varying functionality in an interface (the Strategy design pattern) is far more flexible than subclassing, as it enables us to modify the mapping strategy used by application classes extending* `MultiActionController` *without modifying the source code by changing superclass. This is a good example of the superiority of composition over concrete inheritance discussed in Chapter 4.*

The default implementation of `MethodNameResolver` (`com.interface21.web.servlet.mvc.multiaction.InternalPathMethodNameResolver`) bases the method name on the request URL. For example, `/test.html` is mapped to a method named `test`; `/foo/bar.html` is mapped to a method named `foo_bar`. However, we will normally want the mapping to be more configurable, as we shouldn't tie controller implementation to mapped URLs.

The `com.interface21.web.servlet.mvc.multiaction.ParameterMethodNameResolver` implementation provides similar behavior to Struts, selecting a method based on the value of an `action` parameter included with the request.

The `com.interface21.web.servlet.mvc.multiaction.PropertiesMethodNameResolver` implementation is much more configurable. This enables the mapping to be held in properties specified in the controller servlet's XML configuration file: the same mechanism as used by our `UrlHandlerMapping` implementation. The following bean definition from the sample application demonstrates this approach:

```
<bean name="ticketControllerMethodNameResolver"
      class="com.interface21.web.servlet.mvc.multiaction.
            PropertiesMethodNameResolver">
    <property name="mappings">
            /welcome.html=displayGenresPage
            /show.html=displayShow
            /bookseats.html=displayBookSeatsForm
            /reservation.html=processSeatSelectionFormSubmission
            /payment.html=displayPaymentForm
            /confirmation.html=processPaymentFormSubmission
            /refresh.html=refreshReferenceData
    </property>
</bean>
```

This object is set as the value of the inherited `methodNameResolver` property on application-specific controllers derived from `MultiActionController` as follows:

```
<bean name="ticketController"
      class="com.wrox.expertj2ee.ticket.web.TicketController" >
    <property name="methodNameResolver"
            beanRef="true">ticketControllerMethodNameResolver
    </property>

</bean>
```

Alternatively, an application can easily supply a custom implementation of the `MethodNameResolver` interface, which may determine method name on custom criteria other than request URL, such as the user's session state.

The `MultiActionController` class is also more sophisticated than the Struts `DispatchAction` in that it provides the ability to invoke methods on another, delegate object, rather than a subclass. (The delegate can also be set as a bean property.) This is useful if there's need to invoke a named method in a class with a separate inheritance hierarchy. The delegate doesn't need to implement any special interface, just expose public methods with the correct signatures.

To illustrate how the "multi action" controller approach works in practice, let's look at some code from the main controller for the sample application. The `TicketController` class extends `MultiActionController`, meaning that it doesn't implement the `handleRequest()` method, which is implemented as a `final` method by `MultiActionController`, but must implement a number of request handling methods that will be invoked by name. This single class implements *all* controller code for the sample application, consolidating trivial methods (that would otherwise consume more space as trivial classes) and exposing configuration bean properties relating to all methods:

```
public class TicketController
    extends com.interface21.web.servlet.mvc.multiaction.MultiActionController {
```

I've omitted the configuration bean properties. However, instance data is available to all methods.

The request handling methods must be public, and may throw any type of exception. Otherwise, they fulfill the same contract as `handleRequest()` methods, returning a `ModelAndView` object. The following three methods correspond to the first three keys in the properties-based mapping shown above. I've shown the implementation of only one of the methods:

```
public ModelAndView displayGenresPage(HttpServletRequest request,
    HttpServletResponse response)  {
  List genres = calendar.getCurrentGenres();
  return new ModelAndView("welcomeView", "genres", genres);
}


public ModelAndView displayShow(HttpServletRequest request,
    HttpServletResponse response)
  throws ServletException, NoSuchPerformanceException {
    // Implementation omitted
}


public ModelAndView displayBookSeatsForm (HttpServletRequest request,
    HttpServletResponse response)
  throws ServletException, NoSuchPerformanceException {
    // Implementation omitted
}
```

The `MultiActionController` class also offers a simple data binding capability. The final parameter in a request processing method (request and response will always be required) will be assumed to indicate that the method expects a command bean. The type of the command can be determined from the method signature, which will look like the following example from the sample application:

```
public ModelAndView processSeatSelectionFormSubmission(
    HttpServletRequest request,
    HttpServletResponse response,
    ReservationRequest reservationRequest);
```

A new command instance will be automatically created using reflection (commands must be JavaBeans with no-argument constructors), and request parameters bound onto its properties. If data binding succeeds (that is, there are no type mismatches), the method will be invoked with the populated command object. Any data binding exceptions will be assumed to be fatal. This approach isn't powerful enough for many data binding applications, but it can be very useful. It's similar to the Struts `ActionForm` approach if we choose to use effectively untyped string parameters, in which case type mismatches are impossible. We'll examine the use of this data binding mechanism in the sample application near the end of this chapter.

The `MultiActionController` class can also detect when subclass methods require session state parameters. In this case, the user's `HttpSession` will be passed as a parameter if a session exists. If no session exists, this will be treated as a workflow violation and an exception invoked, without invoking the subclass method.

Another feature offered by the `MultiActionController` lacking in the Struts `DispatchAction` (or indeed the Struts framework as a whole) is support for "last-modified" HTTP headers to support browser or proxy caching of dynamic content. This support is used in the sample application and is discussed in Chapter 15.

This "multi-action" approach has the following advantages, compared with the one-controller-per-request model:

❑ It may be easier to maintain, as there are only a few larger classes instead of many tiny classes

❑ It is a more intuitive model in some cases

❑ It is easier to configure a few more complex classes than many trivial classes, so application configuration is likely to be simpler

This approach has the following disadvantages:

❑ An alternative model to learn: the model of one controller per request type is more familiar, as it's long established by the Servlet specification as well as frameworks such as Struts 1.0. (However, this may change as Struts 1.1 comes into use.)

❑ We lose the advantage of compile-time checking. It's possible that subclasses contain invalid method definitions, which we'll only learn about when the application starts up, and the `MultiActionController` superclass fails to find the necessary request handling methods. However, the `MultiActionController` implementation provides good error information about probable errors in subclass method signatures.

❑ By using individual methods, rather than objects, we lose the ability to catch exceptions in a common superclass and eliminate common request handling code. Exception handling becomes more problematic. When we look at the sample application's implementation below, we'll see how the `MultiActionController` class enables subclasses to catch exceptions thrown from request handling methods.

The choice essentially comes down to the philosophical choice between compile time and run time. A method-based approach is a good choice if it makes an application easier to maintain, and a poor choice if it's used to build huge controllers that group functionality that isn't related and doesn't depend on the same configuration properties.

Of course, it's possible to mix the two models: for example, using single classes to handle actions that require more complex control logic, and multi-action classes to handle groups of simple related actions.

This is by no means a comprehensive tour of this framework's capabilities. See the Interface21 web-demo download for illustrations and explanations of other capabilities.

Web-Tier Session Management

Regardless of which MVC framework we use, our approach to session management can have a big impact on performance and scalability. By holding server-side state on behalf of users we can simplify application code and may improve performance by caching data that may be used later in a user session. However, there is a tradeoff involved as holding server-side state can reduce scalability.

When we need to maintain session state, there are basically two options:

❑ Use the standard J2EE infrastructure to have the server handle state transparently (usually the best option)

❑ Try to hold state in the browser to avoid the need for server-side state

Let's consider each in turn.

Session State Managed by the J2EE Server

The Servlet API provides a simple means of holding state in a `javax.servlet.http.HttpSession` object. An `HttpSession` is essentially a map of name-value pairs, with the `setAttribute()` and `getAttribute()` methods analogous to a Map's `get()` and `put()` methods. A web container will hide the details of session object lookup, holding a unique key for a session in a cookie or special request parameter.

Clustering and Replication

In an application that runs on a single server, there is no problem in holding session state in an `HttpSession` object, managed transparently by the web container; the benefits in code simplification and performance come without any cost attached. As we noted in Chapter 10, this approach is usually preferable to using a stateful session EJB.

However, when we have a cluster of servers, such session state will need to be replicated by the server to ensure failover and to minimize server affinity. Replicated session state data is often stored in a database to ensure robust persistence: a major performance hit. This also means that all objects placed in an `HttpSession` must be serializable, to allow the server to store them in a database or file system.

Simple Optimizations

Due to the potential load of state replication, it's important to apply the following optimizations when using server-managed state:

❑   Don't create session state unless necessary

❑   Minimize the volume of data held in server-side session state

❑   Use fine-grained, rather than large monolithic, session state objects

❑   Consider optimizing the serialization of session data

None of these optimizations compromises application design. Let's consider each optimization in turn.

Don't Create Session State Unless Necessary

It's important to avoid the creation of session state (and hence the need to replicate it in a cluster) until it's necessary. For example, in the sample application, it's only during the booking process that we need to hold session state for users. The majority of user activity will involve browsing genre, performance, and show information and availability, so by creating session state only when users attempt to book we can avoid unnecessary state replication.

When we use JSP as the view technology, we must beware of a trap here. By default, every JSP creates a new `HttpSession` object if none exists, in case there is a JSP bean with session scope bound on the page. This is often undesirable behavior. We can override the default with the following JSP directive:

```
<%@ page session="false" %>
```

I recommend the use of this directive on every JSP. Views shouldn't access or manipulate session state; a controller component should make all data available to the JSP with request scope. A controller can copy session attributes to the data model as necessary, to make them accessible to JSP pages that aren't session-aware.

> **Always switch off default JSP session creation with a page directive. This avoids needless creation of session state, and avoids the risk of JSP pages accessing and manipulating session state, which is inappropriate for views.**

Another reason to avoid JSP pages accessing session objects is that it breaks the important rule that views should only work with data included in the model. Many views (such as XSLT views) may be unable to access session state. However, if necessary session state is included in the model, any view can access it like other model data, and view substitutability is preserved.

Minimize the Volume of Data Held in Server-side Session State

It's important to minimize the volume of data held in a user session. Holding unnecessary data will slow replication and will waste resources on the server. If too much session data is held in memory, the server will need to swap session data into a persistent store, resulting in a large performance hit when passivated sessions are reactivated.

Reference data that can be shared between users should always be held at application level. Data that is unlikely to be reused should probably just be retrieved again if it's ever needed. For example, a primary key might be held instead of a large volume of data retrieved from a database; this is a good sacrifice of performance in rare cases for a real benefit in scalability.

Use Fine-grained, Rather than Large Monolithic, Session State Objects

It's usually best to break session state into a number of smaller objects than one large, composite object. This means that only those objects that have changed will need replication in a cluster.

As there's no easy way to establish whether the state of a Java object has changed, some servers, such as WebLogic, only replicate session state in a cluster when an object is rebound in an `HttpSession`, although the Servlet 2.3 specification doesn't specify what behavior is expected here. (The Servlet 2.4 specification may define standard semantics for session replication.) Such selective replication can deliver a big performance gain when objects stored in a session are updated at varying rates. Thus, to ensure correct replication behavior, always rebind a session attribute when the session data is changed. This won't pose a problem in any server.

Consider Optimizing the Serialization of Session Data

Sometimes by overriding the default serialization behavior, we can greatly improve the performance and reduce the size of serialized objects. This is a specialized optimization that is rarely necessary. We'll discuss serialization optimization in Chapter 15.

Session State Held in the Browser

Some session state must always be held in the user's browser. As HTTP is a stateless protocol, a J2EE server can only retrieve a user's session object if it finds a cookie or a special request parameter containing a unique key for that user's session.

By holding session state in the browser, we lose the advantage of transparent server management of session state, but can achieve greater scalability and simplify clustering.

Session State Management with Cookies

In this approach, we use cookies to hold session state. The Servlet API makes it easy to set cookies, although we must be aware of the restrictions on the characters allowed in cookie values.

The advantage of this approach is that it allows us to make an application's web tier stateless, which has the potential to improve scalability dramatically and simplify clustering.

However, there are several disadvantages that often rule out this approach in practice:

❑ Users must accept cookies. This isn't always feasible, as we don't have control over the client browser and often have little control over user behavior.

❑ By rejecting server state management, we must build our own infrastructure for encoding state into cookies. Typically this involves using reflection to extract object properties, and using an ASCII-encoding algorithm to put that state into legal cookie values. (There are restrictions on the characters allowed in cookie values.) Theoretically such support could be added to a web application framework, but I've not seen this done in practice.

- The amount of state that can be held in a cookie is limited to 2K. We could choose to use multiple cookies, but this increases the complexity of this approach.

- All session data must be sent to and from the server with each request. However, this objection isn't so important in practice, as this approach isn't appropriate if there's a lot of state, and the page weight on typical web sites dwarfs anything we might put in cookies.

Sometimes this approach can be used with good results. In one real application, I successfully used cookies in place of session state where user information consisted of three string values (none longer than 100 characters) and three Boolean values. This approach delivered business value because the application needed to run on several geographically dispersed servers, ruling out replication of server-managed session state. I used an infrastructure class to extract property values from the session object using reflection and generate an acceptable ASCII-encoded cookie value.

Session State Management with Hidden Form Fields

Another time-honored approach to session state management, which also isn't J2EE-specific, involves an application trailing hidden form fields from page to page containing session state.

I don't recommend this approach. It has several serious disadvantages:

- It's relatively hard to implement.

- It makes application logic vulnerable to errors in views such as JSP pages. This can make it harder to ensure a clean separation of the roles of Java developer and markup developer.

- Like cookie state management, it requires session data to be stored purely as strings.

- It makes it impossible to use ordinary hyperlinks for navigation within a site. Every page transaction needs to be a form submission. This usually means that we must use JavaScript links (to submit the form containing the hidden fields) instead of ordinary hyperlinks, complicating markup.

- As with the use of cookies, bandwidth is consumed sending hidden form field values to and from the server. However, as with cookies, this objection is seldom a major problem in practice.

- The user can easily see session state by viewing the page source.

- Session state may be lost if the user leaves the site temporarily. This problem doesn't affect server state management or the use of cookies.

> In some applications, session state can be held in cookies. However, when we need session state it's usually safer – and much simpler – to rely on the web container to manage **HttpSession** objects, ensuring that we do all we can to ensure efficient replication of session state in a clustered environment.

Processing User Input

One of the most tedious tasks in implementing web interfaces is the need to accept user input from form submissions and use it to populate domain objects.

The central problem is that all values resulting from HTTP form submissions are strings. When domain object properties aren't strings, we need to convert values, checking parameter types as necessary. This means that we need to validate both the type of parameter submissions and their semantics. For example, an age parameter value of 23x isn't valid as it isn't numeric; but a numeric value of -1 is also invalid as ages cannot be negative. We might also need to check that the age is within a prescribed range.

We also need to check for the presence of mandatory form fields, and may need to set nested properties of domain objects.

A web application framework can provide valuable support here. Usually we want to take one of the following actions on invalid data:

❑   Reject the input altogether, treating this as an invalid submission. This approach is appropriate, for example, when a user could only arrive at this page from a link within the application. As the application, not the user, controls the parameters, invalid parameter values indicate an internal error.

❑   Send the user back the form allowing them to correct the errors and resubmit. In this case, the user will expect to see the actual data they entered, regardless of whether that input was valid or invalid, or even of the correct type.

The second action is the most commonly required and requires the most support from a web application framework.

The discussion in this section concentrates on the submission of a single input form, rather than "wizard" style submissions spread over several pages. Many of the principles applicable to single form submission apply to wizard style submission, although it is naturally harder to implement multi-page forms than single-page forms (it may be modeled as several individual form submissions onto different JavaBeans, or multiple submissions updating different properties of the same bean stored in the session).

Data Binding and Displaying Input Errors for Resubmission

Often, rather than perform low-level processing of individual request parameters, we want to transparently update properties on a JavaBean. The operation of updating object properties on HTTP form submission is often called **data binding**.

In this approach, a JavaBean – typically a command – will expose properties with the same names as the expected request parameters. Web application framework code will use a bean manipulation package to populate these properties based on the request parameters. This is the same approach as that used by the <jsp:useBean> action, although, as we've noted, this doesn't provide a sophisticated enough implementation. Ideally, such a command bean will not depend on the Servlet API, so once its properties are set it can be passed as a parameter to business interface methods.

Many frameworks, such as Struts and WebWork, use data binding as their main approach to request parameter processing. However, data binding isn't always the best approach. When there are few parameters, it may be inappropriate to create an object. We may want to invoke business methods that don't take arguments, or take one or two primitive arguments. In such cases, application controllers can themselves process request parameters using the getParameter(String name) method of the HttpServletRequest interface. In such cases, creating a command object would waste a little time and memory, but – more seriously – make a very simple operation seem more complex. With a pure data-binding approach, if we have a separate command per bean, as in Struts, we can easily end up with dozens of action form classes that add very little.

Also, sometimes dynamic data to a request isn't contained in request parameters. For example, sometimes we might want to include dynamic information in a virtual URL. For example, a news article URL might include an ID in the servlet path, without requiring a query string, as in the following example:

```
/articles/article3047.html
```

This approach may facilitate content caching: for example, by a servlet filter or in the browser.

Note that processing individual request parameters places the onus on application controller code to check that parameters are of the required type: for example, before using a method such as Integer.parseInt(String s) to perform type conversion.

Where data binding does shine is where there are many request parameters, or where resubmission is required on invalid input. Once user data is held in a JavaBean, it becomes easy to use that object to populate a resubmission form.

Approaches to Data Binding in MVC Frameworks

There seem to be two basic approaches to data binding in Java web application frameworks, both based on JavaBeans:

❑ **Keep the data (valid or invalid) in a single JavaBean, allowing a resubmission form's field values to be populated easily if necessary**
This is the Struts ActionForm approach. It has the disadvantage that the data in the ActionForm bean isn't typed. Since all properties of the ActionForm are strings, the ActionForm can't usually be a domain object, as few domain objects hold only string data. This means that when we've checked that the data the ActionForm contains is valid (and can be converted to the target types) we'll need to perform another step to populate a domain object from it.

In this model, validation will occur on the form bean, not the domain object; we can't attempt to populate a domain object from the form bean until we're sure that all the form bean's string property values can be converted to the necessary type. Note that we will need to store error information, such as error codes, somewhere, as the form bean can store only the rejected values. Struts holds error information for each rejected field in a separate ActionErrors object in the request.

❑ **Keep errors in a separate object**

This approach attempts to populate the domain object, without using an intermediate holding object such as an "action form". The domain object we're trying to bind to will have its fields updated with the inputs of the correct type, while any inputs of an incorrect type (which couldn't be set on the domain object) will be accessible from a separate errors object added to the request. Semantic (rather than syntactic) validation can be performed by domain objects after population is complete.

WebWork uses a variant of this approach. If a WebWork action implements the `webwork.action.IllegalArgumentAware` interface, as does the `webwork.action.ActionSupport` convenience superclass, it will receive notification of any type mismatches when its properties are being set, making it possible to store the illegal value for display if necessary. In this model, type mismatches are transparently handled by the framework, and application code doesn't need to consider them. Application validation can work with domain objects, not dumb storage objects.

Since WebWork combines the roles of command and controller (or "action" in WebWork terms), a WebWork controller is not a true domain object because it depends on the WebWork API. However, this is a consequence of WebWork's overall design, not its data binding approach.

The second approach is harder to implement in a framework, but can simplify application code, as it places the onus on the framework to perform type conversion. Such type conversion can be quite complex, as it can use the standard JavaBeans `PropertyEditor` machinery, enabling complex objects to be created from request parameters. The second approach is used in the framework for the sample application, although this framework also supports an action form-like approach like that of Struts, in which string properties are used to minimize the likelihood of errors.

JSP Custom Tags

How do we know what data to display on a form? Usually we'll want to use the same template (JSP or other) for both fresh input forms and resubmissions, as the prospect of different forms containing hundreds of lines of markup getting out of synch is unappetizing. Thus the form must be able to be populated with no object data behind it; with data from an existing object (for example, a user profile retrieved from a database); or with data that may include errors following a rejected form submission. In all cases, additional model data may be required that is shared between users: for example, reference data to populate dynamic lists such as dropdowns.

In such cases, where data may come from different sources – or simply be blank if there is no bean from which to obtain data – JSP custom tags can be used to move the problem of data acquisition from template into helper code behind the scenes in tag handlers. Many frameworks use a similar approach here, regardless of how they store form data.

If we want to perform data binding, the form usually needs to obtain data using special tags. The tags in our framework with the sample application are conceptually similar to those with Struts or other frameworks. Whether or not the form has been submitted, we use custom tags to obtain values.

For each field, we can use custom tags to obtain any error message resulting from a failed data-binding attempt along with the rejected property value. The tags cooperate with the application context's internationalization support to display the error message for the correct locale automatically. For example, the following fragment of a JSP page uses cooperating custom tags to display an error message if the e-mail property of the user bean on the page failed validation, along with a pre-populated input field containing the rejected value (if the submitted value was invalid) or current value (if there was no error in the e-mail value submitted). Note that only the outer `<i21:bind>` tag is specific to this framework. It exposes data to tags nested within it that enable it to work with JSP Standard Tag Library tags such as the conditional `<c:if>` and output `<c:out>` tags. This means that the most complex operations, such as conditionals, are performed with standard tags. (We discuss the JSTL in detail in the next chapter.)

```
<i21:bind value="user.email">
    <c:if test="${bind.error}">
        <font color="red"><b>
            <c:out value="${bind.errorMessage}"/>
        </b></font><br>
    </c:if>

    <input type="text" length="2" size="30" name="email"
        value="<c:out value="${bind.value}" />"  />
</i21:bind>
```

The `<i21:bind>` tag uses a `value` attribute to identify the bean and property that we are interested in. The bean prefix is necessary because these tags and the supporting infrastructure can support multiple bind operations on the same form: a unique capability, as far as I know. The `<i21:bind>` tag defines a `bind` scripting variable, which can be used anywhere within its scope, and which exposes information about the success or failure of the bind operation for this property and the display value.

The tag arrives at the string value to display by evaluating the following in order: any rejected input value for this field; the value of this attribute of a bean with the required name on the page (the same behavior as the `<jsp:getProperty>` standard action); and the empty string if there was no bean and no errors object (the case on a new form with no backing data). The `bind` scripting variable created by the `<i21:bind>` tag also exposes methods indicating which of these sources the displayed value came from.

Another convenient tag evaluates its contents only if there were data binding errors on the form:

```
<i21:hasBindErrors>
    <font color="red" size="4">
        There were <%=count%> errors on this form
    </font>
</i21:hasBindErrors>
```

We'll look at custom tags in more detail in the next chapter, but this demonstrates a very good use for them. They completely conceal the complexity of data binding from JSP content.

Note that it is possible to handle form submission using Struts or the framework designed in this chapter without using JSP custom tags; custom tags just offer a simple, convenient approach.

Data Validation

If there's a type mismatch, such as a non-numeric value for a numeric property, application code shouldn't need to perform any validation. However, we may need to apply sophisticated validation rules before deciding whether to make the user resubmit input. To ensure that our display approach works, errors raised by application code validation (such as age under 18 unacceptable) must use the same reporting system as errors raised by the framework (such as type mismatch).

Where Should Data Validation be Performed?

The problem of data validation refuses to fit neatly into any architectural tier of an application. We have a confusing array of choices:

- ❑ Validation in JavaScript running in the browser. In this approach, validity checks precede form submission, with JavaScript alerts prompting the user to modify invalid values.

- ❑ Validation in the web tier. In this approach a web-tier controller or helper class will validate the data after form submission, and return the user to the form if the data is invalid, without invoking any business objects.

- ❑ Validation in business objects, which may be EJBs.

Making a choice can be difficult. The root of the problem is the question "*Is validation business logic?*" The answer varies in different situations.

Validation problems generally fall into the categories of **syntactic** and **semantic** validation. Syntactic validation encompasses simple operations such as checks that data is present, of an acceptable length, or in the valid format (such as a number). This is not usually business logic. Semantic validation is trickier, and involves some business logic, and even data access.

Consider the example of a simple registration form. A registration request might contain a user's preferred username, password, e-mail address, country, and post or zip code. Syntactic validation could be used to ensure that all required fields are present (assuming that they're all required, which might be governed by a business rule, in which case semantics is involved). However, the processing of each field is more complicated. We can't validate the post or zip code field without understanding the country selection, as UK postcodes and US zip codes, for example, have different formats. This is semantic validation, and approaching business logic.

Worse, the rules for validating UK postcodes are too complex and require too much data to validate on the client-side. Even if we settle for accepting input that *looks like* a UK postcode but is semantic nonsense (such as Z10 8XX), JavaScript will still prove impracticable if we intend to support multiple countries. We *can* validate e-mail address formats in JavaScript, and perform password length and character checks. However, some fields will pose a more serious problem. Let's assume that usernames must be unique. It is impossible to validate a requested username without access to a business object that can connect to the database.

All the above approaches have their advantages and disadvantages. Using JavaScript reduces the load on the server and improves perceived response time. If multiple corrections must be made before a form is submitted, the load reduction may be significant and the user may perceive the system to be highly responsive.

On the other hand, complex JavaScript can rapidly become a maintainability nightmare, cross-browser problems are likely, and page weight may be significantly increased by client-side scripts. In my experience, maintaining complex JavaScript is likely to prove much more expensive than maintaining comparable functionality in Java. JavaScript being a completely different language from Java, this approach also has the serious disadvantage that, while Java developers write the business logic, JavaScript developers must write the validation rules. JavaScript validation is also useless for non-web clients, such as remote clients of EJBs with remote interfaces or web services clients.

> **Do not rely on client-side JavaScript validation alone. The user, not the server, controls the browser. It's possible for the user to disable client-side scripting, meaning that it's always necessary to perform the same checks on the server anyway.**

Validation in the web tier, on the other hand, has the severe disadvantage of tying validation logic – which may be business logic – to the Servlet API and perhaps also a web application framework. Unfortunately, Struts tends to push validation in the direction of the web tier, as validation must occur on Struts `ActionForm` objects, which depend on the Servlet API, and hence *cannot* be passed into an EJB container and should not be passed to any business object. For example, validation is often accomplished by overriding the `org.apache.struts.action.ActionForm` validate method like this:

```
public final class MyStrutsForm extends org.apache.struts.action.ActionForm {

...

   public ActionErrors validate(ActionMapping mapping,
      HttpServletRequest request) {

   ActionErrors errors = new ActionErrors();

   if (email == null || "".equals(email)) {
      errors.add("email", new ActionError("email.required"));
   }

   return errors;
   }
}
```

I consider this – and the fact that `ActionForm` objects must extend a Struts superclass dependent on the Servlet API – to be a major design flaw.

Struts 1.1 also provides declarative validation, controlled through XML configuration files. This is powerful and simple to use (it's based on regular expressions), but whether validation rules are in Java code or XML they're still often in the wrong place in the web tier.

> **Validation should depend on business objects, rather than the web tier. This maximizes the potential to reuse validation code.**

However, there is one situation in which validation code won't necessarily be collocated with business objects: in architectures in which business objects are EJBs. Every call into the EJB tier is potentially a remote call: we don't want to waste network roundtrips exchanging invalid data.

Thus the best place to perform validation is in the same JVM as the web container. However, validation need not be part of the web interface logical tier. We should set the following goals for validation:

❑   Validation code shouldn't be contained in web-tier controllers or any objects unique to the web tier. This allows the reuse of validation objects for other client types.

❑   To permit internationalization, it's important to separate error messages from Java code. Resource bundles provide a good, standard, way of doing this.

❑   Where appropriate we should allow for parameterization of validation without recompiling Java code. For example, if the minimum and maximum password lengths on a system are 6 and 64 characters respectively, this should not be hard-coded into Java classes, even in the form of constants. Such business rules can change, and it should be possible to effect such a change without recompiling Java code.

We can meet these goals if validators are JavaBeans that don't depend on web APIs, but may access whatever business objects they need. This means that validators must act on domain objects, rather than Servlet API-specific concepts such as HttpServletRequests or framework-specific objects such as Struts ActionForms.

Data Validation in the Framework Described in this Chapter

Let's look at how this approach works in the framework described in this chapter, and so in the sample application. All validators depend only on two non web-specific framework interfaces, com.interface21.validation.Validator and com.interface21.validation.Errors. The Validator interface requires implementing classes to confirm which classes they can validate, and implement a validate method that takes a domain object to be validated and reports any errors to an Errors object. Validator implementations must cast the object to be validated to the correct type, as it is impossible to invoke validators with typed parameters in a consistent way. The complete interface is:

```
public interface Validator {
  boolean supports(Class clazz);
  void validate(Object obj, Errors errors);
}
```

Errors are added to the Errors interface by invoking the following method:

```
void rejectValue(String field, String code, String message);
```

Errors objects expose error information that is used to back display by the custom tags shown above. The same errors object passed to an application validator is also used by the framework to note any type conversion failures, ensuring that all errors can be displayed in the same way.

Let's consider a partial listing of the Validator implementation used in the sample application to validate user profile information held in RegisteredUser objects. A RegisteredUser object exposes e-mail and other properties including postcode on an associated object of type Address.

The `DefaultUserValidator` class is an application-specific JavaBean, exposing `minEmail` and `maxEmail` properties determining the minimum and maximum length acceptable for e-mail addresses:

```
package com.wrox.expertj2ee.ticket.customer;

import com.interface21.validation.Errors;
import com.interface21.validation.FieldError;
import com.interface21.validation.Validator;

public class DefaultUserValidator implements Validator {

  public static final int DEFAULT_MIN_EMAIL = 6;

  public static final int DEFAULT_MAX_EMAIL = 64;

  private int minEmail = DEFAULT_MIN_EMAIL;
  private int maxEmail = DEFAULT_MAX_EMAIL;

  public void setMinEmail(int minEmail) {
    this.minEmail = minEmail;
  }

  public void setMaxEmail(int maxEmail) {
    this.maxEmail = maxEmail;
  }
```

The implementation of the `supports()` method from the `Validator` interface indicates that this validator can handle only `RegisteredUser` objects:

```
public boolean supports(Class clazz) {
  return clazz.equals(RegisteredUser.class);
}
```

The implementation of the `validate()` method from the `Validator` interface performs a number of checks on the object parameter, which can safely be cast to `RegisteredUser`:

```
public void validate(Object o, Errors errs) {
  RegisteredUser u = (RegisteredUser) o;
  validateEmail(u.getEmail(), errs);
  // More check method invocations omitted
}

private void validateEmail(String email, Errors errs) {
  if (email == null || "".equals(email)) {
    errs.rejectValue("email", "emailRequired",
                     "E-mail Address is required");
    return;
  }

  if (email.length()< this.minEmail|| email.length()> this.maxEmail){
    errs.rejectValue("email", "emailLengthInvalid",
                     "E-mail Address is invalid");
```

```
        return;
    }
    // Other checks omitted, including checks on min
  }
}
```

The validator's bean properties are set using the same file format we discussed in the last chapter, meeting our goal of externalizing business rules:

```
<bean name="userValidator"
      class="com.wrox.expertj2ee.ticket.customer.DefaultUserValidator" >
      <property name="minEmail">6</property>
      <property name="maxEmail">64</property>
  ...
</bean>
```

Thus we can validate RegisteredUser objects, regardless of what interface we use (web or otherwise). Error information in interface-independent errors objects can be displayed in any interface we choose.

Let's now look at how we can use our web framework to invoke this validation code.

The com.interface21.web.servlet.mvc.FormController superclass is a framework web controller designed both to display a form based around a single JavaBean and to handle form submission, automatically returning the user to the original form if resubmission is necessary.

Subclasses need only specify the class of the form bean (passed to the superclass constructor). The name of the "form view" and "success view" should be set as bean properties in the bean definition (shown below).

The following simple example, from our MVC demo, shows a subclass of FormController that can display a form based on a RegisteredUser object, allowing the user to input postcode (from the associated Address object), birth year, and e-mail address properties. Postcode and e-mail address will be text inputs; birth year should be chosen from a dropdown of birth years accepted by the system:

```
package form;

import java.util.HashMap;
import java.util.Map;
import javax.servlet.http.HttpServletRequest;
import com.interface21.web.servlet.ModelAndView;
import com.interface21.web.servlet.mvc.FormController;
import com.wrox.expertj2ee.ticket.customer.RegisteredUser;

public class CustomerInput extends FormController {
```

By default, FormController will use Class.newInstance() to create a new instance of the form bean, whose properties will be used to populate the form (the form bean must have a no argument constructor). However, by overriding the following method, we can create an object ourselves. In the present example, I've simply pre-populated one property with some text: we would normally override this method only if it were likely that a suitable object existed in the session, or we knew how to retrieve one, for example, by a database lookup:

```
protected Object formBackingObject(HttpServletRequest request) {
    RegisteredUser user = new RegisteredUser();
    user.setEmail("Enter your email");
    return user;
}
```

This method will be invoked if the controller is handling a request for the form, rather than a form submission.

If there are validation errors – type mismatches and/or errors raised by the validator object – subclasses will not need to do anything. The `FormController` class will automatically return the user to the submission form, making the bean and error information available to the view.

We must override one of several overloaded `onSubmit()` methods to take whatever action is necessary if the object passes validation. Each of these methods is passed the populated domain object. In our simple example, I've just made one of the object's properties available to the view; a real controller would pass the populated command to a business interface and choose a view depending on the result. Note that this method doesn't take request or response objects. These are unnecessary unless we need to manipulate the user's session (the request and response objects are available through overriding other `onSubmit()` methods): the request parameters have already been extracted and bound to command properties, while by returning a model map we leave the view to do whatever it needs to do to the response:

```
protected ModelAndView onSubmit(Object command) {
    RegisteredUser user = (RegisteredUser) command;
    return new ModelAndView(getSuccessView(),
                        "email", user.getEmail());
    }
}
```

We may wish to override the `isFormSubmission()` method to tell `FormController` whether it's dealing with a request to display the form or a form submission. The default implementation (shown below) assumes that an HTTP request method of `POST` indicates a form submission. This may not always be true; we might want to distinguish between two URLs mapped to this controller, or check for the presence of a special request parameter:

```
protected boolean isFormSubmission(HttpServletRequest request) {
    return "POST".equals(request.getMethod());
}
```

If the form requires shared reference data in addition to the bound object, this data can be returned as a map (like a model map in our framework) from the `referenceData()` method. In this case, we return a static array of the birth years displayed on the form, although reference data will usually come from a database:

```
private static final int[] BIRTH_YEARS = {
    1970, 1971, 1972, 1973, 1974 };

protected Map referenceData(HttpServletRequest request) {
  Map m = new HashMap();
```

```
    m.put("BIRTHYEARS", BIRTH_YEARS);
    return m;
}
```

This is all the application-specific Java code required. This controller is configured by the following bean definition in the servlet's XML configuration file. Note the highlighted line that sets the validator property inherited from the `FormController` generic superclass to a reference to the validator bean, and how the inherited `beanName`, `formView`, and `successView` properties are set:

```
<bean name="customerController"
      class="form.CustomerInput" >
      <property name="validator" beanRef="true">customerValidator</property>
      <property name="beanName">user</property>
      <property name="formView">customerForm</property>
      <property name="successView">displayCustomerView</property>
</bean>
```

Let's now look at the listing for the complete form, using the custom tags shown above. Note that the bean name of "user" matches the bean name set as a property on the controller. As postcode is a property of the `billingAddress` property of the `RegisteredUser`, note the nested property syntax:

```
<form method="POST">

<i21:hasBindErrors>
      There were <%=count%> errors
      <p>
</i21:hasBindErrors>

Postal code:
<br>
<i21:bind value="user.billingAddress.postcode">
        <c:if test="${bind.error}">
              <font color="red"><b>
                      <c:out value="${bind.errorMessage}"/>
                 </b></font>
                 <br>
           </c:if>

<input type="text" length="16" name="billingAddress.postcode"
            value="<c:out value="${bind.value}" />">
</i21:bind>
```

The `birthYear` property should be set to a choice from a dropdown of birth years populated by the reference data returned by the `referenceData()` method. We use a nested JSTL conditional tag to select the value from the list that the bind value matches. If the bind value is blank (as it will be when the form is first displayed) the first, "Please select," value will be selected:

```
      Birth year:
      <br>
      <i21:bind value="user.birthYear">
            <c:if test="${bind.error}">
```

```
                    <font color="red"><b>
                        Birth year is required
                    </b></font>
                    <br>
                </c:if>

        <select size="1" name="birthYear">
            <option value=""/>Please select</option>
            <c:forEach var="birthYear" items="${BIRTHYEARS}">
                <option value="<c:out value="${birthYear}"/>"
                    <c:if test="${bind.value == birthYear}">SELECTED</c:if>
                        > <c:out value="${birthYear}"/>
                </option>
            </c:forEach>
        </select>
    </i21:bind>
```

The e-mail address field requires similar code to the postcode text field:

```
Email:
<br>
<i21:bind value="user.email">
    <c:if test="${bind.error}">
            <font color="red"><b>
                    <c:out value="${bind.errorMessage}"/>
            </b></font>
            <br>
        </c:if>

        <input type="text" length="2" size="30" name="email" value="<c:out
value="${bind.value}" />"  />
</i21:bind>
```

When the user requests cust.html, which is mapped onto the controller, the form will appear with the e-mail address field pre-populated from the formBackingObject() method. The postcode field will be blank, as this field was left null in the new bean, while the first (prompt) value will be selected in the birth-year dropdown:

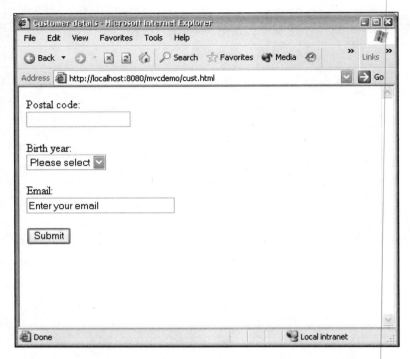

On invalid submission, the user will see error messages in red, with the actual user input (valid or invalid) redisplayed:

If we want more control over the validation process, our framework enables us to use the data binding functionality behind the `FormController` ourselves. (Most frameworks don't allow "manual" binding.) It's even possible to bind the same request onto several objects. The following code from the sample application shows such use of the `com.interface21.web.bind.HttpServletRequestDataBinder` object:

```
RegisteredUser user = (RegisteredUser) session.getAttribute("user");
...
HttpServletRequestDataBinder binder = null;

try {
  binder = new HttpServletRequestDataBinder(user, "user");
  binder.bind(request);
  validator.validate(user, binder);

  PurchaseRequest purchaseRequest = new PurchaseRequest(reservation, user);
  binder.newTarget(purchaseRequest, "purchase");
  binder.bind(request);

  // May throw exception
  binder.close();

  // INVOKE BUSINESS METHODS WITH VALID DOMAIN OBJECTS
```

```
        }
    catch (BindException ex) {
        // Bind failure
        return new ModelAndView("paymentForm", binder.getModel());
    }
```

The HttpServletRequestDataBinder close() method throws a com.interface21.validation.BindException if there were any bind errors, whether type mismatches or errors raised by validators. From this exception it's possible to get a model map by invoking the getModel() method. This map will contain both all objects bound (user and purchase) and an errors object. Note that this API isn't web specific. While the HttpServletRequestDataBinder knows about HTTP requests, other subclasses of com.interface.validation.DataBinder can obtain property values from any source. All this functionality is, of course, built on the com.interface21.beans bean manipulation package – the core of our infrastructure.

The validation approach shown here successfully populates domain objects, rather than web-specific objects such as Struts ActionForms, and makes validation completely independent of the web interface, allowing validation to be reused in different interfaces and tested outside the J2EE server.

Implementing the Web Tier in the Sample Application

We've already covered many of the concepts used in the web tier of our sample application. Let's summarize how it all fits together.

Note that we won't look at JSP views: we'll look at view technologies in detail in the next chapter.

Overview

The web interface we'll discuss in this section is based on the business interfaces we've considered thus far, such as the Calendar and BoxOffice interfaces.

It uses a single controller, com.wrox.expertj2ee.ticket.web.TicketController, which extends the MultiActionController framework superclass, discussed above, to handle all application URLs. Views are JSP pages, which display model beans returned by the controller, which aren't web specific, such as the Reservation object. These JSP pages don't perform any request processing and include few scriptlets, as the controller makes all major decisions about view choice.

Framework configuration involves:

❑   Defining the ControllerServlet (with name ticket) and ContextLoaderServlet in the web.xml file. (We've shown this above.)

❑   Creating the ticket-servlet.xml XML application context definition file defining the beans – business objects, web application framework configuration objects, and the application controller – required by the controller servlet. This includes:

- Definitions of business object beans (we saw some of these in the last chapter).

- Definition of the `TicketController` web controller bean, setting its bean properties. Bean properties are divided into properties that parameterize its behavior – for example, by setting the booking fee to add to purchases – and properties that allow the framework to make application business objects available to it.

- A `HandlerMapping` object that maps all application URLs onto the controller bean

Let's look at the complete definition of the `TicketController` bean again. Like all the XML fragments below, it comes from the application's `/WEB-INF/ticket-servlet.xml` file:

```
<bean name="ticketController"
    class="com.wrox.expertj2ee.ticket.web.TicketController" >
    <property name="methodNameResolver" beanRef="true">
        ticketControllerMethodNameResolver
    </property>
    <property name="calendar" beanRef="true">
        calendar
    </property>
    <property name="boxOffice" beanRef="true">
        boxOffice
    </property>
    <property name="availabilityCheck" beanRef="true">
        availabilityCheck
    </property>
    <property name="userValidator" beanRef="true">
        userValidator
     </property>
    <property name="bookingFee">3.50</property>
    <property name="minutesToHoldReservations">1</property>
</bean>
```

Mappings from request URL to controller bean name are defined using a standard framework class as follows:

```
<bean name="a.urlMap"
      class="com.interface21.web.servlet.UrlHandlerMapping">
      <property name="mappings">
            /welcome.html=ticketController
            /show.html=ticketController
            /bookseats.html=ticketController
            /reservation.html=ticketController
            /payment.html=ticketController
            /confirmation.html=ticketController
      </property>
</bean>
```

As the one controller handles all requests, all mappings are onto its bean name.

The `methodNameResolver` property of the `TicketController` class is inherited from `MultiActionController`, and defines the mapping of request URLs to individual methods in the `TicketController` class. There is a mapping for each URL mapped onto the `TicketController`:

```
<bean name="ticketControllerMethodNameResolver"
    class="com.interface21.web.servlet.mvc.multiaction.
          PropertiesMethodNameResolver">
    <property name="mappings">
          /welcome.html=displayGenresPage
          /show.html=displayShow
          /bookseats.html=displayBookSeatsForm
          /reservation.html=processSeatSelectionFormSubmission
          /payment.html=displayPaymentForm
          /confirmation.html=processPaymentFormSubmission
    </property>
</bean>
```

Handling a Seat Reservation Request

We've already seen the skeleton of the TicketController object. Let's conclude by looking at one complete request handling method, which will try to reserve a seat for a user.

This method will process the selection form for a particular seat type in a particular performance, shown below:

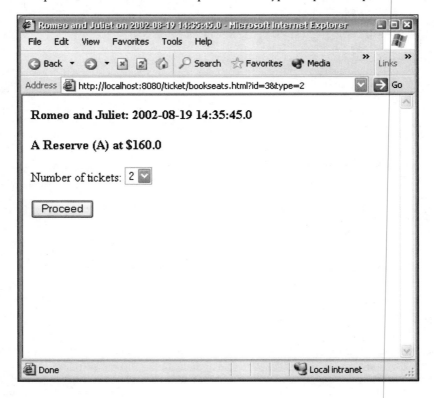

When processing this form we can discount the likelihood of invalid form fields or type mismatches: two of the parameters are hidden form fields (performance ID and seat type ID) written by the application, and the user can only enter a number of seats from the dropdown, ensuring that all values are numeric. The result of form submission should be the following screen, if it is possible to reserve enough seats for the user:

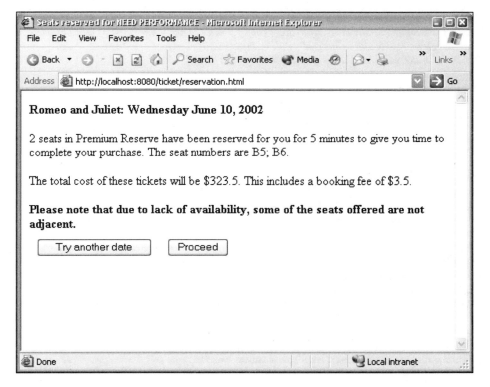

If there aren't enough seats to fulfill the request, the user will be prompted to try another date, and a separate view will be displayed.

The business requirements state that in the event of a successful booking, the resulting Reservation object should be stored in the user's session. The user probably won't have an HttpSession object before this form is submitted. If the user refreshes or resubmits this form, the same reservation should be displayed.

The method's name is reservation, matching the request URL reservation.html in our simple default mapping system.

As error handling on invalid input isn't an issue, we can use the automatic data binding capability of the MultiActionController superclass. This will automatically create a new object of type ReservationRequest using Class.newInstance() and bind request parameters onto it. Thus the very invocation of this method indicates that we have a ReservationRequest containing the appropriate user information.

Note that we simply declare this method to throw `InvalidSeatingRequestException` and `NoSuchPerformanceException`. These are fatal errors that cannot occur in normal operation (in fact they're only checked exceptions because we can't safely throw unchecked exceptions from EJB business methods). The `MultiActionController` superclass will let us throw any exception we please, and will throw a `ServletException` wrapping it.

> *We actually get a chance to handle the exception by implementing an exception handler method taking the exception or any of its superclasses (up to `java.lang.Throwable`) as a parameter. Such handler methods will be invoked on all methods in a `MultiActionController`. However, in this case there's little need for this functionality.*

Note that it *isn't* usually a good idea to declare request handling methods simply to throw `Exception`; it's good to have to decide which application exceptions to catch and which to leave to the superclass, and to make this clear in the contract of the method, as we do here:

```
public ModelAndView processSeatSelectionFormSubmission(
    HttpServletRequest request,
    HttpServletResponse response,
    ReservationRequest reservationRequest)
    throws ServletException,
           InvalidSeatingRequestException,
           NoSuchPerformanceException {
```

Once this method is invoked, the `ReservationRequest` object's properties have been successfully populated from request parameters. This method's first task is to add to the user-submitted information in the reservation request – performance ID, seat type ID, and the number of seats requested – standard information based on our current configuration. All the following instance variables in the `TicketController` class are set via the bean properties set in the XML bean definition element:

```
reservationRequest.setBookingFee(this.bookingFee);
reservationRequest.setReserve(true);
reservationRequest.holdFor(this.minutesToHold);
reservationRequest.setSeatsMustBeAdjacent(true);
```

With a fully configured `ReservationRequest` object, we can check any user session to see if there's a reservation that matches the request already, indicating resubmission of the same form data, which should prompt redisplay of the "Show Reservation" view. Note that we invoke the form of the `request.getSession()` method that takes a boolean parameter with a value of `false`: this doesn't create a session if none exists. Note that I've implemented the check whether a reservation satisfies a request in the `Reservation` class, not this web controller. This will enable its reuse in another interface; as such a check isn't web-specific:

```
Reservation reservation = null;
HttpSession session = request.getSession(false);
if (session != null) {
    reservation = (Reservation) session.getAttribute(RESERVATION_KEY);
    if (reservation != null) {
        if (reservation.satisfiesRequest(reservationRequest)) {
            return new ModelAndView("showReservation", RESERVATION_KEY,
                                    reservation);
```

```
      } else {
        reservation = null;
        session.removeAttribute(RESERVATION_KEY);
      }
    }
  }
```

If this doesn't send the user straight to the "Show Reservation" view, we'll need to invoke the `BoxOffice` business object to try to create a `Reservation`. The `TicketController`'s `boxOffice` instance variable is set via a bean property on application startup, so there's no work in looking up a `BoxOffice` implementation. The `BoxOffice` object's `allocateSeats()` method will either return a `Reservation` or throw a `NotEnoughSeatsException`, which we will catch and which will prompt the display of a different view. On creation of a successful reservation, we place the `Reservation` object in the user's session, creating a new session if necessary by calling `request.getSession(true)`:

```
  try {
    reservation = boxOffice.allocateSeats(reservationRequest);
    session = request.getSession(true);
    session.setAttribute(RESERVATION_KEY, reservation);
    return new ModelAndView("showReservation", RESERVATION_KEY, reservation);
  }
  catch (NotEnoughSeatsException ex) {
    return new ModelAndView("notEnoughSeats", "exception", ex);
  }
}
```

This request handling method contains no presentation-specific code. It deals only with business objects and model data: the "Show Reservation" view is free to display reservation confirmation any way it pleases, using any view technology. This method doesn't contain business logic: the rules it applies (such as "redisplay a reservation on receipt of a repeated form request") are tied to the user interface. All business processing is done by the `BoxOffice` interface.

In the next chapter we'll look at using different technologies, including JSP, XSLT, and WebMacro, to render the view for this screen.

Implementation Review

So, how did we do, overall, at meeting the goals we set ourselves for the web tier of our sample application?

Did we achieve a *clean web tier*, with control flow controlled by Java objects and separated from presentation, handled by templates?

There's no markup in Java code, and views such as JSP pages need to perform only iteration. As we'll see in the next chapter, views can be implemented without using scriptlets.

We have not committed to a particular view technology, although we'll use JSP as the view technology because it's always available and there's no compelling reason to use another technology.

Did we achieve a *thin web tier*, with a minimum code volume and the best possible separation of web interface from business logic?

Our web tier Java code consists of a single class, `com.wrox.j2eedd.ticket.web.TicketController`, which is under 500 lines in length. No other classes depend on the web framework or Servlet API, and no other classes are likely to be relevant only to a web interface. Input validation code is not dependant on web application framework or Servlet API. Were the number of screens in the application to grow, this controller might be broken into individual controllers. We even have the option of introducing additional controller servlets in really large applications. However, there's no benefit in using a greater number of classes now.

Summary

In this chapter we've looked at why it's crucial to separate presentation from control logic in web interfaces, and why it's equally important that a web interface is a thin layer built on well-defined business interfaces.

We've looked at the many shortcomings of naïve web application architectures such as the "JSP Model 1" architecture, in which JSP pages are used to handle requests. We've seen that Java objects are the correct choice for handling control flow in web applications, and that JSP is best used only as a view technology.

We've looked at how the MVC architectural pattern (also known as "Model 2" or "Front Controller" architecture) can help to achieve our design goals for web applications. We've seen the importance of decoupling controller components (which handle control flow in the web tier) from model components (which contain the data to display) and view components (which display that data). Such decoupling has many benefits. For example, it enables us to use domain objects as models, without necessarily creating web-specific models. It ensures that presentation can easily be changed without affecting control flow: an important way to minimize the likelihood of functional bugs being introduced when a site's presentation changes. It achieves a clear separation of the roles of Java developer and presentation developer – an essential in large web applications. We saw that complete "view substitutability" (the ability to substitute one view for another displaying the same data model without modifying controller or model code) is the ideal level of decoupling between controller and view components. If we achieve this (and it *is* achievable, with good design), we can even switch view *technology* without impacting on control flow.

We've examined three open source MVC frameworks (Struts, Maverick, and WebWork), and seen how real MVC implementations share many common concepts. We've examined the design of the MVC framework used in the sample application, which combines some of the best features of the three. This framework is intended for use in real applications, and not merely as a demonstration. It is built on the JavaBean-based infrastructure we discussed in the last chapter, which makes it easy to configure and makes it easy for web-tier components to access application business objects without depending on their concrete classes.

We looked at the problem of web-tier state management. We looked at strategies to ensure that applications maintaining stateful web-tiers are scalable, and considered the alternatives of holding session state in the client browser and in hidden form fields.

We looked at the problem of data binding in web applications (the population of Java object properties from request parameter values), and how web application frameworks address the problem of form submission and validation.

Finally, we looked at the design and implementation of the web tier in the sample application, showing how it meets the design goals we set ourselves for the web tier.

So far we've paid little attention to view technologies such as JSP or XSLT. In the next chapter we'll look more closely at web-tier views, and how we can display model data when using an MVC approach.

13

Views in the Web Tier

In the last chapter we focused on how web applications should handle control flow and access business objects. In this chapter, we'll look closely at view technologies for J2EE web applications.

The choice of view technologies can – and should – be largely independent of web application workflow. We'll begin by looking at the advantages of decoupling views from controller components. We'll then survey some leading view technologies for J2EE web applications. We'll look at the advantages and disadvantages of each, enabling you to make the correct choice for each project.

While it is essential that the J2EE standards define at least one approach to markup generation, the special recognition given to JSP in the J2EE specifications has some unfortunate consequences. JSP is a valuable way of rendering content, but merely one of many valid alternatives. Hopefully, the previous chapter has made a convincing case that servlets and delegate Java objects ("controllers"), *not* JSP pages, should be used to control workflow in the web tier. By bringing much of the power of the Java language into presentation templates, JSP introduces as many dangers as benefits. When we use JSP pages, it's vital to adopt strict standards to ensure that these dangers don't create serious ongoing problems.

In this chapter, we'll take an open-minded look at JSP and some leading alternative view technologies for J2EE applications and how to decide which view technology is best to solve a given problem. We'll look at the strengths and weaknesses of each of the following view technologies, and look at them in use:

❑ JSP. We'll look at traps that must be avoided in using JSP, and how best to use JSP pages to ensure that web applications using them are clean and maintainable. We'll look at the new **JSP Standard Template Library (JSTL)**, which provides valuable assistance in helping JSP pages function as effective view components.

❑ The Velocity template engine. This is a simple, easy-to-learn templating solution that isn't tied to the Servlet API. This is an important bonus, as it can enable templates to be tested outside an application server.

❑ Approaches based on XML and XSLT. XSLT offers very powerful content rendering and a good separation between presentation and content, at the cost of a potentially complex authoring model and a substantial performance overhead.

❑ XMLC, a DOM-based content generation approach introduced in the Enhydra application server, which enables dynamic pages to be created from static HTML mockups.

❑ Solutions enabling the generation of binary content. While these aren't alternatives to the markup-oriented view technologies listed above, any well-designed web application must be able to generate non-markup content if necessary. We use the example of PDF generation – a common requirement that illustrates the challenges posed by the generation of non human-readable and binary formats, and how we can overcome them in an MVC design.

> **Whatever view technology we use, we should not need to modify code in controllers. If we adopt the MVC web architecture we looked at in Chapter 12, controllers and views are completely decoupled.**

Choosing the right view technology for a project is important because it can make it a lot easier to meet presentation requirements. However, the choice can – and should – be made largely independently of the rest of the application code.

The deciding factors are likely to be:

❑ How well the given solution fits the problem. A good guide here will be the volume and complexity of code required for each solution.

❑ Performance considerations. We'll consider some major performance issues in this chapter, while in Chapter 15 we look at benchmarks for some of the view technologies discussed here.

❑ Skills in the project team. For example, if a team has strong JSP skills and little experience of alternative view strategies, JSP is the obvious choice. If any team members come from a Microsoft ASP background, JSP will be likely to prove familiar. On the other hand, in a team with XSLT experience, XSLT might be preferred. If there is no JSP or XSLT experience among content developers, a simple template language such as Velocity may be the best choice, as it has a negligible learning curve.

> **Remember that page layout in all but very simple web applications will be maintained by HTML developers, not Java developers. Thus we must consider their skills and preferences when selecting view technology. Real J2EE development involves multi-disciplinary teams, not just Java developers.**

Throughout this chapter we'll use one of the views from the sample application as an example. As we examine each view technology, we'll implement this view to provide a practical example.

We'll also look at the important concept of **view composition**: building complex pages through combining the outputs of other views or page components. View composition is an essential technique in building the complex pages required on real web sites. We'll examine two common approaches to view composition, with practical examples.

This chapter isn't intended as a guide to using each of the view technologies discussed, but as an overview of how to use each in MVC web applications and a high-level view of the strengths and weaknesses of each. Each section contains references to further information on the technology in question.

Although most of the examples use the MVC web application framework introduced in Chapter 12, the concepts discussed are relevant to all web applications, and especially those using Struts and other MVC frameworks. This chapter concentrates on what you need to do in application code to use each of the view technologies discussed, with a minimum of framework-specific content. See Appendix A for more detailed information on how to install and configure each of these view technologies, and the implementation of the framework's built-in support for each.

Decoupling Controllers and Views

Decoupling controllers from views is the key to the freedom in implementing views that this chapter describes.

This decoupling rests on the following two principles:

❏ The use of a model that contains *all* data resulting from handling the request. This means that views are never required to invoke business operations, but merely to display a complete model.

❏ The **named view strategy** discussed in the last chapter. This layer of indirection allows a controller to select a view by name without knowing anything about the view's implementation. The framework infrastructure can "resolve" the view name to find the shared instance associated with that name at run time.

Decoupling controllers from views brings many benefits. For example:

❏ It is the best way to ensure separation of the roles of Java developers and markup developers. Such separation is essential in all but small-scale web development, as each of these roles requires specialist skills.

❏ It enforces discipline in applying the MVC pattern, ensuring that the responsibilities of controller, model and view are clearly defined.

❏ It ensures that a site's presentation can be changed without affecting its control flow or breaking functionality.

❏ It allows for view composition, in which the output of multiple views or page components is combined, without impacting Java code.

❏ It allows controllers and models to be tested in isolation.

❏ It enables us to support *any* view technology, without changing Java code.

Performed correctly, such decoupling adds no complexity.

> **Views in an MVC J2EE web application should be to JavaBean models what XSLT is to XML. With clear separation of responsibilities, different views can easily present the same data in different formats, while views can be edited by specialists without knowledge of Java programming.**

In the framework that we discussed in the last chapter, the `com.interface21.web.servlet.View` interface delivers this decoupling, providing a standard Java interface that the controller servlet can invoke once a controller returns model data. The notion of view interface is not unique to this framework. For example, the Maverick framework uses a comparable view interface (to which I was indebted in designing the present framework).

The most important method in the `View` interface is the following, which builds the response given the model data returned by the controller:

```
void render(Map model, HttpServletRequest request,
    HttpServletResponse response)
    throws IOException, ServletException;
```

The following sequence diagram illustrates how the controller selects a view, returning the view name and model data to the controller servlet. The controller servlet uses a `ViewResolver` object to find the view instance mapped to the view name, and then invokes that object's `render()` method with the data model returned by the controller:

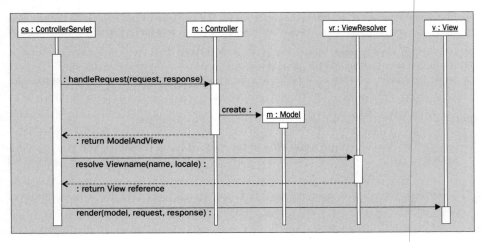

Implementations of the view interface must fulfill some basic requirements:

❑   Wrap a particular page structure, often held in a template in JSP or another template language.

❑   Accept model data provided by the controller in non view-specific form, and expose it to the wrapped view technology.

❑   Use the Servlet API `HttpServletRequest` and `HttpServletResponse` objects to build a dynamic page.

There is one threadsafe, shared view definition for each view. Views are normally JavaBeans, allowing their configuration to be stored outside Java code.

As well as dynamic model data provided by controllers, it is possible to set **static attributes** on views in our framework. Static attributes are set at initialization time and are part of the definition of a particular view instance. Static attributes can be used to set presentation-specific values that does not vary with model data. A typical use of static attributes is to define page structure in template views composed of multiple components (we'll discuss this use under *View Composition and Page Layout* later in this chapter). As static attributes are associated with views, not models or controllers, they can be added or altered without changing any Java code.

To enable the framework to resolve view names, there must be a **view definition** for each view name. Most MVC frameworks provide a means of mapping view names to definitions.

The present framework allows great flexibility in how view definitions are stored. This depends on the implementation of the `ViewResolver` interface being used. In the default `ViewResolver` implementation, used in the sample application, view definitions are JavaBean definitions in the `/WEB-INF/classes/views.properties` file. The properties-based bean definition syntax is defined in Chapter 11.

In Appendix A we look at the implementations of the `View` interface included with the framework, which support all the view technologies discussed in this chapter.

Constructing the View for the Reservations Page

As we examine different view technologies in this chapter, let's consider a simple dynamic page as an example. Last chapter we examined the controller code in the `processSeatSelectionFormSubmission()` method of the `com.wrox.expertj2ee.ticket.web.TicketController` class. This method handles submission of a form that allows the user to request the reservation of a number of seats of a specified type (such as "Premium Reserve") for a particular performance.

Information Presented and Required Formatting

Two views can result from processing this request:

❑ A view displaying the newly created reservation, and inviting the user to proceed to purchase the seats (the "Show Reservation" view)

❑ A view informing the user that there weren't enough free seats for the performance to satisfy their request (the "Not Enough Seats" view)

In this chapter, we'll use the "Show Reservation" view as an example. The "Not Enough Seats" view is completely distinct. Part of the point of using a controller to handle a request is that it enables us to choose one of several possible views depending on the outcome of the necessary business operations. The "Show Reservation" screen looks like this:

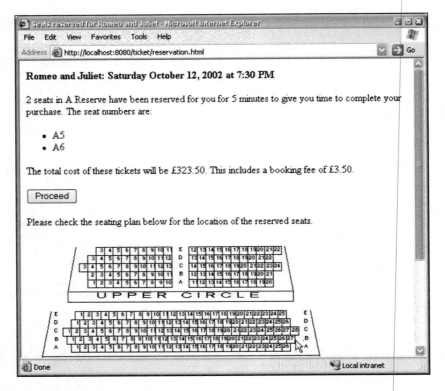

It displays the following dynamic information:

- ❏ The name of the show being performed and a graphic of the seating plan for that show
- ❏ The date of the performance
- ❏ The number of seats reserved, the lifetime of the reservation (how long before other users can reserve these seats if the current user fails to continue to purchase them), the names of the seats, and the cost of purchasing these seats, including the booking fee

Currency display and date and time display should be appropriate to the user's locale.

There is one variant of this view, which is displayed if there were enough seats to satisfy the user's request, but they are not adjacent. In this case, the user should be given the opportunity to abandon this reservation and try to book on another date. We need to add an additional section highlighting the potential problem and providing a link to try to book for another performance. Whatever view technology we use must be able to handle this simple conditional: this is the same view with a minor, presentational, difference, not a distinct view like the notEnoughSeats view.

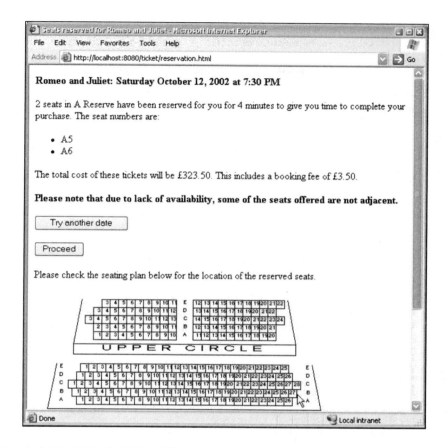

The Model Behind this View

The model returned by the controller's processSeatSelectionFormSubmission() method when it chooses the "Show Reservation" view contains three objects:

❑ performance
An object containing information about the performance and its parent show. This is of type
com.wrox.expertj2ee.ticket.referencedata.Performance.

❑ priceband
An object displaying information such as the name (in the above screenshots, "Premium Reserve") and price of the type of seat requested. This is of type
com.wrox.expertj2ee.ticket.referencedata.PriceBand.

❑ reservation
An object containing information about the user's reservation, such as the seats reserved the quoted price and whether or not the seats are adjacent. This is of type
com.wrox.expertj2ee.ticket.boxoffice.Reservation.

The performance and priceband objects are reference data, shared among all users of the application. The reservation object is unique to the current user.

The three types are interfaces, not classes. The returned objects will be of implementation classes that expose methods that allow some of their state to be manipulated. This is best concealed from views, so we choose not to code views to the mutable classes (views should treat models as read-only). The use of interface-based design also allows the potential for different implementations.

Let's look at some of the important methods in each of these interfaces in turn. Please refer to the sample application source code for a complete listing of each.

Both the `Performance` and `PriceBand` interfaces are part of an abstract inheritance hierarchy based on `com.wrox.expertj2ee.ticket.reference.ReferenceItem`, which exposes a numeric `id` and a name or code as follows:

```
public interface ReferenceItem extends Serializable {
   int getId();
   String getName();
}
```

It's worthwhile ensuring this basic commonality between reference data objects as it saves a little code in concrete implementations, which use a parallel inheritance hierarchy, and makes it easy to treat objects consistently. For example, reference items can be indexed by id whatever their subtype, to allow for rapid lookup.

The following UML class diagram illustrates the inheritance hierarchy:

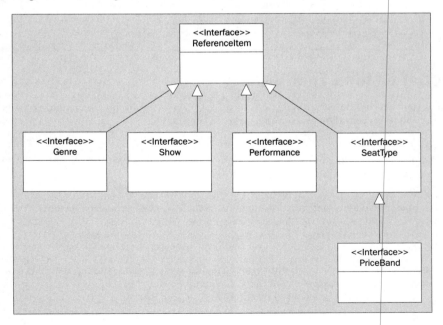

The following diagram shows how reference data instances of the types shown above are assembled into a tree at run time. Each object provides methods to navigate downwards, through its children (for the sake of simplicity, I've only expanded one Show and one Performance:

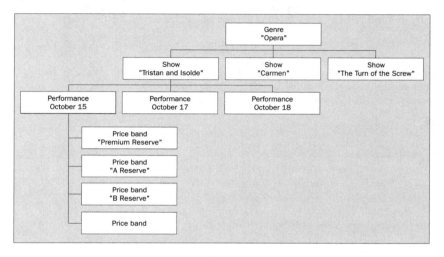

The Performance interface, part of the model for the "Show Reservation" view, extends ReferenceItem to expose a link to the parent Show object, as well as the performance's date and time and a list of PriceBand objects for that performance:

```
public interface Performance extends ReferenceItem {
  Show getShow();
  Date getWhen();
  List getPriceBands();
}
```

PriceBand objects add seat price to the information about seat types such as the name or code (such as **AA**) and description (such as **Premium Reserve**) exposed by the SeatType interface. The following is a complete listing of these two simple interfaces:

```
public interface SeatType extends ReferenceItem {
  int getSeatTypeId();
  String getDescription();
}

public interface PriceBand extends SeatType {
  public double getPrice();
}
```

The com.wrox.expertj2ee.ticket.boxoffice.Reservation interface exposes user-specific information. A Reservation object is created when seats are reserved for a user, and contains a reference to the ReservationRequest object (a command generated by the user) that caused the reservation to be made. A Reservation isn't reference data, but dynamic data created when a user successfully completes the first step of the booking process. Note that a Reservation is serializable. We will need to put Reservation objects in a user session: we need to ensure that this is possible in a clustered environment.

523

I've highlighted the methods relevant to views:

```
public interface Reservation extends Serializable {
```

The following method returns an array of the Seat objects reserved for the user:

```
Seat[] getSeats();
```

The following method indicates whether or not these seats are adjacent. As we've seen, presentation logic may depend on this information, but determining whether or not a set of seats is adjacent isn't presentation logic, as it will involve understanding of the relevant seating plan:

```
boolean seatsAreAdjacent();

int getMinutesReservationWillBeValid();

double getTotalPrice();

ReservationRequest getQuoteRequest();
```

The following methods are used only by controllers:

```
long getTimestamp();
String getReference();
boolean isReserved();
boolean satisfiesRequest(ReservationRequest r);
}
```

Please refer to these listings as necessary to understand the view code shown below.

None of these model objects is web-specific. In fact they're not even UI-specific, which means that we can easily write test harnesses that check for expected results, and could easily use these objects as the basis of a web services interface.

Model Principles

The design of these models raises some important points relating to all models that may be used in web applications:

❑   Models should be JavaBeans, to ensure that they provide the maximum value to views. Note that all the methods exposed by these classes for display follow JavaBeans naming patterns: for example, the Reservation interface exposes a totalPrice property via a getTotalPrice() property getter, not a totalPrice() method. If we expose methods, rather than bean properties, JSP and some other view technologies may have limited ability to access model information.

❑   Some simple calculations are done in the model, even though they could be done by the view. For example, it's possible to work out the number of minutes before a Reservation object expires from the holdTill property of the ReservationRequest object it contains and the system date. Thus the minutesReservationWillBeValid property of the Reservation object is, strictly speaking, redundant.

However, not all view technologies may allow easy access to the system date or implementation of the necessary calculation. If there were to be several views of this model object, each would need to implement its own version of the calculation – redundancy that's likely to have serious implications. Model design is a very different problem to relational database design: there are no prizes for avoiding redundancy. However, processing that involves locale-specific information, such as number formatting, normally *should* be done in views, because this is purely a presentational issue.

❑ Similarly, there's no culling of redundant information in the model. For example, the `PriceBand` object is also, strictly speaking, redundant. It would be possible for a view to navigate to the relevant `PriceBand` object among all the `PriceBand` children of the `Performance` object by comparing each seat type id to the `seatTypeId` request parameter resulting from the form submission.

However, there are good reasons for supplying this "redundant" information in the view. Accessing request parameters trespass on control logic (inappropriate in views). Furthermore, not all views *can* access request parameters: for example, a JSP view can, while an XSLT stylesheet cannot. Views should be able to get all the information they require from the data model, without needing to check the request or any user session. As the `PriceBand` object in the model is a reference to one of the `PriceBand` objects held by the `Performance` object, we've merely moved the lookup inside the controller, rather than wasted memory on an unnecessary object.

Since the web application framework introduced in Chapter 12 enables us to return a `Map`, rather than a single object, as model, we don't need to create a single container object to hold all this information in one object. Such an object would be unique to this page, so by not needing to create one we've avoided creating what would be a web interface-specific object.

> **Model objects used in web interfaces don't need to – and *should not* – be web-specific.**
> **For example, they should never expose markup or other formatting information.**

Following a few golden rules will ensure that model objects provide maximum value to views, whatever the view technology used:

❑ **Model objects should be JavaBeans**
Views should be able to get all the data they need by accessing bean properties and should not need to invoke methods on model objects.

❑ **Model objects should be smart so that the views that display them can be dumb**
This doesn't mean that model objects should perform any data retrieval; this should have been done before the model was returned, by business objects invoked by web tier controllers. It means, however, that models should go the extra mile to make things easy for views; for example, by performing non-trivial calculations and exposing the results, even if the inputs to the calculation are available to views from the model's other bean properties.

❑ **Models should expose all the information required by the view**
There should be no need – and therefore, no excuse – for views to access `HttpRequest` or `HttpSession` objects. The use of incomplete models will constrain view implementations to those technologies, such as JSP, that facilitate access to the underlying Servlet API objects.

❑ **Views, not models, should usually handle locale-specific issues**
Model objects are not necessarily display-specific, and so shouldn't need to handle localization issues.

Sometimes the second of these four rules can best be followed by creating an **adapter** bean: a value object that caches and exposes all model data needed by one or more views in a way that makes it simple to access. For example, an adapter might expose via bean properties data retrieved by method calls on several non-bean objects with complex interfaces. In such cases, the adapter simplifies the data interface available to views and suppresses unwanted, distracting information. We have no need for this adapter approach in the sample application, as domain objects such as the Reservation object are naturally suited to use as models without any design compromises being necessary.

If an adapter bean is used, it should be created by the relevant controller, not the view. Although it is easy for JSP pages to create adapter beans, and this approach is sometimes advocated, this breaks the principle of view substitutability.

JSP Views

JSP has come to be the dominant view technology for J2EE web applications, largely because it is blessed by Sun as a core part of J2EE.

JSP views offer the following benefits:

❑ They're easy to develop. Recompilation on request (at least during development) means rapid develop-deploy cycles.

❑ The use of Java as a scripting language makes it easy to access Java application objects such as models.

❑ Good performance, because JSP pages are compiled into servlets. However, as we'll see in Chapter 15, we shouldn't assume that this means that JSP will always be the highest-performing view option.

❑ JSP is one of the J2EE standards. There's a wealth of literature on JSP authoring, and substantial tool support. Many developers are familiar with JSP.

❑ JSP's support for **custom tags** (discussed below) means that third-party tag libraries are available for a variety of purposes and that the capabilities of JSP can be extended in a standard way.

Standardization is usually a good thing. However, there is a danger that a flawed solution can be used too widely merely because it is a standard. JSP also has such significant drawbacks as a view technology that is questionable whether it would have survived with Sun's imprimatur:

❑ JSP's origins predate the use of MVC for web applications and it shows. The JSP programming model owes much to Microsoft's Active Server Pages (ASP), which dates back to 1996. ASP uses similar syntax and the same model of escaping between executable script and static markup. Microsoft has recently moved away from this model, as experience has shown that ASP applications become messy and unmaintainable.

- ❑ **Scriptlets** (blocks of Java code in JSP pages) can be used to perform complex processing, including EJB tier access, rather than just support view rendering. This is not a positive. It's too tempting to abuse this power. This is one of the central arguments against JSP. If a facility exists and is easy to use, someone is bound to use it, regardless of the long-term consequences.

- ❑ The temptation exists – again, because it is so easy – to use JSP pages to handle control logic. JSP pages provide infrastructure for request handling, including mapping request parameters onto JavaBeans, that's more harmful than helpful in practice.

- ❑ JSP syntax is relatively clumsy and error-prone. This shortcoming can, however, be offset by appropriate use of JSP tag libraries and authoring tools.

- ❑ Syntax errors in JSP pages can produce confusing error output. JSP pages can encounter both translation-time and runtime errors. The quality of error messages varies between web containers.

- ❑ As JSP syntax includes characters illegal in XML, it's impossible to guarantee that JSP documents will generate well-formed markup. Generating well-formed markup may be an important consideration. The JSP specification defines an XML syntax for JSP, but it's not intended for hand authoring.

- ❑ JSP pages are hard to test in isolation, because they're not proper Java classes and because they depend on web container infrastructure at translation time and runtime as well as the Servlet API. Thus we can usually only test JSP pages as part of acceptance testing of a web application.

In practice, the negatives associated with JSP are surprisingly harmful. For background reading on the drawbacks of JSP pages, see the following articles among the many that have been published on the subject:

- ❑ http://www.servlets.com/soapbox/problems-jsp.html. An early and often-quoted contribution to the JSP debate by Jason Hunter, the author of several books on servlets.

- ❑ http://jakarta.apache.org/velocity/ymtd/ymtd.html. This is basically a plug for the Velocity templating system (which we'll discuss below), but makes many valid criticisms of JSP.

In the remainder of this section, we'll look at how to enjoy the advantages of JSP without suffering from its disadvantages. Essentially, this amounts to minimizing the amount of Java code in JSP pages.

The following is a discussion of how to use the JSP infrastructure in maintainable web applications, not a tutorial on the JSP infrastructure itself. Please refer to reference material on JSP if necessary.

> An indication that JSP pages are being used correctly is when JSP pages do not violate the substitutability of views discussed in Chapter 12. For example, if a JSP is (inappropriately) used to handle requests, a JSP view could not be replaced by an XSLT view without breaking the functionality of the application.

What We Want to Avoid

To demonstrate the consequences of misuse of JSP, let's look at an example of a JSP that isn't merely a view, but uses the power of Java to handle incoming requests ("Model 1" style) and uses J2EE APIs.

As the control logic behind the "Show Reservation" view would make a JSP Model 1 version too lengthy, I've used a simple page that enables us to query seat availability by performance ID and seat type. A more realistic version of this page would present dropdowns allowing the user to input these values, but for the sake of the example I've neglected this, along with concern about the user entering non-numeric values.

This JSP, `model1.jsp`, both displays a form allowing the user to input performance and seat type, and processes the result. If the request is a form submission, the number of seats available will be displayed below the form; otherwise just the form will be displayed. The output of this page will look as follows:

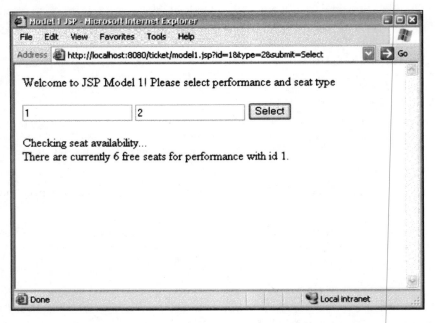

The listing begins with imports of the Java objects used (both J2EE and application-specific). Note that we must use the JSP error page mechanism in the highlighted line to avoid the need to catch every exception that may occur on the page.

```
<%@ page errorPage="jsp/debug/debug.jsp" %>

<%@ page import="javax.naming.InitialContext" %>
<%@ page import="com.wrox.expertj2ee.ticket.boxoffice.BoxOffice" %>
<%@ page
    import="com.wrox.expertj2ee.ticket.exceptions.NoSuchPerformanceException" %>
<%@ page import="com.wrox.expertj2ee.ticket.boxoffice.ejb.*" %>
```

Next we declare a simple bean with properties matching the expected request parameters, so we don't need to work directly with the request. The Model1Bean class is included in the source with the sample application: it simply exposes two int properties: id and type. Note the use of the `<jsp:setProperty>` standard action to populate these properties from request parameters. For the sake of the example, we won't worry about the user entering non-numeric input:

```
<jsp:useBean id="queryBean"
  class="com.wrox.expertj2ee.ticket.web.Model1Bean"
  scope="session">
  <jsp:setProperty name="queryBean" property="*" />
</jsp:useBean>
```

Next there's a little template data:

```
<html>
<head>
<title>Model 1 JSP</title>
</head>
<body>
Welcome to JSP Model 1!
Please select performance and seat type
```

Whether processing a form submission or not, we will display the form. The form's fields will be prepopulated with the bean's property values, which will both be 0 on first displaying the page:

```
<form method="GET" >
  <input type="text" name="id"
         value="<jsp:getProperty name="queryBean" property="id" />" />
  <input type="text" name="type"
         value="<jsp:getProperty name="queryBean" property="type" />" />
  <input type="submit" name="submit" value="Select" />
</form>
```

If this JSP isn't invoked by a form submission, this is all the content we'll see. If it is processing a form submission, which we can tell by checking for the presence of a `submit` request parameter, the scriptlet in the rest of the page takes effect.

The scriptlet performs a JNDI lookup for the `BoxOffice` EJB. Once it obtains it, it queries it for the availability of seats for the performance id and seat type held in the bean. We make no effort to catch JNDI or EJB API errors, but let the JSP error page mechanism handle such errors. Adding additional `try/catch` blocks would be unacceptably complex.

The output generated will vary whether or not there *is* a performance with the specified id. If there isn't, the `BoxOffice getFreeSeatCount()` method will throw a `NoSuchPerformanceException`, which the JSP catches, to provide an opportunity to generate different output. I've highlighted the lines that generate output, which account for less than half the source of the JSP:

```
<% if (request.getParameter("submit") != null) { %>

    Checking seat availability...<br>

<%
  int freeSeats = 0;
  InitialContext ic = new InitialContext();
  Object o = ic.lookup("java:comp/env/ejb/BoxOffice");
  BoxOfficeHome home = (BoxOfficeHome) o;

  BoxOffice boxOffice = home.create();
```

```
try {
   freeSeats = boxOffice.getFreeSeatCount(
                       queryBean.getId(), queryBean.getType());
%>
       There are currently <%=freeSeats%> free seats
       for performance with id <jsp:getProperty name="queryBean" property="id" />.

   <% } catch (NoSuchPerformanceException ex) { %>

       There's no performance with id <jsp:getProperty name="queryBean"
       property="id" />.
       <br>Please try another id.

<% }
} %>
```

Finally, some closing template data is displayed in any case:

```
</body>
</html>
```

Although this JSP doesn't fulfill a realistic function, it does display problems seen in reality. Most experienced J2EE developers have seen – and had to clean up the problems caused by – many such JSP pages.

What's wrong with this, and why will such JSP pages always prove a maintainability nightmare in real applications? The many problems include:

❑ This JSP has two roles (displaying an input form and displaying the results of processing it), making it confusing to read.

❑ The constant escaping between template data and JSP is confusing. Although JSP authoring tools will help prevent unmatched <% and %>s, there is no way of making the combination of Java control structures (if, try/catch) and markup generation in this page readable. It's impossible to understand the content this JSP will produce without some knowledge of Java (for example, Java exception handling).

❑ This JSP is coupled to the EJB implementation of some business objects. If we choose to move away from EJB, we would need to change all such JSP pages, even if we wanted to retain the same presentation. Even changing the JNDI name of the EJB would require a change to all such JSP pages.

❑ The structure of the JSP doesn't reflect the content it will generate. In each of its roles the output will be different.

❑ The exception handling is primitive. We may encounter errors when it's too late to do anything about them, while we're generating dynamic content. Any error will lead to the error page: it will be too late to perform appropriate control flow on particular classes of error.

❑ It would be difficult to add checks that the inputs supplied were numeric, and warn the user accordingly. The page would become even more unreadable.

❑ There's so much Java code in the scriptlets that it's difficult to envisage the markup that will be generated.

❑ With JSP pages like this, changing presentation might easily break the business logic.

In short, there's no separation between presentation and workflow: the one JSP handles everything, making it completely unintelligible to an HTML developer who might be asked to modify the appearance of the generated markup.

How to Use JavaBeans in JSP Pages

After this salutary negative example, let's look at how to write JSP pages that *are* maintainable.

The data displayed in JSP pages normally comes from one or more JavaBeans declared on the page using the `<jsp:useBean>` standard action. In an MVC architecture, these beans will have been set as request attributes before the view is invoked. In some frameworks, controllers will set model data as request attributes. In our framework, an implementation of the `View` interface will expose model attributes as request parameters before forwarding to a JSP. The syntax for appropriate use of the `<jsp:useBean>` action within an MVC web application is as follows:

```
<jsp:useBean
  id="performance"
  type="com.wrox.expertj2ee.ticket.referencedata.Performance"
  scope="request"
/>
```

The value of the `id` attribute will be the name of the bean object, available to expressions, scriptlets, and actions.

Note the `scope` attribute, which determines whether the bean value is set by an attribute value from the local JSP `PageContext`, the `HttpRequest`, the `HttpSession` (if one exists), or the global `ServletContext`. There are four values for scope: `page`, `request`, `session`, and `application`, of which only one (`request`) is compatible with correct use of JSP in an MVC web application, as views shouldn't access (and potentially manipulate) session or application-wide state.

> *A bean of page scope is a local object, used within the current JSP. There are some situations in which this is appropriate, although I prefer to avoid object creation in JSP pages altogether.*

You might notice that I've omitted the optional `class` attribute, which specifies the fully-qualified bean implementation class, rather than the relevant *type*, which may be interface, as specified by the `type` parameter that I have used. By only specifying the type, and not the bean class, we've deprived the JSP of the ability to instantiate a new bean if none is found in the specified scope. It will throw a `java.lang.InstantiationException` instead.

This is good practice, as unless the bean has been made available to the JSP as part of the model, the JSP should not have been invoked: we don't want it to fail mysteriously after automatically creating a new, unconfigured object in place of the missing model object. By specifying only the type, we retain flexibility in the controller (which can supply a model object of any type that implements the interface), and restrict the JSP's access to the bean to the most limited interface that's relevant: another good practice if interface inheritance is involved, or if the object is of a class that not only implements the interface but exposes other properties that are irrelevant to the view in question.

> Never allow the `<jsp:useBean>` action to create an object if none is found in scope by specifying the `class` attribute. A JSP *should* fail if required model data is not supplied. Use only `request` scope with the `<jsp:useBean>` action. This means that, as the default scope is `page`, we must always specify `request` scope explicitly.
>
> JSP pages should not access session or application objects; merely model data exposed by a controller. Even if some model data is also bound in the user's session, or shared with other users (and perhaps bound in the `ServletContext`), the controller should pass it to views as part of the model. Using this approach enables us to use any view technology, and to test views in isolation.

As I noted in Chapter 12, the JSP request property-to-bean mapping mechanism is too naïve to be usable in most real situations. It's also a danger to good design. Unfortunately, there is confusion in the way in which beans are supported in the JSP specification. A bean should really be a model for the page, but the mapping from request parameters onto bean properties means that beans can also be used as a way of helping the JSP handle the request. This is a JSP Model 1 approach, incompatible with an MVC architecture. It seemed plausible when the first version of the JSP specification was drawn up; experience has since shown this to be fatally flawed.

JSP Custom Tags

The most significant enhancement in JSP 1.1 was the introduction of **custom tags**, also known as **tag extensions**. These greatly enhance the power of JSP, but can be used inappropriately.

Custom tags offer the following benefits:

- ❏ They provide a neat way of moving code that would otherwise be in JSP pages into tag handler classes. For example, they can conceal the complexity of iteration over model data from JSP pages that use them.
- ❏ Custom tags are portable. They're packaged in a standard way, and promote reuse.
- ❏ Libraries of custom tags are available to solve many common problems, both in open source and commercially.

However, custom tags also pose some dangers:

- ❏ Custom tags add further temptation to use JSP for purposes other than as views. Far better than moving code out of a JSP to a custom tag is designing the web tier so that JSP pages don't need to contain code.
- ❏ The XML-based custom tag syntax is not always appropriate.
- ❏ As of JSP 1.2, custom tags are implemented in Java. While in some cases this is appropriate, it's problematic when custom tags are purely presentation, as the whole point of using JSP is to avoid the need for Java code to manipulate content.
- ❏ Each custom tag carries a lot of baggage. Implementing a custom tag requires at least one Java class to be written, as well as an XML tag library descriptor.
- ❏ Heavy use of custom tags can slightly reduce the performance of a JSP. However, this is usually a minor concern in practice.

❑ As custom tags can parse their body content, rather than letting the JSP engine evaluate it, it's possible for custom tags to produce unexpected behavior (for example, a custom tag could provide an interpreter for a unique language that could be used as its body content). This is another example of the potential within JSP to achieve functionality that's best avoided.

Custom tags have proven very popular, and they're now central to how JSP is used.

Before we look at specific uses of custom tags, let's consider what role they should play in the MVC web application architecture we've described.

> **If JSP pages are to be used as views, custom tags are *view helpers*. They're neither models nor controllers; they will principally be used to help display the models available to the JSP view.**

We shouldn't use custom tags to do things that are outside the role of views. For example, retrieving data from a database may be easy to implement in a tag handler, but is not the business of a JSP view. Moving the code into a tag handler class won't improve the fundamentally broken error handling. In general, enterprise access (such as EJB access and JNDI access) shouldn't be performed in tags. For this reason, I feel that tag libraries that offer simple database access and the like are dangerous, and should not be used in well-designed web applications.

It's also not usually a good idea to use tags to output markup. Sometimes there's no alternative, but there are several reasons why it's best avoided:

❑ If a custom tag generates markup, it limits the situations in which it can be used. It's the role of JSP pages that use the tag to control the appearance of the page.

❑ Tag handlers are Java components. As experience has shown since the early days of servlets, generating markup from Java code is messy. JSP pages, on the other hand, are natural template components and well suited to generating markup.

Fortunately, custom tags can define scripting variables, letting JSP pages handle output formatting.

The Java Standard Tag Library

Since I started work on this book, there has been a major milestone in JSP usability: the release of the **JSP Standard Tag Library (JSTL 1.0)**. I consider this as more important than the release of JSP 1.2, which was a minor incremental step in the evolution of JSP.

The JSTL offers the following:

❑ An **Expression Language (EL)** that simplifies access to JavaBean properties and offers nested property support. This can be used in attributes passed to the tags in the library.

❑ "General purpose action" tags that can output the value of expressions, create and remove scripting variables and perform error handling.

❑ "Conditional action" tags analogous to Java `if` and `switch` statements or (if you prefer) XSLT's `<xsl:if>` and `<xsl:choose>`.

❏ "Iterator action" tags, which offer a consistent syntax for iteration over Java arrays, Collections, Iterators, Enumerations, Maps, and tokens (as in CSV strings).

❏ "URL related action" tags, which conceal URL encoding and "URL rewriting" when creating URLs and allow easy "importing" of content from resources either inside or outside the current web application.

❏ "Internationalization action" tags that allow easy access to messages in the appropriate locale, kept in standard Java resource bundles.

❏ "Formatting action" tags that allow easy, localizable formatting of dates and numbers.

❏ "SQL action" tags that allow RDBMS operations to be performed easily from JSP pages.

❏ XML tags that support XPath expressions, XML parsing and XSLT transformations on XML data.

Of course none of these tags is original. The JSTL is a codification of the many variants of such tags many developers (including myself) have written since the release of JSP 1.1, but it's exciting because:

❏ It's a standard, and thus is likely to become a *lingua franca* among JSP developers

❏ It's an elegant, well-thought-out and well-integrated whole, based on wide experience

❏ It's a relatively small set of tags without confusing duplication

❏ The JSTL Expression Language is to be incorporated in JSP 2.0

I've seen and implemented many tag libraries, and my instinct is that JSTL has got it right: these tags are simple yet powerful, and intuitive to use.

The only one of the JSTL tag libraries that is questionable is the SQL tag library. As the designers of the JSTL recognize, this shouldn't be used in well-designed applications. Its use is best restricted to prototypes or trivial applications.

I won't discuss individual JSTL tags here, as I'll demonstrate the use of some of the most important in sample application code later in this chapter. The examples shipped with the Jakarta implementation are worth careful examination, displaying most common uses.

The sample application uses the Apache implementation of the JSTL, available from http://jakarta.apache.org/taglibs/. I've found it very usable, although with a tendency to throw `NullPointerExceptions` that occasionally makes debugging more difficult than it should be.

It's hard to overemphasize the importance of the JSP Standard Tag Library. This effectively adds a new language – the JSTL Expression Language – to JSP. As there were a lot of problems with the old approach of using Java scriptlets, and the JSP standard actions were inadequate to address many problems, this is a Very Good Thing.

If you use JSP, learn and use the JSTL. Use the superior JSTL Expression Language in place of the limited `<jsp:getProperty>` standard action. Use JSTL iteration in place of for and while loops. However, don't use the SQL actions: RDBMS access has no place in view code, but is the job of business objects (not even web tier controllers).

Other Third-Party Tag Libraries

The Jakarta TagLibs site is a good source of other open-source tag libraries, and a good place to visit if you're considering implementing your own tag libraries. Many of the tags offered here, as elsewhere, are incompatible with the responsibility of JSP views, but they can still be of great value to us.

Especially interesting are caching tags, which can be used to boost performance by caching parts of JSP pages. Jakarta TagLibs has such tags in development, while OpenSymphony (http://www.opensymphony.com/) has a more mature implementation.

Implementing Your Own Tag Libraries

Although it's fairly easy to implement application-specific tag libraries, don't rush into it. Now that the JSTL is available, many application or site-specific tags are no longer necessary. For example, the JSTL Expression Language renders many application-specific tags designed to help display complex objects redundant (JSTL tags using the Expression Language can easily display complex data).

I suggest the following guidelines if you are considering implementing your own tags:

- ❑ Don't duplicate JSTL tags or the functionality of existing third-party tags. The more unique tags an application uses, the longer the learning curve for developers who will need to maintain it in future.

- ❑ Try to wear a content developer's, rather than Java developer's, hat when designing tags. Clever programming won't necessarily produce benefits; simple, intuitive usage patterns will.

- ❑ Design tags to co-operate with JSTL tags, recognizing that the JSTL tags provide a good, standard, solution to many common problems. For example, don't write conditional tags; ensure that your tags expose scripting variables that can be used with JSTL tags. The i21 tag library included with the framework code accompanying the sample application illustrates how new tags can be designed to co-operate with JSTL tags.

- ❑ Make tags as configurable as possible. This can be achieved through tag attributes and using nesting to provide context. Optional attributes can be used where default values can be supplied.

- ❑ Use the JSP 1.2 declarative syntax to define scripting variables, rather than the JSP 1.1 TagExtraInfo class mechanism, which is more complex and seldom necessary.

- ❑ Avoid generating HTML in tag handlers unless absolutely necessary. Tags can usually be designed to allow the JSP pages that use them to control markup generation.

- ❑ When tags handlers *must* generate HTML, ensure that the generated HTML can be used in a wide variety of contexts: try to avoid generating <html>, <form>, and other structural tags. Consider reading the HTML from a properties file.

- ❑ Use tags to declare scripting variables to help JSP pages format markup.

- ❑ Avoid making custom tags do unexpected things to the request and response. Just because tag handlers *can* access these objects through the PageContext doesn't mean that it's a good idea. How obvious will it be to a reader of a JSP using a custom tag that the tag may redirect the response? Unless the tag's documentation is scrupulous, figuring this out might require plunging into the tag's Java implementation.

> Don't implement your own JSP custom tags without good reason. Especially given the power of the JSTL, many application-specific custom tags are no longer necessary. The more your own JSP dialect diverges from standard JSP plus the JSTL, the harder it will be to maintain your applications.

Guidelines for Custom Tag Use

Here are some guidelines for using custom tags, application-specific and standard:

❑   *Do* use the JSTL: it almost always offers a superior alternative to scriptlets. JSTL will soon be universally understood by JSP developers, ensuring that pages using it are maintainable.

❑   *Don't* use proprietary tag libraries – such as the Struts logic tags – or implement your own tags if JSTL tags can be used to achieve the same result.

❑   *Don't* use tag handlers to do things that views shouldn't do, such as retrieve data. Tag handlers are view helpers, not control components.

❑   *Don't* use tag handlers to perform complex iteration involving deep nesting. This means creating a non-standard XML scripting language, and is likely to make JSP pages hard to understand. I've seen cases where JSP pages using deeply nested custom tags proved harder to maintain than JSP pages using ordinary scriptlets might have.

❑   *Don't* implement your own custom tags without good reason.

> A custom tag should be used as a refactoring of view logic out of a JSP view. It shouldn't conceal the implementation of tasks that are inappropriate in views.

Guidelines for JSP Use

Let's finish with some overall recommendations for using JSP. The following guidelines may seem overly restrictive. However, the chances are that if you can't see how a JSP could work within them, it is probably trying to do inappropriate work and needs to be refactored.

❑   Uses JSP pages purely as views. If a JSP does something that couldn't be accomplished by another view technology (because of the integration with Java or the sophisticated scripting involved) the application's design is at fault. The code should be refactored into a controller or business object.

❑   Place conditional logic in controllers rather than in JSP views. If a substantial part of a JSP varies according to a condition, the JSP is a candidate for refactoring, with a controller forwarding requests to two separate pages, each of which includes the common parts. In contrast, if only a small part of a JSP varies, as in our example's check as to whether the allocated seats are adjacent, it is correct to place the conditional inside a JSP.

❑   Consider placing JSP pages under the /WEB-INF directory, so that they can't be requested directly by clients. The Servlet 2.3 specification is unclear on whether it's legal for a RequestDispatcher to forward to resources under the /WEB-INF directory. This may not work in all J2EE 1.3 web containers, although the confusion is cleared up in favor of allowing it in the Servlet 2.4 specification (section 9.5).

❑ Turn off automatic session creation with the following directive:

```
<%@ page session="false" %>
```

This will improve performance, and enforces good design practice. Views shouldn't be given access to session data, as they might modify it, subverting good design. It's the job of controllers, not views, to decide whether a user should have server-side state in an HttpSession object.

❑ JSP pages should not directly access request parameters. Controllers should perform request processing and expose processed model data to JSP pages and other views. Accessing request parameters requires careful error checking; this is likely to be overlooked in JSP pages, and will complicate them if it is not.

❑ All beans used by JSP pages should have request scope.

❑ Avoid using the JSP inheritance mechanism. JSP pages can subclass a custom superclass that implements the javax.servlet.jsp.HttpJspPage interface, rather than the implementation provided by the container, as occurs by default. The inheritance mechanism is another powerful but questionable piece of the JSP infrastructure, for which I'm yet to see a legitimate application. Using inheritance is also likely to reduce performance, as containers normally provide optimized implementations of the HttpJspPage interface.

❑ JSP pages should not use enterprise APIs such as JNDI or JDBC.

❑ Don't use the standard mechanism of mapping request parameters onto JSP bean properties. It's not powerful enough to solve real-world problems, yet subverts good design practice.

❑ Avoid code duplication in JSP pages. The need for code duplication is an indication of poor design. Refactor the duplicated functionality into an included JSP, bean, or custom tag to make it reusable.

❑ Avoid using out.println() to generate page content. Using this syntax encourages thinking of JSP pages as programs rather than web pages, and is likely to confuse an HTML designer editing a JSP.

❑ Try hard to avoid scriptlets, through appropriate refactoring and use of the JSTL. There are situations in which scriptlets cannot be avoided; accept these, but only after considering all genuine alternatives.

❑ Don't use the <jsp:forward> standard action. It's the JSP equivalent of the dreaded goto, and can make page behavior hard to comprehend. Forwarding violates the principle that a JSP is a view; if the JSP does not know how to respond to the request it was passed, there is an error in the design of the system. The choice of view is a matter for a controller, not a JSP view.

❑ In general, declarations or scriptlets shouldn't be used to create variables referred to throughout a JSP. State within a JSP should be held within beans. Custom tags may, however, legitimately declare scripting variables.

❑ Don't use custom tags to enable JSP pages to do things such as database access that aren't appropriate to views.

❑ Hidden comments should be used to prevent comments bloating HTML output. Document not only the handling of dynamic content, but also any complex markup. This may cause more confusion to readers than appropriately used expressions and custom tags.

❑ Avoid exception handling in JSP pages. In an MVC web application, there should be no need to use `try/catch` blocks in JSP pages or even the standard error page mechanism, as JSP pages shouldn't encounter recoverable errors at runtime.

❑ Don't override the `jspInit()` and `jspDestroy()` methods in a JSP. Using these methods makes a JSP more like a servlet (a program) and less like a web page. Acquiring and relinquishing resources is the business of controllers, not JSP views, so there should be no need for cleanup in JSP pages.

❑ Don't define methods, constants or inner classes in JSP pages. This is another JSP capability that is best avoided.

Looking Ahead: Implications of JSP 2.0

This book is about what you can use right now to build real applications. However, when major changes are signaled well in advance, there can be implications for design strategy.

JSP 2.0 – in proposed final draft at the time of writing – will bring major changes to JSP authoring. In particular, it integrates the Expression Language introduced in the JSTL into the JSP core, simplifies the authoring of custom tags and adds a more sophisticated inclusion mechanism based on **JSP fragments**.

> **JSP 2.0 will bring the most major changes in the history of JSP, although it will be backward compatible. Many of these changes tend to formalize the move away from Java scriptlets that most experienced Java web developers have already made. JSP 2.0 will bring the JSTL Expression Language into the JSP core, allowing easier and more sophisticated navigation of JavaBean properties. It will also allow for simpler custom tag definitions, without the need for Java programming.**
>
> **By avoiding scriptlets and learning to maximize use of the JSTL it's possible to move towards the JSP 2.0 model even with JSP 1.2.**

A JSP View for the Example

The only code we need to write as part of our application is the JSP exposing our model. However, first we'll need to create a view definition enabling the framework's view resolver to resolve the "Show Reservation" view name to our JSP view.

The `com.interface21.web.servlet.view.InternalResourceView` class provides a standard framework implementation of the `View` interface that can be used for views wrapping JSP pages or static web application content. This class, discussed in Appendix A, exposes all the entries in the model `Map` returned by the controller as request attributes, making them available to the target JSP as beans with request scope. The request attribute name in each case is the same as `Map` key. Once all attributes are set, the `InternalResourceView` class uses a Servlet API `RequestDispatcher` to forward to the JSP specified as a bean property.

The only bean property we need to set for the `InternalResourceView` implementation is `url`: the URL of the JSP within the WAR. The following two lines in the `/WEB-INF/classes/views.properties` file define the view named `showReservation` that we've taken as our example:

```
showReservation.class=com.interface21.web.servlet.view.InternalResourceView
showReservation.url=/showReservation.jsp
```

This completely decouples controller from JSP view; when selecting the "Show Reservation" view, the `TicketController` class doesn't know whether this view is rendered by `showReservation.jsp`, `/WEB-INF/jsp/booking/reservation.jsp`, an XSLT stylesheet or a class that generates PDF.

Let's now move onto actual JSP code, and look at implementing a JSP view for the example. We won't need to write any more Java code; the framework has taken care of routing the request to the new JSP.

We'll do this in two steps: first implement a JSP that uses scriptlets to present the dynamic content; then implement a JSP that uses the JSTL to simplify things. These two JSP pages can be found in the sample application's WAR named `showReservationNoStl.jsp` and `showReservation.jsp` respectively.

In each case, we begin by switching off automatic session creation. We don't want a JSP view to create a session if none exists – session management is a controller responsibility:

```
<%@ page session="false" %>
```

Next we make the three model beans available to the remainder of the page:

```
<jsp:useBean id="performance"
  type="com.wrox.expertj2ee.ticket.referencedata.Performance"
  scope="request"
/>

<jsp:useBean id="priceband"
  type="com.wrox.expertj2ee.ticket.referencedata.PriceBand"
  scope="request"
/>

<jsp:useBean id="reservation"
  type="com.wrox.expertj2ee.ticket.boxoffice.Reservation"
  scope="request"
/>
```

Note that as recommended above, I've specified the type, not class, for each bean, and each is given `request` scope.

Now let's look at outputting the data using scriptlets, to demonstrate the problems that will result.

The first challenge is to format the date and currency for the user's locale. If we simply output the when property of the performance, we'll get the default `toString()` value, which is not user-friendly. Thus we need to use a scriptlet to format the date and time parts of the performance date in an appropriate format. We use the `java.text.SimpleDateFormat` class to apply a pattern intelligible in all locales, ensuring that month and day text appears in the user's language and avoiding problems with the US and British date formatting convention – mm/dd/yy and dd/mm/yy respectively. We'll save the formatted text in a scripting variable, so we don't need to interrupt content rendering later:

```
<%
  java.text.SimpleDateFormat df = new java.text.SimpleDateFormat();
  df.applyPattern("EEEE MMMM dd, yyyy");
  String formattedDate = df.format(performance.getWhen());
  df.applyPattern("h:mm a");
  String formattedTime = df.format(performance.getWhen());
%>
```

We need a similar scriptlet to handle the two currency values, the total price and booking fee. This will use the `java.text.NumberFormat` class to obtain and use a currency formatter, which will prepend the appropriate currency symbol:

```
<%
  java.text.NumberFormat cf = java.text.NumberFormat.getCurrencyInstance();
  String formattedTotalPrice = cf.format(reservation.getTotalPrice());
  String formattedBookingFee =
cf.format(reservation.getQuoteRequest().getBookingFee());
%>
```

Now we can output the header:

```
<b><%=performance.getShow().getName()%>: <%=formattedDate%>
at
<%=formattedTime%>
</b>
<br>
<p>

<%= reservation.getSeats().length %> seats in
<%=priceband.getDescription()%>
have been reserved
for you for
<jsp:getProperty name="reservation"
                 property="minutesReservationWillBeValid" />
minutes to give you time to complete your purchase.
```

Since the `<jsp:getProperty>` standard action can't handled nested properties, I've had to use an expression to get the name of the show, which involves two path steps from the Performance bean. I also had to use an expression, rather than `<jsp:getProperty>`, to get the PriceBand object's description property, which is inherited from the SeatType interface. The Jasper JSP engine used by JBoss/Jetty 3.0.0 has problems understanding inherited properties – a serious bug in this implementation of JSP, which is used by several web containers.

Now we need to iterate over the Seat objects in the seats array exposed by the Reservation object:

```
The seat numbers are:
<ul>
<% for (int i = 0; i < reservation.getSeats().length; i++) { %>
  <li><%= reservation.getSeats()[i].getName()%>
<% } %>
</ul>
```

This is quite verbose, as we need to declare a scripting variable for each seat or invoke the `getSeats()` method *before* specifying an array index when outputting the name of each seat.

Since we declared the `formattedTotalPrice` and `formattedBookingFee` variables in the scriptlet that handled date formatting, it's easy to output this information using expressions:

```
The total cost of these tickets will be <%=formattedTotalPrice%>.
This includes a booking fee of
<%=formattedBookingFee%>.
```

A simple scriptlet enables us to display the link to allow the user to select another performance if the `Reservation` object indicates that the allocated seats were not adjacent. This isn't much of a problem for readability, but we do need to remember to close the compound statement for the conditional:

```
<% if (!reservation.getSeatsAreAdjacent()) { %>
  <b>Please note that due to lack of availability, some of the
  seats offered are not adjacent.</b>
  <form method="GET" action="payment.html">
  <input type="submit" value="Try another date"></input>
  </form>
<% } %>
```

We can work out the seating plan image URL within the WAR from the show ID.

> *There is one image for each seating plan in the `/static/seatingplans` directory, the filename being of the form `<seatingplanId>.jpg`. Note that building this URL in the view is legitimate; it's no concern of the model that we need to display a seating plan image, or how we should locate the image file. We'll include static content from this directly whichever view technology we use.*

We can use a scriptlet to save this URL in a variable before using the HTML `<img>` tag. This two-step process makes the JSP more readable:

```
<% String seatingPlanImage = "static/seatingplans/" +
       performance.getShow().getSeatingPlanId() + ".jpg"; %>
<img src="<%=seatingPlanImage%>" />
```

This version of the JSP, using scriptlets, isn't disastrous. The use of the MVC pattern has ensured that the JSP has purely presentational responsibilities, and is pretty simple. However, the complete page is inelegant and wouldn't prove very easy for markup authors without Java knowledge to maintain.

Let's now look at using the JSTL to improve things. The following version of this page is that actually used in the sample application.

Our main aims will be to simplify date and currency formatting and to address the problem of the verbose iteration over the array of seats. We will also benefit from the JSTL's Expression Language to make property navigation more intuitive where nested properties are concerned.

We will begin with exactly the same page directive to switch off automatic session creation, and the same three `<jsp:useBean>` actions. However, we will need to import the core JSTL tag library and the formatting library before we can use them as follows:

```
<%@ taglib prefix="c" uri="http://java.sun.com/jstl/core" %>
<%@ taglib prefix="fmt" uri="http://java.sun.com/jstl/fmt" %>
```

I'll start the listing where things differ.

We can use the `<c:out>` tag and the JSTL expression language to output the value of nested properties intuitively. Note that now that we don't need to use scriptlets, we don't need the get prefix when accessing properties or the parentheses, making things much neater, especially where nested properties are concerned:

```
<b><c:out value="${performance.show.name}"/>:
```

As the above fragment illustrates, the Expression Language can only be used in attributes of JSTL tags, and expression language values are enclosed as follows: `${expression}`. The use of special surrounding characters allows expressions to be used as a part of an attribute value that also contains literal string content. The JSTL expression language supports arithmetic and logical operators, as well as nested property navigation. The above example shows how nested property navigation is achieved using the . operator.

Date formatting is also a lot nicer. We use the same patterns, defined in `java.text.SimpleDateFormat`, but we can achieve the formatting without any Java code, using the format tag library:

```
<fmt:formatDate value="${performance.when}" type="date" pattern="EEEE MMMM dd,
yyyy" />
at
<fmt:formatDate value="${performance.when}" type="time" pattern="h:mm a" />
</b>
<br/>
<p>
```

The JSTL doesn't allow method invocations through the expression language, so I had to use an ordinary JSP expression to display the length of the seats array in the reservation object (an array's length isn't a bean property):

```
<%= reservation.getSeats().length %>
seats in
<c:out value="${priceband.description}"/>
have been reserved
for you for
<c:out value="${reservation.minutesReservationWillBeValid}" />
minutes to give you time to complete your purchase.
```

Iterating over the array of seats is much less verbose using JSTL iteration, because it enables us to create a variable, which we've called `seat`, for each array element. Things are also simplified by simple nested property navigation:

```
<c:forEach var="seat" items="${reservation.seats}" >
  <li><c:out value="${seat.name}"/>
</c:forEach>.
```

Currency formatting is also a lot nicer with the JSTL formatting tag library. Again, there's no need to escape into Java, and nested property access is simple and intuitive:

```
The total cost of these tickets will be
<fmt:formatNumber value="${reservation.totalPrice}" type="currency"/>.
This includes a booking fee of
<fmt:formatNumber value="${reservation.quoteRequest.bookingFee}"
type="currency"/>.
```

For consistency, we use the JSTL core library's conditional tag, rather than a scriptlet to display the additional content to be displayed if the seats are not adjacent. Using markup instead of a scriptlet isn't necessarily more intuitive for a conditional, but again the Expression Language simplifies nested property access:

```
<c:if test="${!reservation.seatsAreAdjacent}" >
  <b>Please note that due to lack of availability, some of the
  seats offered are not adjacent.</b>
  <form method="GET" action="payment.html">
  <input type="submit" value="Try another date"></input>
  </form>
</c:if>
```

Finally, we use a nested property expression to find the URL of the seating plan image. Note that only part of the `value` attribute is evaluated as an expression – the remainder is literal String content:

```
<img src="
  <c:out value="static/seatingplans/${performance.show.seatingPlanId}.jpg" />"
/>
```

The two versions of this page use the same nominal technology (JSP) but are very different. The second version is simpler and easier to maintain. The example demonstrates both that JSTL is an essential part of the JSP developer's armory and that the JSTL completely changes how JSP pages display data. A JSP 2.0 version of this page would be much closer to the second, JSTL version, than the standard JSP 1.2 version shown first.

JSP Summary

JSP is the view technology defined in the J2EE specifications. It offers good performance and a reasonably intuitive scripting model. However, JSP must be used with caution. Unless strict coding standards are applied, the power of J2EE can prove a grave danger to maintainability.

The JSP Standard Template Library can make JSP pages simpler and more elegant, through its simple, intuitive Expression Language, and by supporting many common requirements through standard custom tags.

> **Don't use just standard JSP. Use JSP with the JSTL. As our example illustrates, using the JSTL can greatly simplify JSP pages and help us to avoid the need to use scriptlets.**

Dedicated Template Languages

If we're only using JSP pages for views, we're using JSP pages as **templates**. If we base our JSP usage on the JSTL, we're largely abandoning the original JSP idea of using Java as the scripting language.

Since we don't want to use the request handling capability of JSP pages or the power of Java scripting JSP pages offer and believe that the availability of these features may actually be harmful, it's reasonable to question why we should be using JSP at all.

There are many alternative template languages to JSP, available in open source (XSLT deserves its own section and is discussed later). Unlike JSP, these are designed purely as template languages. Each has its own merits and flaws, but there is much similarity between them. First let's consider the big picture, and the pros and cons of using a template solution, rather than JSP.

Common Concepts

The templating solutions we'll discuss in this section share the following basic concepts:

❑　A template is purely a view. It is restricted to simple conditional logic and iteration and does not attempt to offer the power of a true programming language.

❑　For this reason, template languages are simple and easy to learn.

❑　Data must be made available to the template by a controller. Unlike JSP pages, templates have no way of obtaining data themselves, for example from the request object or any user session. Exactly how a model is made available to the template varies with the individual product.

❑　Using a template involves a two-step process, using a template-manager specific API: Obtain a template instance from the file system or classpath, and use the template with the given model data to generate output and write it to the response.

Why might we choose to use a template language for web tier views in place of JSP?

❑　Using a template language promotes good design. As we've seen, JSP makes it easy and tempting to use an inadequate "Model 1" architecture or to subvert MVC architecture. By using a template language, the role of a view is made explicit.

❑　Most template languages do a better job of matching the appearance of a template page to that of the markup it generates than JSP. This makes life easier for page designers.

❑　Template languages offer simpler syntax than JSP. JSP scriptlet syntax is messy, while JSTL and other custom tags require the use of markup, which is not the most natural way to handle control flow to either a Java developer or a markup author.

❑　Most template languages are not tied to the Servlet API. This means that they can be used in other situations to leverage the investment in adopting them (for example, generating static pages), and that template development and testing can be done without running a J2EE server.

However, there are also disadvantages in using a dedicated template language:

❑ In contrast to JSP and the JSTL Expression Language, no template language is a recognized standard. Given that most template languages are very simple and there's no significant learning curve required, this is not as major a stumbling block as it appears. Furthermore, JSP pages are often edited by markup developers with a very sketchy grasp of Java and JSP syntax. However, the political reality is that in many projects it will simply be impossible to achieve acceptance of technologies outside the J2EE standards for which a "standard" alternative exists, regardless of the grounds for preferring them.

With appropriate choice of templating technology, there is little risk of committing to a template language that will not survive (the classic argument in favor of "standard" solutions): there is little doubt that leading template languages, such as Velocity, are viable and here to stay.

❑ We need to distribute runtime libraries as part of our application. JSP is guaranteed to be available in any J2EE-compliant web container, although it's presently necessary to distribute the binaries for JSTL. However, WARs give us a standard way to include library classes, so this isn't a major problem.

While JSP pages, which are compiled into servlets, might be expected to outperform templating solutions, the reverse may be true in practice. We'll discuss view performance in Chapter 15.

Let's look at some popular templating solutions.

WebMacro

WebMacro is one of the oldest and best-known Java-based template languages.

The following excerpt from WebMacro documentation, quoted with the author's permission from http://germ.semiotek.com/README.html, highlights the differences from JSP and makes the case for using a specialized templating solution instead of JSP:

"WebMacro is similar in many ways to JSP/ASP and other projects in many ways, but differs from those according to our biases:

❑ We think it is wrong to use markup for a scripting language

❑ We think it is wrong to embed programs on a web page

❑ We think it is wrong for web scripts to look like hard programming

❑ We feel that an API like WM should make it easy to do the things you need to do when designing and deploying applications

❑ We believe that programming and graphical page designs are separate tasks

WebMacro uses a simple syntax that doesn't require escaping into and out of scripts, as does JSP pages. Not being markup based, the syntax is more intuitive than using JSP custom tags. The following example shows how WebMacro can be used for a conditional statement, based on a JavaBean property. Note that the bean scripting variable is prefixed with a $:

```
#if ($bean.GoldService) {
   <font size="4">Welcome to our Gold Service!</font>
} #else {
   <font size="4">Welcome!</font>
}
```

JavaBeans are made available to WebMacro templates by being placed in a WebMacro **context**, which contains objects used similarly to the use of `HttpServletRequest` attributes in JSP pages.

Like JSTL, WebMacro supports nested property paths such as `person.spouse.name`. It is also possible to create new variables, perform iteration, calculations etc.

While the syntax differs slightly, the concepts are virtually the same as those of Velocity, discussed below, so I won't discuss the WebMacro template language here. Please refer to http://webmacro.org/WebMacroBasics for more information.

WebMacro is proven on real web sites. Since January 2001, AltaVista, one of the most heavily trafficked sites on the web, has been using WebMacro as its primary page generation technology. WebMacro is available from http://webmacro.org, and is free under the Gnu GPL.

> *The framework code with the sample application includes an implementation of the* `View` *interface,* `com.interface21.web.servlet.view.webmacro.WebMacroView`, *which allows the MVC framework we discussed in Chapter 12 to be used with WebMacro templates. Use this class (remembering to include the WebMacro JAR file in your WAR's* `/WEB-INF/lib` *directory) to use WebMacro templates with this framework without any need to change controller or model code. This view implementation is very similar to the Velocity implementation we'll discuss below, so I won't discuss it here.*

Velocity

Jakarta **Velocity** is essentially a re-implementation of WebMacro with a distinct codebase and some new features. For a discussion of Velocity's relationship to WebMacro, see http://jakarta.apache.org/velocity/differences.html. Velocity has more comprehensive documentation than WebMacro, is published under a different license and the Velocity project seems more active.

In this section we'll look at Velocity's basic concepts, and see how our example view can be rendered by a Velocity template.

Velocity Concepts

Velocity is purely and simply a template engine. This makes Velocity easy to learn and avoids the common problem of a framework providing its own implementations of concepts that are already well handled by other products. The Velocity template engine does not depend on the Servlet API, meaning that it can be used for applications other than web applications, and that Velocity templates can be tested outside a servlet container (a significant advantage over JSP).

The heart of Velocity is the **Velocity Template Language (VTL)**, Velocity's equivalent of the WebMacro language. VTL looks very like the WebMacro template language. There is no need to escape expressions or "scriptlets". The # character is used to prefix directives (control statements), and the $ character to prefix variables. Both these characters can be escaped if they are part of static template data.

Velocity has a slightly different philosophy to WebMacro, aiming to keep the set of core directives to a minimum, while allowing users to extend Velocity's capabilities for their applications by defining **Velocimacros**: reusable template segments that can be used like Velocity directives. Macros can define any number of arguments to be passed on invocation. The following simple macro, with a single argument, outputs an HTML-formatted list of squares from one up to a given maximum value, and illustrates the basic Velocity syntax:

```
#macro( squareList $upTo )
  <ul>
  #foreach ( $item in [1..$upTo] )
    #set ($square = $item * $item)
    <li>$square
  #end
  </ul>
#end
```

This macro can be invoked within a Velocity template as follows:

```
#squareList(6)
```

Velocity macros can be declared "inline" in Velocity templates (although this can be disabled if desired) or collected in **template libraries**, analogous to JSP tag libraries. Velocity macros are in some respects what JSP custom tags should have been: simple and defined without the need to program in Java (JSP 2.0 will introduce simpler tag extension definitions that are closer to this).

As with WebMacro, model objects used in Velocity templates must be made available to Velocity in a **Velocity context** object. Templates can easily expose bean properties, including nested properties, for objects placed in a Velocity context.

Unlike JSP pages, but like WebMacro templates, Velocity templates don't declare model objects required in their context using a comparable mechanism to `<jsp:useBean>`. Variable references that can't be resolved in the context will appear as literals, making it easy to rectify typos (for example, if there is no model object called `nothing`, `$nothing` will appear as a string literal in the template output). The absence of variable declarations and type checks may be off-putting to a Java developer, but web tier presentation templates aren't intended for Java developers to edit.

Velocity comes with a JSP custom tag that interprets its body content as VTL. When using Velocity, there's little reason to use JSP as a wrapper, and mixing JSP and VTL allows all the negatives of JSP plus a mixture of technologies to make maintenance still harder. However, there are a few situations when the Velocity tag library might be useful:

❑   Where the overall page *must* be generated by JSP.

❑   Where you want to use a feature of JSP that Velocity doesn't offer, but which is a valid view operation. For example, if you want to use a particular tag library.

I won't attempt to describe VTL syntax in detail here. A good, concise VTL reference guide is included with the Velocity distribution. Instead, let's look at using a Velocity template to display our sample view.

A Velocity Template for our Example

Our MVC web framework provides standard support for Velocity views. We can define a Velocity view bean for the sample page in /WEB-INF/classes/views.properties using the com.interface21.web.servlet.view.velocity.VelocityView standard View implementation. This standard View implementation will obtain and cache the associated Velocity template on startup. When asked to render a model to the response, it creates a Velocity context with an attribute corresponding to each entry in the model. This is analogous to the way in with the InternalResourceView copies model entries to request attributes. It then uses Velocity to write output to the response, given the template and context data.

> *See Appendix A for information on how this view is implemented, and how to install and configure Velocity.*

The most important bean property to set on the VelocityView class is the templateName property, which identifies a Velocity template within the WAR. We can define our sample view as follows:

```
showReservation.class=com.interface21.web.servlet.view.velocity.VelocityView
showReservation.templateName=showReservation.vm
showReservation.exposeDateFormatter=true
showReservation.exposeCurrencyFormatter=true
```

Note that this bean definition also sets the two format helper properties to true, which causes the VelocityView class to add DateFormat and NumberFormat helpers with the names simpleDateFormat and currencyFormat to the Velocity context, which the template can use to format dates and currency amounts. This functionality, provided by the VelocityView framework class, is necessary since Velocity 1.3 (surprisingly) provides no standard support for date and time formatting (this issue is discussed further in Appendix A).

The first task in writing the Velocity template (found in the sample WAR at /WEB-INF/classes/showReservation.vm) is to set the pattern used by the date helper and to create variables containing the formatted dates and times. As we're reliant on Java support for this, the code we'll use is similar to that used in our JSP example:

```
<!--
$simpleDateFormat.applyPattern("EEEE MMMM dd, yyyy")
#set ($formattedDate = $simpleDateFormat.format($performance.when) )
$simpleDateFormat.applyPattern("h:mm a")
#set ($formattedTime = $simpleDateFormat.format($performance.when) )
-->
```

Note that I've placed the Velocity "scriptlet" in an HTML comment. It won't actually generate output, but this will avoid it upsetting HTML editing tools. The #set directive enables us to declare variables used later in the template.

Once this is out of the way, the rest of the template is easy and intuitive to write. Note the simple access to nested properties. Our model objects, once placed in the Velocity context, can be accessed by name:

```
<html>
<head>
<title>Seats reserved for $performance.show.name</title>
</head>
```

We can now output our formatted date and time:

```
<body>
<b>$performance.show.name:
$formattedDate at $formattedTime
</b>
<br/>
<p>
```

Although Velocity allows us to invoke methods, as well as get property values (by using parentheses, even if methods take no arguments), it doesn't allow us to find the length of an array. Fortunately the number of seats is also available from the quoteReservation property of the Reservation object, so we can take a roundabout route:

```
$reservation.quoteRequest.seatsRequested
seats in
$priceband.description
have been reserved
for you for
$reservation.minutesReservationWillBeValid
minutes to give you time to complete your purchase
```

Velocity shines in iterating over the seat array. Like JSTL (but not JSP scriptlets) Velocity exposes each item in turn as a variable, making this code very simple. Velocity's syntax is simpler and more intuitive than the JSTL markup-based syntax:

```
The seat numbers are:
<ul>
#foreach ($seat in $reservation.seats)
    <li>$seat.name
#end
</ul>
```

Velocity also allows us to find the position in the list through the value of the velocityCount *predefined variable, although we don't need this capability in the example.*

We use the NumberFormat helper object to format the currency amounts, meaning that we don't need to supply currency symbols. The NumberFormat class will always return the one appropriate for the request locale:

```
The total cost of these tickets will be
$currencyFormat.format($reservation.totalPrice).
This includes a booking fee of
$currencyFormat.format($reservation.quoteRequest.bookingFee).
```

Conditionals such as our check as to whether the seats are adjacent use the Velocity if directive. Note the closing #end directive:

```
#if (!$reservation.seatsAreAdjacent)
  <b>Please note that due to lack of availability, some of the
```

549

```
     seats offered are not adjacent.</b>
     <form method="GET" action="payment.html">
       <input type="submit" value="Try another date"></input>
     </form>
  #end
```

Displaying the seating plan image URL involves another nested property. Note the use of what Velocity documentation calls **formal notation** (with the variable name enclosed in curly brackets), which enables us to distinguish the part of the string that is a variable from literal text in the same way as we used the JSTL $ { } expression delimiter:

```
<img src="static/seatingplans/${performance.show.seatingPlanId}.jpg" />
```

Comparing this with the JSTL alternative shows the similarities between accessing bean properties in JSTL and Velocity and the disadvantages of markup-based scripting. The JSTL version involves nested <img> and <c:out> tags, while the output, of course, will include only the <img> tag we're actually trying to generate:

```
<img
  src="<c:out
  value="static/seatingplans/${performance.show.seatingPlanId}.jpg" />"
/>
```

Note how both are less verbose and error-prone than the standard JSP way, which is awkward, even when broken into one scriptlet and an expression:

```
<% String seatingPlanImage = "static/seatingplans/" +
        performance.getShow().getSeatingPlanId() + ".jpg"; %>
<img src="<%=seatingPlanImage%>" />
```

Velocity Summary

Velocity offers a very simple, high-performance, template language that is well suited to exposing JavaBean properties. Velocity isn't web-specific.

Property navigation syntax in Velocity is much like that in the JSTL. The simple Velocity scripting language uses special characters to identify directives, rather than escaping to and from embedded code, as in JSP scriptlets, or markup, as in JSP custom tags. Thus the Velocity template for our example is more concise and easier to read than even the JSP version using JSTL.

While the J2EE-standard argument for JSP is compelling, personally I find that comparing at a Velocity or WebMacro template with a JSP presenting the same information shows how verbose and unintuitive the JSP syntax is, and that custom tags (and the prospect of JSP 2.0) merely reduce the gap. While Java developers tend not to question the readability of JSP pages, in my experience HTML developers, who will have to work with them, find them awkward and alien.

Both WebMacro and Velocity are good, usable solutions that enforce a clean separation between control logic and view template. Although I've chosen to use JSP as the main view technology for the sample application, as the above example shows, using Velocity would probably result in simpler, more readable view templates.

FreeMarker

FreeMarker is conceptually similar to WebMacro and Velocity in that a template is obtained using the provided API and used to render a model constructed using method calls. The FreeMarker template language has a more markup-oriented syntax to WebMacro and Velocity, but is comparable in power.

However, unlike WebMacro, Velocity, and JSP, FreeMarker attempts to avoid the use of reflection to obtain model values, presumably because of concerns about the performance of reflection. This means that adapters must be written as part of application code to expose data to FreeMarker (these adapters are analogous to Swing models). While it's possible to add any JavaBean into a WebMacro or Velocity Context and access its properties and methods without writing any additional Java code, FreeMarker requires explicit coding.

The FreeMarker equivalent of a WebMacro or Velocity context is a "data model tree", in which the root must implement the `freemarker.template.TemplateModelRoot` interface and each subnode must implement another subinterface of `freemarker.template.TemplateModel`. What this means is that, when exposing an object graph, an adapter class will need to be written for each application class. String data can be exposed more easily, using the `freemarker.template.SimpleScalar` convenience class. The Guestbook sample application supplied with FreeMarker shows the use of adapters for each application class. There are 114 lines of code in adapter classes in this trivial application.

I've yet to see reflection prove a performance problem in this kind of situation, so I think that forcing such additional work on application developers to avoid using reflection in a framework is a poor design trade-off. However, not everyone agrees: see http://www.javaworld.com/jw-01-2001/jw-0119-freemarker.html for an article praising FreeMarker's design. The FreeMarker download includes separate packages that enable FreeMarker templates to access XML documents and JavaBeans using reflection, like templates in other products.

FreeMarker is also open source, and is published under the Gnu GPL. It is available at http://freemarker.sourceforge.net/.

XSLT

XSLT, the XML transformation language, is more "standard" than JSP. Unlike JSP, XSLT is purely intended to **transform** data to another format – for example, for display to users – and not to acquire data. Thus in a web application, XSLT stylesheets transform content for presentation, but can't be used to handle user requests. For some tasks, XSLT is more capable than any alternative view technology. It ensures an elegant division between data and presentation.

However, before we leap to the conclusion that XSLT is the ultimate way to render web content, we must consider some significant negatives. XSLT is complex for the uninitiated. XSL transformations are slow (sometimes *very* slow), compared to the other rendering techniques we've discussed. In Chapter 15 we'll look at some benchmarks to quantify the performance issues. We will probably need to convert Java objects to XML before we can transform them, incurring additional complexity and performance overhead. However, we may be able to minimize these disadvantages by using only those features of XSLT that simplify application code.

The following section isn't an introduction to XSLT or XML. Please refer to a good reference such as Michael Kay's excellent *XSLT Programmer's Reference* from *Wrox (ISBN 1-8-6100506-7)* if any of the concepts discussed are unfamiliar.

When to Use XSLT

Adopting XSLT as a view technology has the following advantages, both technical and practical:

❑ XSLT is a standard in its own right. XSLT skills are not J2EE or Java-specific. For example, XML and XSLT are widely used in the Microsoft developer community. This means that we may be able to recruit XSLT authors with experience of our industry or type of site, rather than limiting ourselves to JSP experts. XSLT may well become a cross-platform standard for web authoring. We may also be able to leverage existing XSLT stylesheets.

❑ XSLT is superior to any other presentation solution for rendering tree structured content. It can even be used to perform the equivalent of SQL joins against reference data.

❑ XSLT has excellent sorting capability.

❑ As XSLT stylesheets are XML documents, using XSLT helps to ensure that generated markup is well formed. For example, crossed tags will be illegal in a stylesheet. This will help to avoid many common browser errors.

❑ Using XSLT forces us to make data available as XML. This may have benefits beyond web presentation.

❑ XSLT isn't web-specific, as long as it isn't used only within other view technologies such as JSP.

❑ Unlike JSP (but like all the other templating solutions we've considered) XSLT is not web specific. An investment in developing XSLT skills in-house can produce benefits in many areas.

Against these we need to balance the following disadvantages:

❑ XSLT has a complex syntax, because XSLT stylesheets are XML documents. As we've seen with JSP custom tags, markup isn't an ideal syntax for a scripting language. Although it's easy to do complex tasks once one understands it, XSLT will seem less intuitive to a page designer (and even to many Java developers) than a simple template language such as VTL, or even JSP. Tool support is still limited.

❑ XSLT performance, although not bad enough to rule out its use for any but the most performance-sensitive applications, is unlikely ever to approach that of JSP or simpler templating solutions.

❑ Even with good XSLT authoring tools (a necessity as XSLT stylesheets often look very different to the output they generate), a project will still need at least one developer with an expert understanding of XSLT. Stylesheet performance, for example, can vary widely depending on how a stylesheet is constructed.

❑ XSLT isn't integrated as smoothly with J2EE as JSP. However, as we'll see, we can use JSP custom tags and an MVC framework to provide the necessary infrastructure.

❑ We will usually need to perform the additional step of converting Java objects into XML elements before we can use XSLT to display the data they contain.

Choosing to use XSLT is more of a strategic decision than, say, choosing between JSP and Velocity, which is essentially a choice between how to display the JavaBean properties of the same objects. The XSLT model significantly differs from most other solutions for presenting data, and adopting XSLT may require significant training.

If data already exists in XML, using XSLT is almost always the best approach. However, getting XML out of an OO, Java-based application is not always so easy. In *Chapter 6* we discussed the idea of "domification": converting JavaBeans to XML documents on the fly. The following example will use the Domify open source package. While the use of reflection will incur a small performance overhead, remember that other template technologies such as Velocity and even JSP also make heavy use of reflection.

What Do We Want from XSL?

It's important to remember that XSLT is built on several separable technologies. The **XPath** expression language, used as a sub-language in XSLT stylesheets, is the key to XSLT's powerful capability for selecting content within XML model data nodes.

Even without adopting XSLT as our main view technology, we may be able to enjoy the benefits of XPath. Using Domify or another library (such as Apache Commons JXPath, available from http://jakarta.apache.org/commons/jxpath/) we can even apply XPath expressions to JavaBean model data, as well as data that already exists in XML form. We can also choose to generate only part of a view using XPath and XSLT: the JSTL, for example, provides standard tags that allow the evaluation of XPath expressions and allow us to embed XSLT processing in JSP pages.

How to Use XSLT in Views

Assuming that we have our data in XML form, how do we approach the task of rendering it in the view itself?

Using XSLT Instead of JSP

The "pure" approach is to perform all rendering and content generation with XSLT. The advantages of a pure XSLT approach are:

❑   By converting *all* model data to XML, we have created a platform-neutral presentation layer.

❑   We *know* that our generated content will always be well formed. Non-matching tags are a common source of errors in HTML tags, and it is impossible to be certain that content generated from a JSP will be well formed under all execution paths.

❑   We standardize on a single view technology.

The disadvantages of a pure XLT approach are:

❑   We are *forced* to convert all model data into XML. There are situations where this may be difficult.

❑   The XSLT mechanisms for importing data are relatively complex, relying on the importation of rules using <xsl:import> and <xsl:include> XSLT elements. However, the <xsl:import> mechanism is very powerful. Included files must be well-formed XML documents. In contrast, JSP and other template languages offer easy inclusion of any kind of content.

❑   We will suffer the maximum possible performance hit from using XSLT, with every byte of data returned to the client being the result of an XSL transform.

Using XSLT from JSP Custom Tags

We can reap some of the benefit of XSLT and XPath by embedding XSLT-like operations and XPath expressions within other templates. The JSTL makes this particularly easy, so we'll focus on using XSLT in JSP pages.

The advantage of this approach is that enables us to "cherry pick" when to use XSLT. For example, if some model data is available as XML, we can expose it more easily and efficiently using XPath and XSLT than using Java scriptlets. The disadvantages are that:

- ❑ It's impossible to guarantee that generated markup will be well formed.

- ❑ We won't have a complete XML representation of our site. This is another key benefit of adopting XML: we don't choose XML for any particular stylesheet, but because exposing XML allows us to use *any* stylesheet and thus expose any XML or other text-based format that we want.

- ❑ Combining technologies may increase complexity.

Let's look at using JSTL to expose a model object, available as a request attribute, which is already in XML form, as an `org.w3c.dom.Node`.

First we must import the XML tag library from the JSTL:

```
<%@ taglib uri="/x" prefix="x" %>
```

This library offers XSLT-like tags that allow us to iterate over, evaluate and perform conditional logic based on XPath expressions. For example, assuming that the request attribute node is an XML node, we can iterate over sub-elements like this:

```
<x:forEach select="$node/reservation/seats/item">
    <x:out select="name"/>
</x:forEach>
```

Only the first element of the path ($node) is JSTL-specific, using the JSTL Expression Language to identify an object containing XML data. The remainder of the expression is an XPath relative to this node, so this tag treats its contents in the same way as the `<xsl:for-each>` tag. This is a trivial example; we can use the full power of XPath in such expressions.

This is a simple and powerful approach when model data exists in XML form. However, the JSTL doesn't provide any support for exposing JavaBean data *as* XML. However, in this case we can use a simple enclosing tag to "Domify" JavaBean data. The following example uses a tag available in the framework code with the sample application that uses the Domify library to expose an object attribute (obtained via a JSP expression) and make it available as a scripting variable named node (see the source of `com.interface21.web.tags.DomifyTag` for the implementation of this tag). This enables use of any of the JSTL XML tags within its scope. The following fragment could be used, after the tag library imports shown, to display the list of seats in the `Reservation` model object on `showReservation.jsp`, without any other changes:

```
<%@ taglib uri="/x" prefix="x" %>
<%@ taglib uri="/i21" prefix="i21" %>
```

```
<i21:domify
   root="reservation" model="<%=reservation%>" >
   <ul>
   <x:forEach select="$node/reservation/seats/item">
        <li/><x:out select="name"/>
        </x:forEach>
   </ul>
</i21:domify>
```

This is simply unnecessary for our sample application's "Show Reservation" view: it's easier to perform such simple iteration using the JSTL <forEach> tag. However, if we required anything like the full power of XPath node selection, it would be a different matter.

The JSTL also provides tags that allow the use of XSLT stylesheets to generate part of a JSP: again, useful functionality when data exists in XML form or when its display requires the power of XSLT.

The JSTL also provides tags that allow the parsing of XML body content for use by other XSLT tags. These should be used with caution: acquiring content is the business of web tier controllers and business objects, not JSP views. The potential for parse errors is also problematic in views.

> **JSTL introduces powerful, standard support for using XPath and XSLT within JSP views. This is often a good compromise, enabling us to use the power of XSLT where it is appropriate, while using JSP as our main view technology.**

Note that JSP isn't our only choice for using embedded XSLT (although, with the JSTL, it's a very good choice): other view technologies, such as Velocity, may also allow us to work with XPath and XSLT within larger, composite views.

Implementing our Example Using a "Pure" XSLT Approach

As J2EE doesn't integrate XML and XSLT as smoothly as it does JSP, the biggest challenge is to use a "pure" XML approach, in which an XSLT stylesheet generates the entire view. Fortunately, our MVC framework provides the necessary infrastructure code. The generic com.interface21.web.servlet.view.xslt.XsltView implementation of the View interface compiles and caches an XSLT stylesheet on initialization. When it is asked to render a model to the response, it automatically uses the Domify package to create an XML Node representing the model's data. It then uses the TrAX API to perform an XSLT transform using the cached stylesheet and this XML data and write the output to the response.

> *The implementation of this class and the extension functions used in this example are discussed in Appendix A.*

All we need to do in our application is to declare a view bean of type XsltView in /WEB-INF/classes/views.properties. We must always set bean properties to specify the document root (the tag name for the root element corresponding to the model) and the template URL (the location of the stylesheet within the WAR). We may also optionally set the excludedProperties property to a CSV string of fully qualified properties we wish to exclude from domification. This can simplify the generated node. In the present case it is essential to prevent a cyclic reference. The definition for our sample view is as follows:

```
showReservation.class=com.interface21.web.servlet.view.xslt.XsltView
showReservation.root=reservationInfo
showReservation.stylesheet=/xsl/showReservation.xsl
showReservation.excludedProperties=
  com.wrox.expertj2ee.ticket.referencedata.support.ShowImpl.performances
```

Note that if we don't specify a stylesheet URL, the output will display the input XML document. This is very useful functionality during development. The XsltView class will also add a special element called <request-info> to the model, which contains locale information it extracts from the request. This can support internationalization within XSLT stylesheets.

Our framework also provides XSLT **extension functions** in the com.interface21.web.servlet.view.xslt.FormatHelper class that simplify formatting dates and currencies. Like Velocity, XSLT currently lack good support in this area. We'll use these extension functions in our stylesheet.

Now we understand how the necessary infrastructure code works and how to configure it, let's look at what we need to develop as part of our application to expose the "Show Reservation" screen using an XSLT stylesheet.

As the data doesn't exist in XML, we're reliant on Domify. Thus it's important to understand the structure of the XML document that Domify will generate from our model, which contains three model objects (Reservation, PriceBand, and Performance) and the RequestInfo object we added in XsltView. Note that nodes in this document are generated only on demand; while this DOM document is an essential reference as we write an XSLT stylesheet, it doesn't give an accurate reflection of what the application needs to do at runtime (so long as our stylesheets are efficient, and don't force exhaustive searching of document nodes).

The following is a complete listing of the generated document:

```
<?xml version="1.0" encoding="UTF-8"?>
```

The root element corresponds to our model map:

```
<reservationInfo>
```

We will have one <item> element per model object, the "key" attribute being the object's name in the model (this is Domify's default behavior on exposing java.util.Map objects). Note that simple bean properties are exposed as sub-elements of the relevant <item> element, their text content being a string representation of their value:

```
<item key="priceband"
  type="com.wrox.expertj2ee.ticket.referencedata.support.PriceBandImpl">
  <name>AA</name>
  <id>1</id>
  <description>Premium Reserve</description>
  <price>102.5</price>
  <seatTypeId>1</seatTypeId>
</item>
```

There's no guarantee about the order in which model objects will be exposed by Domify. In this case, the second of the four model objects is the `<request-info>` object added by the `XsltView` class to expose locale information. Note that this contains standard language and country codes:

```
<item key="request-info"
  type="com.interface21.web.servlet.view.RequestInfo">
  <language>en</language>
  <country>GB</country>
</item>
```

The remaining elements expose the `Reservation` and `Performance` objects. Note that the `Reservation` object contains nested objects with their own bean properties. These are exposed in a natural, hierarchical XML structure:

```
<item key="reservation"
  type="com.wrox.expertj2ee.ticket.boxoffice.support.ReservationImpl">
  <timestamp>1027419612736</timestamp>
  <reference>AA</reference>
  <totalPrice>10.0</totalPrice>
  <quoteRequest>
    <performanceID>1</performanceID>
    <seatsRequested>2</seatsRequested>
    <seatsMustBeAdjacent>false</seatsMustBeAdjacent>
    <bookingFee>3.5</bookingFee>
    <holdTill>
      <date>23</date>
      <time>1027419912736</time>
      <year>102</year>
      <month>6</month>
      <hours>11</hours>
      <minutes>25</minutes>
      <seconds>12</seconds>
      <day>2</day>
      <timezoneOffset>-60</timezoneOffset>
    </holdTill>
    <classID>1</classID>
    <reserve>true</reserve>
  </quoteRequest>
  <seats>
    <item type="com.wrox.expertj2ee.ticket.boxoffice.Seat">
      <name>A1</name>
      <id>1</id>
      <seatClassId>1</seatClassId>
      <left>0</left>
      <right>0</right>
    </item>
    <item type="com.wrox.expertj2ee.ticket.boxoffice.Seat">
      <name>A2</name>
      <id>2</id>
      <seatClassId>1</seatClassId>
      <left>0</left>
      <right>0</right>
    </item>
```

```
            </seats>
            <seatsAreAdjacent>true</seatsAreAdjacent>
            <reserved>true</reserved>
            <minutesReservationWillBeValid>4</minutesReservationWillBeValid>
        </item>
        <item key="performance"
            type="com.wrox.expertj2ee.ticket.referencedata.support.PerformanceImpl">
            <name>1</name>
            <id>1</id>
            <show>
                <name>Romeo and Juliet</name>
                <id>1</id>
                <seatingPlanId>1</seatingPlanId>
                <seatTypes/>
            </show>
            <when>
                <date>23</date>
                <time>1027419612746</time>
                <year>102</year>
                <month>6</month>
                <hours>11</hours>
                <minutes>20</minutes>
                <seconds>12</seconds>
                <day>2</day>
                <timezoneOffset>-60</timezoneOffset>
            </when>
            <priceStructureId>1</priceStructureId>
        </item>
    </reservationInfo>
```

Now let's look at the stylesheet for displaying this information.

The XSLT authoring model is also quite different to that for JSP and template engines such as Velocity. Instead of executing sequentially, XSLT templates are usually based on **rules** that are applied to elements in the XML input.

We begin by declaring a namespace for the extension functions in the `FormatHelper` class:

```
<?xml version="1.0" encoding="UTF-8"?>
<xsl:stylesheet version="1.0"
    xmlns:xsl="http://www.w3.org/1999/XSL/Transform"
    xmlns:format="com.interface21.web.servlet.view.xslt.FormatHelper"
>
```

As we'll access the locale codes in the "request info" item, we declare a global variable to shorten the path and possibly improve performance:

```
<!-- Make this available globally -->
<xsl:variable name="reqInfo" select="/reservationInfo/item[@key='request-info']"/>
```

In such a simple stylesheet, we could use a number of approaches to displaying the content. XSLT guru Michael Kay distinguishes between four common types of XSLT stylesheet in *XSLT Programmer's Reference*. In this case we can choose between what he calls a "Fill-in-the-blanks" stylesheet and a "Rule-based" stylesheet.

A Fill-in-the-blanks" stylesheet looks like the generated content, using XPath expressions and iteration to select dynamic content. Such stylesheets execute in down-the-page order and use a similar structure to JSP or Velocity templates. "Rule-based" stylesheets define rules for content elements, so don't mirror the structure of the output document. This is less intuitive at first sight, but can prove very powerful.

I've chosen to use a simple Rule-based stylesheet for the example, as it is a little more concise than a Fill-in-the-blanks stylesheet and demonstrates the classic XSLT model.

We begin by defining a rule for the root element. This prompts the application of the rule for all `<item>` elements in the XML input with a key attribute value of "performance". In the present example, we know there will only ever be one such `<item>` element. Note that this effectively disables automatic application of rules as elements are encountered. As we don't know the order of input elements, this isn't very useful in the present case, but it can be very powerful in other situations:

```
<xsl:template match="/*">
  <xsl:apply-templates select="item[@key='performance']"/>
</xsl:template>
```

The template for `<item>` elements with a key value of "performance" can assume such an element as its **context node**. This means it can work with XPaths relative to such an element. I've highlighted the use of the `dateTimeElement()` extension function:

```
<xsl:template match="item[@key='performance']">
  <html>
    <head>
    <title>Seats reserved for <xsl:value-of select="show/name"/></title>
  </head>

  <body>
  <b><xsl:value-of select="show/name" />:
  <xsl:apply-templates select="format:dateTimeElement(when/time,
   $reqInfo/language, $reqInfo/country)"/>
  </b>
  <br/>
  <br/>
```

The only tricky thing here is how we handle the information about seat allocation and the price of seats. This information comes from the `Reservation` object, although the rest of the content comes from the `Performance` and `PriceBand` elements. We handle this by invoking the appropriate template for the `ReservationInfo` object data, *providing an XPath from the root of the document, not the context node*:

```
<xsl:apply-templates select="/reservationInfo/item[@key='reservation']" />

<form method="GET" action="payment.html">
  <input type="submit" value="Proceed"></input>
</form>

Please check the seating plan below for the location of the reserved seats.
<br/>
<br/>
```

```
    <xsl:variable name="seatingPlanImage">static/seatingplans/<xsl:value-of
     select="show/seatingPlanId"/>.jpg</xsl:variable>

    <img src="{$seatingPlanImage}" />
    </body>
    </html>
</xsl:template>
```

The template for the reservation information is pretty straightforward, save for the need to display the description of the PriceBand object, obtained from the root element (highlighted):

```
<xsl:template match="item[@key='reservation']">

    <xsl:value-of select="quoteRequest/seatsRequested" />
    seats in
    <xsl:value-of select="/reservationInfo/item[@key='priceband']/description"
    />
    have been reserved
    for you for
    <xsl:value-of select="minutesReservationWillBeValid" />
    minutes to give you time to complete your purchase.
    The seat numbers are:
```

XSLT makes light work of iteration over the array of reserved seats:

```
<ul>
<xsl:for-each select="seats/item">
    <li/><xsl:value-of select="name" />
</xsl:for-each>
</ul>

<p/>
The total cost of these tickets will be
<xsl:value-of select="format:currency(totalPrice, $reqInfo/language,
$reqInfo/country)" />.
This includes a booking fee of
<xsl:value-of select="format:currency(quoteRequest/bookingFee,
$reqInfo/language, $reqInfo/country)" />.
```

XSLT conditional syntax is quite like that of JSTL:

```
<xsl:if test="not (seatsAreAdjacent='true')" >
    <b>Please note that due to lack of availability, some of the
    seats offered are not adjacent.</b>
    <form method="GET" action="payment.html">
      <input type="submit" value="Try another date" />
    </form>
</xsl:if>
</xsl:template>
```

Finally, we need a rule to display the <formatted-date> element created by the dateTimeElement() extension function:

```
<xsl:template match="formatted-date">
    <xsl:value-of select="day-of-week"/><xsl:text> </xsl:text>
    <xsl:value-of select="month"/><xsl:text> </xsl:text>
```

```
        <xsl:value-of select="day-of-month"/>,
        <xsl:value-of select="year"/>
        at
        <xsl:value-of select="hours"/>:<xsl:value-of select="minutes"/>
        <xsl:text> </xsl:text>
        <xsl:value-of select="am-pm"/>
    </xsl:template>

    </xsl:stylesheet>
```

The good news is that if this stylesheet is evaluated successfully, we *know* that the generated output is well-formed.

There's no need to change controller code, and the output rendered to the browser will look exactly as that generated by JSP and Velocity. A user would have no way of telling that XSLT was being used.

It is possible to perform XSLT transformations in the client browser, providing both XML document and stylesheet on the server. However, this approach, which has the potential to move processing load from server to client, is problematic in the real world, as not all browsers offer standard or dependable XSLT support. A special View *implementation could add support for this in our MVC framework without changing controller or model code.*

> **The XSLT stylesheet for our simple view is arguably more complex and harder to understand than the approaches we've seen so far – although it's simple given an understanding of XSLT. It would be hard to justify using XSLT as the view technology for the sample application as its business requirements stand.**

However, XSLT is a very powerful language, which comes into its own with more complex presentational requirements, which it can often handle with ease. For example, if the welcome page of our sample application needed to display a tree structure of genres, shows and performances (rather than just genres and shows, as at present) and sorting or filtering was required, XSLT would be a very good choice, and the necessary XSLT stylesheet would almost certainly be simpler than a JSP generating the same output.

Fortunately we don't need to commit to a "pure" XML approach to enjoy some of the benefits of XSLT. We can embed XPath expressions and XSLT transforms within JSP pages using the JSTL.

> **XSLT and XPath are best used when data already exists in XML form, but it's relatively easy to convert JavaBean models to XML, as in our example.**

Alternative Approaches to Markup Generation

All the approaches we've considered so far are templating solutions, in which a template language renders content made available to it by a Java view adapter. This is not the only valid approach for views. Let's now consider some approaches in which the view is built using Java code. In our framework, this means that there will be a distinct implementation of the com.interface21.web.servlet.View interface for each page that will actually generate content.

HTML Generation Libraries

One approach is to use what I'll refer to as an **HTML generation library**: a set of Java classes that enables us to construct HTML documents using Java code. In this model, rather than use a view template such as a JSP or Velocity template, we use Java code to construct an HTML document as an object composed of objects representing text, formatting, form fields etc before writing the generated markup to the response. The HTML generation library ensures that the generated markup is well formed, and conceals the complexity of the eventual output. This concept is quite old, and the earliest implementations predate JSP, although none has become very popular.

Most generation libraries are HTML-specific. However, some concepts can be shared between different output formats. The iText library, which we'll discuss below, allows some commonality between generating HTML and PDF, for example.

The advantages of object generation libraries are:

❑ It's a more object-oriented approach than using JSP pages or a template language.

❑ It is likely to perform well.

❑ It may help to avoid problems such as typos, as complex output generated, rather than coded by developers.

❑ It may support multiple output formats, hiding their details behind an abstraction layer. However, in my experience, this advantage is more theoretical than real, as different output formats don't share enough concepts to make such generalization worthwhile.

The disadvantages include:

❑ Who changes the presentation? Is a Java developer required for every change? If Java resources are always required, it will be a serious problem, even if Java developers are freed of the need to handle fine markup details.

❑ Problematic authoring model. How can HTML mockups, which are often produced during design of a new interface, be turned into Java code to generate it? Some solutions, such as XMLC, address this problem.

❑ Many libraries are too tightly bound to HTML. What if we need to generate WML, for example? This will be a fatal problem if the generation library we're using doesn't support WML; it may call for major code changes even if it does.

❑ We are inviting the central problem with HTML – the fact that, unlike, XML, it doesn't cleanly distinguish between content and presentation – right into our Java code.

❑ HTML is a human-readable format. If we need to generate complex formats such as PDF, using a generation library makes sense. In the case of HTML, however, markup interspersed with a few dynamic statements – as in a well-written JSP or a template – will be more readable than Java code that calls a class library.

Probably the most highly developed object generation library was BEA's **htmlKona**. See http://www.weblogic.com/docs51/classdocs/API_html.html for a description of its capabilities. This was a closed-source, proprietary product bundled with WebLogic server. In WebLogic release 6, htmlKona was deprecated, in favor of JSP – an indication that the HTML generation library didn't prove a runaway success. The Jetty servlet engine also includes an HTML generation library that can be used separately. See http://jetty.mortbay.com/jetty/index.html#HTML.

Later we'll look at an example of using iText to generate PDF. This illustrates a similar authoring model to HTML generation libraries.

> **I dislike HTML generation libraries and can't think of a reason I would choose to use them. However, their use is compatible with good MVC design, and can be supported by our web application framework like any other view technology.**

XMLC

The only way to address the most serious problems with HTML generation libraries – the need for a Java developer to make *any* presentational change, and the difficulty in turning an (X)HTML mockup into Java code to generate it – is to automate the generation of Java code to create or manipulate a predefined output format.

One technology to achieve this is **XMLC**. It was originally developed by Lutris as part of the Enhydra application server, but is now in open source. XMLC is a very different approach to view generation to any we've seen so far. XMLC preserves some of the advantages of HTML generation libraries, while almost eliminating the basic problem of creating holding template structure in Java code.

XMLC drives the generation approach from the markup. A page designer first creates a mockup site with static HTML. XMLC will "compile" the mocked up HTML pages, resulting in Java source code and/or classes. These classes, "XMLC objects", using the W3C DOM, represent the HTML content in Java, and allow programmatic manipulation of the HTML before it is output.

Content from the static mockup can be changed if it is within a tag with an `id` attribute. For example, a page title can be given an `id` attribute to allow it to be changed. When larger sections of markup need to be changed, an HTML `<span>` or `<div>` tag can be introduced to enclose it (these standard structural tags are defined in the HTML 4.0 specification). The XMLC object, and the HTML it represents, can be manipulated either through the standard DOM interfaces (which allow retrieval and modification of elements) or using convenience methods added by XMLC.

Thus Java developers fill in the blanks and add or delete context to the static templates with dynamic content. So long as the blanks don't change, the designers and Java developers can continue to work independently, with revised mockups resulting the generation of new Java objects. The HTML mockups are effectively a contract, defining the dynamic content of the view.

Thus at design time the XMLC approach involves the following steps:

1. Create HTML content with placeholders for dynamic data

2. "Compile" the HTML content to XMLC objects (Java classes) with XMLC

3. Write Java code to manipulate the XMLC objects before output

At run time the XMLC approach involves the following steps:

1. Construct a new instance of the "XMLC object" for the view in question

2. Manipulate the state of that object, for example by adding elements, deleting elements or setting dynamic element content

3. Use XMLC to output the object's final state to the `HttpServletResponse`

XMLC offers the following advantages:

- XMLC is good at generating XML, as well as HTML.
- XMLC is not tied to the Servlet API.
- Prototyping is easy. Templates are pure HTML: they contain nothing to confuse a browser. XMLC allows the designer to insert mockup data, which can be excluded from the compiled class. This means that XMLC templates usually look more complete – when viewed in a browser – than templates using any of the other technologies we've discussed. For example, tables can include multiple rows of mockup data that will be replaced by real data at run time. This is a unique feature, which makes XMLC very attractive in some situations. However, there are two catches:
  - Output data displayed according to conditional logic is problematic. We can add or remove content from the generated XMLC object, but the content needs to be templated somewhere. The usual solution is to have the markup template include all conditionally output data. Data will be suppressed at run time as the conditions are evaluated. This doesn't pose a technical problem, but it does mean that templates may look nonsensical to designers and business users.
  - Static includes will not show up at design time unless the templates are served on a web server that understands server side includes.
- XMLC will work better than other technologies with the unreadable HTML generated by many popular web authoring tools. However, the designer must be able to assign id attributes to dynamic content, and to create `<span>` and `<div>` elements as necessary. XMLC is the only technology we've looked at in which it doesn't matter if the markup is human readable.

The disadvantages of XMLC include:

- Using the DOM API to manipulate XMLC-generated classes is clumsy. However, XMLC generates additional convenience methods to access elements that go some way towards addressing this problem.
- The XMLC model is unusual, and doesn't share many of the concepts shared by other view mechanisms. This may make its introduction difficult in an organization, as it requires the adoption of a model that's likely to be unfamiliar.
- The HTML templates maintained by page designers literally hold the keys to the Java code. Any change to them requires regeneration of the associated XMLC object. This is normally no problem, but if careless change deletes or corrupts the ids required by XMLC, the XMLC object will no longer work. So it's not quite magic: some care is needed in maintaining pure-HTML templates.

An XMLC Template for Our Example

The template is standard HTML, without any XMLC-specific tags. In fact, I started work on it by saving the dynamic output of the Velocity view.

The only special requirement is that elements with dynamic content must be given an id attribute, using an enclosing `<span>` or `<div>` tag if necessary. Note that the values inserted in template will be visible when the template is viewed in a browser.

The title is given an id, enabling us to append the performance name to its initial content of template text. We could also use a `java.text.MessageFormat` here:

```
<html>
<head>
<title id="title">Seats reserved for </title>
</head>
```

With the name, date, and time of the performance we must introduce `<span>` elements, as there's no markup element we can manipulate like the `<title>` element in the opening fragment:

```
<body>
<b><span id="performanceName">Hamlet</span>:
<span id="date">January 1, 1983</span>
at
<span id="time">7:30 pm</span>
```

Note that the contents of the `<span>` elements in the template will serve as placeholders, making the template display meaningfully in a browser. We adopt the same approach for the reservation information:

```
<span id="seatsRequested">2</span>
seats in
<span id="seatType">Seat Type</span>
have been reserved
for you for
<span id="minutesHeld">5</span>
minutes to give you time to complete your purchase.
```

Displaying the list of seat ids involves creating a template list id (the `<li>` tag can be given an id, so we don't need a `<span>` or `<div>` tag to enclose it). Note that I've also added two rows of mockup data, identified with a class of "mockup". These elements will help make the template's appearance in a browser realistic, but can be deleted by XMLC before the generation of the XMLC object:

```
The seat numbers are:
<ul>
    <li id="seat">Z1</li>
    <li class="mockup">Z2</li>
    <li class="mockup">Z3</li>
</ul>
```

Displaying price information simply involves using `<span>` tags to identify potentially dynamic content. Note that we don't *need* to change these values: in some cases, we might be happy with the defaults, and only change them occasionally:

```
The total cost of these tickets will be
<span id="totalPrice">totalPrice</span>.
This includes a booking fee of
<span id="bookingFee">bookingFee</span> .
```

As the content displayed if the seats reserved aren't adjacent includes a nested `<form>` element, we must use a `<div>` element, rather than a `<span>` element, to enclose it:

```
<div id ="nonAdjacentWarning" >
<b>Please note that due to lack of availability, some of the
seats offered are not adjacent.</b>
```

```
<form method="GET" action="otherDate.html">
    <input type="submit" value="Try another date">
</form>
</div>
```

The only remaining dynamic data is the URL of the seating plan image. We give this element an id to allow manipulation, and give it a relative URL that will enable the template to display in a browser:

```
<img alt="Seating plan" id="seatingPlanImg"
  src="../../static/seatingplans/1.jpg" />
```

This certainly separates template from Java code. The best thing about the whole process is that this HTML template looks *exactly* like the dynamically generated page, unlike any template we've seen. The list of seat names is populated with dummy entries, while other dynamic content has placeholder values. The only snag is the inclusion of the non-adjacent seating warning, which won't appear on most pages (we'll have to remove the unwanted branch programmatically at runtime). The following screenshots displays this template in a browser:

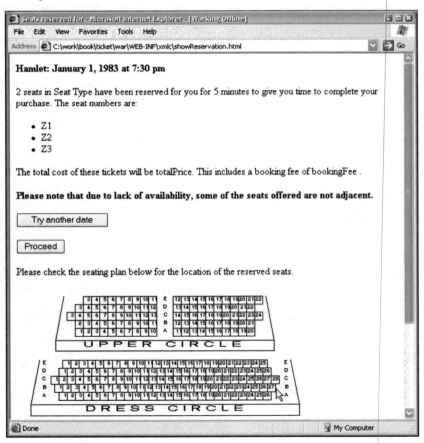

Compiling the Template

Before we can write Java code to implement the "Show Reservation" view, we need to generate an XMLC object. We can run the `xmlc` command shipped with XMLC, but I've chosen to use Ant to make the task repeatable. As only a single HTML file in the sample application is compiled using XMLC, I've hard-coded its name. However, it would be easy to make the Ant target more sophisticated:

```
<target name="xmlc">
  <java
    classname="org.enhydra.xml.xmlc.commands.xmlc.XMLC"
    fork="yes">
  <classpath>
    <fileset dir="${lib.dir}">
      <include name="runtime/xmlc/*.jar"/>
    </fileset>
  </classpath>

  <arg value="-keep"/>
  <arg value="-nocompile"/>
  <arg value="-dump"/>
  <arg value="-ssi"/>
  <arg line="-sourceout src"/>
  <arg line="-delete-class mockup"/>
  <arg line="-class
    com.wrox.expertj2ee.ticket.web.xmlc.generated.ShowReservationXmlcObject"/>
  <arg value="war/WEB-INF/xmlc/showReservation.html"/>
  </java>
</target>
```

The most interesting content is in the flags to XMLC:

❑   The `-keep` flag tells XMLC not to delete the Java source code (it defaults to leaving only a `.class` file).

❑   The `-nocompile` flag tells XMLC not to compile the generated source file. We choose to make this part of our build process, rather than the XMLC compilation process.

❑   The `-dump` flag tells XMLC to display the structure revealed by its analysis of the HTML input. This can be useful if XMLC doesn't generate the convenience setter methods we expect.

❑   The `-ssi` flag tells XMLC to process server-side includes (it doesn't by default).

❑   The `-sourceout` flag tells XMLC where to put the generated Java class. We choose to put it in our `/src` directory, along with our own classes.

❑   The `-delete-class` flag tells XMLC to delete elements with class `mockup`. This will delete the dummy list data we included in the template to make it appear more realistic when viewed in a browser.

❑   The `-class` flag specifies a fully qualified name for the Java class (the default is to generate a class with the same name as the template, in the default package).

❑   The last value is the path to the template.

When this is complete we should have a class called
`com.wrox.expertj2ee.ticket.web.xmlc.generated.ShowReservationXmlcObject`, which is
the Java representation of the template HTML. We won't edit this class, but we will use its methods to
manipulate its state. If generated XMLC objects are placed along with ordinary source code where an
IDE can find them, an IDE should be able to provide context help on their methods, which is likely to
prove very useful.

Manipulating the XMLC Object Generated from the Template

Let's now look at implementing the `com.interface21.web.servlet.View` interface for XMLC.

In the XMLC object, as with a code generation library, we need a distinct Java object for each view. At
runtime the HTML template is no longer required, but we need one view implementation for each
XMLC-generated view.

We don't need to start from scratch. Our MVC framework provides a convenient superclass for XMLC
views – `com.interface21.web.servlet.view.xmlc.AbstractXmlcView` – which uses the
template method design pattern to conceal the necessary plumbing from subclasses and leave them only
the task of creating manipulating the relevant XMLC object. Subclasses need to implement only the
following protected method:

```
protected abstract XMLObject createXMLObject(
    Map model,
    HttpServletRequest request,
    HttpServletResponse response,
    XMLCContext context)
    throws ServletException;
```

Like most XMLC view subclasses, the concrete implementation that we use in the sample application
doesn't expose any bean properties. Thus the entire bean definition in `/WEB-INF/classes/views.properties` is as follows:

```
showReservation.class=
  com.wrox.expertj2ee.ticket.web.xmlcviews.ShowReservationView
```

> See Appendix A for information on installing and configuring XMLC, and a description of the
> implementation of the
> `com.interface21.web.servlet.view.xmlc.AbstractXmlcView` framework class.

Now let's move to our specific example,
`com.wrox.expertj2ee.ticket.web.xmlcviews.ShowReservationView`. We begin by
extending `AbstractXmlcView`:

```
public class ShowReservationView extends AbstractXmlcView {
```

There are no bean properties, and don't need to provide a constructor. We implement the required
protected abstract method as follows:

```
protected XMLObject createXMLObject(
    Map model,
```

```
HttpServletRequest request,
HttpServletResponse response,
XMLCContext context)
throws ServletException {
```

We begin by constructing a new XMLC object. We can do this with a no-argument constructor, but it's more efficient to use the XMLC context argument to provide an object:

```
ShowReservationXmlcObject showReservationXmlcObject =
  (ShowReservationXmlcObject) context.getXMLCFactory().create(
    ShowReservationXmlcObject.class);
```

We now extract our model objects from the map, so we perform type casts once only:

```
Reservation reservation = (Reservation)
  model.get(TicketController.RESERVATION_KEY);
Performance performance = (Performance)
  model.get(TicketController.PERFORMANCE_KEY);
PriceBand priceBand = (PriceBand)
  model.get(TicketController.PRICE_BAND_KEY);
```

Next we use similar code to that we've seen before to use standard Java internationalization support to format dates and currency amounts, based on the request locale:

```
SimpleDateFormat df = (SimpleDateFormat)
  DateFormat.getDateInstance(DateFormat.SHORT, request.getLocale());
df.applyPattern("EEEE MMMM dd, yyyy");
String formattedDate = df.format(performance.getWhen());
df.applyPattern("h:mm a");
String formattedTime = df.format(performance.getWhen());
NumberFormat cf = NumberFormat.getCurrencyInstance(request.getLocale());
String formattedTotalPrice = cf.format(reservation.getTotalPrice());
String formattedBookingFee =
  cf.format(reservation.getQuoteRequest().getBookingFee());
```

Now we can begin modifying dynamic content in the elements with an id attribute. XMLC spares us the ordeal of using DOM to do this, as it generates convenience manipulation methods. Setting dynamic text is very easy:

```
showReservationXmlcObject.setTextTitle(
  showReservationXmlcObject.getElementTitle().getText() + " " +
    performance.getShow().getName());
showReservationXmlcObject.setTextPerformanceName(
  performance.getShow().getName());
showReservationXmlcObject.setTextSeatsRequested("" +
  reservation.getSeats().length);
showReservationXmlcObject.setTextSeatType(priceBand.getDescription());
showReservationXmlcObject.setTextMinutesHeld("" +
  reservation.getMinutesReservationWillBeValid());
showReservationXmlcObject.setTextDate(formattedDate);
showReservationXmlcObject.setTextTime(formattedTime);
showReservationXmlcObject.setTextTotalPrice(formattedTotalPrice);
showReservationXmlcObject.setTextBookingFee(formattedBookingFee);
```

569

To build the list of seat names, we need to obtain the prototype list item, clone it for each row of data in our model, and then delete the prototype row itself. This is a very different approach to any we've seen. It's not difficult, but it isn't particularly intuitive:

```
// Get template node for seat list
HTMLElement seatEle = showReservationXmlcObject.getElementSeat();
for (int i = 0; i < reservation.getSeats().length; i++) {
  showReservationXmlcObject.setTextSeat(
    reservation.getSeats()[i].getName());
  seatEle.getParentNode().insertBefore(seatEle.cloneNode(true), seatEle);
}
// Remove template node
seatEle.getParentNode().removeChild(seatEle);
```

However, remember that this part of the XMLC authoring process is performed by Java developers, not markup developers (who are done when they've provided mockup HTML). So it's safe to assume the necessary programming skills. Remember that the "mockup" list data elements were ignored when XMLC generated a Java object from the HTML template:

We handle the conditional display of the adjacent seats warning by deleting this element if it's not needed:

```
if (reservation.getSeatsAreAdjacent()) {
  Element adjacentWarning =
    showReservationXmlcObject.getElementNonAdjacentWarning();
  adjacentWarning.getParentNode().removeChild(adjacentWarning);
}
```

Finally we obtain the <img> element that displays the seating plan graphic and set its source URL, before returning the configured XMLC object for the superclass to use to build the response:

```
HTMLImageElement graphicEle = (HTMLImageElement)
  showReservationXmlcObject.getElementSeatingPlanImg();
graphicEle.setSrc("static/seatingplans/" +
  performance.getShow().getSeatingPlanId() + ".jpg");

return showReservationXmlcObject;
}
```

> **XMLC offers a very different way of separating presentation template from dynamic code to most view technologies. Its strengths are that the standard-HTML templates it works with can display in a browser *exactly* as they will appear at runtime, populated with dynamic data; and that it can cope with HTML that isn't human-readable. However, it requires an additional "compilation" step in the development process and requires a greater learning effort than simpler technologies such as Velocity.**

Further Reading on XMLC

See the following resources for further information about XMLC:

- http://xmlc.enhydra.org/software/documentation/xmlcSlides/xmlcSlides.html: A simple introduction to XMLC

- http://staff.plugged.net.au/dwood/xmlc-tutorial/index.html: The XMLC Tutorial

- http://xmlc.enhydra.org/software/documentation/doc/xmlc/user-manual/index.html: The XMLC user manual

- http://www.java-zone.com/free/articles/Rogers01/Rogers01-1.asp: Overview of XMLC and comparison with JSP

Generating Binary Content

So far we've considered the generation of markup. What if we want to generate binary content?

The template technologies we've looked at are unsuited to generating binary content. None of them, for example, gives us enough control over generated white space.

We may, however, be able to use an XML approach. XSL-FO (XSL Formatting Objects) is the other half of the XSL specification (other than XSLT), and defines an XML format describing layout. In the future, XSL-FO may be understood by browsers and other GUIs. Presently XSL-FO must be converted into another layout format, such as PDF, for display. For more information on XSL-FO see http://www.ibiblio.org/xml/books/bible2/chapters/ch18.html. See http://xml.apache.org/fop/ for Apache FOP, one of the few existing products that can convert XSL-FO to displayable formats. Apache FOP supports PDF and SVG, among other formats.

Sometimes we might work with the `HttpServletResponse` object directly. For example, we could implement our `View` interface to get the `ServletOutputStream` from the response object and output binary data. The binary data might be contained in the model provider by the controller.

However, often we can use a helper classes that provide an abstraction for the binary format we wish to generate: for example, if the format is well known and publicly documented, such as image formats or PDF. Let's illustrate this approach by examining PDF generation.

Generating PDF with iText

Strictly speaking, PDF isn't a binary format. However, it isn't human-readable and it can contain ASCII-encoded binary data such as image data, so it must be approached in the same way as binary formats.

PDF is publicly documented. It's commercial creator, Adobe, sells PDF tools, but shares the specification. Thus there are several open source Java libraries that can be used to generate PDF documents.

I used iText version 0.93, a PDF generation library written by Bruno Lowagie, and published under the GNU GPL. It is available from http://www.lowagie.com/iText/, which also offers excellent documentation and many examples of Java code using iText. iText also provides a similar model for generating (X)HTML, XML and RTF, although its primary focus is PDF generation.

PDF generation is a perfect application for the "generation library" approach that I rejected to generate HTML. This is a complex format, for which no template language can be used and which it's essential that Java application code doesn't need to handle without a high-level abstraction.

571

Using iText to generate PDF is simple and reasonably intuitive. As with XMLC, we'll need an application-specific class to generate each PDF view.

As usual, we begin by creating a View definition in /WEB-INF/classes/views.properties. As with XMLC, there are no required bean properties, although we can specify properties to customize page size and other output parameters. The complete view definition is as follows:

```
showReservation.class=
    com.wrox.expertj2ee.ticket.web.pdfviews.ShowReservationView
```

As for XMLC, our MVC framework provides a convenient superclass – in this case, the com.interface21.web.servlet.view.pdf.AbstractPdfView abstract class – using the Template Method pattern to simplify application-specific PDF generation classes. Subclasses must implement the following protected abstract method to write model data to the iText PDF document passed as the second parameter. The request and response objects won't normally be used, but we include them in case the view needs locale information or to write a cookie:

```
protected abstract void buildPdfDocument(Map model,
    Document pdfDoc,
    HttpServletRequest request,
    HttpServletResponse response)
    throws DocumentException;
```

> *Please see Appendix A for information on how to install iText and on the implementation of the* com.interface21.web.servlet.view.pdf.AbstractPdfView *framework superclass.*

The application-specific PDF view to display a reservation begins by subclassing AbstractPdfView:

```
public class ShowReservationView extends AbstractPdfView {
```

Next we define the data and font constants we'll use as we generate output. Ideally, this content should be held in a ResourceBundle, allowing the view implementation to use the appropriate ResourceBundle to the request locale. Note that as we can't use a template language, our Java code will be forced at least to manipulate variables containing output strings:

```
private static final String MESSAGE1 =
    "{0} tickets have been reserved for you for " +
    "{1} minutes to give you time to " +
    "complete your purchase. The seat numbers are: ";
private static final String COSTING =
    "The total cost of these tickets will be {0}. " +
    "This includes a booking fee of {1}.";
private static final String ADJACENT_WARNING =
    "Please note that due of lack of availability, some " +
    " of the seats offered are not adjacent";
private static final Font HEADLINE_FONT =
    new Font(Font.TIMES_NEW_ROMAN, 15, Font.BOLD, Color.red);
private static final Font HEADING_FONT =
    new Font(Font.HELVETICA, 13, Font.ITALIC, Color.black);
private static final Font TEXT_FONT =
    new Font(Font.HELVETICA, 11, Font.BOLD, Color.black);
private static final Font WARNING_FONT =
    new Font(Font.HELVETICA, 12, Font.BOLD, Color.black);
```

We must implement the `buildPdfDocument()` protected abstract method to generate content:

```java
protected void buildPdfDocument(Map model, Document pdfDoc,
    HttpServletRequest request, HttpServletResponse response)
    throws DocumentException {
```

As with the XMLC view, we begin by extracting the required model objects from the map. As their controller must have made these available, we don't need to check that they're non-null. We can simply allow a `NullPointerException`, as this amounts to an assertion failure (in Java 1.4 each controller method could conclude with an assertion that the necessary model keys were non-null):

```java
Reservation reservation = (Reservation)
    model.get(TicketController.RESERVATION_KEY);
Performance performance = (Performance)
    model.get(TicketController.PERFORMANCE_KEY);
PriceBand priceBand = (PriceBand)
    model.get(TicketController.PRICE_BAND_KEY);
```

Next, we use the same code we've seen before to format dates and currency amounts according to the request locale:

```java
SimpleDateFormat df = (SimpleDateFormat)
    DateFormat.getDateInstance(DateFormat.SHORT, request.getLocale());
df.applyPattern("EEEE MMMM dd, yyyy");
String formattedDate = df.format(performance.getWhen());
df.applyPattern("h:mm a");
String formattedTime = df.format(performance.getWhen());
NumberFormat cf = NumberFormat.getCurrencyInstance();
String formattedTotalPrice = cf.format(reservation.getTotalPrice());
String formattedBookingFee =
    cf.format(reservation.getQuoteRequest().getBookingFee());
```

Now we can begin to generate dynamic content. This takes the form of adding new objects representing document content to the `Document` object:

```java
String title = "Reservation for " + performance.getShow().getName();
pdfDoc.add(new Paragraph(title, HEADLINE_FONT));
String when = formattedDate + " at " + formattedTime;
pdfDoc.add(new Paragraph(when, HEADING_FONT));
pdfDoc.add(new Paragraph());
String note = MessageFormat.format(MESSAGE1, new String[] { "" +
    reservation.getSeats().length,
    "" + reservation.getMinutesReservationWillBeValid()});
pdfDoc.add(new Paragraph(note, TEXT_FONT));
```

In this model, iteration is handled by ordinary Java code, making it straightforward:

```java
List list = new List(false, 20);
list.setListSymbol(new Chunk("\u2022",
    new Font(Font.HELVETICA, 20, Font.BOLD)));
for (int i = 0; i < reservation.getSeats().length; i++) {
```

573

```
        list.add(new ListItem(reservation.getSeats()[i].getName()));
      }
      pdfDoc.add(list);

      pdfDoc.add(new Paragraph());
      note = MessageFormat.format(COSTING, new String[] {
        formattedTotalPrice, formattedBookingFee });
      pdfDoc.add(new Paragraph(note, TEXT_FONT));
      pdfDoc.add(new Paragraph());
```

Likewise, the conditional inclusion of the warning about seats not being adjacent involves a simple Java if:

```
      if (!reservation.getSeatsAreAdjacent()) {
        pdfDoc.add(new Paragraph(ADJACENT_WARNING, WARNING_FONT));
      }
    }
  }
```

This is pretty simple, given the complexity of PDF, but it shows why such an approach isn't such a good idea for generating HTML. Having Java code manipulate text content is inelegant, and it's hard to get a feel for what the completed document will look like. A template-based approach is much more natural if it's an option.

The PDF document we've just created will look like this:

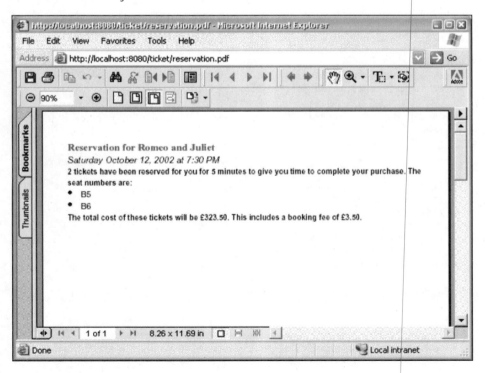

iText supports adding images to PDF documents, so we could display the seating plan graphic as well. Please refer to iText documentation for further information.

View Composition and Page Layout

You may well be thinking, "This is all very well, but the example HTML is very simple. In our site we need to use headers, footers, and navigation bars, not just a single content page".

View structure can get far more complex than the simple HTML document model we've seen. However, as I'll try to demonstrate, this doesn't pose a problem for MVC design or our approach to views.

All the templating technologies we've discussed allow us to **compose** views from multiple dynamic and static blocks. In JSP, for example, this is done via the include directive and include standard action, while both WebMacro and Velocity provide include directives.

There are two basic approaches, which I'll term **content page** inclusion and **template page** inclusion. In content page inclusion, each page of content includes other elements: often, a header and footer. In template page inclusion, a layout or template page includes pages of content as required. The one layout page may be used for an entire application, including different content wells, headers, footers etc. in different contexts. Multiple templates can be easily defined if necessary.

Template page inclusion is much more flexible than content page inclusion. It allows a model in which page fragments are components, which the template page is responsible for assembling. It also allows easy global changes to page structure, simply by changing the template page. With content page inclusion, we will need to change many individual pages to make a consistent change.

Since JSP 1.2 rectified the serious problems with the JSP 1.1 dynamic include mechanism, JSP has provided good support for template page inclusion. However, a higher level of abstraction is really needed. Struts, for example, provide the "template" tag library to handle this.

The present framework addresses template page inclusion through the use of **static attributes** on views. Static attributes are data available to views that doesn't need to come from the model provided by the controller. Thus they may be presentation-specific, and may provide valuable support for template pages. Static attributes will be overridden by model values with the same name, and so can also be used to provide default values.

Let's illustrate the point by looking at a JSP implementation of a simple layout that involves a header and footer.

Content page inclusion would mean that each page included a header and footer, like this:

```
<%@ include file= "header.jsp" %>

Content well content for this page

<%@ include file= "footer.jsp" %>
```

Note that as we know the name of the included page in each case, we can use JSP static includes (via a directive rather than the `<jsp:include>` standard action). This is a simple and intuitive approach, but it's not usually viable for large and complex web applications. While changes to the included header and footer JSP pages would automatically affect all pages including them, what if we wanted to add additional template content in a separate included JSP? Such changes would require the modification of all JSP pages. The basic problem is that each JSP contains the same, redundant, layout information.

In contrast, template page inclusion would involve a single template that would include the header and footer and the content well, which would vary at runtime. Page layout would be defined once only, in the template. A simple template might look like this:

```
<%@ include file= "header.jsp" %>

<jsp:include page="<%=contentWell%>" />

<%@ include file="footer.jsp" %>
```

The `contentWell` variable would need to be provided to the template page as a request attribute or by some other method. Note that a JSP dynamic include is the only option when we don't know what page we need to include. This simple example uses static includes for the header and footer, but of course any of the includes could be parameterized.

The dynamic versus static include issue was far more important in JSP 1.0 and 1.1 than in JSP 1.2, as the `<jsp:include>` action always flushed the buffer, which wasn't always acceptable. JSP 1.2 removes this limitation. This means that there's now only a minor speed penalty for using dynamic (rather than static) includes.

Each content well page would contain just the output relevant to its business purpose. This content, however, would need to be legal HTML at the point at which it appeared in the template, placing some restrictions on layout composition using this technique.

Now let's look at a realistic implementation of template page inclusion using static attributes to provide the necessary information to the template. Remember that the `com.interface21.web.servlet.view.AbstractView` class, from which all our views are derived, gives us the ability to set string static attributes in a CSV string. We can set three static attributes: `header` (the URL within the WAR of the header); `contentWell` (the URL of the content well); and `footer` (the URL of the footer). These static attribute values will be available to all templates, whatever the dynamic model, and define the layout of the composed view.

This inherited support means that we can use the `InternalResourceView` as with any JSP. When we use template page inclusion, we switch the URL in the view definition to that of the template page, but set the original URL (`/welcome.jsp`) as the value of the content well static attribute. Note that the footer is a static HTML resource, as this approach works with any resource inside a WAR:

```
welcomeView.attributesCSV=  header=[/jsp/header.jsp],\
        contentWell=[/welcome.jsp],\
        footer=[/jsp/footer.htm]
```

The first and last character of each attribute value is ignored to allow the , or = characters to be included within it if necessary. While the present example uses [and] characters to enclose each value, any other pair of characters could be used. Note the use of the \ character as described in `java.util.Properties` documentation to break up a single property value for readability.

These three static attribute values will appear in our model as though they were data provided by the controller. This means that, when we use JSP, they will be available as request attributes, and that we can declare JSP beans of type string to access them.

The file /jsp/template.jsp in our sample application is the template file. After disabling automatic session creation (which should be the first task in any JSP), it declares the three beans:

```
<%@ page session="false" %>

<jsp:useBean id="header"
    type="java.lang.String"
    scope="request"
/>

<jsp:useBean id="contentWell"
    type="java.lang.String"
    scope="request"
/>

<jsp:useBean id="footer"
    type="java.lang.String"
    scope="request"
/>
```

Now it's trivial to use these values to structure the output and control the inclusion of the constituent parts:

```
<html>
<head>
<title>Could also parameterize this</title>
</head>

<jsp:include page="<%=header%>" />

<hr>
<jsp:include page="<%=contentWell%>" />

<hr>
<font size="2">
<jsp:include page="<%=footer%>" />
</font>

</body>
</html>
```

Let's try this template page with the welcome page from the sample application. The view definition in /WEB-INF/classes/views.properties used to be as follows:

```
welcomeView.class=com.interface21.web.servlet.view.InternalResourceView
welcomeView.url=/welcome.jsp
```

Now – without any change to controller or model code or welcome.jsp – our welcome page will appear like this:

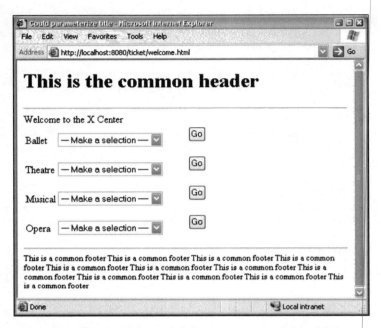

In practice, we would need to ensure that included page components didn't include <html> or <body> tags, so this is a slight oversimplification.

This approach – using a view implementation and "static attributes" – has a significant advantage over custom tag based view composition such as the Struts template tag library provides or that used in the Java Pet Store sample application (which are both based on the same concepts) in that it will work with view technologies other than JSP, such as WebMacro and Velocity.

It's also possible to combine the output of multiple views in Java code, rather than using a template technology. For example, the RequestDispatcher interface provides an include() method as well as the forward() method we've seen so far, which could be used by a custom View implementation to include the output of multiple JSP pages or other resources within a WAR. Alternatively, we could provide a CompositiveView implementation of the View interface that output the result of rendering several views – possibly of different types – in succession (I have successfully used the composite view approach with JSP 1.1 to get around the limitations of dynamic includes).

However, JSP 1.2, Velocity and other templating technologies make view composition so easy that it's hard to justify doing it in Java.

> **When view composition is involved – as in the use of a template page – the details should be concealed in view code. They are not the concern of controllers or models.**
>
> **Whichever J2EE view technology you choose, remember to follow the same principle of separation of presentation from content in the markup layer itself. If using XML and XSLT, this won't be an issue. When generating HTML, make sure that the HTML uses CSS stylesheets to ensure that dynamically generated content is kept apart from rendering information.**

Summary

In the example used throughout this chapter, taken from the sample application accompanying this book, we've seen how good MVC design practice makes it possible to change view technology without changing a line of controller or model code.

JSP, although one of the core J2EE specifications, is only one of many choices for view technology. In this chapter, we've looked at JSP along with several leading alternatives, considering the advantages and disadvantages of each and when you might choose to use it. We considered the following alternative view technologies, demonstrating how they can be integrated with MVC web applications in practice:

- ❑ WebMacro
- ❑ Velocity
- ❑ XML/XSLT approaches
- ❑ XMLC
- ❑ PDF generation using the iText library, and the generation of binary content

None of these view technologies is perfect and none is right for all projects. In addition to the inherent strengths and weaknesses of each technology, the availability of skills will be an important consideration on a project-by-project basis.

JSP has the advantage of inclusion in the core J2EE standards. It is an excellent view technology, so long as its use is subject to strict discipline. We've looked at coding standards to ensure that JSP pages are maintainable. Strict coding standards are essential, as the consequences of abusing JSP are severe, and often seen in practice. The release of the JSP Standard Template Library in 2002 is a huge advance for JSP, and the JSTL should be viewed as an essential part of JSP, to be used in every application using JSP. JSP 2.0 will move this library's expression language into the JSP core, and introduce further enhancements that move the JSP model away from the largely discredited reliance on scriptlets typical of most JSP pages in the past.

The Velocity template language is a simple, effective view technology that is a good choice for many applications. It's simpler than JSP and easier for HTML developers to learn, offering only the features needed to implement clean views, and none of the temptations that still afflict JSP. Velocity macros are particularly neat, providing a simple and effective way of reusing common content without the need for Java coding. As we'll see in Chapter 15, Velocity offers excellent performance.

XSLT and XMLC provide two very different models to JSP and template languages such as Velocity, each providing good separation of presentation from dynamic content generation. Their appropriateness in a project will depend on the overall authoring strategy.

As we've seen, it's even possible to mix different view technologies in the one application. We considered the use of XSLT within JSP pages. There's also no reason why we can't use, say, Velocity for some views and JSP pages for others. This may allow us to benefit from the strengths of individual technologies to solve specific problems. However, the downside to such mixing is that it complicates deployment and increases the range of skills required to develop and maintain an application. Certainly there is no difficulty in a well-designed application in generating a few views using different technologies – for example, to make some content available in the form of PDF documents.

> Remember that the choice of view technology shouldn't have a profound impact on application design. Sometimes the choice of view technology may flow naturally from the application's business requirements and architecture. For example, if data exists within the application as XML, XSLT views may be an obvious choice. However, in general it should be possible to choose between view technologies without changing the application's architecture. Business logic components and even web tier controllers should be unaffected by a change of view technology.

A personal note: Before the release of the JSP Standard Tag Library, I'd come to question whether JSP was a wise choice for most applications. The JSTL negates a lot of the valid criticisms leveled at JSP in the past, and provides a sound basis for application views. While XML-based scripting (as offered by all JSP custom tags, including JSTL tags) can still be clumsy, JSP with JSTL offers a powerful, relatively simple, solution for most requirements.

> Whatever view technology you choose, remember to document the model objects exposed by your web tier controllers thoroughly. This amounts to a contract between controllers and views.

We also looked at **view composition**: the building of complex views from multiple building blocks, which may be the output of other views or page components such as included JSP pages. We saw how this can be achieved using our MVC framework, regardless of the view technology we use.

In the next chapter, we'll look at deployment issues. In Chapter 15, we'll look at the important topic of performance tuning and testing, including benchmarks for some of the view technologies discussed in this topic and the issue of HTTP caching.

14

Packaging and Application Deployment

In this chapter we'll look at packaging J2EE applications and deploying them onto application servers. This is an area in which we require server-specific knowledge, and in which portability between application servers is presently limited.

As application servers use different approaches to class loading, we may need to package applications differently for different application servers. Even standard deployment units such as EARs may not be wholly portable. We'll also need to follow server-specific conventions to define resources such as JDBC DataSources, which applications require. As we'll see, the standard J2EE deployment descriptors do not provide all necessary information, meaning that we normally require additional, proprietary, deployment descriptors. Although the J2EE specifications describe the structure of standard deployment units, no standard deployment process is (as yet) mandated.

As the details of application deployment differ between application servers, I'll aim to provide an introduction here, highlighting areas in which you'll need to research the behavior of your target server. After working through this chapter, you should have a feel for the commonality between application deployment on different servers, and the steps necessary to package and deploy a typical J2EE application on any server.

We'll illustrate the concepts discussed by looking at what we need to do to get the sample application running in JBoss 3.0. Please check the download accompanying this book for information on deploying the sample application to other servers.

Deployment options can have an important impact on performance, so it's vital to explore them throughout the application lifecycle, not merely get your application running on your chosen server.

Packaging

Let's begin by looking at how to package J2EE applications.

Deployment Units

The two most commonly used deployment units in J2EE applications are **Web ARchives (WARs)** and **EJB JAR** files. These are JAR-format files that contain:

❑ The implementation classes, binary dependencies, document content (such as JSP pages, static HTML and images) and deployment descriptors of a web application. If we don't use EJB, a WAR can contain all code and binaries required by a J2EE web application.

❑ The implementation classes and deployment descriptors of an EJB deployment, which may include multiple EJBs.

Typically, each of these deployment units will include both standard J2EE and proprietary, application server-specific deployment descriptors.

WAR and EJB JAR deployment units comprising an application using the entire J2EE stack can be included in a single J2EE deployment unit, called an **Enterprise Archive (EAR)**. EAR files contain an additional deployment descriptor, `application.xml`, which identifies the J2EE **modules** composing the application. In this book we've considered the WAR and EJB JAR file module types, which are used most often in practice. It is also possible to include Java application clients and **J2EE Connector Architecture (JCA)** Resource Adapters in an EAR.

Where collocated applications are concerned, EAR deployment is usually the best option, providing convenient deployment and accurately reflecting the semantics of the application. Hence we'll use it for the sample application.

However, EAR deployment may be less appropriate for distributed applications. It's pointless to adopt a distributed architecture if web-tier components on each server always use EJBs on the same server. Thus in a distributed application, the EJB client components (WARs) in an EAR are likely to communicate at runtime with EJBs running on another server, rather than the EJB instances on the same server. One of the key arguments in favor of adopting a distributed architecture is the potential to devote additional hardware to known bottlenecks – for example, EJBs that perform time-consuming processing. In such cases, EAR deployment of all components on all servers may be wasteful and misleading, as the aim is not for all servers to run all application components.

The alternative to EAR deployment for distributed applications is to separate web applications from EJB deployments, as we know that EJBs will be invoked via RMI. However, deployment in separate modules may be more complex. We will need to include the EJB client views (home and component interfaces, but not EJB implementation classes and any helper classes they use) in both EJB and web deployments.

As we noted in Chapter 2, it's possible to run the J2EE Reference Implementation's Verifier tool against an EAR, WAR, or EJB JAR deployment unit, to check compliance to the J2EE specifications. The sample application's Ant build script includes a target to run the verifier. Such verification should be performed regularly, to ensure that applications are specification-compliant and because it provides an easy pre-deployment check for errors. The verifier tool reports problems such as missing classes or invalid deployment descriptors in a detailed and consistent manner. This may provide clearer information on the cause of a deployment failure than the output of some J2EE servers.

Expanded Deployment Units

Most servers allow deployment units to be deployed in "expanded" or "exploded" form: that is, as a directory structure, rather than an archive in a fixed directory structure. Expanded deployment is typically most useful in development; we will want to roll out single deployment units into production.

The advantages of expanded deployment in development are that it often enables individual files to be updated without full redeployment. For example, it's unacceptable to have to redeploy an entire application to modify a JSP during development. The sample application's Ant build script includes a target to deploy the application as an EAR containing an EJB JAR file, but an expanded WAR. This makes it possible to modify JSP pages and other web content, without redeploying the application.

Understanding J2EE Class Loading

Perhaps the toughest issue in packaging J2EE applications relates to class loading in applications consisting of multiple modules, this affects:

❑   How we package applications, and especially where we include classes used by both EJB JAR and WAR modules.

❑   Portability between application servers. Differences between class loading behavior in different application servers can be a real problem for portability, and can mean that an EAR that works on one server may not work in another, even if it is coded within the J2EE specifications.

> Unless we understand how J2EE server class loading is likely to work and draw the appropriate lessons (we can only say "likely" as it differs between application servers), we risk encountering mysterious `ClassNotFound` or `ClassCastExceptions`.

While there are good reasons for class loading to work the way it does, unfortunately the complexity of J2EE class loading can impact application developers and reduce productivity. Thus it is important to understand the issues involved, complex though they are.

The following discussion concentrates on packaging applications in an EAR (the commonest approach in practice), rather than packaging EJB JAR and WAR modules separately.

Java Class Loading Concepts

Let's first look at how Java 2 class loading works. The following two basic principles will always apply:

❑   Each class retains an association with the class loader that loaded it. The `getClassLoader()` method of `java.lang.Class` returns the class loader that loaded the class, which cannot be changed after the class is loaded. This is the class loader that will be used if the class attempts to load classes by name.

❑   If the same class is loaded by two class loaders, classes loaded by the two class loaders will not be type compatible (although serialization will work).

The documentation of the `java.lang.ClassLoader` class further defines the following behavior for class loaders:

❑ Class loaders are hierarchical. When a class loader is asked to load a class, it first asks its parent class loader to try to load the class. Only if the parent (and parent's ancestors) cannot load the class, will the original classloader attempt to load the class. The top of the class loader hierarchy is the **bootstrap** loader built into the JVM, which loads `java.lang.Object()`.

❑ Although a class loader can see classes loaded by its parent(s), it cannot see classes loaded by its children.

As it's possible to implement a custom class loader (and most application servers provide several), it is possible to depart from the hierarchical behavior described in the last two bullets.

Class Loading in J2EE

J2EE servers use multiple class loaders, largely because this allows dynamic application reloading. Clearly we don't want to reload all the application server's own classes on redeploying an application. This would mean that the application server would always need to be restarted. So application servers use different class loaders for application code to those they use for their own standard libraries, for example. Typically one or more new class loaders will be created for each application deployed on a server.

However, multiple class loaders are not usually used for different application-specific classes in the same application unless we use EJB (JSP pages may be given a separate class loader, but this doesn't usually affect application code).

As I've previously mentioned, using EJB considerably complicates the deployment model, compared to that for a pure web application. This is also true of class loading. In a WAR, we can simply include all binary dependencies in the `/WEB-INF/lib` directory. However, things get more complicated when WARs access EJBs.

To see why, let's consider a common approach to implementing class loading in application servers. In an application deployed as an integrated enterprise application in an EAR, the EJB class loader is often the parent of the WAR class loader. Orion and WebLogic, for example, both use this approach. This is a natural implementation approach, as WARs will typically access EJBs (and therefore need to be able to see at least EJB client classes), while EJBs do not access web components.

> **However, it's not the only valid implementation approach, so the following discussion doesn't apply to all application servers.**

The resulting class loader hierarchy will look as shown in the following diagram. Actually more class loaders may be involved, but these are the three class loaders most significant to application code.

In this diagram the class loader hierarchy is represented by enclosing boxes. The parent-child relationship is represented by an enclosing box:

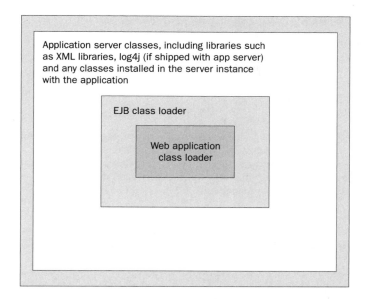

Assuming standard J2SE hierarchical class loading behavior, such a hierarchy will mean that any class can access classes in boxes that enclose its class loader. However, classes associated with the outer boxes cannot load classes in the inner boxes. Thus web application classes can see classes deployed in the application's EJBs and system classes. However, EJB classes cannot see web application classes, and classes installed at server-wide level cannot see any application-specific classes.

Class Loading in Integrated Enterprise Applications

Surely this is all of interest only to implementers of J2EE application servers? Unfortunately, application developers can't afford to ignore, or be ignorant of, the implications of J2EE class loading.

Assuming the class loader hierarchy described above, let's consider a plausible scenario. Imagine that an application class or a framework class used in both EJB and web components attempts to load a class within a WAR. Imagine, for example that a `BeanFactory` implementation used in the EJB container is also used by code within a WAR to load classes by name and manipulate them. Even though this infrastructure class is visible in the WAR, it cannot load WAR classes. Since it was loaded by the EJB class loader it cannot see classes in the WAR, which were loaded by a descendant class loader.

We can't always solve this problem simply by holding class definitions in both WEB and EJB JAR file, because this may cause class cast exceptions, if the two class loaders end up independently loading one or more classes.

Thus there are two basic problems relating to J2EE class loading, in the common case where EJB and web modules are included in the same enterprise application:

❑   Where do we hold the definitions of classes used in both EJBs and web applications?

❑   How do we ensure that two class loaders don't end up holding independent versions of the same class, resulting in class cast exceptions?

587

The Servlet 2.3 Specification's Class Loading Recommendations

Not only do implementations of class loading differ, but different J2EE *specifications* differ regarding class loading.

The Servlet 2.3 specification (9.7.2) states that "It is recommended also that the application class loader be implemented so that classes and resources packaged within the WAR are loaded in preference to classes and resources residing in container-wide library JARs".

This clearly conflicts with the standard J2SE class loading behavior, as described in the Javadoc for the `java.lang.ClassLoader` class. As the WAR class loader must be a dynamic class loader, it must be the child of another class loader provided by the application server. Hence the Servlet 2.3 recommendation is the opposite of normal Java 2 class loading behavior, which clearly states that classes will be loaded from the child class loader (in this case the WAR class loader) only if they cannot be resolved by the ancestor class loaders.

This recommendation (note that it is not a requirement) is also unclear on where EJBs fit into the proposed class loading model. EJBs are presumably not considered to be "classes and resources residing in container-wide library JARs", in which case the requirement does not apply to them.

The contradiction between the Servlet 2.3 and normal Java 2 class loading behavior is underlined by the fact that Sun's J2EE 1.3 Compatibility Test Suite fails on servers that default to implementing Servlet 2.3-style inverted class loading. For this reason, many servers either don't implement the Servlet 2.3 recommendation, or offer it only as a configuration option. The JBoss/Jetty bundle used in the sample application defaults to using normal Java 2 class loading behavior, although it can be configured to use Servlet 2.3 WAR-first behavior. Oracle iAS takes the same approach.

The main merit of Servlet 2.3-style class loading is that it can allow us to ship any patched libraries an application requires as part of the application, without altering the server installation. For example, the XMLC 2.1 web content generation technology discussed in Chapter 13 requires patched versions of XML libraries shipped with some application servers. With Servlet 2.3 class loading, we can include the necessary patches in the `/WEB-INF/lib` directory, without any need to modify overall server configuration or any risk of conflict with other applications.

The Java 1.3 Extension Mechanism Architecture in J2EE

We also need to take into account further J2SE class loading refinements. Changes in J2SE 1.3 make it possible for JAR files to specify dependencies on other JAR files, by specifying a space-separated list of relative file paths in a `Class-Path` header in their `/META-INF/MANIFEST.MF` file. Section 8.1.1.2 of the J2EE 1.3 specification requires that application servers support this for EJB JAR files. The following example from the sample application's `ticket-ejb.jar` file's `MANIFEST.MF` file illustrates the use of this mechanism in the sample application:

```
Class-Path: log4j-1.2.jar i21-core.jar i21-ejbimpl.jar i21-jdbc.jar
```

This declares that the application-specific classes in the `ticket-ejb.jar` file depend on four infrastructure JARs, meaning that the EJB JAR file doesn't need to include any third party classes. These paths are relative. All these JAR files are included with the EJB JAR file in the root directly of the application EAR, as the following listing of the EAR's contents shows:

```
META-INF/
META-INF/MANIFEST.MF
META-INF/application.xml
i21-core.jar
i21-ejbimpl.jar
i21-jdbc.jar
ticket-ejb.jar
ticket.war
log4j-1.2.jar
```

Some application servers support the manifest classpath mechanism for WAR and EAR deployment units, but as these are not loaded directly by class loaders this is not required by J2SE 1.3 or the J2EE 1.3 specification. For example, see documentation at http://otn.oracle.com/tech/java/oc4j/htdocs/how-to-servlet-warmanifest.html on how to enable WAR manifest classpaths on Oracle 9iAS Release 2. (This support is disabled by default.) WebSphere 4.0 also supports manifest classpaths for WAR files, and IBM documentation (see http://www-3.ibm.com/software/webservers/appserv/doc/v40/aee/wasa_content/060401.html) recommends using this when WARs and EJBs reference the same classes. Orion and Oracle will also load manifest classpaths in EARs by default. Note that JBoss/Jetty does *not* appear to respect manifest classpaths in WARs, so I haven't relied on this non-portable feature in packaging the sample application. The J2EE Reference Implementation also ignores manifest classpaths in WARs.

The Servlet 2.3 specification requires that web containers respect the manifest classpaths of library files included in a web application's /WEB-INF/lib directory. However, this is problematic in integrated EAR deployment, as it's unclear what the relative path should be where a WAR is involved. What is the meaning of a relative path from a nested directory inside an archive file? For example, if a .war file is included in the root directory of an EAR, along with the EJB JAR files it references, which of the following two plausible relative paths should library JARs use?

❑   ../../other-jar-file.jar, which navigates to the WEB-INF directory and then the root of the WAR, and assumes that the library JAR(s) are in the same directory as the root of the WAR.

❑   ../../../other-jar-file.jar, which navigates one directory higher, assuming that the .war file will have been extracted into its own directory under the root of the EAR, an approach that most servers will use.

Neither alternative works in JBoss/Jetty. Thus using manifest classpaths in JARs in a /WEB-INF/lib directory is not portable. Perhaps for this reason, the J2EE 1.3 specification (section 8.1.1.2) suggests that it is necessary to include shared libraries in the /WEB-INF/lib directory even if they are included elsewhere in the same EAR file.

Section 8.1.1.2 of the J2EE specification does not require the resolution of classes external to the EAR file, such as libraries installed at a server level. This may work in some servers, but is non-standard. If an application depends on external binaries, it's usually better just to use your server's way of installing binaries at server-wide level. (This is also non-portable, but simpler.)

Despite these limitations, the J2SE Extension Mechanism Architecture has important implications for J2EE application packaging. It allows an approach to J2EE packaging in which we use multiple JAR files to avoid the need to include the same class definitions in multiple modules within an EAR. This is particularly important when application classes depend on in-house or third-party libraries. For example, we can use JAR files containing library classes required by multiple EJBs, while EJB JAR files contain only application-specific EJB implementation classes. See http://www.onjava.com/lpt/a/onjava/2001/06/26/ejb.html for an article by Tyler Jewell of BEA discussing the use of manifest classpaths.

> **Especially in EJB JAR files, use J2SE 1.3 manifest classpaths to avoid the need to include the same class definitions in multiple modules. However, remember that not all application servers support manifest classpaths in EAR or WAR deployment units. Also, remember that manifest classpaths only affect where a class definition is held, and do not resolve problems resulting from which class loader first loads a class (for example, the problem of a class loaded by an EJB class loader being unable to see classes within a WAR in many servers).**

Thread Context Class Loader

It's also possible to try to resolve class loading problems by using the Java Thread API to obtain a class loader programmatically. Section 6.2.4.8 of the J2EE 1.3 specification requires all J2EE containers to support the use of the `getContextClassLoader()` method on `java.util.Thread`.

The J2EE specification isn't entirely clear regarding context class loading. However, the intent appears to be to allow portable classes, such as value objects, to load application classes in whatever container (such as EJB or web container) they may run in. In practice, the context class loader appears to be in the context of the current container. To clarify this behavior, let's consider the effect of the following two calls, made by a helper class that is loaded by the EJB class loader but used in both EJBs and classes running in the web container:

- ❏ `Class.forName(classname)`: Will use the class loader of the helper class: in this case, the EJB class loader. This means that, if the EJB class loader is the parent of the WAR class loader, the helper will never be able to load classes in the WAR by name.

- ❏ `Class.forName(classname, true, Thread.currentThread().getContextClassLoader())`: Will use the current container's class loader. This means that the helper will behave differently wherever it is running. If the EJB class loader is the parent of the WAR class loader, when the helper is used in the EJB container, it will only be able to load EJB classes and classes loaded by higher class loaders. If the helper is used in the WAR, it will be able to load WAR classes as well.

Many frameworks, such as WebWork, use this approach to avoid problems caused by hierarchical class loading. However, it's not usually required in application code, which should normally only load classes by name using an abstraction layer that should conceal any use of the context class loader.

Server Check List

As no two servers implement class loading in exactly the same way, and class loading behavior can even change between successive releases of the same server, let's conclude with a check list of things that you should find out to understand class loading in your application server:

❑ What is your server's runtime class hierarchy? For example, is the EJB class loader the parent of the WAR class loader?

❑ Does your server support Servlet 2.3-style class loading (WAR first) for web applications?

❑ Does your server provide manifest classpath support for EAR and WAR deployment units, not merely JARs such as EJB JAR files? If so, is it necessary to change server configuration to enable it?

❑ Is your server's class loading behavior fixed, or is it possible to configure it? In some servers, for example, it's possible to choose between normal Java 2 and Servlet 2.3 class loading behavior.

❑ What is the relationship, if any, between classes in different applications deployed on the same server? In JBoss 3.0, for example, which uses an unusual, flat, class loader structure, special configuration is required to deploy two different versions of the same class on the same server (otherwise the two versions of the class will conflict). In many other servers, different applications will be entirely independent.

Recommendations

Although the different behavior of different application servers makes it impossible to advance hard and fast rules where packaging and class loading are concerned, I recommend the following guidelines:

❑ **Only include application-specific classes in EJB JAR files and** /WEB-INF/classes **directories**
EJB JAR files that depend on reusable infrastructure classes should use manifest classpaths to indicate their dependency on other classes within the EAR.

❑ **Binaries required only by a web application should be included in the** /WEB-INF/lib **directory**
In pure web applications, simply include all required JAR files in this directory.

❑ **Binaries used by both EJBs and web applications should be included in JAR files in application EARs**
If your application server supports manifest classpaths for WARs, these can be used to declare a dependency on the JAR files in the EAR. If your application server doesn't support this, the JAR files will also need to be included in the /WEB-INF/lib directory of each WAR module. This duplication is unfortunate, but the J2EE 1.3 specification implies that it is necessary for portable applications.

❑ **Consider the implications of loading classes by name carefully**
Try to ensure that classes that load other classes are by name are loaded only by the class loader of the module they will be used in (for example, it is possible to use distinct subclasses of a common superclass when similar functionality is required in a WAR and EJB JAR). Alternatively, you may be able to use the thread context class loader to get a class loader to load classes with. This problem should normally be concealed by infrastructure classes, and thus shouldn't normally affect application code.

❑ **Server-wide classes such as JDBC drivers and JDO implementations should be installed in at server, not application level**
For example, in JBoss 3.0 such JARs or zips can be placed in the /lib directory of the current server; in Orion, they can be placed in Orion's /lib directory. This approach can sometimes be used to solve problems with application-specific class loading (for example, to guarantee that certain application classes are available in all modules of an application), but it's an inelegant last resort. It means that the application server can't dynamically reload these classes, and that deployment units are no longer self-contained, which violates the J2EE specifications.

591

❑ **If necessary, run tests to establish the class loader hierarchy of your application server** The `com.interface21.beans.ClassLoaderAnalyzer` class in the infrastructure included with the sample application contains methods to show the class loader hierarchy for a given class or `ClassLoader`. I've found such diagnostics very useful in tracking down class loading problems.

In complex applications, it can be difficult to devise packaging that is portable across application servers. In some cases portable packaging may add little business value, but may be very time-consuming to achieve.

Concentrate on the target application server when packaging applications. But remember the issues discussed above, and especially the likely implications of hierarchical class loaders in applications using EJBs.

Further Information

J2EE class loading is a very complex topic. See the following resources for further information:

❑ http://kb.atlassian.com/content/atlassian/howto/classloaders.jsp. Clear, concise description of Orion server's class loading behavior, with references to other resources.

❑ http://www.javageeks.com/Papers/ClassForName/index.html. Excellent, detailed discussion of Java 2 class loading behavior, with some (now dated) reference to J2EE.

❑ http://www.theserverside.com/resources/articles/ClassLoading/article.html. Article on application server class loading article by Brett Peterson, which discusses the implementations in WebLogic 6.1, WebSphere 4.0 and HP-AS 8.

❑ Your application server's documentation. This is usually the most important resource. If it's not entirely clear, run a diagnostic tool such as the `com.interface21.beans.ClassLoaderAnalyzer` class included in the download to display the server's class loader hierarchy.

Packaging the Sample Application

The sample application isn't distributed, and contains a web application and one EJB. Thus we will need to create WAR, EJB JAR, and EAR deployment units, and the application will normally be deployed as an EAR. We use Ant to build each of these deployment units.

First we need to understand how to package the generic infrastructure classes the application uses, which may also be used in other applications. As the infrastructure discussed in Chapter 9, Chapter 11, and Chapter 12 – notably, the bean factory and JDBC abstraction packages – is used in both EJBs and web components and needs to load classes by name, it's important that it can be packaged so as not to complicate application-specific class loading.

Thus the framework classes discussed in this book are packaged in four separate JAR files, which can be included in application deployments and referenced using J2SE 1.3 manifest classpaths. The implementation and packaging of this framework takes care to ensure that class loading by name will work, even in application servers that use complex class loader hierarchies.

The framework classes are divided into the following JARs, built by the `/framework/build.xml` file in the download, which is invoked by the sample application's `build.xml` file in the download's root directory. You should adopt a similar multi-JAR strategy if you create your own library packages for use across multiple applications:

- ❑ `i21-core.jar`
  Core framework packages including the `com.interface21.beans` package discussed in Chapter 11; logging support and nested exceptions discussed in Chapter 4; string, JNDI and other utility classes. None of these classes loads other classes by name, although subclasses of some of them will. This JAR file will be used in both EJBs and web applications. All other JAR files depend on the classes in this JAR.

- ❑ `i21-web.jar`
  Framework packages required only in web applications, which should be included only in the `/WEB-INF/lib` directory of WAR files. This JAR includes:

- ❑ Bean factory implementations used only in web applications, such as `com.interface21.beans.factory.support.XmlBeanFactory`. Since these implementations are loaded by the WAR class loader, not the EJB class loader, they are guaranteed to be able to see application classes included in the WAR.

- ❑ The "application context" infrastructure discussed in Chapter 11, which isn't required by EJBs.

- ❑ The MVC web framework discussed in Chapter 12, including custom tags and validation infrastructure.

- ❑ EJB client classes, such as superclasses for business delegates and service locators.

- ❑ JMS abstraction classes. These are never required in EJBs, as we can use MDBs to solve the same problems in a standard way.

- ❑ `i21-ejbimpl.jar`
  EJB superclasses and the JNDI bean factory implementation, which is not used by WARs, and so can be loaded by the EJB class loader.

- ❑ `i21-jdbc.jar`
  The JDBC abstraction layer and generic data access exception packages discussed in Chapter 9. The classes in this JAR do not use reflection, and are likely to be used by both web applications and EJBs.

All that we need to do to assemble an application is to ensure that the necessary JARs are available to EJB and WAR modules. The same Interface21 JARs required to compile application-specific classes must be available to the relevant deployment unit at runtime.

The EAR will contain all the infrastructure JARs except `i21-web.jar` in the root directory, as follows:

```
META-INF/
META-INF/MANIFEST.MF
META-INF/application.xml
i21-core.jar
i21-ejbimpl.jar
i21-jdbc.jar
ticket-ejb.jar
ticket.war
log4j-1.2.jar
```

The EJB JAR module uses a manifest classpath declaring its dependence on `i21-core.jar`, `i21-ejbimpl.jar` and `i21-jdbc.jar`, as we've seen above:

```
Class-Path: log4j-1.2.jar i21-core.jar i21-ejbimpl.jar i21-jdbc.jar
```

The WAR includes `i21-core.jar`, `i21-web,jar` and `i21-jdbc.jar` in its `/WEB-INF/lib` directory, as the following partial listing of its contents shows:

```
WEB-INF/lib/log4j-1.2.jar
WEB-INF/lib/jstl.jar
Other library classes omitted

WEB-INF/lib/i21-core.jar
WEB-INF/lib/i21-jdbc.jar
WEB-INF/lib/i21-web.jar
```

In a server such as Orion or WebLogic, in which the EJB class loader is the parent of the WAR class loader, we would only need to include `i21-web.jar` here. However, in JBoss, which does not use this hierarchical class loading structure, all these JARs are required. If we knew that our server supported manifest classpaths in WARs, we could simply declare a manifest classpath in the WAR.

The `ticket-ejb.jar` file and the `/WEB-INF/classes` directory of the WAR will contain only application-specific classes.

Now that we know what must go into our deployment units, we can write Ant scripts to build them.

Ant provides useful standard tasks to build WAR and EAR deployment units. The `war` task is an extension of the `jar` task, allowing easy selection of deployment descriptors destined for the WAR's `WEB-INF` directory, JAR files destined for the `WEB-INF/lib` directory and application classes destined for the `/WEB-INF/classes` directory. The `webxml` attribute of the `<war>` element selects the standard deployment descriptor; the `<webinf>` sub-element selects other files, such as proprietary deployment descriptors, for inclusion in the `/WEB-INF` directory; while `<lib>` and `<classes>` sub-elements select binaries and classes respectively.

The following is the target used in the sample application:

```
<target name="war" depends="build-war">

    <war warfile="${web-war.product}"
         webxml="${web-war.dir}/WEB-INF/web.xml">

        <fileset dir="${web-war.dir}" excludes="WEB-INF/**"/>

        <webinf dir="${web-war.dir}/WEB-INF">
            <exclude name="web.xml"/>
        </webinf>
```

Here we ensure that application-specific classes, compiled into the directory specified by the `classes.dir` Ant property, go into the `/WEB-INF/classes` directory:

```
        <classes dir="${classes.dir}">
            <include name="**/*.class"/>
        </classes>
```

I've used several `<lib>` sub-elements of the `<war>` element to select the runtime libraries required for the different view technologies demonstrated in Chapter 13, as follows:

```
<lib dir="${lib.dir}/runtime/common" />
<lib dir="${lib.dir}/runtime/jsp-stl" />
<lib dir="${lib.dir}/runtime/velocity" />
<lib dir="${lib.dir}/runtime/xmlc" />
<lib dir="${lib.dir}/runtime/itext-pdf" />
```

The following subelement includes the Interface21 infrastructure JARs in the `/WEB-INF/lib` directory. If the application server supported manifest classpaths for WARs, we could omit the first two of these JARs, and provide a manifest referring to these JARs in the WAR's root directory:

```
<lib dir="${dist.dir}" >
        <include name="i21-core.jar"/>
        <include name="i21-jdbc.jar"/>
        <include name="i21-web.jar"/>
    </lib>
  </war>
</target>
```

The Ant EAR task is also easy to use. We simply need to specify the location of the `application.xml` deployment descriptor and specify the archives to be included using `<fileset>` sub-elements. In the sample application's directory layout, the deployment descriptor is in the `/ear` directory, and the WAR and EJB JAR files are in the `/dist` directory. Note that this task depends on the EJB JAR file and WAR being up to date:

```
<target name="ear" depends="ejb-jar,war">
    <ear earfile="${app-ear.product}" appxml="ear/application.xml">
        <fileset dir="${dist.dir}">
            <include name="ticket.war"/>
            <include name="ticket-ejb.jar"/>
```

We include the EJB JAR file's dependencies in the root directory of the WAR:

```
            <include name="i21-core.jar"/>
            <include name="i21-ejbimpl.jar"/>
            <include name="i21-jdbc.jar"/>
              </fileset>
                <fileset dir="lib/runtime/common">
                <include name="log4j*.jar"/>
              </fileset>
        </fileset>
    </ear>
</target>
```

The optional Ant EJB tasks are less useful, at least in my experience. Unlike WAR and EAR deployment units, EJB JAR files are ordinary JAR files, with deployment descriptors in the `/META-INF` directory. Accordingly, I've used the standard `jar` task to generate the EJB JAR file. This is simply a matter of specifying the contents of the `/META-INF` directory of the generated JAR file (the standard `ejb-jar.xml` and any proprietary deployment descriptors) and selecting the classes by setting the `basedir` attribute to the root of the directory containing the compiled application-specific EJB classes:

```
<target name="ejb-jar" depends="build-ejb">

    <jar jarfile="${ejb-jar.product}"
            basedir="${ejbclasses.dir}"
            manifest="${ejb-jar.dir}/manifest"
    >
    <metainf dir="${ejb-jar.dir}">
                <include name="*/**"/>
    </metainf>
    </jar>
</target>
```

Note the use of the `manifest` attribute of the jar task, which specifies the file to use as the JAR's manifest, enabling us to specify the manifest classpath shown above.

Like the WAR target, this EJB target takes *all* files from the deployment descriptor directory, not just `ejb-jar.xml`. Proprietary deployment descriptors, such as `jboss.xml` or `weblogic-ejb-jar.xml` must also be included in the deployment unit.

> To use the library classes included in this book in your own applications, you will need to include **i21-core.jar** and either **i21-ejbimpl.jar** or **i21-web.jar**, depending on whether you're implementing EJBs or a web module. Note that **i21-web.jar** should be included in a **/WEB-INF/lib** directory: it should not be loaded by an EJB class loader. If using the JDBC abstraction described in Chapter 9, which can be used in both EJBs and web applications, **i21-jdbc.jar** is required.

All these JAR files are found in the `/dist` directory of the download. The complete Ant build file discussed above is named `build.xml` in the root directory of the download.

Application Deployment: Common Concepts

Beyond standard packaging, there are three distinct tasks before we can make a successful deployment:

❑   We need to prepare the application server by setting up server-wide resources such as connection pools, which our applications rely on.

❑   We need to write the required proprietary deployment descriptors for our target application server and include them for packaging with our application.

❑   In some servers, we may need to perform additional steps to prepare a deployment unit for the target server, such as generating and compiling EJB home and component interface implementation classes.

Let's look at each task in turn.

Configuring a Server to Run the Application

Let's look at some of the most important server-wide configuration issues we're likely to encounter. These involve creating the services the application will rely on at runtime, and ensuring that any dependencies are satisfied.

Creating Connection Pools

In most J2EE applications, we'll need to perform RDBMS access. This means that we must configure a `javax.sql.DataSource` and ensure that it is bound in the server's global JNDI naming context. This usually involves creating a connection pool, the details of which will be server-specific, and defining a server-specific `DataSource` that exposes it. `DataSource` objects can be used by code running in either the EJB or web container.

Typical configuration parameters we will need to set when defining a connection pool are:

❑ The JDBC driver class. This is normally a class supplied by the RDBMS vendor, such as `oracle.jdbc.driver.OracleDriver`.

❑ The JDBC URL. The format will depend on the driver.

❑ Username and password, assuming that the container, not the application, will perform authentication (the commonest option in J2EE applications).

❑ The maximum size of the connection pool. This may have a significant effect on performance, as threads will block while waiting for connections if all connections are in use. However, an excessively large pool size may waste valuable database resources, especially if multiple J2EE servers access the same RDBMS server.

❑ The initial size of the connection pool. Sometimes it's best to allocate several connections on startup, if we know that an application will make heavy use of the connection immediately on starting up.

❑ Pool maintenance settings such as the time until inactive connections are closed.

We'll also need to ensure that the necessary database driver is available at application server (rather than application) level, as connection pools are independent of applications.

Creating JMS Destinations

JMS destinations are another example of server-wide resources. These are not limited to any single application. In fact, they can be used for inter-application communication.

In JBoss 3.0, the `$JBOSS_HOME/deploy/jbossmq-destinations-service.xml` file defines the default JMS topics and queues, setting their JNDI names. In Orion the same role is performed by the `/config/jms.xml` file.

Setting up Authentication

Different application servers have different approaches to authentication, but we will need to provide the application server some way of checking user credentials against a persistent store. This usually involves specifying a class, which may be provided by the application server or may be custom, which checks users and role information. Most application servers define a fairly simple interface such classes must implement. User information is usually held in an RDBMS.

In Orion, authentication can be configured at an application level, but in WebLogic and JBoss, it's server-wide.

Installing Libraries

We may wish to install binaries used by multiple applications at server level, rather than distribute them as part of each application. We can do this if necessary by modifying the command that invokes the application server by adding additional classpath elements, although it's more elegant to follow server conventions. In JBoss, we can simply copy the necessary .jar or .zip files to the /lib directory of the relevant server.

Note that when we install libraries at a server-wide level, it will be impossible to modify them without restarting the application server; the application server will be unable to load them in a dynamic classloader such as it may use for application code.

In general, it's better to keep applications self-sufficient, by shipping all required binaries within J2EE deployment units. However, the following are typical cases when we might choose a server-wide approach:

❑   When the binaries in question relate to the server, rather than a specific application. Database drivers are in this category. They cannot usually be included in applications, as servers typically start connection pools before starting applications, and therefore need the drivers before loading applications.

❑   For products such as JDO implementations that will be used by all applications, and which may require server-wide JNDI bindings.

❑   When we need to replace or patch a server-side library, and Servlet 2.3 WAR-first class loading (discussed above) won't solve our problem. For example, JBoss 3.0.0 ships with Log4j. Including a later version of Log4j with an application will produce no effect, as the version loaded with the server's class loader will always take precedence. Thus the only way to update the version of Log4j would be to replace it at a server level.

> **Don't update or patch libraries used by an application server unless it's essential, as it risks affecting the behavior of the application server.**

Occasionally it may be necessary to deploy some classes at server-wide level to avoid class loading problems between WAR and EJB deployments. However, as we've seen, this often reflects poor design of the classes in question, and is a last resort, rather than a positive choice.

Writing Proprietary Deployment Descriptors for an Application

In additional to server configuration, we will need to add proprietary information for inclusion in deployment units.

Proprietary deployment descriptors are required to provide additional information that fills gaps left by the standard deployment descriptors and to configure implementation-specific parameters. For example, proprietary deployment descriptors must be used to:

❑   Tell the server where to find resources the standard deployment descriptors identify. For example, the standard deployment descriptors require declaration of the JNDI names used in application code to access resources such as DataSources, but don't specify how these should be mapped onto server-wide data sources created during server configuration.

❑ Specify how stateless session EJB pooling should work. Stateless session bean pool size is an important configuration parameter, normally specified in proprietary deployment descriptors. However, as the implementation is vendor-specific, `ejb-jar.xml` rightly doesn't describe configuration parameters.

The structure of proprietary descriptors varies, but there's much commonality between their content. The settings I'll discuss below are common to all servers I've worked with.

Entity beans with CMP often require complex proprietary deployment descriptors, the format of which varies between application servers. As I don't advocate use of entity beans, I won't attempt to cover this here. If using CMP entity beans, please refer to documentation about proprietary descriptors for your application server. Plan to use tools to manage the complexity of such deployment descriptors; manual editing is not a viable option for the necessary `ejb-jar.xml` elements and proprietary descriptors.

EJB-Specific Configuration

Usually the most complex parameters relate to EJBs. We'll always need to provide mappings for the JNDI names declared in `ejb-jar.xml`. However, other settings may include:

❑ Stateless session bean pooling options.

❑ Replication options for stateful session beans.

❑ Other cluster-related options, such as routing algorithm within a cluster.

❑ In applications that use EJBs with remote interfaces, whether EJB invocations within the same JVM should be optimized to use call-by-reference. This is the default in most servers, and will greatly improve performance, but may cause unexpected results if the EJBs were coded with the expectation of call-by-value.

❑ Transaction timeouts for CMTs.

❑ Transaction isolation levels to be applied to methods using CMT. In some servers these can only be set for entity beans; in WebLogic, they can be set for any type of EJB.

Note that we don't always need to override the defaults, which may ensure appropriate behavior for most applications.

Web-Tier Configuration

Web-tier configuration is usually simpler than EJB-tier configuration, because the relevant container infrastructure is simpler, because there are fewer gaps in `web.xml`, and because using an MVC framework (such as Struts or the framework we discussed in Chapter 12) tends to move much of the configuration of web-tier components into framework-specific deployment descriptors.

Typically we'll need only to provide mappings for the JNDI names declared in resource references in `web.xml`. However, we may be able to set options such as the following (configurable in `weblogic.xml`):

❑ JSP compilation options, such as which compiler to use, special command-line arguments, and whether all JSP pages should be precompiled when the application starts up

❑ Session tracking options

❑ How to store session data (to a flat file, RDBMS etc.)

❑ Session replication configuration

Deploying an Application

The steps in deploying an application will vary between servers.

Web applications don't generally require any special steps besides making the WAR available to the server, as a web container merely needs to load the relevant servlet classes and make the necessary resources available through JNDI.

EJB deployments, however, may be more complex, as the EJB classes implemented as part of the application don't implement the bean's `EJBObject` and home interfaces. The server must provide implementations of these interfaces, invoking application classes to perform business logic.

Some servers use dynamic proxies to implement EJB component and home interfaces, wrapping application classes. However, many servers, such as WebLogic, require a compilation step, in which the container generates and compiles the necessary classes. The use of container-generated classes may produce marginally better performance by minimizing the need for reflection, although it's unlikely that any such gain will be significant in most applications. Until J2SE 1.3 introduced dynamic proxies, container-generated classes were the only available deployment strategy.

In WebLogic's case, the proprietary `ejbc` tool is used to generate container-specific classes and add them to the EJB JAR file before deployment to the server. WebLogic can automatically perform this step on deployment of a standard EJB JAR file, but it unnecessarily wastes server resources and may make it harder to track down deployment errors, by combining the operations of building the WebLogic-specific EJB JAR file and deploying it on a running server.

> If a server-specific "compilation" step is required, use an Ant target to invoke it and ensure that it occurs before deployment.

Deployment Parameters for the Sample Application

Now we know enough to list the essential tasks required to configure *any* server to run our sample application and add the necessary deployment descriptors to our application. Only how we accomplish these tasks will differ between servers:

- ❑ Create a server-wide `DataSource` for our Oracle database.
- ❑ Create the server-wide JMS topic for reference data update messages.
- ❑ Make the `DataSource` available to the `BoxOffice` EJB through a proprietary deployment descriptor.
- ❑ Make the `DataSource` and JMS topic available to components running in the web container through a proprietary deployment descriptor.
- ❑ Make the `BoxOffice` EJB available to code running in the web container.

Deploying the Sample Application on JBoss 3.0

The following instructions for deploying the sample application begin with a "factory" install of JBoss 3.0. This can be created simply by extracting the distribution archive, `jboss-3.0.0.zip`, into an appropriate location, which I'll refer to as `$JBOSS_HOME`.

This ZIP is the JBoss distribution with the Jetty web container. JBoss is also distributed in a bundle with the Tomcat web container, which is the Reference Implementation for J2EE web technologies. However, Jetty appears to offer superior performance. (The sample application has been tested with JBoss/Tomcat).

Understanding the JBoss Directory Structure

The final release of JBoss 3.0 moves towards a multiple server concept, as used by WebLogic 6.0 and above.

The root directory of the JBoss installation contains a `/server` directory, which in turn contains a directory for each of any number of independent JBoss server configurations. In the following example, I've used the `/default` server, which is started by the default startup script. The directory of the server to start can be set as the value of the system property `jboss.server.name` when invoking the JBoss boot class.

The JBoss startup JARs, used by all servers, are found in the `$JBOSS_HOME/lib` directory.

Each server directory, such as `$JBOSS_HOME/server/default`, contains the following subdirectories relevant to application deployment:

❑ `/conf`
Contains global configuration information for this server, such as authentication configuration and default EJB deployment settings.

❑ `/lib`
Contains the binaries used by the server, including JBoss and standard J2EE libraries. JAR and ZIP files in this directory are automatically loaded by the server. Database drivers required by applications are typically placed in this directory.

❑ `/log`
Server and HTTP request log files

❑ `/deploy`
Contains deployment units (EARs, WARs, EJB JAR files and Resource Adapters) that will automatically be deployed by JBoss, and **service definition** files.

Service definition files are XML files that define JBoss services in the form of JMX MBean definitions. Any file with a name ending with `-service.xml` which is placed in a server's `/deploy` directory will be treated as containing MBean definitions. Each file must include a number of <mbean> elements in a <server> element. However, the attributes applicable to each MBean vary with the relevant class. The way in which MBean classes and properties are set is analogous to, although more complex than, the XML bean factory definition we saw in Chapter 11. As with the bean factory approach, it provides a consistent way of defining different objects, meaning that it's only necessary to learn the basic concepts to understand how it can be used with any MBean implementation.

Since several MBeans, concerning different aspects of server configuration, can be included in the one service definition file, it is often possible to specify all the configuration required for an application in a single XML file, making deployment particularly easy. We use this approach in the sample application.

JBoss doesn't restrict us to defining standard MBeans, shipped with JBoss. For example, we can use the same mechanism to add our own custom classes, or third-party classes, to the global JNDI context when JBoss starts up.

Configuring a JBoss Server to Run the Sample Application

Following the steps we described above, we begin by defining the `DataSource` used by the application.

Creating a Connection Pool

JBoss includes example definitions for several databases, including Oracle, in the `$JBOSS_HOME/docs/examples/jca` directory. A wider range of examples is available in the JBoss CVS repository at http://cvs.sourceforge.net/cgi-bin/viewcvs.cgi/jboss/jbosscx/src/etc/example-config/. However, as these files are under active development, finding the correct version can be a challenge. (Check the CVS tags carefully.)

I took the `oracle-service.xml` file from the examples directory as a basis for the definition of the Oracle connection pool for the sample application.

Here is the complete MBean definition. I've highlighted the lines of the database connection definition that set the URL, driver class, username, and password of my Oracle database. Change them as necessary in your environment:

```
<server>
  <mbean
      code="org.jboss.resource.connectionmanager.LocalTxConnectionManager"
      name="jboss.jca:service=LocalTxCM,name=OracleDS">

    <depends optional-attribute-name="ManagedConnectionFactoryName">
      <mbean
          code="org.jboss.resource.connectionmanager.RARDeployment"
          name="jboss.jca:service=LocalTxDS,name=OracleDS">

        <attribute name="JndiName">OracleDS</attribute>

        <attribute name="ManagedConnectionFactoryProperties">
          <properties>
            <config-property name="ConnectionURL" type="java.lang.String">
                jdbc:oracle:thin:@127.0.0.1:1521:rj
            </config-property>
            <config-property name="DriverClass" type="java.lang.String">
                oracle.jdbc.driver.OracleDriver
            </config-property>
            <config-property name="UserName" type="java.lang.String">
                SYSTEM
            </config-property>
            <config-property name="Password" type="java.lang.String">
                MANAGER
            </config-property>
```

```
                </properties>
            </attribute>

            <depends optional-attribute-name="OldRarDeployment">
                jboss.jca:service=RARDeployment,
                name=JBoss LocalTransaction JDBC Wrapper
            </depends>
        </mbean>
    </depends>

    <depends optional-attribute-name="ManagedConnectionPool">
        <mbean code="org.jboss.resource.connectionmanager.
                    JBossManagedConnectionPool"
               name="jboss.jca:service=LocalTxPool,name=OracleDS">

            <attribute name="MinSize">1</attribute>
            <attribute name="MaxSize">20</attribute>
            <attribute name="BlockingTimeoutMillis">5000</attribute>
            <attribute name="IdleTimeoutMinutes">15</attribute>
            <attribute name="Criteria">ByContainer</attribute>
        </mbean>
    </depends>
    <depends optional-attribute-name="CachedConnectionManager">
            jboss.jca:service=CachedConnectionManager
    </depends>
    <attribute name="TransactionManager">java:/TransactionManager</attribute>
    <depends>jboss.jca:service=RARDeployer</depends>
    </mbean>

</server>
```

Note that this example uses the default administration login to Oracle. This should be changed to a user account with the privileges appropriate for the application.

Before the connection pool will work, we must make the Oracle driver available to JBoss, by copying the `classes12.zip` *file included with Oracle to the* /lib *directory of the JBoss server.*

Creating JMS Destinations

Next we create the JMS topic used by the application, through the following MBean definition. See the `jbossmq-destinations-service.xml` file included in the default JBoss installation for examples of JMS MBean definition syntax:

```
<mbean code="org.jboss.mq.server.jmx.Topic"
       name="jboss.mq.destination:service=Topic,name=data-update">
    <depends optional-attribute-name="DestinationManager">
        jboss.mq:service=DestinationManager
    </depends>
    <depends optional-attribute-name="SecurityManager">
        jboss.mq:service=SecurityManager</depends>
    <attribute name="SecurityConf">
        <security>
          <role name="guest" read="true" write="true"/>
          <role name="publisher" read="true" write="true" create="false"/>
          <role name="durpublisher" read="true" write="true" create="true"/>
        </security>
    </attribute>
</mbean>
```

To gain a slight improvement in JBoss startup time, I deleted the `jbossmq-destinations-service.xml` file in the default server's `/deploy` directory, which defines JMS destinations used by the JBoss test suite and sample JMS applications.

As with `DataSources`, topics can be defined in any file with a name of the form – `service.xml` in the `/deploy` directory.

Installing the Service Definition File

Both these MBean definitions need to be included in a service definition file. I put both definitions shown above in the same file: `ticket-service.xml`. This file is in the `/deploy/jboss` directory of the download, and must be copied to the default server's `/deploy` directory on application deployment. The `jboss` task in the sample application's Ant build script performs this automatically. It also ensures that the Oracle driver is copied to the JBoss server's `/lib` directory. The location of the JBoss server and the name of the deployment unit are parameterized as Ant properties. The complete task is listed below:

```
<target name="jboss" depends="ear">
      <copy todir="${jboss.home}/server/${jboss.server}/lib"
            file="lib/oracle/classes12.zip"/>

      <copy todir="${jboss.home}/server/${jboss.server}/deploy"
            file="deploy/jboss/ticket-service.xml"/>
      <copy todir="${jboss.home}/server/${jboss.server}/deploy"
            file="${app-ear.product}"/>
</target>
```

Reviewing Configuration

JBoss 3.0.0 uses the JMX Reference Implementation's simple web interface to expose the JMX MBeans running on the server. By viewing the default page on port 8082 we can see the `DataSources`, JNDI topics, and other global resources available to applications. This can be invaluable during troubleshooting:

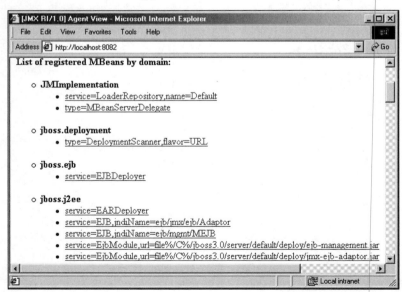

JBoss 3.0.1 introduces its own JMX HTML adapter. The WebLogic console is also JMX-based, and provides a more sophisticated interface. No other configuration changes are required to the JBoss server to run the application.

Writing JBoss Deployment Descriptors for the Sample Application

As our sample application doesn't use entity beans, and uses only one session EJB, EJB configuration is straightforward.

The necessary configuration is held in the `jboss.xml` proprietary deployment descriptor, which must be included in the EJB JAR file's `/META-INF` directory along with the standard `ejb-jar.xml` deployment descriptor. The `jboss.xml` file enables us to fill the gaps in the standard descriptor and provide further, JBoss-specific information.

For reference, the complete `<session>` bean element from `ejb-jar.xml` is:

```
<session>
      <ejb-name>BoxOffice</ejb-name>

      <local-home>
            com.wrox.expertj2ee.ticket.boxoffice.ejb.BoxOfficeHome
      </local-home>
      <local>
            com.wrox.expertj2ee.ticket.boxoffice.ejb.BoxOfficeLocal
      </local>
      <ejb-class>
            com.wrox.expertj2ee.ticket.boxoffice.ejb.BoxOfficeEJB
      </ejb-class>
      <session-type>Stateless</session-type>
      <transaction-type>Container</transaction-type>

   <env-entry>
         <env-entry-name>beans.dao.class</env-entry-name>
         <env-entry-type>java.lang.String</env-entry-type>
         <env-entry-value>
            com.wrox.expertj2ee.ticket.boxoffice.support.
            jdbc.JBoss30OracleJdbcBoxOfficeDao
         </env-entry-value>
   </env-entry>

   <env-entry>
          <env-entry-name>beans.creditCardProcessor.class</env-entry-name>
          <env-entry-type>java.lang.String</env-entry-type>
          <env-entry-value>
             com.wrox.expertj2ee.ticket.boxoffice.support.
             DummyCreditCardProcessor
          </env-entry-value>
    </env-entry>

       <resource-ref>
```

```
                <description/>
                <res-ref-name>jdbc/ticket-ds</res-ref-name>
                <res-type>javax.sql.DataSource</res-type>
                <res-auth>Container</res-auth>
        </resource-ref>
    </session>
```

We must use `jboss.xml` to provide a mapping from the `DataSource` JNDI name used in code and declared in `ejb-jar.xml` (`jdbc/ticket-ds`) to the JNDI name of the server-wide connection pool we created above (`java:/OracleDS`). We also specify the JNDI name of the bean, although this is strictly unnecessary as it defaults to the value of the `<ejb-name>` element, which indicates which EJB defined in `ejb-jar.xml` this configuration element applies to. The following is the complete `jboss.xml` file for the sample application:

```
<jboss>
  <enterprise-beans>
    <session>
            <ejb-name>BoxOffice</ejb-name>
            <jndi-name>BoxOffice</jndi-name>

            <resource-ref>
                    <res-ref-name>jdbc/ticket-ds</res-ref-name>
                    <jndi-name>java:/OracleDS</jndi-name>
            </resource-ref>
    </session>
  </enterprise-beans>
</jboss>
```

The `jboss.xml` deployment descriptor can be used to configure many aspects of EJB behavior, including the chain of "interceptors" used to intercept calls on EJBs. JBoss uses one of a number of standard interceptors to handle each aspect of server-managed functionality, such as thread and transaction management. The `jboss.xml` deployment descriptor even allows us to specify our own custom interceptors to perform application-specific behavior, although this goes well beyond the present scope of the EJB specification and isn't required by most applications.

The downside of all this configurability is that overriding simple configuration parameters such as EJB pool size is harder in JBoss than in many servers. Most servers do not offer comparable ability to customize any aspect of EJB invocation, but do provide a simpler way of specifying common settings.

Each JBoss server's default EJB and other configuration settings are defined in the server's `/conf/standardjboss.xml` file, so another option is to override them on a server-wide basis there. The default stateless session bean pool size maximum is 100. Although this is far more than will be required for our single bean, as it is a *maximum* value, and the server will not need to create this many instances at runtime, so overriding it is unnecessary, either at server or at bean level.

The `jboss-web.xml` deployment descriptor has the same relationship to the standard `web.xml` as `jboss.xml` has to `ejb-jar.xml`. Fortunately the configuration involved is much simpler. All we need to do for the sample application is to provide the same mapping between JNDI names used in code running in the web container (declared in `web.xml`) and the JNDI name of the server-wide objects we created in the server configuration step above. The resource references are defined in `web.xml` as follows:

```
<resource-ref>
      <res-ref-name>jms/TopicFactory</res-ref-name>
      <res-type>javax.jms.TopicConnectionFactory</res-type>
      <res-auth>Container</res-auth>
      <res-sharing-scope>Shareable</res-sharing-scope>
</resource-ref>

<resource-ref>
      <res-ref-name>jms/topic/data-update</res-ref-name>
      <res-type>javax.jms.Topic</res-type>
      <res-auth>Container</res-auth>
      <res-sharing-scope>Shareable</res-sharing-scope>
</resource-ref>
```

The following is a complete listing of jboss-web.xml, showing how these are mapped onto the JNDI names we declared for the data source and JMS topic:

```
<?xml version="1.0" encoding="UTF-8"?>
<jboss-web>
    <resource-ref>
            <res-ref-name>jdbc/ticket-ds</res-ref-name>
            <res-type>javax.sql.DataSource</res-type>
            <jndi-name>java:/OracleDS</jndi-name>
    </resource-ref>

    <resource-ref>
            <res-ref-name>jms/TopicFactory</res-ref-name>
            <res-type>javax.jms.TopicConnectionFactory</res-type>
            <jndi-name>java:ConnectionFactory</jndi-name>
    </resource-ref>

    <resource-ref>
             <res-ref-name>jms/topic/data-update</res-ref-name>
             <res-type>javax.jms.Topic</res-type>
             <jndi-name>topic/data-update</jndi-name>
     </resource-ref>

</jboss-web>
```

Note a JBoss-specific naming convention here for JMS destinations. We declared the topic as follows:

```
<mbean code="org.jboss.mq.server.jmx.Topic"
       name="jboss.mq.destination:service=Topic,name=data-update">
```

The server-wide JNDI name resulting from this MBean definition, and specified in the <jndi-name> element above, is /topic/data-update.

Deploying the Application

Once the server is configured and we have a packaged deployment unit, deployment on JBoss is very simple. We merely need to copy the packaged deployment unit to the /deploy directory of the appropriate JBoss server and define any services that it requires. As JBoss uses dynamic proxies to implement EJB home and EJB object interfaces, there is no need to generate container-specific classes, and deployment is fast.

We've already seen the `jboss` target in the sample application's Ant build script which copies the EAR deployment unit and necessary service definition file to the JBoss deploy directory, after rebuilding the EAR if necessary.

Finally, we can start JBoss by issuing the relevant command from the /bin directory under the JBoss root:

```
run.sh
```

or:

```
run.bat
```

As JBoss starts up, log output will initially appear on the console. The sample application will be deployed automatically.

Summary

In this chapter we've looked at packaging J2EE applications and the issues involved in deploying applications to an application server.

We've seen that the most complex issues in application packaging relate to class loading when we use EJB. J2EE servers use multiple class loaders. Many application servers use a separate class loader for EJBs and web application classes, meaning that we may face problems with classes used in both EJB JARs and WARs. Differences in class loading behavior between application servers mean that deployment units are not always portable.

We've examined class loading behavior as defined by J2SE and the J2EE specifications. We've also considered class loading behavior in several application servers.

We've seen several practical options for application packaging, and concluded that the best approach is usually to use the J2SE 1.3 manifest classpath mechanism to enable JAR-format files such as EJB JAR files to declare dependencies on other, library, JAR files. We've illustrated this by looking at the packaging of the sample application, and how the infrastructure classes discussed in previous chapters can be packaged into four JAR files referenced by application deployment units.

We've also looked at the server configuration required to underpin any J2EE deployment, such as the definition of RDBMS data sources and JMS destinations.

We've seen how we typically need proprietary, server-specific deployment descriptors to map resources referenced in the standard deployment descriptors onto resources defined in server configuration.

Finally, we've taken a practical look at deployment through the process of deploying the sample application on JBoss 3.0. We've seen how the Ant build tool can be used to automate and simplify all aspects of application packaging and deployment.

> *The J2EE Deployment API Specification (http://java.sun.com/j2ee/tools/deployment/) may make application deployment more consistent between application servers, but does not address packaging issues or standardize the definition of resources such as* `DataSources`*.*

Performance Testing and Tuning an Application

So far we've talked a lot about performance and scalability at a theoretical level. In this chapter we'll take a more practical look at how to avoid common causes of performance problems, and how to address any performance problems before they prove costly to a project.

We'll look at basic performance and scalability concepts, and why performance and scalability are critical considerations throughout the project lifecycle. If we ignore these issues until an application is functionally complete (a common mistake) we are courting disaster.

We'll look at the importance of an empirical approach to meeting performance requirements, and how we can gather the necessary evidence by load testing and profiling key application functionality. We'll look at tools for load testing web applications and ordinary Java classes, and the JProbe profiler.

We'll look at techniques for addressing any performance problems identified through testing and profiling. We'll consider how to ensure efficient use of J2EE container services, the benefits (and potential problems with) caching frequently used data, and code-level optimizations.

We'll illustrate these techniques, and use of the performance testing tools discussed in this chapter, by analyzing and improving the performance of one of the key use cases of the ticketing sample application. We'll look at why ensuring satisfactory performance in distributed applications is a special challenge, and how we can overcome it by minimizing the overhead of remote method invocation.

We'll also consider some performance issues relating to web applications. We'll look at benchmarks of some of the alternative view technologies discussed in Chapter 13. We'll see how we may be able to minimize load on web applications by using HTTP headers to enable proxy and browser caching.

Finally, we'll look at some common causes of performance and scalability problems in J2EE applications, enabling us to avoid making costly mistakes.

Strategic Issues and Definitions

High-level design largely determines the efficiency of a J2EE application. Code-level optimization can help to eliminate known bottlenecks, but will seldom produce a comparable return on effort. J2EE provides a wealth of design choices, at many levels. Perhaps most important is the question of whether to use a distributed architecture. If we do adopt a distributed architecture, **application partitioning** – the question of which components run where – will largely determine performance and throughput. As J2EE offers a wide variety of component types, it's also important to consider the performance implications when modeling our applications. For example, should we perform a particular data operation using entity beans, or using JDO or JDBC? Do we really need to use EJB, which delivers many services but adds overhead?

We must balance performance considerations with other issues. For example, should we use high performing but non-portable features of our initial target database? Should we complicate design and implementation by adding our own caching services or using third-party caching software not supplied without our application server? Such decisions may involve tradeoffs. Performance considerations will often be critical to decision making, but good design and a maintainable codebase remain essential. Fortunately, as we'll see, there's often no need to make sacrifices to achieve good performance: good design often leads to good performance, and provides the flexibility essential to implement caching and other worthwhile optimizations.

It's essential to remember that *satisfactory performance is a critical business requirement.* If an application doesn't deliver adequate performance, it doesn't matter how elegant it is or how many design patterns it uses. It's a failure, because it doesn't satisfy the needs of the business. Too many J2EE developers (and too much J2EE literature!) seem to forget this, leading to inflexible pursuit of inherently inefficient designs.

Due to the risks to a project of unsatisfactory performance or insufficient throughput, we should consider performance implications throughout the project lifecycle. We should be prepared to run performance and load tests as development progresses. For example, we may need to implement a "vertical slice" early in the project lifecycle to verify that the design will result in satisfactory performance before we are too heavily committed.

Performance and throughput should be tested as early as possible in a project lifecycle through implementing a "vertical slice" or "spike solution". If such metrics are left until an implementation is functionally complete, rectifying any problems may require major changes to design and code.

Often the vertical slice will implement some of the functionality that we suspect will have the worst performance in the application and some of the functionality that will be most heavily used in production. However, we should try to back suspicions about likely performance problems with evidence. It's not always possible to predict where problem areas will be.

Performance and Scalability

Performance and **scalability** are quite distinct.

When we speak of an application's performance, we are usually referring to the time taken to execute its key use cases on a given hardware configuration. For example, we might measure the performance of an application running in a single application server instance on a server on which it will be deployed in production. A performant application appears fast to its users.

However, performance doesn't necessarily measure the application's ability to cope with increased load, or the application's ability to take advantage of a more powerful hardware configuration. This is the issue of scalability. Scalability is often measured in terms of the number of concurrent users that can be served by the application, or transaction throughput.

Scalability encompasses scalability on a given hardware configuration (for example, the maximum number of concurrent users that can be handled by a given server), and maximum scalability (the absolute maximum throughput that can be achieved in any hardware deployment). Achieving maximum scalability will require the hardware configuration to be enhanced as necessary as the load increases. Usually, a growing **cluster** of servers will underpin scalability. Maximum scalability will usually be limited in practice, as the overhead of running a cluster will grow with the cluster's size, meaning that return from adding additional servers will diminish.

A special case of scalability concerns data volume. For example, a recruitment system might support user searches efficiently with 500 jobs in its database, covering one industry in one city. Will it still function efficiently with 100,000 jobs, covering many industries across several countries?

Performance and scalability are not only different concepts – they're sometimes opposed in practice.

Applications that perform badly are also likely to have poor scalability. An application that thrashes a server's CPU handling the requirements of 5 users is hardly likely to satisfy 200.

However, applications can be highly performant under light load, yet exhibit poor scalability. Scalability is a challenge that can expose many flaws in an application, some very subtle. Potential problems include excessive synchronization blocking concurrent threads (a problem that might not be apparent under light load, when the application might appear very responsive), leaking of resources, excessive memory use, inefficient database access overloading database servers, and inability to run efficiently in a cluster. Failure to scale to meet demand will have grave consequences, such as spiraling response times and unreliability.

Both performance and scalability are likely to be important business requirements. For example, in the case of a web site, poor performance may drive users away on their first visit. Poor scalability will eventually prove fatal if the site *does* succeed in attracting and retaining users.

Adopting J2EE does not allow us, as application architects and developers, to assume that performance and scalability requirements have been taken care of for us by the gurus at BEA or IBM. If we do, we're in for a nasty surprise. While the J2EE infrastructure can help us to achieve scalable and performant applications if used correctly, it also adds overhead, which can severely impact the performance of naively implemented applications. To ensure that our applications are efficient and scalable, we must understand some of the overheads and implementation characteristics of J2EE application servers.

Setting Clear Goals for Performance and Scalability

It's important to be precise about what we want to achieve with performance and scalability.

Scalability is likely to be essential. If an application can't meet the demands of the user community – or growth in the user community – it will be judged a failure.

However, performance may involve more of a tradeoff. Performance may need to be balanced against other considerations such as extensibility, portability, and the likely cost of maintenance. We may even need to trade off within the performance domain. For example, some use cases may be critical to the application's acceptance, whereas others are less important. This may have implications for the application's design.

Clearly such tradeoffs, determining the way in which an application should attempt to meet its business requirements, should be made up front.

> It's important to have specific performance and scalability requirements for applications, rather than the vague idea that an application should "run fast and cope with many users". Non-functional requirements should contain targets for performance and throughput that are clear enough to enable testing to verify that they can be met at any point in the project lifecycle.

Design Versus Code Optimization

Major design issues in J2EE applications are likely to have a performance impact far outweighing any code-level optimizations. For example, making two remote calls in place of one in a time-critical operation in a distributed application because of poor design may impact on performance far more severely than can be addressed by any amount of code optimization.

It's important to minimize the need for code-level optimization, for the following reasons:

- ❑ Optimization is hard
- ❑ Most optimization is pointless
- ❑ Optimization causes many bugs
- ❑ Inappropriate optimization may reduce maintainability forever

Let's consider each of these points in turn, as they apply to J2EE development.

Few things in programming are harder than optimizing existing code. Unfortunately, this is why optimization is uniquely satisfying to any programmer's ego. The problem is that the resources devoted to such optimization may well be wasted.

Most programmers are familiar with the 80/20 rule (or variants), which states that 80% of execution time is spent in 20% of an application's codebase (this is also known as the Pareto Principle). The ratio varies between applications – 90/10 may be more common – but the principle is borne out empirically. This means that optimizing the wrong 80 or 90% of an application's codebase is a waste of time and resources.

It *is* possible to identify the bottlenecks in an application and address specific problems (it is best to use tools, rather than gut feeling, to identify bottlenecks; we'll discuss the necessary tools below). Optimizing code that isn't proving to be a problem will do more harm than good. In the J2EE context, optimization may be especially pointless, as bottlenecks may be in application server code, invoked too heavily because of poor application design. Remember that much of the code that executes when a J2EE application runs is part of the application server, not the application.

Optimization is a common cause of bugs. The legendary Donald Knuth, author of *The Art of Computer Programming*, has stated, "We should forget about small efficiencies, say about 97% of the time: premature optimization is the root of all evil." If optimization makes code harder to understand (and many optimizations do), it's a serious worry. Optimization causes bugs directly, when something that once worked slowly, works only some of the time, but faster. Its effect on quality is more insidious: code that is hard to understand is easy to break and will consume excessive resources *forever* in the course of application maintenance.

Any tradeoff between performance and maintainability is critical in J2EE applications, because enterprise applications tend to be mission critical and because of the ongoing investment they represent. There is no conflict between *designing* for performance and maintainability, but optimization may be more problematic. In the event of a conflict, it may be appropriate to sacrifice performance for maintainability. The fact that we choose to write software in Java, rather than C or assembly language, is proof of this. Since maintenance accounts for most of the cost of a software project, simply buying faster hardware may prove cheaper than squeezing the last ounce of performance out of an application, if this makes it harder to maintain. Of course, there are situations where performance outweighs other considerations.

> **Minimize the need for optimization by heading off problems with good design. Optimize reluctantly and choose what to optimize based on hard evidence such as profiler results.**

Some authorities on optimization recommend writing a simple program first, and then optimizing it. This approach will usually only work satisfactorily in J2EE *within components*, after component interfaces have been established. It is often a good approach to provide a quick implementation of an interface without concern as to performance, and to optimize it later if necessary. If we attempt to apply the "optimize later" approach to J2EE development as a whole, we're in for disappointment; where distributed J2EE applications are concerned, we're heading for disaster. The single area in which we can achieve significant performance improvement in J2EE applications after we've built a system is caching. However, as we shall see, caching can only be added with ease if an application's design is sound.

Tools for Testing Performance and Throughput

To test application performance and throughput, at whatever stage in the development process, we'll need to use appropriate tools and have a clear test plan. It's vital that tests are repeatable and that test results can be filed for future reference.

Usually we'll begin with load testing, which will also indicate performance in the form of response times for each concurrent test. However, we may also need to profile individual requests, so as to be able to optimize or eliminate slow operations.

Preparing to Benchmark

Benchmarking is a form of experimentation, so it's vital to adopt a good experimental method to ensure that benchmarks are as accurate as possible and are repeatable. For example, the application must be configured as it will be in production.

❑ The application should be running on production hardware or the closest available hardware to production hardware.

❑ Logging must be configured as in production. Verbose logging, such as at the Java 1.4 FINE level or Log4j DEBUG level, can seriously affect performance, especially if it results in the generation of log messages that are generated only if they will be displayed. Log output format can also be important. Log4j, for example, provides the ability to display the line number of each logging statement for which output is generated. This is great for debugging, but so expensive (due to the need to generate exceptions and parse their stack traces) as to seriously distort performance outcomes.

❑ Configure third-party products for optimum performance, as they will be deployed in production. For example:

  ❑ MVC web frameworks may have debug settings that will reduce performance. Ensure that they're disabled.

  ❑ The Velocity template engine can be configured to check templates for changes regularly. This is convenient in development but reduces performance.

  ❑ The application server should be configured to production settings.

  ❑ RDBMSs should be set to production settings.

❑ Disable any application features that will not be used in a particular production environment, but may affect performance.

❑ Use realistic data. Performance of a system with only the data for a few hundred test users loaded may be very different from that with the thousands or millions of records used in production.

It's also vital to ensure that there are no confounding factors that may affect the running of the tests:

❑ When running load testing or profiling software on the same server as the J2EE application, check that it's not distorting performance figures by hogging CPU time. If possible, load test a web interface from one or more separate machines.

❑ Ensure that no other processes on the machine(s) running the application server are likely to reduce resources available to the application. Even innocent monitoring tools such as top can consume surprising amounts of CPU time; virus scans and the like can be disastrous in long test runs.

❑ Ensure that there's enough RAM available on the application server and machine running the load testing software.

> Remember that benchmarking isn't a precise science. Strive to eliminate confounding factors, but remember not to read too much into a particular number. In my experience, it's common to see variations of 20-30% between successive test runs on J2EE applications, especially where load testing is involved, because of the number of variables, which will also apply in production.

Web Test Tools

One of the easiest ways is to establish whether a J2EE web application performs satisfactorily and delivers sufficient throughput under load is to load-test its web interface. Since the web interface will be the user's experience of the application, non-functional requirements should provide a clear definition of the performance and concurrency required.

Microsoft Web Application Stress Tool

There are many tools for testing the performance of web applications. My preferred tool is Microsoft's free **Web Application Stress (WAS) Tool** (http://webtool.rte.microsoft.com/).

For a platform-neutral, Java-based alternative, consider Apache JMeter (available at http://jakarta.apache.org/jmeter/index.html) or the Grinder (discussed below). However, these tools are less intuitive and harder to set up. Since it's generally best to run load testing software on a separate machine to the application server, there is usually no problem in finding a Windows machine to run the Microsoft tool.

Configuring Microsoft's WAS is very easy. It simply involves creating one or more **scripts**. Scripts can also be "recorded" using Internet Explorer. Scripts consist of one or more definitions of application URLs to be load-tested, including GET or POST data if necessary. WAS can use a range or set of parameter values. The following screenshot illustrates configuring WAS to request the "Display Show" page in the sample application. Remember to change the port from the default of 80 if necessary for each URL. In this example, it is the JBoss/Jetty default of 8080:

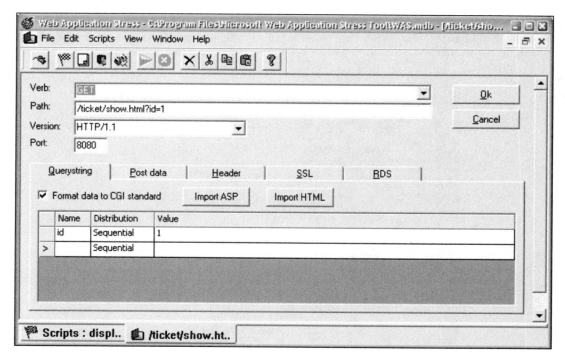

617

Each script has global settings for the number of concurrent threads to use, the delays between requests issued by each thread, and options such as whether to follow redirects and whether to simulate user access via a slow modem link. It's also possible to configure cookie and session behavior. Each script is configured via the following screen:

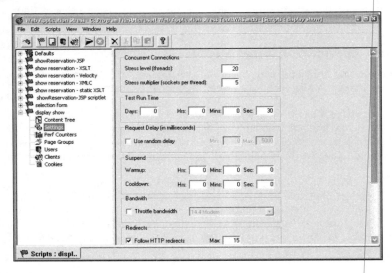

Once a script has been run, reports can be viewed via the Reports option on the View menu. Reports are stored in a database so that they can be viewed at any time. Reports include the number of requests per second, the amount of data transmitted and received, and the average wait to receive the first and last byte of the response:

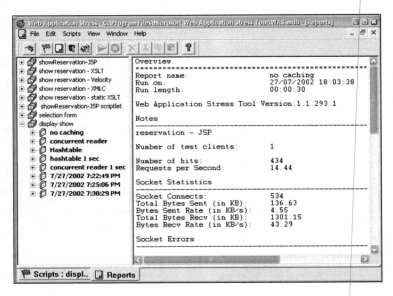

Using the Web Application Stress Tool or any comparable product, we can quickly establish the performance and throughput of a whole web application, indicating where further, more detailed analysis may be required and whether performance tuning is required at all.

Non-Web Testing Tools

Sometimes testing through the web interface is all that's required. Performance and load testing isn't like unit testing; there's no need to have performance tests for every class. If we can easily set up a performance test of an entire system and are satisfied with the results, there's no need to spend further time writing performance or scalability tests.

However, not all J2EE applications have a web interface (and even in web applications, we may need a more detailed breakdown of the architectural layers where an application spends most of its time). This means that we need the ability to load-test and performance-test individual Java classes, which in turn may test application resources such as databases.

There are many open source tools available for such testing, such as the Grinder (http://sourceforge.net/projects/grinder), an extensible load tester first developed for a Wrox book on WebLogic, and Apache JMeter.

Personally I find most of these tools unnecessarily complex. For example, it's not easy to write test cases for the Grinder, which also requires multicast to be enabled to support communication between load-test processes and its console. Unlike JUnit, there is a learning curve involved.

I use the following simple framework, which I originally developed for a client a couple of years ago and which I've found to meet nearly all requirements with a minimum of effort in writing load tests. The code is included with the sample application download, under the /framework/test directory. Unlike JMeter or the Grinder, it doesn't provide a GUI console. I did write one for an early version of the tool, but found it was less useful than file reports, especially as the tests were often run on a server without a display.

Like most load-testing tools, the test framework in the com.interface21.load package, described below, is based on the following concepts:

- ❑ It enables a number of **test threads** to be run in parallel as part of a **test suite**. In this framework, test threads will implement the com.interface21.load.Test interface, while the test suite is usually a generic framework class.

- ❑ Each test thread executes a number of **passes**, independent of the activity of other threads.

- ❑ Each thread can use a random delay of up to a maximum number of milliseconds between test passes. This is essential to simulate the unpredictable user activity likely to be experienced at run time.

- ❑ Each thread implements a simple interface that requires it to execute an application-specific test for each pass (the random delay between test passes is handled by the framework test suite).

- ❑ All threads use a single test **fixture** exposing the application object(s) to test (this is analogous to a JUnit fixture).

Periodic reports are made to the console and a report can be written to file after the completion of a test run.

The following UML class diagram illustrates the framework classes involved, and how an application-specific test thread class (circled) can extend the `AbstractTest` convenience class. The framework supplies a test suite implementation, which provides a standard way to coordinate all the application-specific tests:

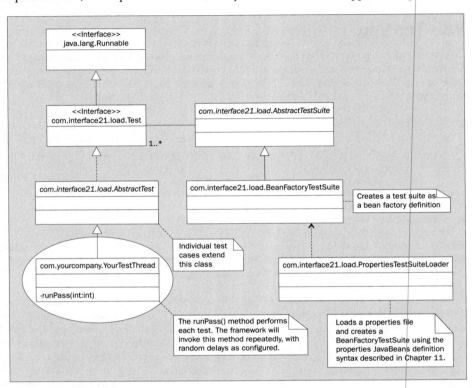

The only code required to implement a load test is an extension of the framework `AbstractTest` class, as shown below. This involves implementing just two methods, as the `AbstractTest` class provides a `final` implementation of the `java.lang.Runnable` interface:

```java
import com.interface21.load.AbstractTest;

public class MyTestThread extends AbstractTest {

        private MyFixture fixture;
```

The framework calls the following method on subclasses of `AbstractTest` to make the shared test fixture – the application object to test – available to each thread. Tests that don't require a fixture don't need to override this method:

```java
        public void setFixture(Object fixture) {
                this.fixture = (MyFixture) fixture;
        }
```

The following abstract method must be implemented to run each test. The index of the test pass is passed as an argument in case it is necessary:

```
protected void runPass(int i) throws Exception {
        // do something with fixture
    }
}
```

Typically the `runPass()` method will be implemented to select random test data made available by the fixture and use it to invoke one or more methods on the class being load tested. As with JUnit test cases, we need only catch exceptions resulting from normal execution scenarios: uncaught exceptions will be logged as errors by the test suite and included in the final report (the test thread will continue to run further tests). Exceptions can also be thrown to indicate failures if assertions are not satisfied.

This tool uses the bean-based approach to configuration described in Chapter 11 and used consistently in the application framework discussed in this book. Each test uses its own properties file, which enables easy parameterization. This file is read by the `PropertiesTestSuiteLoader` class, which takes the filename as an argument and creates and initializes a test suite object of type `BeanFactoryTestSuite` from the bean definitions contained in the properties file.

The following definitions configure the test suite, including its reporting format, how often it reports to the console during test runs, and where it writes its report files. If the `reportFile` bean property isn't set, there's no file output:

```
suite.class=com.interface21.load.BeanFactoryTestSuite
suite.name=Availability check
suite.reportIntervalSeconds=10
suite.longReports=false
suite.doubleFormat=###.#
suite.reportFile=c:\\reports\\results1.txt
```

The following keys control how many threads are run, how many passes or test cases each thread runs, and how long (in milliseconds) is the maximum delay between test cases in each test thread:

```
suite.threads=50
suite.passes=40
suite.maxPause=23
```

The following properties show how an application-specific test fixture can be made available to the test suite, and configured via its JavaBean properties. The test suite will invoke the `setFixture()` method on each test thread to enable all test thread instances to share this fixture:

```
suite.fixture(ref)=fixture
fixture.class=com.interface21.load.AvailabilityFixture
fixture.timeout=10
fixture.minDelay=60
fixture.maxDelay=120
```

Finally, we must include bean definitions for one or more test threads. Each of these will be independent at run time. Hence this bean definition must not be a singleton, so we override the bean factory's default behavior, in the highlighted line:

```
availabilityTest.class=com.interface21.load.AvailabilityCheckTest
availabilityTest.(singleton)=false
```

The default behavior is for each thread to take its number of passes and maximum pause value from that of the test suite, although this can be overridden for each test thread. It's also possible to run several different test threads concurrently, each with a different weighting.

The test suite can be run using an Ant target like this:

```
<target name="load" >
        <java
                classname="com.interface21.load.PropertiesTestSuiteLoader"
                fork="yes"
                dir="src">
                <classpath location="classpath"/>

                <arg file="path/mytest.properties"/>
        </java>
</target>
```

The highlighted line should be changed as necessary to ensure that both the `com.interface21.load` package and the application-specific test fixture and test threads are available on the classpath.

Reports will show the number of test runs completed, the number of errors, the number of hits per second achieved by each test thread and overall, and the average response time:

```
AvailabilityCheckTest-0    40/40    errs=0  125hps avg=8ms
AvailabilityCheckTest-1    40/40    errs=0  95hps   avg=10ms
AvailabilityCheckTest-2    40/40    errs=0  90.7hps avg=11ms
AvailabilityCheckTest-3    40/40    errs=0  99.8hps avg=10ms
AvailabilityCheckTest-4    40/40    errs=0  110hps  avg=9ms
*********** Total hits=200
*********** HPS=521.3
*********** Average response=9
```

The most important setting is the number of test threads. By increasing this, we can establish at what point throughput begins to deteriorate, which is usually the point of the exercise. Modern JVMs can cope with very high numbers of concurrent threads; I've successfully tested with several hundred concurrent threads. However, it's important to remember that if we run too many concurrent test threads, the work of switching execution between the test threads may become great enough to distort the results. It's also possible to use this tool to establish how the application copes with long periods of prolonged load, by specifying a very high number of passes to be executed by each thread.

This tool can be used for web testing as well, by providing an `AbstractTest` implementation that requests web resources. However, the Web Application Stress Tool is easier to use and provides all the flexibility required in most cases.

Locating Performance or Scalability Problems

> Only if we are sure that there *is* a performance problem – as the result of benchmarking a vertical slice or a whole application – should we devote resources to tracking down problem areas.

It's important that the process of finding problems is empirical. While experience and knowledge help to develop strong instincts, there is no substitute for hard evidence.

Let's look at two basic techniques we can use to establish where in a J2EE stack a known performance or scalability problem lies:

- ❑ Try to test the performance of each tier of the architecture in isolation, or without going through higher architectural tiers.

- ❑ Test the entire application using a profiling tool.

Testing in Layers

Good design should enable us to test each architectural tier of a J2EE application independently. Good design will ensure that the application is divided into distinct tiers with distinct responsibilities. Such layered testing will be impossible, for example, if JSP pages perform database access.

This enables us to perform tests such as the following (beginning at the lowest level of a typical application):

- ❑ Test RDBMS queries and updates using database tools. This should involve testing the behavior of concurrent activity in separate transactions.

- ❑ Test JDBC operations by testing Data-Access Objects with a test data source, outside a J2EE application server.

- ❑ Test business object performance. Business objects may be tested in isolation (using mock objects in place of components used for connecting to resources such as databases) and with the real application backend.

- ❑ Test web-tier performance using dummy business objects that respond instantly with test data, enabling us to see web-tier performance in isolation.

Where EJBs are involved, such testing will be harder; we may need to run tests within the application server.

Note that we will normally have test cases for most of these layers as the result of sound development practice. Thus, writing performance and load tests should not require much additional infrastructure, beyond one of the tools discussed above. It's good practice to write and run performance and load tests along with functional tests during application development, to identify potential problems before they can pose serious risk.

This layered approach is particularly useful where load testing is involved, as it makes it very easy to test how any architectural layer performs under load.

Profiling Tools

We can also use tools, rather than our own effort, to establish where the application spends its time. Although this is not a substitute for "layered testing" – especially where throughput is concerned – it can provide hard evidence to replace hunches regarding bottlenecks, potentially saving wasted effort. Profiling can also clarify an application's run-time behavior, through revealing call stacks.

However, there are some problems with profiling that we must be aware of:

- ❏ Profiling severely reduces application performance and sometimes stability. Thus, we may not be able to perform load testing against an application running under a profiler and may be limited to looking at the performance of individual requests. Thus, profiling may not be much help in tracking down scalability problems such as locking (although other specialized tools may help in this area).

- ❏ Profiling may require JVM settings to be changed from those used in production, which can sometimes produce anomalous results. For example, we may need to disable the optimized HotSpot JVM.

JVM Profiling Options

Most JVMs offer a profiling option. For example, starting a Sun Java 1.3 JVM with the following arguments will cause it to dump profile output when it quits:

```
-Xrunhprof:cpu=samples,thread=y
```

The most useful information is contained in the final section of the generated `java.hprof.txt` file, which shows methods ordered by the time they took for execution. It also shows the number of invocations of each method:

rank	self	accum	count	trace	method
1	26.67%	26.67%	12	57	java.net.SocketInputStream.socketRead
2	11.11%	37.78%	5	107	java.net.SocketInputStream.socketRead
3	4.44%	42.22%	2	83	oracle.jdbc.driver.OracleConnection.privateCreateStatement
4	4.44%	46.67%	2	32	java.io.Win32FileSystem.getBooleanAttributes
5	2.22%	48.89%	1	114	java.net.PlainSocketImpl.socketClose
6	2.22%	51.11%	1	130	java.lang.System.currentTimeMillis
7	2.22%	53.33%	1	43	java.net.InetAddressImpl.getLocalHostName
8	2.22%	55.56%	1	34	oracle.jdbc.ttc7.TTC7Protocol.connect
9	2.22%	57.78%	1	17	com.interface21.beans.BeanWrapperImpl.setPropertyValues
10	2.22%	60.00%	1	122	java.lang.ClassLoader.findBootstrapClass
11	2.22%	62.22%	1	87	java.lang.Class.forName0
12	2.22%	64.44%	1	79	oracle.security.o3logon.O3LoginClientHelper.<init>
13	2.22%	66.67%	1	47	java.lang.Throwable.fillInStackTrace
14	2.22%	68.89%	1	77	oracle.jdbc.ttc7.TTC7Protocol.logon

Several free tools can be used to view profiler output files and extract more information about call stacks.

I've successfully used JVM profiling in the past, but it's a very basic solution. It slows applications to a crawl and can cause frequent crashes. For example, JDK 1.3.1_02 seems to have problems starting JBoss 3.0.0 with profiling enabled on Windows, and I've previously had severe problems getting JDK 1.2 profiling working on Solaris.

If you have a real need for profiling, you need something more sophisticated. I don't know of any really satisfactory free or open source products; given the cost of performance problems to projects, a small investment in a commercial product is well worthwhile.

The JProbe Profiler

Sitraka's JProbe (http://www.sitraka.com/software/jprobe/) is the best-known commercial profiler, and has led the market for several years. JProbe isn't the only choice, but it's very good and not overpriced. It's possible to download a free evaluation copy that will work for 10 days – long enough to establish whether it's likely to be a wise investment for a project. The JProbe suite contains several products. I'll only talk about the profiler here.

> *In this section we'll focus on JProbe 4.0, but most of the concepts discussed will apply to any profiler.*

Using JProbe requires first configuring JProbe to run the application with the necessary instrumentation. For server-side applications, the "application" from JProbe's perspective is the J2EE application server, running user applications. While the application is running, JProbe can take "performance snapshots" for immediate or offline analysis.

Integrating JProbe with an Application Server

The JProbe 4.0 distribution comes with settings to integrate it with most commercial application servers. However, I had to manually integrate it with JBoss 3.0, which took a few minutes.

The JProbe installation process prompts to integrate JProbe with a J2EE server via the "JProbe Application Server Integration" dialog. Any of the supported servers can be selected in the dropdown on the left. To integrate with a new server, such as JBoss 3.0, follow the following steps:

1. Select _Other Server from the dropdown.

2. Press the Create button.

3. Customize the settings in the right-hand pane, including setting Advanced Options. This includes setting the IntegrationID to a meaningful name (such as JBoss).

The most important settings in the right-hand pane are:

❑ Server directory. This is normally the home directory of the server.

❑ The server class. The Java class that contains the server's main() method.

❑ The server classpath. JBoss uses a minimal "bootstrap" classpath and loads further binaries from within its directory structure, so this is very simple to configure for JBoss.

❑ The JVM executable to use.

❑ The JVM arguments. It took some experimentation here to arrive at the "Java options" shown below, which were based on the WebLogic integration parameters supplied with JProbe. Without setting the heap size, startup was too slow and JBoss often hung on startup.

The appropriate value for most of these settings can be found in the default JBoss startup script: $JBOSS_HOME/bin/run.sh or $JBOSS_HOME/bin/run.bat, depending on your operating system. The following screenshot displays the JProbe integration settings I used for JBoss 3.0:

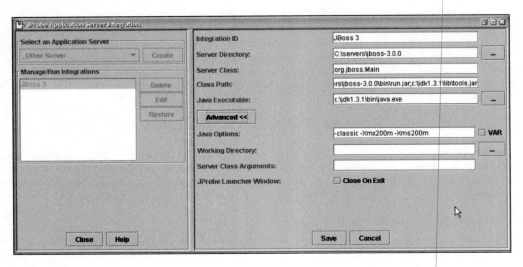

One JProbe installation can use integration definitions for multiple J2EE servers.

Setting Filters

It's also essential to configure settings for each JProbe analysis "session". This determines which application server integration definition will be used, what the profiler will look for, and how the profile data will be collected and viewed. Settings can be defined via the Open Settings option on the main JProbe window. Multiple settings can be defined, allowing choice of the most appropriate definition for a particular profile run.

The most important setting is the packages to filter, shown in the central pane of the dialog opposite. We don't normally want performance information for application server or standard Java or J2EE packages (although this might be useful if we suspected that a performance problem lay outside our own code). Thus we normally filter to restrict profile information to our own classes. Activate filtering by specifying package prefixes and selecting a Detail Level for each from the right column. Note that information will be collected for all packages whose names begin with the given string: for example, specifying com.wrox as the screenshot will result in the collection of profile data for all packages in our sample application.

I found it useful to uncheck Record Performance from Program Start. We don't usually want to slow down application server startup by profiling it. The following screenshot shows the session definition I used for the profile runs in this chapter:

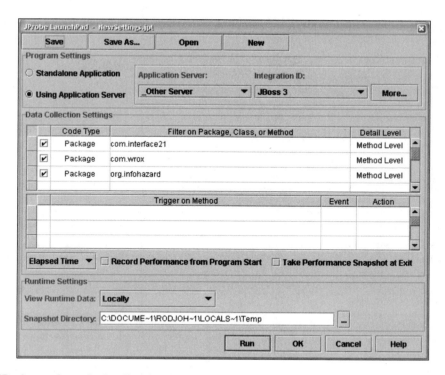

Running JProbe on Sample Application Use Cases

Now we're ready to start a profile run. First we need to start JBoss running under JProbe. We do this from the main JProbe Profiler window, through the **Program** menu, as shown below:

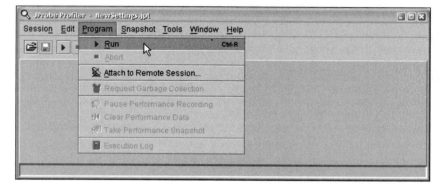

Assuming that our application has been deployed on JBoss, when JBoss starts up, it will start as usual. Note that JBoss will take much longer than usual to start up and to deploy our application, so a little patience (or a very fast machine) is required. Monitor the JBoss and application-generated log files and CPU usage to ascertain when the application has started up. It's a good time to make or buy a coffee.

Now it's time to start recording performance data. We do this by selecting **Resume Performance Recording** from the **Program** menu as shown below:

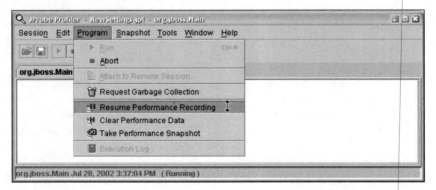

Now we execute the application use case we wish to profile. Again, this will take much longer than usual. When the use case is complete, we select **Take Performance Snapshot** from the same menu. A new snapshot icon will appear in the main JProbe window: the default name is snapshot_1, but we can rename it on saving it. Saving it makes it available for use in the future, independent of whether we're running the profiler to collect new data.

We can right-click on any snapshot and select **Open in Call Graph**. We will see a window like the following, which displays methods ordered in descending order by cumulative execution time (the time they and their subtrees took to execute):

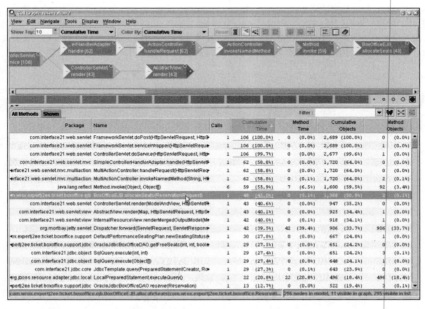

The following screenshot shows the same data, ordered in descending order by method time (the time taken within each method):

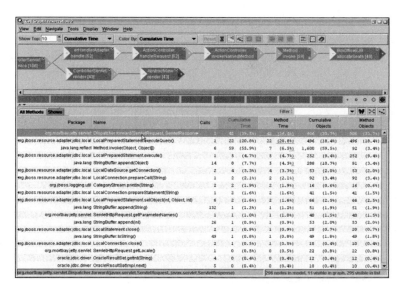

The "call graph" in the upper pane isn't very useful in this example, but can be useful for providing a color-coded display of bottlenecks and allowing easy navigation of data.

For each method, we can quickly get a display of what methods invoke it, what methods it invokes, and how its execution time breaks down.

For example, by double-clicking on BoxOfficeEJB.allocateSeats, which JProbe indicates to have cost 45% of our execution time, we see the following information (the allocateSeats() method is always invoked reflectively by Method.invoke() because JBoss uses dynamic proxies instead of generated classes to implement EJB component interfaces):

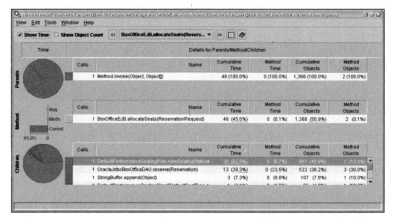

In this case, this is very interesting. It shows that the stored procedure invoked by the OracleJdbcBoxOfficeDAO.reserve() method is faster than the select for update to check for available seats (possibly because the select is against a view based on an outer join). We discussed the data access code running here in Chapter 9.

Select Clear Performance Data from the Program menu before following the same procedure to profile another use case.

Snapshots can be saved for future use. This is very handy to separate the collection of data from analysis (two very different tasks), and to enable comparison of progress in addressing a problem through design and code changes.

We'll look at using JProbe while addressing a real performance issue a little later.

> A good profiling tool such as JProbe can be invaluable, enabling us to base designs on evidence, rather than gut feeling. Sophisticated profiling tools can also quickly reveal useful information about an application's runtime call stack.
>
> Even if there's no great performance problem, it's a good idea to run a single profile run on each use case, to ensure that there's no wasteful activity – for example, in unnecessary string manipulation methods, which will be obvious from a profile run.
>
> It's important, however, to avoid obsession with profiling. It's tempting to use repeated profiler runs to achieve smaller and smaller performance savings. This is a waste of time, once any major issues have been addressed.

Addressing Performance or Scalability Problems

Once we know where our performance problems are, we can look at addressing them. The earlier they are brought to light, the better our chance of eliminating them without the need for major design changes or reworking existing code.

There are many techniques for addressing performance or scalability problems. In this section we'll consider some of the most useful.

Server Choice and Server Configuration

Before looking at design modifications or code changes, we should ensure that the cause of the problem isn't external to the application.

Choice of application server and server configuration will have a vital influence on application performance.

It's vital to *tune* the application server to meet the needs of the applications it runs. Unless your code is particularly bad, this will usually produce a better return than optimizing code, at no cost in maintainability.

The performance tuning parameters available differ between application servers, but they typically include the following, some of which we've discussed in previous chapters:

❑ Thread pool size. This will affect both the web container and EJB container. Too many threads will result in the JVM running into operating system limitations on how many threads can efficiently run concurrently; too few threads will result in unnecessary throttling of throughput.

❑ Database connection pool size.

❑ JSP recompilation support. Often, this can be disabled in production for a slight performance gain.

- ❑ State replication mechanism (if any) for HTTP sessions and stateful session EJBs.

- ❑ Pool size for all EJB types.

- ❑ Locking and caching policy for entity beans (relevant only if using entity beans).

- ❑ Locking and caching policy for any other O/R mapping layer, such as a JDO implementation.

- ❑ JMS options such as whether messages are saved to a persistent backing store.

- ❑ The transaction manager used. For example, it may be faster to disable two-phase commit support in the common case where we only use a single transactional resource.

Tuning JVM options and operating system configuration is another productive area. Usually the tuning should be that appropriate to the application server, rather than any particular application running on it, so the best place to look for such information is in documentation supplied with your application server. Important JVM options include initial and maximum heap size and garbage-collection parameters. See http://java.sun.com/docs/hotspot/gc/ for detailed information on Sun 1.3 JVMs.

It may also be possible to disable unused application server services, to make more memory available to applications and eliminate unnecessary background thread activity.

Application server vendors tend to produce good guidelines on performance tuning and J2EE performance in general. Some good resources are:

- ❑ WebLogic
  http://edocs.bea.com/wls/docs70/perform/

- ❑ IBM WebSphere
  http://www-4.ibm.com/software/webservers/appserv/ws_bestpractices.pdf

- ❑ SunONE/iPlanet
  http://developer.iplanet.com/viewsource/char_tuningias/index.jsp

Database configuration is equally important, and requires specialist skills.

Dispensing with Redundant Container Services

While J2EE application servers provide many valuable services, most of these services are not free. Using them unnecessarily may harm performance. Sometimes by avoiding or eliminating the use of unnecessary container services we can improve performance. For example, we can:

- ❑ Avoid unnecessary use of EJB. All EJB invocations – even local invocations – carry an overhead of container interception. Thus the use of EJB where it doesn't deliver real value can reduce performance.

- ❑ Avoid unnecessary use of JMS. Generally, JMS should be used when business requirements dictate the use of an asynchronous model. Use of JMS in an attempt to improve performance can often backfire.

- ❑ Avoid use of entity EJBs where they don't add value, and where JDBC access is a simpler, faster alternative.

- ❑ Avoid duplication in container services. For example, if we're relying on the web container to manage `HttpSession` objects, we may not need also to rely on the EJB container to manage stateful session beans; it will often prove more scalable to pass session state to stateful session beans as necessary, or avoid the use of EJB.

631

By far the most important performance gain is likely to be in avoiding unnecessary remote invocation; we discuss this further below.

A simpler design is often a more performant design, and often leads to no loss in scalability.

Caching

One of the most important techniques to improve performance in J2EE applications is **caching**: storing data that is expensive to retrieve to enable it to be returned quickly to clients, without further retrieval from the original source.

Caching can be done at many points in a J2EE architecture, but is most beneficial when it results in one architectural tier being able to avoid some calls to the tier beneath it.

Caching can produce enormous performance gains in distributed applications, by eliminating remote calls. In all applications it can avoid calls from the application server to the database, which will probably involve network round trips as well as the overhead of JDBC. A successful caching strategy will boost the performance even of those parts of the application that don't directly benefit from cached data. Server response time will be better in general because of the reduced workload, and network bandwidth will be freed. The database will have less work to do, meaning that it responds faster and each database instance may be able to support a larger cluster of J2EE servers.

However, caching poses serious design challenges, whether it is implemented by J2EE server vendor, application developer, or a third party, so it should not be used without justification in the form of test results and other solid evidence.

If we implement a cache in application code, it means that we may have to write the kind of complex code, such as thread management, that J2EE promised to deliver us from. The fact that J2EE applications may be required to run in a clustered environment may add significant complexity, even if we use a third-party caching solution.

When to Cache

Before we can begin to cache data, there are several questions we should ask. Most relate to the central issues of staleness, contention, and clustering:

- ❑ How slow is it to get the data without caching it? Will introducing a cache improve the performance of the application enough to justify the additional complexity? Caching to avoid network round trips is most likely to be worthwhile. However, as caching usually adds complexity, we shouldn't implement caching unless it's necessary.

- ❑ Do we know the usage and volatility of the data set we want to cache? If it's read-only, caching is an obvious optimization. As we move along the continuum towards write-only, caching becomes less and less attractive. Concurrency issues rise and the benefit of avoiding reads diminishes.

- ❑ Can we tolerate stale data? If so, how stale? In some cases this might be several minutes, making the return on caching much greater. In other cases, data must always be up-to-date, and no caching is acceptable. Business requirements should indicate what degree of staleness is permissible.

- ❑ What is the consequence of the cache getting it wrong? If a user's credit card might be debited by an incorrect amount (for example, if cached price information was out of date), an error is obviously unacceptable. If, on the other hand, the occasional user on a media site sees a news headline that is 30 seconds out of date, this may be a perfectly acceptable price to pay for a dramatic boost in performance.

❑ Can we cope with the increased implementation complexity required to support caching? This will be mitigated if we use a good, generic cache implementation, but we must be aware that read-write caching introduces significant threading issues.

❑ Is the volume of data we need to cache manageable? Clearly, if the data set we need to cache contains millions of entities, and we can't predict which ones users will want, a cache will just waste memory. Databases are very good at plucking small numbers of records from a large range, and our cache isn't likely to do a better job.

❑ Will our cache work in a cluster? This usually isn't an issue for reference data: it's not a problem if each server has its own copy of read-only data, but maintaining integrity of cached read-write data across a cluster is hard. If replication between caches looks necessary, it's pretty obvious that we shouldn't be implementing such infrastructure as part of our application, but looking for support in our application server or a third-party product.

❑ Can the cache reasonably satisfy the kind of queries clients will make against the data? Otherwise we might find ourselves trying to reinvent a database. In some situations, the need for querying might be satisfied more easily by an XML document than cached Java objects.

❑ Are we sure that our application server cannot meet our caching requirements? For example, if we know that it offers an efficient entity bean cache, caching data on the client may be unnecessary. One decisive issue here will be how far (in terms of network distance) the client is from the EJB tier.

The Pareto Principle (the 80/20 rule) is applicable to caching. Most of the performance gain can often be achieved with a small proportion of the effort involved in tackling the more difficult caching issues.

Data caching can radically improve the performance of J2EE applications. However, caching can add much complexity and is a common cause of bugs. The difficulty of implementing different caching solutions varies greatly. Jump at any quick wins, such as caching read-only data. This adds minimal complexity, and can produce a good performance improvement. Think much more carefully about any alternatives when caching is a harder problem – for example, when it concerns read-write data.

Don't rush to implement caching with the assumption that it will be required; base caching policy on performance analysis.

A good application design, with a clean relationship between architectural tiers, will usually facilitate adding any caching required. In particular, interface-based design facilitates caching; we can easily replace any interface with a caching implementation, if business requirements are satisfied. We'll look at an example of a simple cache shortly.

Where to Cache

As using J2EE naturally produces a layered architecture, there are multiple locations where caching may occur. Some of these types of caching are implemented by the J2EE server or underlying database, and are accessible to the developer via configuration, not code. Other forms of caching must be implemented by developers, and can absorb a large part of total development effort.

Let's look at choices for cache locations, beginning from the backend:

Location of cache	Implemented by	Likely performance improvement	Complexity of implementation	Notes
Database.	RDBMS vendor	Significant. However, database cached in the RDBMS is still a long way from a user of the application, especially in a distributed application.	No J2EE work required. Some database configuration may be required. Index creation is simple. We may also be able to use more efficient table types, depending on our target database.	RDBMS caching is often forgotten by J2EE developers. Most RDBMSs cache execution paths for common statements and may cache query results. RDBMS indexes amount to caching ahead of time, and can produce dramatic performance improvements. We looked at the use of PreparedStatements in application code in Chapter 9: this can ensure that the RDBMS can perform effective caching. Whatever the caching our J2EE server offers, and whatever caching we implement, the database cache should still be a help.
Entity bean cache.	EJB container vendor or vendor of CMP implementation	Varies. Can be very significant if it greatly reduces the number of calls to the underlying database. However, this presumes a highly efficient entity bean implementation: in a clustered environment, the cache will need to be distributed, raising problems of transactional integrity and replication. An entity bean cache is still a long way from the client: network round trips may be necessary to get to the EJB tier in the first place. Thus I feel that the value of entity-bean-caching is often overrated in distributed applications.	Nil, or very little.	The J2EE specification does not guarantee caching, meaning that an architecture that performs satisfactorily only with efficient entity bean caching is not portable. However, a third-party persistence manager might be used with multiple application servers.

Location of cache	Implemented by	Likely performance improvement	Complexity of implementation	Notes
Data cache in data access tier – that is, web container or EJB container – other than entity bean cache. For example, a JDO implementation or third-party O/R mapping solution such as TopLink.	Third-party vendor	Benefits similar to an entity bean cache. Also similar problems: will break in a clustered environment unless it is distributed, meaning that only high-end products will be suitable for scalable deployments.	Little.	Introduces dependence on another product besides the EJB container. However, we may have opted for a third-party O/R mapping tool for other reasons.
Session EJBs.	Developer	Depends on how expensive the retrieval of cached data was. Doesn't eliminate network round trips to the EJB container in distributed applications.	Little-to-Moderate.	It's difficult to use the Singleton design pattern in the EJB tier, so cached data may be duplicated in stateless session bean instances, with the caches potentially in different states. However, cached data will benefit all users of a stateless session bean . Stateful session bean s can only cache data on behalf of a single user. The `ejbCreate()` method is the natural place to retrieve data. However, it is easy to use lazy loading, retrieving resources only when first required in a business method, because EJBs can be implemented as though they are single threaded. Thus there is no need to perform synchronization, or worry about race conditions. The `ejbRemove()` method should be used for freeing resources that can't simply be left to be garbage collected. We discussed data caching in session beans in Chapter 10.

Table continued on following page

Location of cache	Implemented by	Likely performance improvement	Complexity of implementation	Notes
Business objects running in the web container.	Developer or third-party solution	Very significant. Eliminates network round trips to the EJB container in distributed applications. Even when EJBs are collocated in the same VM, an invocation on an EJB will be slower than an invocation of a local method.	Moderate-to-high.	Quick wins, such as caching reference data, will produce big returns. However, careful thought is advisable before trying to implement more problematic caching solutions. The J2EE infrastructure cannot help address concurrency issues. However, we may be able to use third-party solutions, two of which are discussed below.
Web tier.	Developer or third-party solution	Very significant.	Moderate-to-high.	There are a host of alternatives here, such as caching custom tags, caching servlets, and caching filters. Caching filters are particularly attractive, as they enable cache settings to be managed declaratively in the web.xml deployment descriptor.
Web tier.	J2EE server vendor	Very significant.	Little-to-moderate.	Similar to the above, but provided by the application server vendor. Web tier caching is provided by WebSphere and iPlanet/SunONE among other servers.
Cache *in front of* the J2EE application server, achieved by setting HTTP cache control headers or "edge side" caching.	Developer, possibly relying on a third-party caching product	Very significant.	Little.	We'll discuss "front" caching for web solutions under *Web Tier Performance Issues* below.

Generally, the closer to the client we can cache, the bigger the performance improvement, especially in distributed applications. The flip side is that the closer to the client we cache, the narrower the range of scenarios that benefit from the cache. For example, if we cache the whole of an application's dynamically generated pages, response time on these pages will be extremely fast (of course, this particular optimization only works for pages that don't contain user-specific information). However, this is a "dumb" form of caching – the cache may have an obvious key for the data (probably the requested URL), but it can't understand the data it is storing, because it is mixed with presentation markup. Such a cache would be of no use to a Swing client, even if the data in the varying fragments of the cached pages were relevant to a Swing client.

> **J2EE standard infrastructure is really geared only to support the caching of data in entity EJBs. This option isn't available unless we choose to use entity EJBs (and there are many reasons why we might not). It's also of limited value in distributed applications, as they face as much of a problem in moving data from EJB container to remote client as in moving data from database to EJB container.**

Thus we often need to implement our own caching solution, or resort to another third-party caching solution. I recommend the following guidelines for caching:

❑ Avoid caching unless it involves reference data (in which case it's simple to implement) or unless performance clearly requires it. In general, distributed applications are much more likely to need to implement data caching than collocated applications.

❑ As read/write caches involve complex concurrency issues, use third-party libraries (discussed below) to conceal the complexity of the necessary synchronization. Use the simplest approach to ensuring integrity under concurrent access that delivers satisfactory performance.

❑ Consider the implications of multiple caches working together. Would it result in users seeing data that is staler than any one of the caches might tolerate? Or does one cache eliminate the need for another?

Third-party Caching Products for Use in J2EE Applications

Let's look at some third-party commercial caching products that can be used in J2EE applications. The main reasons we might spend money on a commercial solution are to achieve reliable replicated caching functionality, and avoid the need to implement and maintain complex caching functionality in-house.

Coherence, from Tangosol (http://www.tangosol.com/products-clustering.jsp) is a replicated caching solution, which claims even to support clusters including geographically dispersed servers. Coherence integrates with most leading application servers, including JBoss. Coherence caches are basically alternatives to standard Java map implementations, such as `java.util.HashMap`, so using them merely requires Coherence-specific implementations of Java core interfaces.

SpiritCache, from SpiritSoft (http://www.spiritsoft.net/products/jms_jcache/overview.html) is also a replicated caching solution, and claims to provide a "universal caching framework for the Java platform". The SpiritCache API is based on the proposed JCache standard API (JSR-107: http://jcp.org/jsr/detail/107.jsp). JCache, proposed by Oracle, defines a standard API for caching and retrieving objects, including an event-based system allowing application code to register for notification of cache events.

> Commercial caching products are likely to prove a very good investment for applications with sophisticated caching requirements, such as the need for caching across a cluster of servers. Developing and maintaining complex caching solutions in-house can prove very expensive. However, even if we use third-party products, running a clustered cache will significantly complicate application deployment, as the caching product – in addition to the J2EE application server – will need to be configured appropriately for our clustered environment.

Code Optimization

Since design largely determines performance, unless application code is particularly badly written, code optimization is seldom worth the effort in J2EE applications unless it is targeted at known problem areas. However, all professional developers should be familiar with performance issues at code level to avoid making basic errors. For discussion of Java performance in general, I recommend *Java Performance Tuning* by Jack Shirazi from O'Reilly (ISBN: 0-596-00015-4) and *Java 2 Performance and Idiom Guide* from Prentice Hall, (ISBN: 0-13-014260-3). There are also many good online resources on performance tuning. Shirazi maintains a performance tuning web site (http://www.javaperformancetuning.com/) that contains an exhaustive directory of code tuning tips from many sources.

> Avoid code optimizations that reduce maintainability unless there is an overriding performance imperative. Such "optimizations" are not just a one-off effort, but are likely to prove an ongoing cost and cause of bugs.

The higher-level the coding issue, the bigger the potential performance gain by code optimization. Thus there often is potential to achieve good results by techniques such as reordering the steps of an algorithm, so that expensive tasks are executed only if absolutely essential. As with design, an ounce of prevention is worth a pound of cure. While obsession with performance is counter-productive, good programmers don't write grossly inefficient code that will later need optimization. Sometimes, however, it does make sense to try a simple algorithm first, and change the implementation to use a faster but more complex algorithm only if it proves necessary.

Really low-level techniques such as loop unrolling are unlikely to bring any benefit to J2EE systems. Any optimization should be targeted, and based on the results of profiling. When looking at profiler output, concentrate on the slowest five methods; effort directed elsewhere will probably be wasted.

The following table lists some potential code optimizations (worthwhile and counter-productive), to illustrate some of the tradeoffs between performance and maintainability to be considered:

Technique	Performance improvement	Effect on maintainability
Minimize object creation, through techniques such as object pooling and "canonicalizing" objects (preventing the creation of multiple objects representing the same value).	Varies. May reduce the work of garbage collection. The performance benefit may not be very great with the sophisticated garbage collection of newer VMs.	Implementing such algorithms may be complex. Code may become harder to read. This is the kind of performance issue that should be kept in mind when writing code in the first place. We shouldn't create large numbers of objects without good reason if there is an alternative, such as using primitives.
Use the correct collection type: for example, `java.util.LinkedList` when we don't know how many elements to expect, and when one will be added at a time, or `java.util.ArrayList` when we know how many elements to expect. Remember all those data structures modules in Computer Science I? Sun have implemented many of the standard data structures as core library collections, meaning we just need to choose the most appropriate.	Varies. May be very significant if the list grows unpredictably or requires sorting.	None. We should access the Collection through its interface (such as `java.util.List`) rather than concrete class (such as `java.util.LinkedList`).
Use an exception rather than a check to end a loop.	Varies with virtual machine.	Likely to make code harder to read. This is an example of an optimization that should be avoided if possible.
Use final classes and methods.	Slight.	It's often good style to use final classes and methods, so we often use this "optimization" for other reasons (see Chapter 4).

Table continued on following page

Technique	Performance improvement	Effect on maintainability
Avoid using `System.out`.	Significant if a lot of output is involved.	In any case, it's vital that an enterprise application uses a proper logging framework. This is discussed in Chapter 4.
Avoid evaluating unnecessary conditions. Java guarantees "short-circuit" evaluation of `ands` and `ors`. Thus we should perform the quickest checks first, potentially avoiding the need to evaluate slower checks.	Can be significant if a piece of code is frequently invoked.	None.
Avoid operations on `Strings`, using `StringBuffers` in preference. As `Strings` are immutable, `String` operations are likely to be inefficient and wasteful, resulting in the creation of many short-lived objects.	May be significant, depending on the JVM.	Due to the significant performance benefit, this is a case where a professional developer should simply get used to reading the slightly more verbose `StringBuffer` syntax. *Note that the HotSpot JVM in Sun's JDK 1.3 appears to perform such optimization automatically; however, it's best not to rely on this.*
Avoid unnecessary `String` *or* `StringBuffer` operations. Even `StringBuffer` operations are relatively slow.	Significant.	None. This is an area where we can safely achieve quick wins.
Minimize the use of interfaces, as they may be slower to invoke than classes.	Very slight.	This is the kind of "optimization" that has the potential to wreck a codebase. The marginal performance gain isn't worth the damage this approach can wreak.

`String` and `StringBuffer` operations can have a big impact on performance. Even `StringBuffer` operations are surprisingly expensive, as use of a profiler such as JProbe quickly demonstrates. Be very aware of string operations in heavily used code, making sure they are necessary and as efficient as possible.

As an example of this, consider logging in our sample application. The following seemingly innocent statement in our `TicketController` web controller, performed only *once*, accounts for a surprisingly high 5% of total execution time if a user requests information about a reservation already held in their session:

```
logger.fine("Reservation request is ["  + reservationRequest + "]");
```

The problem is not the logging statement itself, but that of performing a string operation (which HotSpot optimizes to a `StringBuffer` operation) and invoking the `toString()` method on the `ReservationRequest` object, which performs several further string operations. Adding a check as to whether the log message will ever be displayed, to avoid creating it if it won't be, will all but eliminate this cost in production, as any good logging package provides highly efficient querying of log configuration:

```
if (logger.isLoggable(Level.FINE))
    logger.fine("Reservation request is [" + reservationRequest + "]");
```

Of course a 5% performance saving is no big deal in most cases, but such careless use of logging can be much more critical in frequently-invoked methods. Such conditional logging is essential in heavily used code.

> **Generating log output usually has a minor impact on performance. However, building log messages unnecessarily, especially if it involves unnecessary `toString()` invocations, can be surprisingly expensive.**

Two particularly tricky issues are **synchronization** and **reflection**. These are potentially important, because they sit midway between design and implementation. Let's take a closer look at each in turn.

Correct use of synchronization is an issue of both design and coding. Excessive synchronization throttles performance and has the potential to deadlock. Insufficient synchronization can cause state corruption. Synchronization issues often arise when implementing caching. The essential reference on Java threading is *Concurrent Programming in Java: Design Principles and Patterns* from Addison Wesley (ISBN: 0-201-31009-0). I strongly recommend referring to this book when implementing any complex multi-threaded code. However, the following tips may be useful:

❑ Don't assume that synchronization will always prove disastrous for performance. Base decisions empirically. Especially if operations executed under synchronization execute quickly, synchronization may ensure data integrity with minimal impact on performance. We'll look at a practical example of the issues relating to synchronization later in this chapter.

❑ Use automatic variables instead of instance variables where possible, so that synchronization is not necessary (this advice is particularly relevant to web-tier controllers).

❑ Use the least synchronization consistent with preserving state integrity.

❑ Synchronize the smallest possible sections of code.

❑ Remember that object references, like `int`s (but *not* `long`s and `double`s) are **atomic** (read or written in a single operation), so their state cannot be corrupted. Hence a race condition in which two threads initialize the same object in succession (as when putting an object into a cache) may do no harm, so long as it's not an error for initialization to occur more than once, and be acceptable in pursuit of reduced synchronization.

❑ Use **lock splitting** to minimize the performance impact of synchronization. Lock splitting is a technique to increase the granularity of synchronization locks, so that each synchronized block locks out only threads interested in the object being updated. If possible, use a standard package such as Doug Lea's `util.concurrent` to avoid the need to implement well-known synchronization techniques such as lock splitting. Remember that using EJB to take care of concurrency issues isn't the only alternative to writing your own low-level multi-threaded code: `util.concurrent` is an open source package that can be used anywhere in a Java application.

Reflection has a reputation for being slow. Reflection is central to much J2EE functionality and a powerful tool in writing generic Java code, so it's worth taking a close look at the performance issues involved. It reveals that most of the fear surrounding the performance of reflection is unwarranted.

To illustrate this, I ran a simple test to time four basic reflection operations:

❑ Loading a class by name with the `Class.forName(String)` method. The cost of invoking this method depends on whether the requested class has already been loaded. *Any* operation – using reflection or not – will be much slower if it requires a class to be loaded for the first time.

❑ Instantiating a loaded class by invoking the `Class.newInstance()` method, using the class's no-argument constructor.

❑ Introspection: finding a class's methods using `Class.getMethods()`.

❑ Method invocation using `Method.invoke()`, once a reference to a method has been cached.

The source code for the test can be found in the sample application download, under the path `/framework/test/reflection/Tests.java`.

The following method was invoked via reflection:

```
public String foo(int i) {
        return "This is a string with a number " + i + " in it";
}
```

The most important results, in running these tests concurrently on a 1Ghz Pentium III under JDK 1.3.1_02, were:

❑ 10,000 invocations this method via `Method.invoke()` took 480ms.

❑ 10,000 invocations this method directly took 301ms (less than twice as fast).

❑ 10,000 creations of an object with two superclasses and a fairly large amount of instance data took 21,371ms.

❑ 10,000 creations of objects of the same class using the new operations took 21,280ms. This means that whether reflection or the new operator is used will produce no effect on the cost of creating a large object.

My conclusions, from this and tests I have run in the past, and experience from developing real applications, are that:

❑ Invoking a method using reflection is very fast once a reference to the Method object is available. When using reflection, try to cache the results of introspection if possible. Remember that a method can be invoked on any object of the declaring class. If the method does any work at all, the cost of this work is likely to outweigh the cost of reflective invocation.

❑ The cost of instantiating any but trivial objects dwarfs the cost of invoking the newInstance() method on the relevant class. When a class has several instance variables and superclasses with instance data, the cost of object creation is *hundreds* of times more expensive than that of initiating that object creation through reflection.

❑ Reflective operations are so fast that virtually any amount of reflection done once per web request will have no perceptible effect on performance.

❑ Slow operations such as string operations are slower than invoking methods using reflection.

❑ Reflective operations are generally faster – and some dramatically faster – in JDK 1.3.1 and JDK 1.4 than in JDK 1.3.0 and earlier JDKs. Sun have realized the importance of reflection, and have put much effort into improving the performance of reflection with each new JVM.

> **The assumption among many Java developers that "reflection is slow" is misguided, and becoming increasingly anachronistic with maturing JVMs. Avoiding reflection is pointless except in unusual circumstances – for example, in a deeply nested loop. Appropriate use of reflection has many benefits, and its performance overhead is nowhere near sufficient to justify avoiding it. Of course application code will normally use reflection only via an abstraction provided by infrastructure code.**

Case Study: The "Display Show" Page in the Sample Application

All benchmarks on the following test were run on a 1 Ghz Pentium III with 512 MB of RAM under Windows XP. Microsoft Web Application Stress Tool, application server and database were running in the same machine. The software versions were JBoss 3.0.0, Oracle 8.1.7, and Java JDK 1.3.1_02. Logging was switched to production level (errors and warnings only).

Let's now look at a case study of addressing the performance requirements of one use case in the sample application. Let's consider requests for the "Display Show" page. This displays information about all bookable performances of a particular show. The "Welcome" page links directly to this page, so most users will arrive here on their second page view, although they may be interested in different shows. Thus it's vital that this page can cope with heavy user activity, that it renders quickly and that generating it doesn't load the system too heavily.

Some of the information displayed on this page is rarely changing reference data: for example, the name of the show and the pricing structure. Other information changes frequently: for example, we must display the availability of each seat type for every performance (with 10 performances of a show displayed and 4 classes of seats for each, this would mean 40 availability checks). Business requirements state that caching may be acceptable if required to deliver adequate performance, but that the availability information must be no more than 30 seconds old. The following screenshot illustrates this page:

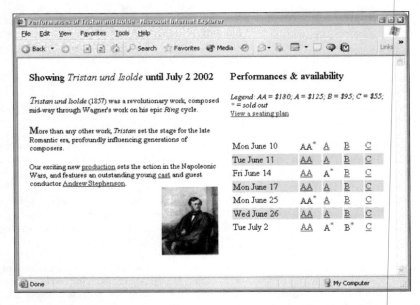

We begin by running load tests without any caching or other optimizations in application code to see whether there is a problem. The Microsoft Web Application Stress Tool reveals that with 100 concurrent users, this page can take 14 hits per second, with an average response time of just over 6 seconds. The load test showed JBoss using 80% of CPU and Oracle almost 20% (it's important to use your operating system's load monitoring tools during load testing).

Although this exceeds our modest performance targets for concurrent access, it does not meet requirements for response time. Throughput and performance could deteriorate sharply if we had to display more than 3 performances of a show (our test data), or if Oracle was on a remote server, as would be the case in production. Of course we would test the effect of these scenarios in a real application, but I have limited hardware and time at my disposal while writing this book. Thus we must implement design and code changes necessary to improve the performance of generating this page.

It's pretty clear from the Task Manager display that the problem is largely in communication with, and work within, the database. However, before we begin amending our design and changing code, it's a good idea to get some precise metrics of where the application spends its time. So we profile two requests for this page in JProbe. The results, ordered by cumulative method time, look as follows:

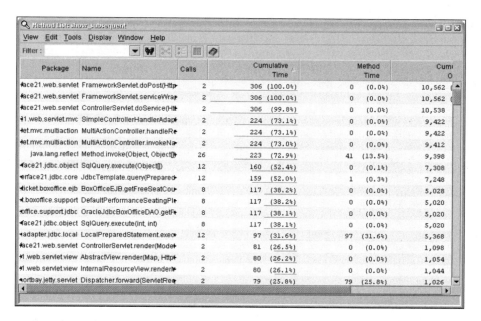

These results indicate that we have executed 6 SQL queries per page view, shown by the 12 invocations of the `SqlQuery.execute()` method, and that these queries accounted for 52% of the total time. Rendering the JSP accounted for a surprisingly high 26% of execution time. However, it's clear that the database access is the main limiter on performance. The 13% spent reflectively invoking methods using reflection via `Method.invoke()` indicates the 12 EJB accesses per page view. Both JBoss and the EJB proxy infrastructure discussed in Chapter 11 use reflection in EJB invocation. 12 EJB invocations per page is also unacceptably high, due to the overhead of invoking EJB methods, so we will also want to address this.

As the queries involved are simple selects and don't involve transaction or locking issues, we can rule out locking in the database or within the application server (we should also check that the database is correctly configured and the schema efficient; we'll assume this to be the case). Since we can't make simple selects more efficient, we'll need to implement caching in business objects to minimize the number of calls to the database. As business requirements allow the data presented on this screen to be as much as 30 seconds out of date, we have room for maneuvering.

Since the web-tier code in `com.wrox.expertj2ee.ticket.web.TicketController` is coded to use the `com.wrox.expertj2ee.ticket.command.AvailabilityCheck` interface to retrieve availability information, rather than a concrete implementation, we can easily substitute a different JavaBean implementation to implement caching.

> **Interface-driven design is an area in which good design practice leads to maximum freedom in performance tuning. While there is a tiny overhead in invoking methods through an interface, rather than on a class, it is irrelevant in comparison with the benefits of being able to reimplement an interface without affecting callers.**

During high-level design, we also considered the possibility of using JMS to fire updates on reservations and purchases, as an alternative to caching, to cause data to be invalidated only when it's known to be changed. As reservations can timeout in the database, without further activity through the web tier, this would be moderately complex to implement: we'd have to schedule a second JMS message to be sent on the reservation's expiry, so that any cache could check whether the reservation expired or had been converted into a purchase. Further performance investigation will reveal whether this option is necessary.

Let's begin by looking at the present code in the implementation of the `AvailabilityCheck` interface to return combined performance and availability information. The highlighted lines use the `BoxOffice` EJB, which will need to perform a database query. This method is invoked several times to build information for each show. Note that the results of JNDI lookups have already been cached in infrastructure code:

```
public PerformanceWithAvailability getPerformanceWithAvailability(
    Performance p) throws NoSuchPerformanceException {

  int avail = boxOffice.getFreeSeatCount(p.getId());
  PerformanceWithAvailabilityImpl pai =
    new PerformanceWithAvailabilityImpl(p, avail);

  for (int i = 0; i < p.getPriceBands().size(); i++) {
    PriceBand pb = (PriceBand) p.getPriceBands().get(i);
    avail = boxOffice.getFreeSeatCount(p.getId(), pb.getId());
    PriceBandWithAvailability pba =
      new PriceBandWithAvailabilityImpl(pb, avail);
    pai.addPriceBand(pba);
  }
  return pai;
}
```

We begin by trying the simplest possible approach: caching performance objects by key in a hash table. As this is quite simple, it's reasonable to implement it in application code, rather than introduce a third-party caching solution. Rather than worry about synchronization – potentially the toughest problem in implementing caches – we use a `java.util.HashTable` to hold a cache of `PerformanceWithAvailability` objects, keyed by integer performance ID.

Remember that the old, pre-Java 2, collections use synchronization on nearly every method, including put and get on maps, while the newer collections, such as `java.util.HashMap`, leave the caller to handle any synchronization necessary. This means that the newer collections are always a better choice for read-only data.

There's no need to set a limit on the maximum size of the cache (another problem sometimes encountered when implementing caches), as there can never be more show and performance objects than we can store in RAM. Likewise, we don't need to worry about the implications of clustering (another potential caching problem); business requirements state that data should be no older than 30 seconds, not that it must be exactly the same on all servers in any cluster.

Since the business requirements state that the seat selection page, generation of which also uses the `AvailabilityCheck` interface, *always* requires up-to-date data, we need to perform a little refactoring to add a new `Boolean` parameter to the methods from the `AvailabilityCheck` interface, so that caching can be disabled if the caller chooses.

Our caching logic will need to be able to check how old a cached `PerformanceWithAvailability` object is, so we make the `PerformanceWithAvailability` interface extend a simple interface, `TimeStamped`, which exposes the age of the object:

```
package com.interface21.core;

public interface TimeStamped {
  long getTimeStamp();
}
```

As the period for which we cache data is likely to be critical to performance, we expose a "timeout" JavaBean property on the `CachedAvailabilityCheck` class, our new caching implementation of the `AvailabilityCheck` interface, which uses a `HashTable` as its internal cache:

```
private Map performanceCache = new HashTable();
private long timeout = 1000L;

public void setTimeout(int secs) {
  this.timeout = 1000L * secs;
}
```

Now we split `getPerformanceWithAvailability()` into two methods, separating the acquisition of new data into the `reloadPerformanceWithAvailability()` method. I've highlighted the condition that determines whether or not to use any cached copy of the performance data for the requested ID. Note that the quickest checks – such as whether the timeout bean property is set to 0, meaning that caching is effectively disabled – are performed first, so that we don't need to evaluate the slowest checks, which involve getting the current system time (a relatively slow operation), unless necessary.

Strictly speaking, the check as to whether the timeout property is 0 is unnecessary, as the timestamp comparison would work even if it were. However, as this check takes virtually no time its far better to run a redundant check sometimes than ever to perform an unnecessary, expensive check:

```
public PerformanceWithAvailability getPerformanceWithAvailability(
      Performance p, boolean acceptCached)
      throws NoSuchPerformanceException {

  Integer key = new Integer(p.getId());

  PerformanceWithAvailability pai =
    (PerformanceWithAvailability) performanceCache.get(key);

  if (pai == null ||
      this.timeout <= 0L ||
      !acceptCached ||
      System.currentTimeMillis() - pai.getTimeStamp() > this.timeout) {

    pai = reloadPerformanceWithAvailability(p);
    this.performanceCache.put(key, pai);
  }
  return pai;
}

private PerformanceWithAvailability reloadPerformanceWithAvailability(
      Performance p) throws NoSuchPerformanceException {
```

```
    int avail = boxOffice.getFreeSeatCount(p.getId());
    PerformanceWithAvailabilityImpl pai =
      new PerformanceWithAvailabilityImpl(p, avail);

    for (int i = 0; i < p.getPriceBands().size(); i++) {
      PriceBand pb = (PriceBand) p.getPriceBands().get(i);
      avail = boxOffice.getFreeSeatCount(p.getId(), pb.getId());
      PriceBandWithAvailability pba =
        new PriceBandWithAvailabilityImpl(pb, avail);
      pai.addPriceBand(pba);
    }
    return pai;
  }
```

Since using a synchronized hash table guarantees data integrity, we don't need to perform any synchronization ourselves. There is a possibility that, at the first highlighted line in the above listing, we will retrieve a `null` value from the hash table, but that before we retrieve the data and insert into the hash table, another thread will have beaten us to it. However, this won't cause any data integrity problems: the occasional unnecessary database access is a lesser evil than more complex, bug-prone code. Clever synchronization is sometimes necessary, but it's best avoided if it doesn't deliver real value.

With these changes, we set the timeout property of the `availabilityCheck` bean to 20 seconds in the relevant bean definition in `ticket-servlet.xml` and rerun the Web Application Stress Tool. The result is a massive improvement in throughput and performance: 51 pages per second, against the 14 achieved without caching. The Task Manager indicates that Oracle is now doing virtually nothing. This more than satisfies our business requirements.

However, the more up-to-date the data the better, so we experiment with reduced timeout settings. A timeout setting of 10 seconds produces runs averaging 49 pages per second, with an average response time well under 2 seconds, indicating that this may be worthwhile. Reducing the timeout to 1 second reduces throughput to 28 pages per second: probably too great a performance sacrifice.

At this point, I was still concerned about the effect of synchronization. Would a more sophisticated approach minimize locking and produce even better results? To check this, I wrote a multi-threaded test that enabled me to test only the `CachingAvailabilityCheck` class, using the simple load-testing framework in the `com.interface21.load` package discussed earlier. The worker thread extended the `AbstractTest` class, and simply involved retrieving data from a random show among those loaded when the whole test suite started up:

```
public class AvailabilityCheckTest extends AbstractTest {

  private AvailabilityFixture fixture;

  public void setFixture(Object fixture) {
    this.fixture = (AvailabilityFixture) fixture;
  }

  protected void runPass(int i) throws Exception {
    Show s = (Show) fixture.shows.get(randomIndex(fixture.shows.size()));
    fixture.availabilityCheck.getShowWithAvailability(s, true);
  }
}
```

It's essential that each thread invoke the same `AvailabilityCheck` object, so we create a "fixture" class shared by all instances. This creates and exposes a `CachingAvailabilityCheck` object. Note that in the listing below I've exposed a public final instance variable. This isn't usually a good idea, as it's not JavaBean-friendly and means that we can't add intelligence in a getter method, but it's acceptable in a quick test case. The `AvailabilityFixture` class exposes three bean properties that enable tests to be parameterized: `timeout`, which directly sets the timeout of the `CachingAvailabilityCheck` being tested, and `minDelay` and `maxDelay` (discussed below):

```java
public class AvailabilityFixture {

  public final CachingAvailabilityCheck availabilityCheck;

  public final List shows = new LinkedList();

  private long timeout;

  private JdbcCalendar calendar = null;

  private long minDelay;
  private long maxDelay;

  public AvailabilityFixture() throws Exception {
    calendar = new JdbcCalendar(new TestDataSource());
    calendar.afterPropertiesSet();
    shows.add(calendar.getShow(1));
    availabilityCheck = new CachingAvailabilityCheck();
    availabilityCheck.setCalendar(calendar);
    availabilityCheck.setBoxOffice(new DummyBoxOffice());
  }

  public void setTimeout(int timeout) {
    availabilityCheck.setTimeout(timeout);
  }

  public void setMinDelay(long minDelay) {
    this.minDelay = minDelay;
  }

  public void setMaxDelay(long maxDelay) {
    this.maxDelay = maxDelay;
  }
```

We're interested in the performance of the caching algorithm, not the underlying database access, so I use a simple dummy implementation of the `BoxOffice` interface in an inner class (again, interface-based design proves handy during testing). This always returns the same data (we're not interested in the values, just how long it takes to retrieve them), delaying for a random number of milliseconds between the value of the `minDelay` and `maxDelay` bean property. Those methods that are irrelevant to the test simply throw an `UnsupportedOperationException`. This is better than returning `null`, as we'll immediately see if these methods ever do unexpectedly get invoked:

```java
private class DummyBoxOffice implements BoxOffice {
  public Reservation allocateSeats(ReservationRequest request)
      throws NotEnoughSeatsException,
            NoSuchPerformanceException,
            InvalidSeatingRequestException {
```

```
        throw new UnsupportedOperationException("DummyBoxOffice.allocateSeats");
    }

    public Booking confirmReservation(PurchaseRequest purchase)
        throws ExpiredReservationTakenException,
               CreditCardAuthorizationException,
               InvalidSeatingRequestException,
               BoxOfficeInternalException {
      throw new UnsupportedOperationException(
        "DummyBoxOffice.confirmReservation");
    }

    public int getFreeSeatCount(int performanceId, int seatTypeId)
        throws NoSuchPerformanceException {
      AbstractTest.simulateDelay(minDelay, maxDelay);
      return 10;
    }

    public int getFreeSeatCount(int performanceId)
        throws NoSuchPerformanceException {
      AbstractTest.simulateDelay(minDelay, maxDelay);
      return 30;
    }

    public int getSeatCount(int performanceId)
        throws NoSuchPerformanceException {
      return 200;
    }
  }
}
```

To use the real, EJB, implementation of the BoxOffice, we'd need to run the tests in the EJB container or access the EJB through a remote interface, which would distort the test results. If we weren't using EJB, we could simply read the XML bean definitions in ticket-servlet.xml in our test suite. The complexity that *any* use of EJB adds throughout the software lifecycle should be considered before choosing to use EJB; in this case using EJB does deliver real value through declarative transaction management, so we can accept greater complexity in other areas.

We can configure our test suite with the following properties file, which is similar to the example we saw above:

```
suite.class=com.interface21.load.BeanFactoryTestSuite
suite.name=Availability check
suite.reportIntervalSeconds=1
suite.longReports=false
suite.doubleFormat=###.#
suite.reportFile=<local path to report file>
```

The crucial framework test suite definitions are of the number of threads to run concurrently, the number of test passes to be run by each thread, and the maximum pause value per thread:

```
suite.threads=50
suite.passes=40
suite.maxPause=23
```

We set the `fixture` object as a bean property of the framework's generic `BeanFactoryTestSuite`:

```
suite.fixture(ref)=fixture
```

The `fixture` is also a bean, so we can configure the `CachingAvailability` object's `timeout`, and the delays in the JDBC simulation methods as follows:

```
fixture.class=com.interface21.load.AvailabilityFixture
fixture.timeout=10
fixture.minDelay=60
fixture.maxDelay=120
```

Finally, we set the properties of each worker thread:

```
availabilityTest.class=com.interface21.load.AvailabilityCheckTest
availabilityTest.(singleton)=false
```

First I set `fixture.timeout` property to 0 to disable caching. This produced throughput of about 140 hits per second, with an average response time of about 360 milliseconds. Setting the thread timeout to 1 second produced a dramatic improvement, without about 7,000 hits per second and an average response time of 7 milliseconds. Increasing the timeout further produced an improvement of 20% or less.

No surprises so far. However I was a little surprised by the results of investigating the effect of synchronization. I began by replacing the `Hashtable` with the unsynchronized `java.util.HashMap`. Unless this produced a substantial improvement, there was no point in putting more effort into developing smarter synchronization. The improvement was at most 10-15% at all realistic load levels. Only by trying hundreds of users simultaneously requesting information about the same show, with an unrealistically slow database response time and a 1 second timeout – an impossible scenario, as the web interface couldn't deliver this kind of load to business objects – did the `Hashtable` synchronization begin to reduce throughput significantly. I learned also that eliminating the potential race condition noted above by synchronization within the `getPerformanceWithAvailability()` method reduced performance around 40% under moderate to heavy load, making it unattractive.

With a little thought, it's easy to explain these results. Although there is an inevitable lock management load in the JVM associated with synchronization, the effect of synchronization on throughput will ultimately depend on how long it takes to execute the synchronized operations. As hash table `get` and `put` operations take very little time, the effect of synchronization is fairly small (this is quite like the Copy-On-Write approach we discussed in Chapter 11: synchronization is applied only to updating a reference, not to looking up the new data).

Thus the simplest approach – the cache shown above, uses the synchronized `java.util.Hashtable` – produced performance far exceeding the business requirements.

Finally, I ran JProbe again on the same use case, with caching enabled, to see what had changed. Note that this is a profile of a single request, and so doesn't reflect synchronization costs in concurrent access:

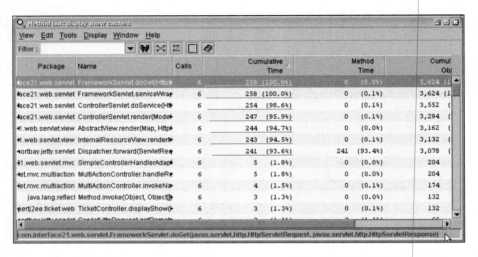

This indicates that 94% of the execution time is now spent rendering the JSP. Only by switching to a more performant view technology might we appreciably improve performance. Further changes to Java application code will produce no benefit. Normally, such results – indicating that we've run into a limit of the underlying J2EE technologies – are very encouraging. However, it would be worth checking the JSP to establish that it's efficient. In this case, it's trivial, so there's no scope for improvement.

It's time to stop. We've exceeded our performance goals, and further effort will produce no worthwhile return.

> This case study indicates the value of an empirically based approach to performance tuning, and how doing "the simplest thing that could possibly work" can be valuable in performance tuning. As we had coded the web-tier controller to use a business interface, not a concrete class, as part of our overall design strategy, it was easy to substitute a caching implementation.

With an empirical approach using the Web Application Stress tool, we established that, in this case, the simplest caching strategy – ensuring data integrity through synchronization – performed better under all conditions except improbably high load than more sophisticated locking strategies. We also established that there was no problem in ensuring that data displayed was no older than 10 seconds, more than satisfying business requirements on freshness of data. Using JProbe, we were able to confirm that the performance of the final version, with caching in place, was limited by the work of rendering the JSP view, indicating no further scope for performance improvements.

Of course the simplest approach may not always deliver adequate performance. However, this example shows that it's wise to expend greater effort reluctantly, and only when it is proven to be necessary.

Performance in Distributed Applications

> Distributed applications are much more complex than applications in which all components run in the same JVM. Performance is among the most important of the many reasons to avoid adopting a distributed architecture unless it's the only way to satisfy business requirements.

The commonest cause of disappointing performance in J2EE applications is unnecessary use of remote calling – usually in the form of remote access to EJBs. This typically imposes an overhead far greater than that of any other operation in a J2EE application. Many developers perceive J2EE to be an inherently distributed model. In fact, this is a misconception. J2EE merely provides particularly strong support for implementing distributed architectures when necessary. Just because this choice is available doesn't mean that we should always make it.

In this section, we'll look at why remote calling is so expensive, and how to minimize its effect on performance when we must implement a distributed application.

The Overhead of Remote Method Invocation (RMI)

Whereas ordinary Java classes make calls by reference to objects in the same virtual machine, calls to EJBs in distributed applications must be made remotely, using a remote invocation protocol such as IIOP. Clients cannot directly reference EJB objects and must obtain remote references using JNDI. EJBs and EJB clients may be located in different virtual machines, or even different physical servers. This indirection sometimes enhances scalability: because an application server is responsible for managing naming lookups and remote method invocation, multiple application server instances can cooperate to route traffic within a cluster and offer failover support. However, the performance cost of remote, rather than local, calling can be hefty if we do not design our applications appropriately.

EJB's support for remote clients is based on Java RMI. However, any infrastructure for distributed invocation will have similar overheads.

Java RMI supports two types of objects: **remote** objects, and **serializable** objects. Remote objects support method invocation from remote clients (clients running in different processes), who are given **remote references** to them. Remote objects are of classes that implement the `java.rmi.Remote` interface and all of whose remote methods are declared to throw `java.rmi.RemoteException` in addition to any application exceptions. All EJBs with remote interfaces are remote objects.

Serializable objects are essentially data objects that can be used in invocations on remote objects. Serializable objects must be of classes that implement the `java.io.Serializable` tag interface and must have serializable fields (other serializable objects, or primitive types). Serializable objects are passed by value, meaning that both copies can be changed independently, and that object state must be **serialized** (converted to a stream representation) and **deserialized** (reconstituted from the stream representation) with each method call. Serializable objects are used for data exchange in distributed J2EE applications, as parameters, return values, and exceptions in calls to remote objects.

Method invocations on remote objects such as EJB objects or EJB homes always require a network round trip from client to server and back. Hence remote calling consumes network bandwidth. Unnecessary remote calls consume bandwidth that should be reserved for operations that do something necessary, such as moving data to where it's needed.

Each remote call will encounter the overhead of **marshaling** and **unmarshaling** serializable parameters: the process by which the caller converts method parameters into a format that can be sent across the network, and the receiver reassembles object parameters. Marshaling and unmarshaling has an overhead over and above the work of serialization and deserialization and the time taken to communicate the bytes across the network. The overhead depends on the protocol being used, which may be IIOP or an optimized proprietary protocol such as WebLogic's T3 or Orion's ORMI. J2EE 1.3 application servers must support IIOP, but need not use it by default.

The following diagram illustrates the overhead involved in remote method invocation:

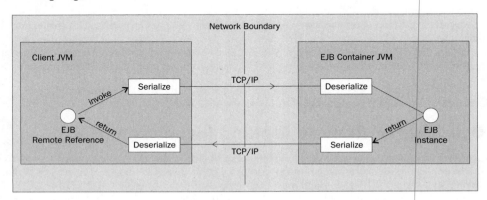

This overhead means that remote calls may be more than 1,000 times slower than local calls, even if there's a fast LAN connection between the application components involved.

> **The number of remote calls is a major determinant – potentially *the* major determinant – of a distributed application's performance, because the overhead of remote calling is so great.**

In the following section, we'll look at how we can minimize the performance impact of remote invocation when designing distributed applications.

Fortunately, we have many choices as architects and developers. For example:

- ❏ We can try to structure our application to minimize the need to move data between architectural tiers through remote calling. This technique is known as **application partitioning**.

- ❏ We can try to move the data we can't help moving in the minimum number of remote calls.

- ❏ We may be able to move individual pieces of data more efficiently.

- ❏ We can collocate components in the same virtual machine so that inter-tier calls do not require remote calling.

- ❏ We can cache data from remote resources to minimize the number of remote calls. We've already considered caching; it will be particularly beneficial in this scenario.

Let's examine these techniques in turn.

Minimizing Remote Calls

The greatest scope for performance gains is in structuring an application so as to minimize the number of remote calls that will be required.

Application Partitioning

Application partitioning is the task of dividing a distributed application into major architectural tiers and assigning each component to one tier. In a J2EE web application using EJB, this means assigning each object or functional component to one of the client browser, the web tier, the EJB tier, or the database. A "functional component" need not always be a Java object. For example, a stored procedure in a relational database might be a functional component of an application.

Application partitioning will determine the *maximum* extent of network round trips required as the application runs. The actual extent of network round trips may be less in some deployment configurations. A distributed J2EE application must support different deployment configurations, meaning that the web container and EJB container may be collocated in the same JVM, which will reduce the number of network round trips in some deployments.

The main aim of application partitioning is to ensure that each architectural layer has a clearly defined responsibility. For example, we should ensure that business logic in a distributed J2EE application is in the EJB tier, so that it can be shared between client types. However, there is also a performance imperative: to ensure that frequent, time-critical operations can be performed without network round trips. As we've seen from examining the cost of Java remote method invocations, application partitioning can have a dramatic effect on performance. Poor application partitioning decisions lead to "chatty" remote calling – the greatest enemy of performance in distributed applications.

Design and performance considerations with respect to application partitioning tend to be in harmony. Excessive remote calling complicates an application and is error prone, so it's no more desirable from a design perspective than a performance perspective. However, application partitioning sometimes does involve tradeoffs.

> **Appropriate application partitioning can have a dramatic effect on performance. Hence it's vital to consider the performance impact of each decision in application partitioning.**

The greatest performance benefits will result from minimizing the depth of calling down a distributed J2EE stack to satisfy incoming requests.

> **The deeper down a distributed J2EE stack calls need to be made to service a request, the poorer the resulting performance will be. Especially in the case of common types of request, we should try to service requests as close as possible to the client. Of course, this requires a tradeoff: we can easily produce hosts of other problems, such as complex, bug-prone caching code or stale data, by making this our prime goal.**

What techniques can we use to ensure efficient application partitioning?

One of the biggest determinants is where the data we operate on comes from. First, we need to analyze data flow in the application. Data may flow from the data store in the EIS tier to the user, or from the user down the application's tiers.

Three strategies are particularly useful for minimizing round trips:

❑   Moving data to where we operate on it.

❑   Moving the operation to where the data is. Java RMI enables us to move code as well as data in order to do this. We can also move some operations inside EIS-tier resources such as databases to minimize network traffic.

❑   Collocating components with a strong **affinity**. Objects with a strong affinity interact with each other often.

Moving Data to Where We Operate on It

The worst situation is to have data located in one tier while the operations on it are in another. For example, this arises if the web tier holds a data object and makes many calls to the EJB tier as it processes it. A better alternative is to move the object to the EJB tier by passing it as a parameter, so that all operations run locally, with only one remote invocation necessary. The EJB Command pattern, discussed in Chapter 10, is an example of this approach. The Value Object pattern also moves entire objects in a single remote call.

Caching, which we have discussed, is a special case of moving data to where we operate on it. In this case, data is moved in the opposite direction: from EIS tier towards the client.

Moving the Operation to the Data

An example of this strategy is using a single stored procedure running inside a relational database to implement an operation instead of performing multiple round trips between the EJB tier and the database to implement the same logic in Java and SQL. In some cases this will greatly improve performance. The use of stored procedures is an example of a performance-inspired application partitioning decision that does involve a tradeoff. It may have other disadvantages. It may reduce the portability of the application between databases, and may reduce maintainability. However, this application partitioning technique is applicable to collocated, as well as distributed, J2EE applications.

Another example is a possible approach to validating user input. Validation rules are business logic, and therefore belong naturally in the EJB tier in a distributed application, not the web tier. However, making a network round trip from the web container to the EJB container to validate input each time a form is submitted will be wasteful, especially if many problems in the input can be identified without access to back-end components.

One solution is for the EJB tier to control validation logic, and move validation *code* to the web tier in a serializable object implementing an agreed validation interface. The validator object need only be passed across the network once. As the web tier will already have the class definition of the validator interface, only the implementing class need be provided by the EJB tier at run time. The validator can then be invoked locally in the web tier, and remote calls will only be necessary for the minority of validation operations, such as checking a username is unique, that require access to data. As local calling is so much faster than remote calling, this strategy is likely to be more performant than calling the EJB tier to perform validation, even if the EJB tier needs to perform validation again (also locally) to ensure that invalid input can never result in a data update.

Let's look at an illustration of this in practice. Imagine a requirement to validate a user object that contains e-mail address password, postcode, and username properties. In a naïve implementation a web tier controller might invoke a method on a remote EJB to validate each of these properties in turn, as shown in the following diagram:

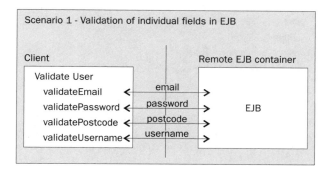

This approach will guarantee terrible performance, with an excessive number of expensive remote calls required to validate each user object.

A much better approach is to move the data to where we operate on it (as described above), using a serializable value object so that user data can be sent to the EJB server in a single remote call, and the results of validating all fields returned. This approach is shown in the diagram below:

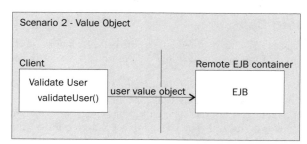

This will deliver a huge performance improvement, especially if there are many fields to validate. Performing just one remote method invocation, even if it involves passing more data, will be much faster than performing many fine-grained remote method invocations.

However, let's assume that the validation of only the username field requires database access (to check that the submitted username isn't already taken by another user), and that all other validation rules can be applied entirely on the client. In this case, we can apply the approach described above of moving the validation code to the client via a validation class obtained from the EJB tier when the application starts up. As the application runs, the client-side validator instance can validate most fields, such as e-mail address and postcode, without invoking EJBs. It will need to make only one remote call, to validate the username value, to validate each user object. This scenario is shown in the diagram overleaf:

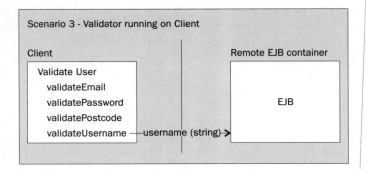

Since only a single string value needs to be serialized and deserialized during the validation of each user object, this will perform even better than the value object approach, in which a larger value object needed to be sent across the wire. Yet it still allows the EJB implementation to hide the validation business rules from client code.

A more radical application of the principle of moving validation code to the data it works on is to move validation logic into JavaScript running in the browser, to avoid the need for communication with the server before rejecting some invalid submissions. However, this approach has other disadvantages that usually preclude its use.

We discussed the problem of validating input to web applications, with practical examples, in Chapter 12.

Consolidating Remote Calls

Due to the serialization and marshaling overhead of remote calls, it often makes sense to minimize the number of remote calls, even if this means that more data must be passed with each call.

A classic scenario for method call consolidation is the Value Object pattern, which we saw in the above example. Instead of making multiple fine-grained calls to a remote EJB to retrieve or update data, a single serializable "value object" is returned from a single bulk getter and passed to a single bulk setter method, retrieving or updating all fields in one call. The Value Object pattern is a special case of the general rule that remote objects should not have interfaces that force clients into "chatty" access.

> **Minimizing the number of remote calls will improve performance, even if more data needs to be passed with each remote call.**
>
> **Each operation on an EJB's remote interface should perform a significant operation. Often it will implement a single use case. Chatty calling into the EJB container will usually result in the creation of many transaction contexts, which also wastes resources.**

Moving Data Efficiently

While minimizing the number of remote calls is usually the most profitable area to concentrate on, sometimes we may be able to reduce the overhead of transmitting across the network data that must be exchanged.

Serialization Optimizations

Since all parameters in remote invocations must be serialized and deserialized, the performance of serialization is critical. While core Java provides transparent serialization support that is usually satisfactory, occasionally we can usefully put more effort into ensuring that serialization is as efficient as possible, by applying the following techniques to individual serializable objects.

Transient Data

By default, all fields of serializable objects other than `transient` and `static` fields will be serialized. Thus by marking as `transient` "short-lived" fields – such as fields that can be computed from other fields – we can reduce the amount of data that must be serialized and deserialized and passed over the network.

> Any "short-lived" fields of serializable objects can be marked as `transient`. However, use this approach only with great care. The values of transient fields will need to be reset following deserialization; failing to do so is a potential cause of subtle bugs.

Primitive Fields

We may also be able to represent the data we need in a more efficient manner. Serializing primitives is much faster, and requires much less network bandwidth, than serializing objects. Thus any object that can be represented as a primitive type is a prime candidate for more efficient representation in a serializable object, saving memory as well as optimizing serialization. The classic example is `java.util.Date`, which can usually be replaced by a `long` system time in milliseconds. If we can represent `Date` objects as `long` in serializable objects, we will usually see a significant improvement in serialization performance and a reduction in the size of the serialized objects. The following table shows the effect of serializing the data in 10,000 dates in three different ways.

Two implementations were used of the following interface:

```
interface DateHolder extends java.io.Serializable {
      Date getDate();
}
```

The first implementation, `DateDateHolder`, held the date as a `java.util.Date`. The second implementation, `LongDateHolder`, used a long to represent the date.

The third row of data is the result of doing away with the 10,000 objects altogether, and using an array of 10,000 longs containing the same information. This produced an even more dramatic improvement in performance:

10,000 serializations, written to a disk file	Time (ms)	Size of file (kb)	Time as percentage of unoptimized case	Data size as % of unoptimized case
Object holding a `java.util.Date` object	370	225	100%	100%
Object holding `long` system time	110	137	30%	61%
Array of `long` system times	5	79	1%	35%

Of course, this kind of optimization may have unintended consequences. If there is a need for repeated conversion to and from a primitive type, its overhead may outweigh the serialization benefit. Also, there is a danger of unduly complicating code. On the whole, it is consistent with good design and often proves a worthwhile optimization.

> **Primitives are much faster to serialize and deserialize than objects. If it's possible to replace an object by a primitive representation, it is likely to improve serialization performance dramatically.**

Serialization Non-Issues

It's also important to realize what we *don't* need to worry about with standard serialization.

Developers sometimes wonder what happens if they serialize a "big" class, which contains many methods. The serialization process does not communicate .class files, so the executable code will not eat up bandwidth. The class will need to be loaded by the receiver, so it may need to be passed once over the network, if it is not locally available; this will be a small, one-off cost.

Serializing a class that is part of an inheritance hierarchy – for example, serializing a class C that extends class B that extends class A – adds a little overhead to the serialization process (which is based on reflection, so will need to traverse all class definitions in the inheritance hierarchy), but doesn't increase the amount of data that will be written out, beyond the additional fields of the superclasses.

Similarly, static fields do not bloat the size of the serialized representation of a class. These will not be serialized. The sender and receiver will maintain separate copies of static fields. Any static initializers will run independently, when each JVM loads the class. This means that static data can get out of sync between remote JVMs, one of the reasons for the restrictions on the use of static data in the EJB specification.

An important optimization of the default serialization implementation concerns multiple copies of the same object serialized *to the same stream*. Each object written to the stream is assigned a **handle**, meaning that subsequent references to the object can be represented in the output by the handle, not the object data. When the objects are instantiated on the client, a faithful copy of the references will be constructed. This may produce a significant benefit in serialization and deserialization time and network bandwidth in the case of object graphs with multiple connections between objects.

Custom Serialization

In some cases it's possible to do a more efficient job – with respect to serialization and deserialization speed and the size of serialized data – than the default implementation. However, unlike the choices we've just discussed, which are fairly simple to implement, this is not a choice to be taken lightly. Overriding the default serialization mechanism requires custom coding, in place of standard behavior. The custom code will also need to be kept up-to-date as our objects – and possibly, inheritance hierarchy – evolve.

There are two possible techniques here.

The first involves implementing two methods in the serializable class. Note that these methods are not part of any interface: they have a special meaning to the core Java serialization infrastructure. The method signatures are:

```
private void writeObject(java.io.ObjectOutputStream out) throws IOException;

private void readObject(java.io.ObjectInputStream in)
    throws IOException, ClassNotFoundException;
```

The `writeObject()` method saves the data *held in the object itself*. This doesn't include superclass state, which will still be handled automatically. It *does* include associated objects, whose references are held in the object itself.

The `readObject()` method is called *instead of a constructor* when an object is read from an `ObjectInputStream`. It must set the values of the class's fields from the stream.

These methods will use the Serialization API directly to write objects to the `ObjectOutputStream` supplied by the serialization infrastructure and restore objects from the `ObjectInputStream`. This means that more implementation work is involved, but the class has control over the format of its data's representation in the output stream. It's important to ensure that fields are written and read in the correct order.

Overriding `readObject` and `writeObject` can deliver significant performance gains in some cases, and very little in others. It eliminates the reflection overhead of the standard serialization process (which may not, however, be particularly great), and may allow us to use a more efficient representation as fields are persisted. Many standard library classes implement `readObject()` and `writeObject()`, including `java.util.Date`, `java.util.HashMap`, `java.util.LinkedList`, and most AWT and Swing components.

In the second technique, an object can gain *complete* control over serialization and deserialization if it implements the `java.io.Externalizable` interface. This is a subclass of the `Serializable` tag interface that contains two methods:

```
public void writeExternal(ObjectOutput out) throws IOException

public void readExternal(ObjectInput in) throws IOException,
    ClassNotFoundException
```

In contrast to a `Serializable` object implementing `readObject` and `writeObject`, an `Externalizable` object is *completely* responsible for saving and restoring its state, including any superclass state. The implementations of `writeExternal` and `readExternal` will use the same API as implementations of `writeObject` and `readObject`.

While constructor invocation is avoided when a serializable object is instantiated as a result of standard deserialization, this is not true for externalizable objects. When an instance of an externalizable class is reconstructed from its serializable representation, its no-argument constructor is invoked before `readExternal()` is called. This means that we do need to consider whether the implementation of the no argument constructor may prove wasteful for externalizable objects. This will also include any chained no argument constructors, invoked implicitly at run time.

Externalizable classes are likely to deliver the biggest performance gains from custom serialization. I've seen gains of around 50% in practice, which may be worthwhile for the serializable objects most often exchanged in an application, if serializing these objects is proving a performance problem. However, externalizable classes require the most work to implement and will lead to the greatest ongoing maintenance requirement. It's usually unwise to make a class externalizable if it has one or more superclasses, as changes to the superclass may break serialization.

However, this consideration doesn't apply to many value objects, which are not part of an inheritance hierarchy. Also, remember that an externalizable class may deliver worse serialization performance than an ordinary serializable class if it fails to identify any multiple references to a single object: remember that the default implementation of serialization assigns each object written to an `OutputStream` a handle that can be referred to later.

The documentation with the JDK includes detailed information on advanced serialization techniques. I recommend reading this carefully before trying to use custom serialization to improve the performance of distributed applications.

Taking control of the serialization process is an example of an optimization that should be weighed carefully. It will produce performance benefits in most cases, and the initial implementation effort will be modest if we are dealing with simple objects. However, it decreases the maintainability of code. For example, we have to be sure that the persistent fields are written out and read in the same order. We have to be careful to handle object associations correctly. We also have to consider any class hierarchy to which the persistent class may belong. For example, if the persistent class extends an abstract base class, and a new field is added to it, we would need to modify our externalizable implementation. The standard handling of serialization enables us to ignore all these issues.

Remember that adding complexity to an application's design or implementation to achieve optimization is not a one-off operation. Complexity is forever, and may cause ongoing costs in maintenance.

Other Data Transfer Strategies

We may not always want to transfer data in the form of serialized objects. Whatever means we choose to transfer large amounts of data, we will face similar issues of conversion overhead and network bandwidth.

XML is sometimes suggested as an alternative for data exchange. Transferring data across a process boundary using serialized DOM documents is likely to be slower than converting the document to a string in the sender and parsing the string in the receiver. A serialized DOM document is likely to be much larger than the string representation of the same document. Bruce Martin discusses these issues in an article in JavaWorld, at http://www.javaworld.com/javaworld/jw-02-2000/jw-02-ssj-xml.html.

Although it is likely, there is also no guarantee that a DOM document will even *be* serializable. For example, the Xalan 2 parser (a variant of which is used by WebLogic 6.1) allows the serialization of DOM documents, while the version of the Crimson parser used by Orion 1.5.2 does not. The `org.w3c.dom` interfaces are not themselves serializable, although most implementations will be. One option that does guarantee serializability is using the JDom, rather than DOM, API to represent the document: JDom documents are serializable (see http://www.jdom.org for further information about this alternative Java XML API).

Thus I don't recommend use of XML to exchange data across network boundaries. As I said in Chapter 6, I believe that XML is best kept at the boundaries of J2EE applications.

Another possibility is moving data in generic Java objects such as `java.util.HashMap` or `javax.sql.RowSet`. In this case it's important to consider the cost of serializing and deserializing the objects and the size of their serialized form. In the case of `java.util.HashMap`, which implements `writeObject()` and `readObject()`, the container itself adds little overhead. Simple timings can be used to determine the overhead of other containers.

However, the idea of communicating data from EJB tier to client in the form of a generic container such as a `RowSet` is unappealing from a design perspective. The EJB tier should provide a strongly typed interface for client communication. Furthermore, processing raw data from the EIS tier such as a `RowSet` may result in the discarding of some data, without it all needing to be sent to the client. This cannot happen if the client is always sent all the data and left to process it itself. Finally, the client becomes dependent on `javax.sql` classes that it would not otherwise need to use.

Collocating Components in the Same JVM

There is one way to eliminate much (but not all) of the overhead of distributed applications without writing a line of code: collocating the components on the same server so that they run in the same JVM. Where web applications are concerned, this means deploying the web tier and EJB tier in the same J2EE server. Most J2EE servers detect collocation and can use local calls in place of remote calls (in most servers, this optimization is enabled by default). This optimization avoids the overhead of serialization and remote invocation protocols. Both caller and receiver will use the same copy of an object, meaning that serialization is unnecessary. However, it's still likely to prove slower than invocation of EJBs through local interfaces, because of the container's need to fudge invocation semantics.

This approach won't work for distributed application clients such as Swing clients, which can't run in the same JVM as a server process. But it's probably the commonest deployment option for EJBs with remote interfaces.

I discussed this approach under the heading *Phony Remote Interfaces* in Chapter 6. As the title implies, it's an approach that's only valid if we know we need a distributed architecture, but the application at least initially can run with all its components collocated in the same JVM. There's a real danger that collocation can lead to the development of applications with RMI semantics that rely on call-by-reference and thus would fail in a truly distributed environment.

> If it's clear that collocation will always be the only deployment option, consider dispensing with the use of EJB (or at least EJB remote interfaces) and doing away with remoting issues once and for all. Flexible deployment is a key part of what EJB provides; when it's not necessary, the use of EJB may not be worthwhile.

Web-Tier Performance Issues

We've already discussed the implications for performance scalability of web-tier session management. Let's consider a few web-tier-specific performance issues we haven't covered so far.

View Performance

In Chapter 13 we looked at using several different view technologies to generate a single example view. We considered authoring implications and maintainability, but didn't consider performance, beyond general considerations.

Let's look at the results of running the Microsoft Web Application Stress Tool against some of the view technologies we discussed.

Note that I slightly modified the controller code for the purpose of the test to remove the requirement for a pre-existing user session and to use a single Reservation *object to provide the model for all requests, thus avoiding the need to access the RDBMS. This largely makes this a test of view performance, eliminating the need to contact business objects, and avoids the otherwise tricky issue of ensuring that enough free seats were available in the database to fulfill hundreds of concurrent requests.*

The five view technologies tested were:

❑ JSP, using JSTL

❑ Velocity 1.3

❑ XMLC 2.1

❑ XSLT using on-the-fly "domification" of the shared Reservation object

❑ XSLT using the same stylesheet but a cached org.w3c.dom.Document object (an artificial test, but one that enables the load of domification using reflections to be compared to that of performing XSLT transforms)

Each view generated the same HTML content. Both WAS and the application server ran on the same machine. However, operating system load monitoring showed that WAS did not consume enough resources to affect the test results. The XSLT engine was Xalan.

The following graph shows the results of running 100 concurrent clients continually requesting pages:

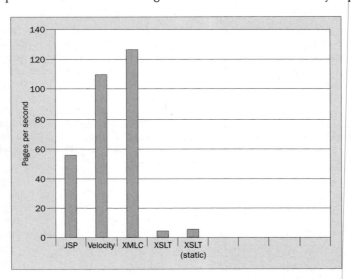

While the actual numbers would vary with different hardware and shouldn't be taken as an indication of likely performance in a production environment, the differences between them are a more meaningful measure.

I was surprised by the very large spread of results, and reran the tests several times before I was convinced they weren't anomalous. JSP achieved around 54 pages per second; Velocity 112; XMLC emerged a clear winner at 128; while both XSLT approaches were far slower, at 6 and 7 pages per second respectively.

The conclusions are:

❑ View technology can dictate overall application performance, although the effect would be less if more work needed to be done by business objects to satisfy each request. Interestingly, the difference between the performance of XSLT and the other technologies was significantly greater than including a roundtrip to the database in the same use case. While I had expected that XSLT would prove the slowest view technology, like many developers I tend to assume that accessing a database will almost always be the slowest operation in any use case. Thus this test demonstrates the importance of basing performance decisions empirically.

❑ JSP shouldn't be an automatic choice on the assumption that it will outperform other view technologies because JSP pages are compiled into servlets by the web container. XMLC proved well over twice as fast, but it does involve commitment to a very different authoring model. To my mind, Velocity emerged the real winner: JSP's perceived performance advantage is one of the essential arguments for preferring it to a simpler technology such as Velocity.

❑ Generating entire pages of dynamic content using XSLT is very slow – too slow to be an option in many cases. The cost of XSLT transforms is far greater than the cost of using reflection to "domify" JavaBean data on the fly. The efficiency of the stylesheet seems to make more difference as to whether "domification" is used. Switching from a "rule based" to "fill-in-the-blanks" stylesheet boosted performance by about 30%, although eliminating the use of Java extension functions didn't seem to produce much improvement.

The figures I've quoted here may vary between application servers: I would hesitate to draw the conclusion that XMLC and Velocity will always be nearly twice as fast as JSP. The Jasper JSP engine used by Jetty may be relatively slow. I've seen results showing comparable performance for all three technologies in Orion 1.5.3, admittedly with older versions of Velocity and XMLC.

The fact that the JSP results were very similar on comparable hardware with Orion, while the new Velocity and XMLC results are much faster, suggest that Velocity and XMLC have been optimized significantly in versions 1.3 and 2.1 respectively. However, these results clearly indicate that we can't simply assume that JSP is the fastest option. Note also that a different XSLT implementation might produce better results, although there are good reasons why XSLT performance is unlikely to approach that of the other technologies.

While it's important to understand the possible impact of using different products, we shouldn't fall into the trap of assuming that because there are so many variables in J2EE applications – application server, API implementations, third-party products, etc. – benchmarks are meaningless. Early in any project we should select an infrastructure to work with and make decisions based on its performance and other characteristics. Deferring such a decision, trusting to J2EE portability, may prove expensive. Thus performance on JBoss/Jetty with Xalan is the only meaningful metric for the sample application at this point.

Web Caching Using HTTP Capabilities

We've discussed the various options for caching data within a J2EE application. There is another important caching option, which enables content to be cached by the client browser or between the client browser and the J2EE application server, based on the capabilities of HTTP.

There are two kinds of web caches that may prevent client requests going to the server, or may reduce the impact on the server of subsequent requests: **browser caches**, and **proxy caches**.

Browser caches are individual caches, held by client browsers on the user's hard disk. For example, looking in the C:\Documents and Settings\Rod Johnson\Local Settings\Temporary Internet Files directory on my Windows XP machine reveals megabytes of temporary documents and cookies. Some of the documents include GET parameters.

Proxy caches are shared caches, held by ISPs or organizations on behalf of hundreds or thousands of users.

Whether or not subsequent requests can be satisfied by one of these caches, depends on the presence of standard HTTP header values, which we'll discuss below. If requests can be satisfied by the user's browser cache, the response will be almost instant. The user may also experience much faster response if the content can be returned by a proxy cache inside an organization firewall, or maintained by an ISP, especially if the server(s) the web site runs on is a long way from the user. Both forms of caching are likely to greatly reduce load on the web application in question, and on Internet infrastructure as a whole. Imagine, for example, what would happen if content from sites such as an Olympic Games or football World Cup site were not proxied!

HTTP caching is often neglected in Java web applications. This is a pity, as the Servlet API provides all the support we need to make efficient use of it.

Cache Control HTTP Headers

The HTTP 1.0 and 1.1 protocols define several **cache control** header options: most importantly the HTTP 1.0 Expires header and the HTTP 1.1 Cache-Control header. Request and response **headers** precede document content. Response headers must be set before content is output to the response.

Without cache control headers, most caches will not store an object, meaning that successive requests will go directly to the **origin server** (in the present context, the J2EE web container that generated the page). However, this is not guaranteed by the HTTP protocols; if we don't specify caching behavior explicitly, we're at the mercy of the browser or proxy cache between origin server and client browser. The default behavior of each of these may vary.

The HTTP 1.0 Expires header sets a date before which a cached response should be considered fresh. This date is in GMT format, not the format of the origin server's or client's locale. Fortunately the Servlet API spares us the details of setting this information. The header will look like this:

Expires: Mon, 29 Jul 2002 17:35:42 GMT

Requests received by the cache for the given URL, including GET parameter data, can simply be served cached data. The origin server need not be contacted again, guaranteeing the quickest response to the client and minimizing load on the origin server. Conversely, to ensure that the content *isn't* cached, the Expires date can be set to a date in the past.

The HTTP 1.1 Cache-Control header is more sophisticated. It includes several **directives** that can be used individually or in combination. The most important include the following:

- The max-age directive specifies a number of seconds into the future that the response should be considered fresh, without the need to contact the origin server. This is the same basic functionality as the HTTP 1.0 Expires header.

- The no-cache directive prevents the proxy serving cached data without successful **revalidation** with the origin server. We'll discuss the important concept of revalidation below.

- The must-revalidate directive *forces* the proxy to revalidate with the server if the content has expired (otherwise caches may take liberties). This is typically combined with a max-age directive.

- The private directive indicates that the content is intended for a single user and therefore should not be cached by a shared proxy cache. The content may still be cached by a browser cache.

Caches can **revalidate** content by issuing a new request for the content with an If-Modified-Since request header carrying the date of the version held by the cache. If the resource has changed, the server will generate a new page. If the resource hasn't changed since that date, the server can generate a response like the following, which is a successful revalidation of the cached content:

```
HTTP/1.1 304 Not Modified
Date: Tue, 30 Jul 2002 11:46:28 GMT
Server: Jetty/4.0.1 (Windows 2000 5.1 x86)
Servlet-Engine: Jetty/1.1 (Servlet 2.3; JSP 1.2; java 1.3.1_02)
```

Any efficiency gain, of course, depends on the server being able to do the necessary revalidation checks in much less time than it would take to generate the page. However, the cost of rendering views alone, as we've seen above, is so large that this is almost certain. When a resource changes rarely, using revalidation can produce a significant reduction in network traffic and load on the origin server, especially if the page weight is significant, while largely ensuring that users see up-to-date content.

Imagine, for example, the home page of a busy news web site. If content changes irregularly, but only a few times a day, using revalidation will ensure that clients see up-to-date information, but slash the load on the origin server. Of course, if content changes *predictably*, we can simply set cache expiry dates to the next update date, and skip revalidation. We'll discuss how the Servlet API handles If-Modified-Since requests below.

At least theoretically, these cache control headers should control even browser behavior on use of the Back button. However, it's important to note that proxy – and especially, browser – cache behavior may vary. The cache control headers aren't always honored in practice. However, even if they're not 100% effective, they can still produce enormous performance gains when content changes rarely.

This is a complex – but important – topic, so I've been able to provide only a basic introduction here. See http://www.mnot.net/cache_docs/ for an excellent tutorial on web caching and how to use HTTP headers. For a complete definition of HTTP 1.1 caching headers, direct from the source, see http://www.w3.org/Protocols/rfc2616/rfc2616-sec14.html.

The HTTP POST method is the enemy of web caches. POST pretty much precludes caching. It's best to use GET for pages that may be cacheable.

Sometimes HTML meta tags (tags in an HTML document's <head> section) are used to control page caching. This is less effective than using HTTP headers. Usually it will only affect the behavior of browser caches. Proxy caches are unlikely to read the HTML in the document. Similarly, a Pragma: no-cache header cannot be relied upon to prevent caching.

Using the Servlet API to Control Caching

To try to ensure correct behavior with all browsers and proxy caches, it's a good idea to set both types of cache control headers. The following example, which prevents caching, illustrates how we can use the abstraction provided by the Servlet API to minimize the complexity of doing this. Note the use of the setDateHeader() method to conceal the work of date formatting:

```
response.setHeader("Pragma", "No-cache");
response.setHeader("Cache-Control", "no-cache");
response.setDateHeader("Expires", 1L);
```

When we know how long content will remain fresh, we can use code like the following. The seconds variable is the time in seconds for which content should be considered fresh:

```
response.setHeader(
      "Cache-Control", "max-age=" + seconds);
response.setDateHeader(
        Expires", System.currentTimeMillis() + seconds * 1000L);
```

To see the generated headers, it's possible to telnet to a web application. For example, I can use the following command to get telnet to talk to my JBoss/Jetty installation:

```
telnet localhost 8080
```

The following HTTP request (followed by two returns) will retrieve the content, preceded by the headers:

```
GET /ticket/index.html
```

Our second code example will result in headers like the following:

```
HTTP/1.1 200 OK
Date: Mon, 29 Jul 2002 17:30:42 GMT
Server: Jetty/4.0.1 (Windows 2000 5.1 x86)
Servlet-Engine: Jetty/1.1 (Servlet 2.3; JSP 1.2; java 1.3.1_02)
Content-Type: text/html;charset=ISO-8859-1
Set-Cookie: jsessionid=1027963842812;Path=/ticket
Set-Cookie2: jsessionid=1027963842812;Version=1;Path=/ticket;Discard
Cache-Control: max-age=300
Expires: Mon, 29 Jul 2002 17:35:42 GMT
```

The Servlet API integrates support for revalidation through the protected getLastModified() method of the javax.servlet.http.HttpServlet class, which is extended by most application servlets. The Servlet API Javadoc isn't very clear on how getLastModified() works, so the following explanation may be helpful.

When a GET request comes in (there's no revalidation support for POST requests), the javax.servlet.HttpServlet service() method invokes the getLastModified() method. The default implementation of this method in HttpServlet always returns -1, a distinguished value indicating that the servlet doesn't support revalidation. However, the getLastModified() method may be overridden by a subclass. If an overridden getModified() method returns a meaningful value, the servlet checks if the request contains an If-Modified-Since header. If it does, the dates are compared. If the request's If-Modified-Since date is later than the servlet's getLastModified() time, HttpServlet returns a response code of 304 (Not Modified) to the client. If the getLastModified() value is more recent, or there's no If-Modified-Since header, the content is regenerated, and a Last-Modified header set to the last modified date.

Thus to enable revalidation support, we must ensure that our servlets override getLastModified().

Implications for MVC Web Applications

Setting cache expiry information should be a matter for web-tier controllers, rather than model or view components. However, we can set headers in JSP views if there's no alternative.

One of the few disadvantages of using an MVC approach is that it makes it more difficult to use revalidation, as individual controllers (not the controller servlet) know about last modification date. Most MVC frameworks, including Struts, Maverick, and WebWork, simply ignore this problem, making it impossible to support If-Modified-Since requests. The only option when using these frameworks is to use a Servlet filter in front of the servlet to protect such resources. However, this is a clumsy approach requiring duplication of infrastructure that should be supplied by a framework. This is a real problem, as sometimes we can reap a substantial reward in performance by enabling revalidation.

The framework I discussed in Chapter 12 does allow efficient response to If-Modified-Since requests. Any controller object that supports revalidation can implement the com.interface21.web.servlet.LastModified interface, which contains a single method:

```
long getLastModified(HttpServletRequest request);
```

Thus only controllers that handle periodically updated content need worry about supporting revalidation. The contract for this method is the same as that of the HttpServlet getLastModified() method. A return value of -1 will ensure that content is always regenerated.

The com.interface21.web.servlet.ControllerServlet entry point will route revalidation requests to the appropriate controller using the same mapping as is used to route requests. If the mapped controller doesn't implement the LastModified interface, the controller servlet will always cause the request to be processed.

The characteristics of a getLastModified() implementation must be:

❑   It runs very fast. If it costs anywhere near as much as generating content, unnecessary calls to getLastModified() methods may actually slow the application down. Fortunately this isn't usually a problem in practice.

❑   The value it returns changes not when the content is generation, but when data behind it changes. That is, generating a fresh page for a client who didn't send an If-Modified-Since request shouldn't update the last modified value.

669

❏ There's no session or authentication involved. Authenticated pages can be specially marked as cacheable, although this is not normally desirable behavior. If you want to do this, read the W3C RFC referenced above.

❏ If a `long` last modification date is stored, in the controller or in a business object it accesses, thread safety is preserved. Longs aren't atomic, so we may require synchronization. However, the need to synchronize access to a long will be far less of a performance hit than generating unnecessary content.

With the `com.interface21.web.servlet.mvc.multiaction.MultiActionController` class we extended in the sample application's `TicketController` class, revalidation must be supported on a per-method, rather than per-controller, level (remember that extensions of this class can handle multiple request types). Thus for each request handling method, we can optionally implement a last modified method with the handler method name followed by the suffix "LastModified". This method should return a long and take an `HttpServletRequest` object as an argument.

The Welcome Page in the Sample Application

The sample application provides a perfect opportunity to use revalidation, with the potential to improve performance significantly. The data shown on the "Welcome" page, which displays genres and shows, changes rarely, but unpredictably. Changes are prompted by JMS messages. The date it last changed is available from querying the `com.wrox.expertj2ee.ticket.referencedata.Calendar` object providing the reference data it displays. Thus we have a ready-made value to implement a `getLastModified()` method.

The welcome page request handler method in the `com.wrox.expertj2ee.ticket.web.TicketController` class has the following signature:

```
public ModelAndView displayGenresPage(
    HttpServletRequest request,
    HttpServletResponse response);
```

Thus, following the rule described above for the signature of the optional revalidation method, we will need to append `LastModified` to this name to create a method that the `MultiActionController` superclass will invoke on `If-Modified-Since` requests. The implementation of this method is very simple:

```
public long displayGenresPageLastModified(
    HttpServletRequest request) {
  return calendar.getLastModified();
}
```

To ensure that revalidation is performed with each request, we set a `must-revalidate` header. We enable caching for 60 seconds before revalidation will be necessary, as our business requirements state that this data may be up to 1 minute old:

```
public ModelAndView displayGenresPage(
    HttpServletRequest request,
    HttpServletResponse response) {
  List genres = this.calendar.getCurrentGenres();
  cacheForSeconds(response, 60, true);
  return new ModelAndView(WELCOME_VIEW_NAME, GENRE_KEY, genres);
}
```

The `cacheForSeconds` method, in the
`com.interface21.web.servlet.mvc.WebContentGenerator` superclass common to all framework
controllers, is implemented as follows, providing a simple abstraction of handling the details of HTTP 1.0 and
HTTP 1.1 protocols:

```
protected final void cacheForSeconds(
  HttpServletResponse response, int seconds, boolean mustRevalidate) {
  String hval = "max-age=" + seconds;
  if (mustRevalidate)
    hval += ", must-revalidate";
  response.setHeader("Cache-Control", hval);
  response.setDateHeader("Expires",
  System.currentTimeMillis() + seconds * 1000L);
}
```

> J2EE web developers – and MVC frameworks – often ignore support for web caching
> controlled by HTTP headers and, in particular, revalidation. This is a pity, as failing to
> leverage this standard capability unnecessarily loads application servers, forces users to
> wait needlessly, and wastes Internet bandwidth. Before considering using coarse-grained
> caching solutions in the application server such as caching filters, consider the option of
> using HTTP headers, which may provide a simpler and even faster alternative.

Edged Side Caching and ESI

Another option for caching in front of the J2EE application server is **edge-side** caching. Edge-side caches
differ from shared proxy caches in that they're typically under the control of the application provider or host
chosen by the application provider and in being significantly more sophisticated. Rather than rely on HTTP
headers, edge side caches understand which parts of a document have changed, thus minimizing the need to
generate dynamic content.

Edge-side caching products include Akamai and Dynamai, from Persistence Software. Such solutions can
produce large performance benefits, but are outside the scope of a book on J2EE.

Such caching is becoming standardized, with the emergence of **Edge-Side Includes (ESI)**. ESI is "a simple
markup language used to define Web page components for dynamic assembly and delivery of Web
applications at the edge of the Internet". ESI markup language statements embedded in generated document
content control caching on "edge servers" between application server and client. The ESI open standard
specification is being co-authored by Akamai, BEA Systems, IBM, Oracle, and other companies. Essentially,
ESI amounts to a standard for caching tags. See http://www.esi.org for further information.

JSR 128 (http://www.jcp.org/jsr/detail/128.jsp), being developed under the Java Community Process by the
same group of organizations, is concerned with Java support for ESI through JSP custom tags. The JESI tags
will generate ESI tags, meaning that J2EE developers can work with familiar JSP concepts, rather than learn
the new ESI syntax.

Many J2EE servers themselves implement web-tier caching (this is also a key service of Microsoft's .NET
architecture). Products such as iPlanet/SunONE and WebSphere offer configurable caching of the output of
servlets and other web components, without the need to modify application code.

The Primary Causes of Performance and Scalability Problems in J2EE Applications

We've discussed all these points previously, but the following is a quick summary, in no particular order, of what I've found to be the primary causes of performance and scalability problems in J2EE applications I've seen.

- ❑ Wrongly configured JVMs, application servers, or databases.

- ❑ Using a distributed architecture when it's inappropriate. Remote invocation is one of the most expensive operations an application can perform.

- ❑ Unnecessarily "chatty" invocation of EJBs in distributed applications.

- ❑ Use of EJB without good reason in collocated applications. Unless using EJB adds real value, it simply adds complexity and significant run-time overhead.

- ❑ Using stateful session EJBs when stateless session EJBs could achieve the same task.

- ❑ Poor performance in a cluster and reduced scalability due to failure to consider the implications of state management. For example: holding unnecessarily large amounts of session state for each user; failure to remove inactive sessions.

- ❑ Use of entity EJBs with BMP, where large result sets must be returned from finder methods.

- ❑ Use of entity EJBs at all in situations where O/R modeling is inappropriate and JDBC would prove much more efficient. As I noted in Chapter 1, J2EE developers tend to be rather doctrinaire about data access; efficiency seems to be prioritized well below the theoretical ideal of a "pure" J2EE architecture.

- ❑ Use of entity EJBs with remote interfaces. With the introduction of local interfaces in EJB 2.0, this can simply be viewed as a design mistake.

- ❑ Failure to leverage the capabilities of the target database. In this common scenario, developers concentrate on *code* portability, when it's better to concentrate on *design* portability, hiding efficient use of performant idioms behind a portable interface. For example, blanket rejection of the use of stored procedures may result in needlessly slow RDBMS access.

- ❑ Blind faith in some "J2EE design patterns" which lead to poor performance. In Chapter 7 we discussed the performance controversy over Sun's Java Pet Store sample application, which demonstrates this danger.

- ❑ Failure to cache resources and data that should have been cached: for example, performing needless JNDI lookups or repeated database access to retrieve reference data.

Summary

Performance and scalability are crucial business requirements that can determine the success or failure of a project. Thus performance expectations must be clearly defined on project inception, and we should consider the performance implications of design decisions throughout the project lifecycle. As this is such an important consideration, I have discussed the performance and scalability implications of each major design choice covered throughout this book. There is usually some scope to improve an application's performance through optimization, even when it is functionally complete, but because high-level design decisions have such an impact on the performance of J2EE applications, it's often impossible to achieve really significant improvements at such a late stage.

We've seen the importance of basing performance-driven design choices on hard evidence, rather than hunches. We've look at using load-testing tools and profiling tools to enable us to gather evidence about performance and throughput, and seen some practical examples. We've seen that such testing should not be left until the end of the project lifecycle, and that "vertical slices" of application functionality should be implemented early to verify that performance targets can be met.

We've looked at some techniques for addressing performance problems, including:

- Ensuring that application server configuration is optimal to the needs of the application.
- Dispensing with redundant container services that add overhead, but are not required to support functionality.
- Implementing caching, or using a third-party caching solution. Caching is particularly important in web applications. Some level of caching is usually essential in distributed applications.

We also discussed code-level optimization, although this will usually produce limited returns in J2EE applications unless application code is particularly inefficient to begin with.

We've looked at the unique performance problems of distributed applications. Remote method invocation is many times slower than local method invocation, so it's vital to minimize the number of remote calls in distributed applications and minimize the total amount of data exchanged across network boundaries.

We've also looked at some web-tier performance issues. We've seen some benchmarks comparing the performance of some of the web view technologies discussed in Chapter 13. We've examined how proxy and browser caching can reduce the load on and improve the performance of web containers, and how we can use HTTP headers to make this more likely.

Finally, we looked at some common causes of performance problems in J2EE applications, and the lessons we should draw from them.

> With a few J2EE projects under your belt, you'll develop a fairly reliable instinct for sniffing out potential performance problems. However, regardless of your level of experience, it's important to base decisions empirically.

16

Conclusion:
Making J2EE Work for You

We've covered a lot of ground in this book. While we haven't attempted to look at the whole of J2EE, we have looked in detail at those features and components that are most useful for building typical real-world applications. While we've focused on web applications, most of the issues discussed are relevant to all client types.

I feel that too much J2EE literature takes a highly theoretical approach that doesn't meet the challenges of real-world enterprise development. In this book, I've tried to take a practical and pragmatic approach to J2EE design and development. In particular, I've emphasized on:

❑ **Simplicity**
To a large extent, adopting a framework such as a J2EE application server is to *simplify* application code.If used correctly, J2EE can help to free developers from some of the most complex of coding tasks.

❑ **Maintainability**
Over 80% of the cost of software is spent on maintenance, rather than development, so it's imperative to develop applications that are easy to maintain.

❑ **Performance**
Performance is an important consideration in most real applications – and especially, web applications. J2EE application servers cannot free us from the responsibility of designing applications to ensure satisfactory performance, and we need to be prepared to make design trade-offs if necessary.

❑ **Productivity**
Applications must be developed in reasonable time. Productivity is a vital consideration, which must be taken into account throughout the project lifecycle.

We've considered not merely the J2EE specifications, but how some important features are implemented in leading servers. J2EE now has several years behind it, and while many features have proven their value, others have not been so successful. We must take this experience into account.

In this chapter, we'll consider some of the lessons that we've drawn.

General Principles

The following is a summary of some of the most important general principles we've discussed:

❑ **Use J2EE: don't let it use you**
Successful software projects treat technologies as tools. J2EE should be used as a means to an end. Each of the many technologies within J2EE should only be used where it delivers demonstrable benefit. Avoid the temptation to use features of J2EE just because (like Everest) they are there; this is likely to add unnecessary complexity, and ongoing expense.

❑ **Don't use EJB unless it delivers real value**
This is perhaps the most important case of the above principle. I feel that far too many J2EE developers assume that EJB is the core of J2EE, and that all enterprise-class applications should use EJB. This is incorrect. EJB is a complex technology that solves some problems well, but adds unnecessary complexity if used inappropriately. When EJBs are used appropriately, they should *simplify* application code by concealing the handling of concurrency issues, transaction management, security management, and remote access. When EJBs don't deliver a simplicity dividend, the decision to use them may be incorrect. The benefits should be obvious, not merely a vague promise of greater scalability.

❑ **Don't use a distributed architecture unless it is necessary to meet business requirements**
Distributed applications, in which application components are distributed amongst multiple servers, are far more complex than collocated applications, in which all application components run in the same JVM. Thus the difficulty and cost of developing and maintaining distributed applications is much greater than that of developing and maintaining collocated applications. We should avoid incurring this cost unless it is necessary. In *Chapter 1* and *Chapter 6* we discussed how to choose when a distributed architecture is appropriate. Note that collocated applications can still be clustered if necessary, with each server in the cluster running all application components. When we use EJB in a collocated application, we should use local interfaces, rather than remote interfaces.

❑ **Don't take an unduly J2EE-centric view of enterprise software development**
Java is a fine language and J2EE is a fine platform for enterprise development. However, enterprise applications involve more than any one language and the technologies around it. A good J2EE developer is literate in the enterprise technologies that J2EE applications interact with, and prepared to seek help from specialist experts when required. A professional developer should also be aware of and open to ideas from alternative platforms such as .NET.

❑ **J2EE isn't merely about specifications**
While it's a great bonus that public specifications describe the functionality of J2EE application servers, it's important to draw lessons from the implementations of them in leading J2EE application servers. For example, we must be aware of the limitations of leading implementations in areas such as stateful session beans and entity beans. We must base our decisions on evidence and evidence can only be drawn from real implementations, not specifications.

❑ **Think carefully about database portability**
Don't try to achieve database portability if it increases complexity or reduces performance, unless there's a real likelihood that you'll require it. There is usually a cost in achieving abstraction between different types of persistent store, such as RDBMSs and ODBMSs. This cost shouldn't be incurred lightly, as data tends to stick where it lands. An RDBMS schema may well outlast a J2EE application.

❑ **JDBC (and SQL) are powerful tools**
Don't be afraid to use them, and learn to use them well. Be skeptical of claims, such as those of the EJB specification, that J2EE can deliver developers from the details of working with relational databases or other enterprise resources. Often this is neither realistic nor desirable. Don't hope to solve the so-called "object-relational impedance mismatch" simply by ignoring how RDBMSs work; try to build OO applications that can use RDBMSs efficiently. Used correctly, JDBC can be highly efficient and easy to work with. In *Chapter 9* we saw a simple abstraction framework that can be used to simplify working with JDBC and help to prevent common errors.

❑ **Don't ignore the capabilities of your target database**
Not only have you already paid for these capabilities: they're the fruits of decades of research and development and should work very well. For example, some tasks can be accomplished much more efficiently in stored procedures than in Java code, and it's frequently possible to harness the performance gain without abandoning good design principles. Don't view an RDBMS as a dumb storage device and also don't ignore the input of DBAs in a fervent quest for a "pure" J2EE solution. The results are likely to be disappointing.

❑ **Try to achieve portability between J2EE application servers if possible**
Regularly use the verifier included with Sun's J2EE Reference Implementation to check your applications' compliance to the J2EE specifications. Sometimes it *is* necessary to use proprietary features of an application server: for example, to maximize the performance of a particularly performance-sensitive operation. However, violations of the J2EE specifications through ignorance or laziness produce no benefit and will be very costly if there is ever a need to port the application to another application server.

❑ **A good application is the simplest possible application**
The XP advice to do "the simplest thing that could possibly work" is especially relevant to J2EE, which provides a wealth of complex options, many of which are required infrequently. Question design decisions that seem to lead to excessive complexity. For example, consider a decision to use JMS to achieve asynchronous calling. While JMS and message-driven beans are very useful in some situations, using them will usually add complexity and make an application harder to debug and maintain compared to using ordinary synchronous calling. Unless this additional complexity delivers real benefit, it's best to eschew it.

❑ **Most of the benefits of EJB can be achieved through stateless session beans**
The trade-offs involved in using stateful session beans and entity beans are more complex, and their benefits less clear-cut. The stateless component model has been proven in many middleware systems, not merely EJB. Stateful session beans and entity beans, on the other hand, are not so well proven in practice. Stateful session beans can limit scalability, if this is a key requirement. Using entity beans makes it difficult to perform many operations efficiently when working with relational databases. Remember that O/R mapping, as provided by entity beans, isn't always appropriate. Also, remember that entity beans are just one approach to O/R mapping, which happens to be defined in the EJB specification; JDO and proprietary O/R mapping products such as TopLink are often superior.

❑ **Think about performance from project inception**
Business requirements should contain clear and measurable targets for performance and concurrency. It's advisable to develop a proof of concept, often called a **spike solution** or **vertical slice**, early in the project lifecycle, to ensure that performance requirements can be met. This allows us to modify application architecture if necessary, without massive waste of effort. Later in the project lifecycle it may be too late to improve performance significantly without expensive changes; in most J2EE applications, we cannot rely on code optimization to deliver significant performance gains. Performance is a real concern in J2EE, as it's often a key business requirement (for example, in web applications) and because some popular J2EE "patterns" produce particularly bad performance. In *Chapter 15* we saw the importance of basing performance-related decisions on hard evidence, obtained from load testing and profiling runs.

❑ **Consider the likelihood and implications of the application running in a cluster of servers, and take this into account in design**
It's possible to design an application that performs well on a single server, but will prove extremely inefficient if it has to run in a cluster – for example, if it holds unnecessarily large amounts of session state, which will need to be replicated between clustered servers. Be wary of such pitfalls if there's a real possibility of the application needing to scale up to a clustered deployment, even if it is initially deployed on a single server.

❑ **When scalability is a crucial priority, as it is in high-volume web applications, try to design using stateless components**
No application server and no technology – J2EE or any other – can prevent the maintenance of server-side state reducing scalability. Consider the example of scalability using geographically dispersed servers. This will prove an enormous problem for replication of server-side state. If server-side state is required, good design should minimize the amount that needs to be held.

❑ **Good J2EE design rests on good OO design**
It's easy to let the details of working with J2EE APIs and components distract us from sound OO practice; this is a costly mistake. The size and complexity of J2EE projects makes it all the more vital to follow good OO practices such as programming to interfaces rather than concrete classes and achieving a consistent level of abstraction within classes. We've also seen how the use of JavaBeans can help us to hold configuration outside Java code, and how interface-based design can help us to ensure portability between application servers.

❑ **Use helper classes to abstract use of low-level APIs such as JDBC, JNDI, and JMS to simplify application code and achieve a consistent level of abstraction**
It's vital that application code concentrates on the problem domain and on implementing business logic. This can only be achieved by ensuring that low-level tasks are concealed by generic infrastructure code, in cases where working with the J2EE APIs directly is too verbose. This doesn't mean that we need to sacrifice efficiency; such an abstraction layer should allow application code to control the use of the underlying APIs. In *Chapter 9* and *Chapter 11* we looked at generic packages that conceal some of the complexity of J2EE from application code. We saw how using these packages significantly simplified the code of the sample application.

❑ **Use the MVC architectural pattern in web applications**
This is probably the single most important piece of high-level design advice for J2EE web applications. The MVC architectural pattern ensures that presentation is separate from control flow and business logic. Experience has proven this to be an essential goal of all real web applications. Use a generic implementation of the MVC pattern such as the Struts framework or the framework discussed in *Chapter 12* of this book. Remember also that the web tier should be as thin as possible, and responsible only for translating user actions into business operations and displaying the results. Business logic should not be web-specific.

Projects

The following is a summary of some of the important guidelines for J2EE projects:

❑ **Base design decisions on what works now, not a promise of brilliant functionality in the future**
Basing a project on a moving target of new server and specification releases is a recipe for failure. The nature of the J2EE specification process, which incorporates community input, but results in specifications being released before production-quality implementations of them, means that specified features are not always proven to work in the real world. This is another area in which J2EE development is about more than specifications.

❑ **Don't read too much into trivial examples**
Most J2EE sample applications, such as Sun's Java Pet Store, are far from production quality, and simply ignore many common problems. So don't assume that all the approaches they use will be relevant to your real-world problems.

❑ **Test your application thoroughly**
Design your application so that it is easily testable and test it at multiple levels. Build unit testing, functional testing, and performance testing into all phases of the development process. Consider writing tests before application code, and keep tests up to date.

❑ **Document your application thoroughly, but keep documentation relevant to application code**
Always provide comprehensive Javadoc comments. Use graphical models and design documents as necessary. However, remember that fat formal documents are likely to be ignored by developers and seldom remain relevant throughout the software lifecycle.

❑ **Adopt a methodology that tackles risk early**
J2EE applications have many moving parts, and must work with disparate resources: a lot can go wrong. Successful projects tackle risks as early as possible.

❑ **Choose an application server early in your project, and develop expertise with it**
Learn about its capabilities and streamline the development, testing and release cycle using it. Although J2EE applications *are* usually portable between application servers, each application server is profoundly different to work with and has different strengths and weaknesses. Deferring a choice of application server will ensure a myriad of irritations, adding substantially to the effort involved in a project. Focus on your organization's needs, rather than marketing material, when choosing an application server.

❑ **Automate the build and testing process early in the project lifecycle**
While IDEs provide valuable functionality, their functionality isn't scriptable. Use IDEs to enhance productivity, but ensure that there's a standard build script in place. Ant is now the de facto standard for building Java applications, and can be used to automate a host of other essential tasks such as unit testing, updating documentation, and deployment.

❑ **Hire a core of experts in J2EE design from the beginning of the project**
J2EE is complex, and doesn't always work as it says on the can. Trying to save money using a team of inexperienced staff will cost more in the end. A core of experts can mentor less experienced developers as the project progresses, gradually building a deeper reserve of expertise.

❑ **Write as little application code as possible**
In particular, avoid reinventing the wheel by understanding and leveraging the capabilities of your application server and using existing frameworks.

❑ **Adopt consistent design and coding standards to ensure good practice**
Its vital that all developers on a project understand and commit to common standards. This helps to ensure good practice, enhances maintainability, and helps to minimize duplication of effort.

Above all, it's vital to take a flexible and pragmatic approach to J2EE design. Ultimately, applications are measured by how well they meet their business requirements and how cost-effectively they are implemented and maintained.

Hopefully, after reading this book you will feel more confident about taking design decisions and making implementation choices in J2EE projects. Good luck!

Implementing View Technologies

This appendix is intended as a reference to accompany Chapters 12 and 13. It discusses how the MVC web application framework discussed in Chapter 12 supports any view technology without the need to modify controller or model code.

It first considers how this framework decouples controllers and views, and then looks at how the framework supports those view technologies discussed in Chapter 13. For each technology we'll look at:

❑　Any installation and configuration required for web applications using it

❑　How our MVC framework supports this technology, and the basic Java code required to integrate with it, whatever framework we use

❑　How to define views of this type in applications using this framework

Finally we look at how new, custom view implementations can be implemented within this framework, to support other view technologies or provide sophisticated, application-specific behavior.

> **Although this appendix is primarily concerned with the MVC web framework introduced in Chapter 12, the information about installing and configuring view technologies applies to all web applications. The code examples illustrating integration with each view technology can also be used as the basis of your own implementation code.**

This chapter contains some lengthy code listings. However, space constraints mean that these aren't all complete. I've tried to show the central code needed to achieve each task (however, please refer to the code in the sample application and accompanying infrastructure packages for complete implementations of the approaches discussed).

Decoupling Controllers from View Technologies Using a View Interface

Let's review the way in which the MVC web application framework described in Chapter 12 decouples controllers from views.

It uses the **named view strategy** to provide a layer of indirection allowing a controller to select a view by name without knowing anything about the view's implementation. This means that all views must implement a common Java interface. Most view technologies hold presentation information such as (X)HTML formatting in **templates** such as JSP pages, rather than Java classes. However, as the details of templates vary between view technologies such as JSP and XSLT, this decoupling depends on different implementations of a Java view interface that manages content rendering using the appropriate technology and template.

I use the term **view interface** to refer to Java objects that provide such decoupling between controller and view, and the term **view** to refer to the resource (such as a JSP page) that holds the actual layout for the page. In some cases, a single Java class may perform both roles.

Implementations of view interfaces are normally multi-threaded, and work on behalf of all users of the application. Typically one instance of a view wraps a particular template, implementing a single, stateless, method that accepts model data and builds a dynamic page. Normally only a template such as a JSP page needs to be provided as part of an application, with the necessary view implementation being a standard class supplied by the framework.

In the framework discussed in Chapter 12, a view interface must implement `com.interface21.web.servlet.View` interface, which is based around the following method, which generates dynamic content given a data model:

```
void render(Map model,
            HttpServletRequest request,
            HttpServletResponse response)
  throws IOException, ServletException;
```

The `model` parameter contains a number of model objects exposed by the controller. In some cases, it will be empty, if a view doesn't require any model information.

The `com.interface21.web.servlet.View` interface also allows **static attributes** to be added to the model exposed by the underlying view technology. This enables additional presentation-specific data (such as arguments to template pages or default page titles) to be added in application configuration without polluting the model returned by controllers, which shouldn't be tailored to any particular view technology.

Static attributes can be added to views only when they are first created. Once a view is in use, its data (including its static attributes) is immutable to ensure thread safety. The AbstractView base class used by the view implementations discussed in this chapter allows static attributes to be defined in CSV format as follows. This property defines three static attributes: header, contentWell, and footer.

```
welcomeView.attributesCSV=header=[/jsp/header.jsp],\
                          contentWell=[/welcome.jsp],\
                          footer=[/jsp/footer.htm]
```

As model data returned by controllers and static attributes are presentation-agnostic, implementations of the View interface can work with *any* view technology.

We'll look at implementations of the View interface in detail below, but let's take a more detailed look at how particular view implementations may fulfill the basic requirements we identified in Chapter 13:

❑ **Wrap a particular page structure**
If a template is required, it can be located and cached when the view object is configured. Some template technologies, such as XSLT, perform much better if views are compiled and cached, although there's no need for view caching with JSP. In some cases, as with XMLC, the view implementation itself will hold the page structure, meaning that we need an implementation of the View interface for each application screen. In most cases; however, the view implementation is a generic framework wrapper for different views using a given technology. For example, each Velocity template in an application can be accessed through a framework Velocity view that takes a template name as an initialization property.

❑ **Expose model data to the underlying view technology**
If the view is a JSP page, model data will be exposed as request attributes. In the case of template engines such as Velocity, model data will be placed in a "context" specific to the template engine. In some cases – such as XSLT – additional pre-processing may be required; for example, to convert Java objects into XML nodes where model data isn't already in XML form.

❑ **Build the dynamic page**
The means of rendering will vary widely. In the case of a JSP page within the same web application, the javax.servlet.RequestDispatcher interface can be used to forward to the JSP page. A RequestDispatcher instance, obtained from the web container, can also be used to forward to an output servlet or a static resource within the sample web application. Template engines such as Velocity provide their own APIs to interpret a template and output data. In the case of XSLT, the TrAX API can be used to perform an XSL transform and write the result to the response.

In our application framework, View objects are normally JavaBeans, configured on application initialization. This means that configuration can be held outside Java code. Typically there is one view instance per view template (such as a JSP page).

How view definitions are stored, depends on the implementation of the ViewResolver interface used. The com.interface21.web.servlet.ViewResolver interface, discussed in Chapter 12, defines the following single method, to return a View instance for a given name and Locale (taken from the request):

```
View resolveViewname(String viewName, Locale locale)
  throws ServletException;
```

It's easy to provide a custom, application-specific implementation of this interface, which might hold view definitions in a custom format or even perform view resolution wholly in Java code.

However, normally we can rely on the default `ViewResolver` implementation, used in the sample application. In this implementation, which we'll use for the examples in this appendix, view definitions are JavaBean definitions in the `/WEB-INF/classes/views.properties` file, or a resource bundle with the appropriate localized name, such as `/WEB-INF/classes/views_fr_ca.properties`, which overrides some or all of the view definitions. As we look at each view technology below, we'll look at the necessary bean definitions for the default `ViewResolver`.

View Implementations

The following UML class diagram shows the view implementations discussed in this appendix, and how all are derived from the `AbstractView` convenience base class. The two classes at the bottom right illustrate how application-specific classes (in this case, classes from our sample application) extend the abstract framework superclasses for XMLC and PDF views:

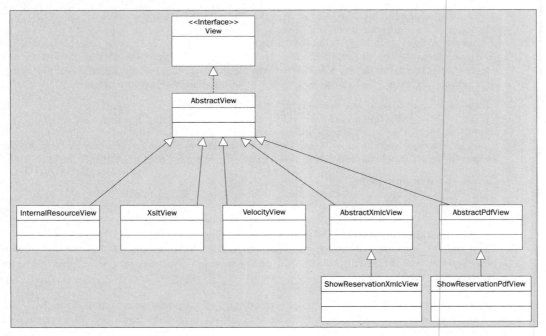

The following framework view implementations are concrete, and can be used without subclassing:

❑ `com.interface21.web.servlet.view.InternalResourceView`
View implementation that can expose model data using JSP, servlet, or other content within the current web application

❑ `com.interface21.web.servlet.view.xslt.XsltView`
View implementation that can expose data using an XSLT stylesheet, converting JavaBeans in the model to XML form if necessary

❑ `com.interface21.web.servlet.view.velocity.VelocityView`
View implementation that can expose data using a cached Velocity template

The following two classes are abstract superclasses for application-specific views. The two view technologies concerned require a Java class to be implemented for each view:

❑ `com.interface21.web.servlet.view.xmlc.AbstractXmlcView`
Abstract superclass for views using XMLC technology. A static HTML template is used at run time, but the application-specific Java class holds page layout at run time.

❑ `com.interface21.web.servlet.view.pdf.AbstractPdfView`
Abstract superclass for views using the iText library to generate PDF. No templates are involved, as all content is generated in Java code.

The `View` interface is simple to implement from scratch, but the `com.interface21.web.servlet.view.AbstractView` superclass provides a convenient superclass for most view implementations, using the Template Method design pattern to conceal the merging of static attributes with model objects supplied by the controller (if a static attribute and a model attribute share the same name, the model attribute will take precedence). Subclasses of `AbstractView` need to implement the following protected method, which has the same contract as the `render()` method from the `View` interface, but works with a merged map of model and static attributes:

```
protected abstract void renderMergedOutputModel(
    Map model,
    HttpServletRequest request,
    HttpServletResponse response)
    throws ServletException, IOException;
```

`AbstractView` invokes this method in a final implementation of the `render()` method as follows. Note that dynamic (model) attribute values will replace static attributes with the same name:

```
public final void render(Map pModel,
    HttpServletRequest request, HttpServletResponse response)
    throws ServletException, IOException {

    // Consolidate static and dynamic model attributes
    Map model = new HashMap(this.staticAttributes);
    model.putAll(pModel);

    renderMergedOutputModel(model, request, response);
}
```

The `AbstractView` class exposes the following bean properties, inherited by all the view implementations discussed here:

Name	Type	Required	Default	Purpose
contentType	String	No	text/html; charset=ISO-8859-1	The content type to write to the response. See the documentation for javax.servlet.Se rvletResponse for more information.
name	String	No	null	The name of this view. Purely for diagnostic purposes.
static AttributesCSV	String	No	null	CSV format string defining the static attributes associated with this view. Used in the default properties view definition syntax. See example above.
static Attributes	java.util. Properties	No	n/a	Properties value defining the static attributes associated with this view. Used if defining views in XML bean definitions (the CSV form is used when defining views in properties files, as it's problematic to have a property value that is itself in properties syntax).

JSP

Let's begin by considering JSP, the commonest view technology in J2EE web applications.

Configuring the JSTL

As JSP 1.2 is part of the J2EE 1.3 specification, it's guaranteed to come with our application server.

However, we do need to include the JSTL libraries.

The sample application uses the Apache Jakarta implementation of the JSTL, available from http://jakarta.apache.org/taglibs. The following JARs from the /lib directory of the Jakarta JSTL distribution are required for using the tags shown in the sample application:

- ❑ jstl.jar
- ❑ standard.jar
- ❑ sax.jar
- ❑ saxpath.jar
- ❑ jaxen-full.jar

The first two JARs define the JSTL API and the implementation of the standard tags; the last three are required by the implementation of the XML tags.

These files are included in the /lib/runtime/jsp-stl directory of the download, and automatically copied to the WEB-INF/lib directory of web applications build by the sample application's Ant build script.

We don't need to include the JSTL TLDs in WARs using it. We can simply import JSTL libraries using their published URLs at java.sun.com, as in the following example, which imports the core library:

```
<%@ taglib prefix="c" uri="http://java.sun.com/jstl/core" %>
```

> **All applications using JSP should use the JSTL, which greatly improves the JSP authoring model. Thus the JSTL binaries should be included with all JSP-based applications.**

The InternalResourceView View Implementation

Let's now look at the framework's implementation of the View interface for use with JSP. The complete listing for this framework implementation can be found in the framework code accompanying the sample application, in the com.interface21.web.servlet.view.InternalResourceView class. The class is named InternalResourceView, rather than JspView, as it can be used for static HTML or servlets within the web application, as well as JSP.

This view implementation copies model entries to request attributes, before using a Servlet API RequestDispatcher to forward to the specified resource within the current web application, identified by a URL provided when the view is initialized.

By extending the com.interface21.web.servlet.view.AbstractView superclass the InternalResourceView class is required to implement only the renderMergedOutputModel() protected abstract method and expose the bean properties necessary to configure view instances.

The following partial listing of the InternalResourceView class omits logging methods and useful functionality to include debug information in the request if the ControllerServlet has set a request attribute indicating that it's in debug mode.

The basic steps to wrap a JSP template are very simple. We will need an instance variable to hold the url property and a property setter to allow InternalResourceView beans to be configured:

```
public class InternalResourceView extends AbstractView {
  private String url;

  public void setUrl(String url) {
    this.url = url;
  }
```

The url bean property must be set to the path to a JSP within the current web application, such as /jsp/myJsp.jsp.

The implementation of the renderMergedOutputModel() method obtains a RequestDispatcher for the cached URL from the web container, and forwards the request to it, after exposing model data as request attributes:

```
public void renderMergedOutputModel(Map model,
      HttpServletRequest request, HttpServletResponse response)
      throws ServletException {

  exposeModelsAsRequestAttributes(model, request);

  try {
   request.getRequestDispatcher(getUrl()).forward(request, response);
  }
  catch (IOException ex) {
    throw new ServletException("Couldn't dispatch to JSP with url '" +
      getUrl() + "' in InternalResourceView with name '" +
      getName() + "'", ex);
  }
}
```

The code to set model attributes as request parameters is refactored into a protected method, in case any subclasses wish to reuse it:

```
protected final void exposeModelsAsRequestAttributes(
    Map model, HttpServletRequest request) {

  if (model != null) {
    Set keys = model.keySet();
    Iterator itr = keys.iterator();
    while (itr.hasNext()) {
      String modelname = (String) itr.next();
      Object val = model.get(modelname);
      request.setAttribute(modelname, val);
    }
  }
}
```

This standard view implementation can be used to wrap any JSP page, servlet, or static content from the same web application. It is not usually necessary to provide application-specific subclasses.

Defining JSP Views for Use in an Application

A typical view definition in `/WEB-INF/classes/views.properties` using the `InternalResourceView` class will look as follows:

```
showReservation.class=com.interface21.web.servlet.view.InternalResourceView
showReservation.url=/showReservation.jsp
```

The only bean property exposed by `InternalResourceView`, beyond those inherited from `AbstractView`, is `url`. This property must be set to a resource URL within the WAR, as shown above. The URL may be under the WAR's `/WEB-INF` directory, as in the following example:

```
showReservation.class=com.interface21.web.servlet.view.InternalResourceView
showReservation.url=/WEB-INF/jsps/protectedJsp.jsp
```

Resources under the special `/WEB-INF` directory are still accessible to `RequestDispatchers`, but are protected from direct user requests.

Velocity

This section discusses how to install and configure Velocity 1.3, and the framework's built-in support for the Velocity template engine.

Installing and Configuring Velocity

Unlike JSP, Velocity isn't part of J2EE and probably won't be shipped with your application server. The `/lib/runtime/velocity` directory of the sample application includes the two JAR files that Velocity 1.3 requires: `velocity-1.3.jar`, and `velocity-dep-1.3.jar`. These must be copied to the `/WEB-INF/lib` of a web application using Velocity. The sample application's Ant build script handles this.

Velocity must also be configured before individual templates can be used. Velocity is highly configurable and exposes many configuration parameters, but the only configuration parameters that we must set tell Velocity where to find templates at runtime. Velocity offers several strategies for loading templates, such as using the file system or the class loader. In the sample application, I've opted for the class loader, as it's more portable between web containers.

The following keys from the sample application's `/WEB-INF/velocity.properties` file tell Velocity to load templates from the classpath (that is, under `/WEB-INF/classes` or `/WEB-INF/lib` within the WAR), and that it should automatically reload altered templates to ease development:

```
resource.loader=class
class.resource.loader.class =
    org.apache.velocity.runtime.resource.loader.ClasspathResourceLoader
class.resource.loader.cache = false
class.resource.loader.modificationCheckInterval = 5
```

> **Velocity template reloading, like JSP compilation, should normally be switched off in production, as it will impact on performance.**

Important optional settings include the paths of Velocity macro libraries to be loaded when Velocity starts, and made available to all templates. The following example specifies the location of a Velocity macro library:

```
velocimacro.library = myMacros.vm
```

Multiple libraries can be included in a CSV list, and they should be located as for ordinary Velocity templates.

We need to apply these properties to Velocity before we attempt to evaluate templates. One way to do this is to use a servlet with a `<load-on-startup>` subelement to ensure it's loaded before our web application receives requests. However, the bean-based framework we discussed in Chapter 11 provides a more elegant alternative. As a "singleton" bean in our application context is guaranteed to be instantiated, even if it's not accessed by user code, we can simply define a bean that will configure Velocity during application initialization. The framework provides the `com.interface21.web.servlet.velocity.VelocityConfigurer` bean for this purpose. The following bean definition from the `/WEB-INF/ticket-servlet.xml` file of our sample application illustrates its use:

```
<bean name="velocityConfig"
      class="com.interface21.web.servlet.view.velocity.VelocityConfigurer">

    <property name="url">/WEB-INF/velocity.properties</property>

</bean>
```

Note the single bean property `url`, which is the location within the WAR of the standard Velocity properties file. The `VelocityConfigurer` bean loads the Velocity properties (in this case from a properties file within the WAR), and uses them to initialize the Velocity singleton as follows:

```
Velocity.init(properties);
```

Velocity 1.2 introduced support for multiple independent instances of Velocity in the same web application, so the Singleton model is no longer the only choice.

Implementing the View Interface for Velocity

Let's look at the framework's built-in implementation of the `com.interface21.web.servlet.View` interface, which exposes model data via Velocity templates.

This framework implementation needs to perform the following steps in its `render()` method:

- ❑ Create a new Velocity context object to build this response.
- ❑ Expose model objects as Velocity context objects, in the same way in which we exposed model objects as request attributes in the `InternalResourceView` class.

❑ Obtain the relevant Velocity template. As each `VelocityView` object will be associated with a single view, the Velocity view can obtain and cache the necessary Velocity template at startup, enabling it to check that the template exists and is free from syntax errors on framework initialization.

❑ Use Velocity to "merge" the template with the context data to write to the `HttpServletResponse`.

Exposing Model Data to a Velocity Template

Please look at the source of the `com.interface21.web.servlet.view.velocity.VelocityView` class in the `/framework` directory of the download for the full implementation. I show the basic steps to achieve each of these steps below.

Like the other view implementations discussed in this chapter, `VelocityView` extends `AbstractView`. The first step in the `renderMergedOutputModel()` method is to is to create a Velocity context to build this response:

```
Context vContext = new VelocityContext();
```

Model objects are exposed to this new, request-specific, Velocity context in the following private method:

```
private void exposeModelsAsContextAttributes(Map model, Context vContext) {

  if (model != null) {
    Set keys = model.keySet();
    Iterator itr = keys.iterator();
    while (itr.hasNext()) {
      String modelname = (String) itr.next();
      Object val = model.get(modelname);
      vContext.put(modelname, val);
    }
  }
}
```

The template can be obtained from the Velocity singleton instance and cached when the view is initialized as follows:

```
private void loadTemplate() throws ServletException {

  String mesg = "Velocity resource loader is: [" +
    Velocity.getProperty("class.resource.loader.class") + "]; ";

  try {
    this.velocityTemplate =
      RuntimeSingleton.getTemplate(this.templateName);
  }
  catch(ResourceNotFoundException ex) {
    mesg += "Can't load Velocity template '" + this.templateName +
        "': is it on the classpath, under /WEB-INF/classes?";
    logger.logp(Level.SEVERE, getClass().getName(), "getTemplate",
```

693

```
                        mesg, ex);
          throw new ServletException(mesg, ex);
        }
        catch(ParseErrorException ex) {
          mesg += "Error parsing Velocity template '" + this.templateName + "'";
          logger.logp(Level.SEVERE, getClass().getName(), "getTemplate",
                        mesg, ex);
          throw new ServletException(mesg, ex);
        }
        catch(Exception ex) {
          mesg += "Unexpected error getting Velocity template '" +
                  this.templateName + "'";
          logger.logp(Level.SEVERE, getClass().getName(), "getTemplate",
                        mesg, ex);
          throw new ServletException(mesg, ex);
        }
      }
```

With a Velocity context populated with model data, we can generate output to the `HttpServletResponse` as follows:

```
    this.velocityTemplate.merge(vContext, response.getWriter());
```

The actual implementation of the `VelocityView` *class uses a more performant, but slightly more complex approach, based on the* `VelocityServlet` *bundled with Velocity. Please see the source for details.*

Providing Support for Date and Currency Formatting

Surprisingly, Velocity 1.3 lacks standard support for date and currency formatting. The Velocity Tools project includes some support, although it still seems to be in development. Thus to ensure that our framework's Velocity view isn't tied to the current locale, we need to help Velocity out in this area.

We could opt to expose formatted dates and currency amounts as string properties in each model, but this subverts good design. Localization is usually better handled in views than in models.

The `VelocityView` class adds `java.text.SimpleDateFormat` and `java.text.NumberFormat` objects to the Velocity context if the view definition indicates that the wrapped template needs to perform date or currency formatting. Java's localizable support for number and currency formatting is simple, familiar is and documented in the `java.text` package Javadocs.

`SimpleDateFormat` and `NumberFormat` objects must be constructed for each request, as Velocity template code may alter their configuration – for example, by setting the formatting pattern. These helpers are exposed only if two bean properties on `VelocityView` – `exposeDateFormatter` and `exposeCurrencyFormatter` – are set to `true` to indicate that a particular `View` instance is associated with a template that needs to format dates or currency amounts (exposing these helper objects to the majority of templates that don't need them would be wasteful). The helpers are initialized using the `HttpServletRequest`'s `locale` property, as follows:

```
    public static final String DATE_FORMAT_KEY = "simpleDateFormat";

    public static final String CURRENCY_FORMAT_KEY = "currencyFormat";
```

```
private void exposeHelpers(Context vContext, HttpServletRequest request) {

    if (this.exposeDateFormatter) {
        // Javadocs indicate that this cast will work in most locales
        SimpleDateFormat df = (SimpleDateFormat)
        DateFormat.getDateTimeInstance(DateFormat.LONG,
            DateFormat.LONG, request.getLocale());
        vContext.put(DATE_FORMAT_KEY, df);
    }

    if (this.exposeCurrencyFormatter) {
        NumberFormat nf =
            NumberFormat.getCurrencyInstance(request.getLocale());
        vContext.put(CURRENCY_FORMAT_KEY, nf);
    }
}
```

We can now manipulate patterns if necessary in Velocity templates and use the objects to format model data as follows:

```
The date of the performance is
$simpleDateFormat.format($performance.when).

The total cost of these tickets will be
$currencyFormat.format($reservation.totalPrice).
```

Defining Velocity Views for Use in an Application

The following example from the /WEB-INF/classes/views.properties file defines a Velocity view bean for the sample page discussed in Chapter 13. Note that it sets the two format helper properties to true, as this page needs to display the performance date and ticket costing:

```
showReservation.class=
    com.interface21.web.servlet.view.velocity.VelocityView
showReservation.templateName=showReservation.vm
showReservation.exposeDateFormatter=true
showReservation.exposeCurrencyFormatter=true
```

The VelocityView class exposes the following bean properties, beyond those inherited from AbstractView:

Name	Type	Required	Default	Purpose
templateName	String	Yes	n/a	The name of the Velocity template to use. The meaning of this property will depend on how Velocity is configured to load templates. The template will normally be located within the WAR.
exposeDataFormatter	boolean	No	false	Should we add a `SimpleDateFormat` object, initialized for the request locale, to the Velocity context?
exposeCurrencyFormatter	boolean	No	false	Should we add a `NumberFormat` object, initialized for the request locale, to the Velocity context?
poolSize	int	No	40	The number of Velocity writers to use to handle this page. Refer to Velocity documentation for further information on this optimization.

XSLT

This section discusses how the MVC web framework supports XSLT views.

Installing Domify

As JAXP is part of J2EE 1.3, the supporting libraries are guaranteed to be in place. However, the framework's built-in XSLT support depends on the open source Domify library (discussed in Chapter 6 and Chapter 13) to expose JavaBeans as XML nodes. The /lib/runtime/common package in the sample application download contains domify.jar, the small JAR file required. This must be copied to the /WEB-INF/lib directory of WARs using XML domification. Again, the Ant build script for the sample application handles this.

Implementing the View Interface for XSLT

As with JSP and Velocity views, we'll need one view instance for each XSLT stylesheet. However, this implementation can be provided by a framework; there is no need for application code to use XSLT directly.

The `com.interface21.web.servlet.view.xslt.XsltView` standard implementation, like the view implementations we've already seen, extends the `com.interface21.web.servlet.view.AbstractView` convenience superclass. It uses Domify to convert JavaBean model data to XML form (if necessary) before performing XSLT transforms using the JAXP standard API.

The underlying XML parser and XSLT transformation engine may vary between servers, as JAXP insulates code using it from the actual implementation. With JBoss/Jetty, the products used are Apache Xerces and Apache Xalan respectively – the commonest choices.

Performing XSLT transforms

The `XsltView` class exposes a bean property enabling the stylesheet location to be set to a URL within the WAR:

```
public void setStylesheet(String url) {
  this.url = url;
}
```

On initialization, each instance of `XsltView` will obtain a new instance of the `javax.xml.transform.TransformerFactory` interface:

```
this.transformerFactory = TransformerFactory.newInstance();
```

It can use this object to create a `javax.xml.transform.Templates` object: a compiled, threadsafe representation of the stylesheet that can cheaply return `javax.xml.transform.Transformer` objects for use with the stylesheet:

```
private void cacheTemplates() {

  if (url != null && !"".equals(url)) {
    Source s = getStylesheetSource(url);
    try {
      this.templates = transformerFactory.newTemplates(s);
    }
    catch (TransformerConfigurationException ex) {
      throw new ApplicationContextException(
        "Can't load stylesheet at '" + url + "' in XsltView with name '" +
        getName() + "'", ex);
    }
  }
}
```

697

The XsltView class's getStylesheetSource() method returns a javax.xml.transform.Source object given a URL. The default implementation uses the ServletContext.getRealPath() method to find the file system location of the URL within the WAR. This works fine in all containers I've tried, but isn't guaranteed to be portable (imagine, for example, a container that extracted WAR contents to a database, not a file system), so this method must be overridden by a custom subclass for use in containers that don't allow such file access:

```
protected Source getStylesheetSource(String url)
    throws ApplicationContextException {

  String realpath = getWebApplicationContext().getServletContext().
                    getRealPath(url);
  if (realpath == null)
    throw new ApplicationContextException(
      "Can't resolve real path for XSLT stylesheet at '" + url +
      "'; probably results from container restriction: " +
      "override XsltView.getStylesheetSource() to use an " +
      "alternative approach to getRealPath()");

    Source s = new StreamSource(new File(realpath));
    return s;
}
```

> Warning: The ServletContext.getRealPath() method is potentially non-portable.
> However, it's so useful in practice that many web application frameworks and packages for use in
> web applications use it.

The actual transformation is accomplished in the doTransform() method, which writes the result to the response. Note that we create a javax.xml.transform.Transformer object from the cached Templates object to perform the transform. We can't cache a Transformer object, instead of a Templates object, as Transformers are not threadsafe. Thus use of a cached Templates object is an essential performance optimization; we don't want to have to create a new Transformer from scratch, requiring the XSLT stylesheet to be parsed and its structure analyzed, for each transform:

```
protected void doTransform(HttpServletResponse response, Node dom)
    throws IOException, ServletException {

  try {
    Transformer trans = this.templates.newTransformer() :
      trans.setOutputProperty(OutputKeys.INDENT, "yes");
    trans.setOutputProperty("{http://xml.apache.org/xslt}indent-amount",
      "2");
    trans.transform(new DOMSource(dom), new StreamResult(new
      BufferedOutputStream(response.getOutputStream())));

  }
  catch (TransformerConfigurationException ex) {
    throw new ServletException(
        "Couldn't create XSLT transformer for stylesheet '" + url +
        "' in XSLT view with name='" + getName() + "'", ex);
  }
  catch (TransformerException ex) {
```

```
        throw new ServletException(
            "Couldn't perform transform with stylesheet '" + url +
            "' in XSLT view with name='" + getName() + "'", ex);
    }
}
```

Although I've set two Xalan-specific properties here, this won't prevent the code working with another XSLT engine; they'll simply be ignored.

The implementation of the `renderMergedOutputModel()` method will expose the contents of our model map as a single XML document, "domifying" JavaBean objects if data isn't already XML:

```
protected void renderMergedOutputModel(Map model,
    HttpServletRequest request, HttpServletResponse response)
    throws ServletException, IOException {

  if (model == null)
    throw new ServletException("Cannot do XSLT transform on null model");

  Node dom = null;
  String docRoot = null;
  Object singleModel = null;
```

If we have a single model object in our model map, we must check whether it already contains XML data. If it does, we simply expose it to the XML view:

```
  if (model.size() == 1) {
    docRoot = (String) model.keySet().iterator().next();
    singleModel = model.get(docRoot);
  }

  if (singleModel != null && (singleModel instanceof Node)) {
    dom = (Node) singleModel;
  } else {
```

If we have multiple model objects or if a single model object isn't in XML format, we'll need to "domify" the entire model map. We use the `docRoot` bean property value to provide a name for the model:

```
    try {
      addRequestInfoToModel(model, request);
      dom = this.domAdapter.adapt(model,
        (docRoot == null) ? this.root : docRoot);
    }
    catch (RuntimeException rex) {
      throw new ServletException("Error domifying model in XSLT view " +
                                 "with name='" + getName() + "'", rex);
    }
  }
```

Now we have XML data in the `dom` object, we can invoke the XML transform:

```
     doTransform(response, dom);
  }
```

This takes care of interaction with the JAXP API. Java application code won't need to perform any XSLT handling or even XML handling unless it's relevant to the application's business requirements.

Date and Currency Formatting Support

The framework's XsltView also solves another common problem. XSLT doesn't provide support for date formatting, so, as with Velocity, we need to help XSLT out in this regard (XSLT 2.0 is likely to add a date formatting capability modeled on Java's java.text.SimpleDateFormat). We also should be able to provide the XLST stylesheet with information about the user's locale, to allow it to initiate date formatting in the correct style. Although the user's locale is available from the HttpServletRequest, it's not part of our data model (and nor should it be).

We add additional information to the model before domification to expose this information as follows:

```
model.put(REQUEST_INFO_KEY, new RequestInfo(request));
```

The com.interface21.web.servlet.view.RequestInfo class, which can also be used for other view technologies, exposes the following properties, each returning a standard two-letter code such as GB or en:

```
public String getCountry();
public String getLanguage();
```

These codes can drive lookups in XSLT or be used as arguments to Java XSLT **extension functions** that provide date formatting functionality to XSLT. XSLT provides a simple **Java language binding** that allows XSLT stylesheets to invoke Java methods using reflection. While Java extension functions can be abused (they offer a small back door towards abuse of XSLT: imagine, for example, what extension functions that performed JDBC operations might do to maintainability), they are occasionally very useful, and are easy to use. The present use – to enhance the capabilities of XSLT view formatting in an area in which it is weak – is a good example of appropriate use.

> *Note that I've borrowed the ideas behind this approach from an excellent article in* Java World *by Taylor Cowan on XSLT extension functions: see* http://www.javaworld.com/javaworld/jw-12-2001/jw-1221-xslt-p2.html.

However, the use of extension functions reduces the portability of stylesheets, which otherwise don't depend on Java, so their use should be kept to a minimum.

The com.interface21.web.servlet.view.xslt.FormatHelper class exposes two static methods that enable us to format dates and currency amounts:

```
public static Node dateTimeElement(long date, String language,
   String country);

public static String currency(double amount, String language,
   String country);
```

The `dateTimeElement()` method returns an XML *Node*, rather than literal content, built using a `SimpleDateFormat` object for the specified locale. (We can use the JAXP API to create nodes in an extension function.) This new node is not included in the XML input document, but will look like this:

```
<formatted-date>
    <month>July</month>
    <day-of-week>Tuesday</day-of-week>
    <year>2002</year>
    <day-of-month>23</day-of-month>
    <hours>11</hours>
    <minutes>53</minutes>
    <am-pm>AM</am-pm>
</formatted-date>
```

Please see the source for the `FormatHelper` class for the implementation of the `dateTimeElement()` method. If we create a stylesheet rule for the `<formatted-date>` element we can now format the information as we desire as follows:

```
<xsl:apply-templates select="format:dateTimeElement(when/time, 'en', 'GB') "/>
```

The `currency()` method of the `FormatHelper` class simply returns a string containing a formatted currency amount, such as £3.50 or $3.50. We can use it like this:

```
<xsl:value-of select="format:currency(totalPrice, 'en', 'GB')" />.
```

To use these extension methods in stylesheets, all we need to do is declare a namespace for them in the root element, as follows:

```
<xsl:stylesheet version="1.0"
    xmlns:xsl="http://www.w3.org/1999/XSL/Transform"
    xmlns:format="com.interface21.web.servlet.view.xslt.FormatHelper"
>
```

Finally we need to be able to customize domification. Domify can't handle cyclic references, such as that between `Performance` and `Show` in our object model: every `Performance` has a parent `Show` that contains a list of `Performance` objects including the original `Performance`. Hence we also need to be able to exclude properties from domification to ensure that infinite loops due to cyclic references are avoided. The `excludedProperties` property of the `XsltView` class is a CSV list of entries of the form `<concrete class>.<property name>` that tells Domify which properties to suppress. We can also use this to simplify the DOM document exposed by Domify. We'll see an example of this below.

Defining XSLT Views for Use in an Application

All we need to do in application code is to declare new view beans of type `XsltView` in `/WEB-INF/classes/views.properties`, specifying the name of the document root, template URL (within the WAR), and any properties we wish to exclude. The definition for our sample view is:

```
showReservation.class=com.interface21.web.servlet.view.xslt.XsltView
showReservation.root=reservationInfo
showReservation.stylesheet=/xsl/showReservation.xsl
showReservation.excludedProperties=
  com.wrox.expertj2ee.ticket.referencedata.support.ShowImpl.performances
```

Note that if we don't specify a stylesheet URL, the output will display the input XML document. This is very useful functionality during development, which I omitted from the code listings above for simplicity:

Name	Type	Required	Default	Purpose
root	String	Varies	null	Root of the generated XML document. Required unless the model contains a single element (in which case the attribute name is used). If the single element is an XML Node, it is used unchanged as the basis for the model, and any value of the root property is ignored.
stylesheet	String	No	Default behavior is to show input XML unchanged	Specifies the location of the XSLT stylesheet within the WAR. If no value is specified for this property, the XML document will be written to the response.
cache	boolean	No	true	Whether the XSLT stylesheet should be cached in compiled form when the view is initialized, or whether the stylesheet should be reread with each response generated. A value of true is useful during debugging, as it enables the stylesheet to be changed without restarting the application, but should not be used in production.
Excluded Properties	CSV-format String	No	n/a	Set of properties (on fully-qualified classes) that should be excluded from "domification". See discussion and example above.

Although the framework's default **XsltView** implementation uses the **Domify** library to convert JavaBean model data to XML form, and TrAX to perform XSL transforms, an alternative implementation could use alternative libraries to achieve this. For example, model-specific implementations (as opposed to the generic implementation described here) could use XML data binding to achieve higher performance.

XMLC

This section describes how to install and configure XMLC 2.1. See Chapter 13 for information on the XMLC authoring model.

Installing and Configuring XMLC

Like Velocity, XMLC doesn't come with J2EE application servers (except Enhydra). Thus we need to distribute it ourselves with our application.

The `/lib/runtime/xmlc` directory of the download contains the binaries for XMLC 2.1. XMLC requires not only supporting libraries such as GNU regular expression library, but patched versions of common products such as the Apache Xerces XML parser.

This directory includes the following files:

❑ `xmlc.jar`: The XMLC binaries

❑ `xerces-1.4.4-xmlc.jar`: A patched version of the Xerces parser

❑ `jtidy-r7-xmlc.jar`: A patched version of the JTidy utilities

❑ `gnu-regexp-1.1.4.jar`: The GNU regular expression library

All these files need to be included in the `/WEB-INF/lib` directory of web applications using XMLC. Again, the sample application's Ant build script handles this.

> *Whether or not the need for patched versions of common libraries causes compatibility problems may depend on your application server. If the application server supports the Servlet 2.3 recommendation for "inverted" class loading (WAR first) discussed in Chapter 14, there's unlikely to be a problem. However, if it follows normal Java language class loading behavior (system classes first) the necessary patches may not be loaded, meaning patching of the application server's own libraries or abandoning XMLC. Hopefully this issue will soon be resolved with later releases of XMLC and the libraries in question.*

Like Velocity, XMLC needs to be configured before it can be used in a web application. Although we were able to configure Velocity using a bean in our application context, we need to use a servlet to configure XMLC. The `XMLCContext` object can only be configured by a servlet; the `ServletContext` isn't sufficient. Our MVC framework provides the `com.interface21.web.servlet.view.xmlc.XmlcConfigServlet` to configure XMLC, which must be set to load on application startup. The `XmlcConfigServlet` configures XMLC as follows:

```
XMLCContext xmlcc = XMLCContext.getContext(this);
```

When using XMLC, the following servlet definition element must be included in each web application's `web.xml` to load the `XmlcConfigServlet` on startup:

```
<servlet>
    <servlet-name>xmlcConfig</servlet-name>
    <servlet-class>
```

```
            com.interface21.web.servlet.view.xmlc.XmlcConfigServlet
      </servlet-class>
      <load-on-startup>3</load-on-startup>
   </servlet>
```

Set the `<load-on-startup>` value according to the number of pre-initialized servlets your application requires.

Implementing the View Interface for XMLC

Let's look at the framework's abstract implementation of the `com.interface21.web.servlet.View` interface for XMLC, which application-specific XMLC views should extend.

With XMLC, as with any generation library approach, we need a distinct Java object for each view. At run time the HTML template is no longer required, but we need one view implementation for each XMLC-generated view.

The framework provides a common superclass for all XMLC views, `com.interface21.web.servlet.view.xmlc.AbstractXmlcView`, which extends `com.interface21.web.servlet.view.AbstractView` and uses the Template Method design pattern to conceal the necessary plumbing from subclasses and leave them only the task of creating and manipulating the relevant XMLC object. The implementation of the protected `renderMergedOutputModel()` method from `AbstractView` uses the `org.enhydra.xml.xmlc.servlet.XMLCContext` object created by the `XmlcConfigServlet`, which can be used to create new templates. The following is a partial listing:

```
   public abstract class AbstractXmlcView extends AbstractView {

      private XMLCContext xmlcContext;
```

The following overridden method from `AbstractView` caches the `XMLCContext`, throwing an exception if XMLC has not been configured:

```
      protected void onSetContext() throws ApplicationContextException {

         this.xmlcContext = (XMLCContext) getWebApplicationContext().
            getServletContext().getAttribute(XMLCContext.CONTEXT_ATTRIBUTE);
         if (this.xmlcContext == null)
           throw new ApplicationContextException(
             "No XMLCContext inited. Use XMLCConfigServlet with loadOnStartup");
      }
```

The implementation of the protected `renderMergedOutputModel()` template method invokes a protected template method to create the application-specific `XMLObject`, before using the `XMLCContext` to output its data to the response:

```
      protected final void renderMergedOutputModel(Map model,
         HttpServletRequest request,
         HttpServletResponse response)
         throws ServletException, IOException {
```

```
XMLObject xo = createXMLObject(model, request, response,
    this.xmlcContext);
response.setContentType(getContentType());
this.xmlcContext.writeDOM(request, response, xo);
}
```

Subclasses must implement the following protected method to create an application-specific `XMLCObject` and manipulate it according to the data in the model parameter:

```
protected abstract XMLObject createXMLObject(
    Map model,
    HttpServletRequest request,
    HttpServletResponse response,
    XMLCContext context)
    throws ServletException;
```

Defining XMLC Views for Use in an Application

As the `AbstractXmlcView` class exposes no bean properties beyond those inherited from `AbstractView`, all we need to do to define an XMLC view is to specify an application-specific concrete subclass, as follows:

```
showReservation.class=
    com.wrox.expertj2ee.ticket.web.xmlcviews.ShowReservationView
```

Of course, subclasses may themselves add view properties, which can then be set in the same way as framework properties. One of the virtues of JavaBean-based configuration is that it automatically works with any class, not just classes that are known to the framework.

Generating PDF with iText

The following section discusses how to use the iText library to generate PDF.

Installing iText

iText is simply a class library, so there's no need to configure the runtime as with Velocity or XMLC. However, we will need to include the binaries in WARs using it. The `/lib/runtime/itext-pdf` directory of our sample application includes the single JAR file required – `iText.jar`. Again, the sample application's Ant build script will copy `iText.jar` to the `/WEB-INF/lib` directory of WAR distribution units it builds.

Implementing the View Interface for PDF Generation with iText

As with XMLC, we'll need one implementation of our View interface for each view that generates PDF.

The basic steps involved in generating PDF using iText involve getting a
`com.lowagie.text.pdf.PdfWriter` instance, adding document content objects to it, and closing the
`PdfWriter` to output the content:

```
PdfWriter.getInstance(document, response.getOutputStream());
document.open();
// Output model data
document.close();
```

However, this simple approach won't work with Internet Explorer, which needs to know the content
length of the generated PDF. Hence in a web application we must use the more verbose code shown
below to perform the same basic steps. We also need to give the requested URL a .pdf extension.
Although the `AbstractPdfView` sets the content type to `application/pdf`, which should be
sufficient, Internet Explorer doesn't always respect this unless we change the extension.

> The use of a **.pdf** extension means that we must also remember to map the relevant
> **.pdf** URL to our controller servlet. Failure to define all necessary mappings in the
> **web.xml** deployment descriptor is a common cause of frustration with any MVC
> framework. If the framework's controller servlet never gets a request in the first
> place, it may be unclear where the problem lies.

Again, the framework uses the Template Method design pattern, providing a convenient superclass for
iText PDF views. The `com.interface21.web.servlet.view.pdf.AbstractPdfView` abstract
class takes care of creating an iText document and writing the complete document to the response in a
final implementation of the `renderMergedOutputModel()` method. It conceals from application code
the complexity of generating the content length and dealing with Internet Explorer's failure to honor the
returned content type. Note that we also set the page size:

```
protected final void renderMergedOutputModel(Map model,
    HttpServletRequest request, HttpServletResponse response)
    throws ServletException, IOException {

Document document = new Document(PageSize.A4);
try {
  ByteArrayOutputStream baos = new ByteArrayOutputStream();
  PdfWriter writer = PdfWriter.getInstance(document, baos);

  writer.setViewerPreferences(
  PdfWriter.AllowPrinting |
  PdfWriter.PageLayoutSinglePage);

  document.open();
```

Now we've created a new document, we need to invoke application code to write content to it. The
following line invokes a protected template method whose definition we'll see below:

```
buildPdfDocument(model, document, request, response);
```

Finally, we output the data to the `HttpServletResponse`, taking care to set the content length using the Servlet API:

```
        document.close();
        response.setContentLength(baos.size());
        ServletOutputStream out = response.getOutputStream();
        baos.writeTo(out);
        out.flush();
    }
    catch (DocumentException ex) {
        throw new ServletException("Error creating PDF document", ex);
    }
}
```

Subclasses of `AbstractPdfView` must implement the following protected abstract method to write model data to the iText PDF `Document` passed as the second parameter. The request and response objects won't normally be used, but we include them in case the view needs locale information or needs to write a cookie:

```
    protected abstract void buildPdfDocument(Map model,
        Document pdfDoc,
        HttpServletRequest request,
        HttpServletResponse response)
        throws DocumentException;
```

Defining PDF Views for Use in an Application

All we need to do to define a PDF view is to specify the application-specific subclass in `/WEB-INF/classes/views.properties`, as follows:

```
showReservation.class=
    com.wrox.expertj2ee.ticket.web.pdfviews.ShowReservationViewExample
```

Additional Views

The following views are included in the framework but not discussed here:

❑ `com.interface21.servlet.web.view.webmacro.WebMacroView`
WebMacro view implementation, similar to the Velocity view discussed earlier.

❑ `com.interface21.servlet.web.view.RedirectView`
View implementation that redirects the response to an external URL, exposing model data as `String` query parameters. This approach works only for simple models, but can be very useful when integrating with third-party sites. The default implementation builds a query string by calling the `toString()` method on each element in the model. Subclasses can customize this behavior by overriding the protected `queryProperties(Map model)` method to return a `Properties` object containing the name-value pairs to be used in the query string. The `RedirectView` class takes care of constructing the query string (using `?` and `&` characters) and the necessary URL encoding.

Custom Views

As the view implementations we've discussed demonstrate, it's easy to implement the `View` interface, especially if we subclass the `com.interface21.web.servlet.view.AbstractView` convenience class.

A custom view implementation can integrate with almost any view technology. We simply need to provide an implementation class, which might be generic or application-specific, and provide a view definition using the standard JavaBean syntax.

The power of the basic approach is shown by the fact that a `View` implementation could easily be written for each of the following, without any need to change controller or model code in the application concerned:

- ❑ A view that causes an XSLT transform to be performed in the client browser (rather than on the server) exposing XML and stylesheet.

- ❑ A composite view that includes the output of other views, possibly even using different technologies.

- ❑ A forwarding view that looks at the user agent string returned by the browser and chooses a delegate view accordingly (for example, if the browser is known to be capable of performing XSLT transforms, control could be passed to a view that initiates a client-side transform; otherwise the XSLT transform could be performed on the server, returning the generated output to the client).

- ❑ A custom view that uses a class library to generate an Excel spreadsheet for numeric model data.

> Using the approach described here, we can define a view for anything that can take model data and generate output. If necessary, we can convert model data into a form other than Java objects.

Index

A Guide to the Index

The index is arranged hierarchically, in alphabetical order, with symbols preceding the letter A. Most second-level entries and many third-level entries also occur as first-level entries. This is to ensure that users will find the information they require however they choose to search for it.

S